MAP OF BUTLER CO. IOWA

History of Butler County

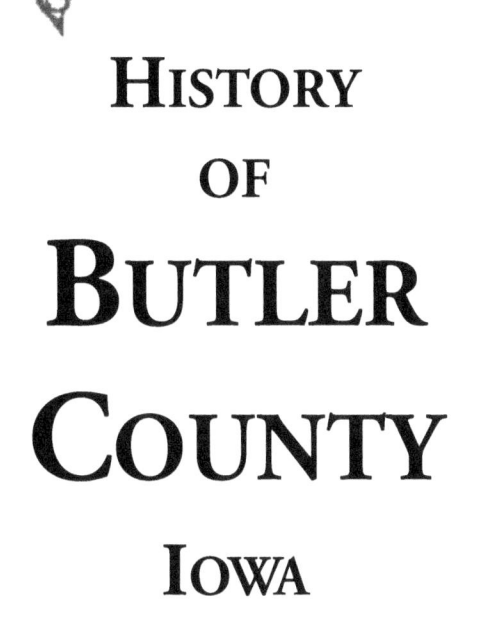

Iowa

Union Publishing Company

HERITAGE BOOKS
2010

HERITAGE BOOKS
AN IMPRINT OF HERITAGE BOOKS, INC.

Books, CDs, and more—Worldwide

For our listing of thousands of titles see our website
at
www.HeritageBooks.com

A Facsimile Reprint
Published 2010 by
HERITAGE BOOKS, INC.
Publishing Division
100 Railroad Ave. #104
Westminster, Maryland 21157

Copyright © 1883 Union Publishing Company

Index Copyright © 1999 Heritage Books, Inc.

— Publisher's Notice —

Many of the pages in this book appear to be missing. The text and information is all there, the missing pages appear to be photographs that were missing from the original. The second half of this book is published in a separate volume titled *Bremer Co., Iowa*.

In reprints such as this, it is often not possible to remove blemishes from the original. We feel the contents of this book warrant its reissue despite these blemishes and hope you will agree and read it with pleasure.

International Standard Book Numbers
Paperbound: 978-0-7884-1343-8
Clothbound: 978-0-7884-8395-0

TO THE PIONEERS

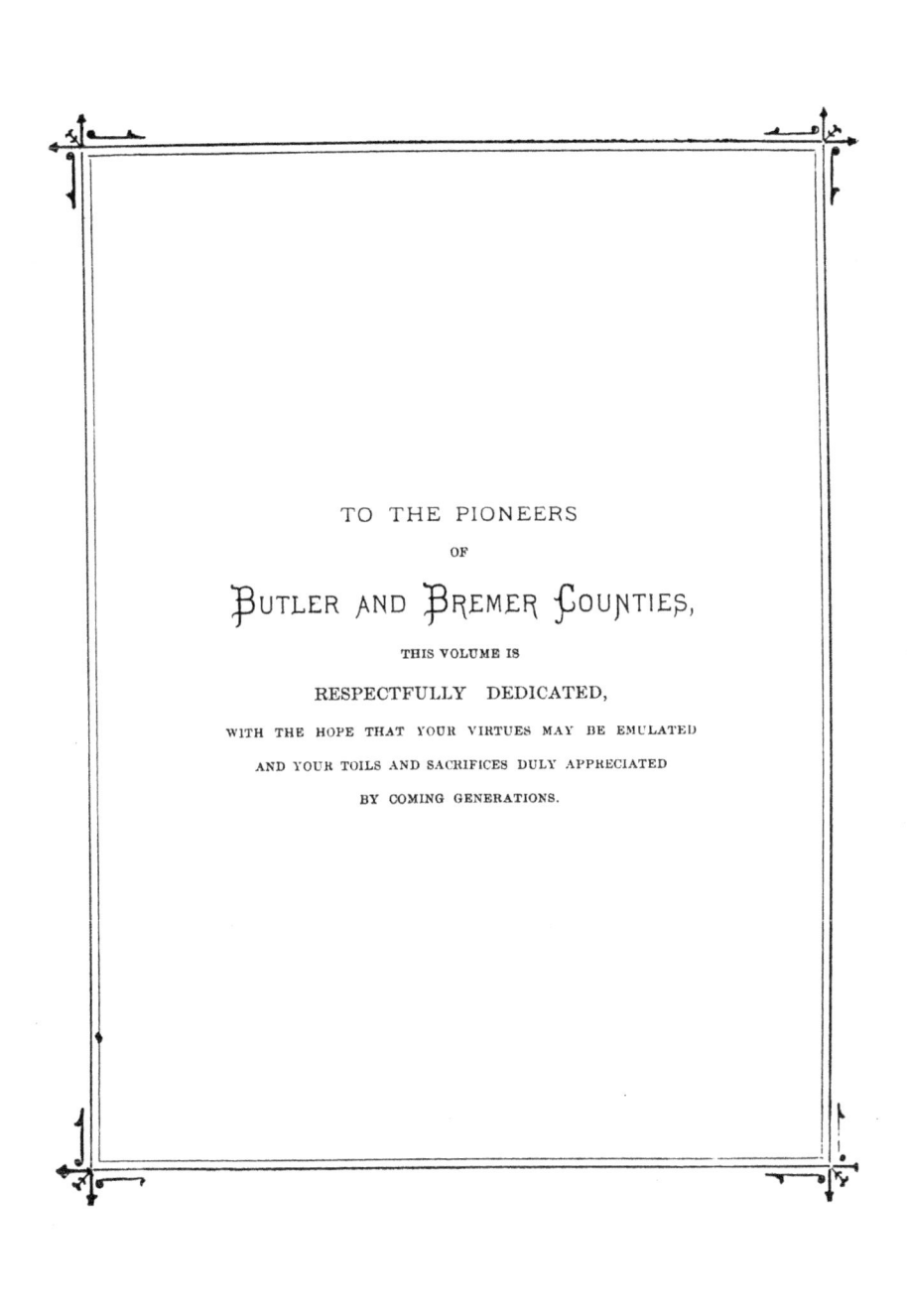

OF

BUTLER AND BREMER COUNTIES,

THIS VOLUME IS

RESPECTFULLY DEDICATED,

WITH THE HOPE THAT YOUR VIRTUES MAY BE EMULATED
AND YOUR TOILS AND SACRIFICES DULY APPRECIATED
BY COMING GENERATIONS.

TABLE OF CONTENTS.

HISTORY OF BUTLER COUNTY.

CHAPTER I.

	PAGE
THE CHANGE	231
Organization of the County	232
Geographical Location and Topography	232
Mount Nero and its Cave	233
Railroads	234

CHAPTER II.

EARLY SETTLEMENT	234
First Things	237
Fourth of July Celebration	238

CHAPTER III.

IN EARLY DAYS	239
The Indian War	240
The Scare in Northern Part of County	242
Hunting by the Pioneers	243
The Prairie Fires	243
The Ferry Lost	244
Hard Times	244
Reminiscence by P. P. Parker	246

CHAPTER IV.

COUNTY GOVERNMENT	250
First Law Suit in Butler County	250
First Court House	252
Officers for 1856	252
Court House Again	253
Railroad Stock	253
Board of Supervisors	254

CHAPTER V.

OTHER OFFICIAL MATTERS	259
Population of Butler County	259
Butler County Sub-divisions	259
Matrimonial	260
Financial	263
Registry of Deeds	264
Vital Statistics	267
County Poor Farm	267

CHAPTER VI.

| POLITICAL | 269 |
| Official Vote | 269 |

CHAPTER VII.

NATIONAL, STATE AND COUNTY REPRESENTATION	287
Congressional	287
Auditor of State	289
Government Appointments	289
General Assembly	289
County Judge	292
County Auditor	293
Treasurer and Recorder	294

	PAGE
County Recorder	294
County Treasurer	295
Clerk of Courts	296
Sheriffs	297
Prosecuting Attorneys	299
Superintendent of Schools	300
County Assessor	300
County Surveyors	300
Drainage Commissioners	300
County Coroners	300

CHAPTER VIII.

COUNTY SEAT STRUGGLES	303
Butler Center as the County Seat	305
Allison the County Seat	306

CHAPTER IX.

THE NEWSPAPER PRESS	307
The Butler Transcript	308
Butler County Jeffersonian	308
Stars and Stripes	308
Butler County Argus	308
The Stiletto	308
The Clarksville Gazette	308
The Star of the West	309
The Clarksville Star	309
Parkersburg Times	311
The Shell Rock Enterprise	311
The Shell Rock News	312
Parkersburg Eclipse	315
Butler County Press	316
New Hartford Bugle	318
The Butler County Standard	318
The Bristow Dial	318
The Allison Tribune	318

CHAPTER X.

JUDICIAL	325
Criminal Convictions	327
County, Probate and Circuit Courts	327

CHAPTER XI.

| THE BAR OF BUTLER COUNTY | 329 |

CHAPTER XII.

THE MEDICAL PROFESSION	345
Reminiscence of Practice in Early Days	346
Allison Physicians	349
Bristow Physicians	351
Clarksville Physicians	352
Greene Physicians	352
New Hartford Physicians	353
Parkersburg Physicians	354
Shell Rock Physicians	354
Aplington Physicians	358
The Butler County Medical Association	359

TABLE OF CONTENTS.

CHAPTER XIII.

AGRICULTURE AND AGRICULTURAL SOCIETIES... 362
First Fair in Butler County... 363
Butler County Agricultural Society... 363
Clarksville Agricultural Association... 364
Farmers' Produce Association, of Greene... 366

CHAPTER XIV.

EDUCATIONAL... 367
County Superintendent of Schools... 369
School Fund Commissioners... 368
Schools in Butler County... 371
Present Condition of Educational Matters... 372
Graded Schools... 376
The Normal Institute... 376
Butler County Teachers' Association... 378

CHAPTER XV.

THE WAR—ITS CAUSES... 380

CHAPTER XVI.

BUTLER COUNTY IN THE WAR... 385
Muster Rolls and History of Regiments... 386
Roll of Honor... 408

CHAPTER XVII.

OLD SETTLERS' SOCIETY... 412
Old Settlers' Meeting... 412

CHAPTER XVIII.

ALBION TOWNSHIP... 414
Early Settlement... 414
Organic... 425
Proctor's Pond... 425
During Early Days... 425
Schools... 429
NEW ALBION... 429
TOWN OF PARKERSBURG... 430
The Beginning and Business Interests... 430
Parkersburg Flouring Mill... 441
Postoffice... 441
Incorporation... 442
Educational Facilities... 444
Religious... 445
Societies... 449
Directory... 450

CHAPTER XIX.

BEAVER TOWNSHIP... 451
Early Settlement... 452
Educational... 455
Organic... 456
VILLAGE OF WILLOUGHBY... 460
NEW HARTFORD... 461
The Beginning... 461
Educational... 463
Religious... 464
Present Business... 466

CHAPTER XX.

BENEZETTE TOWNSHIP... 475
Early Settlement... 476
Religious... 481
Educational... 482
Official Organization... 483

CHAPTER XXI.

BUTLER TOWNSHIP... 492
Early Settlement... 492
Organic... 527
CLARKSVILLE... 528
The Beginning... 530
Educational... 539
Religious... 542
Business of Clarksville... 546

CHAPTER XXII.

COLDWATER TOWNSHIP... 548
Early Settlement... 548
Interesting Items... 555
Official... 556
Coldwater During the War... 557
Educational... 557
Religious... 571
Directory... 575

CHAPTER XXIII.

DAYTON TOWNSHIP... 576
Early Settlement... 577
Characteristic Settlement... 579

CHAPTER XXIV.

FREMONT TOWNSHIP... 587
Early Settlement... 588
Organic... 596
Educational... 597

CHAPTER XXV.

JACKSON TOWNSHIP... 598
Early Settlement... 598
Organic... 600
Educational... 601
Religious... 601

CHAPTER XXVI.

JEFFERSON TOWNSHIP... 610
Topography... 610
Historical Items... 610
Organic... 615
Early Settlement... 616
BUTLER CENTER... 621

CHAPTER XXVII.

MADISON TOWNSHIP... 625
Early Settlement... 625
Historical Items... 627
Organic... 628
Religious... 628
Educational... 628

CHAPTER XXVIII.

MONROE TOWNSHIP... 634
Early Settlement... 635
Historical Items... 647
Organic... 647
TOWN OF APLINGTON... 650

TABLE OF CONTENTS.

IX

CHAPTER XXIX.

	PAGE
PITTSFORD TOWNSHIP	657
Early Settlement	657
Organization	668
Schools	668
Mails and Postoffices	671
Town of Dumont	681

CHAPTER XXX.

RIPLEY TOWNSHIP	686
Early Settlement	686

CHAPTER XXXI.

SHELL ROCK TOWNSHIP	692
Early Settlement	692
Town of Shell Rock	706
Incorporation	714
Business	715

CHAPTER XXXII

	PAGE
WASHINGTON TOWNSHIP	727
Early Settlement	728
Official	740
Educational	740

CHAPTER XXXIII.

WEST POINT TOWNSHIP	741
Early Settlers	742
Organic	752
Town of Allison	753
Town of Bristow	767

CHAPTER XXXIV.

MISCELLANEOUS	777
The Storm King	781
Constitutional Amendment	781
Biographical	782
Diphtheria	783

BIOGRAPHICAL.

	PAGE		PAGE		PAGE		PAGE
Ackerman, David	584	Bisbee, Wm	653	Carpenter, Volney	235	Cross, J. J	588
Adair, Wm	722	Bishop, C. B	761	Carter, Lemuel	580	Cross, Solomon C	515
Adair, Geo. W	695	Bishop, W. H	297	Carson, J. H	727	Crouse, Wm. F	401
Ahrens, Henry	677	Blackmer, E. L	358	Caul, Charles	645	Cronin, William	599
Allen, J. W	699	Blake, G. G	700	Cass, Hollis	751	Crowell, R. G	245
Anderson, John D	371	Blaisdell, E. B	513	Caswell, Chas. H	604	Critzman, Aug	474
Apfel, Henry	709	Bolton, J. F	470	Caywood, David	422	Culp, Joshua R	423
Arends, John P	655	Bomell, E	751	Chamberlin, Cyrus D	479	Cummings, Edward	485
Ashton, M. W	474	Boggs, John N	579	Chamberlin, Ira A	479	Curtis, W. A	350
Atkinson, Henry	504	Boisgardner, F	633	Chapel, Thurman S	424		
Auner, John S	725	Bonnell, Wm. H	580	Chapin, F. W	506	Dubn, F. E	656
Austen, Albert	679	Bonwell, S	588	Chapman, Chauncey	474	Daggett, J. M	755
Austen, Lewis J	686	Bonwell, John	607	Cheever, S. W	603	Daily, Christian	744
Austin, Wm	731	Bonwell, Charles	607	Chesley, Nathaniel	419	Daniels, Richard	416
Austin, Henry	731	Boomer, J. H	342	Christy, John	703	Davis, Timothy	287
		Bourquin, Eugene	463	Chrystie, Alex	653	Davis, E. J	578
Baker, Otis	436	Bowen, John	701	Clark, A. G	294	Davis, James W	339
Bailey, Martin	622	Boyd, John	608	Clark, Thomas	730	Dudley, E. H	357
Baldwin, S. M	620	Boyd, John E	474	Clayton, Walter	414	Dunson, P. E	619
Balsley, W. E	595	Boyan, Isaac	742	Clayton, Walter	635	Dearmon, S. R	674
Bannon, Charles A	382	Bragg, Lafayette	584	Cline, Alexander	679	Deering, N. C	288
Barker, Samuel	590	Bremer, John	343	Codner, Joseph	417	Dellinger, P. N	599
Barker, John	420	Brook, James	645	Collar, James	453	Demoss, Thomas	678
Barnett, Benj. H	485	Brown, H. C	685	Collins, Joseph	440	Dumont, S. B	683
Barkelew, Stephen	606	Brownell, Joseph H	490	Conn, Thomas W	439	Dodge, Frank L	322
Barrett, A. C	514	Burbank, Jerome	350	Coon, August	417	Dodge, Fred A	316
Beals, A. H	567	Burbank, F. E	351	Corson, E. B	703	Dopking, Geo. M	754
Bell, Hiram	750	Burlett, A. J	565	Corwin, C. W	782	Doty, Aaron	603
Bellows, E. C	445	Burke, James E	505	Converse, Alonzo	341	Doty, Cyrus	606
Bement, J. P	717	Burnett, Herman D	473	Connolly, James	771	Downey, Daniel	421
Beninga, Daniel	731	Burt, T. J	436	Copeland, T. G	470	Downing, Simeon	597
Bennett, Edward	595	Burton, H. F. L	537	Courtwright, O. B	344	Downing, John E	480
Benson, Geo	774	Burnham, J. J	732	Coryell, G. J. H	418	Dreyer, Henry	645
Berlin, Frederick	619	Burroughs, S. E	350	Cotton, Wm. R	655	Drum, John	697
Best, A	515	Burdick, W. H	344	Cortright, S. S	472	DeVries, P	733
Bettesworth, Thos	552	Burk, John E	333	Coyle, Peter	630	Early, T. M	673
Bickley, J. E	609	Burdick, W. H	297	Coyle, Edward	630	Eastman, O. L	707
Billhimer, Christopher	525	Burton, W. E	296	Combs, Harrison	734	Eastwood, W. C	716
Billhimer, Henry	520	Byerly, O	351	Craig, George M	343	Ebersold, P. J	580
Billings, James V	422			Cramer, Miss Dr	352	Eichar, J. J	524
Billson, G. W	473	Caldwell, J. M	636	Cramer, James D	440	Eikenberry, J. F	574
Birney, V. C	352	Carr, Clark	604	Cramer, Samuel	417	Ellsworth, J. F	342
Birkbeck Brothers	756	Carpenter, Harrison	235	Croot, Samuel	732	Ensign, Charles	454

TABLE OF CONTENTS.

Name	PAGE	Name	PAGE	Name	PAGE	Name	PAGE
Ensign, E. W.	470	Hilton, Seth	236	Linn, Joseph	642	Nettleton, Henry	699
Etter, F. G.	549	Hilton, D. C.	294	Lobdell, Charles S.	443	Newcomb, O. S.	708
		Hodgson, Asa	519	Lockwood, John H.	483	Newbury, F. E.	773
Eustis, M. D.	733	Hodson, James	519	Lockwood, R. B.	774	Newman, Hiram	518
Evans, Oliver	479	Hollenbeck, Michael	297	Logan, Michael	645	Nichlaus, P.	646
		Horr, R. R.	441	Logan, James	678	Niece, Michael	417
Failing, C. M.	336	Hostetler, David	500	Long, Perry	632	Niece, M. D. L.	309
Fairfield, W. B.	324	Houston, J. M.	519	Long, Norman	632	Norris, Robert	499
Fassett, R. E.	525	Hovey, Elias S.	424	Lovell, Wm.	486	Norton, Selden	526
Feltus, James	526	Hoovey, Lewis	429	Lucas, J. E.	763	Nugent, Michael	644
Feltus, George	525	Howe, John	518	Lucas, W. V.	289		
Ferris, S. W.	680	Howard, L. W.	700	Lyford, Wm. H.	586	Olmstead, Aaron	453
Ferguson, Jarvis E.	586	Howonstein, W. M	434			Olmstead, Nathan	452
Fetters, Samuel	470	Hubbard, A. W.	288	McCrery, W. L.	603	Orr, Jackson	288
Fifield, J. R.	469	Huckins, C. C.	352	McCrery, Samuel	603	Orvis, L. A.	340
Findley, S. B.	653	Hughes, R.	723	McDonald, Robert	726	Owen, L. D.	419
Fisher, Irving M.	763	Hull, L. O.	310	McIntyre, George A.	342	Owen, Henry	419
Fisher, George	532	Hunt, Thomas	514	McKerman, Robert	689	Owens, Edward	646
Fitzgerald, Stephen	584	Hunt, H. D.	519	McKinney, James W.	673	Otthoff, Ottze	646
Fletcher, J. E.	332	Hunt, W. T.	727	McMahon, Peter	638	Overturf, Samuel	681
Flood, William	517	Hunter, R. F.	621	McMannes, S.	684		
Flora, Abraham	551	Hunter, W. M.	473	McRoberts, Samuel	551	Packard, Joseph	585
Foote, S. A.	434	Husband, G. T.	704	Mihee, F. D.	562	Paley, J. H	717
Foote, William M	336	Hyde, Willis	296	Manley, N. T.	432	Parker, J. D.	442
Forney, C. H.	583			Major, Wm.	519	Parker, James F	442
Forney, Alexander	586	Ilgenfritz, C. H.	297	Marts, D. J.	336	Parker, Pascal P.	416
Freeman, M. J.	604	Ilgenfritz, A. J.	535	March, Samuel	525	Parker, Patrick	732
Frowe, Frederick	696	Ilgenfritz, Henry	536	Martin, Robert	734	Parker, Frank	733
				Markle, George	525	Parris Brothers	433
Gabby, A. M.	526	Jackson, Frank D.	341	Margretz, J. S.	696	Parriott, R. R.	734
Gabby, Thomas B.	529	Jamison, W. R.	334	Marquand, E. D.	606	Pattee, William W.	296
Gates, Johnson	507	Jamieson, L. W.	473	Mason, D. W.	336	Patton, J. E.	724
Gibson, J. R.	701	Jaquis, Elihu	421	Mason, D. W.	342	Patterson, William	605
Giblin, John	620	Johnson, Charles	702	Mason, George	585	Patterson, A. B.	607
Gilger, J. W.	336	Johnson, Wm. R.	680	Mather, Charles T.	583	Paulger, John	469
Gleason, Martin	697	Johnson, A. K.	353	Mather, Daniel	501	Peet, George R.	530
Gleason, Charles L.	424	Johnson, N. T.	344	Maxwell, Francis	486	Perrin, Jeremiah	495
Glodery, Andrew	568	Jones, John R	268-503	Maxwell, John	486	Pfaltzgraff, Philip	685
Gough, William	749	Jones, Charles A.	705	Maxwell, E. S.	471	Pfaltzgraff, Fred	651
Goodale, Jonathan	433	Jones, Charles L.	771	Mayberry, L. V.	490	Playter, John B	771
Graham, George	370	Jones, Frank A.	771	Meade, Geo. E.	725	Playter, H. J.	768
Graham, J. A.	725			Meade, John H.	704	Poisal, George W.	501
Graham, W. H.	723	Keenan, James	730	Mead, R. P.	642	Poisal, Byron L.	515
Graves, Zur	340	Keister, William A.	478	Merrill, Richard	369	Pomeroy, Charles	288
Green, K. S.	631	Kemmerer, Jacob	416	Messerschmidt, H.	633	Powers, M. I.	354
Greene, C. M.	741	Kent, F. P.	490	Meyer, Albert	490	Pratt, Henry O	288
Greene, G. P.	714	Kenison, Sevedra	773	Miles, John	681	Prescott, R. D.	342
Greene, H.	701	Kenefick, Patrick	730	Miller, Joseph	550	Price, W. H	585
Griffith, James	308	Kennedy, Samuel	718	Miller, Charles	491	Priest, Benjamin	602
Groat, James M	439	Kephart, T. E.	536	Miller, Philip	744	Prince, Charles S.	654
Gue, W. H.	370	Kerns, J. H.	641	Miner, Richard	565		
		Killen, Gawn S.	489	Mitchell, Wellington	508	Quinn, Rachel	729
Hagey, William H. H.	353	Kilson, Louis	743	Monroe, George W., Jr.	569		
Hale, J. H.	294	Kimmins, John	517	Montgomery, W. S.	342	Ramsy, Charles	587
Hall, J. R.	507	Kincaid, Edwin	688	Moore, Wm.	552	Ransom, C. M.	608
Hall, Jacob	417	Kingery, Wm.	549	Moore, Elihu	552	Ray, John	501
Hart, John M	549	Klinetob, C. P.	605	Moore, W. H.	516	Ray, John W	296
Harlan, James	673	Knapp, J.	422	Moore, J. W.	528	Reed, J. P.	314
Harlan, Jehu	674	Knapp, Horace	520	Moore, Fletcher	555	Reed, W. J.	726
Harter, Aaron M	491	Knipe, Jacob R.	443	Moorehead, J. G.	687	Reints, H. W.	655
Harmon, C. R.	471	Kocher, Jeremiah	768	Morrill, Frederick	586	Renken, R. G.	436
Hartson, A. E.	631	Krebbs, Jacob	351	Morton, John H.	369	Ressler, Amos	637
Hartness, John	538	Kremer, G. K. D	633	Moss, Jacob	490	Ressler, Elias	704
Hartness, Moulton	538	Kublank, J. H.	727	Mott, C. I.	434	Rice, Sylvester	698
Hartgraves, N.	630	Kyle, Adam	489	Mott, E. E.	604	Rice, Orson	332
Haven, E. M.	774			Moulton, David	536	Richmond, George A.	533
Hawley, G. C.	698	Ladd, William A.	590	Mullen, J. M.	723	Richmond, John F	555
Hays, Wm.	616	Lafaver, Geo.	656	Mullen, J. H.	724	Riden, W. A.	505
Haynes, T. L.	712	Lamson, C. T.	688	Mullarkey, Hugh	617	Riefe, Henry	556
Haynes, William H	712	Landis, Felix	550	Mundinger, Jacob	423	Riggs, J. S.	349
Hazen, L. P.	637	Landphere, J. D.	697	Murray, W. W.	713	Robinson, John	589
Hazlett, Gilbert	299	Lathrop, W. A.	339	Myers, Jacob R.	722	Roberts, J. D.	513
Heery, John	502	Leavens, Bainbridge	518			Robbins, Benjamin	703
Henderson, D. B.	288	Lee, A. W.	288	Nash, Thomas	641	Rockwell, J. G.	729
Hersey, Wm.	422	Lott, A. N.	609	Neal, James	588	Root, Milton R.	585
Hesulroad, Wm.	552	Lenhart, Samuel	517	Neal, John P.	525	Root, George C.	608
Hewitt, John	743	Levally, Lafayette	551	Neal, Joseph N.	751	Rozell, C. A. L.	335
Hicks, Joseph	235	Lewis, Baldwin D.	471	Neal, John H	773	Royce, Orlin	417
Hickle, John	505	Leverick, James	297	Needham, B. C	677	Russell, Thomas	418
Hickman, John B	607	Leybrig, Emanuel	551	Needham, Silas	678	Russell, Geo. L	418
Hill, C. H.	644	Linn, Nathan	620	Nelson, Chas. B	601	Russell, F. M	608

TABLE OF CONTENTS.

	PAGE		PAGE		PAGE		PAGE
Santee, Joseph L	688	Sproul, Rev. O. H	1314	Tilford, J. Y	517	Weed, Phineas	700
Scallon, H. G	731	Stannard, Asa	696	Tindal, John	490	Weeks, Henry	423
Scott, Oscar, H	343	Stewart, John W	370	Tobey, Elisha	729	Wemple, Henry B	415
Scobey, John	354	Stevenson, John	608	Tompkins, A. J	293	Whaley, A. M	291
Scofield, J	605	Stewart, J. L	707	Town, E	722	Wheeler, O. J	698
Schoolcraft, D. W	439	Stock, Wilhelm	632	Tracey, Edward S	551	Wheeler, Horace A	773
Schellenger, C. G	508	Stockdale, Chas	738	Trinde, George	750	Whipple, Nelson H	472
Seaver, J. W	474	Stonebreaker, A. G	716	Trotter, James A	619	Whitehead, James	699
Seitz, A	558	Stoughton, Wm	335	Trotter, Henry	688	Wick, D. M	353
Shafer, Wm.W. R	585	Strout, A. O	354–782	Trumbull, M. M	330	Weichman, E	733
Shafer, Thomas	552	Sturtz, Solomon	552	Turner, Abel	414	Wilson, Elwood	294
Shannon, John A	583	Straight, A	643	Turner, E. Leroy	351	Wilcox, A. C	608
Shadbolt, Jerome	516	Strickland, R. D	469			Wilson, Milton	476–782
Sill, Samuel	723	Surfus, C. V	744			Wilkes, John	750
Sill, E. E	358	Swan, H. M	508	Vandever, William	287	Wilkinson, E. A	520
Slimmer, Lewis	535	Sweitzer, H. L	696	VanVlack, William	621	Williams, Samuel	619
Slosson, Henry	518			VanVleck, G. O	724	Williams, James W	586
Smith, W. C	590	Tammen, Mr	439			Williams, E. H	324
Smith, Samuel	632	Taylor, Morrison A	236			Winne, Jurian	732
Smith, A. J	543	Taylor, Sylvanus H	418	Wade, Michael	489	Winsett, J. K	756
Smith, G. B	654	Taylor, J. R	516	Wait, Daniel	605	Woodworth, Wm. P	679
Smith, Orrin C	480	Taylor, W. R	519	Walker, H. N	624	Wrey, Wm	491
Smith, L. L	472	Temple, Julius	585	Walker, Joseph	608	Wright, J. F	711
Smith, W. H	358	Tennyson, John	606	Walter, Elias	526	Wright, Wm	643
Smith, A. E	536	Tharp, Washington	702	Walrath, James	514		
Smith, J. M	537	Thorp, E. L	357	Wamsley, Henry	586		
Smith, Robert	749	Thomas, Edward S	295	Wamsley, John M	590	Yost, Jacob	689
Snyder, Peter B	353	Thomas, Hugh	580	Wamsley, M. V	604	Young, E. J	717
Soesbe, E. W	319	Thomas, Chas. N	590	Wamsley, M. B	493	Young, Wm	352
Soesbe, S. W	336	Thompson, J. D	324	Wamsley, W. S	493	Younker, George	415
Speedy, M. B	620	Thompson, Thomas	618	Wamsley, W. C	513	Younker, Wm. F	415
Speaker, John	710	Thompson, N. C	618	Warner, A. C	643		
Spencer, A. M	440	Thompson, N. A	618	Watson, Wolcott	613		
Spencer, James W	293	Thompson, Charles	750	Waters, Isaac	418		
Spoor, Isaac	555	Thorington, James	287	Watson, Alvin	632	Zell, August	631

PORTRAITS.

	PAGE		PAGE		PAGE		PAGE
Adair, Wm	695	Early, T. M	735	Jackson, F. D	563	Perrin, Jeremiah	498
		Ensign, S. B	356	Jamison, W. R	373	Perrin, Mrs	499
Baldwin, S. M	612			Jones, J. R	391	Priest, E. F	779
Baldwin, Mrs. S. M	613						
Brown, H. C	283	Fisher, I. M	746	Lathrop, W. A	337	Riden, W. A	510
		Fisher, Mrs. I. M	747	Lee, A. W	502	Riden, Mrs. W. A	511
Cayle, Peter	467			Lee, Mrs. A. W	593		
						Stroot, A. O	427
Davis, J. W	265	Harlan, John	665	Needham, B. C	675	Sturtz, Solomon	553
Dodge, F. L	758	Hull, L. O	320			Surfus, C. V	409
Dodge, Mrs. F. L	759	Hunt, H. D	522	Parker, P. P	437	Whaley, A. M	301
Dumont, S. B	247	Hunt, Mrs. H. D	523	Peet, George R	533	Wilson, Milton	477

HISTORY
OF
BUTLER COUNTY,
IOWA

CHAPTER I.

THE CHANGE.

AS the changes of less than half a century are contemplated, one can scarcely realize or comprehend that the wonderful results of time's marvel-working hand are the achievements of a period so brief as to be within the remembrance—almost—of the present generation.

Let us turn back, as it were, the leaves of time's great book to but a quarter of a century ago, and the stranger would have gazed upon a landscape of great beauty; selected by the Sioux and Dakotahs as their camping-ground, with that singular appreciation of the beautiful which nature made an instinct in the savage. These vast and rolling prairies were as green then as now; the prairie flowers bloomed as thickly and diffused their fragrance as bountifully. We are in the haunt of the red man, with scarcely a trace of civilization. But what a contrast! Then all was as nature formed it, with its variegated hues of vegetation; in winter a dreary snow-mantled desert, in summer a perfect paradise of flowers. Now all traces of the primitive are obliterated; in place of the tall prairie grass and tangled under-brush, one beholds the rich waving fields of golden grain. In place of the dusky warrior's rude cabins are the substantial and often elegant dwellings of the thrifty farmers, and the "iron horse," swifter than the nimble deer, treads the pathway so recently the trail of the red man. Then the sickle of fire annually cut away the wild herbage and drove to its death the stag; now it is the home of the cereals and nourishes on its broad bosom thousands of tons of the staple products of the great Hawkeye State. Then the storm drove the were-wolf to its hiding place; now the blast drives the herd of the husbandman to comfortable shelter. The transformation is complete.

ORGANIZATION OF THE COUNTY.

In early days, Butler county was merged into and made a part of Buchanan, for judicial and local government purposes. It was, however, so sparsely settled at the time that it never took any part in the councils of that county, nor is there any record showing that polls were opened at any point for the election of officers for the "consolidated county," so that the territory was called a part of Buchanan more for convenience than owing to the fact. The whole of Butler was then considered one township.

In 1853 enough settlements had been made to warrant an attempt to organize the county. Accordingly, in May of that year, Judge Roszell, of Buchanan county, appointed John T. Barrick, D. C. Overman and William G. Payne as commissioners for that purpose, and for the location of the county seat. They selected Clarksville, as narrated elsewhere. In the following August the same magistrate ordered an election for Butler county, which was then under his judicial jurisdiction. This election was for organization and county officers. The officers were elected, among whom was George W. Poisal, County Judge; but none qualified, because there was "no money in it."

Soon after this Butler was detached from Buchanan county and attached to Black Hawk, which had been recently organized. Pursuant to the order of Judge Knapp, of Black Hawk county, a second election was held in August, 1854, when the following officers were chosen: John Palmer, County Judge; W. E. Burton, Clerk; Abner G. Clark, Treasurer and Recorder; James Griffith, School Fund Commissioner; Robert T. Crowell, Sheriff; Harlan Baird, Prosecuting Attorney; John H. Morton, Surveyor. Baird failed to qualify, and Aaron Van Dorn was appointed to fill the vacancy. The permanent organization was affected on the second of October, 1854, and on the 28th of the same month the first taxes were levied, amounting to $698.50.

GEOGRAPHICAL LOCATION AND GEOGRAPHY.

Butler county is one of the centre of the Northeastern Iowa counties, being contiguous to Floyd county on the north, Bremer and Black Hawk on the east, Grundy on the south, and Franklin on the west. It comprises the territory of townships 90 to 93 north inclusive, of range 15 to 18 west of the fifth principal meridian inclusive, containing an area of 576 square miles, or 368,640 acres. This forms a perfect square of 24 miles each way, and is divided into 16 townships of 36 square miles each.

The general inclination of the surface is a slope to the east and south, and is made up of rolling prairie, with no abrupt break of ground sufficient to be detrimental to agriculture, except in the vicinity of the streams where the surface is often quite broken. This region is known as the "valley of the Cedar and Shell Rock," and has a wide reputation as the "Garden spot of Iowa," while the rivers are frequently called the "gems of Iowa waters," there being in the estimation of many, little, if any choice between them.

The territory of Butler county is diversified with belts of timber and streams of very pure water. These streams take southeasterly courses, with one exception—

that of Beaver creek—which flows almost directly east through the southern tier of townships, and empties into the Cedar just above Cedar Falls. The source of this stream is in the southern part of Franklin county. Its flow of water is not great, but constant, being fed by many springs and tributaries, which increase its flow so that by the time it reaches Parkersburg a good water power is furnished. This is the southern of the three important streams which cross the county. North of this stream another water-course, taking its rise in Cerro Gordo county, passes nearly diagonally through Butler county from northwest to southeast. This is the West Fork of the Cedar. It is sluggish in its flow, more so than the Beaver, and the bed is of a sandy and muddy nature. The land for quite a distance back from the bed, is inclined to be marshy, and is among the best grazing and hay land in the county. There are many small streams which help to swell this body of water at different points. The next is the most important stream in the county, and one of the most prominent in Iowa—the Shell Rock. It is one of the most beautiful streams in the west. Its banks from its source in Minnesota, to its confluence with the Cedar, are of limestone, and its pure sparkling waters flash along with a rapidity far exceeding any other stream in the State, even the "Clasic Cedar," of which, so much has been said and written, is a poor comparison. It enters the county from the north at about an equal distance from the east and west county lines, flows in a southeastern direction, and leaves to enter Bremer county at a point in the southeastern part of Shell Rock township. The width of the river will average about three hundred feet between the banks, and the flow of water is capable of propelling a vast amount of machinery at any season of the year, affording a power every five miles.

A minute description of soil and surface features, or local peculiarities, will be found in connection with the history of the various townships,

MOUNT NEBO AND ITS CAVE.

In the township of Coldwater is a ridge or hill, known as Mount Nebo. Under this is a miniature cave or cavern, which has interesting points connected with it. An attempt was made to explore it in 1875, and, in speaking of the adventure, a local writer said: "This cave has been known for several years, and there are some legends connected with it. One is that it was once used as a place of habitation; another is that a mysterious well of great depth exists somewhere within its bounds. A few days ago a party went down to explore it, but all backed out but J. Dexter and Mr. Barker, whose curiosity was greater than their caution. The place of entrance was small, but they soon found rooms in which they could stand erect, and some from eight to twelve feet high. Passages from one room to another were usually small, some so small that the explorers found difficulty in passing from one to another. After visiting numerous rooms in search of the well, and proceeding three or four hundred feet from the entrance, they returned without finding it. In several places there were supporting pillars, and along the walls resemblances to stalactites. The limits were not reached, and there is still room for adventurers to gratify their curiosity.

RAILROADS.

There are three lines of railway traversing the territory of Butler county, in all directions, and connecting it with the eastern markets. Besides those that cross the country, there are lines of railway within easy reach of the producers of Butler county, just over the line, both east and west. It will thus be seen that shipping facilities are excellent.

The following is the course and location of the various roads:

The Burlington, Cedar Rapids and Northern railway enters the county from the southeast, and follows the Shell Rock valley across the northeastern part of the county. It was built in 1871.

The Iowa Division of the Illinois Central Railroad line crosses the county from east to west, through the southern tier of townships, having been constructed in 1865.

The Dubuque and Dakota railroad crosses the county in the same direction; entering with the Shell Rock river it follows the valley northward to Clarksville, where it makes an abrupt curve to the west, crosses the country in the second tier of townships from the north. This road was graded through in 1875, by the Iowa and Pacific Railroad Company. This company failed, and the road came into the possession of the Dubuque and Dakota Railroad Company, composed of capitalists in Dubuque. The track was laid and trains running through Butler county in 1879. The line is not by any means completed, only running from Sumner, in Bremer county, to Hampton, in Franklin county.

CHAPTER II.

EARLY SETTLEMENT.

Long before there was even any thought of permanent settlement in this region, and while the confines of civilization were yet resting midway between the Mississippi and Ohio, the valley of the Shell Rock and Cedar rivers had been made the resort of trappers and hunters, whose territory knows no bounds. They had followed both of these famous streams from mouth to source, in quest of mink and beaver, and it is not strange that the first settlers stationed themselves along the banks in their tracks. The Shell Rock valley, which traverses the eastern portion of the county, was the scene of the earliest settlement.

There are differences of opinion as to who was the first to make permanent settlement in the county, and it is a hard matter to settle conclusively, as there is no one now living, who can be interviewed, who positively knows. It can only be given as tradition hands it down.

Late in the fall of 1850, two hunter brothers, Harrison and Volney Carpenter, and D. C. Finch, wended their way up the valley of the Shell Rock in quest of game. They had come from Linn county, where they had also stopped for a time. It was a magnificent country, and game of all descriptions abounded. Upon arriving at the point on the river where the village of Shell Rock now rests, they determined to make that spot a temporary home, while they scoured the country for game. A little log cabin was accordingly erected, in which they took up their abode, and for about one year made this a sort of a "huntsman's rendezvous," when Volney, who was a married man, moved his family there. The whereabouts of any of the party at present, or whether they are yet alive, we are unable to state. The grove afterward took the name of Carpenter's Grove.

The first *permanent* settler in the county was Joseph Hicks, who, in December, 1850, tediously made his way up the Shell Rock, and located near the present site of the town of Clarksville, erecting his little log cabin about one mile to the west. Robert T. Crowell came at this time to bring the family of Hicks, and then returned to Wisconsin. Hicks, during this winter, was obliged to personate a pack mule, and carry provisions on his back from Cedar Falls, then a small trading post. The nearest neighbor of Hicks' was James Newell, who, a short time previous, had settled in the forks of the Cedar, about twenty miles to the southeast. Until spring Hicks spent most of his time in hunting, fishing and trapping, and then cultivated a small piece of ground which he planted to corn and vegetables. His wife was a true western heroine, and could "talk injun,"-or shoot a rifle equal to "any other man;" it being a common belief that she could shoot a rifle ball between the lids of a deer's eye on a run. They came from Rock county, Wisconsin, and the grove in which they settled afterward took the name of Coon's Grove. At this time the Shell Rock also went under the name of English river. When the latter name was dropped is unknown.

In the spring of 1851, Joseph's father, Henry Hicks, came on from Rock county, Wisconsin, and locating with his children, he erected a blacksmith shop where he hammered away and forged the first iron in the Shell Rock Valley, until he was called upon to pay the debt of mortality, in 1854.

The first piece of land that a patent was received for was that upon which John Heery, of Milton, Wisconsin, located in 1850. It lies just in the bend of the Shell Rock river, adjoining Clarksville on the southwest. Heery returned to Milton the same season, making the trip both ways on foot, and returned to his claim some years later.

R. G. Crowell, who is mentioned as having come to this county in December, 1850, bringing the family of Joseph Hicks, returned to Wisconsin, and in the spring of 1852 came back and took a claim which was afterwards purchased by Alexander Glenn. Crowell remained here a number of years, and was the first Sheriff of Butler county. He finally sold his excellent farm and went to California. He was not satisfied there, however, and again returned to Clarksville, and settled upon a farm a few miles northeast of town. He is now at Spirit Lake.

In the spring of 1851, two brothers from Ohio—Malon B., and William S. Wamsley—came and took claims a short distance northwest of Clarksville. They were honored and respected citizens, and are mentioned frequently elsewhere in this work.

During the summer and fall of 1851, a number of additions were made to the meagre settlement in this part of the county, among whom were Morrison A. Taylor, E. Ensley and Jeremiah Perrin.

Morrison A. Taylor came with his family in September, 1851, and settled a short distance east of Clarksville, where he commenced valuable improvements, but he was called by death from the midst of a loving family, on the 30th of December, 1856. He was a man of sterling integrity, and his loss made a lasting impression on the little community.

E. Ensley came the same summer and located about two miles from where the town now is. He left some years ago.

Jeremiah Perrin, with his family, made their appearance in September, 1851, and commenced pioneering on a place a short distance from where he is now comfortably fixed. His estimable wife died in 1865, mourned by all.

Seth Hilton, Sr., first came in December, 1851, but did not move his family until March 23, 1852. He erected a small log cabin about fifty rods southwest of where the depot, at Clarksville, now stands. In April, 1853, he erected a cabin on what soon after became the town plat. He came from Southern Illinois. In that State he was also a pioneer, always in advance of railroads. He never saw a locomotive or train of cars until those of the B. C. R. & N. R. R. run across his farm. He is now over eighty years of age, as fine an old gentleman as any one would wish to meet. In 1852 a number of others came, and the settlement thus started in the eastern part of the county branched out and began to embrace not only the eastern tier of towns, but Jackson and Jefferson also had received a few settlers.

George W. Poisall came in July, 1853, and went into quarters on the brow of the hill east of the old Stone School House at Clarksville. Here he remained until 1854, when he sold to Dan. Mather, moved a short distance further north and laid out "Poisall's addition" to Clarksville. Uncle George, as he is familiarly called, still lives.

John T. Baughman, Alfred Elam, Hiram Beard, John Armstrong, C. N. Burton, W. E. Burton, and W. R. Butler, all came this year and located in the neighborhood. John Heery, who has been previously mentioned, brought his family this year.

The Clark brothers also came and located near the present town.

The above were about all of the very earliest settlers in this region, and all of those who are yet alive are in comfortable circumstances.

During the spring, summer and fall of 1854, a number more came in rapid succession, among whom the names of the following are remembered: O. A. Strong, John H. Morton, John Palmer, David Blakely, A. VanDorn, T. T. Rawson, J. J. Eichar, M. M. Trumbull, William Brandon, R. Hardy, Abner Farlow, J. M. Vincent and Daniel Mather.

The settlement spoken of embraced the eastern part of the county. In the meantime the northern part of the county had received its first settlers, and neighborhoods began to spring up. Among the pioneers of this region, irrespective of order as to the time they came in, were, Mr. Laken, Comodore Bennett, John Fox, Lum Coleston, James Griffith, John and Aaron Hardman, John H. Miller, John Boggs, John M. Hart, Dave Miller, Elias Miller, John and William Strong, Felix Landis, R. W. Butler, Levi Burress, James Blake, P. J. Ebersold, William Gough, Hugh Thomas, P. Ebersold, Delano McCain, J. F. Eikenberry, John V. Boggs, McCarty and Nelson Bement, James G. Temple, Robert Renfrew, Shadrach Bonnell, John Lainhart, J. J. Cross and Milton Wilson.

In the western part of the county among the pioneers were, W. R. Jamison, John, James, Asa and Isaac Boylan, Philip Miller, George Lash, Benjamin Needham, Messrs. Early, Parks, McKinney, Rust and Nichols, Ancel Durand, and Dr. Sprague.

The southern portion of the county was also being settled, and among the pioneers there, were, Charles and Titus Ensign, Louis Hammond, Nathan Olmstead, J. M. Caldwell, Clayton Mullarky, P. P. Parker, Messrs. Wilbur, Cramer, Parriott, Nash, the Quinns, Rube Russell, R. R. Parriott and others.

These are the names of all of the earliest pioneers who can be remembered at present writing. The different localities are taken up, in regard to early settlement, and treated at length in the history of the various townships.

FIRST THINGS.

The first postoffice established in Butler county was at Coon Grove, now Clarksville, in 1853, with Abner G. Clark as postmaster.

The first birth in the county, occurred in March, 1852, and ushered into existence a son of Jeremiah and Elizabeth Perrin. The child was named William, and only lived about six months.

The first death occurred in the fall of the year previous, 1851, and carried away Joseph Kirker, aged forty years. His death occurred at the house of W. S. Wamsley.

Malon B. Wamsley was appointed the first justice of the peace in the county in the fall of 1853, by the county court of Black Hawk county.

The first religious society incorporated in the county was the Methodist Episcopal Church, of Shell Rock, who filed their articles of incorporation on the 26th of June, 1855.

The first civic society was a Masonic Lodge, established in Clarksville early in June, 1857.

On the 24th of the same month William Hicks, an Englishman, was the first foreigner in the county to renounce his allegiance to the British crown and declare his intention to become a citizen of the United States. John Palmer and William Glass took like steps toward citizenship the same day. William Gough, a native of England, who had declared his intention in Bremer county, was the first foreigner admitted to full American citizenship in Butler county, which was accomplished on the 6th of October, 1857. Patrick Hayes was the next person naturalized, at the same term of court. Pat was an Irishman.

The first school in the county was opened in a little log cabin at Clarksville, in 1855. The first term was taught by Miss Malinda Searles.

The first sermon preached within the limits of Butler county, was in the fall of 1851, at the house of Malon B. Wamsley, near the present town of Clarksville. The preacher was a Methodist, but his name is lost from memory.

The first lawyer in the county was M. M. Trumbull, now of Chicago. See history of bar.

The first physician in the county was Dr. James E. Walker, a native of Maine. He was county clerk for a number of years; but has long since returned to his native State.

The first marriage license was issued by Judge Palmer to Greenberry Luck and Susan Williams, on November 1st, 1854, and they were married the same day. They were at last accounts living in Beaver township, and had a family of nearly one dozen children. This marriage license precedes all others on the record books in the clerk's office, although two others bear earlier dates. They are given elsewhere.

FOURTH OF JULY CELEBRATION IN 1857 AT NEW HARTFORD.

The villagers and citizens of the surrounding country felt the necessity of helping to save the Union, so far as manifesting their patriotism was concerned, and on the fourth day of July, 1857, the anniversary of the Nation's independence, was celebrated in grand style. The officers of the day were: Martin Bailey, President; E. S. Shaw, Marshal; Judd Bradley, Assistant Marshal, and Alonzo Converse, Orator.

At this time the subject of moving the county seat from Clarksville was being considerably agitated, and the southern portion of the county were advocating the nomination of Mr. Converse for County Judge, who was known to be favorable to said removal. When it was known that Mr. Converse was to deliver the oration at this celebration, quite a large number from other parts of the county were in attendance to see "what manner of man this removal candidate" was. Everything passed off very pleasantly and patriotically, and those who participated went home feeling in good spirits and that the day had been profitably spent.

Mr. Converse—we will say right here—was elected the following August, and during the campaign promulgated the generally accepted "silver rule" of "Do unto others as they do unto you."

This was the first celebration in the county, so far as the historian can find.

CHAPTER III.

IN EARLY DAYS.

The following account of personal matters is given to show the disadvantages under which the hardy pioneers procured the homes, which now seem so comfortable. Whatever of romance adhered to the hardy colonists, was abundantly compensated for by hard work. Contrast the journey of that devoted party through the roadless and bridgeless tract between their destination and Chicago, with a party on a like journey to-day. Instead of weeks of labor and toil, privation and suffering, with cold and hunger, a seat is taken in a palace car, at noon, in Chicago, an unexceptional supper is partaken without leaving the train, the passenger retires upon a downy couch, and in the morning awakes to find himself at his point in central or northern Iowa, having lost only half a day on the journey. Those who enjoy these blessings would be less than human if they were not filled with gratitude to these early settlers, who paved the way, and actually made the present condition of things possible. At that time the confines of civilization were on the lakes; Chicago had not many thousand people, Milwaukee was just beginning to be a village and Dubuque was a mere vidette, as an outpost of civilization. There was nothing in the now great State of Iowa, except the intrinsic merit of the location, to attract people from their more or less comfortable homes in the East, or on the other side of the water. The hope as to the future, which "springs eternal in the human heart" was what lured them on, and although those that came were usually regarded by the friends they left, as soldiers of fortune, who, if they ever returned at all, would indeed be fortunate. They were a sturdy race, who realized the inequality of the struggle in the old States or countries, and resolved to plant themselves, where merit would not be suppressed by traditions.

The men who came were, as a rule, enterprising, open-hearted and sympathizing, they were good neighbors, and so good neighborhoods were created, and they illustrated the idea of the brotherhood of man more by example than by quoting creeds, with a bravery that never blanched in the presence of the most appalling danger, they nevertheless were tender, kind and considerate in the presence of misfortune, and their deficiency in outward manifestations of piety was more than compensated by their love and regard for humanity. And if this meed of praise is justly due to the men, and it certainly is, what shall be said of the heroic women who braved the vicissitudes of frontier life, endured the absence of home, friends and old associations, whose tender ties must have wrung all hearts as they were severed. The devotion which would lead to such a breaking away, to follow a father, a husband or a son into the trackless waste beyond the Mississippi, where gloomy apprehensions must have arisen in the mind, is above all praise. The value of the part taken by the noble women who first came to this uninhabited region cannot be over estimated. Although by nature liberal, they practiced the most liberal economy, and often at critical times preserved order, reclaiming the men from despair during gloomy periods; and their example of industry constantly admonished him to renewed exertion; and the instincts of womanhood constantly encouraged integrity and manhood.

As to the effects of frontier life upon those who have secured homes west of the Mississippi, a few observations may not be inappropriate.

Years ago the Rev. Dr. Bushnell, a noted divine in the east, preached a sermon on the barbarous tendencies of civilization in the West, and on this the Reverend gentleman predicted an urgent—and we almost said, frantic—appeal to Christianity to put forth renewed and strenuous efforts to save the west from a relapse into barbarism. This tendency was supposed to result from the disruption of social and religious ties, the mingling of heterogeneous elements, and the removal of the external restraints, so common, and supposed to be so patent in older communities. Dr. Bushnell did not have a sufficiently extended view of the subject, for in looking over the history of the past, we find that in a nomadic position there is never any real progress in refinement. Institutions for the elevation of the race must be planted deep in the soil before they can raise their heads in beauty and majesty towards Heaven, and bear fruit for the enlightenment of nations The evils of which Dr. Bushnell was so afraid are merely temporary in their character, and will have no lasting impression. What actually happens is this, at first there is an obvious increase of human freedom, but the element of self government everywhere largely predominates, and the fusion of the races which is inevitable, will in due time create a composite nationality, or a race as unlike as it must be superior to those that have preceded it. Even now, before the first generation has passed away, society in the west has outgrown the irritation of the transplanting, and there are no more vicious elements in society here than in the east, as the criminal statistics will abundantly show.

THE INDIAN WAR.

To W. L. Palmer's well written "History of Clarksville," we are indebted for the following graphic description of this memorable time:

"In the spring or early part of the summer of 1854, the nerves of the whole population of North-central Iowa were set into a terrible flutter by the announcement, heralded throughout the country, that the noble 'red men' were greatly incensed by the appearance of numerous pale faces within their, to them, legitimate territory, and that they proposed to massacre, at one fell swoop, every man, woman and child. Had the shock of an earthquake, or the coming of a second deluge been announced, with as much probable certainty, the panic could not have been more successful, and for days and nights, the most timid might have been seen rapidly running toward the south. In some instances everything was left in the rear except sufficient to sustain life until a 'heavier settlement' could be reached. But all did not act thus. The bugle was sounded, the standard unfurled, and courageous volunteers rallied to its support.

Colonel Abner Eads, at that time Superintendent of Public Instruction for the State, happened to be in Cedar Falls. Having been an officer in the army during the war with Mexico, he was immediately elected impromptu commander-in-chief of all the forces that were about to engage in the prolonged and bloody campaign, and promptly set himself about organizing, drilling and reviewing two companies of volunteer 'dragoons.' During the organization, M. M. Trumbull, who was a sergeant of artillery in the Mexican war, and who had distinguished himself in the battles of Palo Alto, Monterey, Chepultepec, etc., was honored, by the Colonel, with the position of Adjutant-General and Chief-of-Staff. Ed. Brown was captain of the company from Black Hawk, and Jerry Farris of that from Bremer. So soon as the roads and weather would permit, 'Brigadier' Eads headed his noble column and boldly struck out for the frontier. When the column had reached Clarksville, its ranks were considerably swollen by the gradual 'falling-in' of strong-hearted recruits from the wayside. At Clarksville it halted for supper, a night's rest and a council of war, after a forced march of twenty-five miles. The refreshments were generously furnished by the remaining citizens, who were so extremely patriotic that they would not 'take a cent;' but, when the troops proceeded the next day, found they had been eaten out of 'house and home.' The decision at the council of war no man knew, save those in authority, but were compelled to 'guess' from the proceedings which followed. A small detachment of 'regulars' was left with the citizens, under orders to erect a fort—on the hill where Mr. Baughman's residence now is—and not delay a moment until its completion. The noble little garrison went manfully to work; detailed two-thirds of their number for picket duty, while the rest began sinking trenches and throwing up breast-works, never stopping a moment except to eat, drink and sleep. During the progress of this work, the main column had proceeded as far northwest as Clear Lake, and frightened a few whites and a number of Winnebagoes almost out of their wits, who thought *them* red-skins. All the excitement was caused by the murder of a 'skinaway' and the scalping of an old 'squaw' belonging to the Winnebago tribe, by a marauding band of Sioux. The troops bivouacked for the night, and many were the disappointed heroes who would be compelled to return the next day bearing the sad tale to their friends that the Indian War was a myth, and that they were not permitted, by kind Providence, to wholly exterminate the very name of 'Injun' from the face of the earth, by pouring out their lifes' blood in defense of their homes and firesides. During the home march of the veterans they were not so careful of their powder as on their northern trip, and occasionally amused themselves by discharging a shot at some wayside object, the reports of which 'panicized' the remaining settlers, who flew to the protection of Fort Eads, at Clarksville. Adjutant-General and Chief-of-Staff Trumbull, when the troops went into camp for the night, strolled away in search of the Shell Rock river for the purpose of bathing. While enjoying the refreshing bath, he chanced to observe a woman, near the bank opposite, washing clothes. An idea struck him. He would rush wildly into camp and report that Indians, thousands of them, were on the opposite side of the river, and were preparing an attack. The disclosure had the desired effect. 'Boots and saddles' was immediately sounded, and the bold soldiers were off in a trice; not toward the enemy, but each upon his own hook, bound to receive shelter behind the protecting walls of the little fortification. When the headlong retreat of the troops, who had all been 'cut to pieces,' was known at the fort by the arrival of the better mounted dragoons—the only ones who escaped with their 'har'—the scenes in the fort could not have been better imagined than described; for there were assembled the women and children! Brave hearts almost ceased to perform their proper functions! Timid women wrung their hands and fainted, while the children wept at beholding the fearful carnage! Quietude was at length restored; a hearty laugh indulged in; the war ended, and all returned to their peaceful homes. Thus closed the Indian massacre of 1854.

THE SCARE IN THE NORTHERN PART OF THE COUNTY.

By W. A. Griffith.

In the early settlement of Coldwater township, when the telegraph was unknown, with no newspaper published nearer than Dubuque, and the nearest postoffice between thirty and forty miles distant, news came rather slowly, and unreliable when it was received; each man had to rely upon his neighbor for intelligence, which very often got mixed, as the following will show:

One stormy night in the month of June, in 1854, when the rain was pouring in torrents and the thunder shaking the very earth, Mr. James Griffith, in Coldwater township, was aroused by a cry of distress, warning himself and family to flee for their lives, as the cruel Sioux were rushing on toward him, massacreing and scalping his neighbors as they advanced. William Choate, his informant, told him he had no time to lose or his scalp, with those of his family, would soon be dangling from the belt of the savage warrior. Mr. Griffith, having no team by which to save his family, concluded to take them to the cabin of John H. Miller, who, being absent from home that night, had left his folks in Mr. G.'s charge. On getting to Mrs. Miller's he found his neighbors all gathered there, preparatory to fleeing the country; but Mr. Griffith, having two families on his hands, persuaded them to halt, and there those brave men decided to face death, defend their wives and little ones, and sell their lives as dearly as possible.

They stood guard all night, hourly expecting to hear the hideous yells of the unmerciful demons, and the breaking in upon them, until at length, after a night of deathly terror, the welcome dawn appeared, when, still as the silent grave, the men gathered their loved ones, ready to flee a country where every bush appeared to hide a lurking enemy, to a place of safety. Mr. John M. Hart, John V. Boggs and James Griffith decided to stand their ground, and not run; but their neighbors told them if they wanted to expose themselves to certain death, they did not, and the greater part of the residents of Coldwater left—some of them never stopping this side of the Mississippi line, and some of them, I fear, are running yet, for they never came back. In the morning, John H. Miller—having returned home in the meantime—and James Griffith, determined to risk their lives, ascertain the danger, and see to what extent the savages had devastated the country. They went up the river as far as "Beelar's Grove"—now Marble Rock —and found the citizens still in bed, unconscious of their danger; so they came back home, and went down the river as far as "Coon's Grove"—now the village of Clarksville—for the purpose of organizing a band for self-protection, and just as they were about to return home, M. M. Trumbull, now Colonel Trumbull, of Dubuque, arrived from the frontier, greatly excited, and on being interrogated about the locality of the Indians, he could not tell the exact locality, but that they were not far off. Some one asked, "Are they at Rock Grove?" His reply was "Nearer than that." "At Beelar's Grove?" "Nearer than that!" "At Coldwater?" And his reply was, "Gentlemen, I was on an Indian trail, and saw their fires this side of there!" Horror! Think of our Coldwater friends! What agony arose in their breasts, to think that their homes were destroyed, and all they held near and dear cruelly butchered or carried away captive. They accordingly mounted their horses, and ran them home. When north of Flood creek they discovered the fires, and marched straight to them; they proved to have been built by Mrs. Levi Burress and girls, who were washing on the banks of the Shell Rock river. They then came home, and found everybody alive and well, which greatly relieved our heroes.

The basis of the scare proved to be that a couple of Sioux and Winnebago Indians had got into a quarrel, which terminated in one of them being sent to the "happy hunting grounds," and the whites had no part whatever in the fight. Such was the great Indian scare of 1854.

HUNTING BY THE PIONEERS.

One of the earliest settlers has kindly written and contributed the following, which will be found interesting:

"When our county was new and thinly settled the settlers had hard times to live; yet this was somewhat relieved and interspersed by the pleasant times passed in hunting buffalos, deer, elk and other animals of the forest and prairie, on which the pioneers chiefly depended for meat, and in connection with their corn-bread, managed to eke out an existence.

From 1851 to 1856, hunting was the main employment of a great many of them, among whom were the Goheen brothers, E. R. and James, and one Tobias Miller, familiarly called 'Tobe,' who could bring down the buck at almost every shot. E. R. Goheen, has been so successful as to shoot twelve deer and one buffalo in a day. At one time he made a contract for furnishing deer for what the hides were worth, as they could shoot them standing on their door-steps. During the winter of 1853 and '54, E. R. and James Goheen surrounded a large buffalo on the present site of the Dunkard church, shot so as to cripple it. It was storming so that the game escaped, but was captured the next morning by Mr. Winchell, of Marble Rock. Thus deer meat was the staple article of food, and the poor pioneers got very tired of it; flour bread being a luxury in which but few indulged. In October, 1853, Mr. John Hart and James Griffith went to the nearest mill, which was located at Cedar Rapids, to get some flour, taking a four-horse team. The trip took one week, and when they got back their families lived in high style on white bread for a time, and it is stated that when 'we could get flour at Cedar Falls we were a happy people.' The pioneer struggled on until he is now reaping his reward, and can have his luxuries without the inconveniences of former times."

THE PRAIRIE FIRES.

The prairie fires during an early period were very damaging, and grew to be a terrible dread to the unprotected pioneers, whose only safety lay in the "fire-break," —a few furrows plowed around their farms

—and often the fire would "jump" the widest of them. Especially is this remembered by the pioneers of the southern tier of townships, as in one of the fires a little girl of Jacob Codner's was burned to death. In the fall of '56, the worst fire ever known to pass over this region, ravaged the country for miles. It started somewhere on the prairies of Grundy county, and the wind, blowing a perfect hurricane, drove the tempest of fire northward with lightning speed, reaping a swath of destruction miles in width. It came into the Parkersburg timber, and killed the greater part of it. Mr. Curtis, who lived just in the north edge, across the Beaver, had to fight for life against the elements. Its progress was not stayed in the least by the stream, and the fire swept around to the north, jumping the West Fork, south of Butler Center, and Samuel Gillard, who had settled in this locality in the fall of '55, was nearly burned to death.

THE FERRY LOST.

The Mr. Curtis, mentioned, came in the fall of 1855, and was one of the earliest settlers of Monroe, living just over the line. He kept the ferry across the Beaver at this point for some years—transporting travelers and mail across the stream. During the wet season of 1857 Mr. Curtis ferried many goods across the stream, and upon one occasion, when he attempted to carry the passengers and mail, he swamped and lost his boat and came near losing his life. As a rule, however, the Beaver could be forded, as it had rather a sluggish flow, and, as one old pioneer suggests, "there was more danger of getting stuck in the mud than being drowned."

HARD TIMES.

Van E. Butler, in his well written history of this township, published in the *Clarksville Star*, says: "This history would be incomplete without reference to the first settlers, who dared the trials and hardships of pioneer life, when they were obliged to haul their supplies from Dubuque or Iowa City. The nearest grist mill was at Independence or Quasxucton, when a barrel of salt was worth $9.00, a bushel of corn $1.50, and a pound of bacon 25 cents. Our people were then compelled to accept what they could get from the mill owners and post agents, who supplied us with the necessities of life, and it was frequently very light returns, as was the case on one occasion, when Phillip J. Ebersold, of Dayton, in company with Charley Angell, of the same town, came home with the grist of twenty bushels of wheat—consisting of only three sacks of flour, and Charley remarked, jocosely: 'you're lucky they didn't chase you clear home for the empty sacks.'"

The same writer, after commenting at length upon various matters, continues:

"In the year 1854, James Blake entered 320 acres on section 25 of Dayton, and erected a cabin. Mr. Blake was born near Augusta, Maine, but in early youth emigrated to Virginia, where he imbibed all the characteristics of the true Virginian; of commanding presence, a man of strong likes and dislikes, either a devoted friend or a bitter enemy; there were no half-ways in his conduct; a man who liked to do everything on a large scale. He gloried in the biggest cattle and the biggest horses in this part of the country, and he was a sight worth seeing, with his four yoke of cattle and a span of mares in the lead that would weigh 3,200, turning over the sod with a thirty-two inch plow.

"As we came to where the old gentleman was one day plowing up the prairie and leaving it very much kinked, we exclaimed: 'Hello, Mr. Blake! Why do you kink the sods so much?' 'Why, you see, the boys like mighty well to shoot chickens, but they ain't worth shucks to take 'em on the wing, so I thought I would kink it enough for 'em to crawl up behind the sods and take 'em a settin.'

"Equally characteristic was the reply to the writer, who one day accosted Mr. Blake as he was plowing a field that had been rented to tenants for a number of years, and consequently was so foul that the last crop was not worth cutting. 'Well, Uncle Jimmy, you're plowing those weed seeds under pretty deep, I see?' 'Yes, I'll plow 'em under deeper'n h——!' And sure enough the next crop was deep enough to satisfy any advocate of deep plowing, even if he wern't ambitious to go quite as deep as Mr. Blake.

"During the rebellion his two oldest boys went into the army, and Uncle Jimmy rented his farm and moved to town, and prided himself much on a neatly kept vegetable garden. While thus employed, the numerous porkers running at large would make frequent raids into his truck patch. He re-nailed his pickets; he remonstrated with the owners of the hogs, all to no purpose. One morning, in making a survey of his 'sass garden,' he caught one of the marauders in the act. He had committed sad havoc among his cabbages; his potatoes looked as though an army of Colorado beetles had swept over them; his peas looked curious; his sweet-corn had soured on him; his tomato vines hung in graceful festoons over the back of the depredator—is human nature perfect? Is philosophy always at hand to guide our actions in the path of right, or is swift justice not sometimes excusable, though it may take a crooked path to strike a well-merited blow? In grim silence he walked to the woodpile; a respectable sized boomerang swept in graceful curves through the air, and the perpetrator of this Carthagenian ruin 'went where the woodbine twineth.' Taking the defunct porker by the leg, he chucked him over the fence, exclaiming, 'There, confound you, if we have a hog law, lets abide by it,' and the recording angel dropped a tear upon the word, and blotted it out forever."

Mr. Butler, the writer of these reminiscences, is an able writer, and was an early settler in the county. In speaking of Henry Trotter, an early settler in Central township, he says:

"Henry Trotter settled in Ripley in the infancy of civilization, and has, perhaps, figured more conspicuously in the politics of Ripley than any other man. He is a Scotchman and a very rare one at that. His good-natured disposition is always apparent wherever you find him. He was for years the member of the Board of Supervisors from Ripley. His puns and jokes at the regular convening of this body were many and good. He took care of the interests of his constituents in a manner satisfactory to their wishes. Not always was he the most elegant in diction. Just a little did he move the risabilities of the board on one occasion, when a committee retired to consult and make report on some matter. They remained absent from the room longer than his business views would permit, and rising to his feet he exclaimed: 'Mr Chairman; *Mr. Chairman!* Where in damnation is that committee? They have been gone long enough to go to h— and back.' He is somewhat sarcastic when he makes an effort, and is very outspoken in his opinion about aspirants for office. As at one time he met an office-seeker, who had before held the office for ten or twelve years, soliciting aid for re-election, when Trotter replied: 'Confound it, can't we make the office hereditary, and let your son have it after you?'"

REMINISCENCES OF SETTLEMENT IN ALBION.

By P. P. Parker.

Way back in the early settlement of Albion township, one, Benjamin Connell, is remembered as coming from Canada and taking up a home. His mind was charged with the belief that the "western pioneers" were all desperate characters, and that to have one "draw a bead" on you was as good as a summons from one who had authority to appear hence—in other words —death. One day while Connell was busy at work in his field, a neighbor, whose name has been forgotten, but who lived at Buck's Grove, chanced to pass by and spoke to Connell about something. Being a little deaf, and not hearing the reply which Connell gave, he dropped his rifle from his shoulder to the hollow of his arm, and stepped nearer so as to catch the words. Mr. Connell at once suspicious, saw blood in the stranger's eye, as he thought. In an instant his past life flashed before him; he knew that in a moment the deadly rifle would be levelled, and expected the leaden bullet to go crashing through his brain. With a gasp of terror he dropped every thing and dug out, never looking behind, making leaps of ten feet at a *jump*, in a zig-zag way, so as to dodge the ball. He did not stop until panting and breathless he reached the house of P. P. Parker, where he reported that an attempt had been made to shoot him down in cold blood. The stranger had followed to learn whether the man was drunk or crazy, and in a short time an understanding was arrived at between the parties, and Connell returned to his work happy.

"Another old settler in this vicinity was an eccentric character under the name of John E. Owen—or as he is more often called—"John Owen, sir." John was the owner of a Black Hawk horse, or, at least he was black, which was the pride of the household and well-known to John's friends. Well, John had to work for him —aside from his wife—an old darkey woman, who, whether considered one of the family or not, took many liberties which John did not like. On one occasion, during the absence of John, the darkey concluded to take a ride on old black, which she did in most approved man-fashion. When John came back he was terribly vexed over the matter, and it is said, gave the wench a terrible booting. Owen said afterward that he found all the hair on the back of the horse scalded so that it fell out—"a fact; sir."

Walter Clayton came to Albion in 1853, and took a claim in section 30. This was shortly afterwards jumped by Tom Mullarpy, and Clayton moved further west, taking a claim east of Aplington. To show how supremely regardless Clayton was of

S. B. Dumont.

law and morality; it was a notorious fact that he had ran away from Wisconsin with a "school marm," leaving a wife and several children, and was here living with the woman, and had several children by her. He afterwards obtained a divorce from the first and married the second.

A few years ago an amusing incident happened, which is worth relating: One election day there chanced to be several gentlemen, among whom were the sheriff, Mr. Bartholomew, and P. P. Parker, standing about a revolving churn discussing various matters. While thus engaged, E. W. Babcock, an old-time settler in the region of Albion, came up and inquired if that was the voting place. Upon being answered in the affirmative, he deposited his ballot in the bung-hole and gave it a punch. Bartholomew gave the crank a turn, and a lonely Democratic vote was lost.

A marriage occurred here which was an interesting affair: A Mr. Ketchum procured a marriage license in Grundy county authorizing his marriage with Miss Mary Wilson. The ceremony was performed in Butler county by Esquire Morse. In several days the groom discovered that he was not legally married, and upon informing his wife of the fact it created quite a panic. The matter was adjusted by procuring a license in Butler county dated back to the time of ceremony.

At an early day human nature was the same as at the present. Peter Cramer became smitten with the charms of Sarah Gaylord, and not being acquainted with the fair one, he called upon a third party to arrange an introduction. All was arranged, and both the charmed and charmer being willing, they met at the little log cabin of the third party, as per agreement. They were introduced; but lo! the difficulty arose that there was only one room in the house, and the family could not stand out of doors while the two were cooing. Finally a slate and pencil was furnished, and the lovers began their wooing. This was used to good advantage, for the next day Peter told his friend that the day had been set. But "true love never runs smooth," as other parties broke up the match.

In the spring of 1854 there was a big Indian scare took possession of the people in this country, and nearly every one ran for their lives. The good people of Janesville lost their wits, and built a stockade of slabs near the old saw mill, on the low ground. Fortunately, it was only a scare, for if there had been an enemy around, every one of the gallant defenders could have been shot from the high ground just east of the stockade.

CHAPTER IV.

THE COUNTY GOVERNMENT.

As stated elsewhere, Butler county prior to organization, was attached to Buchanan for judicial purposes, and Judge Roszell ordered an election in August, 1853, for chosing officers and effecting an organization. The election was held and George W. Poisal was elected county judge, but for reasons not given, did not qualify. The same date Mr. Seth Hilton, Sr., was appointed justice of the peace, and filled the office until his successor was elected and qualified in August, 1854. This attempt to organize the county was a failure, and was finally given up. No records are in existence.

At this time the local government of counties throughout the State was vested in what was termed the "county court," which consisted of a judge, clerk, and the sheriff. In August, 1854, an election was held which resulted in the organization of Butler county, substantially, and from which dates the history of it, as a distinct local government. John Palmer was elected county judge; William E. Burton, clerk of court; and R. T. Crowell, sheriff. These officers constituted the "court," which attended to all the legal matters pertaining to the county. The other officers elected were A. G. Clarke, treasurer and recorder; James Griffith, school fund commissioner, and others who are noted elsewhere.

The records of the county court commence with the October term, 1854, held in Clarksville, which was then the county seat. The court was held in a little log hut in which Mr. Clark sold groceries. The first entry is as follows, dated October 2, 1854:

"Ordered, that the following taxes be and are hereby levied: For State purposes, one and one-fourth mills on the dollar; for county purposes, five mills on the dollar; for school purposes, one mill on the dollar; for road purposes, one mill on the dollar; poll for county purposes, fifty cents; poll for road purposes, $1.00.
[Signed.] JOHN PALMER,
County Judge."

The second entry was made on the 11th of October, 1855, and appoints Charles Mullin to survey a certain tract of land on the west side of the Shell Rock, or English river. This, while the record shows "1855," undoubtedly means "1854," as the very next entry bears the date of the 12th of October, 1854, and is the proceedings of the court in

THE FIRST LAW SUIT IN BUTLER COUNTY.

It seems that David W. Ingham made application for a writ of injunction against Daniel D. Myers, who lived at Shell Rock, restraining him from selling a certain piece of land in section two of Shell Rock township, on the west side of the river;

and having filed his petition and a bond in the sum of $100 with the clerk of court, the writ was issued and placed in the hands of R. T. Crowell, sheriff, who served it by leaving a copy at the residence of the defendant. This took place on the 12th and 13th days of October, 1854, and on the 19th, notice was given to the plaintiff, Mr. Ingham, that on the first day of January, 1855, a motion would be made to dissolve the injunction; but upon further consideration between the parties the matter was postponed until early in February, 1855.

On the date mentioned, the case was called up by the court, with M. M. Trumbull as attorney for Mr. Myers, and A. VanDorn for Mr. Ingham. After calling to order, the motion to dissolve the writ of injunction was sustained by the judge for the reason "that the writ was not issued by an officer authorized to issue the same." Then Mr. Myers, by his attorney, moved the court to assess damages against the defendant in the amount of $100. This was overruled, because no damages had been proven. A motion, which was sustained, was made to allow evidence to prove damages. A jury of six was then summoned, composed of T. T. Rawson, J. V. Hicks, D. C. Hilton, M. B. Wamsley, James Ford and R. W. Butler; and, to use the words of the record: "Jury empannelled and sworn. Case stated by M. M. Trumbull, when the following witnesses were examined on part of Myers: Charles Leverich, A. M. Elam, W. E. Burton, A. Van Dorn and John Palmer, who, being cross-examined by the defense, the case was submitted to the jury, who, after retiring to consider, brought into court the following verdict: 'We, the undersigned jurors, do agree that the said Solomon W. Ingham pay to said Daniel D. Myers the sum of twenty-five cents, with cost.' (Signed by members.)

Defendant gave notice of an appeal to the district court in reference to the injunction and verdict."

This ended the case, so far as the county court was concerned. The costs were $5.90.

The next law suit appears under the date of December 9, 1854, wherein Rufus S. Hardy said, on oath, that one William Casterline had threatened to beat, wound and murder him, and was afraid of his life. Thereupon, a warrant was issued, Casterline arrested, and upon examination, was held to bail in the sum of $100 to keep the peace and answer at the next term of the district court. When the district court convened, the charges were withdrawn, and the case was dismissed.

Immediately following the record of this case, is an entry which will explain itself, as follows:

"STATE OF IOWA, } ss.
   Butler County, }

On this day, to-wit, October 27th, A. D. 1854, the plat of the village of Clarksville, with the acknowledgments of Thomas Clark, Elizabeth Clark, Jeremiah Clark, Maria Clark, D. C. Hilton, Seth Hilton, Elizabeth Hilton, Dan Mather and Roxana Mather, proprietors of the land upon which the above mentioned village is situated; that the same is with their free consent and in accordance with their desire. And the court being satisfied that the requirements of the law have been complied with, it is therefore ordered that the same be placed on the records of Butler county, as the law requires.

                  JOHN PALMER,
                      County Judge."

Hugh F. L. Burton was appointed deputy clerk of the district court, and gave bonds in the penal sum of $5,000. On the same day, M. M. Trumbull qualified as deputy treasurer and recorder. Aaron Van Dorn was appointed and qualified as prosecuting attorney. Also, John H. Morton as county surveyor. The first county warrant issued is recorded as follows:

"November 20th, 1854, warrant No. 1; to W. E. Burton, for assessing Butler precinct and attending election board, for $37.75."

Warrant No. 2, was issued to John Palmer, county judge, for $5.00, and bore the date of December 9th, 1854. No. 3 was issued to Greene & Brother, of Linn county, for $22.25. No. 4 to George R. Allen, for $1.00. No. 5 to an Indianapolis firm for stationery, in the sum of $25.00. No. 6, to M. B. Wamsley, for $1.00, etc., etc.

On the fourth of January, 1855, Thomas Clark presented a receipt signed by John G. Barrick, D. C. Overman and William W. Payne—locating commissioners, who located the county seat of Butler county at Clarksville—dated Barrick's Ford, May 16, A. D. 1853, for the sum of $24.00, and George W. Poisal was produced as witness that the said amount had been paid by Clark. In accordance, a county warrant was issued to Mr. Clark for $24.00.

The following entry appears on the minute book, bearing date of the 29th of March, 1855:

"On this day George W. Adair and Elizabeth Adair presented the plat of the town of Shell Rock, in the county of Butler, situated in the northwest quarter of section 11, in township 91, range 15, west of the fifth principal meridian. And having acknowledged the same as required by law, it was ordered that the whole be recorded as the law directs.

JOHN PALMER,
Judge."

The next session of the court, held during April, 1825, is taken up with attending to the returns of the election throughout the county, and in this connection is given the notice that Aaron Van Dorn has qualified according to law as prosecuting attorney, Walker H. Bishop as sheriff, John H. Morton as county surveyor, and William R. Jamison and Thomas Clark as justices of the peace.

THE FIRST COURT HOUSE.

In an entry on the court minute book, dated the fourth of June, 1855, it is ordered "that sealed proposals for building a court house, on the court house square, in the village of Clarksville, of the dimensions as follows: 40x40 feet, two stories high, the first to be nine feet and the second nine and one-half feet in height, to be made of good and durable material, either of wood or brick."

This building was erected the following year, and is now in use as the school house, in the village mentioned.

OFFICERS FOR 1856.

The records immediately following the election of August 6, 1855, show that David C. Hilton qualified as Treasurer and Recorder; Thomas T. Rawson, as County Surveyor, and Walker H. Bishop as Sheriff.

The county court for this year opened with Aaron Van Dorn, judge, and the sheriff, clerk and prosecuting attorney.

During the March term, in 1856, the matter of township boundaries was taken up, and resulted in a re-division of the county.

On September, 9th, 1856, an entry states that William H. McClure presented the plat of Willoughby village, and "the court being satisfied that the pre-requisites of the law had been complied with," it was ordered recorded. The record does not state the location of this village, but it was in Beaver township.

COURT HOUSE AGAIN.

On the third of November, 1856, the court ordered that on account of insufficiency of means, want of time and material to complete or enclose it for protection against the winter, further progress of building be laid over until the spring of 1857, when it would be resumed and prosecuted to final completion. It was stated that the sum of $25.00 had already been paid in county warrants on building.

In March, 1857, a petition signed by D. N. Root and others, for the removal of the county seat from Clarksville, was overruled by the judge.

In 1857 there seemed to be a panic among the county officials, for at the March term the judge said: "Whereas the office of drainage commissioner has become vacant by the death of the late incumbent, and also the offices of county clerk, surveyor and coroner, by resignation, a special election was ordered to take place on the first Monday in April, 1857."

RAILROAD STOCK.

A special election was ordered and held in Butler county on the 12th day of September, 1857, for the purpose of voting on the question whether or not the county should subscribe for stock in the Chicago, Iowa & Nebraska Railroad Company to the amount of $200,000, the proviso being that the company should build its Cedar Valley Branch through the county within one mile of Clarksville and Shell Rock; bonds payable in twenty years, to be issued therefor. The canvassing board, consisting of C. A. Bannon, John M. Vincent and Asa Ward, reported after official count, that the proposition had carried by a vote of 244 to 187; there being 431 votes cast.

At the August election, in 1857, the officers elected are recorded as appearing and taking the required oath. D. C. Hilton, qualified as treasurer and recorder for the two ensuing years; Walker H. Bishop, as sheriff; John Loomis, as deputy sheriff; Jeremiah Ellis, as county surveyor. It seems that there was some difficulty or controversy arising from this election, as the following entries upon the records indicate, and which explain themselves. The first appears under the date of September 29, 1857:

"D. W. Miller, of Coldwater township, presented his bond and was duly qualified for the office of county judge."

Then, upon the next page of record appears the following entry, under the date of the fifth of October, 1857, viz:

"At a hearing, before Hon. J. D. Thompson, in the matter of judgeship between A. Converse and D. W. Miller, it was ordered that D. W. Miller deliver the office and books pertaining thereto to A. Converse. Witnessed by JAMES E. WALKER, clerk."

Then, to complete the story, at the next term of court, in November, 1857, the record says here were present:—Hon. A.

Converse, judge; James E. Walker, clerk; and W. H. Bishop, sheriff. John Palmer was appointed prosecuting attorney. This case is treated in another place.

At the February session of the court in 1858, the plat of the village of Aplington was presented and ordered recorded.

On the 4th of March, 1858, the township of Bennezette was set off from the territory of Coldwater, and organized, Samuel Overturf being authorized to call the first election. On the 13th of the same month, Pittsford was set apart from West Point, and organized, A. C. Needham calling the first election.

At an election on the fifth of April, 1857, a proposition was submitted to the people as to the question of the county borrowing $20,000 by issuing bonds payable in five years, for the purpose of building bridges in Butler county, as follows:

For bridge at Shell Rock	$3,000
Two bridges at Clarksville	3,000
Bridge at Coldwater	3,000
Bridge at West Fork	1,500
Bridge at Mason's Ford	1,000
Bridge at McConnell's Ford	1,000
Bridge at New Hartford	1,500
Bridge at Olmstead's Ford	200
Bridge at Union road	500
Bridge near R. R. Parriot's	1,500
Bridge near W. Curtiss'	300

This proposition as above stated was voted upon and carried by 346 in favor of and 274 against it—620 votes in all. These bonds were issued on the 10th of August, 1858, in series numbered from one to forty-eight, inclusive, of denomination of $500 each, bearing ten per cent. interest, to S. M. Townsend & Co., Asa Low and D. N. Root & Co.

During the proceedings of the county court, in 1859, the record shows that it consisted of A. Converse, judge; James W. Davis, clerk, and W. H. Bishop, sheriff.

In September, 1860, Judge Converse set off and authorized the organization of the new townships, Washington, Dayton and Madison. Fremont had been set off and organized the year previous.

BOARD OF SUPERVISORS.

In 1859 an act was passed by the General Assembly, which changed the form of local government in the various counties throughout the State. By it a body termed the "Board of Supervisors," superceded the old system of county court, and was vested with nearly all the authority formerly held by the latter body. The board consisted of one supervisor from each organized township, making sixteen members in all, as the county was at this time divided, and the townships organized the same as at the present writing.

Pursuant to law, the first meeting of the "new dispensation" took place on the seventh day of January, 1861, at Butler Center, and the following supervisors were on hand and qualified: Peter Coyle, G. W. Stoner, O. Rice, W. R. Jamison, Thomas Haggarty, J. Gilbert, M. Aldrich, W. H. Long, S. Bonwell, J. Wilson, Milo Hard, J. Hoffman, S. H. Taylor, Wells A. Curtis, and A. J. Thompkins. An organization was effected by the choice of Peter Coyle as temporary chairman; James W. Davis, clerk, and Messrs, Hard, Jamison and Haggarty, as the committee on credentials. This committee reported the following persons as supervisors elect from their various townships, viz:

Jefferson township....................O. Rice
Shell Rock township............James Wilson
Dayton township..................Thomas Haggarty
Beaver township....................Milo Hard
Ripley township.............George W. Stoner
Coldwater township............Moses Aldrich
West Point township...........Julius Hoffman
Jackson township............Jonathan Gilbert
Madison township..................Peter Coyle
Washington township..............W. H. Long
Pittsford township...............W. R Jamison
Fremont township...................S. Bonwell
Albion township..................S. H. Taylor
Monroe township..............Wells A. Curtis
Bennezette township............Milton Wilson
Butler township..................C. A. Bannon

The new board then took the organizing steps by balloting for chairman for the ensuing year; W. R. Jamison received four votes, Peter Coyle nine, and the latter was declared elected. James W. Davis presented his bond as clerk, and it was approved.

Then appears the following item extracted from the records:

"Motion was then made that the members proceed to draw lots for their term of service, according to law. The motion was carried, and the members drew their terms as follows, viz: Messrs. O. Rice, Milo Hard, Julius Hoffman, J. Gilbert, S. Bonwell, W. A. Curtis, C. A. Bannon and Milton Wilson, each one year; and Messrs. James Wilson, G. Haggarty, G. W. Stoner, M. Aldrich, Peter Coyle, W. H. Long W. R. Jamison and S. H. Taylor, each two years.

Thus was the new system inaugurated, and a mile post in the history of the county auspiciously passed.

At the next session, the chairman appointed nine standing committees on different matters, which are too lengthy to give specifically.

A matter of interest came before the board in January, 1861. A petition signed by D. W. Miller and 400 others was presented, asking that the matter of changing the county seat from Butler Center to Clarksville be submitted to a vote of the people; but this was squelched by the committee appointed to investigate, consisting of Milo Hard, G. W. Stoner and J. Gilbert, who reported adverse to it. The latter named gentleman, however, on behalf of the minority of the committee, as opposed to the other two, presented a report favoring the petition, and advising that the matter be submitted to a vote; but it was of no avail as it was out-voted as soon as it reached the main body. The balance of the year was spent by the board in attending to routine business, nothing of special interest transpiring.

In the year 1862, the board convened on the 7th of January, and organized by the election of Peter Coyle as chairman for the ensuing year. The supervisors elect, and who were present to answer the roll call, were as follows, with the townships they represented opposite their respective names:

Fremont...........................S. Bonwell.
Coldwater.....................Moses Aldrich.
Dayton................Thomas Haggarty.
Bennezette....................Milton Wilson.
Pittsford..............William R. Jamison.
West Point........................J. Hoffman.
Jackson............................J. Gilbert.
Butler....................James R. Fletcher.
Shell Rock.....................James Wilson.
Jefferson......................W. A. Lathrop.
Ripley....................George W. Stoner.

Madison..........................Peter Coyle.
Washington.....................W. H. Long.
Monroe...........................J. J. Criswell.
Albion............................S. H. Taylor.
Beaver............................Milo Hard.

The matter of the re-location of the county seat again came up, indicating that Butler Center, as the shiretown of the county, gave much dissatisfaction. The record of the first session of the board of supervisors for 1862, states that "C. A. Bannon, Esq., appeared, and as the attorney of the petitioners, presented a petition of certain voters of Butler county, asking for the granting of a vote upon the question of a re-location of the county seat and the removal of the same from Butler Center, the present county seat, to Clarksville." This petition was signed by 440 voters, of which about 42 were deducted by the committee appointed to investigate. This petition was soon followed by a remonstrance, signed by about the same number of citizens. The county had been thoroughly canvassed by the active champions of each point in question, and the population was about equally divided. The committee in whose hands the matter was placed, did not recommend any action in the matter, but made a plain statement of the case. Their report was accepted, and the board listened to the arguments of the attorneys on both sides, after which Supervisor James R. Fletcher, presented a lengthy resolution, setting forth that the petition had been signed by one-half the legal voters of the county, as per the census of 1859, and ordering that at the April election of 1862, the matter be submitted to a vote. Then appears the following, which explains itself:

"The yeas and nays were called for upon the amendment of W. A. Lathrop, which was as follows: 'Strike out all of Mr. Fletcher's resolution after the word 'resolved,' and insert 'that the facts as set forth by the committee on county seat do not show that the petitioners are entitled to a vote, therefore the prayer be not allowed.'"

The amendment was carried by a vote of ten to six. But the matter was brought up again the following day by the presentation of a resolution rescinding the above vote, and was again beaten by a majority of six.

During this year the board is recorded as having audited and allowed numerous claims for bounty on wolves and wildcats killed.

An extra session of the board was held on the 20th of August, 1863, pursuant to a call signed by W. A. Lathrop, W. H. Long, S. H. Taylor, M. Hard, James Wilson, J. R. Fletcher, S. Bonwell, J. J. Criswell and G. W. Stoner, requesting a meeting to consider and take action upon a proposition offering a bounty by Butler county to the volunteers raised under the call of the President, for 300,000 men. The meeting was called to order by Peter Coyle, and W. A. Lathrop offered a resolution granting $20 to each volunteer; but this was tabled by a motion from J. Hoffman that the whole matter be postponed until the September meeting of the board. The vote upon the matter stood eleven yeas and five nays.

At the September meeting the matter was again brought up, and in lieu of the whole a resolution was adopted instructing all the supervisors to act as relief commit-

HISTORY OF BUTLER COUNTY.

tees for their various towns and supply the wants of the families of volunteers. However, at subsequent sessions, Butler county nobly did her share in quelling the rebellion, appropriating about $53,000 in all.

The board of supervisors met on the 5th of January, 1863, and organized by choosing Peter Coyle chairman for the ensuing year. The board consisted of the following gentlemen from the various townships:

S. H. Taylor..........................Albion
William J. Nettleton................Coldwater
John M. Nichols...................Pittsford
John C. Hites.........................Ripley
Peter Coyle..........................Madison
M. Hollenbeck.....................Shell Rock
H. A. Tucker......................Washington
S. Bonwell...........................Fremont
W. A. Lathrop......................Jefferson
J. J. Criswell........................Monroe
Milo Hard............................Beaver
J. Gilbert.............................Jackson
J Hoffman..........................West Point
Milton Wilson.....................Bennezette
C. Forney.............................Dayton
J. R. Fletcher........................Butler

The name of the last mentioned supervisor drops from sight after the January session, as he was elected county judge, and A. J. Tompkins appears with credentials of appointment, and takes his seat.

Again the county seat matter comes up by a petition to re-locate it at Shell Rock, signed by 486 voters. It was soon followed by a remonstrance. The matter was laid over until the September session, when it was again taken up and defeated.

The balance of the year was spent in attending to routine business.

For several years following, nothing of special interest was brought before the board, therefore the names of the officers serving, alone are given:

FOR 1864,

the supervisors were the same as the year previous, except from the towns named below, who were represented by the gentlemen named.

J. J. Criswell..........................Monroe
J. A. Chamberlain................Bennezette
J. Lawyer...........................West Point
William Rosebrough...............Beaver
E. B. Allen..........................Jefferson
Thomas G. Copeland............Shell Rock
Mr. Wamsley.........................Jackson

THE YEAR 1865.

The changes in the board for this year is recorded as being Thomas Haggerty, from Dayton; Joseph Miller, Coldwater; James Harlon, Pittsford; H. F. L. Burton and E. Fowler, Butler; W. S. Wilson, Shell Rock; W. A. Lathrop, Jefferson; J. P. Bullis, Ripley, Peter Coyle, Madison; R. R. Parriott, Washington; R. W. Shaw, Albion; the chairman chosen was Peter Coyle.

IN 1866.

The record reveals the changes for this year as follows, and the gentlemen named qualified and took their seats:

S. J. Booram.........................Fremont
J. Lawyer...........................West Point
M. B. Wamsley......................Jackson
Edwin Fowle..........................Butler
Stephen Morse.....................Jefferson
Oliver Evans......................Bennezette
J. G. Scoby........................Shell Rock
James Collar..........................Beaver

Chairman for the year, Peter Coyle.

In 1867 the first meeting was held on the 7th of January, and organized by choosing Edwin Fowle chairman. The members who answered the roll call, were S. J. Booram, J. V. Boggs, J. Griffith, O. Evans, S. B. Dumont, J. Lawyer, M. B. Wamsley, E. Fowle, J. G. Scoby, S. Morse H. Trotter, G. W. Smith, M. F. Whitney, Isaac Hall and A. Converse.

In 1868 the board met on the 6th of January, and elected S. B. Dumont chairman for the ensuing year; the members elect were S. Bonwell, J. V. Boggs, O. Evans, B. F. Garrett, M. B. Wamsley, J. Lyle, J. Palmer, J. J. Criswell and Amos Nettleton.

The following year the same chairman was elected, and Messrs. Bonwell, Newhard, Miller, Dumont, Garrett, Wamsley, McEachron, Trotter, Smith, Criswell Hersey Converse and Kenefick, were the newly elected members.

In 1870 the board met on the 3d of January, and was composed of the following members: S. B. Dumont, chairman; James McEachron, M. B. Wamsley, W. H. Hersey, E. Day, Isaac Hall, G. Smith. A. Converse, H. Trotter, B. F. Garrett, J. R. Jones, I. F. Newhard, J. Preston, James Griffith and W. A. Keister.

This was the last meeting of the county legislature, or supervisors made up of one member from each township. The General Assembly, by an act, changed the manner of local government; and the board of supervisors was re-arranged so as to be composed of three, who were to be elected at large throughout the county. The first board, under this law, which is yet in force, convened on the second day of January, 1871, the members being M. B. Wamsley, H. C. Brown and A. Chrystie. The oath of office was administered by the Auditor, and the new board organized by the election of Alex. Chrystie chairman.

The members of the board from that time until the present writing are as follows:

COUNTY SUPERVISORS SINCE 1871.

1871—Alex. Chrystie, chairman; M. B. Wamsley and H. C. Brown.
1872—Alex. Chrystie, H. C. Brown and S. Bonwell.
1873—Same as above.
1874—Same.
1875—Alex. Chrystie, H. C. Brown and N. H. Larkin.
1876—Alex. Chrystie, N. H. Larkin and G. Hazlet.
1877—Same.
1878—Alex. Chrystie, G. Hazlet and A. N. Leet.
1879—Alex. Chrystie, A. N. Leet and Milton Wilson.
1880—A. N. Leet, M. Wilson and J. J. Burnham.
1881—Same.
1882—A. N. Leet, J. J. Burnham and C. L. Jones.
1883—A. N. Leet, C. L. Jones and J. M. Groat.

CHAPTER V.

OTHER OFFICIAL MATTERS.

Following are presented various matters, compiled from records and elsewhere, which will be of interest to all readers. They are given as full as space would permit, the subjects being of such a nature that to go into detail would be impossible.

POPULATION OF BUTLER COUNTY.

The census of 1880 gives Butler county a total population of 14,293, which is divided as follows:

Males	7,604
Females	6,689
Native	12,043
Foreign	2,250
White	14,262
Colored	31

BUTLER COUNTY'S SUB-DIVISIONS.

After the organization of the county nothing was immediately done as to the division of its territory into townships. It soon became evident that to facilitate the successful government, this must be done, and therefore, on the 6th day of February, 1855, the county judge, John Palmer, proceeded to make the division, and the following entry, as to the territory to be embraced by the various towns, is made upon his records:

"The township of Butler to consist of Congressional townships 92 and 93, range 15, and township 92 and the east half of 93, range 16.

The township of Coldwater, of Congressional township 93, range 17, and the west half of township 93, range 16.

The township of Ripley shall consist of Congressional townships 90, 91, 92, range 17, and townships 90, 91, 92 and 93, range 18.

The township of Beaver to consist of Congressional townships 90 and 91, in range 15, and townships 90 and 91, in range 16."

Thus, it will be seen that the first division made the county as composed of four townships. Butler comprised the territory now known as Jackson, Fremont, Butler, and one-half of Dayton. Coldwater embraced, in addition to what it now has, the west half of Dayton. Ripley consisted of what are now the townships of Bennezette, Pittsford, Madison, Washington, Monroe, Ripley and West Point. Beaver was then made up of the four towns which are now the southeastern corner ones of the county, i. e., Jefferson, Shell Rock, Albion and Beaver.

On the 15th of February, of the same year, a warrant was issued to Lyman Norton to organize the townships of Beaver. On the 26th, William R. Jamison was appointed to organize Ripley; and Aaron Hardman to effect that of Coldwater. At the same time the judge made out notices and delivered them to the sheriff, notifying the electors of the different townships of the election on the second of April, 1855.

In this shape the county remained until the third of March, 1856, when a second division of townships was made. Butler remained as in the former division; Coldwater remained the same with the addition of Bennezette. At this time a new town was formed, called West Point, which included within its limits Pittsford. The boundaries of Ripley were changed, taking in its present limits and also the town of Madison. Another new town, Shell Rock, was formed at this time, which included the present township of that name and the territory now belonging to Jefferson. Beaver and Albion were merged together as Beaver, and Monroe consisted of its present area and Washington.

In March, 1857, the townships of Shell Rock and Beaver were divided, and from the former, George A. Richmond was authorized to organize Jefferson; from the latter, Alonzo Olmstead was authorized to organize the township of Albion.

The townships were made to include their present boundaries under the jurisdiction of Judge Converse, who came into office on the fifth of October, 1857. The county court appointed judges of election for the various new towns. On the 11th of March, 1858, the township of Jackson was formed and named after Jackson because it was Democratic, and E. D. Marquand was appointed judge of the election, which was held at the house of John H. VanDyke, on the fifth of April, and permanent organization effected.

The townships which were then set off, and represent the sub-divisions of the county, making a total of sixteen towns, were as follows:

Fremont, embracing all of township 93 north, range 15, west of fifth principal meridian.
Butler, all of township 92, range 15.
Shell Rock, all of township 91, range 15.
Beaver, all of township 90, range 15.
Dayton, all of township 93, range 16.
Jackson, all of township 92, range 16.
Jefferson, all of township 91, range 16.
Albion, all of township 90, range 16.
Coldwater, all of township 93, range 17.
West Point, all of township 92, range 17.
Ripley, all of township 91, range 17.
Monroe, all of township 90, range 17.
Bennezette, all of township 93, range 18.
Pittsford, all of township 92, range 18.
Madison, all of township 91, range 18.
Washington, all of township 90; range 18.

MATRIMONIAL.

When Adam was created and placed in the garden of Eden a helpmeet was provided for him in the person of Eve. This, therefore, is the natural state of man. The marriage state is a solemn one and should be sacredly protected. "What God has joined together let no man put asunder." In various lands the marriage rite is solemnized in different ways and by different ceremonies. In all, the acts of the contracting parties must be understood by each and by the community in which they live as being a mutual agreement to hold the relations toward one another as man and wife. In this State a license has always been required

The first marriage that appears on the record books of this county was solemnized on the 10th of September, 1854, more than twenty-eight years ago. The parties were Daniel W. Kinsley and Mary Farlow. They were married by A. M. Elam, justice of the peace, by virtue of a license issued on the 8th of September under the official seal of the clerk of the county. It was the first marriage solemnized in the county subsequent to its organization.

In the early days young men and maidens were not married in the grand style which usually characterizes marriages of the present time. They did not wait for riches to come before marriage, as is generally the present custom, but married and lived in simple and comfortable style, and generally lived happy and gained the respect of their neighbors by attending to their own business. There were no "diamond" weddings in those days, and the extravagance that often now attends the marriage ceremony was unheard of. The old folks were plain, economical and hospitable people, and the young folks were imbued with the same attributes that characterized their fathers and mothers. They were willing to commence housekeeping in a style corresponding with their means, trusting to the future for larger houses and more expensive furniture.

There are many amusing anecdotes connected with some of the earlier weddings, most of which find their proper places in the various township histories—how the rustic, blushing bride, left the kitchen, unbuckled her apron, and throwing on her sunbonnet climbed into the lumber box wagon and started off with "John," who yet had his pants in his boots and overalls on, for their wedding tour—to hunt up the "squire" and get "jined." An incident is called to mind which is unlocated and cannot properly be placed in any of the townships. It is said that on one occasion way back in the fifties, a country couple made their way to one of the little villages in the county in quest of some one who was authorized to tie the hymeneal knot. They went to a young storekeeper, who, in the way of a practical joke, referred them to the postmaster, stating that the government authorized him to officiate upon such occasions. When the postmaster was seen he disclaimed any knowledge of such authority, and said that he had only been in the employ of the government a short time and was not yet "quite up to snuff." But if the merchant said he could, he supposed it was so. Accordingly the couple were ranged up in front of the postmaster, who in the most approved style impressed them with the solemnity of the occasion, warned them to "let no man put asunder what he had j'ined," and in closing "pronounced them Mr. and Mrs., etc., according to the postal laws of the United States. And you may go in peace. (Only $1.00 apiece, please)."

It would doubtless be of interest to many to give the record of marriages for the first ten years of the county's existence, but they are too numerous, therefore only the first three years are given, as taken from the record in the office of the clerk of the court.

Greenberry Luck and Susan Williams, by Rev. W. P. Holbrook, on November 1, 1854.

Comfort Williams and Ducilla Smart, by Rev. W. P. Holbrook, on November 1, 1854.

Daniel W. Kinsley and Mary Farlow, by Justice of the Peace A. M. Elam, on the 10th of September, 1854.

Samuel E. Taylor and Julia E. Armstrong, by A. M. Elam, Esq., on the 21st of September, 1854.

James W. Goheen and Mary Burrows, by J. H. Miller, Esq., on the 19th of December, 1854.

Robert T. Crowell and Lucretia Burton, by Judge John Palmer, on the 24th of December, 1854.

George Moore and Lorinda Poisal, by Rev. Elijah Kindall, on the 15th of March, 1855.

Orville G. Nelson and Amanda Searles, by Rev. James M. Phillips, on the 1st of April, 1855.

Moses J. Davis and Nancy J. Hall, by Thomas Clark, Esq., on the 17th of June, 1855.

Michael Fague and Elizabeth Plant, by the Rev. Levi Wells, on the 5th of July, 1855.

Randolph Mann and Christinia Lowman, by Rev. B. Holcomb, on the 3d of January, 1856.

The following are those who were married during 1856, without going into particulars as to dates:

Pascal P. Parker, and Martha McEwing.
John Eichar and Eliza Vincent.
George W. McClellan and Eliza Billhimer.
Richard Kellar and Catharine P. Temple.
Seth Strong and Mrs. Mary Cannon.
George W. Armstrong and Miss E. Stacy.
Thomas Hunt and Nancy Farlow.
Noah Hartgraves and Hulda M. Stacy.
Jonathan H. Allen and Elizabeth Harlan.
Henry Thomas and Louisa M. Olmstead.
Charles Leverich and Betsy Dixon.
William Poisal and Rachael L. Burton.
Charles Clark and Harriett Dryer.
John Spowar, aged sixteen, and Rebecca Shaffer, aged fourteen.
William R. Taylor and Nancy M. Martin.
Jacob Wopple and Mary Elizabeth Edwards.
Samuel Vim and Hannah Hollenbeck.
John Dickisson and Hester A. Stone.
William Flood and Delia V. Angel.
James Boylan and Frances Strong.
Nathaniel Chesley and Elizabeth Brown.
Samuel Sewell and Annie C. Hush.
Richard Parriott and Miss Lilly M. Coldwell.
Martin V. Wamsley and Frances J. Griffith.
John P. Davis and Hannah J. Brink.
D. C. Hilton and C. M. Riddle.
M. E. Spower and Jesse Best.

The names and titles of those who performed the marriage ceremonies during 1856, in the cases mentioned, are as follows: Judge Aaron Van Dorn; Reverends B. Holcomb, Samuel Wright, D. Blakely, Hiram Hoode, and James Murphy; Justices of the Peace, W. R. Jamison, Ancel Durand, J. H. Smith, M. Hollenbeck, Asa Low, Harvey Smith and Joseph Embody.

During the last few years of the records of marriages, we notice the names of many, both ladies and young gentlemen, who are sons and daughters of the parties mentioned above, who have themselves taken partners to their joys and sorrows. Thus, a new generation sets in.

The following table shows the number of marriages contracted from the year 1854 to 1882, inclusive:

Year	No.	Year	No.
1854	6	1869	71
1855	6	1870	58
1856	27	1871	85
1857	20	1872	82
1858	28	1873	93
1859	20	1874	75
1860	4	1875	109
1861	32	1876	89
1862	20	1877	101
1863	24	1878	113
1864	33	1879	107
1865	51	1880	137
1866	75	1881	116
1867	73	1882	111
1868	65		
		Total	1833

A glance at the foregoing figures shows conclusively that the matrimonial market is affected by the state of the times. In 1854, and for the first few years the county was too sparsely settled to furnish any indication of it. In 1858 banks suspended and a season of depression set in, and there were fewer marriages contracted for several years, although this county was not visibly affected until 1860, when there were only four marriages. Again, in 1874, hard times caused a visible decrease in this respect. The war, too, caused a falling off in the number of marriages annually contracted, but in 1866, when the boys got home, there were a larger number of licenses issued by the county clerk than in any prior year.

FINANCIAL.

The condition of a county in this respect is always the result of the management it has received, whether to its credit or otherwise. We have collected the principal items in this regard as to Butler county, and they will speak louder than words as to the county's condition.

The first levy of taxes was made on the 28th of October, 1854, by John Palmer, the county judge at that time. The total amount of tax for the year was only $698.50.6. During the following year the amount of taxes collected was $855.63.4. This shows, by comparison, the growth of the county. Only about twenty-five years ago $855.53 covered all the tax raised, and to-day $85,000 is annually levied and collected. It has been truthfully observed that in those days county officers did not grow very fat out of the treasury of Butler county—if speculation in real estate was a profitable business.

From the time the county was organized, in 1854, the issue of county warrants commenced and served as a path by which the county soon became involved in debt. As a rule they were marketable readily, as they drew a fair rate of interest, the discount averaging about 15 to 20 per cent, but at various times they were purchased at as low as 50 cents on the dollar, ranging between this and 95 cents. By the year 1861 there were outstanding about $12,000 of these warrants.

In 1858 the county bonded itself of $24,000, with interest at the rate of 10 per cent, for the purpose of building and repairing bridges. The interest on these bonds was allowed to accumulate for several years, but during the years 1862 and 1863 a tax was levied sufficient to pay both principal and interest, and the bonds were lifted.

This bridge loan served as one of the thorns which rankled the public spirit. The bridges which were erected (specified in the article upon county government) with this money were all of such cheap material and so poorly erected that it is said two of them lasted but one year. The funds appropriated were sufficient to have built substantial and lasting bridges; but this was one of the instances and modes by which new counties, to use a common expression, were "leached."

Then came the war, acompanied by the stringency in the money market and decreasing valuation of property. The county nobly did its part, issuing bounties to volunteer soldiers to the amount of about $40,000, besides a relief fund which amounted to about $13,000. This was all raised by taxation, and paid in money about 1866 or 1867.

From the year 1862 until 1870, a steady and successful effort was made to pay off the debt and keep the current expenses from creeping up. With what success is shown by the fact that $100,000 of debt was raised, and the county had a balance in its favor, in 1869, of about $2,000. It has kept out of debt ever since.

The first county warrant was issued on the 20th of November, 1854, to W. E. Burton, for assessing Butler precinct and attending election board; it was for the sum of $37.75. Warrant No. 2 was issued to Judge John Palmer, for $5.00, and bore the date of December 9, 1854.

The county is to-day entirely out of debt, with no bonds of any description hanging over it. By the recapitulation of the statement of finances made by the auditor in June, 1882, it will at once be seen that the county is in the best financial shape, and has money on hand for the various funds, as follows:

RECAPITULATION.

State fund	$425 00
County fund	4,974 68
County School fund	357 44
Teachers' fund	9,019 73
School house fund	1,061 64
Bridge fund	8,554 15
Road fund	1,687 89
Railroad fund	161 43
Insane fund	3,654 19
Permanent school fund	2,652 34
Temporary school fund	4,001 32
Contingent school fund	3,772 53
Incorporation fund	573 46
Institute fund	193 18
Special State railroad fund	46 21
Board of Health fund	5 79
War and defense bond fund	58
Condemned school house sites	51 50
Total cash on hand June 1, 1882	$41,194 25

The total amount of tax collected in Butler county, in 1881, was $84,662.25. This gives an average of $5,290.76 from each township. The whole amount was divided up as follows:

State tax	$6,643 78
County tax	19,937 35
Special railroad tax	193 37
Bridge tax	9,965 67
County school tax	3,321 89
School house tax	4,591 00
Teachers' fund tax	22,760 75
Contingent fund tax	7,850 02
Road tax	5,699 35
Board of health tax	224 41
Poll tax	1,636 00
Corporation tax	1,245 66
Total	$84,662 25

REGISTRY OF DEEDS.

The records of this office consist of about 140 books in all, of which the "Books of Deeds" are 61, having run

Jas. W. Davis.

through all of the letters and up to number 34, which number they are at present using. There are 20 books of real estate mortgages, running to "T;" there are 25 books of chattel mortgages, running to "W;" three books of record of mortgages of town lots, about fourteen indexes, and the rest are miscellaneous records.

The records pertaining to this county commence in 1853, and were made in Black Hawk county, having been, after Butler was organized, transcribed into the proper books.

The first article recorded is in the shape of a conveyance of land dated September the 4th, 1854, of a piece of land containing forty acres in Albion township, then not organized, from Noah Hartgraves to S. P. Wemple and J. S. Robbins, for a consideration of $300. It was witnessed by William H. McClure and recorded by A. G. Clark. This was the first entry upon the books of Butler county. About the same time, or a little later, is recorded the deed of conveyance of an eighty acre piece of land in the same township, for $250, from Peter and Bridget Comer to Jesse D. Butts. This is witnessed by H. C. and W. F. Overman.

The first village platted and recorded in the county was Clarksville, which bears the date of the 27th of October, 1854.

The first mortgage on record was made on the eighth day of January, 1855, in which Robert T. Crowell and wife mortgages to James Griffith, school fund commissioner, in the sum of $298.14, an eighty acre claim in section 15, of what is now Butler township. This mortgage was satisfied in the presence of D. C. Hilton, recorder, to John H. Morton, the commissioner, on the 22d of April, 1857.

The early records, unlike those of the most of counties, are not literary curiosities, therefore there is no necessity in presenting any of the entries, as they would be of no interest. In fact, the first entries upon the books are as neat and as well written as any at the present day.

VITAL STATISTICS.

The record books of the births and deaths in the hands of the clerk of court, commence in July, 1880, so that prior to that nothing can be learned concerning it.

The first birth recorded is that of Bernard, a son of W. W. and Emma J. Pattee, on the 13th of July, 1880. During the balance of the month of July there were eight reported, and in January, 1881, the records showed 136. From July, 1880, until August, 1882, there had been 530.

The death record commences at the same time, July, 1880, and has since been kept up, giving the name and nationality of the deceased, and cause of death. Up to January, 1881, inclusive of the time from July, 1880, there were 62 deaths reported, and from that time until October, 1882, when the last entry was made, there had been 125 deaths. Number of deaths from July, 1880, until October, 1882, inclusive, 187.

THE COUNTY POOR FARM.

A home for the friendless is always a subject which calls to mind various and conflicting thoughts, and at the same time a surge of feeling of pity. How many, in this wide land of ours, the footstool of the Almighty, for the brotherhood of man, have shuddered at the thought, and shrunk from the mention of the name of the "poor house." Yet, again, thousands have, when forsaken by friends, forgotten by relations, and alone in the world, hailed the name and place with joy and thanksgiving, as a Providential escape from starvation and death. Around the name cluster thoughts of pity and sadness for the poor unfortunate beings who are obliged to become inmates; and at the same time a feeling of gratitude creeps o'er us that we live in an age and land where such eleemosynary institutions are established and supported.

The poor farm of Butler county is located in section 34 of Jackson township. In 1876 the county purchased the northeast quarter of the section named for the purpose, and at once laid plans for the erection of suitable buildings. The contract for building the house was let to Wilkinson & Harvey, for the sum of $4,000, and this firm at once commenced the work, completing the building by the first of June, 1877. The size of the main part of the building is 28 by 44 feet, with a wing 28 by 32, two stories high. The wing is used by the superintendent and family, and the main part for the poor. The main part stories are divided into convenient rooms, the first floor being taken up by the kitchen and dining room, and the upper divided into twelve sleeping apartments. The house was opened to the poor on the 15th of February, 1877, at which time there was but one to put in an appearance and make this a home. At this time, however, there were about forty being supported by the county, but they preferred to take care of themselves. Up to the first of November, 1882, there had been over fifty different paupers on the list at the farm; at present there are but ten.

The county has increased the original purchase from 160 to 320 acres, and the farm is about self-sustaining. There are good buildings on the place for farm purposes—a barn 28 by 32 feet, and a large shed 16 by 100 feet. The salary of the superintendent is $35 per month. Joseph Scofield is the superintendent.

The house is now being arranged so that the county can take care of its insane, instead of having them sent to the asylum at Independence.

CHAPTER VI.

POLITICAL.

The political history of Butler county is more fully and much more authentic in giving the abstract of votes for the various years, than in any other manner, and for convenience of reference it will be appreciated. Any difficulties arising from contested and doubtful elections, or any peculiar features of a campaign, will appear in the following chapters, entitled County, State and National Representation, in connection with the article upon the office that occasioned it.

The first matter presented will be the—

OFFICIAL VOTE OF THE COUNTY FOR EVERY YEAR SINCE ORGANIZATION.

As no records were kept of the first two elections held in the county, we are unable to give the number of votes cast. The first election was ordered by Judge Roszell, of Buchanan county, as Butler was at that time annexed to that and several other counties, for judicial purposes. This was called in 1853, the election being held in August, and was the first attempt made at organization. Geo. W. Poisal was elected county judge, but did not qualify.

In October, 1854, the next election was held, and the organization of the county effected. It resulted in the election of John Palmer, county judge; W. E. Burton, clerk; A. G. Clark, treasurer and recorder; R. T. Crowell, sheriff; and James Griffith, school fund commissioner. These officers are all treated at length in their proper places.

It is likely that the record of the first two elections held here, was entered upon the books of Black Hawk county; but they have never been transcribed to Butler county books. The election records of Butler county commence with the election in April of 1855, and below we present the abstract, as follows:

April, 1855.

Prosecuting Attorney.
A. VanDorn.............................81—81

Drainage Commissioner.
John H. Miller, Rep................... 74—61
George Lash, Dem......................13
M. B. Wamsley, Dem....................1
O. A. Strong, Rep.....................3

Surveyor.
John H. Morton, Rep...................61—14
Thos. T. Rawson, Rep..................47
M. Marquest, Dem......................1

Sheriff.
W. H. Bishop, Rep.....................66—45
D. G. Hilton, Rep.....................21
Orson Rice, Rep.......................13

Coroner.
D. W. Kensley, Rep....................52—49
T. Miller.............................3
O. A. Strong, Rep.....................1

August, 1855.*

County Judge.
Aaron VanDorn, Rep............... 76—11
William R. Jaminson, Dem............. 65
D. B. Mason, Rep..................... 19
John Palmer, Rep..................... 1

Sheriff.
W. H. Bishop, Dem..................123—43
R L. Olmstead, Rep................... 80
Harlan Raid, Rep..................... 30
S. Moots, Dem........................ 2

Recorder and Treasurer.
A. G. Clark, Dem..................... 60—5
D. C. Hilton, Rep.................... 55
J. A. Barker, Rep.................... 39

Surveyor.
John H. Morton, Rep...............135—105
T. T. Rawson, Rep.................... 30
James McKinney, Dem.................. 2

Coroner.
Daniel Kensley, Rep.................. 89—57
Aaron Moore, Rep..................... 32
H. A. Early, Rep..................... 26

[* NOTE—This appears in record as "1855," but probably should be "1856."]

April, 1857.

Drainage Commissioners.
Limon Norton, Rep...................268—56
G. W. Dollison, Dem.................212

Clerk of Court.
James E. Walker, Rep................273

Surveyor.
George McClellan, Rep...............318—154
Jeremiah Ellis, Dem.................164

Assessor.
W. R. Cotton, Rep...................249—9
R. R. Parriott, Dem.................240

Coroner.
J. V. Boggs, Rep....................232—43
E. P. Dunson, Dem...................189

Prohibitory Hog Law.
For the law........................267—205
Against the law..................... 62

Court House Loan.
For the loan.......................304—139
Against the loan...................165

The Bridge Loan.
Against the loan...................312—180
For the loan.......................132

August, 1857.

County Judge.
Alonzo Converse, Rep...............181—8
G. W. Poisal, Dem..................173

Treasurer and Recorder.
D. C. Hilton, Rep ....413—341
I. H. Smith, Dem................... 72

Surveyor.
J. Ellis, Dem......................254—8
George McClellan, Rep..............246

Sheriff.
W. H. Bishop, Dem..................217—43
William Fitzgerald, Dem............174

Coroner.
J. A Barker, Rep...................297—155
E. Butterfield, Dem................142

Special Election, September, 1857.

County Judge.
D. W. Miller, Rep..................229—54
Alonzo Converse, Rep...............175
George A. Richmond, Dem............ 6
H. D. Hunt, Rep.................... 1
"Mother" Smith (Burlesque)......... 4

The above result was declared void upon contest of Alonzo Converse, as stated in another place.

Whether the County Should Subscribe for $200,000 Stock in the C. I. & N. R. R.
For the proposition................245—58
Against the proposition............187

HISTORY OF BUTLER COUNTY.

October, 1857.

Governor.
Ralph P. Lowe, Rep.....................196—46
B. M. Samuels, Dem...................150
George Hawker, Rep.................... 1

Lieutenant-Governor.
Oran Faville, Rep.....................197—48
George Gallaspie, Dem................149

Representative.
M. M. Trumbull, Rep..................172—6
J. C. Bishop, Dem....................166

April, 1858.

Superintendent of Schools.
D. W. Mason, Rep....................296—28
S. M. Chase, Dem 268
J. W. Davis, Rep..................... 72
George McClellan, Rep............... 4

Prosecuting Attorney.
W. R. Jamison, Dem..................338—101
O. Rice, Rep 237
Scattering............................ 20

The Bridge Loan.
For the loan.........................346—72
Against the loan.....................274

Re-location of County Seat.
For Clarksville......................327—7
For Georgetown.......................320

Special Election, June, 1858.

The General Banking Law.
For the law..........................141—57
Against the law...................... 84

Question of the State Bank of Iowa.
For the State bank...................226—216
Against the bank..................... 10

October, 1858.

Secretary of State.
Samuel Douglas, Dem.................347—102
Elijah Sells, Rep...................245

State Treasurer.
John W. Jones, Rep................. 348—104
Samuel L. Lorah, Dem...............244

State Auditor.
Theodore S. Parvin..................348—103
J. W. Cattell, Rep..................245

Attorney-General.
Samuel A. Rice, Rep.................346—101
James M. Elwood, Dem 245

Register State Land Office.
James M. Reid, Dem..................348—103
A. B. Miller, Rep...................245

Congress.
William Vandever, Rep...............345—98
W. E. Leffingwell, Dem 247

District Judge.
Elias H. Williams, Rep..............334—77
W. McClintock, Dem..................257

District Attorney.
M. McGlathery, Rep..................345—99
Elijah Odell, Dem...................246

April, 1859.

Re-locating the County Seat.
For Butler Center...................385—21
For Clarksville.....................364

October, 1859.

County Judge.
Alonzo Converse, Rep................360—62
M. M. Trumbull, Rep.................298
L. Converse......................... 2

County Treasurer and Recorder.
J. H. Hale, Rep.....................271—73
Asa Stannard, Rep...................198
D. C. Hilton, Rep...................197

Sheriff.
William R. Jamison, Dem.............360—65
James Leverich, Dem.................295
W. H. Bishop, Dem................... 4

School Superintendent.
I. R. Dean, Rep.....................368—73
M. D. L. Niece, Rep.................295

Surveyor.
Judd Bradley, Dem..............661—660
D. C. Hilton, Dem....................... 1

Drainage Commissioner.
R. R. Parriott, Dem..............343—19
Isaac Boylan, Dem..................324

Coroner.
John A. Barker, Rep..............333—2
David W. Miller, Rep..............331

October, 1861.

Judge of Supreme Court.
R. T. Lowe, Rep..................440—349
N. Elwood, Dem..................... 91

Representative.
C. A. L. Roszell, Dem..............297—33
Alonzo Converse, Rep..............264
F. Digman, Dem..................... 1
Nathan Moon, Dem................... 20

County Judge.
C. A. Bannon, Rep..................507
John Palmer, Rep..................... 2
Mr. Case, Rep....................... 1
V. Rice............................. 1
"Mrs. Jerome" (Burlesque)............ 3
M. Bailey, Rep...................... 15
A. Farlow, Dem...................... 1
H. H. Margretz, Rep................. 7
John Braden, Rep.................... 4
P. Cinnamon, Dem.................... 1
G. E. Fitch, Rep.................... 1
L. Hammon, Rep...................... 1
N. Olmstead, Rep.................... 1
C. A. L. Roszell, Dem............... 1

Treasurer and Recorder.
J. H. Hale, Rep..................389—83
D. C. Hilton, Rep..................306
John Palmer, Rep.................... 3
W. H. Bishop, Dem................... 1
M. Bailey, Rep...................... 1

Sheriff.
W. H. Bishop, Dem..................415—213
G. G. Hawker, Rep..................202

School Superintendent.
R. Merrill, Rep..................316—22
M. Bailey, Rep..................294

Surveyor.
G. McClellan, Rep ....608—607
R. Merrill, Rep....................... 1

Drainage Commissioner.
N. Olmstead, Rep..................305—28
H. A. Earley, Rep..................277
M. Aldridge, Dem................... 1
P. Robin........................... 2
C. S. Root, Rep.................... 1

Coroner.
J. A. Barker, Rep..................320—46
M. Aldridge, Dem...................274
O. Rice............................ 1

October, 1862.

State Auditor.
J. W. Cattell, Rep................339—32
John Brown, Dem...................207

Register State Land Office.
J. A. Harvey, Rep..................338—34
F. Gottschalk, Dem................206

State Treasurer.
W. H. Holmes, Rep ....339—132
S. L. Lorah, Dem..................207

Attorney-General.
C. Nours, Rep......................330—128
B. J. Hale, Dem...................202

Congress.
A. W. Hubbard, Rep................339—135
J. W. Duncomb, Dem................204

10th District Judge.
Elias H. Williams, Rep..............498—489
L. L. Ainsworth, Dem................ 9
A. Durand, Rep...................... 2

District Attorney.
Milo McGlathery, Rep..............509

Member Board of Education.
G. H. Stevens, Rep..................515

HISTORY OF BUTLER COUNTY.

County Judge.
J. R. Fletcher, Dem..................221—67
W. A. Lathrop, Rep..................154
A. J. Thompkins, Rep 154
A. J. Thompson, Rep.................. 2
W. S. Lathrop........................ 1
G. G. Hawker........................ 1

Clerk of Court.
J. W. Davis, Rep........ ....522—521
Elias Oxford, Rep..................... 1

Drainage Commissioner.
H. A. Early, Rep. .... 67—11
Alonzo Norris, Rep................... 56
E. S. Shaw, Dem..... 33
Scattering.... 53

Coroner.
James A. Gurthie, Rep................ 52—21
A. Durand, Dem...................... 31
Asa Overcracker...................... 28
Scattering......... 65

October, 1863.

Governor.
William M. Stern, Rep...............495—250
J. M. Tuttle, Dem...................245

Lieutenant-Governor.
E. W. Eastman, Rep..................494—259
J. F. Duncomb, Dem.................235

Judge of Supreme Court.
Hon. John Dillon, Rep............. ...501—264
Hon. Charles Mason, Dem............287

State Senator.
C. F. Clarkson, Rep..................487—237
S. P. Brainard, Dem..................250
G. F. Clarkson, Rep................. 1
H. Seymour.......................... 1

Representative.
W. A. Lathrop, Rep... ....488—251
N. B. Chapman, Dem.................287
John Smith........................... 1
N. P. Chapman................. 13

County Judge.
Ancel Durand, Rep...................401—75
J. R. Fletcher, Dem 326
A. Phillips........................... 1
J. Bradley........ 1

Treasurer and Recorder.
John Palmer, Rep....................484—227
J. Gilbert, Dem............ 257
J. Spincer........................... 1

Sheriff.
M. Hollenbeck, Rep..................465—183
W. H. Bishop, Dem..................282

School Superintendent.
Richard Merrill, Rep..... ....487—278
J. Bradley, Dem.....................209
A. F. Townsend, Rep................. 15
J. Palmer, Rep....................... 1
William Rosebraugh........ 1
"Old Notts".... 1

County Surveyor.
A. F. Townsend, Rep ....519—493
Scattering......................... ... 26

Coroner.
E. W. Metzgar, Rep..................483—259
R. Daniels, Rep......................224
Dawson............................. 1

Drainage Commissioner.
T. G. Copeland, Rep.................455—198
G. W. Adair, Dem....................257

October, 1864.

President of United States.
Abraham Lincoln, Republican.........539—318
George B. McClellan, Dem............241

Secretary of State.
James Wright, Rep...................558—316
John H. Wallace, Dem................242

State Treasurer.
W. H. Holmes, Rep..................558—316
J. B. Lash, Dem.................... ..242

State Auditor.
John A. Elliott, Rep.................558—315
E. C. Hendershott, Dem.............243

Register State Land Office.
J. A. Harvey, Rep................558—323
B. D. Holbrook, Dem 235
E. B. Holbrook...................... 7

Attorney-General.
Isaac L. Allen, Rep................558—316
Charles M. Dunbar....................242

Judge of Supreme Court
Chester C. Cole, Rep ....559—318
Thomas M. Monroe, Dem............241

Congress.
A. W. Hubbard, Rep................558—316
L. Chapman, Dem 242

Judge of 12th Judicial District.
William B. Fairfield, Rep............560—345
Cyrus W. Foreman, Dem............215

District Attorney.
John E. Burke, Rep ....559—344
M. P. Rosencrans, Dem.............215

Clerk of Court.
James W. Davis, Rep................575—377
M. B. Wamsley, Dem................198
Abram Smith, Rep.................... 27

County Recorder.
J. H. Hale, Rep....................573—373
Milton Wilson, Dem..................200
P. S. Canfield....................... 27

Coroner.
E. B. Allen, Rep....................568—355
James Aplington, Dem...............213

October, 1865.
Governor.
W. M. Stone, Rep..................454—222
T. H. Benton, Dem..................232
Col. G. Benton 3
W. T. Shaw......................... 1

Lieutenant-Governor.
B. F. Gue, Rep....................489—288
W. W. Hamilton, Dem...............201
S. G. VanAnda, Gr.................. 6

State Senator.
J. B. Powers, Rep..................498—299
S. N. Packard, Dem.................199

Representative.
L. D. Tracy, Rep...................478—286
P. J. Hagerty, Dem.................192
A. Converse, Rep.................... 14

Judge of Supreme Court.
G. G. Wright, Rep..................493—286
H. H. Trimble, Dem.................207

State Superintendent.
Oran Faville, Rep..................494—287
J. W. Sennett, Dem 207

County Judge.
A. J. Thompkins, Rep..............484—299
Alonzo Converse, Rep..............185
James Wilson, Rep.................... 1

County Treasurer.
John Palmer, Rep...................489—304
John J. Eichar, Dem................185
Scattering.......................... 4

Sheriff.
M. Hollenbeck, Rep.................493—295
W. H. Bishop, Dem.................198

School Superintendent.
W. H. Gue, Rep....................495—296
Richard Merrill, Rep...............199
R. Herd, Rep........................ 1

Coroner.
George Murphy, Rep................496—297
E. R. Goheen, Dem.................199

County Surveyor.
M. D. L. Neice, Rep...............495—294
Judd Bradley, Dem.................201
L. B. Raymond, Dem................ 2

Drainage Commissioner.
W. C. Thompson, Rep..............503—305
R. Parriott, Dem...................198

October, 1866.
Secretary of State.
Ed. Wright, Rep....................673—435
S. G. VanAnda, Dem................238
J. F. Duncombe, Gr................. 24

HISTORY OF BUTLER COUNTY.

State Treasurer.
S. E. Rankin, Rep............ ....673—436
George A. Stine, Dem................237
N. G. Sales 24

State Auditor.
J. A. Elliott, Rep.....................674—436
R. W. Cross, Dem....................238
R. S. Higgins.......................... 24

Register State Land Office.
C. C. Carpenter, Rep............ .....674—436
L. P. McKennie, Dem................238
D. Stoddard............................ 24

Attorney-General.
F. E. Bissell, Rep....................675—437
W. Ballinger, Dem....................238
C. Negus........................ 23

Reporter of Supreme Court.
E. H. Stiles, Rep....................674—618
A. Stockdale, Dem.................... 56

Clerk of Supreme Court.
C. Linderman, Rep.................. 675—621
F. Goluchalk, Dem.................. 54

Congress.
A. W. Hubbard, Rep...... ....675—441
J. D. Thompson, Dem. 234

Clerk of Court.
James W. Davis, Rep.................674—472
Tracy M. Bishop, Dem................202
Dunson, Dem......................... 1
Capt. Jones, Rep..................... 1

County Recorder.
J. H. Hale, Rep......................695—508
Abram Surfus, Rep....................187
J. W. Davis, Rep...... 2
M. Bailey,... 1

October, 1867.

Governor.
Samuel Merrill, Rep...................678—372
Charles Mason, Dem........ 306
William Muffley....................... 2

Lieutenant-Governor.
Col. John Scott, Rep.................680—340
D. M. Harris, Dem................... 340

Attorney-General.
Henry O'Conner, Rep.................673—361
W. T. Barker, Dem.................: 312

Judge Supreme Court.
Joseph M. Beck... ....513—206
John H. Craig.......................307
James M. Beck....... 165

State Superintendent.
D. F. Wells........................ ......531—220
Martin L. Fisher.......................311
B. F. Wells..........................151

State Senator.
W. A. Lathrop, Rep..................406—70
Marcus Tuttle, Rep...................336
C. A. L. Roszell, Dem 236

Representative.
J. A. Guthrie, Rep...... ....623—312
James W. Wood, Dem...............311
A. Converse, Rep..................... 10
B. Codner........................... 1
N. Pray............................ 1

County Judge.
A. J. Thompkins, Rep.............. ...680—390
W. R. Jamison, Dem............ 290
J. W. Davis, Rep..................... 1

Treasurer.
J. F. Wright, Rep....................660—349
M. B. Wamsley, Dem...................311
J. Palmer, Rep..................... 3
M. Bailey, Rep....................... 4

Sheriff.
L. L. Smith, Rep....................572—208
W. H. Bishop, Dem...................364
M. Hollenbeck, Rep..................... 9

School Superintendent.
W. A. Lathrop. Rep..................381— 81
George Graham, Rep..................300
Milton Wilson, Dem...................279

Coroner.
E. W. Metzgar, Rep..................671—366
J. H. Smith, Rep.....................305

Surveyor.
O. W. McIntosh, Rep................629—615
O. H. McIntosh....................... 14
Scattering............................. 10

Drainage Commissioner.
E. D. Butler, Rep....................670—670

October, 1868.
President.
U. S. Grant, Rep...................1,118—694
Horatio Seymour, Dem............... 424

Secretary of State.
Ed. Wright, Rep...................1,117—705
David Hammer, Dem................ 412

State Auditor.
J. A. Elliot, Rep...................1,118—707
H. Dunlary, Dem.................... 311

State Treasurer.
S. E Rankin, Rep..................1,117—706
L. McCarty, Dem.................... 411

Register State Land Office.
C. C. Carpenter, Rep...............1,116—705
A. D. Anderson, Dem................ 411

Attorney General.
Henry O'Conner, Rep..............1,116—705
J. E. Williamson, Dem............... 411

Congress.
Charles Pomeroy, Rep.............1,094—664
C. A. L Roszelle, Dem............... 430

District Judge.
W. B. Fairfield, Rep...............1,093—679
Cyrus Foreman, Dem................ 414

District Attorney.
I. W. Card, Rep...................1,115—705
W. W. Stow, Dem................... 410
C A. L. Roszelle, Dem............... 1

Circuit Judge.
Geo. W. Ruddick, Rep.............1,116—707
R. N Matthews, Dem................ 409

Clerk of Court.
James W. Davis, Rep..............1,104—697
Milton Wilson, Dem................. 407

County Recorder.
George M. Craig, Rep..............1,112—704
Richard Gonzales, Dem.............. 408

Surveyor.
Joseph Conn, Rep.................1,116—706
J. G. Scobey, Dem.................. 410

October, 1869.
Governor.
Samuel Merrill, Rep................687—441
George Gillaspy, Dem...............246

Lieutenant-Governor.
M. M. Walden......................688—442
A. P. Richardson...................246

Judge of Supreme Court.
John S. Dillon.....................689—445
W. B Brannom.....................244

State Superintendent.
A. S. Kissell.......................688—442
H. O. Dayton......................246

State Senator.
R. B. Clarke, Rep..................676—442
William Pattee, Dem................234
A. J. Thompkins, Rep............... 1
A. Converse, Rep................... 5

Representative.
S. B. Dumont, Rep.................968—723
P. J. Haggarty, Dem................245

County Auditor.
A. J. Thompkins, Rep..............682—435
Thomas Shaffer, Dem...............247
M. B Wamsley, Dem................ 2

County Treasurer.
J. F. Wright, Rep..................683—438
M. B. Wamsley, Dem...............245

Sheriff.
L. L. Smith, Rep...................675—422
Henry Sweitger, Dem...............253
Isaac Hall......................... 1

School Superintendent.
W. A. Lathrop, Rep ....634—369
J. A. Holmes, Dem 265
W. H. Merrill...................... 4

HISTORY OF BUTLER COUNTY.

Surveyor.
O. W. McIntosh, Rep...............685—444
J. G. Scoby, Dem......................241

Coroner.
T. G. Copeland, Rep..................681—436
J. M. Caldwell, Dem..................245

Drainage Commissioner.
E. D. Button, Rep....................686—446
P. Dunson, Dem.......................240

Special Election, April, 1870.

Senator, to fill vacancy.
J. R. Fletcher, Rep..................873—815
Emmons Johnson, Rep.................. 58
J. M. Caldwell, Dem.................. 1
Mrs. Winne........................... 3
George Poisal, Dem................... 1

October, 1870.

Judge of Supreme Court.
C. C. Cole..........................1,138—716
J. C. Knapp.......................... 422
R. Noble............................. 54

Same, to fill vacancies.
William E. Miller...................1,209
P. N. Smith.......................... 425
J. G. Day...........................1,209
R. Noble............................. 426

Secretary of State.
Ed. Wright..........................1,212—788
Charles Doerr........................ 424

State Auditor.
John Bissell........................1,211—786
W. W. Garner........................ 425

State Treasurer.
S. E. Rankin........................1,211—787
W. C. Jones.......................... 424

Attorney General.
Henry O'Conner......................1,210—784
H. M. Mortin......................... 426

Register State Land Office.
Aaron Brown.........................1,211—787
D. F. Ellsworth...................... 424

Supreme Court Reporter.
E. N. Stiles........................1,211—1,012
C. H. Bone........................... 199
J. L. Sheeon......................... 225

Congress.
Jackson Orr, Rep....................1,213—789
G. C. Smeltzer, Dem.................. 424

District Judge.
G. W. Ruddick, Rep..................1,209—1,202
H. Shaver............................   7

Clerk of Court.
J. W. Davis, Ind..................... 878—184
Van E. Butler, Rep................... 694

County Recorder.
G. M. Craig, Ind..................... 359—124
J. H. Hale, Rep...................... 735
William Douns........................   3

County Supervisors.
M. B. Wamsley, Dem..................1,285
H. C. Brown, Rep....................1,379
A. Chrystie, Rep....................1,387
J. Proctor, Rep...................... 244
P. E. Denison, Dem................... 246
E. P. Day, Dem....................... 329

As to increasing Supervisors to seven.
Against the proposition............. 962—585
For the proposition................. 377

October, 1871.

Governor.
C. C. Carpenter, Rep................1,127—799
J. C. Knapp, Dem..................... 328
C. H. Forney.........................   1

Lieutenant-Governor.
H. C. Bullis, Rep...................1,127—799
M. M. Hannom, Dem.................... 328

Judge of Supreme Court.
James G. Day........................1,094—759
J. L. Duncan......................... 345

State Superintendent.
Alonzo Abernethy....................1,127—799
Edward Mumm......................... 328

State Senator.
A. Converse, Rep............1,072—1,028
C. A. L. Roszell, Dem............... 44
J. W. Davis, Rep.................. 31

Representatives.
S. B. Dumont, Rep............1,129—962
J. M. Caldwell, Dem.......... 167
C. A. L. Roszell, Dem............... 20

County Treasurer.
W. C. Thompson, Rep..........1,323—1,287
J. F. Wright, Rep................ 36

Auditor.
R. L. Chase, Rep.............. 797—195
A. J. Thompkins, Rep............ 602
W. C. Thompson, Rep............ 1

Sheriff.
J. R. Jones, Rep................ 978—678
M. Hollenbeck, Rep.............. 300
Scattering....................... 16

Drainage Commissioner.
Henry Trotter, Rep..................1,296

School Superintendent.
J. W. Stewart, Rep............1,296—1,294
W. A. Lathrop, Rep.............. 2

Surveyor.
M. D. L Niece, Rep............ 958—946
J. G. Scobey, Dem............... 12
O. W. McIntosh, Rep............ 1

Coroner.
T. G. Copeland, Rep............1,285—1,273
E. W. Metzgar, Rep.............. 12

Supervisor.
S. Bonwell, Rep...............1,102—766
M. B. Wamsley, Dem............. 336

Judge of Circuit Court.
R. G. Renegar, Rep..................1,157

November, 1872.

President.
U. S. Grant, Rep...............1,433—1,002
Horace Greeley, Lib.............. 431

Secretary of State.
J. T. Young....................1,442—996
E. A. Guilbert................... 446
Charles Baker 5

State Auditor.
John Russell...................1,442—994
J. P. Casady..................... 448

State Treasurer.
William Chrysty................1,444—998
M. J. Rohlfs.................... 446
D. B. Beers..................... 5

Register State Land Office.
Aaron Brown....................1,443—999
Jacob Butler.................... 444
David Sherwood.................. 5

Attorney General.
M. E. Cutts....................1,444—993
A. G. Case...................... 451

Congress.
H. O. Pratt, Rep...............1,445—999
A. T. Lusch, Dem................ 446

District Judge.
G. W. Ruddick, Rep.............1,434—981
W. A. Lathrop, Rep.............. 453

Circuit Judge.
R. G. Reiniger, Rep............1,442—907
W. C. Stanberry, Dem............ 445

District Attorney.
L. S. Butler, Rep..............1,446—1,008
J. W. Woods, Dem................ 438

County Clerk.
William Burdick, Rep...........1,415—949
Edwin Fowle, Rep................ 466
Martin Bailey, Rep.............. 6

Recorder.
Elwood Wilson, Rep.............1,415—929
W. I. McLean, Dem............... 486
William Griffith, Rep........... 1

County Supervisor.
H. C. Brown, Rep............... 1,234—616
M. B. Wamsley, Dem.............. 638
.....Wamsley.................... 4

October, 1873.
Governor.
C. C. Carpenter, Rep.............1,200—998
Jacob B. Vale, Dem............... 202
Lieutenant-Governor.
Joseph Dysart, Rep.............1,209—1,013
C. E. Whitney..................... 196
Judge Supreme Court.
J. M. Beck.....................1,207—1,013
B. J. Hall........................ 194
State Superintendent.
A. Abernethy..................1,214—1,024
D. W. Prindle..................... 190
Representative.
C. A. L. Roszell, Dem............. 761—103
N. N. Beals, Rep.................. 658
County Treasurer.
W. C. Thompson, Rep............1,341—1,315
Martin Bailey, Rep................ 26
G. M. Craig, Rep.................. 1
Auditor.
R. L. Chase, Rep..................1,390
Sheriff.
J. R. Jones, Rep..................1,372
Superintendent.
J. W. Stewart, Rep................1,366
Supervisor.
Alex Chrystie, Rep................1,379
Surveyor.
J. G. Rockwell, Rep...............1,374
Drainage Commissioner.
E. D. Button, Rep.................1,149
Coroner.
E. W. Metzgar, Rep................1,354

October, 1874.
Secretary of State.
J. T. Young....................1,082—743
David Morgan..................... 339
State Auditor.
B. R. Sherman..................1,055—688
J. M. King....................... 367

State Treasurer.
W. Christy.....................1,055—689
H. C. Hargis..................... 366
Register State Land Office.
David Secer...................1,055—688
R. H. Roderamel.................. 367
Attorney General.
M. E. Cutts...................1,051—683
John Keatley.................... 368
Clerk of Supreme Court.
E. J. Holmes..................1,054—687
G. W. Ball...................... 367
Reporter of Supreme Court.
J. S. Runnells................1,054—691
J. M. Weart..................... 363
County Recorder.
E. Wilson, Rep...................1,244
Clerk of Courts.
W. H. Burdick, Rep............1,240—1,222
Van E. Butler, Rep............... 18
Supervisor.
N. N. Larkin, Rep................1,160

October, 1875.
Governor.
S. J. Kirkwood................1,375—751
S. Leffler...................... 624
Lieutenant-Governor.
J. G. Newbold.................1,367—733
E. B. Woodward.................. 634
Supreme Judge.
Austin Adams..................1,372—741
W. H. Knight.................... 631
State Superintendent.
A. Abernethy..................1,366—736
I. Doane........................ 630
State Senator.
A. C. Hitchcock..................1,220
Representative.
John Palmer, Rep..............1,059—148
C. A. L. Roszell, Dem........... 911

HISTORY OF BUTLER COUNTY.

County Auditor.
R.L.Chase, Rep................1,329—663
M.Bailey, Ind...................... 666

Treasurer.
E.Thomas, Rep................1,061—123
M.B.Wamsley, Dem.............. 938

Sheriff.
J.R.Jones, Rep.................1,089—191
M.M.Hollenbeck, Ind............ 898

School Superintendent.
J.W.Stewart, Ind................1,293—628
Mrs.Jean L.Smith, Rep.......... 665

Surveyor.
J.G.Rockwell, Rep..............1,205—407
Charles Fitch, Dem............... 798

Drainage Commissioner.
E.D.Button, Rep................1,186—376
James M.Caldwell, Dem......... 810

Supervisor.
G.Hazelet, Rep..................1,147—297
Milton Wilson, Dem.............. 850

Coroner.
C.A.Murray, Rep................1,179—372
E.L.Blackmore, Dem............. 807

Shall there be seven Supervisors?
No................................. 691—289
Yes................................ 402

November, 1876.
President.
Rutherford B.Hayes, Rep........1,829—1,049
S.J.Tilden, Dem.................. 780
.... 22

Judge of Supreme Court.
W.H.Seevers....................1,846—1,087
W.Hayes........................... 759
Charles Negus..................... 4

State Auditor.
B.R.Sherman, Rep..............1,841—1,083
W.Groneneg 758
Leonard Brown..................... 4

Secretary of State.
J.T.Young, Rep.................1,840—1,082
J.H.Stubenranch.................. 758
A.McReady........................ 4

State Treasurer.
G.W.Bemis.....................1,840—1,081
W.Jones........................... 759
G.C.Fry........................... 4

Register State Land Office.
David Secor....................1,840—1,081
N.C Ridenour 759
G.M.Walker....................... 4

Attorney General.
J.F.McJunkin..................1,840—1,081
J.C.Cook.......................... 759

State Superintendent.
C.W.VonColln..................1,840—1,836
J.A.Nash.......................... 4

Congress.
N.C.Deering, Rep..............1,841—1,045
Cyrus Foreman, Dem.............. 796

Circuit Judge.
R.G.Reiniger, Rep..............1,895—1,352
C.S.Root, Dem.................... 543
J.M.Elder, Greenb................ 106

District Judge.
George W.Ruddick, Rep.........1,799—1,051
C.A.L.Roszelle, Dem.............. 748

District Attorney.
J.B.Cleland, Rep...............1,908—1,274
John Cligget, Dem................ 634

State Senator.
W.W.Blackman, Rep............1,853—1,413
A.G.Case, Dem.................... 440
Lucius Lane, Greenb.............. 211
Cyrus Lane........................ 95

Clerk of Courts.
W.H.Burdick, Rep..............1,945—1,417
C H.Ilgenfritz, Dem.............. 528

County Recorder.
Elwood Wilson, Rep.............2,074—1,534
E.Jordan, Dem.................... 540

Supervisor.
Alex Chrystie, Rep.............1,907—1,367
Henry Sweitzer, Dem............ 540

Court House Tax.
No..............................2,244—2,113
Yes............................. 131

October, 1877.
Governor.
John H. Gear...................1,453—695
John P. Irish.................. 758
D. P. Stubbs................... 19
Elias Jessup................... 95

Lieutenant-Governor.
Frank T. Campbell..............1,565—805
W. C. James.................... 760
A. Macready.................... 10

Judge of Supreme Court.
J. G. Day......................1,568—807
H. E. J. Boardman.............. 761
John Porter.................... 10

State Superintendent.
C. W. Von Coelln ....1,567—805
J. G. Cullison................. 762
S. T. Ballard.................. 10

Representative.
A. M. Whaley, Rep ....1,199—143
C. A. L. Roszelle, Dem.........1,056
C. H. Forney................... 29

County Auditor.
J. McElvain, Rep..............1,487—662
R. L. Chase, Ind. Rep 825

Treasurer.
E. S. Thomas, Rep..............2,293

Sheriff.
M. B. Speedy, Rep..............1,343—386
J. R. Jones, Ind. Rep.......... 957

School Superintendent.
J. W. Stewart, Rep.............2,237—2,223
J. R. Wagner, Rep.............. 14

Coroner.
H. J. Playter, Rep.............1,307—310
E. C. Beasmont, Dem............ 997

Surveyor.
S. G. Rockwell, Rep............1,013—62
O. W. McIntosh, Rep............ 951
J. D. Rockwell................. 346

Supervisor.
A. N. Leet, Rep ....1,296—275
Chas. Fitch, Dem...............1,021

October, 1878.
Secretary of State.
John A. T. Hull................1,046—118
John A. Hull................... 928
J. A. Hull..................... 167
J. A. T. Hull.................. 62
E. M. Farnsworth............... 156

State Auditor.
Buren Sherman..................1,261—372
B. R. Sherman.................. 889
Joseph Erboeck................. 167
G. V. Sweringen................ 41

State Treasurer.
Geo W. Bemis...................1,428—502
M L Devin...................... 926

Register State Land Office.
James R. Powers................1,430—502
M. F Farrington 928

Attorney General.
J. F. McJunkin.................1,429—541
John F. Gibbons................ 888
C. H. Jackson.................. 41

Judge of Supreme Court.
J. H. Rothrock.................1,408—457
J. C. Knapp.................... 951

Clerk of Supreme Court.
E. J. Holmes...................1,312—383
E. H. Holmes................... 929
Alex Runyon.................... 118

Reporter of Supreme Court.
J. S. Runnels..................1,430—701
J. B. Elliott.................. 729
J. P. Elliott.................. 128
John Elliott................... 31
George W. Rutherford........... 41

HISTORY OF BUTLER COUNTY.

Congress.
N. C. Deering, Rep..................1,405—679
W. V. Allen, Dem..................... 726
L. H. Weller, Greenb.................. 228

Clerk of Courts.
C. H. Ilgenfritz, Dem............... 1,248—138
W. H. Burdick, Rep..................1,110

County Recorder.
W. W. Pattee, Dem..................1,177—5
D. H. Sessions, Rep..................1,172

Supervisor.
Milton Wilson, Dem.................1,234—7
G. Hazlet, Rep......................1,227

October, 1879.
Governor.
J. H. Geer..........................1,726—921
N. N. Trimble 805
Daniel Campbell..................... 60
D. R. Dungan........................ 59

Lieutenant-Governor.
F. T. Campbell......................1,783—980
J. A. O. Yeoman..................... 803
M. N. Moore......................... 62

Judge of Supreme Court.
J. M. Beck..........................1,777—968
R. Noble............................ 809
M. N. Jones......................... 61

State Superintendent.
C. W. VonCoelln.....................1,739—939
Edwin Baker......................... 800
J. N. Nash.......................... 114

State Senator.
W. P. Gaylord, Rep.................1,789—1,655
N. L. Root, Dem..................... 134

Representative.
A. M. Whaly, Rep...................1,647—674
H. H. Markley, Dem.................. 973

Auditor.
James W. Spencer...................1,645—672
E. Jordan, Dem...................... 973

Treasurer.
John W. Ray, Rep...................1,830—1,020
Cyrus Dotty, Dem.................... 810

Sheriff.
Gilbert Hazlet, Rep................1,666—709
Charles Fitch, Dem.................. 957

School Superintendent.
J. W. Stewart, Rep.................1,678—1,143
H. M. Swan, Ind..................... 535

Surveyor.
J. G. Rockwell, Rep................1,612—700
O. W. McIntosh, Rep................. 912
Hugh Mullarky, Dem.................. 93

Coroner.
H. J. Playter, Rep.................1,520—732
Hugh Mullarky, Dem 788

Supervisor.
J. J. Burnham, Rep.................1,654—666
James Kennedy, Dem.................. 988

Drainage Commissioner.
Noble Thompson, Rep................1,755—881
M. Morris, Dem...................... 574

November, 1880.
President.
James A. Garfield, Rep.............2,072—1,135
W. S. Hancock, Dem.................. 937
Gen. J. B. Weaver, Gr............... 43

Secretary of State.
J. A. T. Hull......................2,075—1,144
A. B. Keith......................... 931
G. M. Walker........................ 37
A. W. Hall.......................... 1

State Auditor.
E. H. Conger.......................2,073—1,137
Martin Blim......................... 936
M. Farrington....................... 47
G. P. Loomis........................ 1

Register State Land Office.
J. K. Powers.......................2,079—1,146
Daniel Dougherty.................... 933
Thomas Hooker....................... 37
M. S. Drury......................... 1

H. C. Brown.

HISTORY OF BUTLER COUNTY.

Attorney-General.
Smith McPherson .... 2,069—1,134
C. A. Clark 935
W. A. Spernier 37
William Wolf 1

Congress.
N. C. Deering, Rep .... 2,029—1,137
J. S. Root, Dem 892
M. B. Doolittle 30
E. J. Dean, Gr 84

Circuit Judge.
Robert G. Reiniger, Rep .... 2,073—1,150
Cyrus Foreman, Dem 923
Scattering 14

District Judge.
G. W. Ruddick, Rep .... 2,069—1,147
John Cliggett, Dem 922

District Attorney.
John B. Clelland, Rep .... 2,063—1,137
A. C. Ripley, Dem 924

Senator.
(To fill vacancy).
A. M. Whaley, Rep .... 1,953—1,131
R. C. Mathews, Dem 822
P. F. Casey, Gr 20
Scattering 9

Clerk of Courts.
C. H. Ilgenfritz, Dem .... 1,741—503
O. B. Courtright, Rep 1,238
Scattering 3

County Recorder.
W. W. Pattee, Dem .... 1,707—411
O. B. Barnum, Rep 1,296

Supervisor.
A. N. Leet, Ind Rep .... 1,650—296
August Critzman, Rep 1,354
Scattering 2

Constitutional Convention.
Yes .... 549—306
No 243

Constitutional Amendment.
Yes .... 630—505
No 125

Re-location of County Seat.
Allison .... 1,529—265
Butler Center 1,264

October, 1881.

Governor.
B. R. Sherman .... 1,138—880
L. G. Kinne 258
G. M Clark 7

Lieutenant-Governor.
O. H. Manning .... 1,007—703
J. M. Walker 304
J. M. Holland 7

Judge of Supreme Court.
Austin Adams .... 1,098—797
H. B. Hendershott 301
W. W. Williamson 6
Scattering 1

State Superintendent.
J. W. Akers .... 1,096—791
W. H. Butler 305
A. M. Swain 7

Representative.
Henry C. Brown, Rep .... 1,333—1,322
Scattering 11

County Treasurer.
John W. Ray, Rep .... 1,328—1,302
Cyrus Doty, Dem 26

Auditor.
James W. Spencer, Rep .... 1,364—1,362
Scattering 2

Sheriff.
Gilbreth Hazlett, Rep .... 1,209—1,040
John M. Court, Ind. Rep 169

Supervisor.
Charles L. Jones, Rep .... 844—289
M. Wilson, Ind. Dem 555
Scattering 1

Superintendent of Schools.
John D. Anderson, Rep .... 1,343—1,336
Scattering 7

Surveyor.
O. W. McIntosh, Rep............1,329—1,319
Scattering....................... 10

Coroner.
W. M. Foote, Rep................1,360—1,342
Scattering....................... 18

Special Election, June, 1882.
Constitutional Amendment.
(To prohibit the manufacture and sale of intoxicating liquors).
For the amendment...............1,669—849
Against the amendment........... 820

November, 1882.
Secretary of State.
J. A. T. Hull....................1,652—775
T. D. Walker.................... 877
W. J. Gaston.................... 65

State Auditor.
J. L Brown......................1,642—759
William Thompson................ 883
G. A. Wyant..................... 65

State Treasurer.
E. H. Conger....................1,653—888
John Foley...................... 825
George Derr..................... 65

Attorney General.
S. McPherson....................1,653—770
J. H. Bremermann................ 883
J. W. Rice...................... 65

Judge of Supreme Court.
W. H. Seevers...................1,653—770
C. E. Bronson................... 883
M. A. Jones..................... 65

Clerk of Supreme Court.
G. B. Gray......................1,653—777
H. F. Bonorden.................. 876
E. N. Clark..................... 65
Scattering...................... 7

Reporter for Supreme Court.
E. C. Ebersole..................1,652—776
L. A. Palmer.................... 876
L. D. Palmer.................... 7
J. H. Williamson................ 65

Congress.
David B. Henderson, Rep.........1,708—895
C. M. Durham, Dem............... 813
G. N. Durham.................... 4
Roswell Foster, Greenb.......... 71

Clerk of Courts.
W. S. Montgomery, Rep...........1,322—97
C. H. Ilgenfritz, Dem...........1,225
Scattering...................... 3

County Recorder.
W. M. Hunter, Rep...............1,284—3
A. Edwards, Ind. Rep............1,281
Scattering...................... 2

Supervisor.
Jas. M. Groat, Rep..............2,458—2,453
Scattering...................... 5

CHAPTER VII.

NATIONAL, STATE AND COUNTY REPRESENTATION.

While unworthy men, at times, may force themselves into office, it cannot but be acknowledged that the great body of officeholders of the country are truly representative men—men of positive force and character. They are of the number that build up and strengthen a town, a county, or a State. In this chapter, as far as possible, is given sketches of all who have served Butler county in the Nation, State or county. Some of the sketches are imperfect, but it is not the fault of the historian that they are not more complete. Some of the parties have passed away, leaving no record from which a sketch could be obtained, while others have left the county and their present place of residence is unknown.

CONGRESSIONAL.

Butler county became a part of the Second Congressional district, on its organization, and was represented in the 33d Congress, from 1853 to 1855, by John P. Cook, of Davenport. Mr. Cook was a native of the State of New York, and in 1836 came west to Davenport. He was elected a member of Congress as a Whig, and held the views of that party until its dissolution. On the breaking up of the Whig party he affiliated with the Democratic party, the principles of which he labored to sustain and promulgate, even to the end of his days. His life had been one of great energy and industry. He was by natural instinct a true western man—a wide-awake, thoroughly active pioneer, who never saw the time when he could lay aside the business harness, and, to all appearances, never wanted to. As a lawyer he had few superiors, was always ready, fluent, and an able advocate, and with these qualities were combined energy, tact and industry; and for years past and up to the day of his demise no law firm in the northwest had stood in better repute than that broken by his death. Mr. Cook died at Davenport, April 17, 1872.

James Thorington, of Davenport, was the next Representative in Congress from the Second district. He was not a man of extraordinary ability, but was a good politician and wire-puller. He is now a Consul in one of the South American States.

Timothy Davis, of Elkader, Clayton county, next served the district from 1857 to 1859, or in the 35th Congress.

William Vandever, of Dubuque, was elected a member of the 35th Congress and re-elected to the 37th. William Vandever is a native of Maryland. In 1839 he came west, locating in Rock Island, where he remained until 1851, when he moved to Dubuque. In 1855 he formed a partnership with Ben. W. Samuels, of Dubuque, in the practice of law. In 1858 he was elected a member of the 36th Congress. He made a useful member of that body. While serving his second term, he abandoned his seat in Congress, returned home, and raised the 9th Iowa Infantry, of which he was made Colonel. In 1862 he was promoted a Brigadier-General, and at the close of the war was brevetted Major-General. Since the close of the war he has held several important public positions.

By the census of 1862, Iowa was entitled to six Representatives in Congress. Butler county, on the State being re-districted, became a part of the Sixth district. Its first Representative from this district was Asahel W. Hubbard, from Sioux City. He was elected in the fall of 1862, and became a member of the 38th Congress. He was re-elected a member of the 39th and 40th Congresses. He was a native of Connecticut, born in 1817. In 1836 he came West to Indiana, and in 1857 to Iowa, locating at Sioux City. He had been in the latter place only one year when he was elected Judge of the Fourth Judicial District. While a member of Congress he served on committees of Foreign Affairs, Public Expenditures and Indian Affairs. He was very attentive to his duties while in Congress, and served his constituents and the State with unqualified satisfaction.

Charles Pomeroy, of Fort Dodge, was the next Representative in Congress from the 6th district. He was elected in 1868 as a member of the 41st Congress, and served one term.

Jackson Orr, of Boonsboro, succeeded Mr. Pomeroy in 1871, and served in the 42d Congress as a Representative from the 6th district. Mr. Orr was re-elected as a member from the 9th district, and served in the 43d Congress.

In 1870 it was found the population of the State had increased to a number entitling it to nine Representatives in Congress. In re-districting, Butler county became a part of the 4th district. It was first represented by Henry O. Pratt, of Charles City, in the 43d Congress. Mr. Pratt was re-elected in the 44th, and thus served until March, 1877. Mr. Pratt is a native of Maine. He was admitted to the bar in Mason City, Cerro Gordo county, Iowa, in June, 1862. Soon afterward a call was made for 600,000 men by the President. He enlisted as a private in Co. B, 32d Iowa Infantry. He became completely broken down in health in less than a year, and was discharged in the spring of 1863. The following summer, while regaining his health, he taught a small school in Worth county, Iowa. His health being restored, Mr. Pratt commenced the practice of law at Charles City. As a lawyer he is very candid in the trial of a case; he never tries to defeat the ends of justice, never resorts to clap-trap, and never forgets the dignity of his calling. He is a fluent speaker, and excels as a jury advocate. His record in Congress was creditable to himself and constituents.

N. C. Deering was the successor of Mr. Pratt. He was elected as a member of the 45th, and re-elected in the 46th and 47th Congresses. He was an influential member.

In the fall of 1882 David B. Henderson, of Dubuque, was elected to represent the district in Congress. He is a lawyer of

HISTORY OF BUTLER COUNTY.

much ability, and promises to make an able representative. The campaign in which he was elected was a heated one, there being two other candidates for Congressional honors. The vote in Butler county stood as follows: D. B. Henderson, 1,708; C. M. Durham, 817; Roswell Foster, 71.

AUDITOR OF STATE.

The present Auditor of State of Iowa, Capt. W. V. Lucas, was for a number of years a resident of Butler county, and was at one time editor of the Shell Rock *News*. Right here we will present a little item taken from that paper which will be of interest and which explains itself. It bears the date of December 21, 1882:

WATCHED.—The many friends of Capt W. V. Lucas, at one time editor of the *News*, now State Auditor, will be glad to learn that his efficient deputy, R. L. Chase, and the other clerks in the auditor's office, presented the big hearted captain with a beautiful gold watch, one day last week, as a token of respect as a man, and for the many courtesies extended to them during the two years of his administration. We know the captain will appreciate such a gift and remember the donors.

DEPUTY AUDITOR OF STATE.

Rufus L. Chase, the present deputy State Auditor, is a citizen of Butler county, and for a number of terms served as County Auditor. He is noticed at length in this chapter under the head of County Auditors.

GOVERNMENT APPOINTMENTS.

There are quite a number of Butler county citizens in the employ of the government in the various departments at Washington. Among them are H. J. Playter, J. R. Fletcher and J. P. Reed.

GENERAL ASSEMBLY OF IOWA.

When Butler county was organized, in 1854, it was associated with the counties of Dubuque, Delaware, Buchanan, Black Hawk, Grundy, Bremer, Clayton, Fayette, Allamakee, Winneshiek, Howard, Floyd, Mitchell and Chickasaw, as a Senatorial district, although at that time they bore no numbers. This district was represented from 1854, for the term of four years, by William W. Hamilton, Maturin L. Fisher and John G. Shields.

In the Representative district, Butler county was a part of the Third, associated with Fayette, Chickasaw, Bremer, Black Hawk, Grundy, Franklin, Cerro Gordo, Floyd, Howard, Mitchell and Worth. From 1853 until 1855 this was represented by Reuben Noble and Lafayette Bigelow. The next term, in 1856 and 1857, this county was connected with the Forty-eighth district and was represented by Edwin R. Gillett.

The Senatorial district at this time was known as district 33, and was represented by Aaron Brown, of Fayette, who held for the full term of four years.

In 1857 Butler county was associated with Mitchell and Floyd counties as the Twelfth district, and at the election this year Matthew M. Trumbull was elected Representative and served the ensuing term of two years. He was a "full-blooded" republican, so to speak, and had a majority of six over his democratic opponent, J. C. Bishop, the vote standing 172 to 166. A sketch of Mr. Trumbull is found in connection with the bar history.

In 1859 Butler county was again a part of the Fifty-fifth Representative district, which embraced Butler, Franklin, Wright and Grundy counties, and was represented by Chauncey Gillett, who served until 1861. At the same time Butler county was connected with Grundy, Black Hawk and Franklin as the Thirty-sixth Senatorial district, and Thomas Drummond was elected for the term of four years.

In 1861 Butler county was in the Fifty-fifth, connected with Grundy and Franklin, and Alonzo Converse was Representative. The campaign of this year was a warm and active one, the contestant against Mr. Converse being Hon. C. A. L. Roszell, of democratic persuasion, and one of the most able men in the State, besides a most efficient politician. The vote stood 297 to 264, F. Digman receiving one vote. At this time, D. C. Hastings is the Senator.

In 1863 the Senatorial district was numbered 39, and embraced Hardin, Grundy, Black Hawk, Butler and Franklin counties. Coker F. Clarkson was elected Senator. The county was associated with Franklin and Grundy counties as Representative district 53, and Willis A. Lathrop was elected to represent it. A sketch of him is found in connection with the bar history.

In 1865 James B. Powers represented the district, of which Butler was a part, in the Senate—the district number was 40, and embraced Black Hawk and Butler. The Representative district was 55, and embraced Butler and Grundy counties. Lorenzo D. Tracy had the honor of representing them for the following two years. His opponents through the campaign were P. J. Haggarty and Alonzo Converse.

In 1867 Butler county, together with Franklin, Grundy and Cerro Gordo, made up the 39th Senatorial district, and Marcus Tuttle was elected Senator. Butler and Grundy counties were together as the 67th Representative district, and J. A. Guthrie was elected Representative.

In 1869 Butler was made a part of the 44th Senatorial district, and R. B. Clark was elected Senator, but before the expiration of his term, died, and Emmons Johnson was elected to fill the vacancy. At this time S. B. Dumont was Representative.

In 1871 Butler county was a part of the 43d Senatorial district, and A. Converse was the successful candidate. In this election C. A. L. Roszell received 44 and J. W. Davis 31 votes. At this time the re-apportionment entitled Butler county to one Representative, and S. B. Dumont was again elected in that capacity.

In 1873 the campaign on the subject of Representative, was unusually active. The candidates were Hon. C. A. L. Roszell, democratic, and N. N. Beals, republican. The former was successful by a majority of over 100, the vote standing 761 to 658.

The year 1875 was another year for the election of a Senator. A. C. Hitchcock was almost unanimously elected to that office. The candidates for Representative were John Palmer, republican, and C. A. L. Roszell, democrat, and resulted in the election of the former.

In 1877 A. M. Whaley was elected by a good majority to the lower house of the Legislature.

In 1879 W. P. Gaylor was elected Senator and A. M. Whaley, Representative.

In 1881 Henry C. Brown was almost unanimously elected Representative, and is the present incumbent. The county is a Representative district in itself and numbers 60.

The present Senatorial district is numbered 46, and embraces the counties of Butler, Floyd and Mitchell. As above stated, W. P. Gaylord was elected in 1879, but died not long after his election. To fill the vacancy so occasioned, Hon. A. M. Whaley, of Aplington, was elected Senator, and still holds that position.

Honorable Alvin Manley Whaley came to Aplington in 1869. Since his advent into public life as a soldier in the Union army, several sketches, together with incidents of his life, have been published in the press, from which we glean the following: He was born in Wyoming county, New York, on the 14th of May, 1838. He received the first rudiments of an education in the district school, and at an early day began to prepare for college. He studied languages for four years. When seventeen years of age he commenced teaching, and continued that in winter seasons. In 1860 he entered Middlebury Academy, at Wyoming. Upon the breaking out of the rebellion in April, 1861, he, with ten other classmates, responded to the first call for troops. A company was formed in Wyoming county, and he was mustered in as second lieutenant. This was the first company that left Wyoming county. It was joined to the 17th regiment New York volunteers and designated as Company K. In about six months he was promoted to first lieutenant, and a few months later to captain. After doing guard duty a while at Washington, the regiment was sent to Alexandria, where they relieved the Ellsworth Guards, and later took part in the Peninsular campaign.

He was dangerously wounded at the battle of Fredericksburg. The Medical and Surgical History of the Rebellion gives this as one of the wonderful cases of the war. On page 283, Vol. III., it says:

"Captain Alvin M. Whaley, Company K, 17th New York volunteers, wounded at the battle of Fredericksburg, Va., December 13, 1862, by a musket ball which fractured the left parietal bone. He walked with some assistance to the hospital of the 3d corps, quite a distance. His voice became thick and had an unnatural hesitancy and slowness. The middle and ring finger of the right hand were paralyzed, but the motion and sensibility in first and fourth fingers were only slightly impaired. His mental faculties were clear. He complained of a slight headache, and his pulse was slow and full. The trophine was applied by Assistant Surgeon Tice, and a disc of bone and several fragments were removed, one of which was three-quarters of an inch in diameter. During the operation blood flowed profusely. One large fragment of the bone, evidently from the inner table, lay exactly beneath, but was too large to be extracted from the orifice. The dura mater was found to be uninjured. The power of articulation returned immediately after the operation, and the numbness of the fingers became less marked. On January 2, 1862, the numbness of the fingers had entirely disappeared, and the wound was slowly healing. The patient was mustered out with his regiment. His recovery was owing to a strong constitution and an invincible determination."

After being discharged from the hospital at Georgetown, he went home on a furlough. He returned to Washington, and was discharged with the regiment and mustered out at New York.

The regiment veteranized, and he was commissioned Quartermaster General; was ordered to Alabama, from there to Vicksburg; was in Sherman's Meridian raid; went via Decatur and Huntsville to Atlanta, where they joined Sherman. In the battle of Jonesboro nearly one-half of his regiment was killed, including its gallant Col. Grower; went to Savannah, where he resigned. After his return home he visited the oil regions of Pennsylvania; stopped a few months; then engaged in farming in his native county. In 1869 he came to Aplington. He bought real estate in the town of Monroe. In 1870, he engaged with S. L. Kemmerer, selling agricultural implements and machinery. In 1872 he bought out a drug store, which he run about one year; then he sold that and opened a collection office. In 1874 he went to Independence, where he bought an elevator, and dealt in grain one and one-half years; then traded with S. L. Kemmerer for an elevator and lumber yard in Aplington and returned. He has since made this his home, dealing in grain, flax and lumber. He is also engaged in the banking business, having opened a bank in 1878.

He is a republican in politics; elected to represent Butler county in the State Legislature, in 1877, and re-elected in 1879. He was chairman of the military committee both terms, and also filled important positions on other committees. He was elected Senator from the 46th Senatorial district, which included Butler, Floyd and Mitchell counties, in 1880, to fill a vacancy caused by the death of W. B. Gaylord. He was also chairman of the military committee in the Senate.

He has served his constituents faithfully—has performed his duties in such a manner as to reflect great credit upon the judgment of his friends who elected him and honor upon himself. His re-election and promotion was certainly a strong endorsement of his course.

In 1871 he married Miss Jane H., daughter of George B. Smith, Esq. They have four boys—Grant, George A., Halsa H. and ———

COUNTY OFFICIALS.

A history of Butler county would, indeed, be incomplete without a record of the county officials, who have served since its organization. There has been much difficulty connected with obtaining material for biographical sketches of those who have died or moved from the county since their official services were performed. Where the mention of men, who, in their time, were prominent, is short, it is because of the meagre material to be secured. The following list, embraces a complete list of the various officers, from 1854 to 1882, inclusive. The most fitting office to commence with is that of

COUNTY JUDGE.

This office, in early days, was the most important of the county, embracing the work of various officers of the present day. It is treated at length under the head of county and circuit courts, in the judicial chapter.

The first county judge was John Palmer, who was elected in 1854, and held for a term of one year.

Aaron Van Dorn was the second, and held the office from 1856 to 1858. He was succeeded by Olonzo Converse, who was elected in the fall of 1857, and commenced official duties in January, 1858. He was re-elected in 1859, and served in all four years.

In 1861 C. A. Bannon was elected.

J. R. Fletcher was elected in 1862, and was the only democrat who ever held the office.

Ancel Durand was elected in 1863, and served for two years.

In 1865 A. J. Thompkins was honored and was re-elected in 1867. This ended the county court system, as the duties devolved upon the circuit court and other officials. This matter is treated at length, and personal sketches given of the various judges under the head above mentioned. The county judge was made ex-officio

COUNTY AUDITOR

at the time of the change, in the spring of 1869, and A. J. Thompkins was the first to serve as such. He was re-elected in the fall of 1869, and served during the two succeeding years. He was a married man, and had a family, who were held in high esteem by all who knew them. At the time of his election he was getting well along in years, probably fifty, which would make him now about sixty-five. He remained in the county until the year 1873, when he removed to near Hot Springs, Arkansas, where he and his family yet live.

The next auditor was Rufus L. Chase, who was first elected in the fall of 1871. Mr. Chase was a native of the Empire State, and came to Parkersburg in the latter part of the sixties, where he began the practice of his profession, dentistry, which he gave up to enter the political arena. He was four times re-elected and served as auditor for eight consecutive years. Chase had a very good business education, and made a satisfactory official. He was a sharp and shrewd politician, and is now Deputy State Auditor, at Des Moines.

In the fall of 1879, James W. Spencer was first elected county auditor, and was re-elected in the fall of 1881, by an almost unanimous vote, there being only two cast against him.

James W. Spencer, the present county auditor of Butler county, has been a resident of this county since January, 1872. He was born in the Province of Ontario, then Canada West, in 1840. His father, whose parents were natives of New Jersey, was born at Lundy's Lane, Canada, and his mother was born in England. They now reside in Delaware, Clinton county, Iowa. Mr. Spencer removed with his parents to Jackson county in 1854; was for some time engaged at clerking in Maquoketa, then in Dubuque, and in 1866 went to Chicago, where he acted in the same capacity for a wholesale dry-goods house. In 1872 he returned to Jackson county, and, as stated above, came to Butler county. For two years he acted as assistant superintendent of the Iowa Central Stock Farm, and in January, 1874, was appointed deputy sheriff under Capt. J. R. Jones, in which capacity he served for six years. In the fall of 1879 he was elected county auditor, and re-elected in the fall of 1881.

Politically, Mr. Spencer is a republican, and an earnest advocate of the principles of that party. Officially, he is an able, affable and popular officer; and socially, an agreeable and entertaining companion. Mrs. Spencer was formally Miss Allie E. Sims, a native of Bucyrus, Crawford county, Ohio.

TREASURER AND RECORDER.

When the county was first organized, and for several years thereafter, the duties now belonging to these two offices were attended to by one officer.

The first to act in this capacity was A. G. Clark, who was elected to the office in 1854. Mr. Clark was a native of Indiana, and came to Clarksville early in the fifties, in company with several brothers. He was a genial, pleasant gentleman, and made an accommodating officer. After his term expired he kept the hotel at Clarksville for a few years, and then removed to Missouri. He was of the democratic faith.

David C. Hilton was the next treasurer and recorder. He was elected in 1855 and re-elected in 1857, serving four years. Mr. Hilton was a first-class business man, and also made a good officer. While out of office he was engaged in real estate business, as he was lame, and obliged to do office work. He was a republican, and a native of Ohio, and came to Clarksville in 1852, where he made his residence until about 1866, when he removed to Missouri.

In 1859 J. H. Hale was elected to this position, and served for two years, when he was succeeded by D. C. Hilton, the latter serving until 1863.

In 1863 John Palmer, formerly county judge, was elected treasurer and recorder. During his term the offices were separated, and he was retained as treasurer, while J. H. Hale, in 1864, was elected

COUNTY RECORDER,

and was the first to fill the office, as it is to-day. Hale was elected first, principally, on the issue of the county seat from Clarksville, he favoring the latter. He was a good, square business man, and gave very general satisfaction. He is now postmaster at Spencer, Clay county, Iowa, where he removed in 1870. He served as recorder four years.

In 1868 George M. Craig was elected recorder, and in 1870 was re-elected, serving with honor to himself and satisfaction to those who had business to transact at the court house. . A sketch of him is found in connection with the bar.

Elwood Wilson was Mr. Craig's successor, being elected in 1872. Two years later he was re-elected, and in 1876 again re-elected.

Elwood Wilson was born in Otsego county, New York, on the 5th day of April, 1840. He is a son of James and Aznba (Stetson) Wilson. His father was a native of New York, and his mother of Massachusetts. The most of his life, until seventeen years of age, was passed in St. Lawrence county, New York, he receiving but a common school education. In 1857 Elwood came to Butler county, Iowa, and his parents soon after followed him. Shortly after his arrival he bought a farm in section 26, Shell Rock township, of a brother, who had entered the land some years previous. Here he now owns a fine place and makes there his residence. In the fall of 1872 he was elected to the office of county recorder, and assumed his new duties the following year; he was re-elected twice—holding the office for the space of six years. He was elected justice of the peace in 1878 and again in 1880 and 1882; he is also engaged in the collection agency and insurance business. In politics Mr. Wilson is a staunch republican; he is a Master Mason and a member of the lodge at Shell Rock. He was married in 1861 to Miss Priscilla C. Courtwright, who was born in the State of Illinois. They have two children—Marcia and Herbert D. Mr. Wilson's father is still living in Delaware county, at the age of 82. His mother died in 1874.

William W. Pattee was elected recorder of Butler county in the fall of 1878 and again in 1880. He is a native of Iowa City, where he was born November 27, 1851. His father, William Pattee, was auditor of the State of Iowa from 1851 to 1855. He was also for some time editor of the Keokuk *Argus*. The family subsequently removed to Bremer county, where Mr. Pattee, Sr., published for a time the *Bremer County Argus*, at Waverly. He is now connected with the State Normal School, at Cedar Falls. William W. Pattee, the subject of this sketch, went to Clarksville in 1871, where he was telegraph operator for the B., C. R. and N. Railroad Company until 1873, when he was transferred to Shell Rock, and served as agent of the railroad company until 1878, when he was elected to the office of county recorder. He has also engaged in a general merchandise business at Allison. His wife was Emma Gould, born at Sheboygan Falls, Wis. They have two children, Annie and an infant daughter. They lost their second child, a son, Bernard.

W. M. Hunter was elected in the fall of 1882, and his duties began on January 1, 1883.

COUNTY TREASURER.

John Palmer was the first to hold this office distinct from all others. He was elected in 1863, although part of the term this office and the recordership were merged into one. A sketch of Mr. Palmer is found in connection with the judicial history.

In 1867 J. F. Wright was elected to the office, and served for two terms. He was from Shell Rock, and still remains at that point, engaged in milling. His official career was satisfactory, as he is a good business man.

W. C. Thompson was Mr. Wright's successor, elected in the fall of 1871 and commencing duties on the first day of January following. Mr. Thompson is a republican, and still lives in Jefferson township. He made an accommodating officer, and at the end of his first term, in the fall of 1873, he was re-elected, and served until 1876. A sketch of Mr. Thompson is found in connection with Jefferson township.

At the fall election of 1875, E. S. Thomas was elected treasurer and served for four consecutive years. A sketch of his life is presented in this connection:

Edward S. Thomas, postmaster at Allison and ex-county treasurer of Butler county, was born in Bradford county, Pa., in 1829, where he lived until eighteen years of age. He learned the trade of a tinner, which he followed for many years. He came to Chickasaw county, in this State, in 1856, thence to Floyd county in the spring of 1860, where he lived until

1871, when he came to Butler county and settled at Greene, his family being the first that settled on the village plat. He was engaged in the hardware business at Greene until he was elected county treasurer in 1875, when he removed to Butler Center. He was treasurer four years. Mr. Thomas came to Allison when the county seat was removed to this place. In 1881 he was appointed postmaster. His wife was Miss R. L. Van Curen, born in the State of New York. They have five children—Charles, Charlotte, Virginia, Levi and Zenas—all of whom are married except the youngest.

John W. Ray, the present county treasurer of Butler county, is serving his second official term, having been elected in the fall of 1879 and again in 1881. He was born in Mahoning county, Ohio, in 1841, where he lived until about eighteen years of age. His father died when he was but a child. He removed to Cedar Falls, Black Hawk county, with his mother's family in 1859, and enlisted August, 1862, in Company B, 31st Iowa Volunteer Infantry, serving three years. The 31st regiment belonged to the 15th Army Corps, and he participated in all the battles in which that famous corps engaged. When nineteen years of age he engaged in J. M. Overman & Co.'s mill, at Cedar Falls, to learn the trade. He removed in 1865 to Shell Rock, where he was engaged in milling up to the time of his election to his present position. He still owns one-half interest in the mill at that place. Mrs. Ray, formerly Mrs. Emma R. Bartholomew, born in Illinois, is his wife. They have four children—William F., Cora A., James F. and Lulu N.

Willis Hyde, of the abstract firm of Lathrop, Hyde & Levis, and the present deputy treasurer of Butler county, was for a number of years a resident of Butler Center, where he was connected with the abstract business. The present firm was formed in 1880. He was born in Connecticut in 1857. His wife was Miss Caroline Digman, born in Ohio. They have one son, a namesake of his father.

CLERK OF THE COURTS.

This office was already established when the county was organized. The first clerk was W. E. Burton, who was elected in August, 1854, and served until 1856. He was a native of Indiana, and came to Butler county and settled in Clarksville at a very early day. His deputy was H. F. L. Burton, who did about all of the office work. He yet lives in Clarksville. W. E. Burton now lives in Grand Forks.

In 1856 the records seem to be incomplete. Some one, whose name has been forgotten, was elected, but in a short time resigned, and a Mr. Leslie was appointed to fill out the term.

In 1857 Dr. James E. Walker was elected and served until 1859, when his successor qualified. Dr. Walker was a noble fellow, well educated and capable. In 1859 he returned to Maine, his native State. A short sketch of him is given in connection with the medical profession.

In the fall of 1858 James W. Davis was elected, and commenced official duties on the 1st of January, 1859. He was re-elected seven consecutive terms, serving fourteen years in the capacity of clerk. He is treated at length in connection with the chapter on the bar of Butler county.

In the fall of 1872 William H. Burdick was elected, in 1874 re-elected, and again in 1876, serving six years. Mr. Burdick was a republican and made a good officer. He was a native of Canada, and came to Butler county and located at Clarksville in the fall of 1856, where he engaged at his trade, blacksmithing. In the spring of 1882 Mr. Burdick removed to Dakota Territory, where he yet remains.

The next clerk of courts was Charles H. Ilgenfritz, who was elected in 1878 and re-elected in 1880.

Charles H. Ilgenfritz, clerk of the courts of Butler county for four years ending December 31, 1882, was born in LaPorte City, Ind., in 1850. He removed with his parents, Henry and Ann Ilgenfritz, to Greene county, Wisconsin, in 1852, and to Clarksville, Butler county, in 1863. During the years from 1868 to 1870 he was a student at the Notre Dame College, Indiana, and from that time to his election as clerk of the courts, in 1878, was engaged in the lumber trade and in banking at Clarksville. A democrat politically, Mr. Ilgenfritz is not so strongly wedded to party as to be governed by prejudice, but sustains for official positions men whom he believes to be honest and possessors of the best principles. His popularity as an official may be inferred from the fact that at his first election his majority was 160, and the second time was over 500.

Mrs. Ilgenfritz was, before marriage, Miss Lulu Walrath. They have two sons —Harry L. and Burr.

In the fall of 1882, after a heated campaign, W. S. Montgomery was elected as successor to Mr. Ilgenfritz, to the office of clerk of the courts, and began the duties with 1883. Mr. Montgomery is a lawyer, who has been in practice, residing at Clarksville, and a further notice of him will be found in connection with the history of the bar.

SHERIFFS.

The first sheriff of Butler county was Robert T. Crowell, who was elected in the fall of 1854, at the organization of the county. He was a genial fellow, and made a good officer. Crowell first came to Butler county in 1850, but not to settle until 1851, and located near Clarksville. He is now in Spirit Lake, Iowa.

The next sheriff of Butler county was Walker H. Bishop, who was first elected in 1855; was re-elected in 1857, and held until 1859. He was a native of Indiana, and had inherited democratic proclivities, which he always retained. He settled in Clarksville in 1854, and remained until the latter part of the sixties, when he and his family removed to Nebraska.

James Leverich was the second sheriff, elected in 1859, and serving for one term. Mr. Leverich was elected as a democrat, was a native of Ohio, and still lives in Shell Rock township. He made an accommodating official.

He was succeeded in the fall of 1861 by W. H. Bishop, who was re-elected, and served another term.

In 1863 Michael Hollenbeck was elected sheriff, and in 1865 re-elected, serving four years. Mr. Hollenbeck is a native of New York, and still lives in Shell Rock, where he first settled in 1854.

Michael Hollenbeck is the youngest son of Michael and Sarah (Chase) Hollenbeck, and was born in Oneida county, New York, September 17, 1822. Both his mother and father died during the year 1846—the latter dying one month later than the former. The son remained in his native county until he had attained his majority, and then came West and settled in Ashtabula county, Ohio, where he lived eight years, and then moved to DeKalb county, Illinois, where he remained but one and one-half years. He was married March 26, 1843, to Miss Elsie Osterhout. In January, 1854, they came to Butler county, Iowa, and entered a farm of 160 acres in section 29, Shell Rock township. Here Mr. Hollenbeck built a small log cabin, into which he moved his family in May, 1854. During the early years of their settlement here they experienced many hardships. Upon their arrival but one five-dollar bill was left, and they lived in their log cabin the first summer with no roof, excepting an elm bark one. In this house the family lived for twelve years, but as time went by it was considerably improved. At the time of their arrival in the State not one railroad was built. Mr. Hollenbeck was supervisor, and a member of the first county board, and was also elected the first justice of the peace of the township, besides which he has held other town offices. He was elected sheriff of Butler county in 1863, and held the office for four years. Eight children have been born to them, six of whom are living—Romanzo, now living in this township; Rozelia, now the wife of George Bass, of Kansas; Alice, now the wife of H. A. Page, of Kansas; Ida, wife of Gen. H. M. Day, of Waterloo; Wait and Eliza. In addition to his property in Butler county, Mr. Hollenbeck also owns a fine farm in Kansas.

To the office of sheriff, L. L. Smith, of New Hartford, succeeded Mr. Hollenbeck, being first elected in 1867, and re-elected in 1869, serving four years.

The next sheriff was Capt. J. R. Jones, of Butler township, who served for eight years.

John R. Jones settled at Shell Rock on the 26th day of May, 1856, formed partnership with George Hawker, and as Hawker & Jones engaged in the manufacture of wagons and plows, This firm built the first wagon manufactured in Butler county, and sold the same to John Kimmins for sixty dollars. The firm continued business until 1862, when J. R. Jones recruited Company E of the 32d Iowa Volunteer Infantry, of which company he was elected Captain and mustered into service, June 30, 1862. Captain Jones was elected Colonel of the regiment over a senior Captain, a Major, and a Lieutenant-Colonel, but as Governor Stone, of Iowa, was a personal friend of the Lieutenant-Colonel, he delayed the commission, and J. R. Jones therefore served as Captain until the close of the service, when he received a complimentary commission of Colonel. He participated in thirteen different battles, was an efficient officer, and highly respected as a soldier and commander.

In August, 1865, Captain Jones returned to Shell Rock, and in March, 1866, purchased his present farm, elevated on section 17, Butler township (the same being the land entered by Morrison Taylor, in 1851), and here he has since resided, surrounded by all the comforts of the best farm life. His residence erected in 1873, is one of the best in the county, and all other improvements made by him are of the same character. His private life is now occupied by careful and wise attention to his money and well-tilled acres.

In 1871 Mr. Jones was elected sheriff of Butler county, and thrice re-elected, thereby serving eight years: and it is safe to say Butler county never had a more efficient officer than Captain Jones. He has also held many minor offices of trust at different intervals. Mr. Jones is a member of the Masonic Fraternity, belonging to the Blue Lodge and Chapter at Clarksville, and the Commandery at Cedar Falls. He has always taken an active interest in the promotion of every public enterprise, and deservedly enjoys the highest regard of his fellow citizens.

John R. Jones was born in Detroit, Michigan, on the 8th day of October, 1831. His parents, John R. and Mary (Jones) Jones, were both natives of Wales; they were married in Liverpool, England, in 1830; at once emigrated to the United States, and soon settled at Detroit. In 1832 the family removed to Huron county, Ohio, and in 1838 to Will county, Illinois, where the father died in 1876, and the mother in 1878.

Captain Jones is the oldest of six children. In 1852 he drove an ox team for John T. Basy to Portland, Oregon; the trip occupying five months and twenty-one days. In 1853 he went into California, where he employed his time principally in wagon making, at which business he was reasonably successful. In the spring of 1856 he returned to Illinois, and on the 1st day of May married Miss Angeline Butterfield, a native of New York, and subsequently came to Butler county. They have had three children, two now living—Mary M., now Mrs. G. A. McIntyre, of Allison, and Carrie S., now the wife of J. P. Reed, editor "Shell Rock *News.*" Mr. Jones is a strong republican. In religion the family are Presbyterians.

Gilbert Hazlet, the present sheriff of Butler county, was born in Mercer county, Pennsylvania, in 1839. His parents removed to Fayette county, Iowa, when he was thirteen years of age. He came to Butler county in 1869, and purchased a farm in Pittsford township, where he located. His father, S. K. Hazlet, is now a resident of that township. Mr. Hazlet was elected as supervisor of Butler county in 1874, and served in that capacity for three years. He is now serving his second term as sheriff, having been elected in the fall of 1879, and re-elected in the fall of 1881. His wife is a native of Ohio; a daughter of William Barnhouse. They have three children—Forrest M., Edwin A. and Dorleska.

PROSECUTING ATTORNEY.

This office was first filled by Aaron Van Dorn, who was appointed by Judge John Palmer, in the fall of 1854. He was elected in April, 1855. A sketch of him is found in connection with the bar history.

The next Prosecuting Attorney was C. A. Bannon, who is also noted among the legal representatives.

In 1858 an interesting occurrence disturbed the usual tranquility of this office. The law provided that in case of the absence of the incumbent for a period of six months, the office should be declared vacant, and an election held to fill the vacancy. Mr. Bannon had left the county, and, as understood, was not coming back. Thereupon, in 1858, William R. Jamison was elected to the office, by two-thirds of the entire vote of the county. When court convened, however, Bannon again unexpectedly put in an appearance, and claimed the office, and Mr. Jamison withdrew.

During Bannon's term the office was abolished by law.

SUPERINTENDENT OF SCHOOLS.

A history of this office, together with that of school fund commissioner, appears in connection with the chapter upon educational matters.

COUNTY ASSESSOR.

This office was created in 1857, to take the place of Township Assessor, and W. R. Cotton was the first and only officer ever elected, as it was abolished, reverting to the former and present system of township assessor.

COUNTY SURVEYOR.

The following is a list of the gentlemen who have held this office. The year following the names is that in which the party was elected, the time of service being until the successor qualified:

J. H. Morton........................... 1855
George McClellan.......................
J. Ellis............................... 1857
Judd Bradley........................... 1859
George McClellan....................... 1861
A. F. Townsend......................... 1860
M. D L. Niece.......................... 1865
O. W. McIutosh......................... 1867
Joseph Conn............................ 1868
O. W. McIntosh......................... 1869
M. D. L. Niece......................... 1871
J. G. Rockwell......................... 1873
O. W. McIutosh......................... 1881

DRAINAGE COMMISSIONER.

J. H. Miller........................... 1855
Liman Norton........................... 1857
Isaac Boylan........................... 1859
N. Olmstead............................ 1861
H. A. Earley........................... 1862
T. G. Copeland......................... 1863
W. C. Thompson......................... 1865
E. D. Button........................... 1867
Henry Trotter.......................... 1871
E. D. Button........................... 1873
Noble Thompson......................... 1879

COUNTY CORONER.

D. W. Kensley.......................... 1855
J. V. Boggs............................ 1856
J. A. Barker........................... 1857
R. T. Lowe............................. 1859
J. A. Barker........................... 1861
James A. Gurthie....................... 1862
E. W. Metzgar.......................... 1863
E. B. Allen............................ 1864
George Murphy.......................... 1865
E. W. Metzgar.......................... 1867
T. G. Copeland......................... 1869
E. W. Metzgar.......................... 1873
C. A Murphy............................ 1875
H. J. Playter.......................... 1877
W. M. Foote............................ 1881

Alvin M. Whaley

CHAPTER VIII.

THE COUNTY SEAT STRUGGLES.

This matter in Butler county has been a source of much trouble and disagreement, and many bitter strifes and quarrels have grown from it. Notwithstanding there are five good towns in the county—all of them prosperous, full of business, and convenient, any of which would make an excellent county seat—when one locality succeeded in getting it, all others would co-operate to have it removed. One reason for this is that, until within the last two years, there has been no village of importance near the center of the county. Greene lies on the extreme northern line; Clarksville and Shell Rock were opposed, because of being too far east; and Parkersburgh too far south. When one of these made an effort to secure the seat of government, all others would join in common cause to defeat the object. It was this petty jealousy which led to the "hub" being located for a number of years at one of the smallest places in the county, to which there was no access by railway, but one must return to the primitive modes of travel, and take a stage. This, however, has finally been remedied, and a better condition of affairs now exists, although it was only accomplished by a "very slight majority."

To commence at the beginning of the matter, we must carry the attention of the reader back to 1853, when the first attempt to organize Butler county was made. This having been a part of Buchannan county, Judge Roszell of that county appointed a board of commissioners to locate the county seat. This board arrived to do as directed in May, 1853, and were met by Messrs. Thomas, and Jeremiah Clark, and W. S. Wamsley, whose residences were about one mile north of the present village of Clarksville, and were prevailed upon to locate the seat of justice on their lands. Or, in the words of a local writer: "The matter was taken into consideration by that august body, and they concluded, for reasons not known, to do as requested." The location being decided upon, the ceremonies had so far proceeded, that one of the commissioners was in the act of driving the peg—of dealing the fatal blow upon the "stake" with an ax, when his attention was arrested by an unearthly yell, not unlike that which at "times like those" might have proceeded from the throats of the aborigines. On lowering the fatal instrument, with the undoubted determination of saving his strength and blows, that they might be more particularly needed in a different quarter, he saw, far to the south, the forms of two of nature's noblemen, who, upon nearing, were recognized as G. W. Poisal and Seth Hilton, Sr. They bade them hold the proceedings—with not too welcome information to Messrs. Clarks and Wamsley—as they knew a much more desirable location for the seat of justice. The commissioners heard their "tale of love," went with them, and in one short hour the solid sliver of oak was driven home, on section 18, township 92, range 15, on the spot where the school-house now stands. However, a conciliation was necessary to be made with the former interested gentlemen, and D. C. Hilton, on whose claim the county seat was located, gave Thomas and Jeremiah a one-half interest in his "forty." This was in May, 1853. In August, 1853, Judge Roszell surveyed the original town, immediately after the survey of the State road to Clarksville. Within a few years (about 1856), a court house was commenced, which was completed in spring of 1858, when the first court was held, and the county offices were moved into it. This building is of brick, 40x60 feet, two stories high, and cost about $20,000. The building is now in use as the School-house in Clarksville, having been sold, after the removal of the county seat, to the school district for $2,800.

Even before the court house was finished, the jealousy of other towns was visible, and the excitement was wrought up to a high pitch, every one having a preference and agitating the question. Finally a town was platted and recorded embracing forty acres, in the geographical center of the county, at the four corners of Jefferson, Jackson, West Point and Ripley townships, as the future county seat of Butler county. This town was called Georgetown, and the plat was the best drawn, and made a better appearance—on paper—than any in the county. The village prospective had not a building, nor a sign of habitation; but was to remain unbuilt until a vote was secured and the matter settled. A large petition was gotten up, extensively signed—except in Clarksville—praying that the matter be submitted to a vote. This was presented to Judge Converse, who granted the request. The matter was voted upon at the April election, in 1858, and resulted in Clarksville receiving 327 and Georgetown 320; leaving a clear majority of "7" for the former, This put a quietus to the fond hopes and anticipations for the promising village of Georgetown, and nothing remains of it, except probably a few corner lot stakes. It is an admirable corn-field.

The matter, however, "would not down," and again, in the latter part of 1858, it was agitated. Finally a partial agreement was made among the outsiders to consolidate and wrest it from Clarksville by all working in the interest of Butler Center, which, although having no railroad connection, was nearly in the center of the county. A petition was circulated and over 400 names secured to it, asking that the matter be submitted to a vote as to the removal of the seat of justice from Clarksville to Butler Center. The petition was granted, and the matter was submitted to popular vote on the 4th of April, 1859.

This was the second attempt at removing the county seat, and resulted in Clarksville receiving 336 votes and Butler Center 357, a majority of 21 for the latter. This seemed conclusive, and the following entry was made on the records of the county court, bearing the date of April 11, 1859, which explains itself:

"Be it remembered that on this 11th day of April, A. D., 1859, the returns from the election from all the townships having been received, the County Judge calling to his assistance George McClellan and John M. Nicholas, two justices of the peace of Butler county, proceeded to canvass the said returns of the vote cast upon the question of the county seat on the 4th day of April, 1859, between Clarksville, the existing county seat, and Butler Center, and it appearing that a majority of all the votes cast were in favor of Butler Center, the point designated in the petition asking for a vote upon the question; therefore, in accordance with the provisions of Chapter 46 of the Acts of the Fifth General Assembly of the State of Iowa, Butler Center is hereby declared to be the county seat of Butler county, Iowa."

At this there was "joy and exceeding rejoicing" among the good folks of Butler Center, who threw up their hats, and it is said, shouted with joy until they were black in the face. But this was suddenly stopped. The Clarksville people sued out a writ of injunction for the purpose of staying the removal voted until certain legal objections on their part could be duly adjudicated. In July following the District Court adjudged the election void, because of certain irregularities in its conduct.

Then the joy changed hands, and Clarksville did an unseemingly amount of jollification. But the people of the Center were not satisfied, and kept at work—agitating —until early in 1860, a petition signed by upwards of four hundred voters was obtained and presented to the Board of Supervisors, asking that the matter be again submitted to vote. This was granted, and on the 2d day of April, 1860, the election was held. The canvass of votes was held on the fourth of the same month, and resulted in the declaration of a majority of over eighty votes in favor of Butler Center over Clarksville. It was therefore declared that

BUTLER CENTER WAS COUNTY SEAT,

And the jollification held over the matter, this time, was not without cause.

The books, documents and county offices were accordingly removed to Butler Center on the 5th day of April, 1860. The court house used at that place is a most unpretentious frame structure, 26x36 feet in size, and two stories high. The upper story, which was always reached by an outside wooden stairway, was, by courtesy, called the court-room; the lower story, divided into three apartments of the most inferior character for such uses, were occupied as county offices. This structure, erected in 1860 at a cost of $2,000, was donated to the county together with about two acres of land appurtenant thereto, by Mr. Andrew Mullarky, of Cedar Falls, since deceased, who owned a large amount of land in the vicinity, and who was greatly instrumental in securing the removal of the county seat from Clarksville.

The seat of justice remained at Butler Center for about twenty years. Every year or two heavily signed petitions for its removal to other points were presented to the board of county supervisors, as will be seen by a glance at the history of their proceedings, elsewhere in this volume; but they were always out voted until the new town of

ALLISON CAME INTO THE FIELD AS A COMPETITOR.

On the transit of the Dubuque and Dakota Railroad across the county, and the commencement of this town within a short distance from the geographical center of the county, silent notice was taken by the public, rather instinctively, that the county seat question would again come before the people, with Allison as the objective point. In the summer of 1880, in anticipation of the presentation of the question, the people of Bristow published a notice, and circulated a petition for the removal of the county seat to that place. But Allison was not to be out done, and was soon in the field with a petition, asking the supervisors to submit the question of removal from Butler Center to Allison. The fight waxed warm, and the pent up bad feelings were vented in stump speeches, the press, and the school houses were filled with the advocates of the towns in contest. It did not last long, however, as the Allison petition got a majority of 400 signatures. At the November election, following, the question of removal to Allison carried by a majority of 265 votes; Allison receiving 1,529 and Butler Center 1,264. It was therefore declared that

ALLISON HAD WON THE COUNTY SEAT.

And by an order of the board of supervisors, at the January, 1881, session, the records were removed to Allison on January 10th. No buildings having been erected for the reception of the records, the clerk, recorder and sheriff were put into quarters in the upper story of a building owned by A. M. McLeod. The auditor and treasurer were stationed in the drug store of Dr. Riggs for a few days, until a small county office building, which had been erected at Butler Center, was moved over, into which they moved.

In the submission of the vote for removal, the Allison Town-site Company, represented by John R. Waller, of Dubuque, filed a bond with the county auditor, in the sum of $25,000, securing to the county, in case of the removal of the county seat from Butler Center, and re-locating the same at Allison, the building of a court house 50x55 feet in size, two stories high, with vaults, court and office rooms, finished in an appropriate way. Also the deeding of ten acres of ground, so long as it should be used for county purposes on which to locate said building. The proposed building was to be of wooden frame with brick vaneer, full specifications and draft of which accompanied the bond.

The removal being voted by the people, the Allison company were on hand ready to fulfill the conditions as above; but it being evident that public opinion favored the erection of a better court house, and one which would be a credit to the county, a compromise was effected between the supervisors, and the Allison company was to deposit to the credit of Butler county $7,000 in cash, and the county to appropriate a sum to be used in connection with the $7,000 in the erection of the house, in the proportion of $1 to $3. In the spring of 1881 the contract was let to L. D. Harvey, of Clarksville, for the sum of $10,680. The building was finished, and the various officers assigned their rooms in October, 1881. It is two stories in height, with a basement story of ten feet. The structure is 50 by 55 feet, and makes an imposing appearance. Thus ended the hard and bitter struggle for county seat honors; and as the bitter feeling occasioned is becoming allayed, Allison will in all probability hold the "county capital."

CHAPTER IX.

THE NEWSPAPER PRESS.

Butler county has had abundant opportunities to test the value of newspapers as aids in building up business centers and making known its resources to the outer world, while the civilizing influence is almost unlimited; and, as a general thing, its citizens have always manifested a liberal spirit or purpose towards the various journalistic enterprises that have been inaugurated in their midst. It must be truthfully said, that in dispensing their patronage to the press, they have been tolerant and magnanimous, as they have been reasonably generous to journals of all parties. It may be difficult to correctly estimate the advantages derived by Butler county in a business point of view, from the influence of the press, which at various times has called into requisition respectable, if not eminent talent in the advocacy of local interests, which have had a tendency to inspire its citizens, as well as friends, far and near, with hope and confidence in its prosperity.

In every community there are shriveled souls, whose participation in the benefits of enterprise is greater than their efforts to promote the public welfare. These are the men who will never subscribe for a newspaper, but will always be on the alert to secure, gratuitously, the first perusal of their neighbors' papers. These are the croakers, who predict evil and disparage enterprise. But, with very few exceptions the press of this region, or the community through which they circulate, has never been cursed with such drones. On the contrary, as patrons of the press, Butler county citizens have established a good name. As records of current history, the local press should be preserved by town and county governments in their archives for reference. As these papers are the repositories wherein are stored the facts and the events, the deeds and the sayings, the undertakings and achievements that go to make up final history. One by one these things are gathered and placed in type; one by one the papers are issued; one by one these papers are gathered together and bound, and another volume of local, general and individual history is laid away imperishable. The volumes thus collected, are sifted by the historian, and the book for the library is ready.

There should be some means devised by which press records might be preserved and made accessible. This of course is attempted in all offices; but as a general thing files are sadly deficient; still by diligent search and much enquiry, enough date has been gleaned to supply a tolerably accurate record of the county press; but if any inaccuracies or omissions are noticeable, they may be attributed to the absence of completeness in the files.

THE BUTLER TRANSCRIPT.

This was the first newspaper established in Butler county. It first saw light in 1858, at Clarksville, which was then the county seat, under the management of Palmer & James. It was republican in politics, and was a spicy little sheet. But the county was too new to support it, and in 1860 it was suspended and the material moved to Wintersett, Madison county, Iowa.

BUTLER COUNTY JEFFERSONIAN.

This paper was the second to be issued in Butler county, and was published at Butler Center, in Jefferson township, so the name seems well bestowed. It was started by William Haddock, in August, 1860, and between that time and October, 1861, only about thirty-six numbers of the paper had been issued. In October, 1861, it was purchased by Martin Bailey, who, in January, 1862, changed the name to the

STARS AND STRIPES,

And for two years it made its appearance regularly, and was one of the most able papers ever published in the county, as Mr. Bailey was a pungent writer and a well educated and well read man. Mr. Bailey then went to the war and the publication of the paper ceased. In August, 1865, the material and office furniture was purchased by McCormack & Francis, who with it established

THE BUTLER COUNTY ARGUS.

They continued this newspaper for about six months, and in February, 1866, sold it to Judge John Palmer, who changed the name to

THE STILETTO.

In the spring of 1866, Judge Palmer's interest in *The Stiletto* became the property of his son, W. L. Palmer, who removed it to Shell Rock. In the fall of 1866 it was consolidated with the Clarksville *Gazette*. A sketch of John Palmer is found in connection with the judicial history. W. L. Palmer was an able writer, and in addition to his newspaper writing compiled a history of Clarksville, which is an interesting little work.

THE CLARKSVILLE GAZETTE.

This newsy representative of the press was brought into existence in the summer of 1866 by the efforts of Van E. Butler, a smooth and pithy writer, and one of the most capable newspaper men who ever handled a "stick" in the county. In the fall of 1866 it was consolidated with *The Stiletto*, which was then being published at Shell Rock by W. L. Palmer, and the publication was continued at Clarksville under the firm name of Butler & Palmer, and title of

THE STAR OF THE WEST.

In the winter following, of 1867 and 1868, the paper changed hands and became the property of Frank C. Case, who changed the name to

THE CLARKSVILLE STAR.

It still retains this name. In April, 1872, Mr. Case disposed of the *Star* to James O. Stewart, a gentleman of much newspaper ability, and who by enterprise and energy soon made it one of the leading newspapers in the county.

Mr. Stewart opened the year 1875 with a determination to let nothing remain unturned to make the *Star* an interesting and instructive paper. About the second issue in January he commenced publishing a complete history of Butler county, which ran through the paper after the manner of a continued story for the greater part of the year. For the historian he secured the services of Mr. Van E. Butler, one of the most able writers who have ever been in this part of the State, who had been a resident of the county since boyhood and was therefore familiar with pioneer life in this part of the great Hawkeye State. The history was not only valuable as a history, but was also very interesting reading. This enterprise was indeed commendable in the *Star*, and was the only attempt at such ever made in the county. The history, too, was appreciated by the readers of the paper, as the writer, in his historical interviews and researches, has often had the matter called to his attention in most complimentary terms.

Mr. Stewart, in closing the year 1875, says:

"With this number we close volume eight of the *Star*, fold it up and lay it away, and count it among the things of the past. How well we have suited our patrons we leave for them to say. We have tried to do so. That we have made some enemies and some friends during the year we are very well aware, but have the consciousness that in either case we have done so in carrying out what we honestly believed; hence we have no excuse or apologies to make. If we have been in the wrong we are willing to lay the ill feeling away with volume eight and the old year 1875, and wish all our patrons a happy new year."

Mr. Stewart continued in management of the paper until in June, 1882, when he sold out to Mr. L. O. Hull, who is the present proprietor. Mr. Stewart in leaving the paper in the new management, in the *Star's* issue of the 29th of June, 1882, said:

Good-by.

With this issue the undersigned surrenders the pencil, scissors and paste-pot and vacates the editorial chair in the *Star* office, in favor of L. O. Hull, of Waterloo. Ten years ago we took charge of the *Star* with some hesitancy as to our ability to give you a readable paper, but with a full determination to do our best, and spare no efforts to do so. How well we have succeeded we leave our many readers to determine. However, we feel we will be pardoned for entertaining the thought that we have reasonably succeeded. What our future has in store we have no idea, but be what it may or where it may, we shall always hold in kindly remembrance the people of Clarksville and Butler county. To our friends we say, God bless you; to the other "fellers," look out for yourselves.

We heartily commend to the *Star* family and the people generally, our successor, Mr. Hull. He is a young man of ability, is a farmer's son, who, by dint of hard work, steady habits and a laudable ambition, has already gained a creditable place in the editorial profession. He is a good writer, and an industrious news-gatherer, and we have no doubt will make the *Star* a much more welcome guest than ever before. We ask for him all the favors you have extended to Yours Truly and Sincerely,
J. O. STEWART.

Mr. Hull, in assuming control, greeted his readers with the following:

Greeting.

With the last issue of the *Star*, Mr. Stewart, who has labored long, earnestly and honorably for the people of Butler county, laid down his pencil, and we have no doubt that our readers will long miss his familiar style. All his friends will join us in the hope that he may live long and prosper, wherever his lot may be cast. The present proprietor asks for a continuance of the favor of all the old friends of the *Star*, and promises his most earnest endeavors to make the paper a worthy representative of the people of Butler county. We have come here to stay and labor with and for the united interests of the whole people. The interests of the people are our interests, and it is our ambition to grow and increase as Butler county grows in population and influence.

The *Star* will be republican in its politics, and, at the same time, will endeavor to treat democratic principles with candor and fairness, and democrats as friends and brothers, having an equal stake in the country.

The *Star* will, in the contest which is imminent as a result of the prohibition election in this State, use its influence in favor of the support and enforcement of law, and also endeavor to "be temperate in all things."

The *Star* believes in Christianity and free thought, and that individual conscience, and not restraining creed, should be the rule and guide of life.

The *Star* will remember its friends, and, if it shall have enemies, will try not to forget to treat them with kindness and generosity.

We cannot close this article without thanking the press for their generous comments on our purchase. The notices given us by papers published in the county are especially gratifying to us. We are also under large obligations, which we will try to repay by earnest work, to many good people of Clarksville and Butler county for a generous and hearty welcome.

Sincerely Yours,
L. O. HULL.

L. O. Hull, son of Lorenzo and Emily (Stewart) Artlip, was born in Illinois, March 18, 1855. When he was thirteen months old his father died, and a few months afterwards his mother also; not, however, until they had given him to Mr. and Mrs. Harvey Hull, by whom he was adopted and whose name he bears. With them he moved to Sheboygan county, Wisconsin, in 1858, settling in a neighborhood of "copperheads." His intercourse with that class of boys at school had considerable to do with the formation of his political character, which is, and always has been, republican. He remained there until twelve years old, when he removed to Fon du Lac county, Wisconsin, settling on a farm. At the early age of fourteen years he demonstrated a natural capacity for editorial newspaper work. As a result of this ability—augmented by a judicious selection of reading matter—at this age he contributed considerably to the pages of the county papers. At the age of eighteen he removed to Fon du Lac. At the same time his parents came to Iowa. He removed to Black Hawk county in the fall of 1873, remained there engaged in various businesses until July, 1881, when upon the solicitation of Matt. Parrot, editor of the *Iowa State Reporter*, he removed to Waterloo, and was given editorial charge of that paper. He came to Butler county in July, 1882, and purchased the Clarksville *Star*. Under his efficient management this paper has already been enlarged from four pages of eight colums, to eight pages of six colums each; is well supported by the public, and in a prosperous concondition.

He was married at Dubuque, Iowa, October 5, 1882, to Miss. Lizzie I. Beck, daughter of Wm. P. Beck, of Sioux City.

Mr. Hull is a member of the First Baptist Church, Waterloo. He is an able writer, a good newspaper man, and will make the *Star* take front rank in the Butler county press.

PARKERSBURGH TIMES.

This paper was started at Parkersburgh, in the spring of 1870, by W. L. Palmer; but as no files of it have been preserved, we are unable to present any particulars as to size. The *Times* had rather a hard existence, and as all the material had been purchased by subscription among the citizens, there were too many managers— the "too many cooks spoiled the broth." In 1871 it was purchased by C. G. Bundy, who finally made up his mind that a change of location was desirable, and in July, 1872, changed the name to the Butler County *Times*, and removed it to Maudeville, which was then the Iowa Central Stock Farm. The paper survived until September, 1873, when it quietly succumbed.

THE SHELL ROCK ENTERPRISE.

This was the first newspaper established at the village indicated in its name. It first made its appearance on the 23d of August, 1872, with J. H. Boomer & Co. as editors and proprietors. It presented a neat and tasty appearance, and indicated that the managers were experienced newspaper men. In the salutatory published in the first number its editor says:

In response to the universal demand for a local paper in Shell Rock, the *Enterprise* makes its appearance to-day. As the name indicates, it is an enterprise of the people of Butler county in general, and of Shell Rock in particular But, be it understood, that, while it is an enterprise, it is no experiment. It has come to stick. Its founders have an abiding faith in the liberality of the people of the Shell Rock Valley, and have staked their bottom dol'ar on its success. It has not been nursed into being by any bonus or pledges, other than the earnest, active support which its merits may demand. We propose to make it a local paper. What we know about the unlimited resources of the Shell Rock Valley will be made known.

Unlike the New York *Tribune*, the *Enterprise* will be "an organ." It will support the republican party and its standard bearer. With Grant and Wilson we propose "to fight it out on that line." The publishers of this paper propose to launch their bark upon the sea of public opinion, relying upon a generous public for support, and success. Shall our anticipations be met? Yours, etc.

J. H. BOOMER & CO.

This firm continued the publication of the *Enterprise* until the 4th of October, 1872, when it was purchased by F. M. Barnard & Co., and two months later the firm name of White, Barnard & Co. appears at the head. In this shape the management remained until the 5th of March,

1874, when it was dissolved, and the partnership of White & Hall took the helm of the paper. In making their introductory bow they say:

The undersigned have formed a co-partnership under the firm name of White & Hall, and will, in the future, carry on the business of publishing the Shell Rock *Enterprise*, and would respectfully solicit a continuance of the liberal business the office has formerly been favored with.

SILAS WHITE,
FRANK HALL.

Early in the month of August, 1874, this firm dissolved, Frank Hall retiring, and Silas White becoming sole proprietor. He continued the publication alone until January 29, 1875, when O. B. Courtwright purchased a half interest and became a partner, under the firm name of White & Courtwright.

It seems that from the number of times the paper changed hands, it did not receive sufficient encouragement, or else lack of good management, for on the 19th of February, 1875, it was purchased by E. A. Kittel, M. D. The Doctor did not have much newspaper experience, but he had ability and "grit." In his salutatory he strikes out boldly from shore, as follows:

A newspaper has become a necessity to every live, enterprising village from one end of the land to the other. It would be a sorry comment on the enterprise and intelligence of this community did they not support a newspaper. If we need a newspaper, then let us have a good one.

The great mass of the community will fully endorse the above, but when we come to speak of the means necessary to attain the result, there is too often a difference of opinion. To begin with, something more is necessary on your part, than merely to subscribe for the paper. It is an easy matter to look over the barren columns of your home paper, with a doleful countenance, and anathematize the editor for not furnishing more news; as though a printing office was an establishment where news can be ground out wholesale from ever ready material. Before you say another word, let us ask, have you ever written a word for the paper? Have you ever stepped one single foot from your path to give the editor a single item that may have taken place under your very nose? Lastly, have you paid for the paper you are so liberal in denouncing? The chief object of a county newspaper is the local news; but how meagre it may be in this particular, if the only items published are such as come to the ears of the editor, who from the necessities of the business, must be immured in the office much of the time. Then don't be a niggard in your views. We shall strive, however, to atone for our inexperience as far as possible by especial, earnest and determined effort, hoping by your aid to publish a paper that shall be a credit to the town. We do not aspire to any independence, so called, which is rather a blind obstinacy. But we wish it distinctly understood that we are not a tail to wag at the will of any man or party.   E. A. KITTEL.

Mr. Kittel was succeeded in the management of the paper by Hazlet & Thorp, who changed the name of the *Enterprise* to

THE SHELL ROCK NEWS.

In a short time the firm name was changed to Lucas & Hazlet.

On the 2d of November, 1876, the property was purchased by George E. Farrar, and he inaugurates his administration as follows:

I have purchased the *News* of Lucas & Hazlet, and shall assume the management of the same. In publishing the *News*, I am, in a great part, entering upon a field new to me, and can only tell you what I intend to do. My one endeavor shall be to furnish the people of Shell Rock and Butler county, as good and as readable a paper as the county affords. In politics, the paper will be in the future, as in the past, a republican sheet, working by all honorable means to advance the principles of the republican party as enunciated by their platform, and supporting Hayes and Wheeler, and republican nominees. How well I shall accomplish what I propose to do, time and your own judgment will tell. The *News* has heretofore been well patronized, and I shall do all in my power to merit a continuance of the same.

Mr. Farrar continued in the management of the *News* until the 6th of September, 1877, when he sold it to E. E. and E. Savage. In his "valedictory," he tersely says:

With this issue we close our editorial connection with *The News,* having sold our interest to Messrs. Savage, to whose tender mercies we consign the business with best wishes for its prosperity and yours. Our connection with *The News* has been one of profit and of pleasure to us. Knowing nothing of the newspaper business when we assumed control of the paper, we are egotistical enough to think we do know something now of how a paper should be managed. Our course has been full of errors, and gross ones, too, which our optics perceive as well as yours, and in which we thank you for your kind forebearance. Towards Shell Rock and its people, we shall ever bear the kindest remembrance as the scene of our first business efforts, and as the pleasant village where we have passed more than two years of our existence. Now as we step down from the stool, and our successors step up, we do so feeling that the news will be an enterprise, that it will pay you to support; for we feel assured that it will be more worthy of your support than it has heretofore been. Once more then we say farewell.

GEORGE E. FARRAR.

In the same issue the new proprietors take the pen and say:

Once again we have the pleasure of making our bow to the world as we mount the editorial tripod.

Being naturally very modest, we do not propose, at this late date, to laud and magnify ourselves, nor to make large promises of what we can do. It has been the subject of remark for some years past, that Shell Rock could not support a newspaper, and from the numerous changes it would seem to be a fact, yet we believe that by careful attention to business and economical management, it will not only be possible for a paper to exist, but that it may be made a profitable investment. To the end that we, Shell Rock and Butler county, may be the better for our coming, we ask the assistance of the people of Shell Rock. It shall be our object to aid every undertaking that has for its chief end the good of Shell Rock. In politics we adhere to the republican party; in morals we endeavor to be upright, and shall try to promote purity in the same. We strongly oppose intemperance, that has lain its blight on so many of the towns of our county. With this brief statement of where we may be found, we salute our readers; *Grand Salaam!*

E. E. & E. SAVAGE.

On the 20th of September, 1877, this firm was dissolved, and the senior member, E. E. Savage, retained possession of the paper. In his few remarks on the change he explains it as follows:

Once again! Again we note a change in the ownership of *The News*, Mr. Ernest Savage having disposed of his interest to the senior member of the firm. *The News* will hereafter be managed by the undersigned. There will be no change as regards politics, or principles, nor as regards business matters. We are thankful for past generous patronage, and solicit a continuance of the same.

E. E. SAVAGE.

Mr. Savage continued to publish the paper until in the latter part of September, 1878, when a financial crash came upon him and he was obliged to abandon *The News*. The office was sold at sheriff's sale, and was purchased by J. P. Reed, the present editor and proprietor.

In November, 1878, Mr. Reed took editorial control, and in his salutatory, speaks thus:

Having chosen the publishing business as a life calling, we purchased the material of the late Shell Rock *News*, and propose to make this beautiful little town of Shell Rock our starting point. We believe we have a correct idea of what a good local newspaper should be, and that idea shall be faithfully our guide. We then, reaching across the editorial table, extend a friendly hand to everybody throughout the country, and especially to every citizen of Butler county. We ask your friendship and assistance, your prayers and words of cheer, for the average newspaper man does not get rich in these days of close competition, and his burdens are often grevious to be borne. We shall always labor to make the *News* a spicy, lively and able exponent of the business and growth of our town and Butler county. We are from principle a republican, and shall adhere to the doctrines of that party; but in these critical times it is essential that every man should be on his guard; and it shall ever be the aim of *The News* to lay bare fraud and corruption whether it be committed by republicans or democrats, and always to be on the alert for the interests of the people. On questions of temperance and morality we shall ever be on the right side, and work for morality in all its phases. We know that the interests of the people are our interests; the people's prosperity our prosperity; and we trust always to advocate the highest good to the greatest number. We hope to make *The News* a household and a welcome visitor to every family in Butler county. With these hasty words of salutation, we now turn to the work at hand, with a faith strong and enduring in the future greatness of the beautiful and picturesque village of Shell Rock.   J. P. REED.

Mr. Reed still manages the newspaper, and has made it one of the leading press advocates in the county. With a large and healthy subscription list it makes a most desirable medium for advertising. Mr. Reed is a well read and well posted man, an able writer and a thorough newspaper man.

J. P. Reed, editor and proprietor of the "Shell Rock *News*, was born in Mercer county, Pennsylvania, November 24, 1851, and is a son of Martin and Elizebeth (Morrison) Reed, who are both natives of Pennsylvania. In 1858 his parents moved west and settled in Stephenson county, Illinois, and here J. P. grew to manhood, and received his education in the common schools of Freeport. In the spring of 1864 he enlisted in Company B, 46th Illinois Volunteers, and served as a private until honorably dischared at Baton Rouge, Louisiana. Upon receiving his dismissal from the army, he returned to Freeport, and learned the "art preservative of all arts," in the office of the "Journal" of that city. In 1869 he came to Cedar Falls, Iowa, and, for a while, clerked in a grocery store of that place, and then formed one of the staff of the *Gazette*, and afterwards of the *Reporter*, of Waterloo. In 1878 he located at Shell Rock, and bought the *News*, of which paper he has since been the proprietor. Mr. Reed was married in September, 1880, to Miss Carrie S. Jones, who was born in Shell Rock, and is a daughter of J. R. Jones.

In December, 1882, Mr. Reed received an appointment in the Treasury Department at Washington.

The *News* says in its issue of December 21, 1882:

"J. P. Reed, editor of this paper, writes us saying, that he secured a clerkship in the Treasury Department at Washington, at a salary of $1,200 a year. He does not say when he will be at home, but the *News* will be issued every week just the same."

PARKERSBURGH ECLIPSE.

This ably managed journal first saw the light August 30, 1872, with the names of Auyer & Edwards, C. D. Auyer and S. T. Edwards appearing as editors and proprietors; terms 2.00 per year. The publication day was Friday, and size of the paper eight column folio, all home print. Its columns are well filled with advertisements. In the salutatory remarks appearing in this issue the editor says:

In presenting the initial number of the *Eclipse* to the public, they will naturally expect us to say something in regard to the position we propose to take in setting forth the political doctrines and policies of the day, and other topics that from time to time engage the public attention. We propose—and shall spare no pains or labor to effect that purpose—to make the *Eclipse* an interesting and reliable newspaper that will reflect the popular spirit of the times, and gather inspiration from western enterprise and progress. The *Eclipse* is dedicated to the interests of Northwestern Iowa, and especially to the future destiny of Butler county.

Politically, the *Eclipse* will be republican, and will advocate the re-election of President Grant. Our knowledge of the republican party, from its organization, has taught us to hold in the highest estimation, the intelligence of its leaders, the purity of its doctrines, justice of its policies, and the noble and loyal men who so largely contributed to make up its rank and file, and while we may earnestly support the measures it may adopt, we shall reserve to ourselves the option of judging whether they be sound in principle, and based upon right and justice. We hold that those who entertain different views, from us, on political or other questions, have the same right to express and maintain them, as we claim for ourselves. Our columns shall not be used for the purpose of venting personal malice, nor will they be controlled by clique or ring to the detriment of any.

These are good and loyal principles, and have been followed and maintained by the *Eclipse* up to the present day, with commendable zeal for the right cause.

With the issue of the *Eclipse* on the 5th of September, 1873, number one of volume two, the size is changed from the folio form to a six column quarto, the inside pages being printed at Chicago. The appearance of it is materially improved. The publication day remains unchanged.

The paper evidently prospered, for in its issue on the 13th of January, 1874, the following item appears:

ENLARGEMENT.—We promised our readers on the beginning of this volume, that we would make some decided improvements, during the coming year, and accordingly on the following week we enlarged and changed the form to eight pages. Now we find it necessary, in order to accommodate our advertising patronage, to re-enlarge, making an addition of 2,036 inches of matter weekly in the *Eclipse*. Furthermore we are furnishing a large variety of interesting original matter, and the generous support we are receiving, is substantial evidence that the *Eclipse* is appreciated by its many readers.

With this edition, the *Eclipse* made its appearance as a seven-column quarto, and was the largest paper ever published in Butler county. The day of publication was changed to Tuesday, and the columns were crowded with "live ad's."

In this shape the paper remained until the hard times, and decreased amount of advertising, made running so large a paper unprofitable, so on the 29th of April, 1874, the *Eclipse* resumed its former size—six column quarto—and Wednesday was again made the day of publication.

On the 23d of September, 1874, the management of the paper underwent a change, and the names of Frank L. Dodge and E. E. Savage, under the firm name of Dodge & Savage, appeared as editors and proprietors. The former proprietors, Auyer & Edwards had, some time previous to this, established a paper at Webster City, called the *Argus*, which they intended to devote their whole attention to. In their farewell article, they state that "they have disposed of the *Eclipse* to Messrs. F. L. Dodge and W. H. Mahanke," but the latter gentleman's name does not further appear. The circulation of the paper at this time, is stated as being about 600.

With its issue on the 16th of December, 1875, the *Eclipse* assumed the form of a seven column quarto—as large as any paper in the State at the time—in defference to the demand for more advertising space. The publication day is Thursday, and the editors state that they "wished to make the *Eclipse* sufficient to *satisfy* its many subscribers;" and its prosperity proves that they succeeded.

In January, 1876, the patent inside system was discarded, and the paper continued as a seven-column folio, "all home print;" and the subscription price reduced to $1.50 per year.

One year from this—in January, 1877—the firm of Dodge & Savage is dissolved, E. E. Savage retiring to devote his attention to the practice of law, and Frank L. Dodge assumes full control. At this time the *Eclipse* was a seven column folio, with patent outsides. Mr. F. L. Dodge continued to manage it alone until 1880, when he took his brother, Fred. A. into partnership, and they still, under the firm name of Dodge Brothers continue in the capacity of proprietors. Within the last year or so the Allison *Tribune* was started by this firm, and is edited by F. L. Dodge, while the *Eclipse* is under the editorial guidance of Fred. A. Dodge, a pungent writer, and a thorough printer. The *Eclipse* has a large and growing subscription list. It is now an eight column folio with "patent outsides," is well got up, and has a large advertising patronage.

Fred. A. Dodge, editor of the *Eclipse*, was born in Dunham Township, McHenry county, Illinois, on December 2, 1858. He was the youngest son of Elisha and Susan Dodge, who settled in that locality in 1839. He was brought up on the farm where he enjoyed the privilege of attending district school until eighteen years of age, when he moved with the family to Howard, Illinois, where he attended the high school until September, 1878, at which date he came to Parksburgh, Iowa, and began work at the printer's trade in the *Eclipse* office, then owned by Frank L. Dodge. In September, 1880, he bought an interest in the *Eclipse*, and when they established the Allison *Tribune*, in the spring of 1881, he assumed editorial control of the *Eclipse*, which position he is now filling, and is also associated with Frank L. Dodge in the publication of the Allison *Tribune*.

BUTLER COUNTY PRESS.

This representative of the newspaper press is published at Green, in the northern part of Butler county, and, although it circulates chiefly in this county, a great many of its readers are citizens of Floyd county. It was established in August, 1873, with H. C. Hammond as editor, the first issue making its appearance as a six-column folio, with "patent insides." The political faith of the paper was proclaimed as republican, and since it first saw the light, it has been steadfast to its first declaration of creed. At the head of the columns appeared the announcement "A Local and General News Journal." Mr. Hammond continued in connection until July, 1874, an interest having been held in it for a short time by Mr. Failing, subsequently by Esquire Soesbe, whose share Mr. Hammond purchased. The first year, as is the case with all papers, was not a financial success, and it is claimed the management was made cumbersome by the fact that there were "too many cooks to season the broth."

In July, 1874, the newspaper became the property of the firm of Wagner & Riner, the *personnel* of which was J. R. Wagner and W. W. Riner; the former now deceased, and the latter is now the affable post master at Greene. The circulation at this time was stated at 13 quires per week, and by March, 1875, this had been increased to a weekly edition of 30 quires, or 720 papers. The files of the paper during its first year of existence, while Mr. Hammond was editor, have not been preserved, so we are unable to review them. The file that has been saved commences with number one of volume two, dated the 26th of August, 1874, neatly bound, well edited and printed. At this date the names of Wagner & Riner appear as editors and publishers, and in a short and able review of the situation, headed "Prospective," they say:

With the present issue the *Press* commences its second year of existence, its second series of visitations. * * * We hope to make it deserving, and its weekly visitation one of pleasant anticipation and welcome to all that give us the encouragement of their patronage. From its past history and liberal patronage we are cheered; with its present prosperity, encouraged; with a promising prospect for the future, we are determined to labor zealously for the end that designates every true lover of excellence, and supply our readers with that which has become an everyday necessity—a good support of wholesome reading.

At that time the *Press* was supporting H. O. Pratt, of Floyd county, the Republican candidate for representative in Congress. In the meantime the paper had been enlarged to a six-column quarto, with "patent insides." In January, 1876, the board of county supervisors designated the *Press* as the official paper of Butler county, and the tax list and other legal county printing appeared in it for the ensuing year. In the latter part of 1876, with the issue of the 14th of October, the form of the *Press* underwent a change, being converted into a seven-column folio, all printed at home, and discarding the "patent-inside" system. This commenced with number seven of volume four, and with the same issue the day of publication was changed from Thursday to Saturday and the subscription price reduced from $2.00 to $1.50 per annum. The week after this reconstruction took place the Shell Rock *News* says:

The Greene *Press* is now all printed at home. It is a seven-column folio and presents a neat appearance. * * * Wagner & Riner get up a good paper. Long may the *Press* live!

In 1877, with the issue of May 24, number forty of volume four, the management of the paper again changed, and the firm of W. W. Riner and George E. De Lavan took the helm, announcing as their motto: "Independent in everything, neutral in nothing." The publication day had in the meantime been changed to Thursday, and in its issue on the 26th of July of the same year the size was enlarged to an eight-column folio and again adopted the "patent-inside" pages, which were printed at Des Moines. In this shape the *Press* continued, enjoying a liberal patronage, until May, 1880, at which time the partnership which had existed between W. W. Riner and George E. DeLavan was dissolved, and the former retired from the newspaper business. Mr. DeLavan is still at the helm of the *Press*, and conducts it in an efficient and able manner, being a pointed and ready writer and a competent business manager. The paper is on a solid and permanent basis, with a large and healthy circulation, and is one of the best advertising mediums in Northern Iowa.

NEW HARTFORD BUGLE.

This was a saucy and piquant little sheet which flourished at New Hartford in the year 1873.

THE BUTLER COUNTY STANDARD.

This was a paper established at Greene, in 1876, by J. B. Adams. It was published at that point for about one year, when it was removed to Clarksville, and continued until the latter part of 1880. It was then moved out of the county to Rockford, Iowa.

THE BRISTOW DIAL,

Was established at Bristow, in 1879, by Mr. Morgan, who ran it until the spring of 1880, when it was purchased by J. Q. Stewart, and continued until the winter following, when it was moved to Sumner, Bremer county.

THE ALLISON TRIBUNE.

This newspaper was first conceived by the Dodge Brothers, of the Parkersburgh *Eclipse*, in December, 1880. At that time they made a visit to Allison, and purchased a lot for the erection of an office building, which they at once commenced, and in May, 1881, was so far along that a full and complete outfit of new printing material and stock was put in, and on the 16th of June, 1881, the *Tribune* first appeared, as an eight column folio, with patent insides, well printed and ably edited. The paper was—and yet is—owned and published by the Dodge Brothers, *en personnel*, Frank L. and Fred. A. Dodge, the editorial management being under the direct control of the former.

In the first issue, the *Tribune* rather trampled upon the old and established custom of newspaper men, in not taking up a half column of space setting forth the principles, convictions and policy to be pursued. But the entire "Salutatory" is condensed into three comprehensive lines, which mean everything, as follows:

"The Allison, Butler County TRIBUNE! Pledged to the right in all things, according to our best understanding.
Very respectfully
DODGE BROTHERS."

In another article, the editors, under the head of "THE TRIBUNE," say:

L. O. Hull

Public servants and educators are subject not only to praise and favorable comment, but also to severe and unsparing criticisms. To step before the public as such, is to acknowledge and accept the situation with all its realities and consequences. This is the first number of the TRIBUNE, and it is certainly a strong and healthy looking infant newspaper. A demand has been made for it from the shaping and turning of events, and in its establishment has been duly considered the perils to which young newspapers are subject; but, here it is, reader, a living reality, the product of heavy expense and hard labor. It is now yours, to assist and to be assisted as a helper in the growing interests of Butler county. The same effort which has brought it forth, will be continued to make it a strong and prosperous exponent of county interests. We wish it to be emphatically a county newspaper, which will reach the firesides of the people, laden with reliable news, advocating honorable and elevating principles. Editorially, we will make no pledges further than that contained in our salutatory, except to say that all shall have fair treatment through our columns. If wrong is condemned, it shall be because of the wrong, and not of the individual who may commit the wrong. Locally, we want the TRIBUNE to be bright and newsy. We want newsy correspondence from all parts of the county, and well written, studied articles, communicated upon important current topics. The educational, moral, political, agricultural and scientific themes of the day, we hope to have fairly and explicitly discussed for the benefit of the TRIBUNE readers, but first of all, may it be a Butler County Newspaper.

And again, as to the political policy to be pursued by the paper, the editor tersely says:

In establishing the *Tribune*, we cannot but choose for its foundation those principles of public policy that stand out boldly as having already achieved enduring victories for the right, and which promise most strongly to advance the circumstances of the people of the age in which we live. In the party struggles through which our nation has passed during the last quarter of a century, reaching every grade of dispute, from the organized campaign of discussion, to the terrible climax of war, we truly believe that the right has triumphed, and on the basic principles through which that triumph has been won, we establish the Allison *Tribune*. We establish it on the principles of our country's present administration, making no compromise with the dictatory factions that would disturb and sacrifice its peace. We do not believe in stereotyping opinions, either politically, religiously, morally or scientifically, but would rather have them advance and grow in spirit and in truth. With this we give you the *Tribune's* party principles.

The above was written at the time of the conflict and rupture between two factions of the republican party, over the nomination of Mr. Robertson as collector of the port of New York; Roscoe Conkling leading the Stalwart faction, and the President's administration backed by the Half-breeds. This is what was meant in the reference to "dictatorial factions," the paper siding with the adminstration.

The first issue of the *Tribune* contained a lengthy review, historical, of the county, and of Allison. In the second issue appears this item:

The first copy of the *Tribune* was printed at 4 o'clock, June 14, 1881. The office being full of citizens who were eager to get and possess it, it was put up at auction, J. W. Spencer auctioneer, and knocked down to the Hon. J. W. Ray, at $3.00. The next hour was spent in giving those present a pull at the lever, each one present printing a paper for himself. * * * * Two pails full of ice cold lemonade were drank to the *Tribune's* health, and three rousing cheers given for its long life and prosperity.

The subscription price of the *Tribune* was first fixed at $2.00; but this has since been reduced to $1.50. The publication day was Thursday, and still is. The paper is neatly printed, well edited, and teeming with local news. Mr. Dodge is a well educated and extensively read man, a deep thinker and is an easy and fluent writer. He has made a paper which is a credit to the county. In this connection it will be well to present a short biographical sketch of the editor in charge.

Frank L. Dodge was born September 10, 1846, in the town of Dunham, McHenry county, Illinois, the sixth of a family of ten children. He was brought up a farmer, educated in common schools, in addition to which he had two terms at a select school, and one term each at the high schools of Harvard and Woodstock, of his native county. He was married, at the age of twenty-two, to Anna A. Hills, of Marengo, Illinois. He taught school winters, and worked on a farm summers, until twenty-five years of age, when he moved to Parkersburgh, Butler county, Iowa. He sawed wood to support his family through the winter of 1871-'72, and in the spring following engaged in carpenter work with his brother, C. B. Dodge, who was among the first settlers of Parkersburgh. In the winter of 1872 he engaged in teaching the first school in the new school house of Parkersburgh, which he taught for five terms, vacating one intervening term in the spring of 1874, during which he worked at bridge building with William Ferguson, who had the contract of bridging the Beaver river at Parkersburgh. In the fall of 1874 he resigned the principalship of the Parkersburgh schools to enter upon the editorial duties of the Parkersburgh *Eclipse*, which work employed his attention until the spring of 1881, when Fred A. Dodge, who became a partner in September, 1880, took editorial control of that paper, and he removed to the new county seat, Allison, to take the initiatory steps of founding the Allison *Tribune*, which he issued for the first time June 16, 1881. The way he came to get into the newspaper business, all started in a joke, while waiting to see a friend off on the midnight train. Auyer and Edwards, the owners of the *Eclipse*, were also waiting to go to Webster City, on the same train, to found a new paper. In conversation with them about getting a buyer for the *Eclipse* Dodge jokingly remarked that may be he had better buy it, and from this insincere remark the newspaper fever caught him, and resulted in a purchase in less than two weeks.

CHAPTER X.

JUDICIAL.

When Butler county was first brought under judicial organization, several years after it had been permanently organized as a county, it was made a part of the Thirteenth Judicial District. This district was created in March, 1857, and was composed of the counties of Butler, Franklin, Grundy, Hamilton, Hardin, Marshall, Story and Wright, to which Webster county was added on the 24th of February, 1858. James D. Thompson, of Hardin county, was the judge elected on the 6th of April, 1857, and commissioned on the 1st of July. Prior to this, there had been no court held in the county, more than what was called the county court, which was virtually the board of supervisors. The district at that time had the same jurisdiction it now has, and was made up of about the same officials.

The first term of district court in Butler county was held in October, 1857, at the Grout school house, in Clarksville. It convened on Monday, the 5th, with the following present: Hon. James D. Thompson, judge; James E. Walker, clerk, and Walker H. Bishop, sheriff.

The following gentlemen were impaneled and sworn as the grand jury: John T. Newhard, foreman; J. M. Vincent, bailiff; William Hoisington, John Braden, James Wood, L. D. Owen, G. T. Root, John Palmer, James Bywater, James McKinney, John Boggs, L. A. Orvis, Judd Bradley, Peter Riley, M. B. Wamsley and A. J. Lewellen. This grand jury first got together soon afterward on the little knoll now occupied by the residence of S. M. Townsend, and organized in the open air, after which they were furnished a room.

The first petit jury consisted of the following gentlemen: A. Van Dorn, foreman; G. W. Stoner, bailiff; Felix Landis, Christian Forney, John M. Hart, Charles Ensign, Aaron Hardman, George Harlan, Samuel McCrery, John Lash, James Blake, J. H. Smith, William Burress, Charles Lusted, A. Glenn and Jacob Shaffer. It seems that enough men could not be obtained for this jury, so the grand jury were ordered to be in attendance for this term of court. Then the clerk makes the entry: "*Amongst other*, the following business was transacted," and on motion of M. M. Trumbull, James R. Fletcher and C. A. Bannon were admitted to practice as attorneys before the court.

The first case to come up was that of the State vs. William Casterline, in which the latter had been accused of threatening to kill some one. He had been tried by the county court and bound over, but before anything was done in regard to it by the district court the charges were withdrawn and the case was dismissed. During this term W. R. Jamison, John Palmer, Orson Rice and George A. Richmond were admitted to the bar as full-fledged lawyers. Considerable other business was transacted at this session, but nothing of particular interest transpired.

Honorable James D. Thompson, the first judge over the district embracing Butler county, was a native of Ohio, and filled the position of judge for one year. He was a man of fair education and a good understanding of the law, always rendering decisions as he thought was just and in accordance with the statutes. He was liked by all and respected by the members of his profession who practiced before him. He was a young man at the time.

The next judge elected was in 1858, Hon. Elias H. Williams was placed on the bench over this district, and held his first term in July, 1859. The district attorney was Milo McGlathery; clerk, James W. Davis; sheriff, W. H. Bishop. Mr. Williams was considered one of the best judges who have ever presided over the district; stern and decisive; a man of few words; yet versed in law and always trying to do justice to all whose cases came before him. He presided for the full term, from 1858 to 1862, and was then re-elected for another term, and held until 1866.

In the meantime the district was divided and Butler county was made a part of the Twelfth District, and the Honorable William B. Fairfield was elected judge. He held his first term in June, 1865. He was a native of New York, a man of commanding appearance, with a noble, open countenance, and was a great deal more genial and unreserved than judges usually are. He had a thorough education, was well read, and had a complete understanding of his profession, although he was, at the same time, a man who liked to take matters easy. He resigned his position of judge in 1870, after holding the June term, and went into the banking business at Charles City. He is now dead.

When Mr. Fairfield resigned, in 1870, Hon. George M. Ruddick, who had been serving as circuit judge, was, upon petition, appointed district judge, and held his first term in October, 1871. In 1872 he was elected, and held until 1876, when he was re-elected, and again in 1880, still being the incumbent.

In May, 1878, a peculiar and aggravating case came before this judge, in which the State was prosecuting Joseph and William J. Good. It had been postponed and deferred until it had cost the county a great deal, and exhausted the patience of the lawyers and judge. Finally the defendants managed to get away—escape—and left the county. When the case came up, Judge Ruddick dismissed it with the following order, which appears on record:

Satisfactory evidence appearing that the defendants have left the country, it is ordered, on motion of district attorney, that this case be dismissed, for fear they may be brought back, or may voluntarily return.

Another rather laughable entry appears on the same page of record, to the effect that—

Hereafter there shall be drawn and "surrendered" twenty jurors, at such and such a term of court.

As a matter of joke, we will state that Mr. William Burdick was clerk at that time.

There are many rich anecdotes told of the courts and judges in early days, but nearly all of them, when traced to their origin, are either mere fabrications or happened in another district. But we will give some of the most plausible ones, hoping they will call to mind to those who were familiar with legal matters in early days the pleasant times had when Butler Center was the seat of justice.

When the county seat was removed from Clarksville to Butler Center it of course necessitated a change on the part of the county officers. The clerk of court, however, did not move at once, and it was a fact that for several weeks every morning he walked from his home in Clarksville to Butler Center, a distance of about fourteen miles, and returned in the evening. This was kept up until the itinerant had traveled about eight hundred miles on foot, when he purchased an old horse, which he rode for a time, then purchased a fine pioneer "barouche," in which he made his trips in style. The following spring he moved to Butler Center. This it is said, was the affable "Jimmy" Davis,

In this connection we are reminded of another little incident with which Mr. Davis figured prominently. Everyone will at once remember that genial, pleasant, jolly and happy German, Frantz, now deceased. Well, Frantz kept a boarding house and hotel, and was therefore on intimate terms with all the county officers and court attenders. He at one time purchased an old, broken-down specimen of dilapidated horse-flesh that would alone grace a bone-yard. The horse had been given up as a lost cause and a forlorn hope by the former owner, and therefore Frantz got it cheap. The horse, in addition to other condemned qualities, had a very bad cold, and as a natural consequence his nose was always in a moistened condition, or in other words was running. On one occasion, shortly after the purchase was made and the ownership of the animal was heralded around among the inhabitants, several of the county officials were standing near the court house, among whom chanced to be Mr. Davis, Mr. Lathrop and others, discussing various matters. Finally Frantz came up from the rear and stood within hearing distance. Mr. Davis at once, pretending not to see him, gave the wink to the others and turned the conversation upon the horse, all the others pretending to be unaware of the presence of the owner of the animal in question Mr. Davis, in the course of his remarks, said: "I tell you, gentlemen, it is absolutely dangerous. The horse has the glanders fearfully, and if allowed to remain in town all the horses in the country are bound to catch it. Now, I propose that we hire a man to silently go to the barn, take that horse and lead him out on the prairie, where he can be riddled with bullets and buckshot before morning. Then we can raise a little purse—" But Frantz waited to hear no more. He lit out for his stable, where he led out the plug and hired a boy to take him nine miles in the country to keep him out of the clutches, as he said, "that —— Jimmy Davis." Of course the matter of glanders and the threat to kill the horse was all a joke, but Frantz took it in earnest, and it was several weeks before he would be convinced and allow the old horse to be brought back. This anecdote is still told with a great deal of gusto by those who were in the vicinity of Butler Center at the time.

One thing of this nature leads to another, and we will digress from our subject heading, and relate another which occurred in early times. When the county seat was still at Butler Center, the county supervisors ordered that vaults be built for the safety of public papers. This was accordingly commenced, and among the men at work was an elderly gentleman named Pelton, disrespectfully called "Old Codger," for short. Court time was coming on, and the German "Frantz," who kept the hotel mentioned in the paragraph above, was preparing to feed the jurors and lawyers. He had fatted up a nice heifer, which he intended to kill. A few weeks before court convened this heifer was missing—some one had stolen it. Frantz searched everywhere, high and low, and stirred up the whole neighborhood in the search. But no heifer could be found, and finally Frantz made up his mind that some of the boys at work on the court house vault were playing a prank upon him. One Saturday he went up to where Old Pelton was at work, and said he had made up his mind to offer a reward to the one that would find his lost bovine, with the remark that if Pelton "found dot creature, he could have half of dot beef." Of course the heifer was found, as Pelton, for a week or more, had known where it was, and it was therefore returned to Frantz on Sunday. The matter ran on for several days and nothing was said about the pay. Finally Pelton said to the German "Frantz," what are we going to do about the beef, where's my half." "Vy, vat you mean by dot?" "What do I mean? Why you promised me half of that beef for finding it; now when are you going to kill it?" "Oh!" says Frantz, "don'd vas going to kill dot heifer, she is in good fatness, und I guess I will keep her for a milk cow." This was too much for the temper of Pelton, and quivering with anger he stepped close to Frantz, and shaking a horny fist under his nose, yelled in his ear, "You can do what you please with your half, but by the jumping Jehovah, I'm goin' to *kill my half for court!*" Friends came up, and the pair finally compromised, by Frantz giving Pelton $3.00 and one week's board.

One time, in years gone by, Frantz got to selling liquor, and as it was against the law, he was obliged to keep the matter very quiet. A number of the most prominent of Butler Center's "floating population" became addicted to the use of the beverage, and were having what they called a "hic—high old time." Finally, it was carried too far, and a constable, living not far away, had a search warrant issued against the old man's hotel. This was duly executed, and the spoils—which consisted of several fine glass decanters, and two or three gallons of whisky—were taken to the county clerk, who was at that time, James W. Davis. This official took charge of the stuff, and held it for several weeks, expecting the old man to come and claim it, and thus lay himself liable to legal punishment. At this time the law provided that in case such matter, so obtained, remained unclaimed for a certain length of time, an order should be issued for the destruction of the bottles and spilling the whisky. After the time described had expired, Mr. Walker issued the order and delivered the property to the proper official, who took them to the corner of the court yard, and over a large stone he whacked the elegant glass bottles, until the smell of whisky made him dizzy. Just at this time Frantz confronted Mr. Davis with the question, "Vere vas dot bottles und dose visky?" Mr. Walker explained the matter to him, and it is said the old man grew black in the face with anger. He abused Mr D soundly, and then left, muttering "I don'd care so much for dot visky as dose bottles—the bottles cost much; but all dot visky only cost about 25 cents."

CRIMINAL CONVICTIONS.

The record of Butler county in this line is about as small as of any county in Iowa. During the year 1880 there were only ten criminal convictions, divided into the various classes as follows: Two for assault and battery; one for assault with intent to commit murder; three for larceny; two for libel; nuisance, one; and one for threats to extort money. The total amount of fines imposed by the district court during the year was $622. The total amount of fines collected and paid into the county treasury during the year was $110. The total expenses of the county, on account of criminal prosecutions, including the amount paid the district attorney, during the year 1880 was $7,070.00. This is considerably lessened in 1881, as the total expense of the county for criminal prosecutions was only $3,098.10; amount of fines imposed by the district court, $110; amount collected and paid into the treasury during the year, $243.10. There were nine convictions.

COUNTY, PROBATE AND CIRCUIT COURTS.

When Butler county was first organized the statutes of Iowa provided for the transaction of all legal matters through what was termed the county court or county judge. The court consisted of the judge, a prosecuting attorney, a clerk and the sheriff. The judge had absolute control and jurisdiction in all matters. He had all the powers now vested in the board of county supervisors; had jurisdiction in all matters of probate; issued marriage license and attended to all financial matters, except that he had nothing whatever to do with the school fund, which at that time was under the supervision of a school fund commissioner, but has since been placed in the hands of the supervisors.

The first county judge who qualified was John Palmer, who was elected at the organization of the county, in 1854. He held the first term of court and transacted the first official business of Butler county. He was a native of Ohio, and had at that time what was considered an education above the average, and a mill-wright by trade; a man, while firm when once convinced, was not over-decisive, nor in any sense aggressive, and was, in the capacity of judge, liked very well by all. He served for one term, and is now in the west engaged at his profession of law.

In 1855 Aaron VanDorn was elected and took the bench, for one term. He was a lawyer of considerable ability, and had a placid and pleasant tenure of office. He is now dead.

The next election for this office was held in 1857, and was very close, considerable feeling being manifested in regard to it. The candidates were Alonzo Converse and George W. Poisal, and the former was elected by a majority of eight. The law provides that in case the judge does not qualify within twenty days after election, the office is vacant. It seems that Mr. Converse did not make his appearance within twenty days, the last day coming on Sunday, and he arrived on the following Monday; but the former judge refused to allow him to qualify, claiming his time had expired, and forthwith issued a call for another election to fill the vacancy. This resulted in the election of D. W. Miller, who at once qualified. Mr. Converse at once commenced a contest, which resulted in his election being sustained, and Miller withdrew. Judge Converse served his first term, was re-elected, and served until 1861. He was an impulsive, quick spirited, and energetic man, and in many respects a man much liked as a judge. He was acting in that capacity at the time of the great county seat struggle, in which it was removed from Clarksville to Butler Center, and, of course, many enemies resulted from it, as the matter affected many in a personal pecuniary way, and such things often blind the eyes of men in regard to true capability and integrity. The judge is now in Dakota engaged in opening a farm.

In the fall of 1861, C. A. Bannon was elected judge, and served for two years, quite satisfactory, as he had been prosecuting attorney for some years, and was well acquainted with the *modus operandi* of the office.

During this year the new system of a board of county supervisors was inaugurated, and took most of the business out of the jurisdiction of the county judge, leaving with that functionary entire control of the issuance of marriage licenses and jurisdiction in all probate matters.

J. R. Fletcher was the next county judge, elected in the fall of 1863, for the term of two years, 1864 and 1865. Judge Fletcher, as a judge, was very well liked, as he was a well read lawyer, and had a good education. He was a man of considerable energy and great integrity. He is now in one of the government departments at Washington, D. C.

Ancel Durand was judge for one term, and had a quiet, uneventful, official career, as nothing of any importance came up. He now resides at Bristow.

In the fall of 1865, A. J. Thompkins was elected judge, and served for one term. He was a man of bitter prejudices, crotchety, and quick tempered, although he made a fair judge, and was well liked. He is now in Arkansas.

The records of this court are lost. They were at the house of Judge Durand, at Bristow, where he had taken them for the purpose of making out his reports, and during his absence the house took fire and before any one could reach it, the books and papers were all destroyed.

CIRCUIT COURT.

On the first Monday in January, 1869, the circuit court was established and took control of the probate business, while the marriage license issuance was left with the clerk of court. The county judge was dispensed with, and made county auditor.

The circuit court district is what is known as the Twelfth Judicial district, the same as district court, and embraces the counties of Butler, Bremer, Mitchell, Worth, Cerro Gordo and 'Hancock.

The first circuit judge was George W. Ruddick, now judge of the district court for this district. He was elected in 1868, commencing official work in January, 1869, and held until after the spring term in 1871, when he received the appointment to his present position. A sketch of him will be found in connection with the article on district court. He was succeeded to the bench of circuit court by Judge Robert Reiniger, a native of Ohio, who still acts in that capacity.

CHAPTER XI.

THE BAR OF BUTLER COUNTY.

There is no class or profession which has more influence in social and political matters than the bar. Even the press, which wields a mighty power among the masses, does not surpass it, as matters treated by them are generally local and varying. The pulpit, a great worker of good, is more devoted to the moral and spiritual welfare of man. But the profession of law embraces all under one grand aim. Upon the few principles of natural justice is erected the whole superstructure of civil law, tending to relieve the wants and meet the desires of all alike. The grand object of law is equal justice to all, not technicality; although the latter must be strictly adhered to, to preserve the supremacy of law. The laws are formed as exigencies arise demanding them, by the representatives of the people. Change is necessary. The wants of the people of to-day, and the lawful restraints to be thrown around us of the present age, differ from those of past years. They are either too lenient or too severe—in one case to be strengthened, in the other modified. The business of the lawyer does not call upon him to form laws, but it lies with him to interpret them, and to make their application to the daily wants of men. Every matter of importance, every question of weight, among all classes and grades, come before him in one form or another, for discussion. Hence, the lawyer is a man of to-day—posted upon all matters pertaining to the age in which he lives. His capital is his ability and individuality, and he cannot bequeath them to his successors. They die with him, or live in the memory of his sayings and deeds.

In early days business was not so great in extent as to occupy the full time of the lawyer. Suits were not so numerous or remunerative as to afford him a comfortable living for himself and family, and often other occupations must be taken in connection to swell the slender income. As a rule the lawyer became a politician, and more of the prominent lawyers of those days went to Congress and the State Legislature than at present. The people demanded their services, and they were glad to accommodate the people. To-day the profession stands at the head, almost, of all others, and the good lawyer must always be prominent, as he is one of the forces which move, control and protect society.

There have been, and still are, able and prominent men practicing before the courts in Butler county—men who were an honor to the profession, and to society and the county. Among those who have located in the county for the practice of law, are the names of M. M. Trumbull, J. R Fletcher, C. A. Bannon, John Palmer, Orson Rice, George A. Richmond, W. R. Jamison, J. W. Davis, Zur Graves, L. A. Orvis, Alonzo Converse, C. A. L. Roszell, W. A. Lathrop, C. M. Failing, J. W. Gilger, John Jamison, D. J. Marts, Soesbe Brothers, C. M. Greene, W. M. Foote, F. D. Jackson, William Norval, R. D. Prescott, Col. Woods, Mr. Burnell, J. H. Boomer, D. W. Mason, George M. Craig, N. T. Johnson, O. B. Courtright, Mr. Ellsworth, A. I. Smith, George A. McIntyre, O. H. Scott, John Bremer, Sawyer Haswell, W. H. Burdick, M. J. Downey, E. E. Savage, B. L. Richards and W. S. Montgomery.

There is much more uncertainty, and a great deal more trouble, than would be imagined, connected with obtaining facts and material for a memoir of those who have been so intimately associated with public matters in practicing before the courts at an early day, but as much is given as could be obtained.

THE FIRST LAWYER.

The first lawyer to locate in Butler county for the purpose of practicing at the profession, was Matthew M. Trumbull. He was a native of England, and came to Iowa in 1852, settling in Linn county, where he pursued his study of law, which he had begun, and was admitted to the bar. In 1854 he came to Butler county and located at Clarksville, and commenced practice. He remained here until the war broke out, when in 1861, he enlisted and went into service as Captain of Company I of the 3d Iowa Infantry. Soon afterward he was promoted to Colonel of the 9th Cavalry. When the war closed he was honorably discharged, and the title of Brigadier-General of Volunteers was conferred upon him for deserving conduct, as he was brave as a lion, and did noble service for his country. Upon his return he settled at Waterloo, Iowa, and there resumed the practice of law. Within a few years he removed to Dubuque, where he was Collector of Internal Revenue for a number of years. Resigning this position he removed to Chicago, where he is yet practicing law,

General Trumbull, when he first came to Butler county, was a man of more than ordinary ability, and had besides a good general education a thorough knowledge of law. He was a kind, generous-hearted man, of good impulses and a great deal of integrity. To illustrate this we will relate an occurrence by which the General had the joke, by accident, turned upon himself:

One time late in the fifties the General had occasion to try a suit before one of the justices of the peace. In those days the justices, or as they were termed, the "squires," were rather illiterate, as a rule not knowing any more of law than they did of geology, and this one was no exception to the rule; but they almost invariably, if not befogged by counsel, made rulings based on common sense, law and the statutes to the contrary notwithstanding. Upon the case in question the opposing counsel was Orson Rice, who receives due attention further on. Mr. Rice was in a sort of contrary mood this morning, and kept making objections to testimony, finding something wrong with proceedings, taking exceptions to the rulings and interrupting his honor and everyone else. After a time the General called the attention of the court to the interruptions of proceedings. Finally his honor straightened up, raised his fist, and bringing it down with a thump on the table exclaimed, pompously: "Mr. Rice, *you* sit down!" Mr. Rice paid no attention, but kept right on talking regardless of anyone. The General saw that the 'squire was getting excited, so he said to him: "I wouldn't stand it; I'd make him keep quiet." Rice paid no attention. This was too much for his honor, who, with blood in his eye and shaking his finger at Rice sinisterly, hissed: "Mr. Rice! You sit down, or I'll put a *quietus* on you!" "Yes," interposed Trumbull, with a twinkle in his eye, "that's just what he wants—a quietus writ will put a stop to it." Rice soon again interrupted; and the justice, now fairly enraged, ordered: "Mr. Trumbull, you make out that *writ of quietus*. at once! We'll see who's bossin' this court." The story leaked out, and the General many times was called upon to answer a joking query as to the *writ of quietus.*

General Trumbull had no difficulty in making friends, and when once made they were fast and sincere. George Poisal and Mr. Trumbull were intimate friends, and often had law business to transact. One day in April, 1857, George came into Trumbull's office, and in the course of conversation, remarked, that he had just received a new litter of pigs. "Well," says the General, "that's just what I want. You had better give me one of them!" "All right;" answers George; you shall have one." The matter ran along for some months, and nothing was said about it. Finally, one day in November, George again chanced to be in the General's office, and stated that he had just killed a lot of fatted hogs. "By the way," remarked Trumbull, "I just happen to think of it. How is that hog you gave me, doing?" "That hog?" exclaimed Poisal, "that is the very litter I've been killing. You never called for it!" "Well," Trumbull answers, "I thought the matter over, and decided to let you fat it on shares." A general laugh was indulged in, and the following morning a fine dressed porker was sent to the General's house.

General M. M. Trumbull was elected to the lower house of the State Legislature in 1858, and was the first member elected from Butler county.

The fall of 1859 is noted by the arrival in Butler county of the lawyers, J. R.

Fletcher and C. A. Bannon, who commenced practice in partnership.

J. R. Fletcher was a native of Pennsylvania, and was educated and admitted to the bar as a lawyer, at Bedford, in that State. He was a young man when he came to Iowa, and his good education made a brilliant future possible. But he liked his ease considerably, and after a few years of limited practice, he began devoting part of his attention to stock. In early days he was a candidate for various county offices, and served one term as county judge. In 1881 he got an appointment to a clerkship in the Pension Bureau, at Washington, and is still retained in that capacity. He is now a man of about fifty years of age.

Charles A. Bannon was of Irish descent, and was possessed of all the ready wit so natural to the descendants of the Emerald Isle. He, also, was brought up and educated in Pennsylvania, and was admitted to practice law at Bedford, in that State. He came to Iowa at the same time Mr. Fletcher did, and they practiced law in partnership, living in Clarksville, until the time of Mr. Bannon's decease, in 1865. Mr. Bannon was a man of good education in law, an excellent orator, and promised to become an ornament to the profession. He was a single man, of about 32 years of age; very genial-hearted, capable of adapting himself to any society, very popular, loved humor, and was a man of great integrity. When the war broke out he left his profession and went as first lieutenant in company G, of the Thirty-second Infantry, of which C. A. L. Roszell was captain, serving through the war, and returning to Clarksville, broken down in health. Brain fever set in, and he was finally called from earthly labor, leaving many true and warm friends and associates to mourn his loss.

The above named lawyers were the only ones in the county until 1857. The first term of court was held this year in October, at Clarksville, and at this term, on the fifth day of the month, John Palmer, Orson Rice and G. A. Richardson were admitted to the bar.

John Palmer was a native of Ohio, coming to Iowa in 1849 or 1850, and locating in Linn county. He was the first judge of the county, and an able lawyer. He is noticed at length in connection with the county and circuit courts.

Orson Rice was a native of Ohio, coming to this State from Illinois, arriving in Butler county in 1854, and taking a claim. He was a man of about 28 years of age, and had a family. He was very illiterate and knew nothing at all of law when he commenced practice; but he was energetic, independent, and entirely reckless as to the language he used. He would murder the English language and grammar in a way that often made him the laughing stock. He remained in the county, practicing law, until 1864 or 1865, when he removed to Spirit Lake, and is still at his profession, having served one term as district attorney, and came very near the Circuit Judgeship.

Many laughable and pithy anecdotes are told of Rice, which illustrate the difficulties, in the way of insufficient education, against which he had to battle in his early practice. Several of these will be presented.

On one occasion Mr. Rice had a case before justice of the peace, J. M. Vincent, with General M. M. Trumbull as opposing counsel. The "Squire" was as illiterate as was Mr. Rice, and in drawing up the notice made a serious mistake. It was a case in which some one claimed $22, and some one else refused to pay. The names of parties have been forgotten, but they are immaterial. The "Squire" in drawing up the notice made the amount read "twenty-too dollars." Rice was quick to see a point, but did not have knowledge to push it. When the case was called, Orson Rice, attorney for defendant, moved to "squash, as there was no specific amount or sum stated." The justice said: "Don't be a fool, Rice, and show how blamed ignorant you are." Rice, however, insisted upon "squashing" the case, and remarked that "everyone knows that there is no sense to 'twenty-too—a child knows it, Now, if it had read 'twenty-t-o dollars,' it would have had some weight. But as it is it must be 'squashed.'" The justice stuck to "too," and said he knew it was right, while Rice as vehemently stuck to "to." Finally they agreed to let outside parties, who were authority on spelling, decide which of the two were right. How it was decided has not been told, but members of the bar tell the story of the squabble over the little word "two" with great relish.

John E. Burk, who was at one time prosecuting attorney for this judicial district, and is now a prominent attorney in Chicago, tells a laughable story on Rice. It seems that Rice at one time had a case before the district court at the time Judge Elias H. Williams was on the bench. Rice squabbled considerably, and had made an appeal for a continuance of the suit. In filing his motion with Judge Williams for continuance, he made several mistakes, and had amended his motion three times. The third time he handed it up to the Judge, looked at him, and shook his head solemnly. Rice gave up, and leaning back in his chair, shaking his head in a way peculiar to him, exclaimed: "My client is a conshiensh man; I am a conshiensh man. Now if the court will suggest what we should put into that motion, we'll both swear to it." The judge did not suggest, but a general laugh ensued.

Rice was a very pugnacious fellow, and when once excited would threaten to thrash the attorneys, clients and the court himself. At one time Rice was pleading a case before 'Squire Margretz, at Butler Center, in which George A. Richmond was the opposing counsel. The two lawyers got into a wordy dispute over some point, and one called the other a liar. Rice leaped to his feet, pulled off his coat and was going to "walk right through" Richmond. The 'squire yelled at the top of his voice: "Order in this court!" Not coming to order, his honor got right in the midst of it and stood between the two. Rice doubled up his fist and made a lunge for the 'squire, who, stepping back aghast, exclaimed in his broken English: "*By ——!* Rice, vas you going do schtruck dis court? Ve can't tolerate such conduct like dose. By shiminey! You can both gonsider yourselves in shail for thirty days." This brought order, and we suppose they considered themselves jailed for thirty days.

George A. Richmond, who is also mentioned as being admitted to practice law during the first term of court, was a native of Pennsylvania, having been raised in the city of Philadelphia. When he came to Butler county, in 1854, and located in Butler Center, he was about thirty years of age—tall, straight, with easy carriage, he made an imposing and fine appearance. He had a good education and was popular. His knowledge of law was all picked up after his arrival in Butler county, as he was engaged in land speculation. He never had much practice at law, and in 1859 he removed to Dubuque, where he enlisted in the army, and for bravery and good service was made colonel of some Pennsylvania regiment. He was a brave soldier and a gallant officer. When the war closed, or shortly afterward, he returned to his native State.

During the first term of district court in Butler county, in September, 1857, W. R. Jamison was admitted to the bar, and was for many years after prominent among the legal representatives of the county. W. R. Jamison was born in Chester county, Pennsylvania, January 12, 1816, and raised from infancy to manhood in Lancaster county, Pennsylvania, being the only son of a family of three; brought up on the farm, laboring faithfully for his father until he arrived at the age of twenty-one, having received only a very limited common-school education. The public school system of Pennsylvania had not gone into effect until after he attained his majority. Being of an inquiring turn of mind and reading all books and papers to which he had access, he early acquired a considerable knowledge of men and matters generally. On becoming of age he wended his way about four hundred miles west, traveling on foot and stopping in Ohio. On reaching his destination he went to work as a farm-laborer, about the first of June, 1837, and about the second day of November of the same year married a lady born and raised in the Buckeye State. He remained a resident of Ohio until 1851, when he with his family removed to near Quasqueton, Buchanan county, Iowa, where he remained until about the first of September, 1853, when he with his family removed to Butler county, Iowa, on the place where he now resides.

During his stay in Ohio he was engaged in various pursuits in order to make a livelihood for himself and family, and in the meantime seeking such information and knowledge of matters and things in general as an inquiring mind will naturally make, and more especially in matters relating to the statutes and laws of the State and the judicial proceedings of the courts of justice. On stopping in Iowa, in November, 1851, he rented a farm, and during the next winter entered three hundred and twenty acres of land. During his stay he made some improvements on the land, at the same time not forgetting to thoroughly acquaint himself with the code and statutes of Iowa and the manner of enforcing them in the courts, together with the general principles of law.

On selling out his land in Buchanan county he removed, about the first of September, 1853, to Butler county, Iowa, where, on the eleventh day of August, 1853, he had entered three hundred and twenty acres of land on sections 19 and 20, in township 92, range 18, which now constitutes Pittsford township, Butler county. From 1853 up until 1857 he was principally engaged in making and improving his farm, at the same time making such progress in the study of matters relating to law as the circumstances seemed to invite and permit. In September, 1857, the first term of the district court in and for Butler county was held by Judge John D. Thompson, at Clarksville, when, after the admission to the bar of several gentlemen as practicing attorneys during that term of court, Mr. Jamison, through the persuasion of several attorneys and friends, though reluctantly on his part, consented that an application might be made to the court to appoint a committee of members of the bar to examine Mr. Jamison as to his qualifications to practice law and as to his admission to the bar. Said motion was presented to the court by Messrs. Fletcher and Bannon, whereupon Judge Thompson announced Attorneys James R. Fletcher, James W. Woods and W. F. Newton as such committee. After having discharged their duties as such committee the application was favorably reported, whereupon the court made an order admitting him to practice as an attorney in all district courts in the State from and after that date. From his admission as an attorney Mr. Jamison has practiced in Butler and some of the adjoining counties, with more or less success, generally having a fair share of the business of the courts to look after, until quite recently, when, desiring to turn his attention more especially to his farming matters, he has persistently refused to do further business as an attorney, and at present declines to engage in any case as an attorney. Mr. Jamison has, during all his residence in Iowa, been principally engaged in farming and improving his farms, and has now over a section of land, mostly in Pittsford township, all improved and under fence, the tillable land being all broken and under cultivation, and is now devoting his time to his duties as a farmer, which requires his whole time and attention.

William Stoughton was one of the lawyers who were admitted to practice in 1859. He left during the war. Stoughton had a very good practice, and was a first rate lawyer; but was too jovial.

D. W. Mason was admitted about the same time. He was a native of New York, came to Butler county young, with his parents, who settled near Butler Center. He was engaged in mercantile and real estate business at Butler Center, and from there removed to Shell Rock, where he lived at the time of his admission to the bar. He was the first superintendent of schools of Butler county, having a good general education, but did not make a success of the profession of law. He went to the war, and on his return removed to Missouri, where he has since served a term as judge.

Captain C. A. L. Roszell is one of the most able attorneys in Butler county. He is among the oldest practicing representatives of the legal profession in the county, having located at Clarksville many years ago. He has a very extensive practice, and is recognized at home and abroad as a lawyer of much reading and ability. He is politically a democrat, has represented this district in the General Assembly of Iowa, and has been on the democratic ticket a candidate for Congress and other important offices.

The first lawyer to locate at Greene was C. M. Failing, Esq., who had formerly lived in Jones county, and commenced practice in Greene in 1872. He only remained a few years when he returned to Jones county. He is now in the southern part of the State, engaged in publishing a newspaper.

J. W. Gilger located at Greene early in the seventies. He was a native of New York State, and was admitted to the bar here, in Butler county. He had a fair practice, and was a good lawyer. In 1880 he removed to Hampton, where he is yet in practice.

D. J. Marts, of Pennsylvania, a man of good general education, but not very well read in law, was admitted to the bar and commenced practice in Greene late in the seventies, but did not continue long. He had been living upon a farm near Greene, and had taught school considerable prior to his admission. He is now in Nebraska.

John Jamison, son of W. R. Jamison, Esq., of Dumont, was another attorney, who located in Greene, remaining here with a very fair practice for about one year, from 1876 to 1877. John Jamison was a native of Ohio, where he was born in 1845, coming to Iowa early in the fifties with his father. He was admitted to the bar at Butler Center, and after practicing at Greene as above stated, he went to Shell Rock, and from there to Belmond, Iowa, where he still follows his profession. He is a very well read lawyer, and good speaker.

William M. Foote, attorney and justice of the peace, also present county coroner, of Butler county, was born in Shelby county, Ohio, in 1822; studied law in Dart county; was admitted to the bar in 1858, at Greeneville, where he resided 'till 1864, when he removed to Clayton county, Iowa, where he was engaged in farming, and also occasionally engaged in attending to a law case. He went to Marble Rock, Floyd county, in 1870; came to Greene the following year. He has done something at the practice of law since he came here, but was elected a justice of the peace in 1872, and has held that office constantly since, the duties of which require most of his time. He was elected coroner in the fall of 1881. Mr. Foote has been twice married; his first wife was Miss Rhoda Swisher, born in Ohio, and died in Clayton county, May 13, 1870. His present wife was Miss Sarah A. Moore, born in Carroll county, Indiana. Mr. Foote had twelve children by his first wife, seven of whom are living. Has two children by second wife.

Soesbe Brothers, attorneys, have been in practice at Greene since 1877. This is a well-known firm. They came here when Greene was in its earliest infancy, and are the oldest practicing lawyers in the town. S. W. Soesbe was born near Mechanicsville, Jones county, Iowa, September 24, 1844. His father, William Soesbe, settled in Burlington, from Indiana, in 1840, but soon after located in Jones county. He died in Anamosa in 1880. Previous to engaging in the practice of law, S. W. Soesbe, Esq., was for a time engaged in bridge building with A. Spaulding & Co., who were afterward known as the "Dubuque Bridge Company." He came to Greene in 1871 and engaged in the real estate business. In the meantime he turned his attention to the study of the law, and was ad-

W. A. Lathrop

mitted in Judge D. S. Wilson's court, at Waterloo, January 5, 1877, and at once entered into the practice of his profession here. His wife was Ella L. Newell, daughter of Lorenzo Newell, an early settler of Benton county.

E. W. Soesbe, Esq., was born near Anamosa, November 11, 1851. He read law with his brother at Waverly; was admitted in that city in March, 1877; married Miss Carrie Cross, whose father, J. J. Cross, was an early settler of Freemont township.

The Soesbe Brothers are good lawyers, intelligent and popular gentlemen. They have a large, increasing business, both in legal practice and real estate business.

W. A. Lathrop, of the firm of Lathrop & Davis; also of the abstract firm of Lathrop, Hyde & Levis, is one of the oldest practitioners in Butler county; in fact, with but one exception—that of Captain Roszell, of Clarksville, who came to the county about the same time—has been longer in practice in this county than any other attorney. Mr. Lathrop is a native of New London county, Connecticut, where he was born in 1826. He is of the old Puritan stock, tracing his lineage back to the Rev. John Lathrop, who came over from England, and settled at Scituate, Massachusetts, September 28, 1634. From this Rev. John Lathrop descended all the Lathrops of this country. One branch of the family settled in Bozrah, New London county, Connecticut, and from this branch of the family the subject of our sketch sprung. He acquired in the common schools of his native State such education as they afforded, after which he took a thorough academical course at Leicester Academy, Worcester county, Massachusetts. He studied law with Judge Dwight Loomis, of the Supreme Court of Connecticut, and was admitted to the bar in 1854. He went to Illinois the same year and engaged in the practice of law in Elmwood, Peoria county, where he remained two years, when he returned to his native State and engaged in teaching. He came to Butler county in 1860, settled at Butler Center, and resided there in the practice of his profession until the removal of the county seat to Allison, when he took up his residence there. Mr. Lathrop is a well-educated gentleman and a successful lawyer. His twenty-two years' practice at the county seat has given him a large experience and a thorough knowledge of the various branches of his profession. He was county superintendent of the public schools of Butler county for four years, two years by appointment of county board and two years by election. He was also a member of the Tenth General Assembly of Iowa, representing the counties of Butler, Franklin and Grundy. Mrs. Lathrop was formerly Miss Adelaide Hyde, a native of Connecticut. They have one daughter, Ethel, wife of Mr. Charles W. Levis, the junior member of the firm.

In 1858 a number of accessions were made to the bar. Among them were J. W. Davis, Z. Graves, L. A. Orvis, and Alonzo Converse.

James W. Davis is a native of Oneida county, New York, where he was born October 28, 1826. He went to Lake county, Illinois, in 1853, where he engaged in teaching until 1856, when he removed to Clarksville, Iowa, and worked at carpentering and teaching until July, 1858, when he was appointed deputy clerk. Was elected clerk of the district court of Butler county, Iowa, in 1858, and was elected for seven successive terms. Studied law under Gen. M. M. Trumbull, then of Clarksville, now of Chicago, Illinois. Was admitted to the bar in 1858, at Clarksville, but did not enter into practice until 1873. He, in the mean time, occupying the position of clerk of the courts of said county.

Mr. Davis, by virtue of his office, was clerk of the board of supervisors of said county, from January, 1861, to January, 1869, and during such time acted as auditor of said county, and in such period an old debt of over $16,000, a bridge bonded debt of $40,000, a bounty to soldiers of over $40,000, and soldiers' relief of some $12,000, was fully paid off and canceled.

Mr. Davis' ancestors settled in Connecticut, his grandfather Davis settled in Washington county, New York. At the commencement of the war of the Revolution he entered the Continental army and was in the army under Gen. Gates, when Burgoyne surrendered. His grandfather Benoni Patten, entered the Continental army at the very commencement of the Revolutionary war and was with it during the terrible winter at Valley Forge, at Trenton, and saw its final success by the surrender of Cornwallis at Yorktown. He was taken prisoner at the battle of New York, and confined six or seven months in a British prison-ship in New York harbor. He used to relate the hardships those prisoners had to undergo while thus confined, half fed, poorly clad, and abused by those in charge.

One incident took place during his imprisonment, that shows the hardships and inconveniences they had to endure at that time. One day, after suffering from hunger for a long time, a large iron kettle, with peas boiled into a soup, was brought to the prisoners, with nothing to eat it with—without spoons, ladels or other utensils, and each had to help himself with such as he could find in that loathsome prison-ship. He, in his hunger after food, took from his foot an old shoe and dipped it into the kettle of pea soup, and drank out of the heel of the shoe.

Mr. Davis has three sons and five daughters living. His wife is a native of Connecticut, a sister of W. A. Lathrop, his law partner.

Zur Graves was a native of New York, and came to Butler county in 1855, settling in Jefferson township, where he remained until 1862, when he went to the war, enlisting in an Illinois regiment. Graves was well educated, and had read considerable law, but he was stuffed with egotism, and had a good deal of nonsense in his composition. It is now said that his admission to the bar was more through sport than anything else. He never had a case.

L. A. Orvis was admitted to the bar also in 1858, and he still lives in Butler county. L. A. Orvis was born in Bradford county, Pennsylvania, December 12, 1815, and is a son of Joseph and Nancy (Atwater) Orvis. His mother is a native of New Haven, Connecticut, and his father of Litchfield county, Connecticut. Five years after his birth, the family moved to Steuben county, New York, where the son received his education, which was acquired in the common schools of the county, and by an attendance of several terms at an academy.

Upon quitting school, he learned the blacksmith's trade, which occupation he afterwards followed for a number of years. During the summer of 1841 he came west and settled in Trumbull county, Ohio, where he followed his trade and farming. In 1852 he moved to Boone county, Illinois, and three years later, came to Butler county, Iowa, where he purchased a farm on section 15, of Shell Rock township, upon which he now resides. During his leisure hours, for many years, he read law, receiving instruction at different times, as he required it, from prominent attorneys where he lived, and in 1857, was admitted to the bar of Butler county, by Judge Murdock. Since 1844, Mr. Orvis has belonged to the republican party—previous to that time he was a democrat. He served for thirteen years as justice of the peace in his county, and has also held several other of the town offices. In 1840 he was married to Miss Fanny L. Hills, who is a native of Steuben county, New York. Eleven children have been born to them, six of whom are now living—Laura L., Frank E., Fletcher L., Samantha M., who is now the wife of N. E. Drury, of Kansas; William H., and Ella A., who is now the wife of Edward C. Downs, Jr., of Dakota. Mr. Orvis was a member of the first grand jury of Butler county, and they were compelled to hold their first meetings in the fence corners and in the woods. His father died in 1823, and his mother, in 1862, at the age of seventy-five years.

Alonzo Converse was admitted to the bar in 1858. He was elected county judge in 1857, and re-elected in 1859, serving with credit to himself. A sketch of him is found in the chapter on judicial matters under the sub-head of county and circuit courts.

Frank D. Jackson, attorney at law, established practice at Greene, July, 1880. Mr. Jackson is also the present secretary of the Senate, having been appointed to that position in January, 1882. He was born in Wyoming county, New York, in 1854. He was for some time a student at the Arcade Academy; came to Iowa in 1867, and was for three years a student at the Iowa State Agricultural College. He graduated at the law department of the State University in 1875; began practice at Independence, where he continued for five years, locating here, as above stated, in 1880, succeeding J. W. Gilger, Esq. Mr. Jackson is a young man of culture, of much native ability, and bids fair to attain prominence in his profession. His wife was Miss Anna F. Brock. They have two children. Mr. Jackson occupies the position of assistant adjutant general of the National Guard, State of Iowa.

C. M. Greene, attorney and counselor at law, has been in practice here since September, 1881. He was born in Oswego county, New York, in 1845. He was for some time a student of Hamilton College, and graduated at the State Normal School, at Oswego, in 1869. He was for many years engaged in teaching; came to Iowa in 1870, and for a time was principal of the Central School, at Keokuk. In 1871 he purchased the "Iowa State Educational Journal," which he published for five years. He came to Greene in 1877; was principal of the school here for four years; while teaching, studied law in the office of Gilmore & Anderson, at Keokuk; was admitted to the bar in 1876 at Ottumwa. His wife was Mary B. Swiggett. They have had four children, two of whom are now living.

During the seventies R. D. Prescott commenced the practice of law, at Shell Rock, remaining for several years, but now of Mitchell, D. T. He was a native of New Hampshire, a good business man, well educated, and made a first rate lawyer.

Col. Woods practiced law at one time before the courts of Butler county, and resided at Butler Center; but has long since left.

Attorney Burnell practiced for a time in Shell Rock. He is now in Palo Alto county.

J. H. Boomer was another of Shell Rock's attorneys, having a lucrative practice for several years. He had lived in Iowa for some years prior to his commencing practice, and still lives in Iowa, at Lansing, Alamakee county. He was active, peppery, well-read, and a good lawyer.

D. W. Mason also practiced law in Butler county for some time, and was also one of the first superintendents of schools of Butler county.

W. S. Montgomery is a young attorney who came to Butler county in March, 1880, and locating at Clarksville, has since been engaged in the practice of his profession.

Mr. Montgomery is the third of a family of seven children of James and Sarah (Glew) Montgomery, and was born on February 16, 1853. His parents are both natives of Pennsylvania, and are yet living upon the farm in Dubuque county, Iowa, on which they settled in 1836. The subject of our sketch received a common school education, and in 1874 entered the Law Department of the Iowa State University, from which he graduated in 1875, and was admitted to the bar. From this time until 1879 he engaged in teaching school, and then entered the law office of J. C. Longueville. Thus when he came to Clarksville he was well prepared for his profession. He was for a time associated with Capt. C. A. L. Roszell, which undoubtedly proved greatly to his advantage. Mr. Montgomery at once became a highly esteemed citizen, so much so, that in 1882 the republican party nominated him as their candidate for County Clerk, and he was elected by a good majority, and entered upon his official duties in January, 1883.

J. F. Ellsworth, a lawyer who located at Bristow about 1875, was from Hardin county. He was well fitted for the profession, and made a good lawyer. About two years since he went to Elizabeth, D. T., where he yet remains.

George A. McIntyre, attorney and counselor at law, has resided at Allison since January, 1881. He is a native of Pawpaw, Lee county, Illinois, where he was born in 1855, removing to Marshall county, Iowa, with his father, when eight years of age. He was educated at the seminary in the village of Albion, engaged in teaching two years. He entered the Law Department of the State University of Iowa, September, 1875, where he graduated the following year. He afterward took a special law course in the same institution, completing the course in June, 1877. He began practice at Marshalltown, where he continued until locating here. Mr. McIntyre was married on the 9th of November, 1882, to

Miss Mary M., a daughter of Captain J. R. Jones.

A. J. Smith, attorney at law, of Allison, is a native of Rensselaer county, New York, where he was born in 1848, but brought up at Monroe, Greene county, Wisconsin. He began the study of law at Hampton, Franklin county, Iowa, with the firm of King & Henry, being admitted to the bar in 1878, at Marshalltown. He formed a law partnership with L. F. Butler, Esq., at Northwood, Worth county, Iowa, with whom he remained about two years. He came to Allison in May 1881. The law firm of Craig & Smith have a large and increasing practice. They also transact a general real estate and abstract business. Mrs. Smith was formerly Miss Marietta Weeks, a native of Massachusetts. Her father, Mr. W. Weeks, is a prominent merchant of Hampton.

George M. Craig, attorney at law—firm of Craig & Smith, of Allison—has been a resident of Butler county since October 11, 1864. He was born in Waukegan, Lake county, Illinois, in 1844. He enlisted as a private August 12, 1862, in the 88th regiment Illinois Infantry, and served for two years. He participated in several engagements, was severely wounded at the battle of Chickamauga, and left on the field in the hands of the enemy, where he lay for several days, when he was paroled and sent through the lines to the Union army for disability, July 30, 1864, and came to Butler county in October of the same year. He was appointed county recorder in June, 1868, and elected to that position in the fall of 1869. In the meantime he attended to the study of law, and was admitted to the bar at Grundy Center,

Iowa, in January, 1873, He formed a law partnership with Lora Alford, Esq., for several years. The firm of Craig & Smith was formed July 1, 1882. Mr. Craig has been twice married, his first wife was a native of Illinois; his present wife was Mary E. Chapline, born in Dubuque, Iowa.

Oscar H. Scott, attorney and counselor, came to Allison in May, 1882. The subject of our sketch was born in Greene county, Wisconsin, in 1855, and removed with his parents to Hampton, Iowa, in 1866. He attended for a number of years the public schools of Hampton, and was for one year a student of Battle Creek College, Michigan; also took a course at Baylies Commercial School, Dubuque. He was engaged in teaching a number of years; was principal of the school at Bristow for three years. He began the study of law at Hampton, in the summer of 1880, with the firm of Dow & Gilger; was admitted to the bar in February, 1882, locating here the following May. Mr. Scott is also engaged in the insurance business, representing several fire insurance companies, including the Home, of New York, and the Farmers' Insurance Company of Cedar Rapids. His wife was Miss Maria Thorpe, a daughter of Jefferson Thorpe, formerly of Clayton county, Iowa, who died in the hospital at Vicksburg, during the rebellion. They have one child, Earnest C.

As to the legal profession in Parkersburgh, it has been represented by various gentlemen. The first attorney here was John Bremer, Esq., who came here in 1868, and continued to practice up to the time of his death, which occurred in 1878.

The present attorneys are Messrs. N. T. Johnson and O. B. Courtright.

N. T. Johnson, Esq., attorney and counselor at law, also notary public and collection agent, dates his coming to Parkersburgh August 17, 1871. He was born in Greene county, Pennsylvania, October 27, 1846. His father, David B. Johnson, was a native of Pennsylvania, and removed with his family to Washington county, Iowa, October 27, 1860, where they lived until their death. Mr. Johnson began the study of law at Cedar Falls, with Powers & Hemminway, October 27, 1869. He is the oldest attorney now here. The late John Bremer, Esq., was here when Mr. Johnson came. Mr. Johnson is a successful lawyer and is having a good practice. His wife was Anna R. Wolf, born in Pennsylvania and brought up in Illinois. They have one son, William F. Johnson.

O. B. Courtright began the practice of law at Parkersburgh in 1878. Mr. Courtwright was born in DeKalb county, Illinois, in 1849; he removed to Rockford, in his native State, and thence to Grundy county, Iowa, with his parents, in 1859. His father, C. G. Courtwright, came to Parkersburgh in 1876, and removed to Kansas in November, 1879, and now lives in Clay county of this State. O. B. returned to Rockford, where he attended school for a time, then entered upon the classical course at Beloit College, Wisconsin, where he remained for three years, pursuing his legal studies at the same time. After the completion of his college course he went to Nebraska, where he remained about two years, and then returned to Iowa and purchased what was then known as the Ackley *Independent*, and changed the name of the paper to the Ackley *Enterprise*, by which name it is still known. He conducted the paper for a year and a half. He was admitted to the practice of his profession at Judge Ruddick's court, in Butler county, in 1877. He located in Parkersburgh and engaged in practice, but on account of ill health discontinued in January, 1881, and removed to Nebraska, but returned in August, 1882, and resumed his practice. His wife was Clara D., daughter of Edwin Whitney, who is a brother of Senator Whitney, of Illinois. Mrs. Courtwright was born in the latter State. They have one son, named Dale.

Judge John Palmer was here for a short time in the early history of Parkersburgh.

W. P. Robertson was also an attorney, who continued practice for a short time.

Sawyer Haswell, Esq., came here from Dubuque in the spring of 1870, and left some years ago for Cherokee.

W. H. Burdick, Esq., established a law office in Parkersburgh in the spring of 1871, but in 1874 was elected county clerk, and served for six years. In January, 1879, Burdick & Savage opened an office again in Parkersburgh; but are now in Dakota.

In 1876, M. J. Downey commenced the practice of law in Parkersburgh and remained for several years, when he removed to Dakota, where he died in December, 1882.

B. L. Richards, a lawyer from Dubuque, came here in 1877, but, however, engaged in banking and practiced but little.

In May, 1882, the subject of organizing a bar association was agitated. A number of Butler county attorneys met at the office of Craig & Smith, in Allison, to discus the matter. C. M. Greene was chosen chairman; and George A. McIntyre secretary. A committee consisting of Mr. McIntyre and W. S. Montgomery was appointed to prepare articles of organization. Nothing further appears to have been done in regard to the matter.

CHAPTER XII.

THE MEDICAL PROFESSION.

It is the general impression that no community could well get along without physicians, and the impression is well founded, although in one sense a little exaggerated. Yet it would be trying and sorry work for any community to attempt to get along entirely without the aid of those who have made the work of healing, curing and administering comfort to the afflicted and allaying their suffering, a life study and a life object. Their worth, when they are needed, is not measured by dollars. Their long years of study, preparing for emergencies where life and death are struggling for supremecy at such times, are above value.

The physician, associated as he is, with life and death, is a subject for study. He is present when members of the human race are ushered into existence, allaying pains; lessening danger; is also there at the bed of the child as it grows upward, and expands toward manhood or womanhood; warding off disease; sustaining the health, and conquering deformities; at middle age he is present; for, along life's pathway are strewn for all, a large share of the ills that flesh is heir to; and while old age has set in, and the once rosy youth or maiden passes rapidly down the plane of declining life, as grandma's and grandpa's; the physician is still at his post; and again, as the steady tread of approaching death is heard, while the eyes dim, and the clammy mantle of that awful messenger covers its victim, carrying the humble life into the great blaze of eternity, the physician is still there, exerting his utmost knowledge to prolong the spark or to ease the suffering. God bless the physician—if honest and sincere he is a blessing to the world.

As to progress, the medical world has made wonderful strides, and, in the future, will undoubtedly keep up its onward march. In this respect, that able man Prof. I. H. Stearns, Health Officer of Milwaukee, and for many years Surgeon of the Soldiers' Home, at that place, once said: "It is doubtful whether it is wonderful that medical doctrine has advanced the way it has, in the past fifty years, or stupidity that the advancement was not made years ago. * * * For instance, years ago—but while the practice of medicine was as old as Rome—the discovery was made that boiled oil was not good for gun and pistol shot wounds. What a discovery! It is handed down to us that on a certain battle-field the surgeon ran out of boiled oil, and so as to not discourage his patients he used cold water, pretending it was oil. It is not strange to us that the water patients speedily recoved with little pain, while the oil patients, if they recovered at all, did so in spite of the oil. * * * " Prof. Stearns continued at length, relating the present mode of treating fever, the giving of plenty of water, which, but a few years ago was absolutely forbidden, and many others which would be of interest, but space forbids.

The first physician to locate in Butler county was James E. Walker, who hung out his shingle at Clarksville, in 1854. He was clerk of courts for one term, and is noticed at length in the chapter on county officers. He left a number of years ago and returned to his native New England home.

REMINISCENCES OF PRACTICE IN EARLY DAYS.

By John Scobey, M. D.

By the solicitation of friends and former acquaintances, I visited Shell Rock in the spring of 1856. The village then numbered from fifteen to twenty families. There were two clergymen and a justice of the peace, There was one small dry goods store, one saw-mill, and a flouring mill being erected. I viewed the Shell Rock river at this place, and thought then, as I do now, that it was the finest stream of pure water I had ever seen. Its hydraulic power at this point was sufficient to drive a great amount of machinery. Its waters were stored with vast numbers of fine fish; its banks crowned with fine timber, and frequently skirted with waving groves of small timber. After viewing the local advantages here, I harnessed my trusty mare, Fanny, and started southwest to take a view of the prairie. Fanny ferried me over the Shell Rock, there being no bridge. It was the last of May; the undulating plains were dressed in nature's gay attire of living green. There were but few, if any, laid-out or worked r ads or bridges in this county. I traveled on, as best I could, avoiding the sloughs, which were very miry. Log cabins were occasionally to be seen, generally near to the groves or timber land, where a few acres were plowed, and a few domestic animals were to be seen; but the most of those rich alluvial prairies were then performing their diurnal and revolutionary movements without a human inhabitant.

After meandering over the county, visiting the different localities, where villages were being started, I returned to the Shell Rock, and located here as a physician. I purchased several town lots, which, like most of the other lots, were in their wild condition, covered with hazel bushes, limbs of trees, decaying logs and mud-holes. The next summer I erected my present cottage house, which is enclosed with two-inch plank spiked into sills eight inches square. This cottage stands the test of moving time, with but few signs of decay. Within a few years I built on my lots two more dwelling houses, which have been occupied by families for several years. In the meantime I purchased fifty acres of land lying contiguous to the town plat, which has been cleared of its timber and underbrush, and for years has yielded splendid harvests of wheat and corn.

My family arrived here from Ohio in September, 1856. They had never seen wild uncultivated prairies before. Why were they brought to such an awful looking place. There was not a well worked street. The town was full of stumps, logs, bushes, under-brush and mudholes. The school-house was but a rude log shanty, and the meeting-house but little better. Soon they discovered squads of Indians rambling up and down the river. Their fears were excited. The torch-fire, the war club, the hatchet and the scalping knife would be raised. They would return to friends in Ohio. They would not stay here to be murdered by Indians, or to be torn to pieces by wild beasts. This prairie country was only fitted for Indians, bears, wolves and ferocious wild beasts. The Indians were peaceable and friendly, and our family fears subsided into friendly donations.

During the first summer and fall my medical ride extended over a large part of this county and into the adjoining counties. My long rides were fatiguing. Chills and fever were frequent, and most of the cabins were increasing their family numbers. In the month of November a dangerous type of typhoid-fever began to rage, which proved fatal in some localities, and continued its ravages during the winter.

For seven years my profession called me over these wild prairies, frequently in mid-night darkness. Often the dwellings were miles apart, and naught but a dim trail to follow. Sometimes I was sloughed down, and the wolves howling not far distant, and rattle-snakes hissing. During these seven years the march of improvement in this county was slow. The wild prairies every season produced a vast amount of grass, which was interspersed with several species of gay roses, pinks and violets, which crowded their footholds among the roots of the high grass, and waved their shining flowered plumes on the zephyr's breeze to the passer-by; filling the air with sweet perfume and arresting the monotony of loneliness.

The fall months passed with but little disturbance; December came in like a roaring lion, fiercely driving the falling snow into drifts. From then to next March, there were but few pleasant days; the snow averaging from three to four feet deep. Many buildings were covered. There was much human and animal suffering. In the spring several families left this section. The spring returned in smiles, and the few crops of the county were good, and have averaged abundantly since.

One of the many winter rides which I experienced during the first seven years of my practice here, before the roads were worked or much land cultivated, I briefly present:

On the 14th of January, early in the morning, I started as usual to visit a number of patients up the river, some fifteen miles away. The northwest wind was blowing very hard and cold and the snow flying. My first call to be made was at Mr. Martin's, east of Turkey Grove, five miles away and two miles east from the Clarksville road. No track was to be seen after leaving the main road. Fanny plunged ahead until we came to the slough, some twenty rods from the house. She could go no farther. I tightened the reins and covered her with blanket and robe. I wallowed across the slough, found the house and prescribed for the patients. Mr. Martin asked me to step with him to his yard, where I think I saw six dead hogs, which had chilled and were frozen by coming out of their pen to eat corn. He showed me a pair of oxen that were chilling badly in their stall. The wind was veering and the air full of snow. I could not see six feet in any direction. I crossed the slough. My sleigh was not there. I traveled, as I supposed, up the slough, down the slough, up and down a number of times, the snow up to my waist. Fanny was not to be found. I stopped, kicked the snow away and stamped my cold feet. Where was Martin's house? I could not see it—in what direction I did not know. My hopes were gone. A cold snow-drift would be my winter tomb; the prowling, hungry wolves would feed upon my physical form. Good-bye to my family and friends. I straightened up and tried to look around. Naught could I see but flying snow.

Oh! for one glimpse of beacon light for me to steer,
To cheer me in my last, my hopeless fear.

In those eternal moments of dark despair, had I owned this globe and the revolving worlds in the solar system, I would gladly have given them all for the privilege of stepping into my sleigh behind Fanny.

In those moments of intense thought that seemed to embrace an eternity of time, all the acts, thoughts and deeds of my past life—of three score years—were presented to my mind. My thoughts did not peer into the future; I saw but the past and present. A thought came, I would start for Martin's though I perished in the attempt. As I was lifting my foot to take the first step, Fanny whinneyed not more than one rod from where I was standing. It was a melodious sound that burst upon my ear through the whirling snow-flakes. My flagging energy revives; I skipped to the sleigh, helped Fanny turn it round, and I steped in. Fanny would soon reach the Clarksville road in the timber. I was now monarch of all I could see; there were none to dispute my right but old boreas. He may rage with all his power in his hydrophobic whirls, and drive his snow minions into fits of desperation, but Fanny and I will win the race without my giving a world or a dime. The road being found, I passed up the river to Clarksville, and went several miles above, making frequent calls to see the sick. In the evening I returned safely home; I enjoyed a quiet rest and started on another pilgrimage the next morning.

A vast progressive change has taken place in this section of country during the last fifteen years. There is probably not one acre of land in Butler county but what is in use, and the largest portion improved by skillful agriculturists. This county is a scientific cultivated field, equaling in its cereal productions, its fine horses, its cattle and hogs, any other county of its size and age in Iowa. There is not a section of land in Butler county but has

HISTORY OF BUTLER COUNTY.

from one to four dwelling houses, barns, out-buildings, gardens and yards, and many of its sections and eighties, fine artificial groves of timber and fruit orchards. Many of its farm-dwellings are two stories high and quite imposing, having bay windows and ornamented porches and side dressings. Butler county is systematically laid out into school districts, and in each district a fine school-house.

The county and township roads are in good condition; the streams being all bridged, the larger ones with iron. There is a fine capacious court house near the center. There are three railroads in active operation, passing through the county, one of them by the court house.

The hydraulic powers are generally brought into active and profitable use.

The old worn farming utensils are being replaced by more scientific inventions of modern date, and our people are traveling on the roads of physical health and spiritual progression.

Here in Shell Rock how changed are the rides and labors of practicing physicians. There has long been three or four practicing physicians located here, all of whom do not travel over more territory in their medical rides than one did between the years 1820 and 1830, when there was not a good road or a safe bridge in the county. Now they can dance their spring buggies or sleighs over smooth roads by day or night. No sloughs in which to mire; no wolves to growl; no prairie fires to dread or flee from; no deep rivers to wade through in the darkness of the night; no drifted sloughs on the lonely, wild prairie, to wallow through in the depth of winter. In this incorporated town, for the last ten years, there has been but few if any thistle or thorn-beds, or wiry brush beds filled with wild, stinging nettles and burdock burrs to tear the clothes and scratch and bleed the doctor's hands, and no filthy mud-holes in which to soil his boots and pants. He winds his way by night or day over well graded streets and well finished sidewalks, calling, as required, at fine brick, stone or wood residences, without opening a log cabin door.

The march of agricultural improvement in Butler county during the last ten years is very satisfactory, as well as the growth of its incorporated towns and villages; but no more so than the intellectual, progressive dawning of scientific knowledge in our institutions of learning and orthodox churches. School teachers for years have not inquired for Dellinsworth nor Webster's spelling books, nor Alexander's nor Murray's grammar, nor for the Westminster catechism, nor often for the Jewish Scriptures, from which to teach in school. Science has erected higher pedestals on which to train the young idea how to shoot and how to climb high up the glorious tree of immortal science.

ALLISON PHYSICIANS.

Allison, the shire town of Butler county, is too young to have given time for the location of as many physicians as have represented the medical profession in most of the towns in the county. The present practicing physicians are Jerome Burbank and Son, and S. E. Burroughs.

Dr. J. S. Riggs, M. D., was the first physician to locate here, coming early in 1880. He started the drug store now owned by J. A. Riggs & Co. He went from Allison to Chicago.

W. A. Curtis, M. D., was the next physician, arriving here and commencing practice on the 10th of April, 1882. He had been in practice in Maiden Rock, Wisconsin, and also in Chicago. His whereabouts at present is unknown.

Dr. S. E. Burroughs arrived in Allison ready for practice in August, 1882. Dr. Burroughs had been in partnership with Dr. Riggs for some time, but was lately from Holland. He is still in Allison, enjoying a lucrative practice.

Jerome Burbank, M. D., is the son of a farmer, Ebenezer Burbank and Abagail Turtelotte, and dates his birth at Smethport, Pennsylvania, March 1, 1837. When he was a year and a half old the family removed to Sardinia, Erie county, New York, remaining there until the spring of 1845, when they removed to Harrison, Winnebago county, Illinois, where both parents died that year, leaving a family of nine children. Jerome was one of the oldest ones, and at eighteen and for two years had the oversight of the family. At twenty he went to an academy in Beloit, Wisconsin, attending the same three or four terms. In the spring of 1848 he commenced reading medicine with Professor G. W. Richards, of St. Charles, Illinois; attended a course of lectures at Rock Island, Illinois, in the winter of 1848–49. He practiced his profession at Mt. Vernon, Iowa, during the summer of 1850, and attended a second course of lectures at Keokuk, Iowa, the following winter, graduating in March, 1851. He settled at Avon, Rock county, Wisconsin, in July, 1851, and practiced there until the summer of 1862, when he was commissioned assistant surgeon of the 22d Regiment Wisconsin Volunteers, accompanied the regiment to the field, and was in active service until September, 1863, when, with health completely broken down, he was obliged to resign. When about to leave, the officers drew up a paper expressive of their high appreciation of untiring and self-sacrificing labors in his line of service, and not only every officer, but every private in the regiment insisted on signing the paper, which the doctor carefully preserved, as an evidence that he did not serve his country in vain. He probably came as near dying from overwork, as any man who went into the army, in any capacity, and came out alive. On returning to his home, at Avon, his health began to improve immediately, and in November, 1863, he was chosen to represent the 6th Assembly District of Rock county, in the legislature, which position he filled creditably to himself, and satisfactory to his constituents In July, 1864 he received a commission as surgeon, unsolicited, and was requested by the governor to join the 33d Regiment of Wisconsin Volunteer Infantry. He accepted the commission, and immediately joined the regiment in the field. In December of that year, his old disease—Chronic Dysentery—renewed its attacks, but he remained at the front until mustered out with the regiment, at the close of the war, often on duty when he ought to have been in bed.

After the close of the war he moved with his family to Waverly, Iowa, where he applied himself as closely to his profession as his impaired health would admit. In the summer of 1881 he erected a fine business block, in Allison, the county seat of Butler county, where he put in a drug store, in May, 1882, with his son, F. E. Burbank, who is also a physician, as partner. His family removed to Allison in October, 1882.

In politics he was originally a "free soiler," casting his first vote in 1848, for the men standing on the Buffalo platform, Martin Van Buren and Charles Francis Adams, and has been a staunch republican from the organization of the party.

He is a Free Mason, and has been an active member of the order for several years, and has held the office of High Priest of a Royal Arch Chapter of Masons, at Clarksville, for several years.

His religious sentiments are with the Baptists.

He bears an irreproachable character. Dr. Burbank has a wife and eight children, four sons and four daughters. Mrs. Burbank was Jerusha Kinney, her father was Joseph Kinney, Jr., one of the pioneers of Wisconsin, and was a member of the Territorial Legislature, also of the Constitutional Convention, and afterward of the State Legislature. They were married at Avon, Wisconsin, on the 1st day of March, 1853.

Frank E. Burbank, M. D., was born in Rock county, Wisconsin, in 1856. He began the study of medicine with his father in 1877, and has attended two courses of lectures at the Medical Department of the Iowa State University. He was engaged in the practice of medicine two years at Knoxville, Nebraska. He married Rosa, daughter of Elias W. Patterson, of Iowa City. He is associated with his father at Allison.

BRISTOW PHYSICIANS.

The first physician to locate here was Dr. Charles McCormack. Dr. H. S. Strickland was another early physician to commence practice in Bristow. The physicians at present are Drs. E. Leroy Turner and Jacob Krebbs.

E. Leroy Turner, M. D., has been in practice at Bristow since July, 1874. Dr. Turner was born in Illinois in 1847. He removed to Butler county, with his father, in 1856. The latter settled in Shell Rock township, being one of its early settlers. He continued to reside there until November, 1881, when he left for Clear Lake, Iowa. Dr. Turner began the study of medicine in 1868, with Dr. Boys, of Waverly, and graduated at Rush Medical College in 1871. He practiced a short time at Shell Rock and then located at Tripoli, Bremer county, where he practiced two years, then locating here, as above stated, succeeding Dr. Charles McCormack. Dr. H. S. Strickland, another Bristow physician, located here after Dr. Turner came and practiced about two years. Dr. Turner is having an extensive practice.

Jacob Krebbs, M. D., located at Bristow, March, 1881. Dr. Krebbs was born in Snyder county, Pennsylvania, in 1857, and removed to Elkhart county, Indiana. He was a student for one year at Notre Dame University, in that State. He then removed to Ogle county, Illinois, and began the study of medicine with Dr. McPherson, of Eagle Point. He graduated from the medical department of the Iowa State University in 1879, and practiced two years at Geneva, coming here from that place. He was married in Illinois to Effie Ormsbee. When Dr. Krebbs came to Bristow he succeeded to the practice of Dr. Strickland, who is now in Missouri.

CLARKSVILLE PHYSICIANS.

The first physician to locate here was Dr. James E. Walker, who is noted in various parts of this work, and is mentioned in the beginning of this chapter as the first physician to locate in the county. He was a native of Maine, and returned long since to his native State. Other early physicians were Doctors Jeremiah Wilcox and J. F. Logan. At present the profession is represented by Drs. A. F. Tichenor, D. S. Byres, M. C. Camp and H. W. Dickenson.

GREENE PHYSICIANS.

The medical profession at Greene has been represented at various times by Drs. Nichols, C. C. Huckins, Miss H. D. Cramer, V. C. Birney, William Young, Woodlin and John Nevins. Those who are still in practice at Greene are Drs. C. C. Huckins, V. C. Birney and John Nevins. The dentistry department is represented by Dr. Peter Snyder.

The first physician to locate here was Dr. Nichols, who had been in the practice of medicine in Iowa for some time, and who came to Greene in 1871. He was an allopathist, and secured a fair practice, remaining for several years, when he removed to Rockford. He was a single man, and socially, was well liked.

V. C. Birney, M. D., has been in practice in Greene since March, 1872. Dr. Birney was born in Canada, in 1849. His father was also a physician, with whom he began the study of medicine. He also practiced with him for a time in Floyd county; attended Rush Medical College, Chicago, in 1872–3; graduated at the College of Physicians, at Keokuk, in 1878. His wife was Ada F. Stickney, daughter of Sydney Stickney, an early settler of Floyd county. They have two children, Nellie and Clenthas. Dr. Birney's father was one of the earliest physicians of Floyd county, where he settled in 1856.

C. C. Huckins, M. D., who has been in practice at Greene since March, 1873, was born in Maine in 1843. He served for a time in the army as a member of the 17th Regiment Maine Volunteer Infantry. Began the study of medicine in 1865; he attended lectures at the Maine Medical School; came west and engaged in practice. In 1877 he attended the College of Physicians and Surgeons. The doctor has an extensive practice. He is a thoroughly educated and popular physician. His wife was Pauline Doore, daughter of Joel Doore. Mrs. Huckins is a native of Maine. They have one daughter, Ethel.

Miss Dr. Cramer, commenced practice in Greene early in the seventies, and continued for a number of years, with good success. She was inclined toward the homœopathic side of the profession. She was from Wisconsin, and went from Greene to Mason City, where she is yet in practice.

William Young, M. D., located in Greene at the same time, and continued up to the time of his death, in 1878. Dr. Young was from Wisconsin, a single man, and was well educated in the allopathic department of medicine, being a graduate. Socially, he was well liked, and many warm friends mourned his loss.

A Doctor Woodlin was also numbered among Greene's physicians. He went from there to Minneapolis, where he has since brought himself into notoriety by shooting a furniture dealer for advertising him as a swindler.

A. K. Johnson, homœopathic physician and surgeon, located here January 1, 1880, was born in Marseilles, Illinois, in 1852; graduated at Hahnemann Medical College, Chicago, in 1878. Practiced at Pontiac, Illinois, for two years before locating here. His wife was Miss F. E. Woodling, widow of Homer R. Woodling.

Dr. John Nevins commenced practice here sometime ago, and enjoys a very fair practice.

Peter B. Snyder, dentist, came to Greene in 1881. He was born in Germany, in 1859; came to the United States when sixteen years of age; studied dentistry with Dr. C. N. Kindall, of Woodstock, Illinois. Dr. Kindall was a graduate of the Dental College, at Cincinnati. Dr. Snyder turned his attention to dentistry at quite an early age, having studied the subject in Germany. He practiced two years in Woodstock before coming to Greene. Dr. Snyder's wife was a native of England.

NEW HARTFORD PHYSICIANS.

The medical profession in New Hartford is represented by Drs. D. M. Wick and W. H. H. Hagey.

Dr. D. M. Wick is a son of Azariah and Amanda (Hughes) Wick, and was born in Whiteside county, Illinois, on the 12th day of November, 1848. His early educational advantages were the district school; however, later he attended Mount Morris Seminary, (Illinois) three years, and Cornell College, Iowa, two years; after which he received his medical education. He studied one year in the medical department of Ann Arbor, Michigan, and two years at the Chicago Medical College, where he graduated in the class of 1874, and for sometime afterwards he was engaged in Chicago, in hospital and city practice. In the spring of 1875 he came to New Hartford, Butler county, Iowa, and has since followed his profession here, and enjoys an extended practice. The doctor is, and was a charter member, of the Butler County Medical Association, and also a member of the Iowa State Medical Society. In 1876 he was united in marriage to Miss Ella Thayer, who was born in the State of Michigan. They have two children, Merton and Rouelle.

Dr. William H. H. Hagey is a son of George and Sarah (Moyer) Hagey, and was born in Trappe, Montgomery county, Pennsylvania, December 5, 1841. In 1855 the family moved to Sterling, Illinois, where the son grew to manhood. His early educational advantages were such as the common schools afforded, and what he could acquire by studying at such times as he could command. In May of 1861, he enlisted in company B, 13th Illinois Infantry, serving as a private about one year, was then honorably discharged on account of sickness. He afterwards re-enlisted in the one hundred day service, 140th Regiment Illinois Volunteers, and served until honorably discharged. Upon returning to civil life, he began the study of medicine, and after sometime entered Rush Medical College, of Chicago, graduating from there in February, 1868. Upon receiving his diploma he practiced for a while in Whiteside county, then four years in the city of Chicago, again in

Whiteside county, and in July, 1881, came to New Hartford, Butler county, where he enjoys an extended practice. In July, 1873, he was united in marriage to Mrs. Ellen Humphrey McKibbin. They have two children, Josie and Charlie.

PARKERSBURGH PHYSICIANS.

The first representative of the medical profession to locate in this little city was Dr. M. I. Powers, who commenced practice here in 1867. The first physician of the homœopathic school was Dr. John Wyatt, who is now gone. At present the profession is represented by Drs. M. I. Powers, E. B. Ensign and A. O. Strout.

M. I. Powers, M. D., is the pioneer physician of Parkersburgh. He came here May 22, 1867. He was born and grew to manhood in the State of New York. He graduated at Berkshire Medical College, Massachusetts, in 1865. After graduating he was located at Colliersville, Otsego county, New York, coming here, as stated, in 1867; has been in practice here since that time, except an absence of two years, which he spent at Independence, in this State, returning in October, 1882. His wife was Ella, daughter of N. T. Manley. They have three children—Joseph, Milton and Jennie.

Dr. S. B. Ensign, homœopathic physician and surgeon, has been in practice here since 1871. He is an early settler of the county, and a brother of Charles Ensign, a prominent early settler of Beaver township. He was born in the town of Delhi, Delaware county, New York, but was brought up in Connecticut. He began practice in this county in 1865, and was probably the first homœopathic physician of the county. He came here, as stated, in 1871, succeeding Dr. John Wyatt, who was the first physician of his school in the town. Dr. Ensign is a successful and popular physician, and has for many years had an extensive and lucrative practice. His wife is a native of Massachusetts. They have an adopted daughter, Hattie R. Ensign.

Dr. A. O. Strout is a native of Portland, Maine, where he was born in 1849. He went to Chicago in 1867, where he was engaged in teaching about five years; began the study of medicine in 1872, and graduated at the Chicago Medical College in 1875. He practiced at Anamosa, Jones county, in this State, for four years, and for three years of that time was a physician to the penitentiary at that place. He came here in September, 1879. His wife was W. A., daughter of A. H. Cole, of Davenport. They have one son, Harry R.

SHELL ROCK PHYSICIANS.

The first physician to locate in this town was Dr. John Scobey, who came here in May, 1855. He continued a lucrative practice until 1875, when he retired from active professional work. He is still a resident of the village where he first hung out his shingle, and is an honored citizen.

The present representatives of the medical profession are Drs. E. H. Dudley, W. H. Smith, E. L. Thorp and E. E. Sill.

Doctor John Scobey, the first physician of Shell Rock, was born in Francistown, New Hampshire, April 19, 1800. His early life was passed in his native State, where he received an academic education, and entered Dartmouth Medical College in the

E. B. Ensign M.D.

HISTORY OF BUTLER COUNTY.

year 1824. He diligently applied himself, and graduated in medicine in 1826. Soon after leaving college, he located at Bethlehem, in Northern New Hampshire, where he practiced his profession for five years, and then removed to Concord, Vermont, where he remained another five years. At the expiration of this time he went to Truxton, New York, where he practiced for two years, and then decided to seek his fortune in the west. He located at Jackson, Ohio, where he lived for twenty years. In May of 1855, he came to Shell Rock, Iowa. He is the oldest living physician of Butler county, and for a number of years after his settlement here, the doctor's ride carried him all over this county, and over portions of adjoining counties. For the past seven years the doctor has almost entirely given up practice, being content, in his ripe old age, with the laurels he has so justly won by his knowledge of and faithful attention to the study of medicine. Mr. Scobey has always taken great interest in the improvement of Shell Rock, and in his younger days was greatly interested in the politics of the country. He was married in 1825 to Miss Nancy Wallace, of Antrim, New Hampshire. Seven children have blessed this union—Joseph, the eldest son, was an attorney of the State of California, and also a member of the legislature of that State. He died there, July 21, 1866; Philomelia is the wife of Phineas Weed, of Shell Rock; Leander is engaged in business at Ackley, Iowa; Daniel, who now resides in Colorado; John, who lives in Shell Rock; Annette, wife of Oscar Eastman, of Shell Rock; Adelaide, wife of William Palmer, of Pierie, Dakota.

Doctor E. L. Thorp was born in Berkshire county, Massachusetts, May 17, 1836, and is a son of H. S. and Emeline (Lacey) Thorp, who also are natives of Massachusetts. In 1838 his parents moved to Kenosha county, Wisconsin, and here the doctor grew to manhood. He attended the academy at Kenosha, and afterwards entered Beloit College, at Beloit, Wisconsin. Here he studied for some time, and then went to Chicago and studied medicine in Rush Medical College of that city. Upon leaving this college he came to Shell Rock, and here in 1865, began the practice of medicine; he continued his practice for some years, and then went to Cincinnati and entered the Eclectic Medical College of that city, and graduated there in 1877. After receiving his diploma he returned to Shell Rock, and again took up his profession which he still practices. In politics, the doctor is a republican, and has held the office of supervisor of the county for one term. He was married in 1857 to Miss Anna Eliza Clarke, who is a native of Kenosha county, Wisconsin. They have two children—Emma, wife of C. E. Skinner, of Shell Rock, and Frank. Mr. Thorp was engaged in the drug business for twelve years in Shell Rock, is the oldest practicing physician of the place, was postmaster of Shell Rock for eight years, and supervisor for one year. He is a member of the State Board of Health.

Doctor E. H. Dudley was born in Rutland, Wisconsin, May 12, 1848. He is a son of S. E. and Cynthia (Chapin) Dudley, who were early settlers of Dane county, Wisconsin. Young Dudley received a classical education at Evansville Seminary, Evansville, Wisconsin, graduating from there in the year of 1868. In April of 1864, at only sixteen years of age, he enlisted from the Seminary into Company C, 49th Wisconsin Infantry, and served as a non-commissioned officer until the close of the war, after which he remained on provost duty until November of 1865, when he was honorably discharged at St. Louis, Missouri. Upon receiving his dismissal from the President, he returned to the seminary, and, as we have said before, graduated in 1868. Soon after leaving school he began the study of medicine, and afterwards entered Rush Medical College, Chicago, where he graduated during the winter of 1874-5. Between his courses he practiced medicine at Broadhead, Wisconsin, with Doctor Boughton, a former preceptor. In 1875 he located at Shell Rock, Butler county, Iowa, where he has since been practicing; he now enjoys a large and well earned patronage. He is one of the charter members of the Butler county Medical Association, and is now president of that society. He is also a member of the State and American Medical Association, and December 1, 1880, he was appointed United States Medical Examiner for pensions. He was married in 1869 to Miss Mary Austin. They have four children—Samuel O., Edward Henry, David Austin, and Jennie Chapin.

Dr. W. H. Smith was born in Sheboygan county, Wisconsin, February 9th, 1851. He is a son of Charles and Margaret (Hazleton) Smith, who were early settlers of that county, and their son W. H. was among the first white children born in Scott township, of Sheboygan county. Dr. Smith's early education was received at home, and he supplemented this with two terms in the graded schools of Hartford, Wisconsin. He then entered Wayland University, at Beaver Dam, Wisconsin, where he completed his classical course in the year 1871. Soon after he began the study of medicine with Dr. Therom Nichols, of Milwaukee, Wisconsin, now of Fort Dodge, Iowa. He entered the Chicago Medical College in 1873 and graduated from there in 1878. After receiving his diploma he practiced at Sheboygan for a short time and then located at Shell Rock, Iowa, where he now enjoys an extended practice. He is a member of the Butler County Medical Association, of which he is now secretary, and is also a member of the State Medical Association. Dr. Smith was married in May, 1878, to Miss Ella A. Mansfield, of Greenbush, Wisconsin.

Dr. E. E. Sill, homœopathic physician, was born in Allegany, Cattaraugus county, New York, October 13, 1858, and is a son of Rev. S. and Mary (Pierce) Sill. Two years after the doctor's birth his parents came west and located at Sharon, Wisconsin, where his father was pastor of the Baptist Church for three years. In 1863 they came to Shell Rock, Iowa, where they remained six years. The doctor's classical education was obtained in Osage, Iowa, at the Cedar Valley Seminary. His medical education, though not yet completed, is good, he having studied for several terms under Drs. Frank Dunton, of Osage, and M. H. Chamberlain, now of Waterloo. He located at Shell Rock in April, 1881, and now enjoys a good practice.

APLINGTON.

E. L. Blackmer, M. D., was born in Stephenson county, Illinois, August 12,

1842. He attended the district school in his younger days, and also three terms at the academy in Durand, Illinois. He commenced the study of medicine with Dr. C. N. Andrews, Rockford, Illinois, remaining in his office one year. He was subsequently in the office of Dr. J. Y. Campbell, of Durand, two years. In 1867 he went to St. Louis and attended a course of lectures at the St. Louis Medical College, and then located in Van Buren county, Iowa. He subsequently graduated from the St. Louis Medical College. In 1868 he located at Butler Center, where he remained until December, 1873, when he removed to Aplington and engaged in the practice of his profession. In 1880 he bought one-half interest in the Aplington mill, and in 1882 became sole proprietor. Dr. Blackmer was united in marriage, in 1872, with Harriet Davis, a native of Connecticut. They have three children— Harriet, Ralph and Auzman.

THE BUTLER COUNTY MEDICAL ASSOCIATION.

The object of this association is in conjunction with the State Medical Association. None are admitted as members except those who are graduates of a college that is recognized by the American Medical Society, and conforms to the code of ethics of that society.

The Butler County Medical Association was organized on the 2d of April, 1878, the first meeting being held at Butler Center. The first officers were elected as follows:

President, I. R. Spooner, of New Hartford.

Vice-President, E. L. Turner, of Bristow.

Secretary, F. H. Boucher, of Clarksville.

Treasurer, H. L. Isherwood, of Shell Rock.

Censors, M. I. Powers, of Parkersburgh; J. H. Brower, of Butler Center; and E. H. Dudley, of Shell Rock.

The charter members were as follows:
F. H. Boucher, of Clarksville.
J. H. Brower, of Butler Center.
E. H. Dudley, of Shell Rock.
H. L. Isherwood, of Clarksville.
M. I. Powers, of Parkersburgh.
I. R. Spooner, of New Hartford.
E. LeLoy Turner, of Bristow.
D. M. Wick, of New Hartford.
William Young (deceased), of Greene.

Since organization the following new members have been added to the association:
Dr. William Robinson, of Cedar Falls.
" A. O. Strout, of Parkersburgh.
" W. H. H. Hagey, of New Hartford.
" W. H. Smith, of Shell Rock.

The Presidents have been as follows, commencing with the first:
Dr. I. R. Spooner, of New Hartford.
" M. I. Powers, of Parkersburgh.
" D. M. Wick, of New Hartford.
" E. H. Dudley, of Shell Rock.

Of the members of this Association, five are members of the State Medical Society, as follows:
Dr. E. H. Dudley, of Shell Rock.
" M. I. Powers, of Parkersburgh.
" William Robinson, of Cedar Falls.
" A. O. Strout, of Parkersburgh.
" D. M. Wick, of New Hartford.
" W. H. Smith, of Shell Rock.

Dr. E. H. Dudley, of Shell Rock, is the only one who is a member of the American Medical Association.

The Butler County Association meets once in four months.

The following is the constitution and by-laws drawn up by the society:

ARTICLE I.—This society shall be known as the Butler County Medical Society, and its members shall be graduates of some respectable regular school of medicine, who possess a good moral and professional reputation.

ARTICLE II.—The objects of this society shall be the advancement of medical knowledge, the uniformity of medical ethics, the elevation of the character and the protection of rights and interests of its members, and the study of the means calculated to render the medical profession most useful to the public and subservient to the interests of humanity.

ARTICLE III.—SECTION 1. Names of candidates for membership, with the date and place of their graduation, shall be prepared in writing by members having personal knowledge of their qualifications, who may add other facts relative to them which may aid the censors in the discharge of their duties.

SECTION 2. The censors shall, after investigation of the character and standing of candidates proposed, report thereon at the next regular meeting, when, if two thirds of the ballots deposited are favorable, they shall be declared duly elected.

SECTION 3. Candidates rejected for membership shall be ineligible thereto for twelve months after such rejection.

SECTION 4. Members-elect shall sign the constitution and by-laws, with the name of the institution of which they are a graduate, and date of graduation, before admittance to the full privileges of the society; and neglect of this provision for one year may involve the forfeiture of membership.

ARTICLE IV.—All resignations of membership shall be made in writing and be accompanied with a certificate from the treasurer, that all dues to the society have been satisfied; but no member shall be permitted to resign while charges are pending against him.

ARTICLE V.—Violations of the laws of this society may be presented to the board of censors in written charges against members accused, who shall be informed of this fact by the board after due investigation. The censors shall report on such charges at the next regular meeting, when sentence of expulsion, suspension or reprimand may be passed, by a two-thirds vote of the society, upon such accused as fail to exculpate themselves.

ARTICLE VI.—The officers of this society shall be a president, vice-president, secretary, treasurer and three censors, elected by ballot, at annual meetings, on second Tuesday of June, and serving till the election and installation of their successors.

ARTICLE VII.—SECTION 1. A fee of not less than $1.00 shall be due from each member, on and after each annual meeting.

SECTION 2. A fee of not less than $2.00 shall be due from each member-elect upon his signing the constitution.

SECTION 3. Non-payment of dues for one year shall be reported to the society by the treasurer, and non-payment of the same for six months thereafter, shall be also reported in like manner, and involve forfeiture of membership.

ARTICLE VIII.—The code of ethics of the American Medical Association is a part of the regulations of this society.

ARTICLE IX.—Alterations of, or amendments to, this constitution may be made at regular meetings, by a three-fourths vote of members present, provided written notice of the same has been given at the previous regular meeting.

In acknowledgement of having adopted the foregoing articles, and of our willingness to abide by them and use our endeavors to carry into effect the objects of this society as above set forth, we have hereunto affixed our names.

M. I. POWERS, Pittsfield, Mass., at Berkshire Medical College, November, 1865.

E. H. DUDLEY, Rush Medical College, Chicago, Ill. Session 1874–5.

D. M. Wick, Chicago Medical College, Chicago, Ill. Session 1874.

I. R. Spooner, Rush Medical College, Chicago, Ill., February, 1867

William Young, Ann Arbor, in year 1868 or 1869; re-graduated at I. S. University in 1875.

H. S. Isherwood, Rush, June, 1877.

F. H. Boucher, Jefferson Medical College, Philadelphia, 1877.

J. H. Brower, Medical College of Ohio, Cincinnati. Session of 1876 and 1877.

E. L. Turner, Rush Medical College, Chicago, February, 1877.

BY-LAWS.

ARTICLE I.—Section 1. Regular meetings shall be held at Butler Center, at 1 p. m , on the first Tuesday of June, October and February, unless otherwise provided by the society.

Section 2. Special meetings may be called by the president, on written request of three members, and shall have cognizance only of such business as is specified in the calls for the same.

Section 3. Seven members shall constitute a quorum requisite to elect officers and alter or amend the constitution and by laws. Three members shall constitute a quorum sufficient for the transaction of ordinary business, and for literary or scientific purposes a quorum shall always be presumed, unless an actual count be demanded.

ARTICLE II.—Section 1. The president shall preside at meetings, and perform the customary duties of his office.

Section 2. The vice-president shall perform the duties of the president in his absence.

Section 3. The secretary shall give notices of meetings, record transactions, have charge of books and papers, and present a report at the annual meeting.

Section 4. The treasurer shall receive and disburse all moneys of the society, under the direction of its officers, and retain vouchers for all expenditures.

Section 5. The censors shall perform the duties required by the constitution.

ARTICLE III.—Non-payment of dues shall involve forfeiture of franchise at annual meeting.

ARTICLE IV.—The regulations of Cushing's Manual, when not conflicting with the laws or precedents of this society, shall be recognized as authoritative.

ARTICLE V.—Alterations of, or amendments to, these by-laws require a two-thirds vote at a regular meeting of this society.

ARTICLE VI.—The following shall be the order of business:

1. Reading of minutes.
2. Report of censors.
3. Election of members.
4. Proposition of candidates.
5. Secretary's report (at annual meeting.)
6. Election of officers (at annual meeting.)
7. Reading of papers.
8. Discussion of subjects.
9. Report of cases.
10. Presentation of specimens.
11. Unfinished business.
12. Reports of committees.
13. Miscellaneous business.
14. Adjournment.

CHAPTER XIII.

AGRICULTURE AND AGRICULTURAL SOCIETIES.

Butler county is acknowledged as being among the best and most prosperous agricultural counties in Iowa. Its people are awake and keep step with the progressive march of the times in all that pertains to a civilization of happiness, industry and culture. Its future possibilities may be set high among the cluster of its hundred sisters, a star of pride to the noble State. The early pioneers did not come loaded with wealth, and in fact few had more than enough to barely get settled upon their lands; but they came with that which was, in those days, equal to it—training in agricultural pursuits, brawny hands that were able and not ashamed to do hard work, and in connection with industrious habits, the energy and determination to win success. The country was new, and there was no alternative but that success must be wrought from the soil—which was their only wealth and their only hope. And, in spite of all the obstacles and inconveniences to be encountered, success has attended their efforts, and the transformation from the primitive to the present comfortable condition of things accomplished. Nor is the end yet reached, but the county still has a mine of agricultural wealth yet undeveloped, which, as years roll on, will grow more and more valuable, and when years of cultivated maturity shall dawn to transform the yet unsubdued prairie to waving fields of growing grain, Butler county will occupy a place among the foremost ranks of Iowa's banner counties.

Early in the development of this country, wheat was the main product, and for a number of years excellent crops were raised with scarcely a failure. At the present time it has partially given up its former place to other cereals, while the farmers find many other avenues at which to devote their time and energies. The general theory—or it might be more properly said—it is known in a general way, that the wheat belt has been traveling westward ever since it was first started at Plymouth, Massachusetts, when the pilgrim fathers landed there over two hundred and sixty years ago. At first it moved on its westward march, not in a very rapid way, until fifty years ago the valley of the Genesee, in New York, was the great wheat raising region. But, when Michigan, Illinois and Iowa were opened up for cultivation, the wheat growing center began its Kangaroo jumps toward the setting sun, and Iowa was for years its resting place; but how long it will be before its now receding line will pass clear beyond the confines of Iowa and land in Dakota and Nebraska, time alone can determine. The gradual increase in stock raising has placed corn in the front rank at present. Flax of late years has been raised quite extensively. Rye, barley and all the cereals common to this latitude do well, and vegetables and small fruits grow abundantly where well cultivated. It was formerly taught that apples could not be successfully raised here, but the county now has many fine and thrifty orchards which have proven the matter quite to the contrary, and have punctured this fallacy. About one-half of the area of the county is under a good state of cultivation.

The following items of statistics of values throughout the county will prove to be of interest:

TABLE OF VALUES.

Lands, exclusive of town property	$2,133,289
Total number of acres	366,025
Total exemptions for trees planted	$105,044
Total, after deducting exemptions	2,028,245
Cattle assessed in the county, 24,516; value	$178,123
Horses assessed in the county, 8,207; value	234,685
Mules assessed in the county, 153; value	4,562
Sheep assessed in the county, 1,929 head, value	1,929
Swine assessed in the county, 19,480 head; value	34,898

VALUES IN THE VILLAGES.

Allison	$10,727
Greene	36,504
Bristow	9,469
New Hartford	8,012
Clarksville	38,808
Shell Rock	36,776
Butler Center	1,660
Aplington	23,235
Parkersburgh	43,471
Aggregate assessment of reality in towns	$208,662
Aggregate value of railroad property as assessed by the executive council, under chapter 5, title X, of the Code of 1873	$304,426
Aggregate valuation of personal property, including horses and cattle	652,273
Grand total valuation in the county	$3,193,606

THE FIRST FAIR IN BUTLER COUNTY.

The first fair held in Butler county was held at Willoughby village, about 1856 or 1857. It was a small affair, but a good time was had. The village at which the fair was held has long since been counted a thing of the past.

BUTLER COUNTY AGRICULTURAL SOCIETY.

This was the first organization of the kind in the county. It came into existence about 1857, with James Collar as first president, and James Davis, first secretary. From the first the public seemed to take an interest in the annual meetings of the society, and with a few exceptions, when weather interfered, fairs have been held annually and premiums paid in full. Upon organization the place of holding meetings was fixed at Shell Rock for twenty years. The nineteenth annual fair was held at Shell Rock on the 28th, 29th and 30th days of September, 1875, and was a success.

The officers at this time were as follows:

Martin Bailey, of Butler Center, president.

T. G. Copeland, of Clarksville, vice-president.

J. O. Stewart, of Clarksville, secretary.

E. Town, of Shell Rock, treasurer.

The board of directors at that time were as follows:

John Hickle, of Clarksville.
James Collar, of New Hartford.
J. H. Carter, of Shell Rock.
A. Doty, of Clarksville.
Richard Hughes, of Shell Rock.
I. E. Bussey, of Shell Rock.
S. Rice, of Shell Rock.

The following rules and regulations were adopted for the government of the society, viz:

RULES AND REGULATIONS, AND PROGRAMME.

Entries may be made at the secretary's office, at the grounds, until 12 o'clock M., of the second day.

Entries, except otherwise specified, limited to producers residing within, and life members residing without, the county. Class 5 open to the world.

Inventors, mechanics and agents not entitled to make entries for premiums, may make entries for exhibition.

Articles entered must be kept on exhibition during the fair.

Unworthy articles will receive no premiums, even though there be no competition.

Draft teams will be tested and plowing match take place in the forenoon of the second day.

Grange race will be called at 10:30 A.M. second day.

In the afternoon of the second day, 3 minute trotting and running race, exhibition of carriage teams, buggy horses and walking horses will take place.

In the forenoon of the 3d day the trial of double teams, saddle horses and roadster stallions, will come off.

At noon, third day, annual election of officers.

In the afternoon of the third day the sweepstake and 3:30 trotting race, and ladies' equestrianship will take place.

A suitable police force will be kept on duty at night to protect the animals, and other property.

Committees will attach emblems to articles examined, and in all cases make their reports to the secretary as early as possible.

Protest made against the action of any committee, must be made in writing, at the secretary's office, on the ground, and no protest made after the close of the fair will be considered.

Premiums not called for in six months after the treasurer gives notice that he is prepared to pay them, will be forfeited to the society.

When there are articles entered in any class, and the committees do not deem them worthy, they shall not award premiums.

All holders of annual tickets shall be entitled, with their wives and members of their families, under fourteen years of age, to all the privileges of the society, at all its fairs, excepting to vote for officers.

Membership fees, as follows: Life membership, $10.00; annual membership, $1 50.

The society is now in prosperous condition, is free from debt, and is efficiently managed by the following, who are the present officers:

J. H. Carter, of Shell Rock, president.
Richard Hughes, of Shell Rock, secretary.
Elwood Wilson, of Shell Rock, treasurer.

CLARKSVILLE AGRICULTURAL ASSOCIATION.

The Clarksville Agricultural Association was organized in 1875, and during the same year the fair grounds were purchased of John Hicks and others, containing twenty-five acres. The incorporators were as follows: E. A. Glenn, G. R. Peet, Ike E. Lucas, L. Bartlett, George Barber, S. McRoberts, Jr., David Crosby, Benjamin Crosby, J. R. Fletcher, and J. O. Stewart. The first officers were as follows: Samuel McRoberts, Sen., president; Ike E. Lucas, secretary; Cyrus Doty, treas-

HISTORY OF BUTLER COUNTY.

urer; J. R. Jones, James R. Fletcher, E. A. Glenn, Lorenzo Bartlett and George R. Peet, directors.

The first fair was held in October, 1876, and proved to be a splendid success.

In 1876 the officers were Cyrus Doty, president; C. H. Ilgenfritz, treasurer; E. A. Glenn, George R. Peet, A. N. Leet, L. Bartlett and J. R. Jones, directors.

In 1877, during the month of October, the second fair was held, and was a very interesting one.

In 1878 the officers were as follows: Cyrus Doty, president; N. H. Larkin, vice-president; J. O. Stewart, secretary; C. H Ilgenfritz, treasurer; board of directors, A. N. Leet, Charles Fitch, James Burke, H. F. L. Burton and C. R. Nelson.

In 1879 no fair was held on account of the drenching rain.

In 1880 the officers who managed the affairs were J. R. Jones, president; Levi Baker, secretary; H. F. L. Burton, treasurer; board of directors, C. R. Nelson, J. H. Hickle, John Shannon, C. H. Forney and W. E. Burton.

For 1881—J. R. Jones, president; O. J. Pope, vice-president; H. F. L. Burton, treasurer; J. O. Stewart, secretary; board of directors, Cyrus Doty, Aaron Doty, John Shannon, John Kephart and Jacob Hickle.

The officers for the year 1882, were as follows: J. R. Jones, president; O. J. Pope, vice-president; J. J. Eichar, secretary; H. L. F. Burton, treasurer; board of directors, Cyrus Doty, William Tennyson, John Shannon, John Kephert and Aaron Doty.

A fair was to be held during the three days, September 25, 26 and 29, but only continued for two days, as the exhibition was not sufficient to warrant it on the third.

BY-LAWS OF THE ASSOCIATION.

The by-laws adopted by the Clarksville Agricultural Association, and which now govern them, are as follows:

BY-LAWS.

SECTION 1. The board of directors shall have entire control of the grounds of the Association.

SEC. 2. Each officer of the Association who shall be absent from the annual fairs of the Association, shall be fined $1.00, unless good cause can be shown for such absence.

SEC. 3. Animals or articles intended for exhibition shall only be admitted by the gate-keeper on showing the secretary's card with the number and class of his entry.

SEC. 4. The secretary shall enter each class in a separate book for the use of the awarding committee.

SEC. 5. No animal or article shall be taken off the fair ground without leave of the president, who, in such case, shall give a check card which shall admit the animal or article when brought back.

SEC. 6. Premiums in no case shall be given unless the judges consider the object worthy.

SEC. 7. All roots, etc. offered in competition shall be cleansed and trimmed, and exhibited in baskets or open vessels. Grain and seeds may be exhibited in sacks.

SEC. 8. The secretary of the Association shall furnish a card with the name of owner and No. of class of the entry thereon.

SEC. 9. Each committee shall be furnished by the secretary of the Association, with a book containing the number and designation of every animal, article, etc. entered for competition in the class to which the committee is appointed.

SEC. 10. Farms, fences and all other objects of competition which necessitate a committee to travel in the county, shall be entered for such competition before or on the 20th of August, and the committee adjudicating thereon shall report in writing by their chairman to the president of the Association on the morning of the second day of the fair.

SEC. 11. All objects entered for competition which shall require a committee to travel in the country, shall be subject to an entrance fee of $2.00 for each object unless they are situated upon the same farm.

SEC. 12. If any stockholder shall at any time fail to heed the call of the board, or pay in any installment, called in as aforesaid, within ten days after being notified so to do, then the board of directors may, at their option, either collect the said installment by law, or declare the stock forfeited to the Association. If, however, at any time within ten days after such forfeiture the delinquent stockholder shall give to the board sufficient and satisfactory reason for his delinquency, the directors may, at any meeting, rescind such forfeiture and receive the payment due, together with ten per cent. damages, as a penalty for such delinquency.

SEC. 13. The by-laws of the Association may be amended or altered at any meeting by a vote of the majority of the stockholders present.

SEC. 14. The board of directors shall have power to call a meeting from time to time for the purpose of assessing the stock of the Association, which assessment shall not at any one time exceed twenty-five per cent. of the capital stock.

SEC. 15. The board of directors may at any time call a meeting of the stockholders by giving ten days notice of the same through the village press.

[Signed.]   IKE E. LUCAS,
Secretary.

FARMERS' PRODUCE ASSOCIATION OF GREENE.

An association under this caption was organized in 1875 for the mutual benefit of the farmers and producers of Butler county. It was incorporated under the general law of Iowa. The following were the founders: J. L. Spaulding, H. Johnson, Wesley Searles, J. M. Packard, A. Palmatier, B. Huskins, John E. Downing, W. Hassell, J. C. Lockwood, E. Hiller, John Gates, M. Wilson, J. B. Dexter, T. F. Heery, G. B. Merrick, O. D. Barnum, H. W. Smith, Martin Gates, Lewis Farthan and E. Lydig. As its articles of incorporation stated, the association commenced business on the 20th day of March, 1875, and was to terminate on the 20th day of March, 1885, unless sooner discontinued by a two-third vote of the stock. The capital stock as advertised was $10,000, which could, by the same vote as above mentioned, be increased to $25,000, and which should be divided into shares of $50 each. The affairs of the association were conducted by a board of seven directors, and until the first election, the following gentlemen were appointed to act in the capacity of trustees, viz: John Gates, Wesley Searles, Hugh Johnson, J. L. Spaulding, J. M. Packard and J. B. Dexter. In the early part of March, 1875, a meeting of the stockholders of the association was held and officers were elected as follows: President, Wesley Searles; vice-president, Thomas F. Heery; secretary and treasurer, J. L. Spaulding; directors, B. Huckins, Wesley Searles, John Gates, J. L. Spaulding, T. F. Heery, H. Johnson and M. Wilson.

In April, 1875, the association purchased the building known as "Warehouse B.," and on the 3d of May, commenced doing business with C. Fortney, attending to the purchasing. Everything went smooth for a time, and the business prospered; for in September, 1875, we find that a dividend of ten per cent. was declared on the stock, and $207.90 was placed to the reserve fund, representing the gain over the dividend for the months of May, June and July. But, in October, the bank of Greene failed, and its cashier, J. L. Spaulding, who was treasurer of the association, lit out for parts unknown, taking what money he could find with him. This so crippled the enterprise that it was finally abandoned, and the warehouse sold to Mr. John Gates, who still owns it, and it is run by Bruce & VanSaum.

This association would have been a great benefit to the farmers and producers, had it been a success, as it was to be run more on the co-operative plan.

CHAPTER XIV.

EDUCATIONAL.

In this respect the facilities in Butler county are fully up to the average of Iowa's counties. The present mode of government of the public schools differs much from early days, and is a great improvement, for as it is with all innovations, the law in this respect has run the gauntlet, and finally arrived at what must be considered as filling about all the requirements. There are, however, some weak points which prove in many cases very inconvenient, if not exasperating. The law provides for the organization of what is termed district townships, which are divided by the local board into sub-districts. The district township, as the name implies, is a township organized for educational purposes. All of the sub-districts are a part of the whole, and the finances and all business matters of one and all are managed by the board of directors or school supervisors, made up of one from each sub-district. Thus one district cannot make up their minds to vote a tax and build a school-house which may be sadly needed, unless the whole township agrees that the tax can be levied; a school teacher cannot be engaged by the sub-district where she is to teach, but the whole township has a voice in it. The board of directors fixed a price to be paid to all teachers in the township, and thus one teacher with a hard school to teach, and fifty pupils, must receive the same compensation as does the teacher with an easy taught school and but five pupils. To partially rectify this opening for injustice, the law provides for the organization of the sub-districts into independent districts, or in other words, gives them power to choose their own board of directors and officers in whom is vested all the powers held by the officers of the district township. It also provides for the erection of school-houses by the independent districts, but modifies this by the declaration that there must be fifteen scholars of school age in the district before this can be done. There is one district of this kind in the northeastern part of the county, which was made independent by all of the sub-districts in the townships agreeing to become independent, and so organizing; and this one only having ten scholars, cannot build, even though it has at the present writing, and has had for some time, money in the treasury appropriated and taxed for the purpose of building a school-house, but they have not the required number of scholars—only having ten—and are therefore at a standstill.

COUNTY SUPERINTENDENT OF SCHOOLS.

A review of educational matters would be incomplete without a history of the office above named.

When Butler county was organized in 1854, the office of superintendent of county schools had not been created, and the educational matters were, to a very limited extent, vested in an officer, termed school fund commissioner. The commissioner, as is implied by the name, only had charge of the school funds. He had power to loan them to private parties on acceptable security, at moderate interest, and in fact, the records show that most of mortgages, in early days, were held by him. Mr. James Griffith was the first school fund commissioner, and was elected in the fall of 1854 for one term. He made a careful and efficient officer, and the first mortgage loan in the county, is recorded as having been made by him.

James Griffith has resided in Coldwater township since 1852. The first settlement in the township was made only a year previous to his coming here; John Fox, L. Colston, Commodore Bennett and Mr. Lakin having taken claims in 1851. Mr. Griffith was born in Kentucky in 1817; he removed to Indiana with his parents when a child, where he lived till thirty-five years of age, or until he came to Butler county in the fall of 1852. He has been twice married. His first wife was a native of Virginia, and died in Indiana. His present wife was Elizabeth A. Landis, a native of Virginia. He has four children—Frances Jane, born in Indiana in 1839; she is now Mrs. Clarke Carr; William A., born in Indiana in 1842, is a graduate of Cornell College, Iowa, graduating in 1865; he is by profession a teacher; Charles W., born in what is now Dayton township, April 21, 1855; he was probably the first white child born in that township; his youngest child, Belle, was born in Coldwater township, February 21, 1863.

He has lost two children in Butler county—Abram P. and James Madison. Mr. Griffith resides on section 13, near the line of Dayton, in fact the principal part of his farm is in the latter township, where he has 160 acres, having but 30 acres in Coldwater, on which his residence stands. Mr. Griffith being one of the pioneers of the county, endured with his fellow pioneers, all the privations incident to a pioneer life. He has seen Butler county progress from a state or nature till it now ranks with the more advanced and important counties of the State. He has been a close observer, and possesses an excellent memory, and is valuable authority on the early history of Butler county.

John H. Morton was the next commissioner of school funds; but before the expiration of his term of office, the office was abolished by law. The duties devolved upon the county judge, and so continued until the county court system was changed to the board of county supervisors, who have since managed the school funds, with the exception of those devoted to holding normal institutes, which matter is treated at length in its proper place.

When, in 1858, the commissioner was dispensed with, the office of

COUNTY SUPERINTENDENT OF SCHOOLS

was created, and D. W. Mason was elected to fill it in the spring of 1858. Mr. Mason was a lawyer, and is noted more fully in connection with the history of the bar of Butler county. He only served a few months, when he resigned, and M. D. L. Niece was appointed to fill the position so made vacant, and filled out the unexpired term. Mr. Niece was one of the early settlers of Butler county, coming here and locating in the township of Pittsford in November, 1856. He was born in Ohio, was brought up to the occupation of farming, and in early manhood engaged in teaching during the winter season. Several men, who have since become noted, attended, in their boyhood, these winter schools. James A. Garfield was a pupil of his during the winter of 1846-7, at Orange, Ohio. Charles E. Henry, ex-Marshall of the District of Columbia, and Emerson E. White, President of Lafayette College, Indiana, were also his pupils. As before stated Mr. Niece came to Butler county in 1856. He has been engaged much of the time in teaching; was county superintendent of schools of Butler county at one time, and has the office of county surveyor.

His brother, Nathaniel Niece, came to Iowa from Ohio in 1839, and settled in Linn county. He came to Butler county, and settled in Pittsford township in 1855. He had entered a farm there the previous year. His wife was Ziprah H. Lewis. They have a family of nine children, five of whom are living. Nathaniel Niece died March 21, 1882; his wife died the day previous, and they were buried in one grave at the same time.

Mr. Niece's term of office expired with 1859, and at the election in the latter part of that year, I. R. Dean was chosen superintendent of schools. Dean had settled at New Hartford at an early day, where he followed preaching the gospel, being of the Baptist faith; but at the time of his election was residing at Shell Rock. His term expired in 1861, and he died a few years later.

In the fall of 1861 Richard Merrill was elected to this office, and served for two terms.

Mr. Merrill was born in Washington county, Pennsylvania, on July 14, 1814. He emigrated in early childhood with his parents to Belmont county, Ohio, where his youth was spent on a farm and attending common schools. After arriving at manhood he undertook the task of obtaining a liberal education. By dint of that dogged perseverance which characterized him through life, and by his own unaided efforts, he prepared himself and entered New Athens College, from which he graduated with credit to himself. After this, being strongly a Presbyterian in his faith, he went to a theological seminary at Pittsford, Pa., and completed the course of study preparing him for the ministry, and commenced preaching the gospel in Carroll county, Ohio. He continued there in the ministry until 1859, when he came to Butler county, where the first few years of his residence were spent principally in preaching the gospel, having charge of congregations at Coldwater, Boylan's Grove and Butler Center. He continued a useful life, and an active worker in every good cause until December 4, 1875, when, at the age of 62 years, he was called from earthly labor to that home beyond the river. He was a man of strong mind. He reasoned vigorously. He accepted no proposition until he had tested it by his logical powers. When it met the approval of his intellect he inflexibly maintained it. As a citizen he interested himself in everything that tended to build up society. As a friend he was warm and abiding. The labor and turmoil of his life is over, and he has gone to his rest. For a number of years prior to his death he resided at Butler Center, and was extensively engaged in agricultural pursuits. His widow still lives there.

In the fall of 1865, W. H. Gue was elected superintendent, but after serving a few months, resigned, and has left the county. Gue was a man of considerable ability. He lived at Shell Rock, and was elected just after his return from the war. W. A. Lathrop was appointed to fill the vacancy caused by his resignation.

George Graham was the next superintendent elected in the fall of 1867. He was a Presbyterian minister, and still resides in Clarksville; he was a good scholar, and made an efficient and accommodating officer. He was succeeded in 1869, for the years 1870 and 1871 by W. A. Lathrop, who also made an excellent officer. A sketch of Mr. Lathrop is found in connection with the history of the bar.

In 1871, John W. Stewart was elected superintendent of the schools of Butler county, and made one of the most thorough and capable officers in the State, elevating the office to a level with that of any county in the State; he held it for ten years.

John W. Stewart is a son of Elizabeth (Crooks) and William Stewart, and was born in Alleghany county, Pennsylvania, November 29, 1837. In 1856 he had completed an academic course at Cochvanton Academy, in Crawford county, and one at Alleghany College, in Meadville, Pennsylvania. In 1856 he came west, and settled in Rock county, Wisconsin, and engaged in teaching. From there he went to Greene county, where he taught until he entered the army. In August, 1862, he enlisted in company K, 22d Wisconsin Infantry, as a private, but was soon promoted to the 1st lieutenancy. In the winter of 1862 he was obliged to resign on account of ill health. He then returned to Wisconsin, and in the fall of 1864 came to Butler county, Iowa, located on a farm four miles south of Shell Rock, and occupied himself with farming and teaching until 1868. At this time he disposed of his farm and engaged in mercantile trade at Shell Rock. In this business he remained until the fall of 1872, when he was elected county superintendent of schools in Butler county, which office he held for ten years.

Mr. Stewart is a stalwart republican; he cast his first vote for Stephen A. Douglas, but when Fort Sumpter was fired upon, changed from the democratic to the republican party. He is a member of the Methodist church. He was married December 29, 1859, to Miss Martha J. Graham, who was born in Pennsylvania. They have three children living—Lillian, now the wife of Wallace Weed; Cornelius William, and Lulu Elizabeth. He is a member of the Escalop lodge of Masons, of Shell Rock.

John D. Anderson, the present county superintendent of public schools of Butler county, is a native of Ohio, having been born in the town of Beverly, Washington county, that State, in 1846. He came to Grundy county, Iowa, in 1874. Mr. Anderson taught several terms of school in that county, and came to Butler Center in 1877, and took charge of the school of that place. He was eminently successful as a teacher, and was elected in the fall of 1881, to succeed Mr. John W. Stewart as superintendent. Mrs. Anderson was formerly Miss Florence Davis, daughter of James W. Davis, Esq., of Allison.

It is not the intention in this review to make an exhaustive treatise upon the methods or work of the office, but we will merely mention a few of the points wherein Butler county has improved upon the general mode of conducting matters relating to this most important office.

One important and decided improvement is in the shape of a manual, entitled "Course of Study for the Public Schools of Butler County," which was prepared by John W. Stewart, in 1881. The object of this is to secure a more uniform classification, and systematic method of teaching, and wherever it has been followed, the best results have been obtained. One of them is kept in each school, and teachers obtaining certificates are required to sign an agreement that, as far as possible, they will follow the course prescribed. In connection with this, the teacher is given a blank to be filled just before the end of the term, which will show to the successor just how far each scholar has reached in studies, and obviates that necessity of spending a week or more in reviews, determining where to place scholars, as in former times. This is termed a report of classification and progress and is very beneficial, as it enables the teacher who follows to at once know the condition of the school.

Another point is this: just prior to the meeting in the spring and fall, of the boards of directors of the various townships, the county superintendent mails to every secretary a statement of the "needs and wants" of his district, as found by the superintendent on his last visit, and this is read to the board at their meeting. It has, in most cases, the effect of keeping the various schools supplied with the necessary apparatus, and the house and grounds in good shape and repair.

SCHOOLS IN BUTLER COUNTY.

By the report of the State Superintendent of Public Instruction, made in 1864, we glean a number of items which will indicate pretty clearly the condition and advancement of educational matters at that day. The county at that time was just ten years old as an organization.

The report states that every township in the county had been organized as district townships, and a total of 66 sub-districts; the total number of children in the county, of school age, was 2,207; total number of schools, 63; average number of scholars in attendance, 609; number of teachers in the county, 101; aggregate cost of tuition per week for each scholar, thirty-five cents; aggregate amount paid teachers during the year, $7,811.

In connection with these items, it is stated that the year previous, 1863, Butler county had 17 districts, and 57 sub-districts; number of children of school age, 2,007; average attendance at the schools, 694; number of teachers in the county, 92; average cost of tuition per week for each pupil, thirty-three cents; aggregate amount paid teachers during the year, $6,239.39. Now, as a means of comparison, we will turn our attention to, and in this connection give some interesting facts concerning the

PRESENT CONDITION OF EDUCATIONAL MATTERS.

J. D. Anderson, the efficient county superintendent, in submitting his first annual report in October, 1882, for that school year, says:

"The schools of our county are in a prosperous condition. Exceptions to this rule are found, of course, but generally in the hands of young and inexperienced teachers * * When our children are in the school room every day of every term, in time for every roll call, they will be able to complete the work of the common school, and will come to maturity with a good, practical education. Our graded schools are presided over by teachers of special merit, who have had professional training, and such schools are in excellent condition. In the county we have none of the higher institutions of learning and depend largely on our graded schools and normal institutes for instruction in methods."

From the same report upon which the above general remarks were made by the superintendent, we glean the following items, which will be of interest,—the figures represent a total for the entire county—viz:

Number of district townships in the county	11
Number of sub-districts	84
Number of independent districts	46
Number of graded schools	9
Number of schools of all kinds in the county	150
Number of teachers employed	148
Average number of months of school each year	7.1
Average compensation of teachers per month—male	$35 15
Average compensation of females	28 70
Number of scholars between the ages of 5 and 21—male	2,540
Same—female	2,422
Whole number of scholars between ages of 5 and 21	4,962
Number of deaf and dumb children, of school age	6
Number of pupils enrolled in the schools	4,397
Average daily attendance	2,474
Average cost of tuition per month for each pupil	$2 14
Average cost of tuition per school year for each pupil	$15 19
Number of school houses in the county	129
Value of school houses	$82,280

W. R. Jamison

Value of apparatus in the schools	$2,047
Number of dictionaries in schools	137
Number of teachers' certificates granted in 1882	225
Of which are males	56
And females	169
Number of applicants rejected—females	54
Males	10
Average age of male teachers	23
Average age of female teachers	20

As to the financial condition of the educational department of Butler county, it could not be better, and in this connection is presented a few items taken from official reports of 1882, for the information of readers, as follows:

SCHOOL HOUSE FUND.

Dr.

Amount on hand per last report	$4,692 96
Received from district tax	5,243 82
Received from other sources	823 67
Total	$10,760 45

Cr.

Paid for school houses and sites	$3,351 73
Paid for apparatus	10 05
Paid on bonds and interest	3,163 60
Paid for other purposes	1,100 47
On hand	3,134 60
Total	$10,760 45

CONTINGENT FUND.

Dr.

On hand per last report	$8,338 12
Received from district tax	9,691 53
Received from other sources	404 51
Total	$18,434 16

Cr.

Paid for rent and repairs on school houses	$2,333 47
Paid for fuel	3,731 91
Paid secretaries and treasurers	1,347 74
Paid for records, dictionaries, etc.	233 02
Paid for insurance and janitors	762 88
Paid for supplies	955 62
Paid for other purposes	1,307 35
On hand	7,762 17
Total	$18,434 16

TEACHERS' FUND.

Dr.

On hand as per last report	$20,850 45
Received from district tax	26,417 24
Received from semi-annual apportionment	5,950 49
Received from other sources	884 30
Total	$54,132 48

Cr.

Paid teachers	$31,815 24
Paid for other purposes	608 88
On hand	21,708 36
Total	$54,132 48
Whole amount paid by districts for school purposes during year	$50,721 96
Whole amount now in hands of district treasurers	32,605 13
Amount reported on hand September, 1881	34,047 38
Amount reported "on hand at last report," September, 1882	33,881 53
Lost in hands of district treasurers	165 85
Amount of institute fund on hand	105 22

During the last year the county superintendent, J. D. Anderson, has visited 132 schools, and made in all 143 visits; and has held twelve public examinations for teachers. Mr. Anderson is an efficient and able officer, untiring in his endeavors to elevate the character of the schools under his charge, and is succeeding admirably with his work.

A history of each of the various schools will be found in connection with the town or locality in which it is located.

BRANCHES TAUGHT AND TEXT-BOOKS.

The branches taught and text-books in use in the schools of Butler county are about as follows, and they are all the most standard and reliable authorities upon the subject of which they treat:

Orthography—Swinton and Watson.
Reading—American and Independent.
Writing—Spencerian.
Arithmetic—Robinson, Ray and Goff.
Geography—Swinton and Harper.
English Grammar—Reed, Swinton and Burtt.
Physiology—Steele and Cutter.
History of United States—Barnes and Swinton.
Algebra—Robinson.
Book-keeping—Bryant and Stratton.

In addition to the above comes the list of reference books for the aid and use of teachers, as follows:

Doty's Manual of Arithmetic; Mark's First Lessons in Geometry; Swinton's Outlines of the World's History; Townsend's Analysis of Letter Writing; Townsend's Analysis of Civil Government; Calkin's Primary Object Lessons; Hooker's Child's Book of Nature; Wickersham's Methods of Instruction and School Economy; Gow's Good Morals and Gentle Manners; Page's Theory and Practice of Teaching; and every teacher is expected to read one educational journal.

GRADED SCHOOLS.

The following is a list of the various graded schools in Butler county, together with the names of the present principal, and salary of the same, viz:

Aplington, employs two teachers and E. T. Bedell, principal, at $405 per annum.

Butler Center, two teachers and Ella Mullarky, principal, at $320.

Bristow, two teachers; Hattie Ripson, principal, salary $320.

Clarksville, four teachers; N. H. Hineline, principal, salary $450.

Greene, four teachers; A. H. Beals, principal, salary $585.

New Hartford, two teachers; William Hunter, principal, salary $405.

Parkersburgh, four teachers; E. C. Bellows, principal, salary $540.

Shell Rock, east, two teachers; V. L. Dodge, principal, salary 360.

Shell Rock, west, two teachers; W. J. Hunt, principal, salary $450.

The graded schools are all in most excellent condition, and are doing good and efficient work. All under the supervision of able and experienced teachers, they are, in Butler county, fully supplying the place of those higher and more expensive institutions which are found in many other counties throughout Iowa. Nearly all of the higher branches are taught, and a young man or woman having passed through one of them by earnest study and application, with success, needs go no farther for education, as they will have already attained sufficient to meet all the diversified conditions and requirements of life.

A history of the graded as well as the common or district schools will be found in connection with the history of the various localities in which they are located.

THE NORMAL INSTITUTE.

By an act passed by the General Assembly of Iowa, in 1873, the county superintendents were required to commence, and each year hold a Teachers' or Normal Institute at some convenient point in each county, for the drill of those who were or who intended to teach. The object or design of this was, and is, to furnish teachers an opportunity to review and enlarge their knowledge of the branches to be taught, to acquaint themselves with improved methods of teaching, to awaken an increased desire for self-improvement in knowledge, skill, and power to control others, and to give them more confidence and ability in managing the affairs of the school. For the purpose of defraying the expenses incident to such gatherings, the Institute Fund was created, to which the State annually pays $50, and it is made up by the $1.00 examination fees paid to the county superintendent, and the fees of $1.00 each charged to each member who attends the institute. This fund is under the exclusive control of the county superintendent, and in Butler county, amounts to about $500 per annum. There is no law compelling teachers to attend the institutes; but each applicant for a certificate is required to show good cause for not having attended. The matter is also greatly assisted by the county seperintendent, who makes all certificates expire on the first day of August, no matter at what time they were issued; thus leaving no excuse for a teacher's absence.

The first institute was held in August, 1874, by John W. Stewart, county superintendent and *ex-officio* manager of Institute; he conducted one each year from that time until his term of office expired in 1881. They were all very successful, and their effect was plainly visible in elevating the character of the schools.

The last institute was held at Clarksville in 1882, commencing on the seventh day of August, and continuing for three weeks, having an enrollment of 24 males and 107 females—total, 131. The average attendance was 105. The officers and conductors of this school were as follows: General Manager, John D. Andrews; conductor, Erwin Baker; instructors, L. S. Bottenfield and C. M. Greene; lecturers, Erwin Baker, State Superintendent, J. W. Akers and W. A. Lathrop. The expense of the institute amounted to about $404.70, and it was considered as being as enjoyable and profitable a session as has yet been held. The next will be held in August, 1883.

The following preface to the course of study for the last Institute contains information as to the method of conducting the gatherings:

To INSTRUCTORS AND MEMBERS.—The design of an Institute drill is to furnish teachers an opportunity to review and enlarge their knowledge of the branches to be taught, to acquaint themselves with improved methods of teaching, to awaken an increased desire for self-improvement in knowledge, skill, and power to control others, and to give them more confidence and ability in managing the affairs of the school.

The county superintendent will assume the business management of the Institute. He will assign members to their proper divisions as soon as enrolled, basing the classification on ability and experience. This classification will be changed only on recommendation of class instructors, approved by the conductor. He expects full reports from class instructors and conductor at close of Institute, of the work best done, and of such things as are most needed to improve the schools of Butler county.

The conductor shall act as principal of the school, and is charged with the execution of the regular daily programme. He shall exercise careful supervision over the work done, and methods employed by the assistant instructors At the close of the Institute he shall make a report to the county superintendent, embracing the items reported by the assistants, and in addition, his own suggestions and observations.

The assistant instructors are expected to do all in their power to make the Institute a unit; dismiss classes promptly, and meet the superintendent and conductor daily to report progress and discuss methods. They are especially requested to encourage members to do ALL the reciting and MOST of the talking. At the close of the session they will make out a report to the conductor, embracing those points in which the teachers were found most lacking, and suggesting the things most needed to develop their teaching powers and improve the schools.

Members of the Institute are expected to conduct themselves as pupils or students. They are earnestly requested to be present at roll-call, both in the morning and afternoon; to give special attention to the *methods* employed by instructors in presenting subjects; to do the work assigned them in the best possible manner, and to remain during the entire session and be present at the examination.

J. D. ANDERSON,
County Superintendent.

BUTLER COUNTY TEACHERS' ASSOCIATION.

At the time of the Normal Institute, held in Clarksville, in August, 1882, the teachers got together and with forty-two charter members, organized the association under the above name. The object declared was the elevation of the profession of teaching by the mental improvement of its members in all correct educational means. A preamble, constitution and by-laws were drawn and neatly printed, and each member was required to deposit 25 cents as fee. The association has grown rapidly in interest and in numbers, now having a membership of about 60, and holds regular meetings four times each year. The first and present officers are as follows:

President, J. D. Anderson, county superintendent; secretary, Emma Sweitzer, of Shell Rock; treasurer, A. H. Beals, of Greene; executive committee, J. D. Anderson, Allison; Emma L. Cole, Greene; N. H. Hineline, Clarksville. The vice-presidents are as follows: Fremont, Carrie E. Howe; Dayton, Sarah Bement; Coldwater, John Wilson; Bennezette, Jennie Wray; Pittsford, George Brown; West Point, Hattie Ripson; Jackson, Mrs. Lina Fowle; Butler, E. L. Palmer; Shell Rock, Florence Meade; Jefferson, Ella Mullarky; Ripley, Alice Barlow; Madison, Helen Slaid; Washington, Bridget Chrystie; Monroe, E. T. Bedell; Albion, E. C. Bellows; Beaver, George H. Cook.

CONSTITUTION AND BY-LAWS.

The constitution and by-laws adopted by the association were as follows:

PREAMBLE.

We, the undersigned teachers of Butler county, feeling that we owe a duty to ourselves as teachers, and to the profession which we represent, and believing that by co-operation we may dignify our calling and unify our efforts, do form ourselves into a Teachers' Association, and for our guidance do adopt the following constitution and by-laws:

CONSTITUTION.

ARTICLE I—NAME.

SECTION 1. This association shall be called the Butler County Teachers' Association.

ARTICLE II—OBJECT.

SEC. 1. The object of the association shall be the elevation of the profession of teaching by the mental improvement of its members in all correct educational means.

ARTICLE III—OFFICERS.

SEC. 1. This association shall have the following officers, whose terms of office shall be from the time of election until the close of the next succeeding county institute: President, vice-president from each township, secretary, treasurer, and an executive committee of three members, one of which shall be the president.

ARTICLE IV—DUTIES OF OFFICERS.

SEC. 1. It shall be the duty of the president to preside at all regular meetings, and to perform the duties usually required of the chairman of an organized assembly.

SEC. 2. It shall be the duty of the secretary to keep a correct record of the proceedings of each regular meeting; keep a record of attendance; notify members who have been placed upon the programme by the executive committee; see that the programme and proceedings are published, and to attend to such other correspondence as shall be necessary for the good of the association.

SEC. 3. It shall be the duty of the treasurer to keep an account of all money received into or paid from the treasury, and to pay no money except on order of the president and secretary.

SEC. 4. It shall be the duty of the vice-presidents to encourage the teachers from each township to attend the association, and to assist the president in making the association a success. It shall be the duty of the executive committee to make out a programme for each meeting and to furnish the same to the secretary at least three weeks prior to the time of its execution. They shall also make any necessary arrangements for holding meetings of the association.

ARTICLE V—DEPOSITS.

SEC. 1. All members shall sign the constitution and shall deposit with the treasurer the sum of twenty-five (25) cents, which shall be returned whenever a member withdraws, minus general assessments.

ARTICLE VI—AMENDMENTS.

SEC. 1. This constitution may be altered or amended at any regular meeting by a majority vote of all the members of the association, notice of such alteration or amendment having been given to the secretary in writing at the previous meeting.

BY-LAWS.

ARTICLE I—MEETINGS.

SEC. 1. This association shall meet four times each year, at such times and places as the executive committee shall direct.

SEC. 2. Each regular meeting shall be preceded by a business meeting, in which Roberts' Rules of Order shall be the guide.

ARTICLE II—HONORARY MEMBERS.

SEC. 1. Any person may be elected an honorary member of this association by a majority vote of all the members, and such person shall not be required to make a deposit.

ARTICLE III—AMENDMENTS.

SEC. 1. These by-laws may be altered or amended at any regular meeting by a majority vote of all the members of the association.

Signed by forty two teachers.

CHAPTER XV.

THE WAR—ITS CAUSES.

From the commencement of government there have been two antagonistic principles contending for mastery, slavery and freedom. Sometimes smoldering and even invisible; but the seeds were there and ever and anon would burst into flames, carrying destruction, death and desolation with it. A repetition of that great conflict which, for ages, has agitated our globe —the conflict between aristocratic usurpation and popular rights. History is crowded with descriptions and scenes of this irrepressible conflict. Two thousand years ago, when the aristocracy of Rome was headed by Cneues Pompey, Julius Cæsar, espousing the cause of the people, unfurled the banner of equal rights, and striding through oceans of flood which tossed their surges over every portion of the habitable globe, overthrew the aristocratic commonwealth, and reared over the ruins, the imperial commonwealth. Again on the field of Pharsalia, the aristocratic banner was trailed in the dust, and democracy, although exceedingly imperfect, became victor. It was aristocracy trying to keep its heel on the head of democracy which has deluged the Roman Empire in blood.

But the nobles regained foothold, and regardless of these lessons, renewed their oppression. Again they commenced sowing the seed which must surely bring forth terrible fruit. Over two hundred years ago the aristocracy of France, housed in magnificent palaces, mounted on war horses, with pampered men at arms ready to ride rough shod on every embassage of violence, trampled upon the suffering serfs, until humanity could no longer endure it. The masses of the people were deprived of every privilege, save that of toiling for their masters. The aristocracy so deprived the people, whose wives and daughters through their brutality were forced to go to the field bare-headed and bare-footed, and be yoked to the plow with the donkey, that they never dreamed that the wretched boors would dare even to look in defiance towards the massive and stately castles whose noblemen proudly strode along the battlements in measureless contempt for the helpless peasantry below. But the pent up vials of vengeance of ages at last burst forth. These boors, these jacks, rose and like maddened hyenas, rushed upon their foes. Imbruted men, who for ages had been subjected to the most outrageous wrongs, rose by millions against their oppressors, and wreaked upon them every atrocity which fiend-like ingenuity could devise. All the brutal and demon passions of human nature held high carnival, and it can truly be said France ran red with blood. But at length disciplined valor prevailed. After one-half of the peasantry of France had perished, the knighted noblemen, the aristocrats resumed their sway, and the hellish bondage, worse than slavery, was again placed upon the people. This war of the jacks, or as it is called in history, *Jacqueri*, is one of the most interesting and warning events of the past; and yet it was all unheeded.

The oppression went on, growing more and more outrageous; the people were kept ignorant that they might not know of their wrongs; poor that they might not resent them. That the lords might live in castles and be clothed in purple, and fare sumptuously, the people were doomed to hovels, rags and black bread. The peasant must not place the bit of dough in the ashes by his fireside—he was compelled to have it baked at the bakery of his lord, and there pay heavy toll. He dare not scrape together the few crumbs of salt from the rocks of the ocean shore, he must buy every particle from his lord at an exorbitant price. "Servants obey your masters," was interpreted to apply to all save of noble birth; and religion was converted into a method for subjecting the masses. Bibles were not allowed to be read by these "boors," lest they learn what the Savior really taught, and a peasant detected with one in his hand, was deemed as guilty as if caught with the tools of a burglar or the dies of a counterfeiter. As associates for lords—the idea would have been considered contrary to nature or reason. Thus Louis XV., surrounded by courtesans, debauchees and the whoredom of his castle, once said: "I can give money to Voltaire, Montesqien Fontinelle, but I cannot *dine* and *sup* with these people." If the peasant with his wife and child toiling in the field, in cultivation of a few acres of land, managed to raise $640 worth of crops during the year, $600 of it went to the King, the Lord and the Church, while the remaining $40 was left to clothe and feed the emaciate family. Thomas Jefferson in the year 1785, wrote from Paris to a friend in Philadelphia:

"Of twenty millions of people supposed to be in France, I am of the opinion that there are nineteen millions more wretched, more accursed in every circumstance of human existence, than the most conspicuously wretched individual in the whole United States."

It was this state of affairs which brought on the war of the French Revolution, inaugurating the most terrific of all Time's battles. Such combats earth never saw before, probably never will see again. Two worlds as it were came clashing together. Twenty millions of people trampled in the mire, rose ghastly and frenzied, and the flames of feudal castles and the shrieks of haughty oppressors appalled the world. All the combined aristocracy of Europe were on the other side to crush the demand of the people for the equality of man. Russia, Prussia, Sweden, Austria, England, Spain—all the kings rallied their armies to the assistance of France in subduing the oppressed masses who, believing they were right, marched heroically to the victories of Marengo, Wagram and Austerlitz. But in the final victories of the despots, aristocratic privilege again triumphed in Europe. In the meantime a similar though less bloody and terrific battle had taken place in England; the same ever rising conflict between the united courtiers and cavaliers under Charles I., and the Puritans under Cromwell. With prayer, fasting, and hymn, the common people who had for ages been under the yoke of servitude, took to arms in defense of their rights, and many cavaliers bit the dust through their sturdy blows. But Charles II., returned to the throne and again aristocracy triumphed. The oppressed were our Puritan fathers; again they were trodden under foot. Then it was that the heroic resolution was adopted to cross the ocean three thousand miles, and there in exile establish and found a republic where all men in the eye of the law should be equal. The result is too well known to need rehearsal. How they fought their way through all the dangers of the savage new world and succeeded in the object. How the aristocracy of England made the desperate effort to again bring the yoke to bear; to tax us without allowing us to be represented in parliament—to place the appointment to all important offices in the hands of the king, who would send over the sons of England's noblemen to be our governors and our judges, and who would fill all the posts of wealth, dignity and power with the children of the lords.

Hence the war of the Revolution. We, the people, conquered, and established our government independent of all the world, placing as corner-stone of the edifice, that "all men are born free and equal, and are alike entitled to life, liberty, and the pursuit of happiness."

Then coming down to the great conflict of America, the Rebellion, it was a continuance of that irrepressible conflict which has shaken the world to its uttermost depths for ages. It was based upon slavery, that which has caused the shedding of oceans of blood, and making millions of widows and orphans.

The Constitution under which we are bound together, is in its spirit and legitimate utterance, doubtless one of the most noble documents ever produced by the mind of man, and even now when the advancement of a century has dawned upon its use, not a paragraph requires changing to make it true to humanity. But yet ingloriously and guiltily we consented to use one phrase susceptible of a double meaning, "held to labor." So small and apparently so insignificant were the seeds sown from which such a harvest of misery has been reaped. In the North these honest words meant a hired man or an apprentice. In the South they were taken to mean slavery, the degradation and feudal bondage of a race. A privileged class assumed that the constitution recognized it, and the right of property in human beings. This class endeavored to strengthen and extend their aristocratic institution, which was dooming ever increasing millions to life-long servitude and degradation. All wealth was rapidly accumulating in the hands of these few who owned their fellow-man as property. The poor whites, unable to buy slaves, and considering labor which was performed by them degrading, were rapidly sinking into a state of frightful misery. The sparse population which slavery allowed, excluded churches, schools and villages. Immense plantations of thousands of acres, tilled by as many slaves, driven to work by overseers, consigned the whole land to apparent solitude. The region of the southern country generally presented an aspect of desolation which Christendom no where else could parallel. The slaveholders, acting as one man, claimed the right of extending this over all the free territory of the United States. Free labor and slave labor cannot exist together. The admission of slavery effectually excluded free men from them. It was impossible for those men, cherishing the sentiment of republican equality, to settle there, with the privileged class who were to own vast realms and live in luxury upon the unpaid labor of the masses. It was on this point that the conflict, in its fierceness, commenced.

From the year 1790 the strife grew hotter and hotter every year. The questions arising kept Congress, both the Senate and House, in one incessant scene of warfare. There could be no peace in the land until this aristocratic element was effectually banished.

The Hon. Mr. Iverson, of Georgia, speaking of the antagonism of the two systems, aristocracy and freedom, said, in the Senate of the United States, on December 5th, 1860:

"Sir, disguise the fact as you will, there is enmity between the Northern and Southern people, which is deep and enduring, and you can never eradicate it—never. Look at the spectacle exhibited on this floor. How is it? There are the Northern Senators on that side; here are the Southern Senators on this side. You sit upon your side silent and gloomy. We sit upon our side with knit brows and portentous scowls. Here are two hostile bodies on this floor, and it is but a type of the feeling which exists between the two sections. We are enemies as much as if we were hostile States. We have not lived in peace. We are not now living in peace. It is not expected that we shall ever live in peace."

Hon. Mr. Mason, of Virginia, in continuation of the same debate said: "This is a war of sentiment and opinion, by one form of society against another form of society."

The remarks of the Hon. Garrett Davis, a Senator from Kentucky, are to the point:

"The cotton States, by their slave labor, have become wealthy, and many of their planters have princely revenues—from $50,000 to $100,000 per year. This wealth has begot a pride, and insolence, and ambition, and these points of the Southern character have been displayed most insultingly in the halls of Congress. As a class, the wealthy cotton growers are insolent, they are proud, they are domineering, they are ambitious. They have monopolized the government in its honors for forty or fifty years with few interruptions. When they saw the sceptre about to depart from them, in the election of Lincoln, sooner than give up office and the spoils of office, in their mad and wicked ambition they determined to disrupt the old confederation, and erect a new one, wherein they would have undisputed power."

Thus the feeling continued growing stronger. One incessant cry became, "Abjure your democratic constitution, which favors equal rights to all men, and give us in its place an aristocratic constitution, which will secure the rights of a privileged class." They insisted that the domestic slave trade should be nurtured, and the foreign slave trade opened; saying, in the coarse and vulgar language of one of the most earnest advocates of slavery: "The North can import jackasses from Malta, let the South, then, import niggers from Africa."

The reply of the overwhelming majority of the people of the United States was decisive. Lincoln was elected and inaugurated despite the conspiracy to prevent it.

Volumes could be and have been written upon these actions, but they are well known. We will merely mention the most prominent features, transpiring until the havoc of war actually set in,

On the 7th of November, 1860, it was known that Abraham Lincoln was elected President of the United States, and was to enter upon his duties on the 4th day of the following March. In the meantime the executive government was virtually in the hands of the slave power. James Buchanan, the President, had been elected to the office openly pledged to pursue the general policy the slave-holders enjoyed. The cabinet were all slave-holders and slave-masters. The United States Navy was scattered all over the face of the earth, leaving only two vessels for the defense of the country; the treasury was left barren; the army was so scattered in remote fortresses in the far west, as to leave all the forts where they would be needed, defenseless; the United States Arsenals were emptied, the Secretary of War sending their guns to the Slave States, where bands of Rebels were organized and drilling, prepared to receive them. One hundred and fifteen thousand arms, of the most approved pattern, were transferred from Springfield, Massachusetts, and from Watervleit, New York, together with a vast amount of cannon, morter, balls, powder and shells were also forwarded to the Rebels in the Slave States.

On the 18th of February, 1861, the inauguration of Jefferson Davis, as President of the Southern Confederacy, took place at Montgomery, Ala. Four days later the collector of customs, appointed by the Confederate Government in Charleston, South Carolina, issued the manifesto that all vessels, from any State out of the Confederacy, would be treated as foreign vessels, and subject to the port dues, and other charges established by the laws of the Confederate States. Thus by a stroke of the pen, the immense commerce of the Northern States was declared to be foreign commerce, beneath the guns of the forts which the United States had reared, at an expense of millions of dollars.

Already a number of States had passed the ordinance of secession.

On the fourth of March, 1861, Abraham Lincoln was inaugurated President, and assumed official duties.

At half-past four o'clock on the morning of the 12th of April, 1861, the rebels opened fire upon Fort Sumter, and, after enduring terrific bombardment from all sides, the heroic defenders abandoned it, and were conveyed to New York. Fort Sumter was the Bunker Hill of the civil war. In both cases, a proud aristocracy were determined to subject this country to its sway. In both cases the defeat was a glorious victory.

On the next Monday, April 15th, President Lincoln issued a call for three months' service of 75,000 volunteers. The effect was electrical. Within fifteen days it is estimated that 350,000 men offered themselves in defense of our national flag.

Thus the civil war had burst upon the United States with almost the suddenness of the meteor's glare. It was, however, but like the eruption of the volcano whose pent-up fires had for ages been gathering strength for the final explosion. The conspirators had for years been busy preparing for the conflict. In the rebel convention, which met in South Carolina to consummate the conspiracy, Mr. Inglis said:— "Most of us have had this subject under consideration for the last twenty years." Mr. Keitt said: "I have been engaged in this movement ever since I entered political life." Mr. Rhett said: "It is nothing produced by Mr. Lincoln's election, or the non-execution of the fugitive slave law. It is a matter which has been gathering for thirty years." But more need not be said; the result is too well known. Call followed call in quick succession, the number reached the grand total of 3,339,748. The calls were as follows:

April 15, 1861, for three months	75,000
May 4, 1861, for five years	64,748
July, 1861, for three years	500,000
July 18, 1862, for three years	300,000
August 4, 1862, for nine months	300,000
June, 1863, for three years	300,000
October 17, 1863, for three years	300,000
February 18, 1864, for three years	500,000
July 10, 1864, for three years	200,000
July 16, 1864, for one, two and three years	500,000
December 21, 1864, for three years	300,000
Total	3,339,748

Many interesting references are made to the events occurring during the breaking out of the war, and also as to the dates on which the various rebelling States seceded, in the War Chapters of Butler and Bremer counties, in this work.

CHAPTER XVI.

BUTLER COUNTY IN THE WAR.

Looking at Butler county to-day we can scarcely realize that when the war broke upon the country, arraying more than a million of men in arms, and which made our Ship of State reel and stagger as if smitten by thunderbolts and dashed upon rocks, that it had not been settled ten years; and Iowa as a State of the American Union was yet in her teens. But, notwithstanding its own soil had not been fully subjugated to man's use, very material aid was promptly offered in subduing the rebellious States. The feeling throughout Iowa was universal that the Union must be preserved, and the sights and sounds that were so noticeable in every village and hamlet north of Mason's and Dixon' line, were duplicated here. The celerity with which men abandoned the pursuits of peace to take up those of war was most marvelous.

The population of Butler county in 1860 was 3,724, and the volunteer enlistments during the year 1861 and 1862 were 293. The quota during that time under the various calls required 179—showing an excess of men furnished of 114. During the war there were about 504 re-inlistments. A few were drafted, but most of them furnished substitutes.

Officially, Butler county nobly did its part, issuing bounties to volunteer soldiers to the amount of about $40,000, besides a relief fund which amounted to about $13,000.

Appended is given a list of the gallant heroes who participated in the war. When possible the list of the various regiments have been submitted to some one familiar with the names.

SECOND VETERAN INFANTRY.

COMPANY F.

Cotton, Charles M, Wilcox, John,
Myers, Campbell,   Wilder, William.
Warner, William E.,

COMPANY K.

Sergeant:
Anderson Edwards.

THIRD INFANTRY.

FIELD AND STAFF OFFICERS.
Lieutenant-Colonel—Matthew M. Trumbull.
Quartermaster Sergeant—Edward H. Mix.

COMPANY I.
Captain:
Matthew M. Trumbull.

First Lieutenant:
John G. Scobey.

Sergeant:
Isaac M. Henderson.

Corporals:
Charles E. Turner,   John Booram,
Henry Martin,   William Burdick.

Privates:
Cotton, Gaylord,   Getchell, William,
Crosby, Spencer S., Gilbert, Tilly G.,
Clousky, Joseph S., Merifield, Willis H.,
DeWitt, Stephen,   Mix, Thomas M.,
Edwards, Anderson,   Parks, George,
Forney, Abraham,   Robison, Albert.
Filkins, William.

THE THIRD IOWA INFANTRY.

The Third Iowa Volunteer Infantry contained men from all parts of the State. The companies forming the command were among those who sprang to arms at the first outbreak of the rebellion.

The Third Regiment, numbering about 970, was sworn into the service of the United States at Keokuk, part on the 8th, and part on the 10th of June, 1861, with Nelson Williams, of Dubuque county, as Colonel; John Scott, of Story, Lieutenant-Colonel; William M. Stone, of Marion, Major.

The regiment remained at Keokuk till the 29th of June, on which day it embarked on steamers for Hannibal, Missouri. The regiment was hastened westward, where lively work was soon expected. They were without means of transportation, without knapsacks, haversacks, canteens, cartridge-boxes or ammunition. The only weapons the men had were empty muskets and bayonets.

From about the 12th of July till the 7th of August, regimental headquarters and seven of the companies were at Chillicothe, a place on the railway something more than half way across the State. The other companies were near by guarding the railroad. On the 4th of August the men drew their accoutrements.

The regiment was marched and counter-marched all through northeastern Missouri, without accomplishing any visible good, and participation in a battle was necessary to remove the weight of despondency from their spirits. Lieutenant Scott, who was then in command, soon made an opportunity by fine audacity, whereby this most desirable result was brought about. This was at the combat of Blue Mills Landing, fought September 17. They marched into ambuscade, and rebel bullets were fatally pattering against it from one end to the other. The Colonel gave orders to fall back slowly. Out of sixteen officers ten had already fallen either killed or wounded. They fell back to a dry slough, where they took a stand, and repulsed the rebels with considerable loss. The combat continued about one hour, and the action of the officers and men was most creditable throughout. The regiment went to Quincy, Illinois, and remained till the 9th of November; they then went to St. Louis, and remained at Benton Barracks till the day after Christmas, when they moved to Mexico, and spent the winter guarding the railroad.

On the night of the 3d of March, 1862, they started to join the forces of General Grant, in Tennessee, and embarked on the 17th, at Pittsburg Landing, and went into camp about a mile therefrom, in the direction of the Shiloh Church, where they remained till the surprise of April 6.

During the battle of Shiloh the Third fought under Hurlburt, where they behaved with great bravery. Colonel Williams was disabled, Major Stone captured, one Captain killed and six others wounded, seven Lieutenants also wounded, while the entire loss to the regiment gave ample attestation to its valor.

The regiment then started on the march to Corinth. In July they went into camp at Memphis till the 6th of September.

At the battle of the Hatchie, the Third added fresh laurels to its wreath of honor, where it carried the bridge over the river, and lost in a few minutes, nearly sixty officers and men. After the battle the regiment returned to Bolivar.

They were at the siege of Vicksburg, and too much cannot be said in praise of the officers and men for their fortitude and courage exhibited during the entire siege. In the campaign which immediately followed the siege of Vicksburg the Third Iowa bore a most conspicuous part, after which they returned to Vicksburg and went into camp for the winter, and about two hundred of the men re-enlisted and went home on furloughs.

The non-veterans were with Banks in his disastrous campaign, after which they received their discharge, and were mustered out.

The veterans were engaged in the battle of Atlanta, where they literally fought themselves out of existence. The remaining members of the organization were consolidated with the Second Iowa. The history of the Third throughout was gallant in the extreme.

THIRD INFANTRY.
COMPANY I.
Trowbridge, Samuel, Wilcox, Jesse B.,
Warner, William E., Wilcox, Alfred M.
Winship, James W.,

ADDITIONAL ENLISTED MEN.
Turner, Charles E., Pauley, Charles,
Wilcox, John, Cotton, Charles M.

SEVENTH INFANTRY.
COMPANY B.
Corporal:
William L. Palmer.

Privates:
Adair, John, Dunham, Alfred E,
Colton, Theodore L., Mason, William H.

VETERANS.
Corporal:
William L Palmer.

Privates:
Adair, John, Mason, William H.

EIGHTH INFANTRY.
COMPANY B.
Brownwell, Schadrac, Castlow, Thomas.
COMPANY C.
Campbell, James E.
COMPANY D.
Dobbins, Rollin, Goodhue, James M.
COMPANY G.
Maynard, Curtis, Murry, Daniel.
COMPANY K.
Beebe, Eli.

NINTH INFANTRY.
COMPANY G.
Privates:
Leverich, Willard, Myers, John M.

VETERAN.
Myers, Philip B.

COMPANY I.
Corporal:
Chester W. Inman.

Privates:
Consadine, Patrick, Parcupile, James H.
Inman, David W.

VETERAN.
Captain:
Chester W. Inman.

(Unassigned.)
Hillusted, Herman, Manwairn, Emery,
Larne, Francis, St. John, Jarmine.

For history, see Bremer county war chapter.

TWELFTH INFANTRY.
COMPANY E.
Sergeant:
William H. Beckwith.

Corporals:
Charles V. Surfus, Joel A. Stewart,
Thomas Boylan.

Privates:
Abrenso, John, Johnson, Charles,
Bird, E. R., Meyers, Alexander,
Bird, Robert L., Margretz, Jeremiah,
Bird, William O., Mason, George,
Carter, John B., Strong, Nelson,
DeMoss, James, Smith, Harvey,
DeMoss, Thomas, Pomeroy, Robert L.,
Hubbard, George, Spears, William,
Hoisington, Hiram, Sharp, Oliver.
Hoisington, John,

VETERANS OF COMPANY E.

Sergeants:
Charles V. Surfus,   Harvey Smith.
Jeremiah Margretz,

Privates:
Bird, E. R.,   Meyers, Alexander,
Bird, Robert L,   Surfus, Nathaniel.

COMPANY F.
Goodell, William H.

TWELFTH INFANTRY.

Very soon after the disaster to the Union arms at Bull Run, in Virginia, the President issued a proclamation calling for additional volunteers, under which several regiments were recruited in Iowa, and among them was the Twelfth Infantry. The companies which formed the regiment were enrolled in the counties of Hardin, Allamakee, Fayette, Linn, Black Hawk, Delaware, Winnesheik, Dubuque and Jackson, and went into rendezvous at Dubuque, where they were mustered into the service during the months of October and November. The organization was completed near the close of the latter month, the last company being sworn in on the 25th, at which time the regiment numbered, rank and file, nine hundred and twenty-six men. J. J. Woods, of Jackson county was commissioned Colonel; John P. Coulter, of Linn, Lieutenant-Colonel; and Samuel B. Brodtbeck, of Dubuque, Major.

A few days after organization the regiment moved to St. Louis, and went into quarters there for drill and discipline, at Benton Barracks. The men composing this fine command were remarkable for their vigorous, manly appearance. But during the winter 1861-2, and especially the months of December and January, the regiment was sadly afflicted with sickness, being scourged at the same time with two dreadful diseases—measles and pneumonia. At one time half of the men were sick, and during this time about seventy-five members of the regiment died, among them Captain Tupper, of Company G.

Having endured the discomforts of these notorious barracks about two months, the regiment moved by rail to Cairo, and thence to Smithland, Kentucky, where it remained a short time, then joined the army under General Grant, which was about to move upon the enemy's works in Tennessee. The regiment was present at the capture of Fort Henry, February 6, 1862, and suffered very much from the extreme, severe weather.

On the 12th the regiment marched from Fort Henry to the neighborhood of Fort Donelson, and on the morning of the next day took position on the left wing of the investing army, being on the left flank of the Second Brigade on the left of the Union lines, a position which turned out to be one both of danger and of honor. In the sufferings, and contests, and final glorious success of the wonderful victory of Fort Donelson, the Twelfth bore its part manfully, and at once won a high reputation among the citizens of Iowa and other States, who read the thrilling details of General Grant's first success. The regiment remained on the field, taking needed rest and recuperating from the effect of the short but arduous campaign.

At the conclusion of this period of rest, the campaign of Shiloh was opened. The Twelfth took steamer on the Tennessee river, proceeded to Pittsburg Landing, where they went into camp about a mile from the hamlet.

At the battle of Shiloh, which took place on the 6th and 7th days of April, 1862, the Eighth, the Twelfth and the Fourteenth Iowa Volunteers composed four-fifths of that little band which held back ten times their force of Rebels, long after all support had fallen away from their right and left, fighting after the last hope of saving themselves had gone, and by sacrificing themselves, saving the army of the Union till Buell and night had come.

As the sun was setting on the army they had saved, these gallant men threw down their guns and surrendered prisoners of war. They had fought all day without flinching, but it made the blood run cold in the veins of the stoutest hearted to see many of their comrades shot down after they had surrendered, and some of them so long after the surrender, that ignorance of the fact could not have been pleaded in excuse of the foul atrocity.

The prisoners were marched five miles to the rear, and spent the stormy night in a corn-field. The next day they marched to Corinth, thence by rail to Memphis, and from there soon afterwards to Mobile, Alabama. The officers with the rank of Captain and above, were sent by steamer to Selma. The Lieutenants and men were taken to various places in Alabama, and confined in loathsome prisons. About half of the men of the Twelfth were released during the month of May, and sent to parole camp, Benton Barracks, Missouri. The rest suffered the hardships and privations of imprisonment during the summer and fall. The officers remained in Selma three months, then were taken to Atlanta for a short time, when they proceeded to Madison, where they were joined by the officers who had been separated from them, where they remained until the 7th of November. They were then sent back to Libby Prison, Richmond, and were paroled on the 13th at Aiken's Landing. The enlisted men were paroled on the 20th at the same place, and all went to the parole camps at Annapolis, Maryland, and thence to St. Louis. During this period, officers and men suffered worse than had been known up to that time among civilized people, from the effects of harsh treatment. Many died in prison, many more died afterwards from the effects of their prison life, while others were compelled to quit the service because they had been rendered unfit ever to perform its duties. About one hundred and fifty members of the Twelfth—men who had been in hospital, or for other causes were not present at the battle of Shiloh, or had escaped from imprisonment—were performing active duties on the field in the "Union Brigade."

The Union Brigade—which was, in fact, rather a consolidated regiment than a brigade—was disbanded, resolved into its original elements. Those parts of it belonging to Iowa Regiments went to Davenport and remained there during the winter of 1862-63, the members of the Twelfth rejoining the regiment about the 1st of April, when it was re-organized. The paroled men had been declared exchanged on the 1st of January, 1863, and about a week afterwards went to Rolla to defend that place against a threatened raid by Marmaduke, but returned to camp without having a fight. They spent the time

J. R. Jones.

between that and the spring campaign at St. Louis.

In this campaign the Eighth, Twelfth and Thirty-fifth Iowa Regiments formed the Third Brigade, Third Division, Fifteenth Army Corps, and moved from Duckport, Louisiana, on the 2d of May, to take Jackson, and then Vicksburg in the rear. The regiments participated in the marches and combats under General Sherman throughout the campaign which resulted in placing the Union army around Vicksburg in regular siege. On the 23d of May, the Brigade to which the Twelfth belonged, took position in the front line about a mile to the right of Fort Hill, and there remained taking full part in the siege about one month, when it marched sixteen miles to the rear of Vicksburg, with the Army of Observation under General Sherman. When, Vicksburg having fallen, the Expeditionary Army on the next day, moved out after the Rebel, General Johnson, the Twelfth Iowa marched with it, and took part in all its operations. On the 20th of July, they again turned their faces toward Vicksburg, and three days afterwards went into camp on Bear creek, fifteen miles east of the city, where they remained encamped on a fine plantation until the tenth of the following October, having only light picket duties to perform. On the 10th of October the regiment went with other troops in the direction of Canton, and had a slight skirmish at Brownsville, with no material loss to either side. The command returned and pitched tents eight miles in rear of Vicksburg, and remained there till the 10th of November.

Having been ordered to report to General Hurlburt, the regiment marched to Vicksburg and proceeded thence by steamer to Memphis, which place they reached about the middle of the month. In two or three days they moved on to Chewalla. Lieutenant-Colonel Stibbs took command of the post, and his regiment had charge of the railroad, as guard, for four miles east, and the same west of Chewalla. Here the regiment remained until near the close of January, 1864.

When, on the 28th of January, the Memphis and Charleston railway was ordered evacuated, the Twelfth moved thereon to its western terminus, and was there assigned again to the Vicksburg campaign, to go with General Sherman on the great Meridian raid. The division was delayed on the river; and when it reached Vicksburg, General Sherman's column had been some time on the forward march. On this account, the division was ordered to encamp near the Big Black river, and go forward with supplies when they should be ordered. The supplies were not ordered, for General Sherman returned from the raid early in March, having levied upon the country through which he passed for all the supplies he needed.

On the 4th of January, while at Chewalla, the regiment had mustered as a veteran organization all the men present with the command except about twenty, though there were others not present, who did not re-enlist, having re-enlisted—"a larger proportion," says Lieutenant-Colonel Stibbs, "than in any other regiment from the State." There being no pressing need of men in the field, they were ordered home for a thirty days' furlough. The regiment reported for duty at Davenport, on the 25th of April, and reached Memphis on the 2d of May, and, on that afternoon, arms, accoutrements and camp equipage were immediately drawn, and five companies marched out on picket the same night. The regiment pitched tents just outside the limits of the city.

The brigade to which the Twelfth regiment was attached, embraced now only one other Iowa regiment—the Thirty-fifth; the Eighth being ordered to remain at Memphis, as provost guard of the city, the Seventh Minnesota taking its place in the brigade, Colonel Woods commanding.

Early in June, the command was ordered to LaGrange, Tenn., repairing the railroad on the way, so that it might be useful as a line of communication to General Smith, about to commence offensive operations against the rebel troopers, Forrest and Lee, in Central Mississippi.

On the 5th of July the army rightwheeled from the railroad, and, marching by Ripley and Pontotoc, reached the vicinity of Tupelo in about one week, where there was fighting much of the time, day and night, on the 12th, 13th and 14th of July. On the 12th, the Twelfth regiment, being at the time guard of the train, was attacked by a brigade of rebels, eager for victory and plunder, and thinking both could be easily gained from the inferior force opposed to them. But never were men more mistaken. The regiment stood like a wall, from which the charge of the troopers rebounded as though springing from a consuming conflagration. No small force repelled a large force more bravely or more completely during the whole war. In the subsequent fighting of this brilliant campaign, wherein the rebels were thoroughly defeated and routed, the regiment bore a prominent part, fighting all the time with marked gallantry and efficiency, losing heavily in killed and wounded, and, at the close of the extended contest, receiving the special commendation of the General commanding the army.

The regiment returned to Memphis on the 24th of July, and there had a week's rest after active operations in the field, which might have entitled it to more, had the men wanted it.

On the 1st of August, the command started on another raid, moving by rail to Lumkin's Mills, and from whence it marched to Holly Springs, of which post, Lieutenant-Colonel Stibbs took command, with the Twelfth regiment on duty there.

Here, Companies A and F, which had been on detached service at the mouth of White river, rejoined the regiment on the 10th. The value of this detachment at this post had been very great to the Union. In consequence of which the rebels determined to attack the post and defeat and capture the garrison. Captain Hunter, in command, had ordered the building of a strong stockade at the post, but it was not completed when he received intelligence which led him to believe he would soon be attacked. The whole force was put to work on the stockade, on the 4th of June, and kept at work till midnight. At three o'clock, the next morning, they were attacked by Marmaduke's men, numbering nearly four hundred, under command of a Colonel. The two companies of the Twelfth numbered just forty-seven muskets. So sudden was the attack, that the men did not have time to dress themselves after the alarm was given, before the enemy was upon them. They sprang at once to arms, and fought in uniform which the wags called "shirt-tail regalia." The enemy delivered the attack with great spirit and determination, and a number of them, by a bold dash, gained the stockade on one side. Their success here would have resulted in the complete defeat of the garrison, but for one of those splendid acts of heroism, for which brave men in the olden times were apotheosized. Sergeant Isaac Cottle and Corporal George D. Hunter, of Company F, armed with revolvers, rushed out of the stockade and boldly attacked the rebels who had gained the works, firing rapidly, and making every shot tell. The enemy, no doubt thinking the sallying party embraced a considerable force, fled in confusion, but a random shot killed Corporal Hunter on the spot, and another wounded Sergeant Cottle, so that he died three weeks afterward. In three-quarters of an hour after the attack commenced, the rebels were repulsed in indiscriminate rout, with a loss of over fifty in killed, wounded and prisoners, the commanding officer being among the killed. Their dead and wounded were left on the field. Besides Hunter and Cottle, the loss of the garrison was four wounded.

The detachment was joyously welcomed back to the regiment in its camp at Holly Springs. The regiment returned to Memphis near the close of August.

On the first of September, intelligence was received that the rebels were blockading White river in Arkansas, and threatening communication with Little Rock and other posts held by our forces. General Mower was ordered to raise the blockade with his division of troops. He embarked on steamers the same day, and sailing down the Mississippi and up the White river to Duvall's Bluff, without meeting the enemy, marched to Brownsville, and here learned Price had gone north. He was ordered to pursue. Leaving Brownsville on the 17th, with ten days damaged rations, he marched by Searcy, Jacksonport and Pocahontas, Arkansas, and Poplar Bluffs, Greenville and Jackson, Missouri, to Cape Girardeau, a distance of three hundred and fifty miles in nineteen days, reaching the Cape on the 5th of October. Rain, mud, swamps, rivers and short rations—these were the obstructions in the way of this remarkable march. As an evidence of its severity, it may be stated that when the Twelfth Iowa, numbering two hundred and fifty rank and file reached Cape Girardeau, five officers and one hundred and one men were in their bare feet. Other regiments were in similar conditions, and perhaps there was not an officer or man in the column, who could have made a respectable appearance on dress parade.

On the 6th, the command embarked on steamers and went to St. Louis, remaining there only long enough to be supplied with clothing and necessary equipage. The troops were ordered to join General A. J. Smith in the pursuit of Price. The Twelfth went by steamer to Jefferson City, arriving there October 19th, and going the same day to Smithton. From this time until the 27th, it was with the army in hot pursuit of Price, most of the time near the enemy, but unable to overtake him, as he would not or could not, stand long enough against our cavalry for the infantry to come up. On the 30th, the countermarch commenced, and on the 15th of November, the regiment reached St. Louis, where Colonel Woods and the non-veterans were mustered out, their time having expired.

Having been ordered to join General Thomas at Nashville, the regiment arrived at that place on the 1st of December, and at once went into position two miles south of the city. It fought with a gallantry, especially on the battle field of the 15th and 16th, and bore its share during the siege against the capitol. The good behavior of the men on this glorious field received warm commendations in the official reports of both brigade and division commanders, which were all the more valuable, from the fact that there was not a commissioned officer in the line. The companies were commanded by Sergeants and Corporals. During the fight the regiment captured two flags from the enemy, for which Luther Kaltenbach, Company F, and private Andrew J. Sloan of Company H, were presented with medals by the Secretary of War.

In pursuit of Hood, the Twelfth proceeded to Eastport, Miss., arriving there on the 7th of January, 1865. Here, it assisted in building quarters and extensive fortifications, and then betook itself to a vigorous and well-earned rest after its active seven months' campaign.

About the middle of February, the Twelfth left Eastport for New Orleans, and there embarked, with the forces under Major-General Canby, on the expedition against Mobile, which resulted so triumphantly to our arms. The regiment was in the front line of battle, on the morning of the 27th of March, when the army advanced against Spanish Fort. During most of the time of the siege — a period of thirteen days and nights — it was exposed to all kinds of missiles, from the minnie-ball and hard grenade up to the hundred-pound shell. Notwithstanding the tremendous cannonading by guns of both heavy and light calibre, not a man was killed, and only eight wounded. The enemy evacuated on the night of the 8th of April, and our army entered Mobile in triumph on the following day. From here they marched to Montgomery, distant 175 miles, where they remained one week, and then marched to Selma, where intelligence was received of the surrender of Lee, and the assassination of the President, in the hour of the Nation's triumph and gladness.

Intelligence of the surrender of Johnson was also soon received, which event having practically closed the war, the active operations of the regiment were forever ended.

THIRTEENTH INFANTRY.

(Unassigned.)
Utley, Matthew S.

FOURTEENTH INFANTRY.

COMPANY C.

Sergeants:
John Braden,　　Henry Beckwith.

Corporals:
Henry P. Consadine,　Theodore L. Cotton,
Frank S. Inman,　　Hudson D. Cook,
Valentine L. Spawr.

HISTORY OF BUTLER COUNTY.

Privates:
Boylan, William H., Dawson, Martin,
Bird, Ely, Halsted, William R.,
Burger, George, Myers, Uriah,
Boylan, Cornelius, Margritz, John H.,
Cummins, John R., McAlister, Asahel P.,
Chitester, Miles, Stewart, Charles,
Cook, Augustus A., Winchell, Lyford H.,
Cook, Hudson D, Wetsel, James T.,
Couch, Manderville, Wetsel, Thomas C.

A history of this regiment is given in connection with the Butler county war chapter.

FIFTEENTH INFANTRY.
COMPANY H.
Allen, David C., Bartholomew, Ezra,
Allen, James W., Park, John W. (or M.),
Webster, Wheeler R.

EIGHTEENTH INFANTRY.
COMPANY H.
Corporal:
Edmon B. Brown.

TWENTY-FIRST INFANTRY.
COMPANY A.
Sergeants:
Daniel Haine, Aaron Moss.
Corporal:
Ransom H. Gile.
Privates:
Hall, William, Inman, Walter,
Hart, Francis, Moss, Jacob,
Sturtz, John.

THIRTY-SECOND INFANTRY.
COMPANY B.
Privates:
Falsom, Jacob G., McDonald, Archibald,
Needham, Edward E.

COMPANY C.
Privates:
Gilbert, Mills B

COMPANY D.
Privates:
Bourguin, Louis

COMPANY E.
Captain:
John R. Jones.
First Lieutenant:
Alonzo Converse.
Second Lieutenant:
John F. Wright.
Sergeants:
John F. Wright, Samuel German,
Marshall Kelly, Ovid Hare,
William H. Guy, Edward A. Glenn,
Samuel E. Hayden.
Corporals:
William M. Martin, Alexander March,
Wesley H. Long, Clark Speedy,
Robert Stanley, Albert O. Royce,
Robert Inman. Jacob Hinkle.
Musicians:
William H. Burham, John Burham.
Wagoner:
Nathan Olmstead.
Privates:
Ackerman, Lawrence, Kimmel, Bacheus F.,
Asprey, Joseph, Ketchem, William H.,
Albright, Elias D., Leverich, James P.,
Broque, Mordecai B., Langdon, John B.,
Blackman, Anson, Lewis, Charles,
Blass, John W., Lewis, Wilbert L.,
Blackman, E. W., March, William,
Bolton, George, Mead, Rollins P.,
Brookman, Albert H., Mix, William N.,
Burgess, Eli S., Mix, Charles E.,
Brannic, Francis, Newcomb, Orlando S,
Billhimer, Henry, Needham, Edward E.,
Copeland, George R, Needham, Perrin O.,
Conner, John N., Olmstead, Robert L.,
Codner, Oliver, Orvis, Franklin E.,

Codner, George G.,
Churchill, James N.,
Collins, Henry C.,
Clayton, Dow,
Dunning, Abram,
Dunning, William H.,
Dodge, Mordecai,
Dickisson, John,
Ede, Richard T.,
Ferris, Theodore H.,
Foster, Francis G.,
Flood, William,
Griffith, John W.,
Hartman, Matthew,
Henderson, David M.,
Hedrick, Moses,
Hannant, Robert,
Howard, James N.,
Hall, Calvin,
Hites, Elijah,
Houck, Thomas,
Hinkle, Jacob,
High, Isaac,
Hough, Nehemiah R.,
Jones, Nathan,
Jones, Henry O.,
Knight, Hinkley,
Kimmel, George W.,
Olmstead, Wallace W.,
Olmstead, Theodore,
O'mstead, Oren P.,
Putnam, Fletcher C.,
Plummer, Daniel C.,
Parrot, Jasper,
Peck, Josiah,
Quimby, John,
Quinn, James W.,
Roberts, Benjamin,
Rockwell, Myron,
Royce, Anos O.,
Sumner, John C.,
Sperry, James N.,
Sowash, George,
Stockdale, William,
Sperry, John,
Smith, James,
Thomas, Henry,
Turner, Jesse,
Whitney, Samuel B.,
Williams, William H.,
Wilson, Ezra S.,
Wilcox, Austin,
Wheeler, Solomon,
Waters, Julius A.,
Williams, George H.,
Zelmer, George E.

COMPANY F.

Champlin, William R., Pierce, Moses,
Yaw, Marcellus.

COMPANY G.

Captain:
Charles A. L. Roszell.

First Lieutenant:
Charles A. Bannon.

Second Lieutenant:
Daniel Haine.

Sergeants:
William Poisall.

Corporals:
John McCain,
Daniel W. Kinsley,
Emanuel Surfus,
Roselle Kane,
Uriah Farlow,
George H. Burton,
James Butler.

Musicians:
Archison Wilson.

Wagoner:
J. Rush Brown.

Privates;
Anderson, Benj.,
Allen, Sylvester,
Allen, William V.,
Allen, George L.,
Bishop, Harvey A.,
Boon, Sylvester M.,
Broogg, Sylvester W.,
Boon, Warren,
Boon, Sidney W.,
Boon, James H.,
Burton, George H.,
Bishop, William C.,
Boggs, Albert,
Babcock, Joseph,
Brooks, Henry,
Beetles, David,
Clawson, Phineas,
Cavo, William R.,
Carter, James H.,
Cline, Michael,
Cosson, Wilbur C.,
Clark, Mortimore O.,
Clark, Daniel N.,
Doty, Aaron,
Davis, Nathaniel W.,
Dockstader, Josiah,
Ellis, Andrew,
Forney, John C.,
Farlow, George,
Farlow, Leander,
Goodhue, James M.,
Goodhue, S. Newell,
Graver, Seth H.,
Harrison, DeWitt C.,
Harter, Aaron M.,
Hardman, James L.,
Kane, Roselle,
Keller, Richard,
Lenhart, John,
Martin, John,
Mafflt, Apollos W.,
Miller, Francis M.,
Miller, Elias,
Miller, James M.,
Muffler, William,
McClellan, George,
Miller, George G.,
Modlin, Isaac N.,
Phillipi, Jehu,
Phillipi, James M.,
Poisall, George C.,
Poisall, Hiram,
Phillips, Joel,
Smith, Henry,
Straum, Jabez,
Strutz, Solomon,
Strutz, Michael,
Strutz, Adam,
Straum, Nicholas,
Svim, John D.,
Sheffer, James M.,
Thomas, Charles N.,
Upps, John,
Warner, Daniel D.,
Wamsly, Martin V.,
Whitted, Oliver P.,
Whitter, Baltzer.

COMPANY H.

Sergeants:
James H. Hall.

Privates:
Beecher, Albert R., Hesse, Stephen,
Considine, Peter, Robinson, Solomon,
Yost, Josiah W.

COMPANY UNKNOWN.
Lenhart, Washington

THIRTY-SECOND INFANTRY.

The companies forming the Thirty-second Infantry, Iowa Volunteers, were recruited in the counties composing the Sixth Congressional District, during the latter part of the summer and early fall of 1862. They rendezvoused at Camp Franklin, near Dubuque. Here, on October 6th, they were sworn into the service of the United States for three years; John Scott, of Story county, being Colonel; E. H. Mix, of Butler, Lieutenant-Colonel; G. A. Eberhart, of Black Hawk, Major; Charles Aldrich, of Hamilton, Adjutant. Here it remained under drill and dicipline till about the middle of the following month. The barracks at Camp Franklin were uncomfortable in cold weather, of which, unhappily, there was much about this time. Measles of a malignant type broke out in camp, the exposed condition of which, the unfavorable weather and the want of sufficient clothing, conspiring to make the disease unusually fatal.

From the 14th to the 18th of November, the regiment, numbering about 920, embarked by detachments for St. Louis, reporting there on the 21st, and going into quarters at Benton Barracks. Here it remained a few days, when, under orders from Major-General Curtis, six companies under Colonel Scott proceeded to New Madrid, Missouri, and the remaining four companies, under Major Eberhart, went no further down the river than Cape Girardeau. The separation of the regiment thus effected on the last day of the autumn of 1862, continued until the spring of 1864.

It was a prolific cause of annoyance and extraordinary labor. The details required of a regiment were frequently demanded from each of these commands; stores sent to the regiment would sometimes go to the detachment, sometimes to head-quarters, when they should have gone just the other way; the mails were in an interminable tangle. The companies at head-quarters were: Company B, Company C, Company E, Company H, Company I and Company K. The companies under Major Eberhart were, A, D, F, and G.

The history of the regiment during this long period of separation must necessarily be two-fold. It will not be improper to write first, an account of the detachment under command of Major Eberhart,

In obedience to the order of General Curtis, they proceeded to Cape Girardeau, and the Major assumed command of that post, on the 1st of December, 1862. The garrison consisted of these companies, and one company of the Second Missouri Heavy Artillery. Here they remained during the winter, performing provost and garrison duties. On the 10th of March the garrison was re-enforced by the First Nebraska Volunteers, and preparations commenced for a march into the interior. On March 14th Major Eberhart marched his detachment to Bloomfield, accompanying a regiment of Wisconsin cavalry, and a battery of Missouri artillery, where they remained until the 21st of April, when they moved to Dallas, forty-six miles northward. The march was by a circuitous route, requiring sixty miles travel.

The Rebel General Marmaduke, now threatened Cape Girardeau with a considerable army. He himself was at Fredericktown, northwest of Dallas, while another was coming up the Bloomfield road. General McNeil, commanding the Union forces, marched at once to Cape Girardeau, by Jackson. The detachment of the Thirty-second, guarding the train, marched from Dallas to Jackson, a distance of twenty-two miles, in less than six hours, and reached Cape Girardeau on the evening of the 24th. The next day Marmaduke, with a force of 8,000 men, invested the place. At 10 o'clock at night he sent a flag of truce, with a demand of unconditional surrender, giving the Union commander thirty minutes for decision. General McNeil, by Colonel Strachan, who received the truce, sent back a flat refusal in one minute, and politely requested a credit of twenty-nine minutes by General Marmaduke. The attack, however, was not commenced until Sunday morning, the 26th, at 10 o'clock, when the rebels retired with considerable loss, just as General Vandever came down the river with re-enforcements for the garrison. In this combat, Major Eberhart's command was posted on the right, in support of a section of Meltfly's. Its loss was but one man, captured on picket. On the 28th the detachment of the Thirty-second was ordered to Bloomfield. Leaving Cape Girardeau at 5 o'clock in the afternoon, it marched fifty miles by dark the next evening, and went into camp near Castor river. Completing the bridge over this stream, it returned to the Cape, reaching that post on the 5th of May. Here it remained on garrison duty till the 11th of July, when it again marched for Bloomfield. Having remained there a few days, at work on the fortifications, it was attached to the Reserve Brigade, First Cavalry Division, Department of the Missouri, and on the 19th started on the memorable march, which ended with the capture of Little Rock, Arkansas.

The command reached Clarendon on the 8th of August. Early on the morning of the 13th the detachment started up White river. The expedition lasted three days, and was quite a brilliant success. The fleet went up White river to the mouth of the Little Red river, and then proceeded up that stream to the town of Searcy, where two steamers were captured and a pontoon bridge destroyed. When ten miles below Searcy, on the return, the fleet was attacked by three hundred rebels, who directed their principal fire on the prize, "Kaskaka," which was manned by half of Company D, under Lieutenant William D. Templin. The steamer was near the shore from which the attack was directed, but made a gallant defense. The rebels were driven off with a loss of more than twenty killed. The loss in Company D was one killed and five wounded. Before reaching White river the fleet was again attacked, but the assailants were quickly driven off, with loss, and without any casualty on board. Large quantities of public property were destroyed, and a number of prisoners captured during the expedition. In the heavy skirmish at Bayou Metoe, on the 27th, the detachment was engaged, losing one killed and two wounded.

The day the command reached "Dead Man's Lake"—the scorching heat of that day, the parched ground marched over, the air at times filled with the flying dust—is one not easily to be forgotten. The stagnant pond bearing that name was covered with a green scum, yet the men, burning with thirst, plunged in and drank greedily of the filthy water.

The two trips from Duvall's Bluffs to Brownsville, as guard to the cavalry train, were trips of hard marching in hot weather, and of suffering for water for man and beast, and from dust and heat. The sick on this march certainly received no extra care—at first shipped to Helena, and then to Clarendon, on the White river.

About the 21st of August a small steamer, a side-wheeler, sailed up the White river loaded with sick and convalescent soldiers. It was one of the hottest of August days in this climate, when she ran from Clarendon to Duvall's Bluffs, forty-five miles, in four hours. Not a spot on that boat, from the border deck to the hurricane deck, but was covered by a sick man. Sick men were piled away on that hurricane deck in the broiling sun, wherever a man could be laid. Is it any wonder, on that run of about four hours, twenty-six men died on that boat?—one of them a corporal of Company G (Carter).

On the 25th of August another march of twenty-six miles across those prairies of Prairie county, Arkansas. About 11 o'clock that night we filed into the little court house yard at Brownsville. Just as we filed in, General Davidson stepped to the fence and said, "Boys, lie down quickly and take some rest, for I will need you at an early hour." Then turning to another officer, he said, "These brave boys have marched 500 miles, and kept up with my cavalry." By 3 o'clock next morning we were astir, and at 4 were in line and on the move. A march of nine miles brought us to the rebel outposts, skirmishing three and a half miles to the brow of the hill, and after manouvering, etc., half a mile to the bank of "Bayou Metaire." The whole movement during the day was only a bushwhacking affair. In the evening we fell back to the top of the hill to support a battery. There dark found us. The battery and all other troops had left. One detachment alone was on the field, with the rebels closing around us, when we withdrew and fell back that night to a corn-field near Brownsville; and about 1 o'clock at night, at the word "halt," the boys dropped on the ground, and lay down between corn rows. No alignment encampment was made. The night was dark, as *dense black clouds* o'respread the sky, and soon the rain came down in torrents; but there the boys lay—what else could they do? About 9 A. M. it broke away; but, oh! the *mud, mud!* We had no rations, but soon found a patch of sweet potatoes, and had a sweet potato breakfast.

The detachment remained two days in camp in the timber near, and then moved to the old cavalry camp north of town, where our sick boys had been kept in a double log house on the edge of the prairie, and at a little grove of a few scattering oaks, and near a pond of stagnant water.

On the 31st of August, 1863, the day was very hot, and hence the train was ordered to go through to Duvall's Bluffs in the night. All the detachment was ordered to go as guard. The whole detachment able to go was ordered on the trip. We could raise only forty men, and some twelve or fifteen of them were unable to march, but were ordered to go, as they could be piled on the wagons, and could use their guns in case of an attack. This was a serious camp-ground to the detachment. A few days and not a well man was in that camp, and not many men able to care for the sick. It had been used as a cavalry camp until the very ground was crawling with filth. Every nook and corner of the old house, every spot on the floor, porch and hall, was covered by a sick man. Everything that could be done under the circumstances was done for the sick. But we were in advance of the main army and supplies. No sanitary or sutler supplies had reached us, and much of the ordinary soldiers' fare was unfit for use. Much of the "hard-tack" had *too much life*. I can now see some boys breaking their hard-tack into small bits, and blowing out the *things* of life.

On the 6th of October, occurred the first death. William A. Spurlin, one of the brightest and best of young men, was laid in an humble soldier's grave. On the 8th he was followed by Henry Cantonwine. On that day we moved to another camp south of town, in a nice little grove. One day's rest there, and the command was ordered to Little Rock. The sick were brought, and laid down on the sand in the hot sun before the old log tavern hospital. That very sand was crawling with "gray backs." As the command moved away, George Macy lay on a cot, under a little tree, dying, and soon another of the young men of our company, Wilson Bond, was added to that group of humble graves. There we laid four of the young men of our company, side by side.

> Their young lives were ended,
> Their young spirits fled,
> And now they are sleeping
> In peace with the dead.

Every spot in that old log tavern that could be occupied, was covered by a sick man. How many of those brave boys were buried in that little graveyard, I never knew.

On the removal of the detachment to Little Rock, it was relieved for a time from all guard or other duty, except the care of its own sick, by order of General Davidson, adding that the care of its own sick in camp, was all it was able to do. But death had then fastened his cold, icy hand upon a number of boys. Calvin M. Sayre, John L. Sayre, Jesse Shultz, Nathan R. Austin and Ira G. Christian were soon numbered with the dead. Little Rock proved to be a very healthy place for us, and while there the company, considering its reduced condition, improved rapidly. It may not be generally known that that Arkansas expedition of General Steele's, was one of the most destructive of life, of any campaign of the war. Steele' started with 1,200 men; he received re-enforcements of at least three brigades, making at least 15,000 effective men; 100 would cover all his loss in killed and wounded, and yet by the time he had possession of Little Rock, and was fairly settled down to his *gambling and horse racing*, he had barely 5,100 effective men fit for duty. And of General Steele I will say that he had no sympathy in common with a Union Soldier, save his opposition to the abstract idea of secession.

General McPherson, Medical Director, afterwards at Vicksburg, said that the sending of our four companies through on that campaign to keep up with the cavalry, was a burning shame, one of the outrages of the war, and no wonder the men were used up; they remained at Little Rock until the middle of October, when it moved to Benton, twenty-five miles distant. It returned to Little Rock, where they remained till January, 1864, when it started to Memphis, which place it reached on the 5th of February. Here it was ordered to report to Brigadier-General A. J. Smith at Vicksburg. It reached Vicksburg on the 9th, and remained there till the 27th, when it marched out to Black river to await the army on its return from the interior.

Meanwhile, Colonel Scott established his headquarters at New Madrid, and assumed command of the post. On the 17th of December, 1862, he sent out a detachment of one hundred men, under Capt. Peebles, who went as far as St. Francis river, bringing back several prisoners, much public property, and valuable information.

On the 28th of December, Colonel Scott destroyed the public property, and evacuated New Madrid, by order of General Davies, after which he proceeded to Fort Pillow, reaching there on the 29th. They remained at Fort Pillow for nearly six months, in the performance of garrison duties. The command embarked for Columbus, Kentucky, on the 17th and 18th of June, 1863, in detachments, and went into camp there on the 19th, and there regimental headquarters remained for more than seven months, Col. Scott being most of the time in command of the post.

On July 10, Union City, in Tennessee, was captured by the rebels. The command hastened to that place, but arrived too late to find the enemy. After burying the dead and caring for the wounded they returned. The command was soon afterward again divided into fractions. Companies B and I, under command of Captain Millier, alone remained at regimental headquarters; Company C was attached to the Fourth Missouri Cavalry; Company E was placed at Fort Quimby, not far from Columbus, whilst Companies H and K, Captain Bensen commanding, proceeded down the river to Island No. 10. From this time forth until January, 1864, the history of each of these detachments, except that of Company C, is devoid of remarkable events. This detachment was actively employed during most of this period, and the labors of officers and men were arduous in the extreme. They scouted a wide extent of country infested by guerrillas, marched oftentimes a considerable distance from Columbus, going out in all weather, by night as often as by day. They braved many perils and endured many hardships.

In the month of January, 1864, these six companies were brought together and soon embarked for Vicksburg, where they were assigned to the Second Brigade. Perhaps there was not a single organization in the whole army under Major General Sherman that so gladly commenced that singular campaign as the one under Colonel Scott. If the battalion left Vicksburg joyfully, its return was still more joyful, for here were found Major Eberhart and his four companies, and the whole regiment was together for the first time since November, 1862. The re-union brought great satisfaction to officers and men. Shortly after, the regiment was ordered to the Department of the Gulf, and there accompanied the disastrous Red river expedition.

In this expedition the Thirty-second Iowa suffered more severely, perhaps, than any other regiment. It formed a part of General A. J. Smith's command, consisting of ten thousand infantry and three batteries of artillery, which left Vicksburg, March 9, on transports, accompanied by gunboats. At the mouth of the Red river this fleet was joined by Admiral D. D. Porter, with a large fleet, including several iron-clads. The fleet entered Red river by the southern stream and passed thence into Achafalaya, proceeding as far as Semmesport, where the troops disembarked on the night of the 13th and immediately commenced a march on Fort De Russey. No halt was ordered till the army had marched some seven miles. It was twenty-eight miles, from here to Fort De Russey. Nevertheless the army marched that distance the next day, constantly harrassed by rebel cavalry; delayed once two hours at a stream over which a bridge had to be made; attacked the fort and carried it by storm before sundown and before the gunboats had arrived. In this assault the Thirty-second was on the right, and "the men on the right took the fort," said the prisoners. Colonel Shaw, commanding the brigade, speaks in unqualified praise of all the officers and men in his command. The loss was slight on either side. Of the Thirty-second, one man was killed and two were wounded.

At Fort De Russey they re-embarked and proceeded to Alexandria, where the troops again disembarked and remained nearly two weeks. At this point the column under General Smith formed a junction with the column which had marched from New Orleans. The boats could not be taken over the rapids while laden, so the troops marched to Cotile Landing, some twenty-five miles up the river. Here our regiment had its first battalion drill, with all the companies in line, since leaving Dubuque, in November, 1862. On April 3 the command again embarked and reached Grand 'Ecore on the next evening, where it remained till the morning of the 7th, when it marched to the front of the battle of Pleasant Hill, where the brigade to which the Thirty-second belonged, commanded by Colonel Shaw, of the Fourteenth Iowa, stood the brunt of the fight, being the first in the battle, fighting longer than any other, in the hardest of the contest, the last to leave the field, and losing three times as many officers and men as any brigade engaged.

"Of Colonel John Scott, Thirty-second Iowa," says the brigade commander, "it is sufficient to say that he showed himself worthy to command the Thirty-second Iowa Infantry—a regiment which, after having been entirely surrounded and cut off from the rest of the command, with nearly one-half of its number killed or wounded, among them many of the best and prominent officers, forced its way through the enemy's lines, and was again in line, ready and anxious to meet the foe, in less than thirty minutes." It is certain no regiment ever fought with a sublimer courage than did the Thirty-second on the battle-field of Pleasant Hill. Its heroism and its sacrifices were worthy of a better fate than a retreat from the scene of its splendid daring and its glory. The fame of its gallant conduct spread all over Iowa, as it would have spread over the whole country had the commanding General accepted the victory which the troops had given him. But sad losses befell the regiment. Lieutenant-Colonel Mix was slain on the field, also many of the officers were either slain or wounded. The regiment lost, in all, two hundred and ten officers and men, killed, wounded and missing; most of the missing were also wounded—any so reported, no doubt slain. Iowa gloried in the fame of her honored sons, and wept for their dead comrades who fell on the stricken field. The following beautiful lines were written by Mrs. Caroline A. Soule, upon hearing of the sad losses sustained by the Thirty-second at Pleasant Hill:

> Cold are the sleepers
> Wrapt in their shrouds—
> Pale are the weepers
> The battle has bowed;
> Softly they slumber,
> Our soldiers in death—
> While hearts without number
> Cry, with hushed breath—
> O God, are they dead!
>
> Pale are the sleepers,
> Like marble they lie—
> Sad are the weepers,
> Tear-stained their eyes;
> Quiet they slumber,
> Soldiers entombed,
> While hearts without number,
> All shrouded in gloom,
> Cry—O, are they gone!
>
> Calm are the sleepers,
> Taking their rest—
> Sad are the weepers,
> Joyless their breasts;
> Softly they slumber,
> Our soldiers to-day,
> While hearts without number
> Cry, only this way
> Can our battles be won?

Colonel Shaw's brigade covered the retreat of the army to Grand 'Ecore, when the Thirty-second Regiment, after a movement up Red river to aid the fleet in escaping from eminent peril, went into encampment. It joined in the retreat down the Red river on the 21st, and frequently met light bodies of the enemy in skirmish. The retreat from Alexandria to the Mississippi was also harassed by the enemy, and considerable skirmishing took place at Bayou La Morge, Marksville and Bayou de Glaize, in both of which the regiments took part. Colonel Shaw in his report of the latter battle, says to "Colonel Gilbert, Twenty-seventh Iowa, Major Eberhart of the Thirty-second Iowa, Captain Crane of the Fourteenth Iowa, and their commands, is due the safety of the army. Had they failed to move into the position assigned them (although a difficult one, that of changing front under fire) with less celerity, or failed to hold it steadily after taking it, our left and rear would have been enveloped by overwhelming numbers, and nothing could have saved us—not even the fighting qualities of the Sixteenth Army Corps."

The regiment reached Memphis on the 10th of June, from there the command moved to Moscow, and thence to La Grange in the latter part of June. From this point it marched with General Smith's forces on the Tupelo campaign. It returned to Memphis, and having encamped there about ten days, joined in the Oxford expedition. The next active campaign in which the Thirty-second took part, was in Missouri in the pursuit of Price. It was a campaign of severe marching, but not of battle. The regiment marched at least six hundred and fifty miles, averaging twenty miles a day. It marched across the State and back again. Halting a few days at St. Louis, it moved to Cairo by steamer, arriving November 27th.

From here it moved to Nashville, which was soon afterwards besieged by the rebel General Hood. In the battle of Nashville, December 15th and 16th, the Thirty-second, fighting in General Gilbert's Brigade, was warmly engaged, and won great credit for daring, efficient behavior. It captured a battery of five guns and many prisoners, and lost about twenty-five killed and wounded. With the pursuit of the defeated rebels, closed the campaigning of the regiment for the year 1864, in face of the enemy.

Early in 1865, the regiment marched to Clifton, Tennessee, whence it moved by steamer to Eastport, Mississippi. Its next and last campaign, was that of Mobile under Major-General E. R. S. Canby. It remained in Alabama some time after the fall of Mobile, and was mustered out at Clinton, Iowa, August 24, 1865. Returning to Iowa, the Thirty-second Iowa was in due time disbanded, the officers and men receiving everywhere along the line of their journey, the kind greetings and hearty welcome of a grateful people, whose hearts had been with them through all their hardships.

THIRTY-EIGHTH INFANTRY.

COMPANY B.
Musician:
Cassius P. Inman.

A history of this regiment will be found in connection with the history of Bremer county.

FORTY-FIRST REGIMENT.

COMPANY A.
Sergeant:
Edward C. Bristol.
Corporal:
Campbell McClen.
Privates:

Baker, Albert C.,
Daily, Anthony,
Gilbert, James W.,
Harris, Benjamin,
Mann, Isaac B.,
Pattee, Adam C.,
Smith, Isaac,
Smith, Benjamin,
Smith, Orrin,
Wemple, Philip.

FORTY-FOURTH INFANTRY.

COMPANY E.
Captain:
Hugh F. L Burton.
Sergeants:
Hiram W. Babcock,
Edward Nutting,
Orin F. Shaw,
George A. Mead.
Corporals:
Amos G. Waters,
William Farlow,
Eliphalet W. Ensign,
John C. Jerome,
Milo E. Mather,
Ezra Winship,
Willet A. Willis.
Musicians:
Henry F. Blakenship, George Adair.
Wagoner:
John L. Eddy.
Privates:

Ackerson, Joseph,
Alexander, Frank E.,
Colver, Walter J.,
Dobbins, George P.,
Edson, William,
Fulsom, Lewis L.,
Fague, Calvin J.,
Goodhue, James M.,
Guthrie, Thomas E,
Gilmore, Samuel,
Hilton, Seth,
Mather, Milo E.,
Mills, Adarian D,
Orvis, Fletcher L.,
Overacker, Ransom P.,
Parthemer, Arthur A.,
Porter, George L.,
Spawn, Marion,
Smith, Oliver J.,
Scribner, John W,
Surdevant, Harvey B.,
Tibbles, James,

Harmon, Charles R., Voltz, Ferdinand,
Hopkins, Harvey H., Wright, Eugene A.,
Hunt, Hiram T., Wieser, Andrew,
Kenison, Solvin S., Wheeler, John,
Kenison, George, Walter, John W.,
Low, Walter W., Willett, Aaron B.,
Maxwell, John E., Wilcox, Jacob.

The Forty-fourth Regiment was one hundred day men, and contained eight hundred and sixty-seven officers and men. It was mustered at Davenport, the 1st of June, 1864, with Stephen H. Henderson as colonel.

FORTY-SEVENTH INFANTRY.

COMPANY E.
Corporal:
Leonidas L. Lush.

SECOND CAVALRY.

COMPANY E.
Corporal:
Herman Margaretz.

COMPANY I.
Surfus, Abraham.

ADDITIONAL TO COMPANY A.
Dunham, Alfred G., Hunter, David H.

SEVENTH CAVALRY.

COMPANY D.
Quartermaster Sergeant—Orville H. Hammond.

COMPANY K.
Privates:
Baker, Albert C., Mann, Isaac B.,
Gilbert, James W., Smith, Isaac A.,
Harris, Benjamin P., Smith, Benjamin,
Leffler, Godfrey, Smith, Orin C.,
Wemple, Philip.

VETERANS.
Sergeant:
Edward C. Bristol.
Corporal:
Campbell McLean.
Privates:
Baker, Albert C., Mann, Isaac B.,
Daily, Anthony, Smith, Isaac A.,
Gilbert, James M., Smith, Benjamin F.,
Harris, Lord M., Smith, Orrin C.,
Leffler, Godfrey, Wemple, Philip.

EIGHTH CAVALRY.

COMPANY G.
Corporal:
James J. Phillips.
Privates:
DeWitt, Charles E. D., Marquand, Charles H.,
Hickle, Alfred, Quillen, William,
Hodgson, Samuel, Tharp, Washington.

NINTH CAVALRY.

COMPANY G.
Captain:
S. B. Cunningham.
Corporal:
Nathaniel N. Simpson.
Privates:
Cramer, Adam W., Daniels, Alfred,
Caldwell, Stephen S., Daniels, Lemuel.

THIRD BATTERY.

The Third Battery, more generally known, perhaps, as the "Dubuque Battery," was organized at the city of Dubuque, in the month of August, 1861.

Captain M. M. Hayden was in command. This battery distinguished itself at Pea Ridge. Afterwards, its principal battle was that of Helena, where it won high praise. It was subsequently engaged in the campaign of Arkansas.

THIRD BATTERY IOWA LIGHT ARTILLERY.

Corporals:
Seymour Brookman, Harvey Quinn.

Musicians:
Joseph Waters, Orvell O. Williams.

Artificers:
Zur H. Graves, William H. Bisbee.

Privates:
Baker, John N., Kelly, John F.,
Brooksland, Albert, Martin, Charles S.
Brown, Andrew H., Maxwell, George W,
Clark, William H. H., Owens, John D,
Daniels, Samuel A., Owens, Ludlow D.,
Davis, William W., Owens, Chancy F.,
Dawson, William, Overacker, Henry D.,
Dockstader, L. F., Richardson, Wm. H.,
Folsom, Daniel, Wright, Samuel J.,
Hyde, Charles B., Wells, Sidney H.,
Hall, Lewis G., Yocum, Christopher.

VETERANS.

Sergeants:
Charles S. Martin, Hiland H. Weaver.

Corporals:
Nathan W. Aplington, William H. Main.

Bugler:
Joseph S. Waters.

Privates:
Brooksland, Albert, Hall, Lewis G.
Bisbee, William H., Owen John D.,
Folsom, Daniel, Quinn, Harvey.

IOWA SOLDIERS IN MISSOURI REGIMENTS.

ENGINEER REGIMENT OF THE WEST.

COMPANY F.

Hawley, Gustave, Mullins, William N.,
Stewart, John L.

ROLL OF HONOR.

The following comprises a list of those gallant soldiers who left their homes, their wives and babies and took up the musket for the defense of their country's honor, never to return, finding graves in southern soil; who laid down their lives in defense of the Union. "It is sweet and honorable to die for one's country," should be engraved over the grave of each in characters that will perpetuate throughout all coming time and proclaim to the future generations their noble sacrifice:

Lieutenant John Braden, died of wounds at Rolla, Missouri. October 31, 1864.
Lieutenant Edward H. Mix, killed in battle, April 9, 1864, at Pleasant Hill, Louisiana.
Ahrens, John, died at Macon, Georgia, September 25, 1862.
Allen, Sylvester E., died September 26, 1863, at Brownsville, Arkansas.
Blackman, Anson, died March 3, 1865, at Nashville, Tennessee.
Burgess, Eli S., died March 7, 1863, at Fort Pillow, Tennessee.
Bird, William O., died at Macon, Georgia, September 29, 1862.
Booram, John, died June 29, 1862, at Corinth, Mississippi.
Blass, John W., killed in battle, April 9, 1864, at Pleasant Hill, Louisiana.
Burton, George H., killed April 9, 1864, at Pleasant Hill, Louisiana.

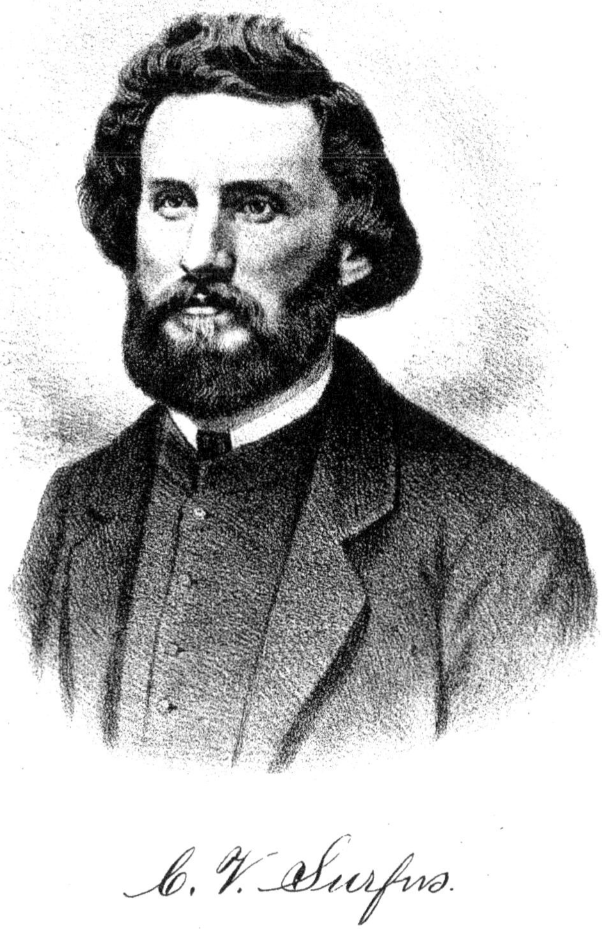

Boon, Sylvester M., died January 3, 1863, at Cape Girardeau, Missouri.

Boon, James H., died September 26, 1863, at Little Rock, Arkansas.

Babcock, Joseph, died June 5, 1864, at Pleasant Hill, Louisiana.

Brooksland, Albert, died September 5, 1865, at Fort Smith.

Considine, Peter, died at Keokuk, December 5, 1862, of typhoid fever.

Champlain, William R., died May 21, 1864, at Pleasant Hill, Louisiana, of wounds.

Clawson, Phineas, died June 5, 1864, at Memphis, Tennessee.

DeWitt, Stephen, killed April 6, 1862, at Shiloh, Tennessee, in battle.

Dodge, Mordecai, died March 5, 1864, at Columbus, Kentucky.

Daniels, Alfred, died March 2, 1864, at Benton Barracks, Missouri.

De Moss, James, died October 10, 1862, at Corinth, Mississippi, of wounds.

Davis, William W., killed July 14, 1863.

Dockstader, Leonard T., died August 24, 1865, at Little Rock, Arkansas.

Ferris, Theodore H., died April 26, 1863, at Fort Pillow, Tennessee.

Farlow, Uriah, died July 1, 1864, at Cedar Falls.

Horsington, Hiram, died at Atlanta, Georgia. June 30, 1862.

Hopkins, Harvey W., died at Memphis, Tennessee, September 19, 1864.

Hogdson, Samuel, died May 7, 1865, at St. Louis, Missouri.

Halstead, William R., died July 8, 1864, at Memphis, Tennessee.

Henderson, David M., died March 12, 1865, at Davenport.

Hites, Elijah, killed April 9, 1864, at Pleasant Hill, Louisiana.

Hough, Nehemiah R., died June 4, 1864, at Vicksburg, Mississippi.

Hesse, Stephen, died February 9, 1863, at Fort Pillow, Tennessee.

Inman, Cassius, died September 13, 1863, at New Orleans, Louisiana.

Johnson, Charles, died September 11, 1862, at Macon, Georgia, of starvation, while prisoner of war.

Kelly, Marshall, died at New Madrid, December 21, 1862.

Kimmel, George W., died March 8, 1863, at Fort Pillow, Tennessee.

Kimmel, Zacheus F., died April 5, 1863, at Fort Pillow, Tennessee.

Leverich, Willard, killed March 7, 1862, at Pea Ridge.

Long, Wesley H., died April 27, 1864, at New Orleans, Louisiana.

Lewis, Charles, died September 16, 1864, at Tyler, Texas, while prisoner of war.

Lewis, Wilbert L., killed April 9, 1864, at Pleasant Hill, in battle.

Mason, George, died at St. Louis, January 25, 1862.

Martin, Henry, killed June 23, 1863, at Vicksburg, Mississippi.

Mix, Thomas M., killed September 17, 1861, at Blue Mills, Missouri.

Myers, Philip B., died of wounds received at Atlanta, Georgia, August 1, 1864.

Myers, John M., killed March 7, 1862, at Pea Ridge, Arkansas, in action.

McCain, John, died September 12, 1863, at Brownsville, Arkansas.

Miller, Francis M., died January 20, 1863, at Cape Girardeau, Missouri.

Miller, Elias G., died December 12, 1863, at Benton, Arkansas.

Nutting, Edmond, died at Memphis, June 29, 1864.

Olmstead, Robert L., died April 20, 1864, at Pleasant Hill, Louisiana, of wounds.

Parks, George, died of wounds received at Matamora, Tennessee, October 18, 1862.

Panley, Charles, died at Huntsville Missouri, February 13, 1862.

Parriott, Jasper, killed April 9, 1864, at Pleasant Hill, Louisiana.

Phillippi, Jehu, killed April 9, 1864, at Pleasant Hill, Louisiana.

Pierce, Moses, died July 14, 1864, at Cairo, Illinois.

Spears, William, died of chronic diarrhœa, November 10, 1864, at Sedalia, Missouri.

Surfus, Emanuel, died at Camp Franklin, November 6, 1862.

Sheffer, James M., died July 8, 1864, at Memphis, Tennessee.

Smith, Isaac A., died March 10, 1865, at Spirit Lake

Stockdale, William, died March 4, 1864, at Mound City, Illinois.

Smith, James, died July 24, 1863, at Columbus, Kentucky.

Sperry, James U., died February 8, 1864, at Vicksburg, Mississippi.

Swim, John B., killed April 9, 1864, at Pleasant Hill, Louisiana.

Sturtz, Solomon, died June 6, 1864, at Vicksburg, Mississippi.

Sturtz, Michael, died November 3, 1864, at Little Rock, Arkansas.

Sturtz, Adam, died May 22, 1864, at Pleasant Hill, Louisiana.

Sturdevant, Harvey B., died August 30, 1864, at Keokuk.

Thomas, Henry, died March 4, 1863, at Fort Pillow, Tennessee.

Winchell, Lyford, died at Shell Rock, Butler county, Iowa, November 12, 1863.

Wilson, Ezra S., died May 19, 1863, at Fort Pillow, Tennessee.

Waters, Julius A., killed April 9, 1864, at Pleasant Hill, Louisiana.

Wamsly, Martin V., died June 26, 1864, at Tyler, Texas, while prisoner of war.

CHAPTER XVII.

OLD SETTLERS' SOCIETY.

This organization was effected in 1882, and is therefore so young that there is not much history connected with it. But we present the proceedings of the last two meetings in this connection, and from this, all information can be gleaned. The best and most prominent men in the county are taking an active interest in the matter, and the result will be that Butler county will have an Old Settlers' organization that will be second to none. All persons who have been residents of Butler county for fifteen years are eligible to membership in the society.

The following are the proceedings of the society at their first meeting.

OLD SETTLERS' MEETING.

Pursuant to a call of the president, the Old Settlers' Society of Butler county met in Clarksville, on Saturday, September 30, 1882.

The meeting was called to order by the president, G. W. Poisal.

It was moved and seconded that the constitution of the society be amended so as to read as follows:

The officers of this society shall consist of a President, sixteen Vice-Presidents (one in each township,) Secretary and Treasurer.
Carried.

The following officers were then elected for the ensuing year:
President, J. R. Jones.
Vice-Presidents:
  Fremont—S. Bonwell.
  Dayton—C. H. Forney.
  Coldwater—J. Hart.
  Bennezette—M. Wilson.
  Pittsford—J. Harlan.
  West Point—C. L. Jones.
  Jackson—Cyrus Doty.
  Shell Rock—J. H. Carter.
  Jefferson—Martin Bailey.
  Ripley—Henry Trotter.
  Madison—E. Coyle.
  Washington—M. Parrott.
  Monroe—J. M. Caldwell.
  Albion—Richard Daniels.
  Beaver—James Collar.
  Secretary, Cyrus Doty.
  Treasurer, G. W. Poisal.

The following resolution was adopted:
Resolved, That the president and vice-presidents appoint a committee to examine and correct the manuscript history of Butler county, which is now being prepared by S. J. Clarke and his corps of historians.

The meeting adjourned to meet at Harrison's Hall, in the village of Clarksville, on Saturday, October 14, 1882, at 1 o'clock P. M.
  Cyrus Doty, *Secretary.*

Shortly afterwards the following call was made for the meeting on October 14th, viz:

The Old Settlers' Society of Butler county will meet at Harrison's Hall, Clarksville, Saturday, October 14th, at 1 o'clock P. M. All persons residents of Butler county fifteen years, are eligible to membership in the society, and are therefore respectfully invited to attend.
  J. R. Jones, *President.*
Cyrus Doty, *Secretary.*

The society met as per adjournment, at Clarksville, and the following appeared as their proceedings:

OLD SETTLERS' MEETING.

On Monday, according to adjournment, the Old Settlers' Association met at Harrison's Hall.

The President called the meeting to order.

Minutes of last meeting read and approved.

The object of the meeting was for the ratification of the constitution and by-laws, and to more fully complete an organization.

J. J. Eichar was elected marshal.

On motion of Joseph Miller, the Old Settlers hold their first re-union at Clarksville on the fourth Thursday in May next, and that it be a basket pic-nic.

A committee of nine was appointed to assist in the revision of the History of Butler County, now being gotten up by S. J. Clarke.

Committee—J. J. Eichar, J. Perrin, J. W. Davis, Milton Wilson, J. H. Carter, Charles Ensign, James Griffith, W. R. Jamison, J. M. Caldwell.
  Cyrus Doty, *Secretary.*

NOTE.—We urge on all of the Old Settlers in the county to send their names to the secretary, or J. J. Eichar, with 25 cents as membership fee, and let us have an organization second to none.

CHAPTER XVIII.

ALBION TOWNSHIP.

This is one of the best townships of Butler county, lying in the southern tier. It is on Beaver river, which passes through it from west to east. Albion is a full Congressional township of about 23,040 acres, and embraces the territory technically known as township 90, range 16.

The land slopes from each way toward the center, and has a rolling tendency. The soil is a rich dark loam underlain with a sub-soil of clay. It is a prairie township, with but little timber; what there is being along the river. There is plenty of brick-clay but no stone. The soil is well adapted to raising the cereals, and the farmers, as a rule, are in prosperous condition. The facilities for stock raising in this vicinity are unexcelled, as the land along the Beaver is somewhat marshy, and furnishes excellent grazing land.

EARLY SETTLEMENT.

Albion township commenced its evolutions toward settlement and civilization in 1853, about the same time the other townships in Butler county. The first to come here with the determination to secure a permanent home, was Walter Clayton, who, in the spring of 1853, laid claim to the southeastern quarter of section 30. He came from Wisconsin, driving through with an ox team. His first work was to erect a little log cabin, where he remained in almost entire solitude, having left his wife in Wisconsin. He lived here for about six months, when Tom Mullarky jumped his claim and Clayton moved over the line into Monroe township, where he died some years ago. Clayton was a good hearted man, but very rough and quick tempered. He procured a divorce from his first wife, and married a woman in Butler county with whom he had been living. To the children of his first wife he was very abusive, and would take them often by the hair of the head and jerk and kick them in a most brutal manner. His ferocious quick temper finally was the cause of his death, producing heart disease. For a number of years he was prosperous, and made considerable money, keeping tavern in his little shanty, where the stages stopped. Often as many as twenty were accommodated in the one room, where, on account of the low ceiling, the guests were obliged to kneel while dressing.

The next settlers in Albion were the Turners, Abel and his father, although Abel was the only one to make this his permanent home. A short sketch of the life of Abel Turner is appended:

Abel Turner was one of the earliest settlers of Butler county, locating on section fourteen of Albion township, in the fall of 1853. He was born in England, March 7, 1818. He lived in England till fourteen years of age, when he came to this country with his father and stepmother, his own mother having died in England, and the family settled in Ohio. Mr. Turner's father also came here and lived with his son. He was killed by the cars while on his way to Ohio, the place of his former residence. Abel Turner was married to Harriet Waters, who is a native of Pennsylvania, and seven children have blessed the union, to-wit: Arthur B., who was born December 23, 1858; Smith W., born May 2, 1860; P. Acorn, born August 19, 1861; Stella, born June 6, 1863; Delia D., born July 12, 1875; Fanny, born May 6, 1872, and Elsie, born April 15, 1876.

During the remainder of 1853 there were no more arrivals. The year 1854 witnessed quite a number of settlements. The third settler, Wilmont Wilbur, arrived in the spring of this year. He came from Canada and settled upon the old Clayton place, on section thirty. He brought his family and remained here for about six months, when he pulled up stakes and left for St. Louis, where he has since been interested in several patent rights. His wife, while on her way to St. Louis to meet him, heard in some way that her husband had been murdered, whereupon she became crazy and so unmanageable that she finally succeeded in jumping from the car window and was killed.

The next settlement was made in June, 1854, when George Younker, W. F. Younker, Jacob Kemmerer and others came and took claims.

George Younker, the first named, has been a resident of the county since his first advent. He was born in Pennsylvania in 1836. His father was Jonathan Younker, who died in Pennsylvania. Mr. Younker has been twice married. His first wife was Mary Williams, daughter of James Williams, an early settler of Beaver township. She died in May, 1872. His present wife, Emma, a daughter of Henry B. Wemple, was born in February, 1855. Mr. Younker has one daughter (Carrie) by his first marriage; he has two daughters by his present wife—Mabel and Lizzie.

Mr. Wemple, father-in-law of Mr. Younker, settled on section 28, in this township, in 1854. He was born in the town of Schuyler, Herkimer county, New York, in 1805, living there until he was twenty-six years of age, when he went to Rome, New York, remaining there five years; thence to Onondaga county, remaining there ten years, removing to the State of Wisconsin about 1848. He was one of the earliest settlers of this township, settling on section 28, in the year 1854. His wife, whose maiden name was Kate Auyer, was born in the same town as her husband. Mr. and Mrs. Wemple have had fifteen children, eleven of whom, three sons and eight daughters, are living— Peter, Philip, Charles, Elizabeth, Susan, Lucy, Frances, Mary, Margery, Lielia and Emma. Mr. and Mrs. Wemple were married January 1, 1827, and have lived together (January, 1883) fifty-six years.

William F. Younker, brother of George, came to Albion in June, 1854, locating upon one hundred and sixty acres of government land, which he has since increased to two hundred and forty acres. He was born in Pennsylvania in 1826. His wife is a native of Wyoming county, in the same State.

Jacob Kemmerer lives on section 33, where he settled in 1854. He was born in Monroe county, Pennsylvania, on December 6, 1813. He married Caroline Younker, April 7, 1842, a native of Northampton county, Pennsylvania, born in 1822. Mr. Kemmerer's chief occupation through life has been farming; though he worked for several years as a millwright and builder. Mr. and Mrs. Kemmerer have two children—Edward, who lives at Oskaloosa, and William who remains at home. They are members of the M. E. Church. At about the same time a number of others arrived and settled in this township, among whom were Richard Daniels, P. P. Parker, Samuel Cramer, Augustus Coon and Michael Niece.

Richard Daniels, the first named, is still living upon a fine farm in section 34 of Albion, and is among the prominent early settlers of Butler county. Mr. Daniels is a native of Montgomery county, New York, where he was born in 1819. His parents were John and Abigail Daniels. His father lost his life by accident; his mother came to this county, where she spent her life. Mr. Daniels was married to Catherine Codner, born in Schoharie county, New York, in 1819. In 1841 Mr. Daniels removed from Herkimer county, New York to Rock county, Wisconsin, where he lived till he came here. He first took up government land. He has 300 acres in his farm. Mr. and Mrs. Daniels have had twelve children, eight of whom are living, to-wit: Samuel, Lemuel, Lida, Frank, Richard, Eugene, Wesley and William E. Alfred, their fifth child, enlisted in the Ninth Iowa Cavalry, and died of disease at Benton Barracks, Missouri, in 1864; another son, John, died in his 14th year. They also lost two children in infancy. Mr. and Mrs. Daniels are members of the M. E. Church. Mr. Daniels has held the position of class leader and exhorter; was licensed to preach in 1860, and ordained as local deacon in 1864. He has always been prominently identified with church work, and its interests have been forwarded by his labors.

The next is Pascal P. Parker, who also came to this township in 1854, and still holds forth upon the place of his choice in pioneer times. It was through him that the first postoffice in this section was established, and in its infancy the name of Parkersburgh was bestowed upon the growing town.

Pascal P. Parker was born in Malone, Franklin county, New York, in 1826. He was brought up at Moore's Junction, Clinton county, in his native State. His parents were Jonas and Deborah Parker. His father was a soldier in the war of 1812, and participated in the important battle of Plattsburg. He held a commission as Captain during the latter part of that war.

Mr. Parker went to Chicago in 1845, but returned to his native State, and again came west in 1853. He came to Butler county August 16th, 1854. He purchased a farm in section 31, of the government, where he still resides. Mr. Parker has been prominently identified with the interests of this township. He organized the township, an account of which will be found elsewhere. He was also the first postmaster. Mr. Parker has been twice married; his first wife was Marian P. McEwen; his present wife being a sister of the first, her christian name is Martha. He had one son by his first wife—Peolah P. His children by his present wife are Philo P., living at Cedar Falls—Marion C., Alvah C., Illion C., and Essie B. Having altogether four sons and two daughters. His farm contains 220 acres, including 40 acres of timber land.

Samuel Cramer was another of the pioneers of 1854, and still resides upon his original place, in section 29, which he bought of the government.

Mr. Cramer was born in Canada, and came to Jackson county, Iowa, in 1853, where he lived but one year, coming to Butler county the following year. Mr. Cramer has been twice married; his first wife was Margaret Nichols, born in Canada; she died here, September 17, 1865. His present wife was Mrs. Deborah (Wilson) Stringer. Mr. Cramer has several children by his first marriage. Mrs. Cramer has a son and a daughter by her former marriage. Another son, Frank Stringer, a stock dealer, was killed by the cars, while en route to Chicago with stock, December 14, 1882.

August Coon came from Wisconsin to Albion in 1854, driving an ox team, and bringing his family with him, and finally dropped anchor on the southeast quarter of section 33. He broke some land and erected a little cabin. In the spring of 1855 Mrs. Coon died, and in a short time he sold his place to W. S. Waters, and went back to New York, his native State.

Michael Niece, a Dutchman, came here from Wisconsin at about the same time as Coon, planting his pioneer stakes around the southwest quarter of section 34. At this time Mike was a single man; he built a little log hut, and afterwards married Miss Ingall. Ten years later he removed to Shell Rock, where he still lives.

In July, 1854, Orlin Royce made his advent from Illinois, bringing a large family, settling on section 35. Here he remained for a time, and then, after occupying another farm for a time, he removed to Dakota Territory, where he still lives. Royce was rather an interesting personage—a great castle-builder, visionary, and a poor financial manager, yet not exactly a spendthrift. Since leaving here he has been entirely broken down once, but is now picking up and doing very well.

Jacob Hall came to Albion at the same time as Richard Daniels, and settled on section 21. He was from Wisconsin, and came across the wild waste lying between that State and this, driving an ox team, bringing his family and camping on the way, as, in fact, did all the hardy pioneers. He remained upon his farm for twelve or fifteen years, when he moved to Grundy county.

In November, of '54, Charles W. McEwen arrived, and took a farm on section 31, but lived with P. P. Parker. He afterward returned to New York; his native State, and has since gone to Oregon.

Joseph Codner, in June, 1854, marched into Albion, and stationed himself over a parcel of Uncle Sam's domain, in section 27. He brought his family from Wisconsin by ox-team, camping on the way. They lived in their wagon while their cabin was in process of erection. Codner remained there until his decease. His wife is also dead. The balance of the family still live on the place. Mr. Codner was a good-hearted, genial man, and very well liked by his neighbors. He was a horse jockey, and made many a dollar in his sharp trades. The ministers often talked to Joe about trying to reform his ways, but Joe's answer always was, "Well, I tell you, I can't be a christian and trade horses."

Isaac Waters resides on section 33. His father, William S. Waters, purchased the east 80 acres of this farm of Mr. Coon, and the west 80 of Charles Mack. William S. Waters was a native of England. He came to this country, with his family, in 1829, settling at Coal Castle, Pennsylvania, and engaging in coal mining. He removed to Rock county, Wisconsin, in the fall of 1848, coming here and settling in 1854. He died January, 1874; his wife died in 1875. Isaac Waters was born in Cornwall, England, in 1827. He worked for many years as a machinist. His father came here from Ozaukee county, Wisconsin, where he had removed from Rock county.

Mrs. Jane (Fairfield) Coryell, widow of G. J. H. Coryell, resides on section 30, where she settled, with her husband, in 1856. Mr. Coryell was born in Canada in 1828, marrying Jane Fairfield, also a native of Canada. They moved here directly from Canada in September, 1856, living here till his death, in June, 1882. The father of Mr. Coryell settled here in 1855. Mrs. Coryell has six children living—Elizabeth G. A., now Mrs. J. Jackson, Fred., Frank N., Abram I., William H. and Lada L. Mrs. Coryell's farm contains 313 acres.

George L. Russell dates his coming to Butler county July, 1856. His father, Thomas Russell, was born near New Haven, Connecticut, and was a descendant of one of the early New England settlers. The family descended from the Rev. John Russell, who came over from England more than two centuries ago. His son, Rev. Samuel Russell, a generation later, was a prominent New England clergyman. Mr. Thomas Russell was born in 1799; he married Cynthia Wooster, who survives her husband. Mrs. Russell was born in Pennsylvania. Her parents also belonged to one of the old Connecticut families. Mr. Thomas Russell removed with his family to the State of New York, thence to Illinois, afterward coming to Iowa, as stated above. He purchased the farm where the family still reside, of Franklin Tewksbury. Mr. Russell died in 1870. Mr. and Mrs. Thomas Russell had six children—Ellen, Caroline, Nelson, Shelden, George L. and Susan. The homestead farm contains 80 acres.

Sylvanus H. Taylor, a settler of 1857, is a native of St. Lawrence county, New York, where he was born, August, 1823. He resided at the place of his birth until fifteen years of age, when he removed to Canada, and thence to DeKalb county, Illinois; coming from the latter place to Butler county. He has lived in the same place ever since he came to this county—his location is on section 31. He purchased his farm of a non-resident, no improvements having been made. He has 146 acres, 40 acres lying within the corporation of Parkersburgh. His wife was Achsah Needham. Her father, B. C. Needham, Sr., was an early settler of Pittsford township, and spent the last years of his life in Parkersburg. Mr. and Mrs. Taylor have four children—Estella L., Willis B., Etta P. and Luella L.

The settlements already treated of are all in the southern portion of the township. In the meantime the northern part of Albion had received its initiatory settlers, and was taking rapid strides in advance.

The first settler in the northern part of Albion was Jacob Brown, who came from Illinois in 1854 with his family, and took a claim of about 1,080 acres lying in Beaver and Albion townships. He remained about one year and then sold to Elder Bicknell, a Baptist preacher. He then removed to section 4, to what is called the "Horseneck," and purchased a farm. He remained on this ten or twelve years, when he removed to Franklin county. He is now in Kansas. Brown was a Methodist preacher, and was considered a good man.

The next settler was Moses J. Conn, who came from Canada in 1855 with his family and erected a cabin in the township of New Albion, remaining here for about nine years, when he moved to Monroe township. He still lives in Butler county.

Henry Owen came to Butler county with his father, Jesse Owen, in 1854. He was born in Broome county, New York, in 1835. He married Catherine Blass, whose father, John Blass, settled in Linn county about 1852. He removed to Waterloo and settled in Beaver township, Butler county, in 1859, where he resided till his death. Mr. and Mrs. Owen have four sons and one daughter—Charles M., Chauncey D., William H., Andrew J. and Lany B. They lost a son and daughter, twins—John J. and Julia—who died when seven years of age. Mr. Owen has one hundred and twenty acres of land, eighty acres of which were entered by his father. The remainder he bought of Henry Jenkins, who entered it as government land. Jesse Owen, father of Henry, now lives in Parkersburg. He settled on section eight, in the summer of 1854. He was born in Ontario county, New York, in 1806. When thirteen years old his parents removed to Broome county. He was married in the State of New York in 1834, removed to Michigan and thence to Indiana, coming to Butler county in 1854. His wife, Lany Kark, was born in the State of New York in 1808. Their children are Henry; John D, who married Lielia S. Wemple; Chauncey F., who married Amanda Brown; Avoline E., married Edward P. Bigelow, who was drowned in the Beaver river, at Parkersburg. She has since married Wm. Hubbard. They lost their second child—Israel.

L. D. Owen was a brother of Jesse Owen and came to Albion at the same time, settling on section eight, where he remained for eighteen or twenty years, when he removed to Parkersburg, where he has since died. His wife also has passed away.

Nathaniel Chesley was another pioneer in the northern part of the township. He came from the State of New York and settled with his large family upon a farm in section three. He remained here for about twelve years, when he removed to O'Brien county, where he died. His great failing was remembrances of the good old times in York State. On one occasion he went to Daniel Downey's for potatoes, and Mr. D. was just digging some of the finest he had ever raised. The yield was enormous. Chesley stood by for a few moments, and then stated that it reminded him of a crop he had once raised in York State. "The field," he said, "was on the side of a hill, and when the potatoes were dug they would roll down and lodge against the fence, which soon filled full, and many bushels rolled over the fence and were lost."

John Barker, a farmer from Illinois, was also one of the pioneers of 1855. He settled on section three and remained ten years. His pathway was not all strewn with roses, as he got into some trouble about running away with property (cattle) in his trust, and was finally convicted and served one term in the Wisconsin Penitentiary.

Marshall Kelley, in 1855, came from one of the eastern States, and took up his abode upon a farm on section 2. Here he remained, respected by all his neighbors until 1861, when the war broke out and he enlisted, dying in the service. He was a good man, honest and industrious.

Asa Overacker came from Indiana in 1855 with his family, and settled on section 8. He is now in Kansas. He was a prominent man in town affairs, and held various offices of trust.

E. W. Babcock was a native of Vermont, and came at about the same time, settling on section 4. He was a scheming money-maker, now living in Dakota.

Widow Ann Jaquis came from Clinton county, New York soon after the last named pioneer, and with a large family settled on section 12. She is now in Kansas, but some members of the family still reside in the township.

Solomon Lashbrook came from the same place in New York State, and also took a claim on section 12.

There were others who came in 1855-6, and who have since gone, but are still remembered. Among them are Mr. Roberts, William Waters, Peter Riley, Lorenzo Perry and Adam Leffler.

Henry B. Wemple and Philip, his son, came to this township and settled in 1855 on section 28. They came from Wisconsin, Rock county; here they remained about twenty years, when they removed to a place adjoining, belonging to George Younker. Henry B. still lives in the township, but Philip moved to Parkersburg.

Edward Dawson came with his family from Ohio, in 1855, and settled on section nine, where he remained two years, and then removed to Waverly. His son now occupies the place.

The following year, Alonzo Perry came and selected a home on section five. He was a Vermonter. He afterward removed from this place to section seven, where he died.

Elijah Brown, who was also a pioneer of '55, settled on section eight, where he remained four or five years, and then removed to Black Hawk county.

Section fourteen also received a settler in 1856 by name of Peter Melindy. He purchased in this vicinity 1,080 acres, remained about one year, and then went to Cedar Falls. He has since been United States Marshal, President of the State

Board of Agriculture, and held other positions of trust.

John Warren settled on section fourteen in 1857, remaining three years, until his death.

One of the prominent early settlers of Albion township was Daniel Downey, who settled here in 1856. Mr. Downey was born in County Cork, Ireland, in 1823, where he was educated in the art of farming. He came to the United States in 1847; lived in Vermont about two years; came to Illinois in 1848, and located in the town of Aurora, Kane county, where he learned the trade of a miller, at which he worked for about six years. He then settled on a farm in Kendall county, in that State, where he resided until he came to Iowa. Mr. Downey bought his first land of Edward Dawson, in section nine, in Albion township. He eventually became one of the most prominent farmers in the township. He increased his first purchase of land to 580 acres, which he still owns. His sons now conduct the farm. Mrs. Downey's maiden name was Catherine Burns. She was born in County Wicklow, Ireland, about 1832, and came to the United States with her brother in 1848. Mr. and Mrs. Downey have seven children—James H., Hattie (wife of Charles Younker), Daniel, Stephen, Kate, Mary and Cora. They have lost two sons—John and Michael J. The latter, their oldest son, was a lawyer by profession and of fine attainments. He was located at Parkersburg for several years, and from there he removed to Dakota, where he died December 18, 1882. The family are members of the Catholic Church. Mr. Downey, with his family, now live in Parkersburg.

Elihu Jaquis has been a resident of Albion township since June, 1856. He first settled on section 12 in this township, on land he had entered two years previously. He now lives on section 3. He bought the first "forty" of his present farm of Samuel Leslie, and the remaining forty of David Davis. Mr. Jaquis was born in Clinton county, New York, in 1840, where he lived till nine years of age, when he removed to Illinois with his parents, Benjamin and Fanny Jaquis. His father went to California in 1852, where he lost his life by drowning. The parents of Mr. Jaquis had six children, five of whom are living—Elizabeth, who lives in Nebraska, Elihu, Ann, in Colorado, Mary, in Idaho, and Sarah, in Nebraska. Elihu married Mary Ann Stuart, born in Maine in 1843. Her parents were Charles and Margaret Stuart. They removed from Maine to Canada, and from thence to this county in 1855. Her father died in Webster City, February, 1881, where her stepmother still lives. Her own mother, Jane (Perry) Stuart, died in Canada. Mr. and Mrs. Jaquis have six children—Charles A., Benjamin H., Libbie M., William H., George L. and Hattie M. They lost two children—a son and daughter. Mr. Jaquis has eighty acres, and made all of his own improvements.

OTHER PROMINENT CITIZENS.

Emerson truly says that "biography is the only true history," and in this connection we present sketches of a few of the representative citizens of the township who settled a little later than those already named, but who also deserve attention:

James V. Billings settled on section 32 in 1864, where he still resides. He purchased of Stephen Morse, who removed to Grundy county, where he died in March, 1881. Mr. Morse purchased the farm of the government. Mr. Billings was born in Montgomery county, New York, March 16, 1811, where he lived till thirty-six years of age. His father, Caleb Billings, was also a native of Montgomery county, and died in the house in which he was born. James V. lived the first thirty-six years of his life in the same house, and a brother of Mr. Billings still owns the homestead of his father. Mr. Billings married Temperance Jane Bunn, also a native of Montgomery county. They removed to Rock county, Wisconsin, in July, 1849, where they lived until they removed to this county. They have eleven children—Earl, born in 1835; William H., born in 1837; Winfield S., born in 1839; Henrietta, born in 1841; George W., born in 1843; J. B., born in 1846; Margaret E., born in 1848; Temperance J., born in 1851; Sarah M., born in 1854; Alice A., born in 1856, and Addie C., born in 1858. They lost one child, Nellie, born in 1860 and died the same year. Mr. Billings' farm contains 220 acres, also seven acres of timber. He formerly owned forty acres within the present limits of Parkersburg. Facilities for emigrating have greatly improved since Mr. Billings began his pioneer life in Wisconsin in 1849. His route to Wisconsin was by way of the Erie canal to Buffalo, and thence to Racine by way of the great lakes. The boat on which he and family took passage from Buffalo was wrecked near Conoatt, Ohio, and sank, but the passengers were all rescued. The entire journey occupied three weeks, two of which were spent on the lakes.

Mrs. Sally S. Hersey, living on section 15, is the widow of William Hersey, who was born in Roxbury, Massachusetts, in 1822. His parents died when he was a boy. He was brought up in Massachusetts; was married at Natick, in that State; removed to Grafton, where he lived ten years, and came to Butler county in 1864 and settled on section 15. Mr. Hersey died May 3, 1877. Mrs. Hersey was formerly Sally S. Felch, a native of Massachusetts. She has nine children, three sons and six daughters—Levi F., Martha L., Sarah F., Lucy E., Mary S., Esther A., Nancy G., William H. and Thomas T. G., all born in Massachusetts. Mr. Hersey was quite a large land owner, and a successful farmer. He owned at one time about 600 acres, a portion of which has been conveyed to the children.

David Caywood resides on section 13, where he settled in 1866. He has been a resident of this county since 1863. Mr. Caywood was born in Tompkins county, New York, but brought up in Chemung county, where he lived from the time he was four years old until he was 38. He was married in Chemung county to Mary Boyer, who died August 9, 1866. His present wife was Susan Davis, born in Lewis county, New York. Mr. Caywood has three sons by his first wife—James, George and Grant. He has two children by his present wife, twins—Mary and Wilbur, born in 1869. Mr. Caywood's farm contains 220 acres.

John Knapp settled on section 8 in 1867, where he now lives. He purchased of Martin Manser. The farm was entered by

E. W. Babcock. Mr. Knapp was born in Steuben county, New York, in 1839. He went to Illinois when 18 years of age; enlisted in the Eighth Illinois Cavalry, Company G. He served two years and three months in the army; was wounded at Beverly Ford, Virginia; being disabled, he was discharged, and came to Iowa in 1865, settling on section 4, in this township. He afterwards removed to section 6, where he lived one year, then to present location in 1867. He made all the improvements on his farm. His father came here in 1866, and died at the residence of his son, in 1874. His mother died September, 1867. Mrs. Knapp's maiden name was Emma Chesley, daughter of Nathaniel Chesley, who settled on section 3, of this township, in 1855. Mr. Chesley was born in Vermont, moving to the State of New York, where he married Phœbe Parish; they moved to Ohio, where they lived eight years, and thence to this county. They had 12 children, eleven of whom are still living, only two of whom are residents of this county—Mary J., wife of Henry Brown, of Monroe township, and Mrs. Knapp; all the others live in Clay and O'Brien counties, except George, who resides in Fall City, Nebraska. Mr. Chesley removed to Clay county, with his family, in 1870. Mr. and Mrs. Knapp have three children—Elon J., Cora A. and Andrew Guy. Mr. Knapp's farm contains 80 acres.

Henry Weeks settled on section 6, in 1866. He bought his farm of Henry Mead, who purchased of Babcock, the original owner of the farm. Mr. Weeks was born in Middlesex county, Massachusetts, in 1823, going to Illinois in 1854, and settling in Ogle county. He married Jane Gibson, a native of Canada. They have three children—Joseph, born February, 1863, Mary E., born here in 1867, and Charles F., born May 29, 1877. Mr. Weeks is the only one of his father's family living in Iowa. Two brothers of Mrs. Weeks, Joseph R. and Theophilus, live in Shell Rock. Mr. Weeks has about 270 acres of land.

Joshua R. Culp, settled on section 29, in the spring of 1869. He bought his farm of W. H. Billings. Mr. Culp was born in Niagara county, New York, January, 1829. He removed with his parents to Coldwater, Branch county, Michigan, when nine years of age. His father, Nicholas Culp, died in Michigan. Mrs. Culp was born in Coldwater, Michigan. Her maiden name was Harriet Gage. Her father, Elias Gage, is now deceased; her mother is still living. Mr. and Mrs. Culp have three children—Orissa, Harry J. and Aurelia. The youngest child was born in Albion township; the others were born in Michigan. Mr. Culp has 80 acres of land. He was the first settler on his place.

Jocob Mundinger lives on section 6, where he settled in 1869. He was born in Michigan, in 1839; when fourteen years of age he removed to Dubuque county, Iowa, with his father, where he lived about ten years. He went to Montana Territory in 1864, and engaged in mining; was absent about five years; returning to Iowa he settled in Jones county. His wife was Phœbe E. Rolston, daughter of David Rolston, who settled in Jones county, in 1853, where he still lives. Mr. and Mrs. Mundinger have five children—Ira, Clarence, Eunice, Frank and Harvey. The parents and a brother of Mr. Mundinger came here in 1876, and reside in the township.

Thurman S. Chapel resides on section 13, where he settled in the fall of 1870. He was born in Erie county, New York, in 1827; he removed from his native State to Illinois, and from thence to Butler county in the fall of 1868; he has been a resident of this township since that time. Mrs. Chapel's maiden name was Ann E. Brown, a daughter of James Brown. Mrs. Chapel has the deed of this farm, which she obtained from her father, who received it of John Bicknell in 1860. Her father never resided here, but six of his children, four sons and two daughters, settled in this township, all of whom have since removed, except Mrs. Chapel.

Mr. Chapel enlisted in 1861, in the Fifty-second Illinois Infantry, Company H, and served in the army three years. He was at the battle of Shiloh, the Siege of Atlanta, and with Sherman's March to the Sea. Mr. Chapel has been twice married; has two children by his first wife—May A., now Mrs. Francis Upton, of Michigan, and Odelbert. Mrs. Chapel has also been twice married; her first husband was Miles P. Dean, by whom she had three children—Mrs. Julia A. Grandon, Anna and Fremont. Mr. and Mrs. Chapel have two children—James W. and Roy. The farm contains eighty acres. They have also 160 acres on sections 11 and 14.

Elias S. Hovey resides on section 2, where he located in 1875. He purchased his land of non-residents, and has made all of the improvements upon it. He was born in the town of Brookfield, Orange county, Vermont, in 1823; but brought up in the town of Albany, Orleans county. He was reared to the occupation of farming; came to Iowa in November, 1855, and settled in Buchanan county, where he purchased an improved farm. In 1867, with his brother, Elijah A. Hovey, he engaged in the well business. Another brother, George Hovey, became a member of the firm in 1871. In 1873 they secured a patent on a drive-well. George, subsequently, became sole proprietor of this patent. It was claimed by Andrews that the invention of the Hovey brothers was an infringement on what is known as Greene's patent for drive-wells. Andrews being the agent employed by Greene to collect royalty on the drive-wells of the country. The case is still pending in the courts. Mr. Hovey is a large land owner and stock dealer. He has 440 acres in a body, where he resides, and 120 acres on section 12. He is the present postmaster of Swanton, though the office is kept at the residence of Mrs. Marcia A. Hovey, in Jefferson township. His wife was formerly Martha M. Fisk, born in Brookfield, Orange county, Vermont. They have three children—Almira M., wife of Charles H. Little; Horace N. and Carrie. The eldest was born in Vermont; the others in Buchanan county, Iowa.

Charles L. Gleason lives on section 28. This farm was entered by H. B. Wemple. Mr. Gleason has lived here since the spring of 1878. He was born in Massachusetts, in 1836. He is the son of Luther H. Gleason of Beaver township, Grundy county, who settled therein 1857, purchasing his farm of N. Drew. Mr. L. H. Gleason was born in Middlesex county, Massachusetts, in 1812; he learned the trade of a shoemaker, which he followed till coming here. He married Mary Felch, a native of Massachusetts. They have four children—Charles L., Etta, Halina, wife of James Daniels; and Martha, wife of Elijah Lamb. Charles L. married Mary Cramer, daughter of Samuel Cramer, born in Canada West, in 1843. They have two children—Grace, born in 1865, and Edith, born in 1868. Mr. Gleason was one of the first business men of Parkersburg; he located there in 1866, being the first who manufactured boots and shoes in that village. His farm contains 128 acres.

ORGANIC.

In 1855 this township was merged into the organization of Beaver, and remained in this connection until 1856, when it was set off by Judge Vandorn, P. P. Parker being authorized to call the first election. This was accomplished, and the first election was held at the house of Stephen Morse, who at that time lived about one mile east of Mr. Parker's. This was in April, 1856; the first officers elected were supervisor, Richard Daniels; justices, Stephen Morse and Jesse Owen; trustees, J. L. Kemmerer, E. W. Babcock and Asa Overacker; Clerk, P. P. Parker; constable, Joseph Codner; assessor, Abel Turner.

Township affairs have been managed in a careful and frugal manner, as efficient officers have always held the helm of local government.

The last annual election was held in November, 1882: Justices of the peace, C. S. Lobdell, N. T. Johnson and William Dawson; trustees, S. H. Taylor, Monroe Brown and James Ray; Clerk, Daniel Downey; constables, S. Bass and J. N. Dawson; assessor, Richard Daniels.

PROCTOR'S POND.

This small body of water is without special historical interest other than the occasion which gave it the name it bears.

The people of Albion township are, and have been, a union loving, law-abiding class—yet in 1864 there were a few who preferred the success of rebel arms, and were outspoken in thesr denunciation of "Lincoln hirelings." A number of these "brave boys in blue" chanced to be at home on a furlough—and these expressions of dislike towards the Union cause came to their ears. They soon traced out the source—and repairing to a wheat-field found Jonas Proctor—the man they had business with, and demanded at once that he "hurrah for Lincoln and the Union;" he positivly refused, whereupon he was taken and given free transportation on a rail to this pond near New Hartford. On the way, a man by the name of Smith, of like tendency, was pursuaded to join the interesting procession. Upon arriving at the water, Smith not desiring a bath, shouted lustily for the Union. Proctor, however, remained sullen and silent, and was ducked; still refusing to comply, the ducking was continued until he was unable to express himself otherwise than by grunts, which he did, indicating also by motion of the hand his willingness; after thus expressing himself he was released. This body of water has been known from that day to this as "Proctor's Pond."

DURING EARLY DAYS.

When the settlement of this township commenced, and for some years after, the nearest mill was at Cedar Falls, and the pioneers made their tedious and often dangerous trips to that place in summer and winter for flour and other eatables. Mullarky & Henderson kept a trading post at this point, and supplied the country for miles around with goods, bartering with the farmers for their wheat or flour. The mill at this time consisted of a little 24-inch burr in the old saw-mill. There was also a little shanty put up at New Hartford, which was kept as a tavern where travellers could obtain supplies. The mail route was established here in 1855, and carried on horseback through to Iowa Falls and Fort Dodge until 1857, when the stage company of Fink & Walker commenced running their heavy ambulances over the line. The stage exchange was established at Mr. Parker's, and remained there until the cars began running through this section.

The first birth in the township occurred in August, 1854, and was a plural affair, twins to Augustus and Catherine Coon, but the event, in one sense, proved a very sad one. Mrs. Coon gave her life in giving birth to the innocent ones. The babies were christened Alonzo and Melisse; Alonzo died in infancy.

The first marriage of parties from Albion took place on the 7th of January, 1856. They were P. P. Parker and Miss Martha McEwen. The ceremony was performed at the house of Adna Thomas, in Beaver township, by the Rev. Samuel Wright.

The first marriage to occur within the township united the future destinies of Mr. Abel Turner and Harriet Waters. The happy affair was solemnized at the house of William S. Waters, by the Rev. John Connell, in 1857.

John Bicknell and Miss Chesley were united in marriage the same year.

The first death in Albion occurred in July, 1854—a sweet little daughter of Mr. and Mrs. Wilbur.

The first death of an adult was Mrs. Moses Lemon, in February, 1855, which is mentioned elsewhere.

Rev. Mr. Burleigh preached at the first religious services held in the township. The meeting was held at the house of William F. Younker, in December, 1854. There are now no churches in the township except those at Parkersburg.

It is well remembered that among the first to dispense the word of God in the township was a man named Willard Dingman, sometimes called "Elder." He and his wife boarded with the family of "Cooney" Gardner. While here he began abusing his wife and acting in a disgraceful manner, forgetting that "decency had to be observed in this community." He carried the matter too far, and finally his relatives turned out for the purpose of tarring and feathering him. No tar could be found, and, as a substitute, they took molasses, and after putting on the necessary coat of this, covered it with feathers, they turned him loose. Not satisfied with all this, the loving relatives followed, and would have killed the poor wretch, had it not been for William Connell, who interceded in his behalf. Dingman left for New York State the following day.

Moses Lemon, an eccentric character, settled in Albion township at an early day, and with his wife commenced pioneering on a claim a short distance from where Mr. Parker now lives. He was not considered of sound mind when he first came,

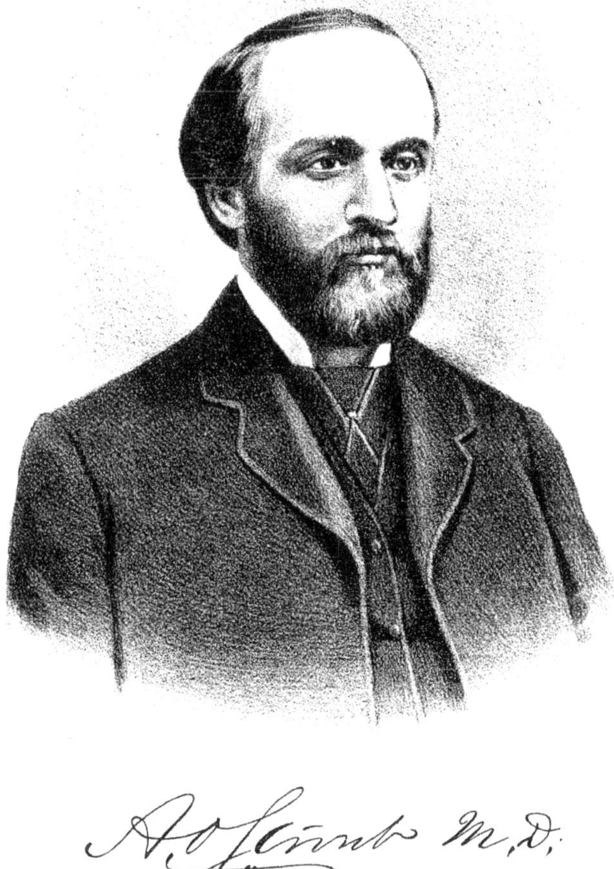

and his wife dying entirely unbalanced his mind. He would perform some of the queerest freaks and pranks imaginable— in fact many of his actions were so far out of the ordinary line that the more timid early settlers became afraid of him. It is also said that many were the little children who were glad to get into bed at the regular time by the remark from the tired mother that she guessed she would "have to call in old Mose Lemon." Another remark which always had a magical effect upon unruly urchins was in the shape of: "Don't do that, or don't meddle there—Old Mose'll get you!" Soon after the unfortunate man settled here his wife died, and he grew a great deal worse. Her death occurred in mid-winter, and so affected him that he was hard to control. During the night following his wife's death he succeeded in escaping from his room and getting out on the prairie, where he took off his shirt, and stark naked and barefooted he took a wild, madman's run of a mile, bounding over the frozen, snow-covered prairie like a deer. He finally brought up at the cabin of Solomon Cinnamon, where he remained through the balance of the night, going back the next morning apparently none the worse for his crazy adventure. In a few days he returned to his original home in New York State, and since then all trace of him has been lost.

SCHOOLS.

The first school taught in the township was by John Bicknell, in the winter of 1855–6, in a little log school-house at New Albion. This was the first school-house erected in the township, and had been put up the fall previous.

The first frame school-house was put up by District No. 1, in the summer of 1856.

There are at present nine school houses in the township, including the one at Parkersburg.

NEW ALBION.

A village by this name was platted about 1856, in the northern part of the township, lying partly in sections 3 and 4. Quite a number of parties were interested in its project, among whom were Jacob Brown, Dr. Wright, Clifford Dawson and Chesley and John Barker. It was at one time quite flourishing, with saw mill, store, post office, etc.

The post office at this point was established a number of years ago. In August, 1857, Mrs. Lorenzo Perry walked to Cedar Falls for the mail, for she, as well as most of the neighbors, had her mail sent to that point. On her return she brought the official documents establishing the post office at New Albion, under the title of Swanton; also a commission for Jacob Brown as the first postmaster, the office being kept at his house. The present acting official in this capacity is Mrs. Marcia A. Hovey. A personal sketch is appended:

Marcia A. Hovey is the widow of Lewis Hovey, who was a brother of Elias S. Hovey, of Albion township. He was born in Albany, Orleans county, Vermont, January 3, 1831. He came to Linn county, Iowa, in 1854, and went to Buchanan county the following January, where he purchased a farm. Mrs. Hovey's maiden name was Marcia A. Nefford; she was born in the town of Glover, Orleans county, Vermont, and went to Linn county, Iowa, in 1855, where she was married to Mr. Hovey. They came to Butler county in November, 1866, and settled at Swanton, in Jefferson township. Mr. Hovey obtained his farm of his brother, T. K. Hovey, one of the early settlers of Jefferson township. The latter now lives in Buchanan county. Mr. Hovey died very suddenly, April 5, 1877. Mrs. Hovey still owns the homestead farm, which is one of the finest in the township. She has two children—Julia I. and Emma P.; the former was born in Buchanan county, the latter in Butler county. The homestead farm contains 300 acres.

TOWN OF PARKERSBURG.

This is one of the best points for trade and business in Butler county. The streets always present an animated appearance, with the well-to-do farmers making their purchases and transacting business; the grain buyers busy, the merchants made happy by thrifty trade, showing a marked contrast between it and the staid older towns. It lies in the Beaver valley, extending into both Albion and Monroe townships, and is at the confluence of the North and South Forks of the Beaver. This stream furnishes a powerful and permanent water-power, which has already been improved and partially utilized. No locality presents a more favorable opportunity for the employment of capital in manufacturing enterprises. Situated upon a division of the Illinois Central Railroad, one of the most important thoroughfares in the country, the town is possessed of most desirable shipping facilities. Back from the river the valley gives way to a gradual slope, which rises to the level of the surrounding country. Parkersburg reminds one of the stories of New England life, and as you view the many white-robed cottages resting so gracefully upon the sloping hillside, you can almost imagine yourselves in some hamlet of the Eastern States.

The site which the town now occupies was formerly covered with a heavy and rank growth of brush, which was hard to penetrate either by man or beast, and was called by some of the early pioneers the "Brush Bed of the Beaver." This, however, soon disappeared. The plat covers the following described portions of land: the southwest quarter and the south half of the northwest quarter of section 30, township 90, range 16; and the northeastern part of the southeast quarter of section 25, township 90, range 17, embracing in all about 240 acres. The plat was surveyed by Engineer Smith, of the Central railroad, an Englishman. The streets are laid out after English fashion, too narrow; they are laid north and south, east and west.

THE BEGINNING AND BUSINESS INTERESTS.

The earliest steps leading to the founding and subsequent development of a town or locality is a matter which must of necessity receive the first attention of the historian, and the collection of such data as will be of interest is attended with much more difficulty and uncertainty than would be supposed by those who have never undertaken the collection of such matter. Even though it be but a decade and a half in the past, the reports are often as different and conflicting as can be imagined, for to the memory—

"Years that have passed
Are but as fleeting hours."

The land upon which the village stands was purchased from the United States government in 1854 by a speculator living in one of the eastern cities, whose name has been forgotten, but he never made any improvements, and it is doubtful whether he ever saw the land. In 1857 John Connell and his son William H. purchased the land and erected a cabin a short distance south of the village. When the railroad survey was made this section of country was skipped as to stations, although Aplington and New Hartford, both east and west of it, had been decided upon and platted; but when the railroad managers realized the natural advantages of the location and the confluence of the North and South Forks, they came to the conclusion that there was a chance for a town here, and accordingly Parkersburg was platted and recorded, receiving its name in honor of P. P. Parker, a prominent and esteemed early settler, and the station was commenced and completed in 1865.

The first sign of life, in a business point of view, commenced at about the same time, when Mr. Thomas Williams erected what was called the Williams House, which he opened in a small way and commenced keeping "tavern." This building was the starting point of what is now the Commercial House, it being at that time about one-fourth as large as at present. It has changed hands a number of times, and has finally become the property of Robert Norris, being run in a satisfactory manner by O. W. Cooley. About the same time that Williams commenced the erection of his hotel, R. T. Jackson—or, as he was familiarly known, "Ring-Tail" Jackson—made his appearance and commenced putting up a store building, which he completed soon after Williams completed his hotel — size twenty by thirty feet, two stories high. He at once had his goods brought, and before his store was enclosed was selling goods from one of the rooms in the Williams Hotel, where everyone made their headquarters. There is a difference of opinion as to how he received his goods, some claiming he had them brought with team and wagon, and others that he got them on the construction train and before regular trains were running. This was the first store in the place, and although the stock of goods was limited a good business was commenced.

In the summer of 1865, before Jackson had settled, and long before he was handling goods over the counter, Benjamin Needham made his appearance, and put up a large building, about 30x40 feet in size, near the depot on the north side of the track. Here he put in a limited stock of general merchandise, and continued to run the store until the time of his death, a few years since, when the business was closed. The building at present is occupied as a tenement by several families. The building of this house was immediately followed by the erection of the store building of N. T. Manley & Son, who put up a substantial building on Depot street, near where the corner drug store now is, and put in the first extensive and complete stock of general merchandise brought to Parkersburg. The building has since been moved to Main street.

The mercantile business of N. T. Manley & Son was established by N. T. Manley in 1867. In 1872 the present partnership was formed, C. I. Manley joining his father in business. N. T. Manly was one of the earliest merchants of Parkersburg; the business which he established is the oldest in town. Mr. Manley was born in Essex county, New York, in 1820. He received a good education, and when a young man was engaged for some time in teaching. He went from the State of New York to Northampton county, Pennsylvania. He was married in Pennsylvania to Miss U. M. Insley, a native of New Jersey. They removed to Fox Lake, Dodge county, Wisconsin, about 1851, where they lived till 1864, when they removed to Plainview, Minnesota, coming to Parkersburg in January, 1867. Mr. Manley built a store, and engaged in business, the same spring; this was the second store in the town, Jackson & Tanner having a small store at that time. The town then contained eleven buildings and about thirty inhabitants. Mr. Manley has not confined himself to mercantile pursuits, but has dealt considerably in real estate during his residence here. He purchased a farm on section 19, near the village, in 1867, paying six dollars per acre, which he still owns. The father of Mr. Manley was a Congregational clergyman, a native of the State of New York, where he died at the advanced age of 92 years. Mr. Manley has been twice married. He lost his first wife in 1857. His present wife was Miss M. L. Cahart. He has three children by first marriage—Ella E., wife of Dr. M. I. Powers; C. I. and Edward I.

C. I. Manley, who is engaged with his father in business, was born in Northampton county, Pennsylvania, in 1850. He was engaged for many years in the store with his father before the present partnership was formed. His wife, Mary E. Howenstein, was a native of Ohio. They have had two children—Insley H., (deceased), and Jennie E.

Edward I. Manley was born in Dodge county, Wisconsin, in 1855. He carried on the homestead farm, on section 19, for eight years, but is now engaged in the store. He married Miss M. D. Strout, daughter of Benjamin Strout. Mrs. Manley is a native of Massachusetts. They have one child—Howard I.

Mr. N. T. Manley has two children by his second marriage—W. E. and Lewis H.

In 1865 the depot was completed and Mr. Joseph Demmick officiated as the first agent. He put up a little building across the track, in which he kept the post office —being postmaster—where he kept a general line of yankee notions, together with a meat-market, grocery, paint shop, wagon works, and, in fact, everything you could think of. He bought the first grain, storing it in the depot. He was soon followed in the grain buying business by B. F. White and Mr. Buswell, who succeeded to the business of grain buying.

"Jake" Young and Frank Shaffer fell into the line of progress, and put up what is now the Eagle House, a building 28 x 30 feet in size. It has since been enlarged and improved, and is now run by Mr. Stone, who makes a most accommodating host. Jake Young, the first mentioned partner, erected a little building, 16 x 24 feet, near the hotel, in which he opened a restaurant or saloon, soon after the hotel was completed, and kept a general stock of liquors. In 1868, Edward Bigelow bought the concern, and in 1869 moved it to where it now stands, on Depot street, near the drug store, at present occupied by Thomas Conn for a grocery store.

Jonathan Goodale came to Parkersburg in the fall of 1868. He built a store the following spring and engaged in general merchandising. He built a residence adjoining his store, both of which were destroyed by fire in March, 1878. Mr. Goodale sustained a loss at this time of $10,000. He rebuilt on the site of his former store the following summer, and now has one of the most extensive general stores in the county. Excellent business qualities and strict integrity have made him successful. He was born in the town of Oppingham, Herkimer county, New York, in 1821. He was educated in the trade of farming and merchandising. His parents were David and Charity (Shaffer) Goodale, natives of New York State, both of whom are deceased. Mr. Goodale was employed in merchandising before he came west. He came to Iowa in March, 1865, and bought a farm in Grundy county, where he engaged in farming till he came here in 1868. His wife was Almira J. Hough, also of the State of New York. They have one daughter, Jennie, born in the State of New York.

Not long after Mr. Goodale had commenced business, and during the same year (1868) Charles Charnock started the first lumber yard with W. M. Howenstein. The latter gentleman, however, did not remain long in the lumber business. In company with Dr. Powers he started a drug store, which business he now runs alone. Charnock remained in the lumber business until 1880, when he sold to E. W. Babcock, who had been running an opposition yard, who soon after sold to the gentleman who now represents the lumber interests, John Voogd. In 1881 another lumber yard was started by a Dubuque firm, which is still doing business.

The first hardware establishment was started in 1866 by James Parker, father of the present postmaster, who put up a building twenty by sixty, on Depot street below the drug store, and put in a stock of hardware. Melvin Dees was associated with him. After a time Joseph Kellogg became interested in the store, and finally purchased the interest of the other partner and removed the stock to a building erected by him on Main street. After changing hands twice—to Parker Bros. and Mr. Nye—it was purchased by the Parris Brothers, who are yet proprietors. Within the last few years Foote & Mott started and still carry on this line of business, as stated further.

Parris Brothers, dealers in hardware and boots and shoes, succeeded Joseph Kellogg in October, 1875. Mr. Kellogg succeeded J. Kennedy & Olmstead, who established the business. George and Fred Parris are natives of England. Their father emigrated from England in 1842 and settled in Stephenson county, Illinois. The brothers came to Parkersburg in 1872 and engaged in the grocery business, which they continued till 1881, when they were succeeded by Sam Norris. Their brother Henry came to Butler county in

1875 and engaged in farming in Monroe township. The wives of George and Fred are natives of St. Louis, Missouri. Fred has four children—Achsah, Willie, Fred and Grace.

Foote and Mott are general hardware dealers. The partnership was formed in the fall of 1878. S. A. Foote, of this firm, is the son of George A. Foote, a native of Delaware county, New York; he removed to Richland county, Wisconsin, with his family in 1856. He was a blacksmith by trade, but engaged in farming in Wisconsin; coming to Butler county in the spring of 1868, he settled on section 13, in Monroe township. He died November, 1877. His wife survives him and lives in Parkersburg, though still owning the homestead farm. S. A. Foote was born in the State of New York, in 1849. He engaged in the live stock business here in 1877, changing to the hardware trade in 1878. His wife was Hattie S. Burnham, born in Wisconsin. Mr. and Mrs. Foote have two children—Dotha and George, both of whom were born in Parkersburg. C. L. Mott, of this firm, is one of the early settlers of Parkersburg; his residence here dating from 1869. He was born in Kalamazoo, Michigan, in 1842, where he lived till nineteen years of age. In 1861 he went to Galena, Illinois, where, with his father, he engaged in keeping a hotel. His parents were Elter and Margaret Mott. In 1868 the family removed from Illinois to this county, and settled at New Hartford. The family removed to Colorado in 1879, where the father died in the fall of 1881. Mr. C. L. Mott went to Ackley, Hardin county, in 1867, where he engaged in the livery business; from Ackley he went to Marietta, coming to Parkersburg in 1869. He established himself here in the mercantile business, which he continued for eight years. While living in Michigan, Mr. Mott had an experience of two years in the banking business, and while in Illinois was engaged in hotel keeping, farming and milling. He married Flora, daughter of George E. Fitch, a prominent early settler of Beaver township. Mr. Mott is the only member of his father's family now living in Butler county.

In 1865 Charles Gleason started the first boot and shoe store, and did the first cobbling. This was in a little house which he rented, east of the Commercial House, and from there he moved to Main street, and continued in business until 1875 or 1876, when he sold to Henry Perry, who sold to Mr. Hiller; finally the business came under the management of Mr. Bohall, who erected the substantial building now occupied by him.

W. N. Allen opened a stock of boots and shoes at an early day in the history of the village, and still continues to run one of the most extensive stores in town.

Henry Ballhousen, in 1877, commenced business, and is still in the boot and shoe trade.

The first harness shop was started in the fall of 1867 by Henry Frank, who employed Val. Lahr as his assistant. Mr. Frank still holds forth in this line. Val. Lahr afterwards started a shop of his own in 1868, and still does a thriving business.

Willis M. Howenstein is the proprietor of the pioneer drug store of Parkersburg. The business was established in 1868, by Dr. M. I. Powers, who conducted the business alone for a short time, when he took as a partner, H. L. Gibbs, who remained in the firm about one year, when Dr. Powers was again alone for a short time. Mr. Howenstein bought one-half interest in the business, November, 1870, and has been connected with the business since that time. After about six months partnership with Mr. Howenstein, Dr. Powers sold his interest to A. J. Whitfield; then the name of the firm became Howenstein & Co., by which it has since been known, though several changes have been made since that time. In 1874 J. D. Burt became the partner of Mr. Howenstein; his present partner is F. P. Ray. Mr. Howenstein was born in Ohio, in 1835. When twenty-one years of age he went to Fort Wayne, Indiana, where he read medicine for a time. He traveled overland to California in 1858, and returned in 1865. He came to Parkersburg, November, 1868, and was for some time in the employ of C. Channock, who started the first lumber yard in Parkersburg. Mrs. Howenstein was formerly Carrie E. Tenent, a native of Wisconsin. They have one daughter, and lost two sons. The drug store now being run by Frank Ray, was established by Mr. Eno Renken, and is now doing a thriving business.

In 1868 Mr. Babcock opened the first furniture store in a building now used for an agricultural warehouse by the Beaver Valley Bank. Mr. Babcock was not very successful, and finally gave up the business. The next one started was by A. S. Burnham. The business is now carried on by Burnham & Bass. One or two others have been started which were of short life. About 1870 Clark Mott rented the Perkins' building and opened a general merchandise establishment, which was run but a few years. Mahanke & Co. started a few years since, and do a large business.

The first blacksmith shop was opened and run by Charlie Dunham, a son-in-law of Mr. Wemple. He only remained here two years, removing to Illinois. The next was by a man called "Rollo," who has long since gone.

The first bank was opened by the Gibbs Brothers, in 1868. They continued for a few years, then sold to J. B. and M. I. Powers, who continued the business until bought out by Wolfe & Son, who are still bankers. The next established was the Beaver Valley Bank, in 1876, by the present proprietors—Parker & Richards.

In 1869 Mr. Benedict erected a building and opened a stationery store. After conducting the business a short time he rented the building to W. W. Cartner, who opened a confectionery store in it; but after a year or more, Mr. Schoolcraft buying the building, the business was discontinued. This line is now represented by D. C. Monte.

About 1869 William Wallace erected a building and started a meat market. This business finally was purchased by Martin Cartner, who still runs it, in company with Mr. Demorest.

The first livery stable was started by Charley Reynolds, in the spring of 1867, in a stable near the Eagle House, but he remained in the business only a short time. Maxwell & Downs commenced the second and carried on the business during one summer. In May, 1869, J. T. Burt opened a stable on a large scale, which he ran for thirteen years. The business is now represented by Otis Baker and Williams & Bailey.

T. J. Burt has resided in Parkersburg since 1868. He was born in England in 1838, and came to this country with his parents when thirteen years of age. His father, William Burt, settled with his family in Carroll county, Illinois, and still lives in that State. His mother is deceased. Mr. Burt came here from Illinois in 1868. He and a sister—Mrs. James Chapman, who resides in Linn county—are the only members of his father's family in Iowa. Mr. Burt was engaged in the livery business here for many years. He built a livery stable on Main street in 1869, which was removed in 1881 to make place for a store. In 1875 he erected the building now used as a drug store, on the corner of Main and Market streets. He also built the structure now used by Sol S. Werner as a clothing store. He built his dwelling house in 1869. Mrs. Burt's maiden name was Mary M. Funk, a native of Maryland.

Otis Baker, proprietor of livery stable, came here November 2, 1870, succeeding Frank Shaver to the present business. He built his present stable in 1875, at a cost of $900. He also built the store now occupied by D. C. Monte, in 1875, and his dwelling house in 1877. He has recently built an ice-house, 26x40 feet, costing about $300. Mr. Baker was born in the town of Hawley, Franklin county, Massachusetts, August 12, 1836. When ten years of age he removed with his parents to the township of Bristol, Dane county, Wisconsin. His father, Ephriam Baker, was born in Massachusetts, in 1807; he still lives in Dane county, Wisconsin.

Mr. Baker removed to the village of Floyd, Floyd county, Iowa, in 1867, coming here in 1870. His wife was Harriet Crowell, a native of the town of Hawley, Franklin county, Massachusetts.

A place known for years as the "Robber's Roost" was put up in 1866 by Jake Young and Frank Shaffer. It was a low flat roofed building covering about a whole lot, where the white residence of Otis Baker is now situated. Many wild and improbable stories cling to the remembrance of this den, about strangers being fleeced and leaving the place penniless; but it is conceded that the manipulators never "went through" any of the citizens. It was a saloon, billiard hall, and gambling house, where all cronies of this "ilk" made headquarters, and was run for seven or eight years. It is said that whenever it rained the billiard tables had to be moved, as the roof only made the water come down in streams.

The first lawyer in Parkersburg was John Beemer, of Floyd county, who arrived here in 1868, and remained until the time of his death, in 1878. The legal profession is now ably represented by Messrs. N. T. Johnson and O. B. Courtright. The first member of the medical fraternity, to practice in the village, was Dr. M. I. Powers. The medical profession at present is represented by Doctors Powers, Strout, Parker and Ensign, the latter representing the homeopathic side of the profession.

Renken & Tammen, general merchants, established their business February, 1878. They have a general stock, including dry goods, boots and shoes, and clothing. R. G. Renken, of the above firm, was born

P. P. Parker.

in Germany, in 1853. His father, R. G. Renken, Sr., died in Germany. Mr. Renkin came here with his brother, Eno Renken, who carried on the drug business here for several years. He is now at Spirit Lake. Mr. Renkin was engaged in selling goods for Mahanke for several years. Mr. Tammen was also born in Germany. Messrs. Renken and Tammen completed, in the fall of 1882, a fine brick store on Main street, at a cost of about $4,500. They are building up an extensive trade. In 1871 Mr. Tammen was married to Miss Mate Renken. They have one child, born in December, 1882.

D. W. Schoolcraft is one of the earlier business men of this place, and has done much toward building up and advancing the interests of the town. He located here May 6, 1869. Mr. Schoolcraft was born in Tioga county, New York, in 1842. His parents removed to Boone county, Illinois, in 1846, where they died. Mr. Schoolcraft came to Iowa in 1866, stopping at Waverly and Monticello, Jones county, for about two years, coming here in the spring of 1869. He was the first to engage in the produce business at this place. After about two years he started in the grocery trade, which he continued two years. He was in the live stock business for several years, also in the grain and coal trade. He is a real estate and insurance agent. He has erected several business houses, the first being the building which was occupied by W. N. Allen, as a boot and shoe store. He built what is known as the Schoolcraft block, in the fall of 1870, at a cost of about twenty-five hundred dollars. His fine residence he built in 1877. Mr. Schoolcraft's wife was formerly Fannie A. Howenstein, a native of Ohio. They were married May 1, 1873. They have two boys—Frank H. and D. Willis.

James M. Groat has been engaged in the grain and coal trade here since August, 1882. He has resided in Butler county since December, 1869, when he settled in Monroe township. Mr. Groat was born in Wyoming county, New York, in 1842. His father, Herman Groat, was a native of Delaware county, New York, where he was born in 1812. He now lives in Wyoming county, is a cabinet maker by trade, and is in business at Attica. James M. Groat went to Carroll county, Illinois, in 1867, and worked at the carpenter's trade. He came to Butler county in 1867, purchased a farm of E. Y. Royce, in Monroe township, section 27, which he still owns. He married Vira Swan, daughter of Z. Swan. They have two children—Luella and Flora. Mr. Groat was a justice of the peace in Monroe township from January 1, 1879, till he came here. He was elected county supervisor in the fall of 1882.

Thomas W. Conn, grocer, is the son of Samuel Conn, an early settler of Monroe township. He was born in Canada in 1852. Married Sarah J. Anderson, daughter of Benjamin Anderson, an early settler of Pittsford township. They have one son—Earl Clarence. Mr. Conn engaged in business here with Robert Smith, succeeding Nanna Rave. He has been alone in trade since February 10, 1881.

Robert Norris was born in Scotland, and came to this country when twelve years of age. He was brought up in Portage, Wisconsin, where he went with his parents in 1849. His father, G. W. Norris, still lives in Portage City. Mr. Norris was engaged on the Wisconsin and Mississippi rivers, as a captain, for about five years. He came to Butler county in 1876, and kept a hotel at Butler Center for about one year. He purchased the Commercial House here in 1877, which he conducted for a time, and still owns the hotel. Mrs. Norris was formerly Mary J. Morrison. They have eight children—Rebecca A., wife of Charles H. Huntington, of Rock Rapids, Wisconsin; Samuel, Martha J., Ettie, Mary I., Robert J., James T. and an infant son. They lost their eighth child, George. Their oldest son, Samuel, is in the grocery, crockery and glassware trade, succeeding Parris Brothers, in August, 1881. He was born in Portage City in 1859.

O. Byerly, photographer, located here in June, 1882. He was born in Chillicothe, Ross county, Ohio, June 29, 1836. He went to Dubuque, Iowa, when a boy, learning the business of photography, in that city, with Frank Pickerel. He engaged in business at Potosi, Wisconsin, for a time, but has spent the greater part of his life in Iowa and Illinois. Mr. Byerly began the business of photography when that art, which has now reached such perfection, was in its infancy. He has kept pace with the improvements that have been made from time to time, and is well informed in all the branches of his profession. A visit to his rooms and an examination of his work proves him an excellent artist. His wife is a native of Vermont. Mr. and Mrs. Byerly have two children—Lilly and Frederick. They lost their oldest daughter at Farley, Iowa.

James D. Cramer was born in Upper Canada in 1814, where he lived till the fall of 1860, when he came to Butler county and settled on section 33, Albion township, on the farm now owned by W. H. Billings. Mr. Cramer kept hotel at his farm house for a number of years. He removed to Parkersburg in 1867, and was the first to open a meat market in that village. He has been engaged in various kinds of business since coming here. He was married to Jane Dixon, born in Scotland in 1825. Her mother died in Scotland. She came to America with her father, James Dixon, about 1833. Her father lived in Canada, where he died. Mr. and Mrs. Cramer were married in 1844. They have six children—Amanda, now Mrs. Edward Kemmerer, who was the first station agent on the Iowa Central Railroad at Ackley, and a resident of that place for eleven years; James D., Margaret, now wife of W. H. Wilson; Robert, Jessie and Lilly. They have lost two children—Charles, who enlisted in the Ninth Iowa Cavalry, in the war of the rebellion, and died during the war, from injuries received, in his twenty-first year—and Jane S.

A. M. Spencer, at present engaged in running the elevator of Mr. Kennedy, has been in Butler county since 1869. He was born in Yates county, New York, in 1842. He removed to Wisconsin with his parents in 1850; enlisting in 1863, in the First Wisconsin Heavy Artillery, and served two years; settled at New Hartford in 1869; came here in 1871. His wife was Clarissa Otterburn, a native of New York. They have six children. His father, Daniel Spencer, came to Iowa, in June, 1878, and died in Osceola county, August, 1881.

Joseph Collins came to Iowa and settled in Grundy county, about three miles south of New Hartford, in 1855, where he took up a farm of government land, which he owned till 1868; since that time he has been a resident of Butler county. In 1860 Mr. Collins went to what is now Leadville, then known as California Gulch, and engaged in mining. He learned the trade of a tanner and currier when a young man, but has generally followed the occupation of farming. In 1868 he purchased a farm and saw-mill in Beaver township, where he lived for several years, and then purchased a farm on section 18, in Albion township, which he still owns. He removed to Parkersburg, December, 1880. His wife was Mary A. Benson, born in Ashtabula county, Ohio. Her parents were William and Caroline (Collins) Benson. Her father was a native of New York; her mother was born in Canada. Mr. and Mrs. Collins have five sons and one daughter — William A., Edward E., Walter H., Joseph A., M. R., wife of S. Conn, and E. B. Mr. Collins' father was born in Vermont; his mother in Massachusetts. His father was in the Revolutionary War, being at that time sixteen years old. He was known as an old Revolutionary Soldier. He died in Illinois at the age of eighty-four.

Recellus R. Horr, one of the early settlers of Monroe, was born in Denmark, Lewis county, New York, April 25, 1837. In 1855 he left home and came to Iowa, locating in Butler county; bought eighty acres of land of L. P. Hazen, who had pre-empted it for him, as at that time he was too young to pre-empt land. He married March 5, 1863, Miss Lena Townsend a native of Ohio. They were blessed with five children—Charles W., Arthur T., Harry W., Lena May and Irena May (twins) Mrs. Horr died when these twins were but eight days old. He married his second wife, Mrs. George Hoey, September 6, 1878, daughter of Raby R. Parriott. They have two children—Jenny and Eva. In 1881 he bought a house and lot in Parkersburg, and now lives there. He has a farm of 320 acres which he rents. He is now living in retirement, except that he speculates in real estate.

PARKERSBURG FLOURING MILL.

This mill was erected in 1879 by Mr. E. Hiller. In June, 1881, it was purchased by the present proprietor, J. R. Russell. The mill building is 50 by 60 feet in size, and is equipped with one set of rollers and three run of stone, giving it a capacity of 75 barrels per day. The mill is propelled by a good water power, obtained from the Beaver river.

PARKERSBURG POST-OFFICE.

This was the first office established in this part of Butler county, and, for the first few years of its existence probably supplied a larger area of country with mail than any other. The luxury was instituted in August, 1855, by the department at Washington, through the influence of Mr. P. P. Parker, who had settled on section 31 of Albion, in 1854. He sent in the application recommending that the name be Albion, as that was the name of the township; but he was notified by the department that there was already one post-office in Iowa, named Albion, and that Parkersburg would be the name of this office, in honor of Mr. Parker, who was to be first postmaster. The first mail was carried through from Cedar Falls to Fort Dodge in the old fashioned saddle bags, on horseback. The mail consisted of about a half dozen letters. In a short time the stage route was established from the terminal points above mentioned, and the ambulances stopped at the door of Mr. Parker's residence, where the office was kept. After retaining the office for several years—until during the war—when he became tired of it, he resigned in favor of Stephen Morse, who received his commission, and in due time the office was removed to his cabin, about half a mile east of Mr. Parker's. This would have been satisfactory except for the fact that the stages refused to stop there, and to get the mail Mr. Morse was obliged to go half a mile to intercept them. It would not work, and finally, after having been postmaster some six months, he resigned, and Thomas Russell took charge, moving the office to his residence, half a mile further east. This made matters worse, and at the end of six months, P. P. Parker was obliged to take the office back to his house, and again become postmaster. Thus the matter remained until the village of Parkersburg was platted and the first train of cars had run up to the depot. At this time, in 1865, Mr. Parker had the office moved to the store or Joseph Demmick, who was depot agent, and appointed deputy; then, as soon as possible, Mr. Parker resigned in favor of that gentleman. Within a few years James Parker was commissioned, and a few years subsequent his son, James F. Parker, the present incumbent, received the appointment. The office is neatly fitted up, and is kept in the same building as the Beaver Valley Bank, on Main street.

DEATH OF J. D. PARKER.

J. D. Parker, who had for three years prior to his death been postmaster at Parkersburg, died, from a species of heart disease, on Saturday, the 21st of September, 1872. He was born in New Bedford, Massachusetts, on the 17th of January, 1820, and was therefore in his fifty-third year. He was a man of most generous impulses, and left many warm friends to mourn his loss. The public lost a faithful servant, and the family a kind and indulgent husband and father.

James F. Parker, postmaster, and cashier of the Beaver Valley Bank, is the son of James D. Parker, who came here in 1867, and engaged in the hardware business with M. Dees. He followed that business until his death. James F. Parker was appointed postmaster as successor of his father. He has been cashier of the Beaver Valley Bank since 1877.

INCORPORATION.

The village of Parkersburg became an incorporated town early in the year 1875, and has since retained its dignity under a very creditable management. The first election was held in the spring of 1875. The following were the first officers, viz.: Mayor, C. S. Lobdell; trustees, N. T. Manley, Joseph Kellogg, Jurgen Renken and F. L. Dodge; recorder, N. T. Johnson; treasurer, J. F. Parker; marshal, W. I. McLean; street commissioner, D. W. Schoolcraft. The first meeting of the council was held on the 4th day of March, 1875, pursuant to a call of the mayor, at the office of the recorder, N. T. Johnson. After the preliminaries usual to such occasions, the new board proceeded to transact their first official business. It was resolved that the recorder be instructed to confer with other incorporated towns in relation to ordinances for the government of the town, and shortly afterward, a long list of effective ordinances were submitted, many of which are still in force.

In relation to the actions and doings of the council, but little has transpired that would be of general interest. A detailed review of their meetings would be dry reading. This community has always been fortunate in obtaining the services of good and competent men to control its municipal affairs. There has been no useless waste or extravagances attending the financial department of its public business. It will, however, be necessary to a complete history of the town to give the names of the various officers who have officiated since the organization, and it is herewith presented.

In the year 1876 the following were the officers: Mayor, C. S. Lobdell; recorder, N. T. Johnson; treasurer, J. F. Parker; marshal and street commissioner, R. T. Bartholomew; trustees, J. Kellogg, F. L. Dodge, T. J. Burt, C. G. Courtright and J. Kennedy.

In 1877—Mayor, N. T. Johnson; recorder, F. H. Rix; treasurer, J. F. Parker; assessor, W. W. Cartner; trustees, J. Kennedy, T. J. Burt, J. Goodale, Charles Charnock and Lewis Davis.

For the year 1878—Mayor, O. B. Courtright; treasurer, J. F. Parker; recorder, M. J. Downey; trustees, J. Kennedy, J. Goodale, F. Parris, Val Lahr and F. H. Rix.

For 1879—Mayor, N. T. Johnson; recorder, M. J. Downey; treasurer, J. F. Parker; street commissioner, N. Goodale; trustees, J. Goodale, O. B. Courtright, Val Lahr, F. Tammen, George C. Parris and J. Kennedy.

For 1880—Mayor, C. S. Lobdell; recorder, W. Smith; treasurer, J. F. Parker; trustees, Lewis Davis, J. Kennedy, George C. Parris, J. Goodale, F. Tammen and Val Lahr.

For 1881—Mayor, William H. Burdick; recorder, A. N. Ferris; trustees, Val Lahr, J. Collins, C. Murray, J. Kennedy and George C. Parris.

The present officers are: Mayor, C. S. Lobdell; recorder, R. G. Renken; treasurer, Frederick Parris; marshal, Martin Cartner; street commissioner, J. D. Cramer; assessor, Lewis Davis; trustees, A. O. Strout, J. Kennedy, J. W. Ray, Joseph Collins, N. T. Johnson and W. A. Smith.

Several years ago a calaboose was erected by the city for a receptacle of refractory persons, which is still in use. It cost less than $100. The City Hall was constructed in 1880, near the lock-up, and is a neat and substantial two-story frame building, size 18 by 28 feet, and cost in the neighborhood of $1,000. Meetings are sometimes held at the hall, although as a rule the mayor's office, on Main street, is made the place for sessions.

As many of the others who have been prominent in town government are noted elsewhere, we here append a biography of the present mayor of Parkersburg:

Charles S. Lobdell, the present Mayor of Parkersburg, is a native of Johnstown, New York, where he was born in 1806. His father, Abijah Lobdell, was a native of Massachusetts, his family being numbered among the early settlers of New

England. His mother was born in the State of New York. Mr. Lobdell has spent many years of his life in the South. In 1829 he went to the parish of Feliciana, Louisiana, where he was for a time studying law with an elder brother, John L. Lobdell, who located there in 1825. In 1832 he engaged in merchandising, which he continued till 1836, when he returned to the State of New York. In 1841 he was elected by the people to the position of postmaster of Johnstown, which he held until a change of administration occurred. He then determined to resume mercantile business, and for the purpose of learning more thoroughly the different phases of trade, he went to New York City, and engaged in clerking for two seasons. He, however, purchased a farm in his native county, and for a time was interested in farming. He afterward was for several years engaged in the manufacture of gloves and mittens. In 1847 Mr. Lobdell returned to Louisiana, and, with a brother, William S. Lobdell, purchased a sugar plantation at West Baton Rouge. This business occupied his attention until the war of the rebellion compelled them to give it up. From 1862 to the close of the war, he was at work buying and selling the produce of the country—cotton, sugar and molasses. After the close of the war Mr. Lobdell removed to the State of Wisconsin, purchased a farm, and engaged extensively in the raising of hops. In 1869 he came to Parkersburg, where he has since resided. He came here when the town was in its infancy, and has always been deeply interested in its growth and prosperity. He has been justice of the peace since 1873, and has served as mayor four years. These positions he still holds. He is a man of generous impulses and kindness of heart; possessing in a high degree the respect and confidence of his fellow citizens. Though long a resident of the south, his sympathies were strongly with the Union during the war; politically he is a republican. His wife was formerly Susan R. Coffin, born in the State of New York. They have no children. In 1874 Mr. Lobdell's attention was called to the subject of spiritualism, by reading a work on that subject by Robert Dale Owen. He began a series of investigations, which continued for a year, when he became convinced of the truth of the spiritual philosophy. Since that time he has given much thought and investigation to the subject, and derives much happiness from the knowledge afforded by this philosophy.

EDUCATIONAL FACILITIES.

The Independent School District of Parkersburg was set off from the district township, and was organized in the spring of 1871, at which time an election was held, and the following officers were declared elected: President, M. I. Powers; secretary, R. L. Chase; treasurer, W. Howenstein. The first meeting of the board was held on the 24th of March, 1871; it was resolved that the secretary and treasurer be required to give bonds in the sum of $1,000 each; the president was authorized to purchase the necessary books and blanks. The members of the board at this time were J. Goodale, W. A. Allen and L. D. Davis. The next meeting was held on the 28th of March, 1871. The length of the summer term was fixed at three months, commencing on the 1st day of

May; the salary of teachers not to exceed $45 per month, which was a little in excess of the amount paid to the prior teacher, F. H. Rix.

In 1872 the question of the district issuing bonds to the amount of $2,500 to assist in building a school-house was submitted to a vote; the project was carried by a majority of 38. Plans were drawn, and a building 24x24, two stories high, was erected in the southern part of the town. In this shape the school building remained until 1878, when the increasing attendance demanded an addition. An "L" was added to it. The building is now 24x36, built by Elliott Brothers, of Grundy county, the contract being let for $1,493. This makes a substantial and neat looking building, a credit to the town, and, for the present, at least, is sufficiently large to accommodate all the departments. The present officers of the district are as follows: President, N. T. Johnson; secretary, Fred. A. Dodge; treasurer, W. M. Howenstein; members of the board, Fred Parris, J. Collins and L. Davis. At present the teachers consists of E. Bellows, principal; Mrs. E. C. Bush, first intermediate; Miss Maggie E. Wicker, second intermediate; Mrs. F. H. Rix, primary.

A list of the various principals who have managed the schools, is as follows: Frank L. Dodge, J. E. Davis, Mrs. W. C. Breckenridge, G. P. Linn and E. Bellows; the latter being the present principal.

E. C. Bellows, principal of Parkersburg graded schools, was born in Janesville, Wisconsin, May 8, 1854. He came to Iowa in 1873, and for three years was occupied in attending a graded school and in studying medicine with Dr. Spooner, of New Hartford. He taught his first term of school in Root's district, Beaver township, beginning May 1, 1876. He remained in the same school the three succeeding terms, completing the year. He taught the school in Jamison's district, in the same township, during the winter of 1877. He then attended the State Normal School at Cedar Falls for about two years; was principal of the school at New Hartford during the fall and winter terms of 1879, and has been principal of the Parkersburg school since the spring of 1880. Mr. Bellows possesses the qualification of a successful teacher—a love for his profession. His methods of instruction are approved by our best educators, and he has the happy faculty of interesting his pupils, while he commands their respect—elements in a teacher which render the important matter of good government comparatively simple.

The Parkersburg schools are second to none in Butler county.

RELIGIOUS.

The facilities for worship in Parkersburg are above the average, there being several thriving and prosperous societies, each with a neat and comfortable church edifice. In this connection is presented a history of the various organizations:

The followers of the Catholic faith have held services in this vicinity for a good many years. The first, it is claimed, was held at the residence of Daniel Downey, on section 9, about the year 1861, at which meeting the congregation consisted of but three families. Services were held at Mr. Downey's residence for about twelve years. The first pastor was the

Rev. John Shields, who officiated for about six years, when he was succeeded by the Rev. T. F. Gunn, who remained four years. Following him was Rev. Peter O. Down, now of Independence; then Rev. Michael Flavien; afterward Father Ryan; next Rev. Patrick Smith, and last Father McKabe, who still presides. During Rev. Smith's pastorate, in the summer of 1877, the church at Parkersburg was erected, at a cost of about $1,300, and was dedicated the following spring. The church is in a most prosperous condition, having a membership of twenty-five families, and is entirely free from debt.

The Methodist Episcopal Church of this place was organized by W. O. Glassner in March, 1869. Among the first members were the following: J. L. Johnson, James Gallard, D. Jay, C. and O. E. Spicer, E. B. Lamb, R. Daniels, C. Kemmerer, B. Brutley, F. C. Burdick, Jesse Owen and others. The first officers of the organization were F. C. Burdick, James Gallard, J. L. Johnson, C. Spicer and J. Goodale. The first religious services were held in the school house. The pastors, from the organization until the present time, are as follows: Rev. W. O. Glassner, one year; Rev. J. A. Kerr, one year; Rev. J. N. Platt, one year; Rev. W. Mitchell, one year; Rev. Bargelt, one year; Rev. George Elliott, one year; Rev. S. Sherrin, one year; Rev. O. H. Sproul, one year; Rev. J. G. Wilkinson, two years; Rev. J. M. Hedges, two years, and Rev. W. F. Barclay, two years. A majority of these divines held revival meetings while in charge. In 1870 the church was built, size 36 by 56, at a cost of $3,000, in which services are at present held. The present officers are C. Stone, J. Bailey, R. F. Shauntz, C. Wolf and W. Howenstein. The membership of the society is now about forty. The church is free from debt and prosperous.

The M. E. Sunday school was organized in 1870, with J. Goodale as superintendent. At present the following are interested in its management: Miss Mately Bush, Miss Anna Goodale and Mrs. J. Spicer. The attendance ranges from forty to sixty, and the school is in excellent order.

The Congregational Church of Parkersburg was organized in 1869 by Rev. J. N. Williams. Its first religious services were held at the depot of the Illinois Central Railroad, and subsequently in the old school house. In 1870 the present church edifice was erected at a cost of $3,500. Rev. Mr. Williams, who organized the church, became its first pastor. He remained some two or three years, and was succeeded by Rev. L. D. Boynton, who remained several years. Rev. H. H. Robbins was the next pastor. At the expiration of two years he was succeeded by Rev. H. M. Amsden, and in turn by Revs. Alexander Parker, G. W. Dorsey, H. M. Sly and J. P. Richards, the latter being the present pastor. The present officers of the church are I. E. Manley, R. R. Horr, and G. A. Warren, trustees; Fred Parrish, clerk; T. Wonderly, treasurer. The Sunday school was also organized in 1869, and is in a prosperous condition.

The Baptist Church of Parkersburg was organized by Rev. T. H. Judson, on the 27th of October, 1870, with seventeen members, as follows: A. Pingrey and wife, M. S. Miller and wife, Samuel Conn and wife, James Hall and wife, John Hall, H. H. Twining, George M. Cooper and wife,

Ruth Cooper, Mrs. S. Lynn, Mary Coryell and W. L. Laurence. The first officers were: Deacons, M. S. Miller and Joseph Collins; trustees, J. Collins, A. Pingrey and A. J. Cummings; clerk, H. H. Twining. The first religious services of this denomination were held at the Congregational Church in Parkersburg, and afterward for a time in district school houses. A hall near the depot was fitted up shortly, in which devotional services were held for two years. After that time, the Union Hall, on Main street, was used until the completion of their church edifice, which was ready for occupancy and dedicated on the 31st of October, 1880, by Rev. J. Sunderland. The first pastor of the organization was Rev. T. H. Judson, who remained from October 22, 1870, to June 28, 1871. He was a man of energy and ability, and did much toward building up the society. He is now at Swan Lake, Dakota. Rev. E. P. Barker next filled the pulpit, and remained until in March, 1872. He is now a resident of Hardin county. Following came Rev. C. Spragg, F. H. Judson and A. E. Simons. During the latter's term the church was erected. He was a man of decided ability and push. In March, 1881, the present pastor, Rev. J. B. Edmonson, took charge of the good work, and is doing effective service. The church is a neat frame structure, which was erected at a cost of about $1,200, and has a capacity for seating an audience of 300. The present officers of the church are as follows: Deacon and clerk, Joseph Collins; trustees, A. J. Cummings, W. H. Burdick and H. H. Twining. The total membership since organization has been 104; present membership, sixty-one.

The Sunday school was organized at the same time as the church, and now enrolls thirty-five members.

SPIRITUALIST SOCIETY.

The Spiritualists of Parkersburg and vicinity met on the 12th of January, 1873, at the residence of W. A. Curtis, pursuant to notice, for the purpose of organizing a society for the promotion of scientific and religious knowledge. The meeting was organized by electing Mrs. Lydia Bawn president, and W. A. Curtis secretary. Resolutions and regulations were adopted, and the following officers were elected: President, P. P. Parker; vice-presidents, Mrs. Lydia Bawn and C. B. Dodge; secretary, W. A. Curtis; treasurer, P. Wemple; trustees, Francis Bawn, Isaac Waters and F. L. Dodge.

The subject is still being agitated by the people.

MASONIC LODGE.

In May, 1868, a dispensation was granted to seven members of the Masonic fraternity, and the first formal meeting of Compass Lodge No. 239, was held May 26, 1868, and ever since then the stated meetings of the Lodge have been held Wednesday evening on or before the full moon of each lunar month. Harley Day was Worshipful Master during the year the Lodge was worked under dispensation. On June 2d, 1869, a charter was issued to Compass Lodge No. 239, by Reuben Michel, Grand Master, and T. S. Parvin, Grand Secretary. M. I. Powers was chosen W. Master of the Lodge. The Lodge has had seven Masters, as follows: Harley Day, M. I. Powers, R. L. Chase, D. W. Schoolcraft,

E. E. Savage, N. T. Johnson, and the present Master, A. O. Strout. The Lodge has had 115 members since its organization, but, as many have demitted and gone to other localities, it now has 55 members. There has been but two deaths—Isaac DePew and J. F. Root—but several former members died after having demitted and removed from here. The Lodge now occupies a fine comfortable hall, is prospering nicely, while peace and harmony prevails.

ODD FELLOWS.

Parkersburg Lodge, No. 258, I. O. O. F., was organized April 26, 1873, by Wellington Russell, D. G. M.; with the following named charter members: James Muncy, Isaac DePew, C. S. Lobdell, Thomas Curtiss and D. W. Currier. Its first officers were C. S. Lobdell, N. G.; James Muncy, V. G.; P. P. Parker, secretary; Isaac DePew, treasurer. The following named have filled the office of N. G.: C. S. Lobdell, James Muncy, N. T. Johnson, F. L. Dodge, H. Wood, D. D. Pierce, H. B. Perry, John Bird, H. Ballhausen, J. E. Kellogg, Wm. Pierce, J. M. Hedges, R. T. Bartholomew, W. H. Beckwith. The following named have died since the organization of the lodge: Isaac DePew, E. L. Galpin, John Erb and S. Morse. The total membership has been 95, with a present membership of 34. The lodge is in a healthy, prosperous condition.

DIRECTORY OF PARKERSBURG.

The following is a complete directory of the present business men of Parkersburg, and will serve as a recapitulation of the history of the town:

Allen, W. N.—Boots and shoes.
Bailey, James—Blacksmith and wagon maker.
Beaver Valley Bank—B. B. Richards and J. F. Parker.
Bohall, H. A.—Groceries, etc.
Brown, Charles—Blacksmith and wagon maker.
Burnham & Bass—Furniture.
Bush, E. C.—Carpenter.
Bird, John—Butcher.
Byerly, O—Photographer.
Connell, J. L.—Groceries and bakery.
Cooley, O. W.—Commercial Hotel.
Crossett, A. E.—Agricultural implements.
Collins Brothers—Creamery.
Conn, Thomas W.—Groceries, etc.
Decker, L. W.—Market.
Dodge Brothers—Proprietors *Eclipse*.
Exchange Bank—A. Wolfe & Son.
Elchleff, H. F.—Blacksmith and repair shop.
Foote & Mott—Hardware dealers.
Frank, M.—Harness maker.
Ferris, A. N.—Dentist.
Goodale, J. & Co.—General store.
Groat, J. H.—Grain and coal.
Howenstein & Co—Drugs.
Jackson, R. T.—Grocery.
Jensen, D.—Blacksmith.
Kennedy, James—Grain buyer.
Kientz, Mrs. Jacob—Restaurant.
Lahr, V.—Harness maker.
Lingleback, W.—Saloon.
Markley, H. H.—Butter dealer.
Mahanke, W. H. & Co.—General store.
Manley, N. T. & Son—General store.
Monty, D. C.—Grocer.
Norris Sam—Grocer.
Owen Mrs. S. E.—Grocer.

Parker & Richards—Agricultural implements.
Parris Bros.—Hardware.
Pierce, H. E.—Blacksmith.
Perkins, H. L.—Bakery.
Porcupile, J. H.—Carpenter.
Ray, Frank P.—Druggist.
Renken, Tammen—General store.
Russell, J. R.—Miller.

Rix, F. H.—Carpenter.
Schultz, E. G.—Jeweler.
Taylor, Mrs. H. F.—Milliner.
Voogd, O. D. & Co.—Lumber dealers.
Wade, Mrs. P. A.—Milliner.
Wolf & Son—Exchange Bank.
Wonderly, E. J. & Co.—General store.
Wheeler, J.—Carpenter.

CHAPTER XIX.

BEAVER TOWNSHIP.

This is the southeast township of Butler county, joined on the east by Black Hawk county, on the south by Grundy, on the north by Shell Rock township and on the west by Albion. In this, as in all the townships of the county, the government survey remains unchanged, this being a full congressional township, embracing the territory of township 90, range 15, containing an area of about 23,040 acres.

There are no very abrupt breaks in the general surface of the township, but through the center, from east to west, there is a ridge of upland. The soil of this upland is a heavy clay, while the lowland varies from a black loam to a light quicksand.

There are two main water courses—the Beaver and the west fork of the Cedar river. The latter enters the township south of the center of section 6, and crossing makes its exit near the middle of section 12. At this point it has the greatest flow of water, and empties almost directly into the Shell Rock. The Beaver—so named because in early days its waters were the resort of this animal—enters the township on section 31, and taking an easterly course finally flows through section 36 into Black Hawk county. Both streams have a number of small tributaries in Beaver township. The supply of timber is good. The main groves follow the course of the streams, with the exception of Beaver grove, which consists of several varieties of hard wood. The bottom land extends well back from the streams. The supply of stone is very meager, but there is plenty of good brick clay. From all these facts it can be seen that Beaver township is well timbered, well watered, and has a good soil. It is an excellent township, with bright prospects.

The Illinois Central Railroad crosses the township from east to west, having been constructed in 1864. The only town in Beaver is New Hartford.

EARLY SETTLEMENT.

Settlements began to be formed in this township in advance of most of the townships of Butler county. Its growth before the war was somewhat slow, but since that time the tide of immigration has been opened and its growth has been very rapid. There is an abundant evidence that the first settler in this township was Barnett Grandon, who came here from Linn county in the fall of 1851, and planted his pioneer stakes around a farm on section 30, where his son, William Grandon, now lives. He remained here until 1859. Returning again in 1860, he remained until 1877, when he removed to Nebraska, where he lived until 1882. Again he returned to this old "stamping ground," and now lives with his son William.

The following spring, Clinton Thomas made his appearance, and commenced farming on section 29. Here he remained until 1870, when he moved to Kansas, and from there to Texas, where he now resides. He was a native of Illinois.

Adna Thomas, Sr., came in the fall of 1852, and also settled on section 29. Here he remained until he died, August 12, 1868.

During the following year, 1853, "Nick." Hartgraves pushed his way within the limits of Beaver, and went into camp on section 30. He afterwards moved to section 29, but has since moved to the West Fork; he still lives in Butler county.

Rev. Nathan Olmstead came the following year. He was born in Wilton, Connecticut, on the 16th day of September, 1809, and is a son of David and Rebecca (Jackson) Olmstead, who were also natives of that State. When Nathan was seven years old the family emigrated to Tompkins county, New York, where they remained about three years, and then moved to Tioga—now Chemung—county, where the son lived until twenty-four years old. At that time he came West, and after spending one year in La Salle county, Illinois, moved to what is now DeKalb county. In 1842 he joined the Protestant Methodist Church, and, soon after, became a minister of the gospel. He followed this calling, as a local preacher, while in that State, and was also ordained a deacon while living there. In 1853 he came to Butler county, Iowa, and settled on section 18, Beaver township, and in January, 1854, entered the land where he now lives. In 1858 he was ordained an elder. Mr. Olmstead was an active worker in the church in the early days of the township. He preached the first sermon here the Sunday following his arrival, and soon afterward organized a church. He believes in republicanism, and has taken quite an active part in the politics of the township. In July, 1831, he was united in wedlock to Miss Julia Ann Knapp, also a native of Connecticut. Ten children have blessed this union, of whom eight are now living—Melissa, now the widow of Henry Thomas; Alonzo, living at Butler Center; Edward, living in Beaver township; Oscar now living in Waterloo; Orvis, now living in Ackley; Julia Ann, widow of Asa Lee, of Ackley; Theodore, who is living at home, and Lydia, wife of L. H. Boyd. In 1881 Mr. and Mrs. Olmstead celebrated their golden wedding. Mr. Olmstead is a genial, whole-souled gentleman, and a man who is greatly beloved and respected by all who have the honor of his acquaintance. Always fearless in doing right, and ready to tread under foot whatever borders on oppression, he is one of those, whose influence for good is felt by all who come in contact with him.

Others crowded in rapidly, among whom were the following named: James Collar, George E. Fitch, S. Hazelton, Charles Knipe, Aaron Olmstead, Peter Rude, John Hartgraves, Titus Ensign and Charles Ensign.

George E. Fitch, in 1857, took his slice of government domain from section 14.

S. Hazleton, in 1854, commenced his settlement on section 3, upon which he still resides.

James Collar located on section 15. He was born in Steuben county, New York, January 17, 1825; and is a son of Calvin and Eunice (Boss) Collar. His father was a native of Connecticut, and his mother of Rhode Island. When James was eleven years of age, his parents moved to Washington county, New York, and here the son grew to manhood on his father's farm, receiving a common school education. In 1853 he was married in that county to Miss Diantha Morton, a native of Massachusetts. In 1856 the young couple came to Butler county, Iowa, and purchased a farm of 240 acres on section 15, and two years later, bought 120 acres more. He afterwards sold his entire farm, and in 1866 purchased land on sections 22 and 23, and settled on the last named section. He now owns 330 acres, all of which is under fine cultivation, and has been brought to this condition by his own labor. Mr. Collar is a model farmer, and everything about his premises is in the best of order. He believes enthusiastically in republicanism. The office of county supervisor has been filled by him, and also the offices of township supervisor, town clerk and other minor township offices. Mrs. Collar is a member of the Baptist Church. One son has blessed this union—Calvin Morton—who is now living at home.

Charles Knipe selected section 10 as his future home, "way back" in 1855.

Aaron Olmstead had the year previous—1854—taken a farm on section 20. He is a son of Isaac L. and Elinor (Owens) Olmstead, and was born in Chemung county, town of Catherine, New York, on the 25th day of June, 1826. When Aaron was ten years of age his parents came west and located in LaSalle county, Illinois, where they remained a short time, and then settled in DeKalb county. Here the son grew to manhood on his father's farm, and afterwards followed the occupation of farming while in that State. In 1854 he came to Iowa and entered a farm of 160 acres on section 20, Beaver township, where he now resides. Mr. Olmstead has held the office of trustee of the township, and has always taken a great interest in school matters. He is a republican, and is a member of the United Brethren Church. In 1850 he was united in marriage with Miss Hulda M. Bagley, who is a native of Pennsylvania. Nine children have been born to them, of whom six are living—

Silas E., who lives near his father's place; Francis L., living at home; Edna H., wife of John Quimby, of Grundy county; Eliza, wife of Lorenzo Farnsworth; Margaret M. and Hattie M.

Peter Rude, in 1854, placed his sign manual upon papers for a farm on section 25.

Charles Ensign, one of the first settlers, came to this township in the fall of 1854, remaining but a short time, then removed to Waverly, Bremer county, where he opened the first school there during the winter following. He came back in 1856, and became a permanent resident. Titus Ensign, his uncle, had arrived here previously.

Charles Ensign is a son of Elias and Clara M. (Benjamin) Ensign, and was born in Colchester, Delaware county, New York, March 29, 1819. His father and grandfather were natives of New Hartford, Connecticut. The latter was a resident of that town eighty-three years, and died there at the advanced age of eighty-nine. He was a soldier in the Revolutionary war. Charles' father died in Walton, Delaware county, New York, in 1832. His mother was born in Columbia county, New York, and died in Castile, New York, in the same State, May 20, 1851. Mr. Ensign's early life was passed in the county of his birth, where he received a common school education, supplemented by three terms at a select school. When he was seventeen years old the family moved to Castile, Wyoming county, New York, where Charles lived for eighteen years. In March, 1854, he started west, and crossed the Mississippi river on the 29th day of that month. His first summer in the west was spent at Rockville, Delaware county, Iowa. In November he came to Waverly, Bremer county, and that winter taught the first school of the town. Here he remained until the spring of 1856, and then settled in New Hartford, Butler county, and during the winter of that year taught the first school in that village In 1855 Mr. Ensign voted for the temperance law. In his younger days he belonged to the whig party, but changed to a republican upon the formation of that party. He has taken an active interest in political matters in his township, and also quite an interest in the politics of the country. The office of township clerk has been filled by him for nineteen years out of the last twenty-four. Besides his business as a farmer, which occupation he has followed until the last year, he has been a notary public for the past twenty-two years. In 1846 he was united in marriage to Miss Nancy Swain, who is a native of Olean, New York. Four children have been born to them, of whom three are now living— Emily A., wife of William Strong, of Grundy county; Laura, who is now a teacher in the Cedar Falls Normal School, and is a graduate of the college in Iowa City. She graduated in the class of 1876, and in June of 1877 took the Diadactive degree, and one year later the Master of Arts degree. To her belongs the honor of being the first lady ever selected from that college to read the Master of Arts oration, Clarissa, the youngest daughter, is a student at the Cedar Falls Normal School.

Among other early settlers were—Baldwin Lewis, Alonzo Converse, Patrick Flinn, Daniel Martin, David Twohig, Michael Rude, H. T. Morris, William Rosebrough, L. B. Corwin, Peter Gunnison, Cassell

Churchhill, C. S. Root, J. B. Hare, Ash Cornwall, Lorin Cornwall, H..H. Weaver, Samuel Petters, Nelson Dowd, Geo. Daniels, Robert Stanley and James Williams.

EDUCATIONAL ITEMS.

The school facilities in Beaver are very good, and are equal in efficiency to those of any of the townships of Butler county.

The first school in the township was taught during the summer of 1855, in a log building, which was Baldwin Lewis' residence, on section 28. The teacher was Miss America Taylor, who died in Grundy county, a short time after her school closed. The land where the school house stood is now owned by C. S. Root.

The second school was taught by Charles Ensign, in New Hartford, in the winter of 1856–7.

The third school was taught in the summer of 1857, at New Hartford, by Mrs. Sarah Dean.

The fourth school in the township was taught at the residence of James Collar, in the southeast corner of section 15, by Mrs. James Collar, during the winter of 1857–8. There were seven pupils in attendance.

The first school house was erected in New Hartford, and was used for both school and church purposes. This was in 1859.

There are now eleven school houses in the township, all frame, and cost about $600 each. The school at New Hartford is noticed at length in the history of that place.

ITEMS OF HISTORICAL INTEREST.

The first marriage ceremony performed in the township was in 1857, the contracting parties being William Dodd and Miss Dowd. They were made one at the residence of William Dowd, the bride's father, on section 15, upon land now owned by Oliver W. Townsend.

The first death in the township was the wife of Joseph Casto, who had come to this vicinity in 1856.

In 1856 and 1857 there was but little advancement in matters here on account of financial stringency. During this time trading was mostly done at Cedar Falls. The land office was at Dubuque, and not a few exciting races were made for that office in 1857.

S. B. Ensign was appointed as the first postmaster. Afterward, through some means, another office was established at Taylor's Hill, about a mile southwest, and for some time mail was brought from Cedar Falls by private conveyance.

The first religious services were held at the house of Adna Thomas, on section 29, in May, 1853, by Rev. Nathan Olmstead. An organization was effected of the Protestant Methodist Church at this time, the members being Jacob Brown, Mrs. Adna Thomas and Alonzo Olmstead, with Rev. Nathan Olmstead as pastor. Services were held at the residence of Mr. Thomas. When a church of the same denomination was organized at New Hartford this little band became a part of the same.

MANUFACTURING INDUSTRIES.

The first saw mill erected within the limits of Beaver, was put up in 1855 by Mr. Marslin. The mill occupied a site on section 9, and for a number of years continued piling up sawdust, but was finally torn down.

The second saw mill erected within the limits of Beaver was put up by Titus and S. B. Ensign. The mill was on section 28. It has since been removed.

A steam saw mill was erected at an early day on section 30, by Alonzo Norris. The machinery, after a few years of active service, was sold and removed to Kansas, and the building rotted down.

Another steam saw mill was erected on section 29, some years ago, by James Williams, which led a roving life. It was first sold to Alonzo Converse, who removed it to section 28, opposite the village. It was next traded to John Shaw, who sold it to parties who removed it to Webster City, and it has since been moved to Tennessee.

CEMETERIES.

The first ground in the township which was used for burial purposes, was located on section 24. The first interment was the wife of Michael Rude, whose death occurred in the fall of 1854.

Oak Hill Cemetery is located on section 28. The first burial here was in December, 1876, when the remains of John Peckham were placed in their last resting place.

Another cemetery is located on section 29, but who was first to receive burial here we are unable to state.

ORGANIC.

According to the first division of Butler county into townships, Beaver embraced just one-fourth of the county, or in other words the territory now comprising the townships of Shell Rock, Jefferson, Albion and its present limits. This was in February, 1855, and the county court appointed Lyman Norton as judge of the first election, held in April of that year. In March, 1856, the county was again divided, by Judge Converse, and the upper half of what had constituted Beaver was organized as Shell Rock. Beaver then embraced the territory of Albion in addition to its present area. About this time one of the trustees elected did not qualify, and there was some difficulty about the funds belonging to Beaver proper, Albion claiming a part of them. Mr. Converse went to Clarksville, which was then the county seat, and drew the funds. Mr. Hammond having been appointed trustee in lieu of the unqualified trustee, a proper distribution was then made of the money.

On the 5th of October, 1857, Beaver was made to include only its present limits. The first election was held at the village of Willoughby.

The officers for the various years since organization have been as follows:

1857—Trustees, Charles Ensign, James B. Hare and Lewis Hammond; clerk, Alonzo Converse.

1858—Trustees, C. S. Root, Hannibal Hammond and Aaron Olmstead; clerk, James Collar.

1859—Trustees, Milo Hard, Thomas B. Hall and James Collar; assessor, C. S. Root; clerk, Charles Ensign; justices, George E. Fitch and Joseph Collins. T. W. Hall resigned as trustee, and James Williams was appointed in his stead.

1860—Justices, Joseph Collins and Loren Cornwell; constables, Lewis Hammond and Samuel Fetters; trustees, James Williams, Milo Hard and Aaron Olmstead; clerk, Charles Ensign; assessor,

Judd Bradley. April 2, 1861, Arthur Boyrie was appointed justice of the peace, Joseph Collins having resigned April 9, 1860. J. P. Wood was appointed to the office of constable in the stead of Lewis Hammond, he having moved from the township.

1861—Justices, J. A. Guthrie and Laren Cornwell; township supervisor, Milo Hard; clerk, Charles Ensign; trustees, C. S. Root, R. L. Olmstead and Aaron Olmstead; constables, Samuel Fetters and J. P. Wood; assessor, J. F. Root.

1862—Milo Hard, township supervisor; James Williams, assessor; Robert L. Olmstead, Aaron Olmstead, and C. S. Root, trustees; J. P. Wood and Samuel Fetters, constables; Charles Ensign and Laren Cornwell, each received an equal number of votes for township clerk, on October 12, 1861, and they determined by lot in the presence of R. L. and Aaron Olmstead, trustees, which should be town clerk, and the lot fell to Laren Cornwell.

1863—James Williams, James Collar and Aaron Olmstead, trustees; L. L. Smith and Laren Cornwell, justices; Samuel Fetters and John Davis, constables; L. Cornwell, town clerk; C. S. Root, assessor. January 23, 1863, C. S. Root was appointed to fill the vacancy caused by the resignation of James Williams, trustee. E. O. Groat was appointed assessor; the assessor-elect failing to qualify. J. P. Wood was appointed constable, that officer not qualifying.

1864—William Rosebraugh, town supervisor; Baldwin D. Lewis, assessor; Charles Ensign, clerk; James Collar, Arthur Boyrie and James B. Hare, trustees; E. D. Allbright, justice; James Hall and Philander Wood, constables. On the 23d of March, 1864, the trustees appointed O. W. McIntosh trustee to fill the vacancy occasioned by the resignation of Arthur Boyrie; also Thomas Wilson in place of Laren Cornwell, who failed to qualify; and Eugene Bourquin instead of L. L. Smith, who resigned. Early in October of the same year, the trustees appointed George E. Fitch township supervisor in place of Mr. Rosebraugh who had resigned.

1865—James Collar, supervisor; H. Smith, J. B. Hare and E. S. Maxwell, trustees; Charles Ensign, clerk; L. L. Smith and A. Vincent, justices; R. D. Smith and J.P.Wood, constables; C. S. Root, assessor.

1866—James B. Hare, E. S. Maxwell, and William Rosebraugh, trustees; Charles Ensign, clerk; Alonzo Converse, supervisor; C. S. Root, assessor; William W. Gibson, justice; Benjamin D. Smith and J. C. Jerome, constables.

1867—Alonzo Converse, supervisor; C. S. Root, assessor; E. S. Maxwell, C. E. Harmon, L. L. Smith, trustees; J. A. Smith and Amos Nettleton, justices; J. C. Jerome and B. D. Smith, constables.

1868—Amos Nettleton, supervisor, W. W. Olmstead, clerk; E. S. Maxwell, J. B. Hare and B. Haskin, trustees; Daniel Pickett, assessor; F. G. Foster and J. C. Wood, constables.

1869—Alonzo Converse, supervisor; William Burdick and George E. Fitch, justices; George E. Fitch, James Collar, and E. Bourquin, trustees; C. S. Root, assessor; Charles Ensign, clerk; J. P. Wood and C. E. Bristol, constables; J. A. Smith, collector.

1870—Alonzo Converse, supervisor; Charles Ensign, clerk; C. S. Root, assessor;

James Collar, J. F. Root and Robert Stanley, trustees; Charles Ensign, justice; E. H. Smith and E. C. Bristol, constables.

1871—J. E. Fitch and J. F. Root, justices; E. C. Bristol and John P. Campbell, constables; Charles Ensign, clerk; James Collar, O. W. McIntosh and J. F. Root, trustees; G. E. Fitch, assessor.

1872—Samuel Fetters, J. B. Hare and E. S. Maxwell, trustees; L. W. Jamison, assessor; Charles Ensign. clerk; J. S. McElwain, justice; J. E. Maxwell and E. C. Bristol, constables.

On March 23, 1873, L. L. Smith was appointed justice in the place of J. S. McElwain, who resigned.

1873—L. L. Smith and O. W. McIntosh, justices; John M. Diltz and Robert Stanley, constables; Charles Ensign, clerk; C. S. Root, assessor; Robert Packard, G. W. Bilson and O. W. McIntosh, trustees.

1874—Charles Ensign, clerk; Robert Packard, C. S. Root and E. S. Maxwell, trustees; G. W. Bilson, collector; James E. Campbell and B. Haskins, constables.

1875—L. L. Smith and August Critzman, justices; James E. Campbell and John Fetters, constables; C. S. Root, James Collar and Robert Packard, trustees; Charles Ensign, clerk; G. W. Bilson, assessor.

1876—J. S. McElwain, C. S. Root and L. W. Jamison, trustees; Melvin J. Pierce, clerk; G. W. Bilson, assessor; W. W. Warner, constable, to fill vacancy.

1877—J. S. McElwain and August Critzman, justices; J. A. Wood and Thomas Houck, constables; Henry Knipe, assessor; Charles Ensign, clerk; C. S. Root, L. W. Jamison and Patrick Grady, trustees.

1878—C. S. Root, L. W. Jamison and John E. Boyd, trustees; Charles Ensign, clerk; Henry Knipe, assessor.

1879—L. W. Jamison, John E. Boyd and R. Packard, trustees; Charles Ensign, clerk; L. W. Jamison, assessor; J. S. McElwain and August Critzman, justices; J. A. Wood and David Diltz, constables.

1880—C. S. Root, trustee, for three years; George F. Root, clerk; G. W. Bilson, assessor.

1881—August Critzman and L. L. Smith, justices; C. R. Harmon, assessor; Charles Ensign, clerk; G. W. Bilson, trustee, for three years, and John E. Boyd, two years.

1882—L. W. Jamison, trustee, for three years.

1883—L. L. Smith and August Critzman, justices; William H. Dwight and J. M. Knipe, constables; J. E. Boyd, trustee, for three years; Charles Ensign, clerk; C. R. Harmon, assessor.

VILLAGE OF WILLOUGHBY.

This village was laid out in the spring of 1855. Its plat occupied the southwest quarter of the northwest quarter of section 9. It was named by the proprietors—Cameron and McClure. The first house was built by this firm in the spring of 1855, and was occupied as a dwelling by G. W. Daniels. This building stood upon the grounds until 1862, when it was torn down.

A store was opened in the fall of 1855 by Cornwell Brothers, who carried a general line of goods. They remained until 1864, when they sold the stock to Mr. Hewart—as near as the name can be remembered—of Clear Lake, and he moved it to that place. A part of the store building was sold to O. W. McIntosh, who used it for a hotel, and the remainder was sold to B. Haskins, who occupied it as a residence for a time. It was afterward burned.

A blacksmith shop was started by Cornwell Brothers in the spring of 1856. After running it three years they sold to other parties.

The first school was taught by Miss Hannah Ensign during the winter of 1857-8, at the residence of Mr. King. The first school-house was erected in 1861, and is still standing.

A church organization of the Protestant Methodist faith was effected in the fall of 1870, and was disbanded two years later.

A hotel was built by the Cornwell brothers during the summer of 1856. They ran it until 1860, and it has since passed through the hands of J. B. Gordon, Robert Olmstead, O. W. McIntosh and H. D. Burnett. The latter gentleman ran it until 1872, when it was closed. A part of it is still upon his farm, and is used for a residence.

The postoffice of Willoughby was established in 1855, and was then on the Cedar Falls and Algona Mail Route. The first postmaster was G. W. Daniels. He was succeeded in turn by A. Cornwell, B. Haskins, O. D. Olmstead, R Stanley, George Burnett, David Diltz, Samuel Fetters and the present postmaster, H. D. Burnett. The office is now kept at his house, and is on the route from this place to Butler Center, mail being carried twice each week.

There are now two houses standing on the town plat aside from the school-house; and Willoughby as a village has ceased to exist.

NEW HARTFORD.

This is the only village of note in Beaver township. It was so named by Titus Ensign after the city of New Hartford, Connecticut, the former residence of some of the pioneer settlers here. The village is very pleasantly located on the northeast quarter of section 33, Beaver township, on the stream bearing the same name as the township, and on the Iowa Division of the Illinois Central Railway, one of the great thoroughfares of the northwest. The surrounding country is an excellent farming locality, and as the farmers are generally well-to-do, New Hartford has a good share of patronage, is a center for trade, and its future seems bright.

THE BEGINNING.

In the spring of 1854 a Mr. Chapman, of Cedar Falls, pre-empted the land where the village now stands, and in August of that year erected a little log house on or near the spot now occupied by the dwelling of Daniel Pickett.

In August, 1854, Titus and S. B. Ensign arrived here from Castile, Wyoming county, New York, and made arrangements to build a mill, after which they returned. Before returning, however, they bought the east half of the section upon which the village is located, and receiving authority from Mr. Chapman to enter it, which annulled his pre-emption claim. In January, 1855, the Messrs. Ensign returned to New Hartford, and pursuant to previous arrangements, erected a mill on the Beaver just north of where the creamery now stands, and the same year built a log house about twenty rods east of the present school building. During the fall, either in October or November, the village of New Hartford was platted by Titus Ensign, the surveyor being Mr. Holmes, who at that time filled the office of county surveyor. The original plat consisted of eight blocks and one public square; each block divided into eight lots, four by eight rods. In the spring of 1856 Judd Bradley made an addition to the village of three blocks on the north side. The streets running east and west were called Main, Water and Saratoga, commencing on the south side.

The first two houses erected in the village were built by Charles and S. B. Ensign, the former on lots 6 and 8, block 6, and the latter on lots 1 and 3, block 11. This was in the spring of 1856. Charles Ensign had the first deed issued after the village was laid out, and had his house ready for occupancy about the middle of May, when he brought his family from Waverly to occupy it—thus being the first resident in New Hartford.

G. W. Ensign came with Titus and S. B. In the spring of 1857 he erected a building on block 6, and put in the necessary machinery for cutting hard wood shingles. This mill he ran for five or six years, when the building was removed to lot 8, block 12, Root's addition, and with some changes is now used for a barn by Dr. Hagey.

Soon after this R. Shaw arrived, and built on lots 2 and 4, block 11; E. L. Shaw, who did the same on lots 2 and 4, block 10; E. M. Shaw, on lots 6 and 8, same block; Nelson Childs, on lots 5 and 7, block 8. E. M. Shaw erected a blacksmith shop on lot 7, block 11. Dr. Joseph Casto erected a house on lots 2 and 4, block 8, where L. L. Smith now lives.

E. O. Stevens bought the house built by S. B. Ensign on lots 1 and 3, block 11, and soon moved into it. Shortly afterward William Jones occupied it for a short time. Late in the summer, or early in the fall, Mr. Jones erected a building just west of the present store of Mr. Bourquin's, and started a saloon.

Martin Bailey, of Cedar Falls, made arrangements to erect a store building on lots 1 and 3, block 1, which was completed and ready for occupancy in August, 1856, at which time he brought his family and goods, and established the first store in New Hartford. He remained until May, or April, 1860, when he removed to Butler Center, where he is still living, engaged in agricultural pursuits.

In the fall of 1856, D. N. and Elijah Root, of Orleans county, New York, bought the west half of the northeast quarter of section 33, of Solomon Lashbrook, and platted what is known as Root's addition to New Hartford. During the winter of 1856-7 an election was held at Martin Bailey's store, to vote on the annexation of said addition, which resulted unanimously in favor of it. The judges of this election were Robert Shaw, Lansing Morrison and Dr. Casto; clerks, Martin Bailey and Charles Ensign.

D. N. Root purchased the building erected by E. L. Shaw on lots 2 and 4, block 10, and enlarged the same for a hotel, it being the first hotel in the township.

After this the immigration set in so rapidly that it is impossible to note them in detail.

HISTORY OF BUTLER COUNTY.

After the Messrs. Root had made an addition to the village, D. N. Root, furnished with a "site of the town on paper," visited the Eastern States and disposed of quite a number of lots, and other parties soon became interested in the welfare of the growing village.

In August, 1860, E. Bourquin arrived here from Dubuque and commenced trading in general merchandise, being the only store in the village at that time. In 1861 Mr. Bourquin sold his stock to a Mr. Welch, who supplied the wants of the people until the next fall, when Mr. Bourquin again bought the stock, and has continued in business ever since—the first ten years in a store building standing in the eastern part of town, but since 1871 on the corner of Main and Packwaukie streets. He does a business of about $30,000 annually.

Eugene Bourquin is a son of J. P. and Elizabeth (Ray) Bourquin, and was born in France in May, 1832. He came to America in 1854, and first located near Detroit, Michigan, where he remained some time, and then moved to Dubuque, Iowa, and engaged in the grocery business. Mr. Bourquin has held the office of school director, and was postmaster for eighteen years. In 1859 he was united in marriage to Miss Josephine Jardee, who is a native of New York State. They are the parents of four children—Afred, Lucien, Lewis and Julia.

HISTORICAL ITEMS.

The first birth in the township was Annie, a daughter of Mr. and Mrs. William Jones, during the time they occupied a part of O. E. Stevens' dwelling, in the latter part of August, 1856.

The second birth was a daughter, Celia, to Mr. and Mrs. Martin Bailey. This occurred on the 30th of December, 1856.

The first death was the wife of Dr. Joseph Casto, who passed away on the 31st of December, 1856. The second was that of a Mr. Hare in the winter of 1856-7. The third was of a daughter of Charles Ensign in July, 1857.

During the winter of 1857 a "singing school" was organized by Robert Shaw, and many pleasant social hours were passed by the lovers of music in this town.

EDUCATIONAL.

The first school was opened about the first of January, 1857, Charles Ensign being the teacher. Mr. Ensign taught for a term of three months, and was again chosen for the summer term. There being no school house in the district, the house of the teacher was used. On account of sickness and death in his family, Mr. Ensign was unable to finish the term. He therefore resigned, and Mrs. Sarah Dean was engaged to finish the term, the school being held at her house for the remainder of the year.

A school house was built during the year 1857, but was soon found to be unsuitable both in size and accommodations, and in 1867 a very good two-story building was erected, both stories being furnished for school use.

Among those who have filled positions in the New Hartford schools, are the following gentlemen: Messrs. Ensign, Huntley, Maxwell, White, Rogers, Stanton, Lucas, Maryatt, Savage, Lyon, Harwood, Atwell, Plummer, McElwain, Campbell,

Enos, Lynn, Bellows, Shepard and Hunter —and the following ladies: Misses Robbins, Rhodes, McGill, Olmstead, Chapman, Caldwell, Maxwell, Converse, Prince, Wolcott, Ricks, Guthrie, Stanton and Currier.

The present building was erected at a cost of about $2,000. There was quite a controversy about this structure, and also as to who should fill the offices. Even in those early days, when political purity was proverbial, there was plenty of wire-pulling and sharp dodges, which would compare very well with modern practices. At one time the schools of New Hartford were considered the most efficient in the county, and had scholars in attendance from all parts of the county. It was set off as an independent district in the winter of 1871-2.

RELIGIOUS.

The citizens of New Hartford had learned, it might be said, from the history of the world that the school house and the church were its greatest civilizers, and arrangements were early made for the preaching of the gospel. In the latter part of 1856, Rev. Nathan Olmstead preached the first sermon in this village, services being held in the store of Martin Bailey.

A meeting was held in the early part of 1857, in the school house (then in Mr. Ensign's house). Mr. Olmstead and Harvey Smith conducted the services, at which a class of the Protestant Methodist denomination was formed. The members were: E. M. and Robert Shaw, with their wives, Nelson Childs and wife, and Charles Ensign and wife. Nelson Childs was chosen as the first class-leader. No church edifice was ever erected by this denomination. Services were held for a number of years, but were finally abandoned, in 1870.

About the same time, in 1857, a Baptist Society was organized. Among the first members were Joseph Collins and wife, E. H. Collins and wife, Eber Dunham, Lois Dunham, Joseph Casto, Norman Devoe, S. B. Ensign and wife, Lewis Hammond and wife, and Daniel Pickett. Joseph Collins and Daniel Pickett were chosen deacons; Norman Devoe, church clerk. The first minister was Rev. I. R. Dean.

A Union Sabbath School was formed in May, 1857, at a meeting held in the school room at Charles Ensign's. That gentleman was chosen superintendent. This school thrived for about five years, after which the Baptist and Methodist Episcopal denominations each had a distinct school.

The Baptist society built a church in 1866, at a cost of $5,500, being the first building of the kind in the county used exclusively for church purposes. They also own a good parsonage, worth $1,500. The present membership of the church is 87. Following Rev. I. R. Dean in pastoral work, were Rev's. Gibbs, A. Orcutt, William Wood, E. G. O. Grout, D. P. Maryatt, Mr. Cox, Judson H. D. Weaver, L. D. Lamkin, William M. Simmons and William C. Pratt, the present pastor.

The present officers of the church are— George M. Bronson, A. V. Sprague, E. S. Philo, Daniel Pickett, deacons. Miss Lottie L. Dwight, church clerk; E. Bourquin, William Strong, A. V. Sprague, trustees.

The Sunday school in connection with this church has a membership of 65, with the following officers: G. M. Bronson, superintendent; Mrs. Jesse H. Pratt, assistant; Frank Bolton, secretary; Trilla Pratt and Julia Bourquin, organists.

METHODIST EPISCOPAL CLASS.

The circuit which originally included this town, embraced a large extent of territory, but in 1857, there being a sufficient number, a class was organized at New Hartford, with E. S. Maxwell for class leader, and having the following members: E. S. Maxwell and wife; Mr. Shaw and wife; Robert Shaw and wife; Mr. Childs and wife. Meetings were held every two weeks in the old log school house. The church experienced from time to time revival seasons, when goodly numbers were added to the society. The first sermon preached by a representative of this denomination was at the residence of Charles Ensign, in 1856. Soon afterward this class was formed and the gospel regularly dispensed. The following ministers have since presided: Rev's. Taylor, George Murphy, Glasner, Ward, McGee, Bargett, McKim, McKee and W. Ward Smith, the present pastor. The membership having largely increased, more room was a necessity, and in 1871 a neat and commodious house of worship was erected, at a cost of $3,000. The dedicatory sermon was preached by Rev. A. B. Kindig. The present membership is 62, with the following named officers: Class leader, Ira Bicksby; trustees, C. Ensign, E. S. Maxwell, W. H. Hunter; stewards, H. G. King, E. S. Maxwell, John Dixon, Mrs. Nancy Ensign and Mrs. Jane E. Crane. A neat parsonage building has just been completed. The church is free from debt, and in a prosperous condition.

SALOONS.

New Hartford has always taken an active part in the temperance cause. Several attempts have been made to carry on the liquor traffic, but none of them have succeeded. About 1862 one Miller, a carpenter by trade and saloon keeper by profession, pursued his dual calling for a short time.

In December, 1857, H. S. Burch opened a stock of intoxicating liquors, and for a short time was allowed to sell the same without open protest. But the evils were not long in manifesting themselves, and the citizens determined to test his lawful right to disturb the peace. Accordingly a search warrant was issued and placed in the hands of Morey J. Hewett, deputy sheriff of the county, who found and took possession of the liquor. When the day of trial came Mr. Burch agreed to the destruction of the liquor and promised not to engage in the traffic in the future.

In March, 1859, M. J. Coon arrived at New Hartford and became a guest at D. N. Root's hotel. It was soon discovered that he had one or more casks of liquor in his wagon, and that he had either sold or given away enough to cause the beastly intoxication of some of the citizens. The inhabitants were incensed at the audacity of the man, and again proceeded to get possession of the liquor on a search warrant issued by Martin Bailey, justice of the peace. The officers executed the warrant, and while the citizens were sending to Clarksville for M. M. Trumbull to prosecute the case some of the principal witnesses placed themselves beyond the reach of subpœnas. When the day of trial came a compromise was made, Mr. Coon getting his liquors again on condition that he leave the county with them and never return to engage in the business, which agreement he has since observed.

POST OFFICE.

In the summer of 1855 the government established a post office in the village called Beaver Grove, and S. B. Ensign was appointed postmaster; but on account of an office established at Taylor's Hill, a mile and a quarter southwest, at about the same time, the government discontinued the supplies for the village office, and the citizens of New Hartford had their mail matter brought from Cedar Falls by private conveyance until arrangements were made for regular supplies.

The office at New Hartford was established in 1858, and was first kept in Root's hotel, D. N. Root being commissioned deputy postmaster. Dr. Joseph Casto, the first postmaster, was succeeded by C. H. Chamberlain, Dr. J. A. Guthrie, J. P. Wood, E. Bourquin and J. S. McElwain, the present incumbent. The office, of course, was changed from one place to another as the officers changed. It was made a money-order office on the 15th of August, 1881, and the first order was sent on that date by David Diltz to William Ewald, of Waterloo, the amount being $10. The first order received was paid on the same date to Dr. Wm. H. H. Hagey, the remitter being W. C. Sackett, of Sterling, Illinois, to the amount of $9.75.

PRESENT BUSINESS.

The business interests of New Hartford at present are represented in all the various lines. The business men are an energetic, enterprising class. We present in this connection a short historical resume of the different establishments.

Martin Bailey has already been mentioned as having started the first store in New Hartford. He now lives in Butler Center.

The business house of E. Bourquin has already been noticed at length.

The New Hartford creamery was established in 1877, by a stock company. In the spring of 1880 E. Bourquin purchased the property, and now does a business amounting to $20,000 annually. The building which it occupies is 24x75 feet, one story in height, a five horse steam engine, and an eight power boiler is the propelling force.

The grain trade is carried on exclusively by J. Paulger & Son. A warehouse was erected by Root & Beckwith a number of years ago, and after running it for about six years, it was sold to E. Bourquin; it was sold again to E. Williams, who was succeeded by the present owners, J. Paulger & Son. The elevator was built by T. Beswick, in 1876, and was afterwards sold to J. Paulger & Son. Its size is 24x40, two stories high.

The drug business was established in the fall of 1880, by Wick Brothers, who are now doing a good business.

The hardware store and the lumber yard of J. Paulger & Son was established by J. Cousins, and was purchased in July, 1882, by the present owners. J. Paulger

Peter Coyle.

& Son established a coal yard in 1870, and still continue the business.

John Paulger, of the firm of Paulger & Son, was born in England, on the 5th day of April, 1825. He was reared on a farm and followed the occupation of a farmer while in that country. Upon his arrival in America, in 1869, he came to Iowa, and settled in New Hartford, Butler county. Soon after his settlement here he became engaged in the coal trade, and at present deals in grain, lumber and hardware, and is one of the "live" business men of the town. He was married in 1848 to Miss Ann Hobson, also a native of England. They have six children—John Hobson, who lives in England; Alice, also living in England; F. W., who is in partnership with his father; Grace Ellen, the wife of G. P. Linn, of Sumner; Frank O., who lives in Nebraska; and Annie, who is still at home.

In the fall of 1860, G. W. Maxwell established a general merchandise store, which he still carries on, doing a good business.

In the fall of 1867, R. D. Strickland opened a general merchandise store in a part of the building he now occupies. He now does a business of $5,000 annually. He is a son of Chandler and Hannah (Willard) Strickland, and was born in Watson, Lewis county, New York, October 19, 1832. There he received a common school education, and spent the first thirty years of his life. In 1862 he moved to Herkimer county, New York, where he lived three years, and thence to Parkersburg, West Virginia, where he engaged in trade for some time. In 1867 he came to New Hartford, Butler county, and engaged in the mercantile business, in which he still continues, enjoying a good trade.

J. R. Fifield was born in St. Lawrence county, New York, on the 10th day of August, 1841, and is a son of Robert and Betsy (Perkins) Fifield. His mother was a native of New York State, and his father of Vermont. J. R. received his education and grew to manhood in his native county. During the first year of our late rebellion, he enlisted in Co. F, 60th N. Y. Infantry, as a color sergeant, and was discharged at Wautchie, Tennessee, in 1863. He afterwards re-enlisted in the veteran volunteer corps—same regiment—and was again honorably discharged at Annapolis, Maryland, in 1865. Upon receiving his dismissal he returned to his native county and engaged in the furniture trade until 1872, when he came to Iowa and settled in New Hartford, Butler county. The year following his arrival he again embarked in the furniture business, and continued in that branch of trade until 1878, when he opened a wagon shop. Mr. Fifield was elected president of the school board in 1882. He was married in 1865 to Miss A. I. Hutchinson, a native of New York. They have two children—Maud A. and Allie.

The Exchange Hotel, the only one in town, was originally built for a store. It has thirteen rooms for the accommodation of guests.

There are three blacksmith shops in town.

OTHER SETTLERS.

Many other persons of more or less prominence have contributed toward the building of this township, and its present prosperity is largely due to their influence. Limited space forbids the mention of all, but the following will be found a sufficient number to show the character of this settlement, which is largely made up of a thrifty, energetic class of intelligent farmers:

J. F. Bolton was born in Botetourt county, Virginia, on the 14th day of January, 1825, and is a son of Peter and Mary (Falls) Bolton. His mother was a native of Pennsylvania, and his father of Virginia. When J. F. was five years old the family moved to Giles county, Virginia; there the son grew to manhood, and received a common school education. In April, 1854, he came to Iowa, and took a claim of 160 acres on section 21, Beaver township, where he still resides. His brother George resides with him. Mr. Bolton's father died in Cedar county, Iowa, in 1858; his mother followed in September, 1878.

Samuel Fetters is a son of Philip and Catherine (Dickerhoff) Fetters, and was born in Stark county, Ohio, September 9, 1827, where he remained until twenty-six years of age. His early life was passed on a farm. He then spent one year in the State of Indiana, and in 1854 moved to Black Hawk county, Iowa; from there he moved to Willoughby, Iowa, where he remained four weeks; then removing to New Jerusalem, Butler county, remaining until the following August, he returned to Willoughby, purchased town lots, and built a house, dwelling there about twelve years; he then purchased and settled on a farm on section 8 of Beaver township, where he now owns 110 acres of land. Mr. Fetters was postmaster at Willoughby two years, and has also held the offices of trustee and constable. In 1850 he was married to Miss Catherine Ann Daniels, a native of Ohio. They have had eight children, five of whom are living—John, Clark, George, Samuel and Ida May, the wife of William M. Olmstead. Mr. Fetters' father died in 1855; his mother followed in 1862.

T. G. Copeland is a son of Joseph and Clarinda (Litchfield) Copeland, and was born in Courtland county, New York, April 8, 1817, where he remained for thirty-nine years, with the exception of one and one-half years spent in Illinois. While young he learned the boot and shoe trade, following that occupation most of the time while in Courtland county. In 1856 he came to Shell Rock township, Butler county, Iowa, and during the spring of 1857 moved into the village of Shell Rock. During the year 1859 he was in partnership with O. S. Newcomb. Early in the year 1865 Mr. Copeland settled on his farm in Butler township, and there resided for eleven years. He then came to Beaver township and settled on a farm on section 9. He held the office of coroner of Butler county for four years. In 1841 he was married to Miss Serepta Couch, who bore him six children, four of whom are now living—George R., Willis D., Charles F. and Horace E. This wife died in 1875, and in 1876 he was married to Hannah A. Couch, widow of Wilson Couch. She had eight children by her first husband, four of whom are now living—Manderville A., Albert A., Adelaide, wife of Burton Hollenbeck, and Ella, wife of Elbert Tabor.

E. W. Ensign is a son of Titus and Lucretia (Belden) Ensign, and was born in

Wyoming county, New York, on the 26th day of June, 1844, where he remained until 1857, when the family moved to New Hartford, Iowa. In May, 1864, E. W. enlisted in the one hundred day service, in Company E, Forty-fourth Iowa Infantry, and served until honorably discharged September 13, 1864. Returning to civil life Mr. Ensign engaged in milling and farming. In 1866 he was married to Miss Martha A. Raymond. They have eight children, all of whom are living—Susan, Jennie, Flora, Charles, Nellie, Harry, May and Lewis.

C. R. Harmon is a son of C. E. and Hannah E. (Smith) Harmon, and was born in Saratoga county, New York, December 31, 1845. When he was ten years of age his parents moved to Ypsilanti, Michigan, where they remained two years, then came to Butler county, Iowa, first settling on the southwestern quarter of section 15. After living here some time they moved to New Hartford village. The son remained at home until nineteen years of age, and then began life for himself by entering E. Bourquin's store as clerk. Here he labored for several years, and finally opened a store of general merchandise in the town of New Hartford. In September, 1881, he settled on his farm on section 17. He now owns 240 acres of land. Mr. Harmon is at present assessor of the township, having previously filled that office two terms. He was married on the 1st of January, 1872, to Miss Mary Childs, also a native of Saratoga county, New York. They have four sons living—Willie J., Fred C., Arthur N. and Harry F. In May, 1864, Mr. Harmon enlisted in the one hundred day service, and after five months of service was honorably discharged.

E. S. Maxwell is a son of Anthony L. and Rachel (Stafford) Maxwell, was born in Saratoga, Saratoga county, New York, December 2, 1818. He remained in that county until 1857, then came west to Iowa, and settled in Beaver township. During his second year here he purchased a farm on which he lived for three years. Since that time he has been in business at New Hartford. Mr. Maxwell has been trustee of the town several times. He was married in 1839 to Miss Amy Quackenbush, also a native of New York State. They have four children—George W., John E., Carrie, wife of Edwin Williams, of Cherokee; and Hattie, who is living at home.

Baldwin D. Lewis (deceased) was born in Erie county, Ohio, March 10, 1830, where he passed his early life, on a farm. He was married in March, 1852, to Miss Elizabeth Phelps, a native of Maryland. When she was eleven years of age her parents moved to Ohio, where the daughter grew to womanhood. In 1857 she, with her husband, came to Iowa and located on a farm on section 19, of Beaver township, Butler county. Six children were born to them, five of whom are living—Adella, the wife of Elias Harmon; Josephine, wife of George Caywood; Milo, Callie and Ida. Mr. Lewis died in September, 1872.

Jacob M. Knipe was born in Montgomery county, Pennsylvania, June 30, 1848, and is a son of John S. and Mary (Mosser) Knipe, who were both natives of Pennsylvania. In 1860 the family moved to Iowa, and settled on a rented farm on section 15, of Beaver township, Butler county. The father afterwards purchased a farm on section 16 of the same township, which, upon his death in 1880, fell to a family of seven children. The mother died in 1878. In 1872 Jacob settled on his farm on section 8, where he now resides, and owns 193 acres. Mr. Knipe is at present one of the constables of the town. He was married in 1872 to Miss Anna Bolton; they have three children—Bertie, Edith and James. For seven successive winters Mr. Knipe taught school in this county.

L. L. Smith was born in Granby, Hampshire county, Massachusetts, May 12, 1830, and is a son of Elisha and Nancy (Goldthwaite) Smith, also natives of Massachusetts. When he was twenty-three years old he came west to Illinois, and settled on a farm in Bureau county, where he remained until 1860. In March, 1860 he came to Albion township, Butler county, and lived on a farm for three years. Afterwards he became proprietor of the hotel at New Hartford, remaining there until he took the office of sheriff, January 1, 1868, which office he held four years, and then returned to New Hartford, afterwards engaged in farming about three years, he finally settled himself in the insurance business. Mr. Smith has held the office of justice of the peace most of the time since 1872. In May, 1864 he enlisted in Company E, Forty-fourth Iowa, and served as First Lieutenant until honorably discharged at Davenport, Iowa, in September of that year. In 1851 he married Miss Adelia Dwight, also a native of Hampshire county, Massachusetts. Six children have been born to them, three of whom are now living, to-wit—William D., who is now principal of the Jackson public schools, Jackson county, Minnesota; Clara and Roscoe D.

Nelson H. Whipple is a son of Josiah and Eunice (Hazen) Whipple, and was born in Summit county, Ohio, December 29, 1832. When Nelson was three years of age, the family moved to Portage county, and afterwards to Ashtabula county, Ohio. Here he remained until twenty-one years old, then moved to Illinois, where he spent one year. In the fall of 1855 he came to Iowa and settled in Grundy county near the Butler county line. The following July he went to Minnesota, and after living in LeSueur county two years, returned to Grundy county, where he spent three more years; he then moved to Beaver township, Butler county, and worked in the Vorris mill. In December of the year 1862, he settled on his present farm on section 29, and engaged in carpentering. Mr. Whipple was married October 21, 1856 to Miss Zillyah Taylor, a native of Ohio. They have five children living—Flora Amelia, wife of C. I. Bolton; Rosella V., wife of William C. Murray; Nelson Adolph, Harry Earl and Jerry Burton.

S. S. Cortright is a son of Cornelius and Catherine (Winter) Cortright, and was born in Wilkesbarre, Luzerne county, Pennsylvania, March 6, 1826. Here he learned blacksmithing, and remained until nineteen years of age; after which he came west and located in Clinton, Rock county, Wisconsin, where he followed his trade. At the end of three years he moved to Boone county, Illinois, where he worked at his trade for fifteen years. In May of the year 1863 he came to Butler county, Iowa, and located at New Hartford, where he followed his trade for two years, and then settled on his farm on section 14. He now owns 240 acres of land on sections 14 and 23. Mr. Cortright was married in 1849 to Miss Eliza A. Covey, a native of New York. They have three children living—Edward J., Alta D., and George C.

Herman D. Burnett is a son of George B. and Electa (Daily) Burnett, and was born in Jefferson, Schoharie county, New York, December 13, 1838, where he remained until twenty-one years old; then came west and settled in Bureau county, Illinois, where he remained until the first year of our late rebellion. At that time he enlisted as a private in Company C, Seventh Illinois Cavalry, and served until honorably discharged at Springfield, Illinois, October 21, 1863. Upon again entering civil life he returned to Bureau county, and there remained until the following spring, when he came to Shell Rock, Butler county, Iowa. This place he made his home until his removal to Beaver township in the year of 1866. He now owns a good farm of 120 acres in that township. Mr. Burnett has been postmaster at Willoughby three years. In April of the year 1864 he was married to Miss Lucy Darrow, a native of Pennsylvania. They have five children—Ella May, Ethel Amelia, Rosaltha, George Eugene and Royal Curtis.

L. W. Jamieson is a son of John and Ann (Remiley) Jamieson, and was born in Lewis county, New York, June 13, 1831. He was reared on a farm, and remained in his native county until the year 1856. At that time he came west and located in LaSalle county, Illinois, where he lived until the spring of 1865. He then came to Iowa and located on the southeastern quarter of section 15, Beaver township, Butler county. Here he now resides and owns 220 acres of land, 200 of which are under cultivation. Mr. Jamieson has held the office of town assessor, and at present is one of the town trustees. He has also been a member of the school board. In January, 1854, he was married to Miss Lucy Peebles, a native of Lewis county, New York. Five children have been born to them—Edward, who now lives in Dakota; Clarence, Charles, Lillie and Coy.

G. W. Billsen is a son of J. N. and Hester M. (Tobias) Billsen, and was born in Tompkins county, New York, in January, 1824. There he remained until he became of age, then moved westward, and settled in Cook county, Illinois, where he remained fourteen years, following the business of railroading. In 1859 he went south, and there lived until the third year of the late war. Having, with so many others, suffered a financial reverse, he decided to return to the North. In 1865 he removed to this State, and bought his present farm, on sections 20 and 21, of Beaver township. He now owns 120 acres of land. After making this purchase he engaged in railroading for several months in Missouri and Wisconsin, and in the fall of the succeeding year, settled on his farm. Mr. Billsen belongs to the republican party, and has taken an active interest in the county politics. He filled the office of assessor four years, and is present trustee of the township. In 1848 he was united in wedlock to Miss Isabel Millen, who bore him one child—J. M.—and died in the city of Chicago, during the year of 1852. In January, of the year 1866, he was married to Hattie A. Chapman.

M. W. Ashton resides on section 15, where he located October 1, 1872. Mr. Ashton was born in Livingston county, New York, July 2, 1832. He was brought up in the town of Mount Morris, in that county. His parents were Sidney and Eliza Ashton. He married Eliza A. Demmon, daughter of Calvin Demmon. Mrs. Ashton was born in Tuscarora, Livingston county, New York, in August, 1833. They were married December 24, 1856; removed to Illinois in 1863, and to Indiana the same year; to their present location from the latter State. Mr. and Mrs. Ashton have two daughters—Minnie, now Mrs. John Knipe, and Cora. Mr. Ashton's farm contains 140 acres.

J. W. Seaver is a son of J. W. and Mary E. (Long) Seaver, and was born in Genesee county, New York, March 15, 1834. When six years of age his parents came west and settled in Walworth county, Wisconsin. Here J. W. grew to manhood and lived until the spring of 1868, when he came to Butler county, Iowa, and settled in Albion township. Here he lived until 1872; then moved to Beaver township and settled on section 18, where he now owns 140 acres of land. In 1855 he married Miss Mary E. Rogers, a native of Washington county, New York. They have two children—Albert VanNess and Arthur E.

John E. Boyd was born in Logan county, Ohio, July 28, 1835, and is a son of James and Margaret (Sullivan) Boyd, who were natives of Virginia. He was reared on a farm and received a common school education. On the 1st day of May, 1864, he enlisted in the one hundred days' service, and served until honorably discharged at Columbus, Ohio, after serving one hundred and fifty days. Upon receiving his dismissal he returned to his home in Logan county, where he remained until the month of October; then came West, and settled on a farm in Grundy county, Iowa. There he lived one year, then moved to Black Hawk county, where he resided about seven years. In the spring of 1872 he came to Beaver township, Butler county, and settled on section 3, where he now resides, owning a fine farm of 200 acres. Mr. Boyd has been a member of the board of trustees for four years. In 1865 he was united in wedlock to Miss Caroline Wheeler, also a native of Ohio. They have seven children—Walter H., Deborah M., Emma May Belle and Rosana May Belle, (twins), Abbie E., Cora Matilda, and Nettie Florence.

Aug. Critzman was born in Germany, February 12, 1848, and is a son of Aug. and Rosalia (Bufleb) Critzman, both natives of that country. In 1857 his father died, and two years after this sad event he and his remaining parent came to America. They settled in Rockford, Illinois, and there engaged in farming for thirteen years. At the expiration of that time Aug. came to Butler county, Iowa, and settled on section 8 of Beaver township, where he now owns a fine farm of 120 acres. His mother died in 1867. Mr. Critzman is present justice of the peace, and has held that office for the past ten years. In 1870 he was united in marriage to Miss Louisa Lake. They are the parents of four children—Oliver, Flora, Maud and Mabel.

Chauncey Chapman was born in Monroe county, New York, November 6, 1809. He remained in his native county until

1842, and then came West, and settled on a farm in McHenry county, Illinois. In 1872 he moved to Iowa, and, in the spring of the following year, settled on section 20, of Beaver township, Butler county, where he now owns 160 acres of land. Mr. Chapman was married in 1835 to Miss Mercy French, a native of New York. Seven children have been born to them, of whom four are now living—Hattie A., wife of G. W. Billsen; Chauncey S., Justus H., and Emma, wife of E. R. Dodd.

W. M. Hunter, the present county recorder, was born in Warren county, Indiana, March 11, 1853, and is a son of James and Caroline (Mears) Hunter. His mother was born in Indiana, and his father in county Antrim, Ireland. Two years after William's birth, the family came to Butler county, Iowa, and settled in Ripley township, where his parents still reside. William grew up on his father's farm, attending school during the winters, until seventeen years old. He then attended the Iowa City Academy seven months, and afterwards Lennox College, at Hopkinton, Iowa, fall and winter, for three years. He taught his first term of school at Pine Creek, Buchanan county, Iowa, at a salary of $28.00 per month; also, a term near Zwingle, Dubuque county. This was during the years he attended college. Mr. Hunter has taught twenty-five terms to the present time, filling the position in the towns of Butler Center, Aplington, Shell Rock and New Hartford. In the spring of 1881 he became principal of the New Hartford school, filling that position with great credit. In 1882 he was the republican nominee for recorder, and was elected. April 22, 1878, he was married to Miss Alice Conn, who was born in Canada. They have one child living—Willie G. Mr. Hunter is popular wherever known, and there doubtless is a bright future before him.

CHAPTER XX.

BENNEZETTE TOWNSHIP.

This township occupies the northeast corner of Butler county. It is bounded upon the north by Floyd county; on the west by Franklin county; on the east by Coldwater township, and on the south by Pittsford. It embraces township 93, north, of range 18, west. The area is 23,040 acres, or 36 square miles.

The land is rolling, consisting mostly of prairie. The soil is a rich, dark loam. There are only two small groves of timber, so whatever timber needed is brought from Coldwater or Franklin county. The main water courses are two small creeks—Hamlin's and Coldwater. These supply a sufficient amount of water for practical purposes. During dry seasons the creeks become very low. Years ago the land was marshy, but now, in ordinary seasons, one can scarcely find a piece of land unfit for cultivation. It is better adopted for stock than almost any township in Butler county, from the fact of it being good grass land.

Most of the trade is carried on with Greene, Dumont and Bristow. The nearest railroad point is in Franklin county for the west side; Greene for the east side, and Dumont and Bristow for the south.

Artificial groves surround nearly all residences, and the various pieces of timber planted and cultivated by the farmers, will soon give the vast prairie the appearance of a timbered country.

EARLY SETTLEMENT.

In early days the township of Bennezette was in the Dubuque Government Land District, as was almost the entire county. The first settler was William A. Keister, who arrived here in 1854, and took his claim in the northeast of the southeast quarter of section 1. Here he erected a dwelling, but after a short time sold the place to William Kingery, and purchased the northeast quarter of the same section where he yet resides. Mr. Keister was born in Montgomery county, Ohio, in June, 1830. When quite young his parents moved to Warren county, Indiana. In February, 1852, he there married Mary J. Miller, a native of Ohio, born in 1833. The following year after marriage he removed to this county and township as stated. In 1862 he enlisted in the Thirty-third Iowa Infantry, and served with it until the close of the war, participating in fourteen engagements. He was honorably discharged at Montgomery, Alabama, July 22, 1865. Returning to his home he resumed farming, and in 1867 erected his present residence. Mr. and Mrs. Keister have eight children living—Annie, Louis A., John A., Milton W., Alfred B., Iona., Ora E. and C. O. Mr. Keister at present holds the office of justice of the peace.

In 1855 John J. Chase came to Bennezette township from Waverly, and drove his stakes on section 4. He remained but a short time.

In 1856 William Kingery, a native of Indiana, purchased the farm of Mr. Keister. He remained there until 1865, when he removed to his present home on section 13 in Coldwater township. At the same time, came Hamblin, a native of Ohio. He took up a claim in the southeast quarter of section 30. In 1863 he removed to Butler Center. His whereabouts at present are unknown.

Another early settler was William Mufley, a native of the Empire State, who claimed the northwest quarter of section 1. He is now living at Osage.

Milton Wilson, a pioneer of 1857, is a native of New York, born in Niagara county, in 1826. His younger days were spent on a farm. On the 17th of April, 1850, he married Adaline Freer, a native of Niagara county, New York. He subsequently moved to Lockport and engaged in the boot and shoe trade. In the fall of 1852 he removed to the town of Cambria, and returned to farm life. In 1856 he sold out, and in the spring of 1857 started west.

Milton Wilson.

Arriving at Buffalo the family took passage in a boat for Milwaukee, from which point they came overland to Butler county, and located a claim on section 15, Bennezette township. Mr. Wilson at once erected a shanty in which the family lived until a more comfortable house was built. For some time they were without a stove, Mrs. Wilson doing her cooking by an open fire. Ten children have blessed the union of Mr. and Mrs. Wilson—George W., E. Frank and R. L., who were born in New York; Mary H., Cora A., Ida L., Douglas, Addie J., John C. S. and Ed. M., born in Iowa. Mr. Wilson has been prominently identified with the interests of both town and county. He was one of the first county supervisors elected in 1859, serving a term of one year; was again re-elected in 1860; elected again in 1878, serving for three years. He has held town offices, and is at present town clerk, an office he has filled several years. In politics Mr. Wilson is a democrat. He cast his first vote for President, for Lewis Cass, of Michigan. He sold his first wheat at Cedar Rapids, 110 miles distant, at sixty cents per bushel. That was the nearest market at the time.

Among those who came in 1857, were Ira A. and Cyrus D. Chamberlin, Oliver Evans, William P. Woodworth, Samuel Overturf, Orin C. Smith, John A. Smith, George O'Brien, Philip, John and Michael McKinney, John and Philip Kelley, John P. Mills, and James H. Morris.

Ira A. and Cyrus D. Chamberlin were natives of Vermont. They both took up claims on section 34; Ira securing his present farm, on the northeast quarter; and Cyrus, the southeast, where he remained until his death, in 1866.

Ira A. Chamberlin was born in Windsor county, Vermont, on the 22d of February, 1831. His younger days were spent in school and on the farm. In 1852 he moved to Illinois, remaining one year in Cook county. He then moved to Michigan, where he spent four years in Ottawa county. In 1857 hs came to Iowa and settled in Bennezette township, Butler county, where he took a claim on section 34. In 1861-2 he built his present frame house, and married, in 1867, Mrs. Hannah, widow of Cyrus Chamberlin. They have had two children—Agnes B. and Martilla J. Agnes died in 1875, in her fourth year.

Cyrus D. Chamberlin, brother of Ira A. Chamberlin, was born in Windsor county, Vermont, May 25, 1827; died of comsumption, in Bennezette township, Butler county, Iowa, in 1866. In 1854 he left his native State, locating in Michigan. In 1857 he moved to Bennezette township, and took a claim on section 34. In 1859, going to California, he engaged in mining until 1862, when he returned to Bennezette township. In 1864 he married Miss Hannah Hall. Mr. Chamberlin was a respected citizen, making friends wherever he went. Sorrow at his death was felt by all.

Oliver Evans was born in Columbia county, New York, September 15, 1825; when but four years of age his father died. His mother soon after married again. In 1840 the family moved to Cayuga county. In 1853 Oliver left his native State and settled on a farm in Ogle county, Illinois. In 1856 he spent a month in Iowa prospecting. The following spring he attended the land sale at Osage. On the 1st day of June, 1857, he arrived in Butler county and made a claim on section 17, township No. 93, north range 18 west, his present home, where he has lived a life of single blessedness. In politics he is a republican; cast his first vote for President, for General Taylor.

William P. Woodworth and Samuel Overturf were natives of Pennsylvania, moving here in 1857. Mr. Woodworth planted his stakes around the southwest quarter of section 35, where he remained until 1872, when he moved out of the county, but subsequently again became a citizen of Butler county by locating in Pittsford township. Mr. Overturf selected the northwest quarter of section 35, but remained here only two years. His present residence is also in Pittsford. These two pioneers named the township "Bennezette," in honor of their native town in Pennsylvania.

Orin C. Smith was an Ohio man; he came here from Michigan, and entered a farm on section 27. When the war broke out he enlisted; and upon his return, settled in the townships just south of this, remaining there until 1882. His present residence is in Wright county. His brother, John A. Smith, was also a pioneer of 1857, settling on section 34. He removed to Pittsford township in 1867, and is now living in Minnesota.

George O'Brien, who came here with his parents in 1857, from Illinois, settling on section 21, was of Irish extraction. In 1876 he removed to Coldwater where he died. His sister, and a brother, John, now live in Coldwater.

The three McKinney brothers, Philip, John and Michael were natives of Ireland, and came from New York State to Illinois. In 1857 they came to Butler county, and took claims on sections 17, 28 and 30, in Bennezette township, where they stayed long enough to prove their claims, then departed; but returned in a few years and sold the land.

John and Patrick Kelley, also natives of Ireland, came from Illinois in 1857. John took the northeast quarter of section 28, and Patrick the northeast quarter of section 23. They soon returned to Illinois, but have never sold this property. John is living in Aurora, Illinois. Philip is dead.

John P. Mills, a native of New York State, came here in 1857. He claimed the northeast quarter of section 8, and remained until 1858, when he left for parts unknown.

James H. Morris was another of the pioneers of 1857, coming from Illinois and settling on section 33. After remaining a few years he removed to West Point township, and has since died.

Among others who settled in the township during this year were Augustus Clukey, Peter Galipo, Warren Caswell and Mr. Ward.

Charles Miller, a native of Pennsylvania, settled on his present homestead on section 35 in 1859.

In 1863 Benjamin Boyd came to the township and settled on the southeast quarter of section 9, where he still resides.

About the same time James Mitchell came and settled on section 34. After remaining here a number of years he removed to his present home in Rock county, Minnesota.

William Hesetroad also came about this time and took a homestead on the southeast quarter of section 10, where he lived one year, when he sold his claim to Alexander Campbell, a native of New York, and bought his present farm in Coldwater township. Mr. Campbell lived here about two years, when he sold the farm to Francis Maxwell, the present owner.

John Maxwell, a brother of Francis, came at the same time and purchased the southeast quarter of section 10, where he still lives.

In 1862 B. H. Barnett, in company with his parents, located their present home on the southwest quarter of section 2.

In 1864 John Calvert came from New York and settled on the northeast of section 16, where he remained about three years; then sold out and moved to his present home in Butler township, where he now resides.

From this time the addition to the settlement was more rapid. J. E. Downing, Richard Parish, John Newborn, John H. Lockwood, A. J. Lockwood, Alfred Tabor, Oliver McGee, Michael Wade, W. J. Adams and others crowded in.

Further on in this chapter will be found a number of "settlers of a later day" treated at length.

FIRST OCCURRENCES.

The earliest birth known was that of Louisa, daughter of William A. and Mary Kuster, born December 29, 1855. In November, 1874, she was married to Harvey Williams, and now resides in Fairbault City, Minnesota.

Another early birth was that of Mary H., daughter to Milton and Adeline Wilson, born May 30, 1858. She was married October 26, 1878, to Philip VanBuskirk, and now resides on section 12 in Bennezette.

The first marriage in the township was that of John Bartlett to Miss Adelia Muffley, in 1859, at the residence of the bride's parents. Elder Moss, of Coldwater township, officiated.

The first deaths occurred in the fall of 1857, when Allen and Sarah L., son and daughter of William Kingery, were called from earth. Their remains were interred in the German burying ground in Coldwater township. Elder Moss officiated at the funeral.

RELIGIOUS.

The first religious services within the limits of Bennezette were held in 1858, by Elder Moss, in the house of William Kingery, on section 1. The Elder was of the German Baptist or Dunkard persuasion, and lived in Coldwater. The neighborhood generally turned out, and meetings were occasionally held, but no society was organized.

A number of Methodists were also among the early settlers, and in 1861 meetings were held at the school house, on section 1, Moses Davis, an itinerant reverend, preaching. Elder Inman, of the Free-Will Baptist; Rev. S. D. Stone, of the United Brethren, and Elders Sheldon and Henry, Disciples, also preached occasionally; but no organizations were effected.

Baptist meetings were also held in Bennezette quite frequently. Elder Button was one of the preachers. The school house of District No. 3 was used, and for two years services were held quite regularly; but no organization was formed, and the citizens who are now of that faith worship in the church, just over the line, in Franklin county.

A Sabbath school was organized in the school house in District No. 1, in 1868, with William Keister as superintendent. It was a Union school, and had quite a good attendance. It did not thrive but a short time.

Another Sunday school was organized in 1878, at the school house in District No. 3, with Mr. Wissler as superintendent. This is still continued at the church in Franklin county.

In 1878 a Methodist class was organized in Bennezette by Elder Sproul, at the school house in District No. 6. John Tindall was class leader, and there were eight members. Preaching is held every two weeks, at present by Elder Camp, from Hansel. This is known as the Bennezette class.

EDUCATIONAL.

This township, for educational purposes, is divided into nine districts, and the schooling facilities are fully up to the average townships of Butler county.

The first school house was built in 1861, in the northeastern part of section 1. It was a frame building and the town was taxed to pay for it. Here the first school in the township was held the winter following, with Miss Mary A. Briggs as teacher, her wages being $14 per month, she to "board herself." There were ten scholars in attendance. In 1873 the present house was erected on section 11. The old house is now in use as Mr. Skillen's granary. This district is known as No. 1.

In 1864, District No. 2 was set off, and during the following year a school house was erected on section 9, in which Dan McDonald, now postmaster at Grand Forks, Dakota, taught the first school, with six pupils in attendance. In 1882 the old school house was sold at auction, leaving this district without a building.

One of the first schools in District No. 2 was taught by Eliza J. Logan, in the winter of 1864, being a four months' term. The teacher is now Mrs. John Jamieson, of Belmond, Iowa.

District No. 3 was set off in 1872, and during the same year a school structure was erected in the southeastern part of section 6, which is still in use. Miss Arvilla Niece first taught in this district.

Shortly afterward, District No. 4 was formed. This district is without a house, and the scholars attend in other districts.

District No. 5 is holding school in a house in the northeastern part of section 21, which was erected in 1882. It is a frame building, and is very neatly furnished. David McKinney taught the first school here.

The school house in District No. 6 was erected in 1874, on section 23, and was a very neat frame building. This building was demolished by the tornado in 1878, and the present building was erected the same year. The first school was taught by Miss Annie Ward. Miss Susie Frisbie taught the first school in the present house.

District No. 7 erected their school house on section 35, in 1882, and the first school was taught by Miss Florence White.

The school house for District No. 8 was erected in 1863, on section 34, and the first school was taught in the winter of 1863-4, by Miss Addie B. Fay. That school house was used until 1882, and the scholars of the district now attend in No. 7.

School District No. 9 erected their school house in 1868, on section 32. In 1873 this house was removed to section 29. The first school was taught in Sylvanus Hamblin's house, on section 30, in 1862, by Mrs. Mary Smith. Two or three terms were taught in this place.

COLDWATER POST OFFICE.

This office was established in Franklin county a number of years ago. About 1875 it was moved to Bennezette township, and John H. Lockwood was appointed postmaster, with the office at his house on section 6. Mail arrived there twice a week from Sheffield and Marble Rock. The office is still in existence at the same place.

John H. Lockwood was born in Saratoga county, New York, November 24, 1817, where he received his education in the district school, with one term at the Schuylerville Academy. In 1865 he came to Iowa and lived for a while with his brother, who was one of the pioneer settlers in Franklin county, just across the line. He bought wild land in the town of Bennezette, on section 6, which he has improved. On December 30, 1846, he married Miss Mary M. Fax. They have seven children—Edwin A., Olive E., Harvey J., Emily F., Eliza C., Ida May and Dora E. Mr. Lockwood was for some years superintendent of schools in his native town of Wilton, as well as teacher in the public schools of New York State and Iowa.

WILSON'S GROVE POST OFFICE.

This was an office established in April, 1878. Milton Wilson was postmaster, with the office at his house on section 15. Mail arrived once a week from Greene during the first year, and after that twice a week from Sheffield. The office was discontinued in the fall of 1880.

INDIAN WAR.

It is said by early settlers in this vicinity that the northern part of Bennezette was once the scene of an Indian battle. The account of the tragedy is somewhat incomplete, as time has marred the memory of those who were cognizant of the facts. It seems that two tribes, the Winnebagos and Sioux, carried their fight into Butler county, and in manœuvering the Winnebagos found a good place for defense on section 5. They threw up earthworks and fortified themselves as best they could. The Sioux discovered them, and greatly outnumbering them rushed down upon the little band. A terrific conflict ensued, in which the Winnebagos were almost annihilated. This is said to have taken place in 1853, and the early settlers used to visit the scene of the combat and pick up many trinkets, such as knives, broken guns, beads and jewelry.

OFFICIAL ORGANIZATION.

According to the first division of the county into townships by Judge Palmer, in February, 1855, Bennezette was made a part of the township of Ripley, then embracing nearly one-half of the county. On the 3d of March, 1856, another division occurred, and the territory now comprising Bennezette was made a part of Coldwater, and merged into the organization of that township. In this shape matters remained for about two years, when on the 4th of March, 1858, it was set off from Coldwater, and ordered organized by Judge Converse, Samual Overturf being authorized to call the first election. This same gentleman bestowed the name of Bennezette upon the township, after his town in Elk county, Pennsylvania.

FIRST ELECTION.

The first election was held at Samuel Overturf's house on section 35, on the 5th day of April, 1858, and the following officers were elected: Clerk, William P. Woodworth; trustees, Ira A. Chamberlin, Milton Wilson, Samuel Overturf; road supervisor, Cyrus D. Chamberlin; constables, Thomas Overturf, Orrin C. Smith.

SECOND ELECTION.

At the regular election, October 12, 1858, the following officers were elected: Trustees, Ira A. Chamberlin, Milton Wilson, Samuel Overturf; clerk, William P. Woodworth; assessor, William A. Keister.

1859—Trustees, Ira A. Chamberlin, William A. Keister, Milton Wilson; clerk, William P. Woodworth.

1860—Trustees, Charles Miller, William H. Muffley, Orrin C. Smith; clerk, William P. Woodworth; assessor, Ira A. Chamberlin.

1861—Assessor, Ira A. Chamberlin; clerk, Oliver Evans; trustees, Sylvanus Hamblin, Milton Wilson.

1862—Clerk, Oliver Evans; trustees, Ira A. Chamberlin, Sylvanus Hamblin, Milton Wilson.

1863—Trustees, Milton Wilson, Charles Miller, James Mitchell; clerk, William P. Woodworth.

1865—Clerk, Milton Wilson.

1866—Trustees, Oliver Evans, Ira A. Chamberlin; clerk, Milton Wilson.

1867—Assessor, William A. Keister; trustees, William A. Keister, Oliver Evans, W. P. Woodworth; clerk, Milton Wilson.

1868—Trustees, Byron S. Adams, James Mitchell, William A. Keister; clerk, Milton Wilson; assessor, Silas Knipe.

1869—Trustees, Byron S. Adams, James Mitchell, Loughridge Barnett; assessor, Ira A. Chamberlin; clerk, Milton Wilson.

1870—Clerk, M. Wilson; justice of the peace, M. Wilson; assessor, W. A. Keister; trustees, L. Barnett, J. H. Lockwood, Ira A. Chamberlin; constable, B. H. Barnett.

1871—Trustees, L. Barnett, J. H. Lockwood, Ira A. Chamberlin; clerk, M. Wilson.

1872—Trustees, Charles Wilkins, E. A. Lockwood, Peter Ebling; clerk, M. Wilson.

1873—Trustees, P. Ebling, Charles Wilkins, John H. Lockwood; clerk, M. Wilson.

1874—Trustees, Ira A. Chamberlin, W. F. Crouse, William Hassell; clerk, M. Wilson; assessor, J. H. Lockwood.

1875—Trustees, William Hassell, W. A. Keister, Ira A. Chamberlin; clerk, M. Wilson.

1876—Trustees, Ira A. Chamberlin, W. Hassell, W. A. Keister; clerk, M. Wilson.

1877—Trustees, J. E. Downing, H. J. Lockwood, W. A. Keister; clerk, M. Wilson.

1878—Trustees, J. E. Downing was elected for three years; William Wray for

NOTE—The records of the clerk's office are lost until 1865.

two years, and G. N. Carpenter for one year; clerk, M. Wilson.

1879—Trustee, G. N. Carpenter; clerk, John F. Clark; assessor, Peter Ebling.

1880—Clerk, M. Wilson; assessor, Ira A. Chamberlin; trustee, William Wray; justices, C. B. Head and W. A. Keister; constables, Peter Ebling, J. A. Keister.

1881—Trustees, J. E. Downing, W. F. Crouse, to fill vacancy; justice, L. L. Mabary, to fill vacancy.

The present officers of the township, who were elected at the November election in 1882, are as follows: Justices of the peace, Ira A. Chamberlain and W. A. Keister; township clerk, Milton Wilson; constables, G. W. Wilson and Peter Ebling; assessor, J. F. Clark; trustee, W. F. Crouse.

SPECIAL ELECTIONS FOR THE REMOVAL OF THE COUNTY SEAT.

An election was held April 5, 1858, for the removal of the county seat from Clarksville to Georgetown. There were twelve votes cast, all in favor of removing the county seat to Georgetown.

April 4, 1859, there was another election held to vote on the removal of the county seat from Clarksville to Butler Center. There were thirteen votes cast—twelve for removal and one against.

On the second day of November, 1880, at the general election, they were again called on to vote for the county seat removal. There were seventy-eight ballots cast. The result was: For Allison, seventy-two; against, six.

SETTLERS OF LATER DAYS.

In this connection is given the personal history of some of the representative citizens of Bennezette who arrived later than those already treated:

Benjamin H. Barnett, a native of New York, was born in October, 1845, in the City of New York. In 1852, when he was but seven years of age, his parents settled in Dubuque county, Iowa, which he made his home until November, 1863, when he enlisted in Company K, Ninth Iowa Cavalry, remaining with the regiment until February 1, 1866, when he was honorably discharged at Little Rock, Arkansas. He then came to Butler county and bought land on section 1, in Bennezette township, which he has since improved. He was married in 1873 to Miss Lulu Crabtree. They have two children—Elsie and Lee.

Edward Cummings, a native of Vermont, was born in Windsor county, August 25, 1824. He attended the district school and one term at Kimball Union Academy, at Meriden, New Hampshire. When quite a young man he went to Ohio, where he spent a year; then returned to Vermont and remained one year with his parents. He then went to Wisconsin, where, on account of ill health, he remained but one year and went to Ohio. In 1844 he located in Iowa county, Iowa, being among the early settlers. He made some improvements on a claim and one year later sold out and returned to Ohio, there learning the carpenter's trade. In 1850 he started across the plains with two horses and five oxen, in company with three others, for California. The company broke up before he got there, and he joined another. He finally sold his interest in the team, and buying a horse and saddle completed his journey on horseback, arriving at Placerville after about one hundred days. He there engaged in mining eight years; then went to Humboldt, where he engaged in the lumber business two years, and then to Los Angelos, where he engaged in farming one year. He then started on his return by the southern route, passing through Arizona and New Mexico, making short stops on the way. He arrived in Texas and spent the winter near Sherman. In the spring he started for Missouri, intending to spend the summer there. As it was in war times, he found it rather hot for him there, so he removed to Iowa, where he spent the summer. In the fall he returned to Ohio, and in the spring went into the government service, in the quartermaster's department, going to Cincinnati; then to Cattlesburg, where they joined Garfield's command; then to Flat Lick, via Louisville. In four months he returned to Ohio. In 1866 he came to Tama county, Iowa, removed from there to Butler county, and bought his present home on section 35, Bennezette township.

William Lovell is a native of England, born December 7, 1817. In 1844 he came to America, landing at Quebec. He spent four months near Toronto, then moved to Michigan. The winter of 1849-50 he spent in Louisiana. In 1857 he settled in Will county, Illinois, remaining there until 1866, when he came to Iowa, and settled in Butler county, buying land in the township of Bennezette, on section 24. In 1875 he built his present home. He married, in 1852, Miss Anna Hart, a native of Yorkshire, England. They were blessed with seven children—Philip, Sarah, Mary, Emma, William M., Frank and Louisa. Louisa died February 14, 1870, three years of age; Emma died May 28, 1875, fifteen years of age; Mary died March 22, 1881, twenty-three years of age.

Francis Maxwell is a native of Donegal, Ireland, born in 1845. In 1863 he left his native land for America. Landing at Quebec, he went to Canada West, and spent a year farming, near Guelph, then moved to Ogle county, Illinois, where he engaged in farming and selling dry goods until 1867, when he came to Iowa, and located in Butler county, buying land in Bennezette township, on section 10. In 1875 he built the nice frame house in which he now lives. On September 13, 1867, he was married, in Illinois, to Miss Jane Dailey, a native of County Monahan, Ireland, but came to America with her parents when quite young. They have one son—Charles L.

John Maxwell, a native of Ireland, was born in Donegal, September 22, 1839. In 1863 he emigrated to America, in company with his brother, Francis, landing at Quebec, and going from there to Canada West, about thirty miles from Guelph, where he remained one year, then located in Cherry Valley, Ogle county, Illinois, where he engaged in farming and selling dry goods, until 1867, when he came to Iowa, and settled in Butler county, buying land in the township of Bennezette, on section 10, which he has improved, building his present fine home in 1880. The two brothers, John and Francis, who came to this country together, now each have a fine farm on the same section. He was joined in marriage, in March, 1869, to Miss Nettie Adams, a native of Jo Daviess' county, Illinois. They have seven children—Willie, Eugene, Ezra, Nellie, Nettie, John, and Grace.

John E. Downing is a native of Ireland, born June 22, 1837. When quite young his father died. In 1849 he came to America with his mother. They landed at Boston, and went to Fall River, where he was employed in the Globe Print Works until 1856, when he went to Michigan, and engaged in the copper mines. He was married there, in 1859, to Catherine Moroney. In 1861 they came to Iowa, and lived in Middlefield, Buchanan county, until 1867, when he bought land in the township of Bennezette, Butler county, on section 26. He soon improved the land, and built his present home. He is the present secretary of the Board of Education, which office he has held since 1877. He has ten children—Patrick J., Josie, Mary A., Ellen A., Michael, John, Theresa, Bridget, William Henry, and Cecelia A.

Adam Kyle was born at Hessian, now a part of Germany, October 1, 1820. His father died when he was but two years old. When nine years of age he came to America, with his mother. They settled in Pennsylvania. In 1842 he settled in Jo Daviess county, Illinois; one of the early settlers. He there bought mining property, and engaged in mining until 1849, when he started for California, crossing the plains with three teams, in company with eight others; taking their camping utensils with them and camping out on the way. They were one hundred and forty days making the trip. They located at Hangtown, now called Placerville, and engaged in mining until 1854. He then went to San Francisco, taking a steamer for home. He crossed the Isthmus, went up the Mississippi river to Rock Island, and there hired a buggy to take him to Jo Daviess county. He soon after started for Wisconsin, where he settled in Grant county, buying a farm one and one-half miles from Lancaster, where he lived until 1870, when he sold it and came to Butler county, Iowa, buying his present farm, on section 16, township of Bennezette, where he now lives. He married, February 22, 1856, Theresa Foak. They have ten children—Maggie and Elizabeth, the oldest, are twins; John, Herman, Veronica, Catherine, Adam, Francis, Joseph, and Theresa. Mr. Kyle's mother is still living with him, in her eighty-seventh year.

Gawn S. Killen, native of Ireland, born in County Down, April 4, 1832. His father was a mason by trade, and he learned that trade when quite young. In 1848 he left his native land for America, landed at New York; went to Batavia, and there worked at his trade, also worked at farming. In 1868 he came to Iowa, and was employed as mason on the Insane Asylum at Independence, three years. He then came to Bennezette, Butler county, and bought a farm on section 1, which he has improved, and built his present home. He married in October, 1858, Miss Jane Livingston. They have three children—John, Robert and James.

Michael Wade was born in Kilkenney, Ireland, in 1831. In 1851 he left his native land for America; landing at New York he went to Kingston, where he engaged in a stone quarry for one year, getting out flag stones; he then went to Charleston, South Carolina, where he stayed seven months; from there he went to Oxford, Massachusetts, working in a woolen mill six months; then returned to Charleston, South Carolina, where he was engaged with the United States Coast Survey, remaining with them eleven years. He then went to Winooski Falls, Vermont, where he was employed in a woolen mill. In 1863 he came to Iowa, and engaged in railroading in Dubuque county until 1868, when he removed to Charles City, remaining in the same business. In 1871 he came to Bennezette, and bought land on section 7, there building his present home. He married in 1858 Miss Mary Breen. They have eight children—John F., Martin E., Catherine, Mary E., William, Margaret and Agnes.

Joseph H. Brownell was born in Erie county, Pennsylvania, February 26, 1834. In 1856 he moved to Winnebago county, Illinois. In 1857 he moved to Iowa, buying land in Black Hawk county. In 1863 he removed to California, where he engaged in freighting and farming for two years, when he returned to farming in Illinois. In 1872 he came to Iowa, buying a farm in Bennezette on section 24, where he built his present home. He married December 2, 1858, Miss Mary Collier, a native of Illinois. They have four children—Florence L., J. Clarence, George W. and Ernestine E.

Franklin Pierce Kent was born in Essex county, New Jersey, September 10, 1852. In 1860 his parents moved to Floyd county, Iowa. In 1863 they moved to Charles City, where he attended school. In 1873 he came to Bennezetté, Butler county, settling on his present home on section 8. He married in 1878, Miss Addie Frisbie; they have three children—Vera E., James F. and Annie D.

John Tindal was born in Sandusky county, Ohio, February 3, 1847. His father, who was a farmer, was one of the first settlers of Tama county, Iowa, moving there in 1852. Here John received his education. In 1876 he came to Bennezette township, Butler county, buying his present farm, on section 16. He was married in 1870, to Miss Margaret Crouse. They have three children—Aggie, John H., and Edwin.

L. L. Mayberry is a native of New Jersey; born in Warren county, May 23, 1834. In 1840 his parents moved to Oakland county, Michigan. In 1847 they moved to Ogle county, Illinois, among the earliest settlers of that county. L. L.'s younger days were spent on the farm. He was married in 1865, to Miss Mary, daughter of Robert Light, Esq., of Ogle county, Illinois. They have four children—William W., Robert R., Margaret E., and James L. March 17, 1877, Mr. Mayberry came to Bennezette township, Iowa, and bought his present farm, on section 31.

Albert Meyer was born in Germany, in August, 1843, where his occupation was farming. In 1866 he emigrated to America. Landing at New York, he started immediately for St. Paul, Minnesota, where he was employed in a packing-house eight years. He then engaged in draying four years. In 1878 he came to Bennezette township, Butler county, Iowa, and bought his present farm, on section 21. He was married in 1864, to Miss Caroline Kath. They have two children—Bertha A., and Helena H.

Jacob, son of Elder Philip Moss, was born in Indiana, February 2, 1845. In the fall of 1855 his parents moved to Coldwater, Iowa, where he attended school; later devoted his time to agricultural pursuits. In 1876 he bought a farm in Bennezette township, on section 11, moving his family there that winter. He was married in 1866 to Miss Catherine J. Sturtz. They have four children—Clarence, Franklin, Owen and Bertha.

Aaron M. Harter was born in Carroll county, Indiana, July, 1841. In 1856 his parents moved to Dayton, Butler county, Iowa, settling on section 19. His father still occupies the original claim. His mother died April 1, 1881, in Vernon County, Missouri. In August, 1862 he enlisted in the Thirty-Second Iowa, Company G. While in the service he lost his eye-sight, and was otherwise disabled; and was honorably discharged July 8, 1865, when he returned home and consulted a physician, with whose assistance his sight was restored. He then commenced studying medicine, and has since practiced, making diseases of the eye a specialty. He has made permanent cures where the patients were totally blind. In 1874 he went to Missouri, where he engaged in mining in Jasper and Vernon counties. In 1875 he returned to Iowa and carried on his father's farm for two years. In 1878 and 1879 he moved to Waterloo, where he practiced medicine. The year 1880 he spent in Greene. In 1881 he moved to Bennezette, and bought his present farm on section 16. He was married in 1868, October 1, to Catherine Earnest. They have two children—Charlie W. and Nora A.

William F. Crouse is a native of Ohio, born in Ashland, March 13, 1841. When in his thirteenth year his father died, and his mother with the family moved to Wisconsin. In 1866 he married Miss Mary C. Crabtree. In 1869 he came to Iowa, and bought a farm in Bennezette, on section 24, which he has since improved. They have nine children, but three of whom are now living—John W., Etta Mabel and Florence May. In 1878 they buried six children in one month. They died of that dread disease, diptheria. Mr. Crouse enlisted in August, 1862, in the Twenty-fifth Wisconsin, Company I. He was with the regiment until the close of the war, and was honorably discharged in June, 1865. He has filled offices of trust in the town, and is at present trustee.

Charles Miller was born in Clearfield county, Pennsylvania, the 7th of April, 1834. In the summer time he was engaged on the farm, and in the winter season he worked in the woods getting out lumber. In 1859 he came to Iowa and settled in Butler county, town of Bennezette, section 35. He improved the land, and in 1875 built a substantial frame house. He married in 1856 Miss Catherine Lewis. They have seven children, all boys— G. William, Robert L., Reno J., Charles G., Daniel B., Orley and Lewis.

William Wrey is a native of Ireland, born in county Tyrone in 1829. In 1847 he emigrated to America, and made his home in Philadelphia, where he was employed in a carpet factory, also in a sugar refinery, and in the Pennsylvania R. R. depot. In 1861 he came to Iowa, buying land in Pittsford township. In 1879 he traded his farm for land in Bennezette on section 31 and 32. He lives on section 31. Isabella Smith became his wife in 1852. She died in March, 1868, leaving eight children. Their names are Margaret, William J., James M., Robert S., Jane, Ulysses G. and Annie J. He married his second wife, Miss Aravilla Niece, in 1875. She has three children— Harry H., Andrew N. and Earl R.

CHAPTER XXI.

BUTLER TOWNSHIP.

This town lies in the eastern part of the county bearing the same name. Bremer county lies on the east, Jackson township on the west; Fremont on the north, and Shell Rock on the south. It comprises township 92, range 15, containing about 23,040 acres of excellent farming land. The Shell Rock river traverses the township from southeast to northwest. Parallel with it are the railway lines of the Burlington, Cedar Rapids and Northern R. R. and the Dubuque and Dakota.

The soil is generally a dark loam with clay subsoil. On the timber uplands it is lighter and mixed with sand in places, and is very productive. There are no very abrupt breaks or bluffs, the surface being nearly level, or generally undulating.

Nearly or quite all the township is in the hands of actual settlers, who have improved it; and there is very little waste land. The main body of timber lies along the Shell Rock river. The population is mixed, many nationalities being represented, but all seem an industrious thriving people.

EARLY SETTLEMENT.

The first permanent settler in Coon Grove was Joseph Hicks, who made his advent in December, 1850, and erected a cabin on a claim one mile west from what is now Clarksville. His nearest neighbor was James Newell, who, a short time previous, settled at the forks of the Cedar, about twenty miles southeast of him. Hicks carried provisions on his back during the winter, for the maintainence of himself and family, from Cedar Falls, which was then but a small trading post. His time was principally occupied until spring, in hunting, fishing, and trapping, when he cultivated a small piece of ground and planted it with corn and vegetables. His wife was a true western heroine, and could "talk injine" or shoot a rifle equal to "any other man." In the spring of 1851 his father, Henry Hicks, arrived from Wisconsin, and erected a blacksmith's shop. It is said of him that he actually charmed the birds of the air with his shrill "whistle," the only luxury he ever indulged in, while he steadily forged the first iron in the Shell Rock Valley. He died in the winter of 1854, was buried on the place; his remains have since been removed to Linwood Cemetery. Joseph Hicks went to Kansas in 1867, where he remained a few years, then returned to the old place. He did not seem contented, however, so started for Mexico, but was delayed on the way near the Solomon river, in Kansas, where he yet remains. He had a brother who came here with his father from Wisconsin, called "John;" he yet remains in the county. The Hicks family do not properly belong to Butler township's early settlement, as the lines are now drawn; but being closely indentified with the earliest settlement of this vicinity they are mentioned in this connection.

R. T. Crowell also came in December, 1850, for the purpose of moving Hicks' family here. He went back to Wisconsin, but returned in the spring of 1852, and took a claim, afterward occupied by Alexander Glenn, where he remained many years. Becoming dissatisfied he disposed of his splendid farm, went to California, but soon returned, and is now in Spirit Lake, Iowa.

M. B. and W. S. Wamsley were also early settlers, just along what is now the line, and had much to do with the early times of this township. M. B. settled in Butler county April 20, 1851, section 1, Jackson township, a claim previously taken up by his brother, John Wamsley. As this place was without improvements Mr. Wamsley built at once a log cabin, 14 x 16, commenced breaking the land, and the first year raised corn, beans, potatoes, and other vegetables, enough for family use. His family consisted of himself, wife and two children. During this season considerable sickness—mainly ague—was experienced. However, he was successful, and in about four years the log cabin gave way to a good, substantial building, which is still in good repair. Mr. Wamsley's health failed him about the year 1870; since then he has been unable to do hard work. In 1878 he removed to the village of Clarksville. He still carries on his farm, also dealing in live stock. Mr. Wamsley is one of the incorporators of the Butler county bank, and was president for ten years. He was born in Adams county, Ohio, October 9, 1826. His parents, John and Sarah (Swim) Wamsley, were both natives of said county. He is the oldest of four children, was brought up to farm life in his native state; was in 1848 married to Miss Milly Cooper, a native of Adams county, a daughter of Samuel and Nancy Cooper. He remained a resident of his native county until he came to Butler county. Mr. and Mrs. Wamsley have had ten children, seven of whom are now living— Henry, Sabia J., now Mrs. Milton Molsberry, Marion, Byron, Bascomb, Mary and Charley. Mr. Wamsley is a democrat, and has associated with that party since he reached his majority. He was the first justice of the peace in his township, and has since held other local offices. He is a member of the Masonic fraternity, belonging to the Blue Lodge and Chapter at Clarksville and the Commandery at Cedar Falls.

W. S. Wamsley was born in Adams county, Ohio, September 19, 1828, his parents being John and Sarah (Swim) Wamsley. When but a small boy he removed with the family, to Iroquois county, Illinois, where the mother died, leaving four children—Malon B., William S., John N., and Melissa J., now the wife of Colonel Harlon Baird, of Dakota county, Nebraska. The family then returned to Adams county, Ohio. The father subsequently married Mrs. Sarah Caroway *nee* Parks. Soon after the four children named, commenced the battle of life alone. William S. worked for a time at farming for different parties. He subsequently entered the employ of Jesse Wykoff—owner of a steam saw mill—whom he served until he reached his twentieh year. Mr. Wamsley being energetic and ambitious, decided to engage in business for himself. He therefore, with his brother Malon B., purchased a one-half interest in the mill, which did not prove a success, and in 1850 William S., accompanied by his younger brother John N., boarded a steamboat at Cincinnati, and started out in search of a location on the western frontier. Arriving at Dubuque, they at once set out on foot, for the Turkey river, where the country, not meeting their expectations, they turned their steps southward and soon arrived in Washington county, Iowa. Here they met Henry Moore, son of Aaron Moore—better known as Uncle Aaron—the early settler of the Shell Rock valley, who wished some help in taking a drove of cattle into Bremer county. As he gave a very glowing description of the country, they concluded to assist him providing he would bear the expense. They found immigration brisk, and during the month of May Mr. Wamsley helped a German erect a cabin a little north of the present site of Waverly—the first cabin in that vicinity. After wandering about a few days Uncle Aaron and W. S. Wamsley concluded to explore "Coon Prairie," of which the former had heard trappers speak. They started on horse-back, and, after a few hours ride, they reached their destination, and finding the country, without doubt, the finest they had ever seen, Mr. Wamsley at once concluded to settle. As the land was not yet in market, he returned to Ohio, leaving his brother in the employ of Uncle Aaron. On the twentieth day of February, 1851, he was married to Miss Ann Eliza Richards, daughter of Sampson and Elsie (Kirker) Richards. In March Mr. Wamsley and bride, accompanied by his half brother, Martin VanBuren Wamsley, better known in Butler county as "Van" Wamsley, started with a team for the western frontier. At Muscatine they met Malon B. Wamsley and family, who had come to that place by steamboat. From thence they journeyed on together, arriving at Uncle Aaron's about April twentieth, and on the twenty-sixth of said month W. S. Wamsley located on the northeast quarter of section 12, Jackson township, where he still resides. W. S. and Malon B. Wamsley were poor men, having but one team of horses and a wagon which they had brought from Ohio. They each purchased a cow, a pig and a few chickens; these, with a few household goods, comprised their personal property. They each also purchased eighty acres of land at $1.25 per acre, and this took the balance of their cash. The summer of 1851 proved to be a very wet season and it was often very difficult to get to market. In June W. S. Wamsley started for Muscatine; when he arrived at Marion it was raining. Purchasing a few goods he started back. He found the streams so swollen that he was compelled to fasten the box onto the running gear to keep it from floating away while crossing. During the summer in order to cross the Cedar River, he often had to take the wagon apart, transfer it across on canoes, and swim the horses to the opposite shore. In the winter of 1851-2 he made a wooden mortar, and in this crushed their corn for bread-stuff. This, with a few potatoes and a small amount of meat, constituted their provisions. After the first year, however, they fared better, as they raised wheat, and this they could get ground at Cedar Falls, but had to do the bolting by hand. Mr. Wamsley has given his attention almost exclusively to farming, and has met with marked success. He now owns over four hundred acres of well improved land. He is one of the founders of the Butler county bank, and for many years served as one of its directors. In politics he is a democrat and has held local offices. Mr. and Mrs. Wamsley have had nine children, six of whom are now living—Didama J., now Mrs. A. J. Ilgenfritz, Alvira, now Mrs. John Neal, Isolina, now Mrs. Fowle; Wylie C., Amy and Ida.

Jeremiah Perrin made his appearance in August, 1851, driving his stakes about one-half mile north of his present handsome residence, which is situated one mile east from Clarksville, on section 17, where he still lives. He made a good selection, and by hard work and strict economy has risen from a poor man to one of the foremost farmers and capitalists in this section.

Morrison A. Taylor, the same date, settled about one-half mile east from Mr. Perrin, and began substantial improvements, but died the 30th day of December, 1856.

Jeremiah Perrin is an Englishman born in North Hamptonshire, November 28, 1820. In January, 1845, with his wife, he emigrated to the United States, and settled in Allegheny county, Pennsylvania. In 1848 he removed to Beaver county, that State. In 1851 he started for the western frontier, traveling by steamboat down the Ohio and up the Mississippi rivers to Muscatine, Iowa. He came west prepared to buy, but his health failing, he rented a farm near Muscatine, where he remained that season. In August he made the acquaintance of Morrison Taylor and E. Ensley, who came from Indiana the previous spring, and were proposing to go west with an ox-team, Mr. Perrin had a good wagon and team of horses, and proposed, if they would bear one-third of the expenses, to drive through. To this they agreed, and the trio started. In a short time Mr. Taylor and Perrin were located on section 17, and Ensley on section 16, Butler township. Perrin and Taylor soon returned to Muscatine and brought their families to their new homes, settling down on the 16th day of September, 1851. Mr. Ensley brought his family in about six weeks. Here they all erected cabins, and made preparations for the coming winter. Mr. Perrin has since followed farming quite successfully, accumulating a large amount of land, and considerable other property. In 1882 he erected the Perrin block, the finest and most costly building in Clarksville. He has been twice married, first in 1844 to Miss Elizabeth Woods. She died in 1865. They had three children, two of whom are now living—Elizabeth, now Mrs. Henry Branlon, and Mary A., now Mrs. W. H. Moore. In June, 1866, he was united in marriage with Miss Ann Hillman, of Rockford, Illinois. They have two sons—Oscar C., and Mark J. Mr. Perrin was formerly a democrat, and voted for Douglas in 1860, but since the rebellion has been identified with the republican party. He has not entered much into politics. He is, however, always ready to assist in putting the right man in office. He is one of the foremost farmers and capitalists of this section.

Mr. Taylor settled about one-half mile east from Mr. Perrin; but on the 30th day of December, 1856, he was called to the better home above.

Mr. Ensley sold out his old place years ago, and his present whereabouts are unknown.

Seth Hilton was also intimately connected with this settlement, but now belongs to Jackson township.

Geo. W. Poisall came in 1853, making his home on the hill east of the old school house. In 1854 he sold it to Dan Mather, and moved a peg further north, laid out "Poisall's Addition to Clarksville." He is now living in the city of Clarksville.

Thomas and Jeremiah Clark came the same year, and took claims about one mile north of Clarksville.

The following named persons entered land in the order named: Alfred Elam settled here in 1851 on Barnard's place, about four miles southeast of the town. Hiram Beard, an old soldier of the Mexican War, took up the claim afterward known as the Mix estate. John Armstrong came in 1851, and took his claim two and a half miles southeast, on section 29. C. N. Burton on section 8, where he died years ago. In 1850 John Heery entered the land adjoining the town plat on the south; he did not move his family until 1853. These are all the earliest settlers we can enumerate, and all who have survived the hardships of life to the present day, are independent. After this time settlers came in rapid succession, among whom were O. A. Strong, John H. Morton, John Palmer, David Blakley, A. VanDorn, J. J. Eichar, T. T. Rawson, M. M. Trumbull, Wm. Brandon, R. Hardy, Abner Farlow, J. M. Vincent and Dan Mather. These came during the spring, summer and fall of 1854.

A. VanDorn was elected county judge in 1855, and died in the fall of 1858, leaving a large family.

T. T. Rawson brought to the county a small stock of goods, sold them out, moved to Hampton, Franklin county; returned and went into the land agency business; eloped with another man's wife, and ruined the happiness of two families.

M. M. Trumbull was a good attorney, a perfect gentleman, and a fine scholar. He was elected to a seat in the lower branch of the legislature, in 1858, which he filled with honor to himself and his constituents.

William Brandon was a genuine backwoodsman. He began life as such in Virginia, from whence his father came to Indiana at an early day, and "Uncle Billy" was reared on rifle, ax, deer and "bar's" meat. His first residence in Iowa was near Rockford, Floyd county; he afterwards moved to Cedar Rapids, and from there to this vicinity.

R. Hardy erected a hewed log cabin on the corner now occupied by the Central House. He kept hotel one winter, but "starved out" and went to Missouri.

J. M. Vincent, an older man among the pioneers, was known as "Squire" for many years. During the summer of 1860 his residence was destroyed by fire; he being in limited circumstances, the citizens contributed liberally and phoenix-like, a new

J. Perrin.

Mrs J. Perrin.

and better edifice soon arose over the ruins. He died a number of years ago in extreme old age.

On the 5th day of July, 1852, George W. Poisal, wife and four children, Thomas Clark and family, Jerry Clark and family and Mrs. Cynthia Clark and family arrived. They made the journey with teams, and were twenty-eight days in coming from Howard and Carroll counties, Indiana. Mr. Poisal and Thomas Clark at once entered one-half of section 18, Butler township, erected a log cabin and commenced pioneer life. As they brought but a small amount of provisions with them, they were soon obliged to purchase. For this purpose, in the month of August, Mr. Poisal took his team and started out. He drove one hundred miles, five miles beyond Marion, and there purchased a load of corn at twenty-five cents per bushel. While on his homeward way he busied himself shelling corn, which task he completed before he reached Cedar Falls, where he had the corn ground. He purchased flour at Cedar Rapids. They had also raised a crop of potatoes, which, with fish and venison, carried them through the winter. In 1853 Mr. Poisal sold his 160 acres to Daniel Mather and purchased the northeast quarter of section 18. In 1855 he laid out a portion of this into village lots as an addition to the village of Clarksville, where he resides. Farming has been his principal business, and although he has not accumulated a large fortune, he has always been able to supply his family with home comforts. Mr. Poisal—or Uncle George, as he is familiarly called—was born in Virginia on the 10th day of March, 1814. His parents, Jacob and Nancy (Smith) Poisal, were also natives of that State. He was reared on a farm, and in 1833 married Miss Mary Ann Burket. She died in 1842, leaving eight children, two of whom are now living—Lucinda, now Mrs. George Moore, and Hiram. In September, 1845, Mr. Poisal married Miss Elizabeth Clark, a sister of Thomas Clark, and by this union has had three children, two of whom are now living—Mary and Maria. Uncle George has always been highly esteemed by his fellow men. He was elected the first judge of Butler county, but did not qualify, for the reason he would be obliged to go to Independence to do so. He is a democrat, and has often held local offices. His religious connection is with the Methodist Episcopal Church. Mr. Poisal is a Mason, being a charter member of the Blue Lodges at Cedar Falls and Clarksville. He is a member of the Chapter at Clarksville and the Commandery at Cedar Falls. He has filled all the offices in the Blue Lodge except master, and for the past four years has been treasurer both of the chapter and Blue Lodge.

John Ray is found among the very earliest pioneers. He settled in Butler township in September, 1852, and with his wife and three children resided with Robert T. Crowell the first winter. Their provisions consisted principally of corn bread and buffalo meat. He has since been a resident of the county, farming being his principal occupation. Mr. Ray was born in Saratoga county, New York, May 1, 1821. August 2, 1845, he married Miss Emma J. Phelps. In 1848 they migrated to Waukesha county, Wisconsin, and two years later to Greene county, residing there until their removal to Iowa. Of his ten children six are now living—Sarah J., Andrew, William E., George W., Mary A. and Ora G. In politics Mr. Ray is a republican, in religion a liberal.

Daniel Mather, upon his arrival in this county in October, 1854, settled in Clarksville, where he purchased land on section 18, from G. W. Poisal; upon this he platted a portion of the town, which is now the south part of Clarksville. He secured the contract for the carpenter work of the court house, the consideration being $1,500. Changes in the plan were afterward adopted, and the contract price changed to $2,750. Mr. Mather was born in Oswego county, New York, September 12, 1796; was brought up on a farm, also learned the carpenter trade, which he followed in his native State until 1825. During this time in 1820 he married Miss Roxa Underwood. In 1825 he moved to Warren county, Pennsylvania, where he remained nineteen years, then removed to Boone county, Illinois. In October, 1854 he came to Clarksville, Iowa. His wife died in 1856, leaving four children—Maria, now Mrs. Charles Nelson; Charles, of Dayton township, Stephen, who resides in Tennessee, and Milo, now in Kansas. Mr. Mather was afterwards married to Mrs. Sally V. Francis; she had one child from her first marriage—Mary, now the wife of Captain C. A. Roszell.

J. J. Eichar, mayor of Clarksville, Iowa, as before stated, was a pioneer of 1854. He is a native of Westmoreland county, Pennsylvania, born October 28, 1829. His parents, Henry and Catherine (Seichtg) Eichar, were both natives of said State. He received an academic education, and subsequently read law for two years. In the fall of 1852 he came to Anamosa, Jones county, Iowa, and engaged as book-keeper for the firm of J. H. Fisher & Son, general merchandise and flouring mills. He held this position until May, 1854, when with G. Dollison he came to Clarksville and engaged in the mercantile business under the name of Eichar & Dollison. The goods had to be drawn in wagons from Dubuque and Muscatine, and the roads many seasons of the year were almost impassable; it sometimes took two weeks to make the trip from Dubuque to Clarksville. Often they were obliged to leave goods by the way, the teams being unable to get through. This firm closed out in 1860. Mr. Eichar then dealt in real estate, also followed farming until 1870. He has acted as justice of the peace, land agent, insurance; has been city mayor for several years, and held other local offices. Mr. Eichar, in January, 1855, married Miss H. E. Vincent, daughter of J. M. Vincent; she died in October, 1876. They had seven children, five now living—May, now Mrs. John Wilhelm; Kate, now Mrs. W. C. Wamsley; Stella, now Mrs. J. Belden; Ada and Frank.

Considerable of the early settlement, and many of the first occurences are identical with those of the city of Clarksville, an account of which appears elsewhere. Sketches of a few representative men of this township are appended, from which may be gathered the character of the settlement.

The first piece of land entered in Butler county, consisted of 160 acres, located on sections 18 and 19, Butler township. This was entered on the 22d day of November, 1850, by John Heery. Mr. Heery at that time resided at Milton, Wisconsin, and was informed in regard to the land along the Shell Rock river by James Newell, who had been trapping along said stream. When Mr. Heery listened to the description as detailed by Mr. Newell, he at once concluded to there procure for himself a home. He therefore on Monday morning, November, 11, 1850, bid his family an affectionate good-by, assuring his wife that he would return one week from the Saturday following. He started on foot for the frontier; upon reaching the Shell Rock he soon found the identical piece of land described by Newell; then he went to Dubuque where he entered the same and returned home, arriving at Milton on Saturday evening. It was a very dark night, and he was obliged to borrow a lantern to light his way, but he reached his home before 12 o'clock. In the spring of 1852, Mr. Heery brought his family to their new home. John Heery is a native of Ireland, born in 1813. In 1845 he married Miss Catherine Leonard. In 1848 he emigrated to the United States. He first settled at Newburg, New York; subsequently he emigrated to Wisconsin. Mr. and Mrs. Heery have reared a family of six children, five of whom are now living—Thomas, John, Peter, Albert and Mary. Mr. Heery is a democrat in politics, and in religion a Roman Catholic.

Captain John R. Jones is of Welsh descent, his father, John R., and mother, Mary Jones, both being natives of Wales, the former born in 1807 and the latter in 1811. They were married in Liverpool, England, in 1830, and shortly afterward emigrated to the United States, locating in Detroit, Michigan, from which place they removed to Ohio in 1832, and from there to Wilmington, Illinois, in 1838. The father died in 1877, and mother in 1879. There were five children, four sons —John R., William G., George W., Robert A.—and one daughter—Margaret.

John R. Jones was born at Detroit, Michigan, October 8, 1831. He removed with his parents to Wilmington, Illinois, where he received a common school education. When eighteen years of age he learned the wagon-maker's trade, following it until 1852, when he drove an ox-team across the plains to Oregon. The following year he went overland to Shasta county, in northern California, where he remained mining and ranching until February, 1856, and then returned by water and rail to Wilmington, Illinois. On May 1, 1856, at Kankakee City, Illinois, he married Miss Angeline Butterfield, the daughter of Egbert and Nancy Butterfield, of Wilmington. On the 26th day of May, 1856, he moved to Shell Rock, Butler county, Iowa. In company with George G. Hawker he engaged in wagon, plow making, and blacksmithing. In the summer of 1862 he raised a company for the Thirty-second Regiment, Iowa Volunteer Infantry, was elected Captain, August 26, 1862, and mustered into the United States service by Captain George S. Pierce, at Camp Franklin, Dubuque, Iowa, October 6, 1862. In November, 1862, he was ordered to St. Louis, from there, in December, to New Madrid, Missouri; from there to Fort Pillow, Tennessee. In February, 1863, he was ordered to Columbus, Kentucky, remaining there until January, 1864, when orders came to move on to Vicksburg, Mississippi, and join General Sherman in his march to Meridian, returning to Vicksburg in March. In the same month he was ordered on the Red River Expedition with General Banks, and took part in the capture of Fort DeRusse, on the 14th of March, 1864. On April 9, 1864, he was engaged in the battle at Pleasant Hill, Louisiana, where his company lost thirty-one out of fifty-three men. In June, 1864, they returned to Vicksburg. On the 30th of June, Mr. Jones was elected Colonel of his regiment, to fill a vacancy caused by the resignation of Colonel John Scott. This was a compliment rarely ever paid, except for most gallant service, as it was a promotion of a Junior Captain over a Senior Captain, Major, and Lieutenant-Colonel. But before his commission could arrive, his regiment had become so reduced in numbers that they were not entitled to a Colonel. In July the regiment was ordered to St. Louis, where they joined General Rosecrans, going with him on his seven hundred-mile-march after Price. They returned to St. Louis in November, and in the same month joined General Thomas at Eastport, Mississippi, from which place they went to Nashville, Tennessee, and on the 16th and 17th of December, 1864, engaged in the battle there, in which rebel General Hood was defeated. In January, 1865, they were ordered to join General Canby at New Orleans, going with him to Blakely, Alabama, and on the 9th of April engaged in battle at that place. From there they marched to Montgomery, where they remained until August, 1865. In same month were ordered to Clinton, Iowa, where he was mustered out on the 24th of August, 1865, arriving at his home, at Shell Rock, Iowa, on the 26th day of August. On April 7, 1866, he moved to his farm, one and a half miles east of Clarksville, where, in 1873, he built a large and beautiful residence, making his home one of the most pleasant and comfortable in the county. In the fall of 1868 he was elected from Butler township as one of the sixteen supervisors of the county. In 1871 he was elected sheriff, and was re-elected in 1873, 1875, and 1877—the only sheriff that has ever held the office for eight years or more than two terms. As a politician he has espoused the republican cause from its beginning.

Mrs. Angeline Jones, wife of Captain John R. Jones, was born in St. Lawrence county, New York, on the 31st day of October, 1836. Her father, Egbert Butterfield, was born October 3, 1810, and her mother, Sally M., January 13, 1816. They moved from New York to Wilmington in 1845. They had three children—two sons —Levi, born January 14, 1839; William, born May 10, 1841; and one daughter, Angeline, born October 31, 1836. She remained with her parents at Wilmington, receiving a common school education, until her marriage on the 1st of May, 1856, to Captain John R. Jones. Of the three children which have blessed this union two are living—Mary M., born March 12, 1857, and Carrie S., born September 6, 1861. Ida A., born June 24, 1859, died September 28, 1860. Carrie S. was married to John P. Reed, of Shell Rock, September 30, 1880. Mary M. was married to George A. McIntyre, of Allison, November 9, 1882.

Henry Atkinson settled at Clarksville in December, 1855. He entered the employ of Daniel Mather, and remained with him for over two years. Subsequently he worked for Robert T. Crowell. He finally rented a piece of land and commenced toiling for himself. In 1860 Mr. Atkinson married Miss Sophia Cloukey, a native of Lower Canada, and in 1863 located on section 12, Butler township. He has been industrious, as well as economical, and now owns 240 acres of fine farming land and thirteen and one-half acres of timber. Mr. Atkinson is a native of England, born in Yorkshire, October 3, 1831. He emigrated to the United States in 1851, and resided in New York and Canada until 1855. He is a republican, but in local politics believes in voting for the best man, regardless of party principles. The children are Alice, Viola, Francis H., May, Samuel L., George A., Clara B. and I. O. W.

John Hickle purchased two hundred acres of land and settled where he now resides in May, 1856. He soon became highly respected among the settlers, as he was ever ready to stretch forth a helping hand to assist a new settler who was battling with pioneer life. There are many of the settlers still in the county who speak in the highest terms of Mr. Hickle for favors shown them during the hard times of 1857-8-9. Mr. Hickle was born in Ross county, Ohio, August 24, 1812. In 1840 he married Miss Hester VanGundy, and in 1846 migrated to Illinois, residing there until his removal to Butler county, Iowa. He now owns 300 acres of land. Of their nine children seven are now living—Jacob, William, David, Warren, Charles, Eliza and Alfred. Mr. Hickle was for many years a trustee of the town. He has been a strong republican ever since the party was organized. When he was nine years of age, his father dying, he was obliged to work his way up in life, and his education was therefore very limited.

The first regular blacksmith shop in Clarksville was opened in the fall of 1855 by W. A. Riden, who continued the business until 1866. He then settled on his farm, 200 acres of which he purchased when he first came to the county, but he now owns 320 acres, all of which is well improved. Mr. Riden was born in Mifflin county, Pennsylvania, in October, 1825. His early life was spent on the farm, but at the age of eighteen years he commenced work at his trade. In 1849 he married Miss Sarah Schnee, of Union county, Pennsylvania. In the spring of 1855 he started westward, and after stopping a few months in Ogle county, Illinois, he came to Clarksville as already stated. Mr. and Mrs. Riden have four children—Mary B., now Mrs. Sutcliffe, and whose husband died in July, 1873; Harvey, Willis E. and Frank A. Mr. Riden is and always has been a democrat. In religion his family were Lutherans.

James E. Burke arrived in Butler county on the 30th day of September, 1858. He lived on rented land on section 33 for one year. In December, 1859, he bought ninety-seven acres of land on section 29, but did not move on to it until March, 1860. In the spring of 1864 he sold out and departed for Kansas, but returned in the fall and purchased the same farm, now having 168 acres of well improved land. Mr. Burke was born in the city of New York, February 12, 1831. His father, William Burke, was a native of Ireland,

and his mother, Eliza, a native of England. They both came to this country with their parents when children. The subject of this sketch grew to manhood in Ohio on a farm, received but a limited education, and remained in Ohio until he came to Iowa. When he went to Kansas he expected to stay, but not finding things satisfactory he returned. Mr. Burke tells of many hardships he had to endure the first year. He got only fifty cents in cash for labor, and was obliged to sell some of his clothes to get food. On the 3d day of February, 1853, he married Miss Mary J. Anderson, a native of Ohio. They have six children living—John, William, Sarah (now Mrs. William Betts), Clifton, and Allie and Alice, twins. In politics Mr. Burke is a strong republican; in religion he is a liberal.

Wellington Mitchell was born in Tompkins county, New York, March 15, 1830. He was bred to farm life, residing in his native State until 1854. He then emigrated to Iowa and settled in Linn county. In 1857 he married Miss Caroline M. Bruce. In 1861 they came to Clarksville, but in 1862 Mr. Mitchell felt it his duty to respond to the call of his country. As his most intimate friends lived in Linn county, he enlisted from there in Company H, of the Twenty-fourth Iowa Infantry, served bravely with his company, and at the battle of Champion Hill, May 16, 1863, gave his life for his country, and was buried on the battle field. His wife, Mrs. C. M. Mitchell, is still a resident of Clarksville, and since 1871 has been postmaster at that place. She is a native of Medina county, Ohio, her parents being Harvey and Mary Jane (Sharp) Bruce. Her only son D. B., also resides at Clarksville.

F. W. Chapin, son of Joel and Lucy Chapin, was born in Jefferson county, New York, February 3, 1833. In 1850 the family emigrated to Illinois, and settled in LaSalle county. Here F. W. learned the carpenter's trade; previous to this he had always worked on the farm, and had received but a common school education. In 1854 the family removed to Greene county, Wisconsin, where he continued his trade, also followed wagon-making and farming. He was married in 1859 to Miss Martha Kellogg, who died in 1861, leaving no children. In 1862 Mr. Chapin came to Butler county, Iowa. He now owns 216 acres of well improved land. In 1865 he married Miss Eliza A. Panley, daughter of Jonathan Panley, a native of Virginia. They have four children—Horace V., Byron E., Fred H. and Elvalette. Mr. Chapin has been justice of the peace in his town for four years, assessor for one year, and a member of the school board for eight or ten years. He is a republican to the back bone; in religion he is a liberal. Joel Chapin (father of F. W.) and family came to Butler county in 1861. There were five children, four of whom are living—Juliaette, F. W., B. W. and Alvira E. Joel Chapin died in 1877, and his wife in 1871.

David Hostetler, a native of Holmes county, Ohio, was born February 4, 1817. His parents, Joseph and Susanna (Mast) Hostetler, were natives of Pennsylvania, but they settled in Ohio in 1807, being among the early settlers of Holmes county, where they both died in 1858 at an advanced age. David was brought up on a farm, and received but a common school education. He is the fourth son of a family of eight, all of whom are living. He resided in Indiana and afterward in Wisconsin, where he married Miss Elizabeth Shafer. In 1862 he came to Iowa and settled on section 36, Butler township. Mr. Hostetler has been identified with the school interests ever since he came to the county, and has been president of the school board for two terms. He has also been trustee of the town for two years. In politics he has been both democrat and republican, but now is an independent, voting for the best man. In religion he is a liberal. His wife died November 7, 1881, at the age of fifty-five years. He has three children—Eugene, Max and Bruno. His two oldest sons are now in the mercantile business in Nebraska, and the other in the State University.

J. R. Hall resides on section 27, Butler township. He came to this county in 1862. His parents, Young and Rachel (Hay) Hall, were both natives of Kentucky, and he was born in that State on the 6th day of February, 1835. While he was yet an infant the family emigrated to Illinois, where the parents still reside, having celebrated their golden wedding November 24, 1879, at which anniversary there were eight persons present who witnessed the marriage fifty years previously. J. R. resided with his parents until 1862, when he came to Iowa, and in partnership with James O. Barnard purchased about one hundred head of cattle, herded them during the summer, and in the fall drove them to Chicago, the trip occupying twenty-one days. In 1863 Mr. Hall married Miss Mary J. Barnard, daughter of William Barnard, now of Butler county, and in 1865 settled where he now resides. He has made farming his business, and now owns about 400 acres of land. The children are G. F., Mittie P., Lida R. and Sylvia E.

Johnson Gates, Jr., settled on section 26, Butler township, in 1864. He was born in Saratoga county, New York, September 16, 1845. His father, Johnson Gates, was of Spanish parentage and a native of Saratoga county, New York. His mother, Caroline Gates, was born in Washington county, New York, in 1818. The family emigrated to Wisconsin in 1850 and settled in Walworth county, where they resided until 1864, when they came to this county. The father died in 1873. His mother still lives and resides with Johnson, Jr., who now owns the homestead. Mr. Gates received a liberal education, completing it at Bryant & Stratton's Commercial College, Milwaukee, in the winter of 1864. He was married December 10, 1873, to Miss Ida M. Gilbert. They have one son—Loran J.

Simeon Downing resides on section 13, and his post office is Shell Rock. He was born in Adams county, Ohio, February 17, 1828, and when ten years of age removed with his parents, William and Susannah (Newman) Downing, to Sciota county, where he helped till the soil until 1844. The family then migrated to Iroquois county, Illinois. Here, in 1850, Mr. Downing married Miss Susannah Williams, also a native of Adams county, Ohio. In 1864 they emigrated to Iowa, lived in Bremer county two years, then came to Butler county and located where they now reside. Mr. Downing has been successful as a farmer, and now owns 180 acres of fine land. In politics he was a democrat up to 1864, since which time he has voted the republican ticket. His religious connections are with the Methodist Episcopal Church. The children are Mattie, now wife of George Sewell, of Dakota; Arthur, Dennis, residing in Dakota, and Flora B. Mr. Downing received but a common school education. His father died in Kansas and his mother in Illinois. The family were of English descent.

James Neal, the sixth of ten children of William and Rebecca (Murray) Neal, was born in Greene county, Pennsylvania, June 18, 1844. He removed with his family to Wisconsin, and helped till the soil until 1863, then went to Montana Territory and followed mining until the fall of 1865, then returned to Wisconsin, and soon afterward came to Butler county, Iowa. When Mr. Neal first came to this county he worked at the carpenter's trade, and, in 1871, in partnership with Wm. Morrison, purchased the old saw mill in the south part of town, running the same until 1879; also continuing his trade. Mr. Morrison then withdrew, and J. E. Gilbert became a partner. In 1881 Mr. Gilbert sold to W. H. Bettenger, and the firm then fitted the mill for grinding feed. In 1882 Mr. Neal became sole proprietor, but soon associated his brother, E. L. Neal, as a partner, and the firm, as Neal Brothers, fitted up the present steam feed mill in Clarksville, which they now operate, and also carry on an extensive flour and feed business. Mr. Neal, in 1870, married Miss Cakturia Taylor, and they now have one son—Albert. In politics Mr. Neal is a democrat, and always has been. He was assessor of the city for one year.

H. M. Swan was born in Cattaraugus county, New York, on the 7th day of June, 1820. He was a resident of western New York until 1856, when he emigrated to Iowa, first locating at Monona, Clayton county, Iowa; subsequently resided two years at Waukon, Allamakee county, from which place he came to Bremer county, and eighteen months later, (in 1867), to this county. He located on section 16, Butler township, where he now owns eighty acres of land. Mr. Swan has taught about forty terms of school. He attended the scientific course at the Western Reserve College, at Oberlin, Ohio, and spent two years at a theological seminary; he graduated from the scientific department in 1853. At about seventeen years of age he commenced to teach. He has taught some in this town, and has been a member of the school board. In politics he is a democrat. His religious connections are with the Congregationalists. On the 25th day of April, 1850, Mr. Swan married Miss Elizabeth Allen, and they now have five children—Chester M., Julius A., Eva M., Jane, and Bertha.

C. G. Schellenger came to Clarksville in 1868, and at once purchased a small stock of hardware, which was being closed out at that time; enlarged the same, and associated George Eck as partner. Geo. Eck & Co. carried on business about one year; the business then changed to Schellenger & Hesse, and continued with marked success until December 14, 1879, when their stock was destroyed by fire. Mr. Schellenger then settled up the business of the firm, and in the fall of 1880

W. H. Riden.

Sarah F. Riden.

engaged in the grocery business. To this he has since added boots and shoes, and now enjoys a good trade. Mr. Schellenger is a native of Lafayette county, Wisconsin; born December 18, 1832. His father, George Schellenger, was a native of New York, and his mother, Beulah (Lamb) Schellenger, of Indiana. He was reared on a farm, but at the age of twenty-one, engaged in general merchandise at Wiota, Wisconsin. Two years subsequently, he came to Iowa, a pioneer of Howard county, being engaged in trade at Oregon until he came to Clarksville in 1868. Mr. Schellenger was married in 1857 to Miss Lauraine McColum, a native of Massachusetts. They have had three children, one son now living— Charles L. Mr. Schellenger is a member of the Masonic fraternity, belonging to the Blue Lodge and Chapter at Clarksville, and Commandery at Cedar Falls. He was Master of the Blue Lodge one year, and High Priest of the Chapter three years. He was one of the charter members of the Chapter and its first secretary. In politics Mr. Schellenger is a republican. His father died in Wisconsin some three years ago, but his mother is still living on the old homestead.

J. D. Roberts resides on section 29, Butler township. He now owns 200 acres of land. He is a native of Ross county, Ohio; born September 10, 1833. His parents, Elijah and Mary (Hickle) Roberts, were both natives of Virginia. In 1847 the family emigrated to Illinois, and engaged in farming. In 1862, J. D. enlisted in Company B, Ninety-fourth Illinois Volunteer Infantry, and served three years, participating in the battles of Prairie Grove, siege of Vicksburg, Brownsville, siege of Fort Morgan, Spanish Fort, etc. He was in six battles, in all, serving as a private; was not wounded, although he saw many of his comrades fall by his side. He then returned to Illinois, and in September, 1868, came to Iowa. In 1864 Mr. Roberts married Miss Maria Oliver. They have six children—William, Oliver, John, Grant, Ida, and Edward. Mr. Roberts cast his first ballot for John C. Fremont, and has been a republican since. He is a member of the Masonic fraternity. His religious connections are with the Baptists. He has been one of the trustees of the town for a good many years.

W. C. Wamsley, son of Allen and Emily Wamsley, was born in Adams county, Ohio, November 6, 1857. He was left fatherless when two years of age; his mother subsequently married W. T. Smith, and in 1869 the family moved to Iowa and settled in Clarksville. Mr. Wamsley's younger days were spent on a farm, but, having a desire to lead a mercantile life, at the age of sixteen he commenced clerking in Clarksville, where he continued for six years. In the year 1877 he graduated at Bailey's Commercial College, of Keokuk, Iowa. He embarked in the mercantile business with Mr. Horton, under the firm name of Wamsley & Horton. Here he continued until 1881, when he disposed of his interest, and has been clerking in the same store for A. C. Smith. He was married December 21, 1881 to Miss Kittie Eichar, daughter of J. J. Eichar, of Clarksville.

E. B. Blaisdell resides on section 13; owns 223 acres of land and is a well-to-do farmer. He is a native of New Hampshire; born March 2, 1822. He remained on a farm until he was nineteen years of age, receiving a common school education. In 1841 he learned the trade of a machinist, and followed the same in New Hampshire and Massachusetts for about ten years. In 1850 he migrated to Wisconsin where he was engaged in mill-wrighting for four years. He then returned to his native State; helped his parents dispose of their property, after which they also migrated to Columbia county, Wisconsin, where they still reside. After returning from the east Mr. Blaisdell followed farming for one year, and then engaged in the stock buying and shipping business, also milling business, in which he continued six years. While in Wisconsin he was justice of the peace for twelve years, and a member of the county board of supervisors for twelve years, also, clerk of the school board during the time of his residence there. At the age of twenty he was married to Miss Olive Wylie. She died at Wyocena, Wisconsin, leaving three children, two of whom are now living—Frances, now Mrs. A. Calvert, and John E. Mr. Blaisdell subsequently married Miss Charlotte Smoke, and in 1869 came to Iowa, and purchased his present farm, and has since been a resident of Butler township. In politics he is a strong republican. He has been secretary of the school board in this township for six years.

James Walrath was born in Madison county, New York, September 3, 1847. His parents, Henry and Elizabeth Walrath, were also natives of said State. In 1849 the family emigrated to Illinois, and in 1863 to Monroe county, Wisconsin; thence in 1871 to Iowa. In 1876 James married Miss Margaret Dixson, of Will county, Illinois. They have three children—Willie J., Mary E. and Carrie Belle. Mr. Walrath is a republican in politics, and at present is assessor of Butler township.

A. C. Barrett, an early pioneer of Bremer county, is a native of Northumberland county, Pennsylvania, born July 1, 1827, his parents being Caleb and Rachel (Cooper) Barrett, both natives of said State. Mr. Barrett's school days were few. He helped till the soil, and in 1847 married Miss Sabulia Bonestein, a native of Northampton county. In 1856 he emigrated to Iowa and settled at Waverly. Mr. Barrett worked at various employments until 1869, when he came to Butler county, and purchased his present farm of 120 acres (the same being raw prairie), and he now has it all well improved; its value is about $35 per acre. The children are Oliver, Alvin, Francis, Richard and Mandus.

Thomas Hunt came to this county in 1854. He was born in Trumbull county, Ohio, October 2, 1832. His father, Samuel Hunt, was born in Pennsylvania, and his mother, Sarah (Faulkner) Hunt, in Ohio. He resided in his native State until he came to Iowa. In 1857 he married Miss Nancy Farlow, and in 1860 settled where he now resides. Mr. Hunt owns 212 acres of land, all of which is under cultivation, and his dwelling erected 1882, is one of the best in the county. He also owns 480 acres in Dakota. Mr. and Mrs. Hunt have seven children—Sarah E., U. F., Charles A., Mary M., Samuel, Lillie B. and Thomas A. Mr. Hunt has been treasurer of the school board for a good many years. He is a republican. In religion a liberal. He was one of the charter members of the Odd Fellows Lodge, is a member of the Masonic Lodge, and has held offices in the same.

Solomon C. Cross was born in Monroe county, New York, in 1819. His parents, Asa and Abigail Cross, were both natives of New Hampshire. In about 1828 the family removed to Cattaraugus county, New York, where Solomon C. helped till the soil until 1855. He then emigrated to Wisconsin, and there married Miss Helen A. Whelan. In 1856 he came to Iowa, and first settled in Bremer county. Here, November 6, 1861, his wife died, and he subsequently married Miss Phœbe A. Whelan. In April, 1870, he came to Butler county, and now owns 235 acres of fine land. Their children are Elida, Edwin, Abbie and Sydna.

A. Best came to the county in 1862, and first lived with his brother, Jesse Best, who came here in 1854, and now resides in Kansas. In June, 1864 he married Miss Catherine McCrery, daughter of Samuel McCrery, of Indiana, and in 1865 settled on section 31, Butler township. He owns 300 acres of well-improved land. Mr. Best was born in New Jersey, July 10, 1836, his parents being Peter and Mary (Trimmer) Best. In about 1839 the family migrated to Knox county, Ohio. Here Mr. Best learned the wagonmaker's trade, and followed the same for three years after coming to Butler county. The children are Jacob S. and John W. The family are all members of the Presbyterian Church. In politics he is a strong republican.

Ruluff Root is a native of Herkimer county, New York, being born at West Schuyler on the 10th day of September, 1827. His father, Ruluff Root, was a native, of Kenyon, Connecticut, and his mother, Fannie (Kent) Root, of Rhode Island. They were married in Herkimer county, New York, and reared a family of seven children, four of whom are now living—Sallie, now Mrs. Horace Richardson, of Oneida county, New York; Mary Ann, now Mrs. E. M. Day, of West Schuyler, New York; George, of Fairport, New York, and Ruluff—the subject of this sketch—who was bred to farm life. In 1859 he came to Iowa and entered one thousand acres of the best land situated in Dayton township, Butler county, then returned to his native state. In 1864 Mr. Root brought his family to Butler county, living on his farm until 1868. The farm where he now lives adjoins the town plat of Clarksville and contains 247 acres. Mr. Root still owns all the land he entered in 1854, and his is the finest stock farm in the county. His real estate amounts to thirteen hundred and forty-seven acres. In 1855 Mr. Root was married to Miss Rula Budlong, a native of Freeport, Monroe county, New York. Her father, Milton Budlong, was also born in the Empire State, and shipped the first carload of cattle over the N. Y. C. & H. R. Railroad. Her mother, Clarissa (Shumway) Budlong, was a native of Massachusetts. Mr. and Mrs. Root have four children—Milton R.; Clara F., now Mrs. Lewis Slimmer; Lida E., now Mrs. William Ladd, and Rula M. Mr. Root is a republican, but takes no more interest in politics than to perform his duty as a citizen.

Byron L. Poisal, only son of William Poisal, was born in Clarksville, August 5, 1859. He was educated in the public schools of that city. He learned the shoemaker's trade at the age of fifteen years, and followed the same until May, 1881. He then entered the employ of H. F. L. Burton, as clerk, and in September, 1882, became a partner in the business, the firm now being Burton & Poisal.

W. H. Moore, a farmer on section 16, was born in Schoharie county, New York, on the 14th day of March, 1841. He spent the days of his youth attending school and helping his parents till the soil. Subsequently he taught school; residing in his native State until 1861. He then emigrated to Wisconsin, continued teaching, and in 1865 enlisted in the Forty-sixth Wisconsin Infantry, and served eight months as a private. In 1866 Mr. Moore came to Iowa, and purchased property in Butler township. He taught school the following winter, and in 1867 married Miss Mary A. Perrin, daughter of Jeremiah and Elizabeth (Woods) Perrin. Mr. Moore now owns 240 acres of land, and is considered a prosperous farmer. He is a republican in politics, and has held local offices. The children are—Ellena, Delmar J., Lizzie, Annie P., and Arthur G.

J. R. Taylor purchased his present farm on the 11th day of October, 1852, and then returned to Indiana. Two years subsequently he returned to Butler township. In 1855 he was married, in Indiana, to Miss Hester Cook. They have four children— Morrison A., John M., Percill A. C., and Rose E. Mr. Taylor is a son of John and Rachel (Robey) Taylor. He was born in Fairfield county, Ohio, in 1829. He removed with the family to Park county, Indiana. After the death of his father he returned with his mother to Ohio, and lived with her in that State until her marriage with Mr. Burton. Mr. Taylor is a highly respected citizen, and an enterprising farmer. He takes little interest in politics, and associates with the Christian Church.

Jerome Shadbolt is one of the pioneers of May, 1855, at which time he settled at Clarksville, and has since spent most of his time in pursuit of his trade—that of a carpenter. He settled where he now resides about 1871. His handsome dwelling, just completed, is one of the finest farm houses in the county. Mr. Shadbolt is a native of Genesee county, New York, born April 9, 1823, and resided in his native county until twenty-four years of age. In 1846 he married Miss Louisa L. Main. In 1847 he emigrated to the Territory of Wisconsin. He had a brother living at Milwaukee, who tried to persuade him to settle at that place, but Jerome did not have enough confidence in the growth of that city. His brother, John Shadbolt, is now a member of the firm of Shadbolt & Boyd, wholesale dealers in carriages, etc., Milwaukee. Jerome Shadbolt went twenty miles north of Milwaukee, locating at Grafton. He purchased a water-power, and engaged in the manufacture of "chair stuff," which business proved a success, and he made money rapidly. He had a partner associated with him, and one day he made him an offer to give or take a certain amount for his interest, which, to the surprise of Mr. Shadbolt, his partner agreed to give. Mr. Shadbolt therefore sold out, came to Iowa, and settled in Butler county, as above stated. In 1864 he was enrolled in the service, joining Company C, Fifteenth Iowa Volunteer Infantry, and served until the close of the war. The children are—Ida, Charles S., Rouen, Albon, and Jessie.

J. Y. Tilford, one of the leading stock farmers, resides on section 19, Butler township. His farm contains 280 acres, and the improvements on the same are valued at about $6,000. Mr. Tilford is a son of John S. Tilford, a sketch of whose life appears in the State Atlas of Iowa. He was from Indiana, and resided there until 1852, when he came to Iowa, and followed farming in Benton county. In 1857 he married Miss Mahala A. Harper. She died January 3, 1862, leaving three children—Cora M., Maggie A., and Minnie. In November, 1862, he married Miss Hattie A. Wilcox. In 1881 he came to Butler county, and has since been engaged in stock farming. By the second marriage he has three children—J. Ethel, Hattie May, and William Alva.

William Flood settled on sec. 28 in May, 1855. Here he has since tilled the soil and now owns 130 acres of land. He was born in Bennington, Vermont, in 1826. At the age of sixteen he commenced work at the blacksmith trade, which he followed in several different states until he came to Butler county. In 1862 he enlisted in Company E, Thirty-second Iowa, and served three years. In 1857 he married Miss Delia Angel. They have seven children—Matilda, George, Asa, Lizzie, Tena, Una and Nettie. In politics he is a republican.

Samuel Lenhart came to Butler county in June 1855 and first settled on the south half of sec. 19, Fremont township, remaining there until 1880, when he purchased 125 acres adjoining the city of Clarksville. Mr. Lenhart has been very successful as a farmer. He owns about eight hundred acres and his improvments are among the best in the county. Mr. Lenhart was born in Somerset county, Pennsylvania, January 30, 1806. In 1833 he married Miss Margaret McMillan. In 1834 he removed to Ohio, in 1845 to Indiana, and in 1855 to Iowa. Mr. and Mrs. Lenhart have had eight children, seven of whom are now living, the youngest having died while on the journey from Indiana to Iowa—John, Henry, Washington, Sarah J., Susan, Almeda and Nancy.

John Kimmins, a well-to-do farmer residing on sec. 23, Butler township, is a pioneer of 1855. He is a native of England, born in Devonshire, February 28, 1819. In 1843 he married Miss Julia Elliott and in 1849 emigrated to the United States. Mr. Kimmins, after coming to the United States, first settled in Lawrence county, Pennsylvania, and engaged in mining. In 1852 his wife died and in 1853 he married Miss Cynthia Veasey, a native of Beaver county, Pennsylvania, born October 31, 1830. In 1855 Mr. Kimmins emigrated to Iowa and after stopping a few weeks in West Dubuque he came to Butler county and settled on sec. 22, of Butler township. For two years afterwards he was afflicted with sore eyes, so that he was nearly blind, and as he was a poor man he experienced many hardships of pioneer life. He resided on the farm he first purchased until 1876, then lived in Clarksville about eighteen months, then settled on sec. 23. He now owns 160 acres of well improved land, has a good farm residence and a pleasant home. Mr. Kimmins is a democrat, but takes no more interest in politics than to perform his duty as a citizen. His religious connections are with the Christian church. He has held some of the minor town offices.

In 1855 John Howe walked from Muscatine to Shell Rock and entered a piece of land, but did not become a resident of the county until 1859. When Mr. Howe settled in Butler county he was an unmarried man, poor in worldly goods, but not afraid to work. He worked for other parties a few years and then improved his land, soon becoming one of the principal farmers. He now owns 240 acres of land. Mr. Howe was born in Philadelphia, Pennsylvania, in 1832, removed to Ohio in 1851, and from thence to Iowa. In February, 1882, he married Miss Hattie Smith, a native of Indiana. Her father was an American and her mother of Irish descent.

Henry Slosson was born in Cayuga county, New York, April 26, 1803, and there learned the trade of morocco dressing, following the same in his native State until 1846, and serving in the employ of one man for twenty years. On February 25, 1843, he married Miss Laurena W. Newton, daughter of Calvin and Mary (Robinson) Newton and grand-daughter of Ebenezer Robinson, a soldier of the Revolutionary war. In 1846 Mr. Slosson emigrated to Cleveland, Ohio, three years later to Illinois, eleven years subsequently to Wisconsin, and in 1865 to Iowa, where he soon became a resident of Butler county, living on section 1, Fremont township, until his death, which occurred October 18, 1872. He left five children— Emma A., Harry H., Isabelle, Rosa L., now deceased, and William W. In 1880 Mrs. Slosson married William Lyon, a native of New Jersey, who came to Iowa in 1866. He died March 21, 1882. Mrs. Lyon now resides in Butler township. Her oldest son, George Francis Slosson, enlisted in 1864, at the age of sixteen years, in the Forty-first Wisconsin, and served 100 days, during which time he contracted disease which led to his death January 27, 1881.

Bainbridge Leavens located on the southwest quarter of section 25, Butler township, on the 7th day of June, 1857, and still resides on the same. He has made farming a business, and has met with marked success, accumulating 500 acres of land, 480 lying in one body, and all under cultivation. Mr. Leavens is a native of Ohio, and was born July 1, 1834. In 1836 the family removed to DuPage county, Illinois, and there followed farming. In 1862 Mr. Leavens married Miss Adaline E. Wheeler. They have three children—Eugene L., Miles W. and Martin B. Mrs. Leavens died December 9, 1882.

Hiram Newman is a native of Adams county, Ohio, and was born September 21, 1826. His father, Barton Newman, was a native of Virginia, and his mother, Catherine (Jones) Newman, of Kentucky. Hiram, who is the fifth of ten children, lived with his parents on a farm, and in 1850 married Miss Amelia Wykoff. She died leaving two children—Franklin and Granville. Mr. Newman subsequently married Miss E. C. Gabby, daughter of Alex. M. Gabby. In 1862 they emigrated to Iowa and settled at Clarksville. Mr. Newman is a democrat in politics and a Royal Arch Mason. By the second marriage there were five children, two now living—Fred and Mamie.

W. R. Taylor, one of the earliest pioneers of this county, was born in Park county, Indiana, June 17, 1834, his parents being John and Rachel Taylor. He was left fatherless when only three years of age. His mother subsequently married Clement Burton, and in 1853 the family removed to Iowa and settled in Butler township, this county. In 1856 W. R. Taylor married Miss Nancy M. Martin. They have five children—Richard, Melissa, Emma, Ada and Lettie. Mr. Taylor is a republican in politics.

Asa Hodgson, son of James and Elizabeth (Probasco) Hodgson, was born in Illinois, in 1850, and when five years of age came with the family to Butler county, and lived on the farm until 1872. He then married Miss Ruvira Walter, daughter of Elias and Rachel Walter, and has since resided on his present farm in Butler township. Mr. Hodgson is a republican, and his religious connections are with the Christian Church.

James Hodgson settled on section 15, Butler township, in 1855, and there followed farming until his death, which took place in March, 1868. He was born in the State of Ohio, in 1821, and in 1831 removed with his parents to Tazewell county, Illinois, where, in the year 1842, he married Miss Elizabeth Probasco, a native of Virginia, born in the year 1819, and continued farming in said county until his removal to Iowa in 1855. Mr. and Mrs. Hodgson had twelve children, six now living—Caroline, now Mrs. Henry Billhimer; Asa, Sarah J., now Mrs. Z. Shaw; William, Emma C., now Mrs. Fletcher Walrath, and James H. Mr. Hodgson at the time of his death owned 300 acres of land.

William Major is a native of England, born in 1812. He came to the United States in 1865, and at first located in Wisconsin, from which State he came to Butler county. In April, 1872 he married Mrs. Elizabeth Hodgson, widow of James Hodgson.

J. M. Houston came to this county in 1857; entered the northeast quarter of section 2, and here commenced pioneer life as a tiller of the soil. In 1861 he moved into the village of Clarksville, and engaged in the grocery business, soon adding general merchandise. He continued in the same until September, 1880, when he sold his stock to Rieffe & Company, and retired from active life. Mr. Houston is a native of Scotland, born August 17, 1817. At the age of seventeen years he embarked as a sailor, and continued the seafaring life for about ten years. He afterwards engaged in mercantile life. In 1851 he emigrated to the United States, and located at Grafton, Wisconsin, continuing in mercantile business until 1856, when his property was destroyed by fire, and he was compelled to begin life anew. Mr. Houston was married in 1850, to Miss Margaret Robinson. They have had four children; two are now living, to-wit— Margaret A., now the wife of Dr. M. C. Camp; and Elizabeth.

H. D. Hunt has been a resident of this county since February, 1853, at which time he purchased 200 acres of land on section 28, Butler township, and still cultivates the same. Mr. Hunt was born in Ohio, January 8, 1826, his parents being Samuel and Sarah (Forkner) Hunt. He was bred to farm life, and resided in his native State until 1852, then came west, and in the early part of the year 1853 settled in Butler county. In 1854 he married Miss Sarah A. Husband, then of Shell Rock, but a native of Westmoreland county, Pennsylvania. They have six children—William J., John H., Charles, Heman D., Herman S. and Florence I. Mr. Hunt has been successful in life, as he came to the county with but $400, and now owns 374 acres of well improved land. He is a republican in politics, and a member of the Methodist Episcopal Church.

Elias Walter is a pioneer of October, 1853, and has therefore witnessed the settlement of the county from its infancy. Mr. Walter is a mason by trade. Upon his arrival here he located at Shell Rock, purchased property, and then erected the first frame house in the village. On the 12th day of February, 1854, he married Miss Rachel Billhimer. The ceremony was performed by M. B. Wamsley, Esq., and was the first in Butler county. Mrs. Walters is a daughter of John and Barbara Billhimer, is a native of Pennsylvania, born on the 28th day of October, 1831. Elias Walter has followed his trade most of the time until 1880, since then his health has not permitted him to perform manual labor. Mr. and Mrs. Walter reared a family of eleven children, eight of whom are now living—James F., Ruvira, George W., Henry E., Clara B., Charley, Lucinda, Fred and Elias B. Mr. Walter is a native of Ohio, born in Muskingum county, June 26, 1831. His parents, Ebenezer and Martha (Parker) Walter, came to Butler county in 1855. Here the father died in 1858. The mother still resides at Shell Rock, at the advanced age of seventy-five years. He is a republican in politics, and a member of the Christian Church.

Henry Billhimer is the fifth of the nine children of John and Barbara Billhimer. He was born in Westmoreland county, Pennsylvania, May 15, 1830, and resided in his native State until 1852, when his parents, with the four younger children, emigrated to Iowa and settled at Shell Rock. Here Henry helped till the soil, and in 1862 enlisted in Company E of the Thirty-second Iowa Volunteer Infantry and served three years. He then returned to Butler county, and in 1865 married Miss Carrie Hodgson, daughter of James Hodgson. They have had two children, one of whom is now living—Minnie. Mr. Billhimer is a republican in politics, and a member of the Masonic fraternity and the Christian church. He now resides on section 22, Butler township, and owns ninety acres of real estate. He lost his health in the war, but as yet does not get a pension. He was in a number of hard-fought battles.

E. A. Wilkinson was born in Oneida county, New York, in March, 1847. In 1869 he removed to Iowa; first stopped in Chickasaw county, afterward in Bremer county, and in 1873 came to Butler county, where he is meeting with marked success. In 1873 he married Miss Ida Markle, daughter of George and Sarah Markle. They have four children—George A., Clara, Iva and an infant.

Horace Knapp, among the first settlers in Clarksville, came to Butler county in 1855, and followed farming a few years. In 1864 he settled on section 6, Butler township, where he now owns 90 acres. Mr. Knapp was born in Rhode Island in

H. D. Hunt.

Mrs. H. L. Hunt.

1832. At the age of fourteen years he emigrated with his uncle, H. K. Stephens, to Joliet, Illinois. He subsequently removed to Michigan, remaining until 1861. In March he married Miss Isabel Shields. They have eight children—Henry D., Nellie, Edith, Rosey, Frank, Isabel and Horace.

John P. Neal was born in Pennsylvania on the 4th day of April, 1846. He removed with the family in 1849 to Greene county, Wisconsin. In 1864 he came to Butler county, Iowa, and remained one year, when he returned to Greene county. In the fall of 1865 the family came to Iowa, settling at Clarksville. The father, William Neal, still lives in the county. The mother, Rebecca (Murray) Neal, died in 1868, leaving nine children—Sarah J., Lindsay E., Delila A., William A., Francis C., James E., John P., Robert J. and Thomas A. In 1873 John P. was married to Miss Alvira Wamsley, daughter of William Wamsley. They have had three children, one now living—Alice M.

George Markle was born in Canada in 1819, came to the United States in 1839 and in 1842, at LaPorte, Indiana, married Miss Sarah Brown. In October, 1860, he located in Butler county and has since made farming a business. Of their ten children seven are now living—Catherine, now Mrs. Reuben Strawhacker; Betsy, now Mrs. Betsy Ryckman; Mary Belle, now Mrs. Joseph Moshier; Ida, now Mrs. Ed Wilkinson; Ellen, now Mrs. Fred Ollinburg, and Charity L.

Samuel March came to Iowa in 1857 and after living a few weeks in Bremer county removed to Butler township, where he has resided with the exception of five years in Black Hawk county. Mr. March was born in Pennsylvania, June 14, 1829, his parents being Abraham and Eliza (Price) March. In 1835 the family migrated to Ohio and settled at Knox. In September 3, 1851, Mr. March married Miss Harriet A. Lewis. They have five children—Evangeline C., now Mrs. H. L. Myers; Chas. L., Alma H., L. G., and H. D.

R. E. Fassett is a native of Steuben county, New York, born November 19, 1835. In 1846 he emigrated with the family to DeKalb county, Illinois. June 8, 1862, he married Miss Philinda Taylor. In 1865 he came to Butler county, Iowa. The children are—Daniel, Nellie, Ellis, Grant and Rosa.

Christopher Billhimer is the eighth of the nine children of John and Barbara Billhimer. He was born July 4, 1835, and in 1852 removed with the family to Butler county. He subsequently drove a team for Alfred Elam to Texas, and from there to Nebraska. In 1864 he enlisted in Company C of the Fifteenth Iowa Infantry, and served until the close of the war. Since then he has followed farming, now resides on section 14, and owns 47 acres. Mr. Billhimer has been twice married. In 1859 to Miss Melinda Hodgson. She died in 1863, leaving two children—Mary E. and Sarah E. In 1865 he married Miss Sarah Probasco, and by this union have two children—Clara and Myrtle.

George Feltus was a native of Ireland, born in 1815. He married Miss Ellen Burroughs, and about 1855 emigrated to the United States, first settling in the State of New Jersey. Mr. Feltus was a moulder by trade, and worked at the same about five years, until he emigrated to Illinois, where he engaged in farming, in Lee county. In 1870 he emigrated to Iowa, and settled on section 20, Jackson township, this county. His death took place August 20, 1880, and his wife died February 22, 1881.

James Feltus, only son of the above, was born in Ireland, on the 14th day of February, 1856. He was educated in the schools of Butler county, also took a course at the commercial college of Sterling, Illinois. He resided with his parents until their death. On October 1, 1881, he purchased the dray, express and transfer business at Clarksville, and is now carrying on the same. No young man in this county has more warm friends than James Feltus.

Selden Norton, who resides in Clarksville, was born in Erie county, Pennsylvania, in 1832, where he lived till eleven years of age. His parents were Nathan and Nabby Norton. They removed from Pennsylvania to Illinois about 1841. Mr. Norton came to Butler county in the fall of 1855, and settled in Clarksville. He settled on a farm in Fremont township, section 32, in 1864, which he still owns. His parents settled in Buchanan county, Iowa, in 1855, where they lived till death. He is the only one of his father's family who settled in this county. He has two brothers in Buchanan county, a brother and sister in Illinois, and a brother and sister in Kansas. Mr. Norton married Sobrina Beebe, born in Ohio. Her parents, Eli and Olive Beebe, came to this county at the same time as Mr. Norton. Mr. and Mrs. Norton have one son—Albert S.

A. M. Gabby was born in Pennsylvania in 1804. He married Miss Nancy Knox, and, in about 1844, emigrated to Adams county, Ohio. In 1865 he came to Iowa, and now resides at Clarksville. Of the six children born to Mr. and Mrs. Gabby, three are now living—John, Thomas B., and Margaret, now the wife of Charles Ramsey.

Thomas B. Gabby was born in Pennsylvania, came with the family to Iowa, and now resides on land purchased by his father and himself in 1865. In 1865 he married Miss Ellen Henney, then of Adams county, Ohio, but a native of Pennsylvania. They have six children—John, Thomas, Mamie, Ella, Flora, and an infant.

David Moulton is a native of New Hampshire; born in the town of Lyman, Grafton county, on the 10th day of August, 1881. His parents were David and Sarah (Knapp) Moulton. He resided in his native State, tilling the soil, until 1848; then, for a number of years, worked on railroad bridges in several different States. In 1855 he was in Illinois, and there gave Albert Reynolds some money to purchase him some land in Butler county, Iowa. In 1857 Mr. Moulton came to Butler county and remained a few months; then returned to Illinois, and subsequently traded most of his land for property in Illinois. In 1865 Mr. Moulton again came to Butler county. He married Mrs. Eliza McClelland, nee Billmiler; has since been a resident of the county. In politics Mr. Moulton was formerly a democrat, but when the rebellion broke out he at once joined the republican ranks, and has since been a strict adherent to the principles advocated by that party. He is a Royal Arch Mason; and has been secretary of the Blue Lodge, at Clarksville, for some time, and as such performs his duties in the most strict and competent manner. The children are Grant and Colfax.

ORGANIC.

The first election was held in a log house built by George Poisal on the corner where the bank now stands. The first township officers elected were during the fall of 1853: Trustee, Jeremiah Perrin; justice, Alfred Elam. The present officers are as follows: Trustees, G. W. Poisal, Henry Atkinson, Thomas Morrow; clerk, Wm. H. Moore; justice, J. J. Eichar; assessor, James Walworth.

The first death in the township was John, son of Jeremiah and Elizabeth Perrin, March 17, 1862.

The first marriage was that of Harlan Beard to Jane Wamsley, sister of M. B. Wamsley, by Justice Elam, in 1853.

The first birth was in 1852, a son to Jeremiah Perrin.

CHRISTIAN CHURCH.

This church was organized at Antioch, Butler county, on the 5th day of July, 1857, by giving themselves to God and one another in full fellowship, the foundation being the Word of God, with the Lord Jesus Christ as the chief corner stone. The organization was completed with the following membership: William McBarnard, P. Barnard, James Hodgson, Elizabeth Hodgson, Hannah P. Davis, Clement N. Burton, T. A. Taylor, Sarah Taylor, Mary Kinsley and Mary P. Burton. During the first year the following persons were added: John Kimmins, Cynthia Kimmins, Francis Probasco, Malinda Hodgson, Christopher Billhimer, Barbara Billhimer, Mary Barnard, Lydia E. Barnard, Alex. March, Charles S. Martin, Samuel March, Abram March, Eliza March, Thomas Houck, Elizabeth Houck, Sarah P. March, Rachel Burton, James M. Burton, Esther A. Taylor, John Farlow, Elizabeth Brown, Mary H. Brown, James R. Taylor, George H. Burton, Alfred Brown, William R. Taylor, Nancy M. Taylor, Joseph Probasco and Mary Rothrock.

November 6, 1858, the following persons were elected to office: Wm. McBarnard and Chas. S. Martin, elders; Samuel Hodgson and J. R. Taylor, deacons, and John T. Davis, clerk. After one year's service they were elected to serve for life. Rev. T. R. Hansberry was the pastor who assisted in the organization. He remained one year, then removed to Nebraska, and is now a resident of Kansas. The church was then supplied from other points by different preachers, among whom were John Kane, N. E. Corey, of Charles City, and N. A. McConnel, of Marion. Thus the time was filled until 1865, when J. W. Moore became their pastor. He remained four and one-half years. Then came U. H. Watson, who took charge September 25, 1870. During this time he also preached at Shell Rock, Coldwater and Finchford, and during the year preached two hundred and eighty sermons. In 1870 J. W. Moore again returned and has since had charge, with the exception of one year (1881), when he was preaching in Linn county. During this year Dr. Hunt had charge. The present officers are: J. R. Hall, elder; J. R. Taylor, deacon and treasurer; Asa Hodgson, deacon, and G. McDonald, deacon and clerk. The present membership is about one hundred.

The first church edifice was dedicated in February, 1877, and cost about $1,200. Previous to that time services were held in the school house near where the church now stands.

The Antioch Sunday School was organized in 1866. The first superintendent, J. W. Moore, was followed by J. R. Hall, Eliza Moore, J. R. Hall, J. W. Moore, M. A. Taylor, Asa Hodgson and Guy Angell. The average attendance is about forty.

Rev. J. W. Moore, pastor of Antioch church, is a native of Tennessee, born December 29, 1825. His parents, Francis and Mary (Gregg) Moore, were both natives of North Carolina. In 1834 the family emigrated to Livingston county, Illinois. Here J. W. Moore followed various employments. In March, 1849, he married Miss Sarah Armstrong, then of Woodford, Illinois, but a native of Clark county, Indiana. Her father, John Armstrong, was a second cousin of Stephen A. Douglas. He then prepared himself for the ministry, and in 1856 emigrated to Green county, Wisconsin. In 1861 he commenced preaching in Wisconsin, but soon returned to Livingston county, Illinois, and there engaged as traveling evangelist for the Missionary Society of the Ninth Missionary District of Illinois. In 1863 he had charge of two churches, and in 1864 took a trip through Iowa, preaching in various places, among which was Butler county. In 1865 he again came to Iowa, and took charge of his present congregation remaining over four years; then spent twenty months in Illinois, and since that time he has had charge of the Antioch church, with the exception of one year, (1881), which he spent preaching in Linn county, Iowa. When Rev. Moore took charge of his present church it had only eighteen members, and the meetings were held in a school house. Now it numbers one hundred members, and has a good church edifice. This, alone, speaks volumes for the work done by Rev. Moore. The children are—William A., John F., Palmer O., and Arthusa A.

CLARKSVILLE.

This is the only town in Butler township, and is one of the largest and most important in Butler county. It is situated upon a second table of perfectly level and dry prairie, about two and one-half by three miles in extent, and is one of the most productive tracts in the whole Shell Rock valley. The farming region is excellent, and the farmers are in good circumstances. Many of the homesteads have been under cultivation for the past thirty years. The river at this point furnishes excellent power, which will support any amount of manufacturing enterprises. Shipping facilities are also excellent, as there are two railroads passing through the village, the B., C. R. & N. and the D. & D.

The original town was surveyed during the month of August, 1853. Soon afterward two additions were made, one on the east by Daniel Mather and one on the south by Seth Hilton. With these additions the town comprised seventeen blocks, and was thus put on record. For the first two or three years the town seemed to flourish and prosper, but in 1857 a damper seemed to be placed upon its enterprise, consequent upon the notably "hard times" of that day. However, a place so favorably located could not long remain unnoticed, but just as life and enterprise seemed to infuse new strength, the "great American conflict" called to arms, and civil war, so disastrous to every undertaking, had its effect upon the embryo village, and but little progress was made for a number of years. The fact that this would soon become a place of some importance was apparent to anyone who would take cognizance of the surroundings, and it was when better times set in, a rapid and substantial growth began. Men of means and brains were attracted hither. This impetus was augmented in 1871 by the advent of the Burlington, Ceder Rapids and Minnesota Railway company, which commenced the construction of a line, taking in this place on its route up the Shell Rock valley, and in a short time Clarksville had easy communication with all inportant points, and her growth and permanence were assured.

It is needless to speak of her strides toward prominence. Suffice it to say that in a short time she outgrew her "village" clothes, and was duly incorporated as a city. The election upon the question was held on the 21st day of September, 1874. The first officers elected were, John Palmer, mayor; S. M. Townsend, H. Ilgenfritz, H. F. Burton, T. Shafer and Edwin Fowle, trustees; E. A. Glenn, recorder. The first meeting of the city council was held at the mayor's office, October 23, 1874. Present—S. M. Townsend, Thos. Shafer and Henry Ilgenfritz, trustees. E. A. Glenn, the recorder elected, having sent in his resignation, H. F. L. Burton was chosen, pro tem. Palmer, Burton, Fowles and Shafer were appointed a committee on ordinances, and Shafer, Ilgenfritz and Townsend a committee on streets and alleys. Hiram Newman was appointed marshal, but did not qualify, and at the next meeting of the council E. Duncan received the appointment. The city officers since elected have been as follows:

In 1877 — J. J. Eicher, mayor; H. F. L. Burton, G. W. Poisal, C. G. Schellinger, F. G. Phillips and J. Palmer, councilmen; Donald McDonald, recorder; William Morrison, assessor; David Moulton, treasurer; E. Duncan, street commissioner. On March 10, the council elected G. W. Wilcox, marshall.

1878—J. J. Eicher, mayor; D. McDonald, recorder; David Moulton, treasurer; M. B. Wamsley, G. W. Poisal, F. G. Phillips, Henry Brandon, Ed. Fowle, jr., councilmen; Ed. Duncan, street commissioner. Council elected Ed. Duncan, marshall.

1879—John Palmer, mayor; O. F. Lush, recorder; David Moulton, treasurer; J. E. Neal, assessor; John Loomis, street commissioner; M. B. Wamsley, Henry Brandon, G. W. Poisal, Geo. Fisher, Wm. Morrison, Frank Hesse, councilmen.

1880—J. J. Eichar, mayor; S. Vale, recorder; D. Moulton, treasurer; M. Wamsley, M. Moore, councilmen; B. Ravenscroft, assessor; E. Duncan, street commissioner.

1881—L. Slimmer, mayor; Ed. Davis, recorder; B. Ravenscroft, assessor; David Moulton, treasurer; E. Duncan, street commissioner; Thos. Shafer, Geo. Fisher, councilmen. At this election the question of license was also submitted, with the following result: For license, 70 votes; against license, 99 votes.

1882—J. J. Eichar, mayor; M. Hartness, recorder; E. Fowle, assessor; T. E. Kephart, A. J. Ilgenfritz, councilmen.

The present councilmen are, M. B. Wamsley, M. Moore, T. E. Kephart, Thos. Shafer, Geo. Fisher.

THE BEGINNING.

The first house built in what is now Clarksville, was a log structure erected by Seth Hilton.

Abner Clark was the first merchant. He erected a store building on the ground where the Tremont House now stands. There he opened a general stock, and continued in trade about two years, when he sold the goods to John Palmer, and they were removed. Mr. Clark then converted the building into a hotel, after which it changed hands a number of times until purchased by "Billy" Brandon. Mr. Brandon run a hotel a short time, and was followed by his son, Henry, who soon took down the building, and in 1874 erected on the ground the present edifice. He continued there the hotel business a little more than a year, then rented to Mr. Ravenscroft, who remained a time; then purchased the property and rented it to Mr. Younger. Mr. Younger remained one year, when Ravenscroft again resumed, and is the present proprietor.

The second store was Palmer & Moneton, in the fall of 1853, on the west side of the court house square, where the residence of John Polly now stands.

The next store was kept by Eichar & Dollison, located on the main street. They remained in the business six years, and sold out.

The first hardware store was opened in this building by Davis & Griffin.

The first blacksmith was John Hardy, who built a log shop and log house where the Peet Hotel now stands. He also kept a hotel at the same place.

The first term of district court was held here October 5, 1857; James D. Thompson, Judge.

The first newspaper in Butler county was published here by Palmer & James, in July, 1858. It was politically republican.

Jeremiah Clark was the first practicing physician, and was followed by Dr. James E. Walker, in 1854.

J. Gilbert opened the first drug store, on the corner where the new bank now stands, in a one story frame building. He is yet in the business in the city.

James Hazelett run a large grocery store a number of years. He is now in Boone.

In 1856 Henry Newman opened a large store and remained a number of years. He built several houses in town, and was an extensive dealer in cattle and hogs. He removed to Oregon.

George Riley Peet came to Clarksville in 1856 and purchased the hotel property, a small building located where the Central House now stands. Some years afterward he erected the Central House, and with the exception of about three years was landlord of the same until his death, which was the result of a sad accident, on Friday, October 10, 1879. On the day mentioned Mr. Peet took the 1 p. m. train, which was somewhat late, for Shellsburg, this State, to attend a stock sale. The engine took water a few rods above the station, and when it stopped for that purpose the rear end of the train rested upon a high bridge. When the train stopped some one, whether a train hand or some passenger, spoke to Mr. Peet, who was lying down at the time, partly asleep, that that was his station. In his usual quick, impetuous manner he jumped up, grabbed his overcoat and walked out of the car, supposing it to be at the station. He stepped off and fell a distance of twelve feet or more to the ground below, breaking his neck. He was immediately discovered by Conductor Loomis and a brakeman, who went to his assistance, and who claim that he said: "Help me on my feet, boys; I feel faint," and then expired in their arms. A surgeon was called, but he was beyond all human aid. His wife was telegraphed the sad tidings and took the 10:35 train, returning on the 3:15, Saturday, with the remains. George Riley Peet was a man of indomitable energy, full of enterprise, public spirited, and a liberal giver, always ready to give time, money and encouragement to public improvements or charitable works. He always worked hard for his town and did much for its advancement. He rendered great assistance to the farming community by bringing in and breeding good stock. He was a man of impetuous disposition, and what he did was with all his might. No man ever went to Riley Peet in distress or need that did not receive aid and comfort, and many a hungry unfortunate has been fed at his table and sent away rejoicing, without money or price. Mr. Peet was born in Courtland county, New York, June 30, 1826; emigrated with the family to Jones county, Iowa, in 1848, and commenced mercantile life as a clerk. Subsequently he went to Marion, Linn county, where he made the acquaintance of Miss Sarah Parsons, who became his wife in September, 1851, and resided in Linn county until he came to Clarksville. Mrs. Peet still runs the Central House. They had five children — Cora, now Mrs. Thomas Heery; Carrie, now Mrs. Frank Newman; Jennie, now Mrs. Samuel Vale; Florence and George.

Others followed representing different lines of trade, but this is enough to show the character of the commencement.

CLARKSVILLE MILLS.

In 1856 J. J. Eichar, Geo. W. Dollison, and O. A. Strong, formed a co-partnership, and as Eichar, Dollison & Strong, erected the Clarksville mill, the first mill in the county. The building is 42 feet long, 32 feet in width, with 32 feet posts, containing three stories besides basement. It was built for three run of stone, but only two run have been put in. Those were brought from St. Louis; the balance of the machinery was obtained at Rock Island. The mill was completed and put into operation in 1857. It is run by water-power, having five feet head, and is situated on the northeast of the northwest quarter of section 19, Butler township, on the east bank of the Shell Rock river. In 1860 the firm changed to Eichar, Dollison & Abbott, and in 1864 this firm sold to Thomas Shafer, who is still operating the mill.

Mr. Shafer has at different intervals had various parties associated with him, and since 1878, Captain C. A. L. Roszell has been his partner, and the firm is Shafer & Roszell. The mill is operated as a custom and merchant mill, and is doing a good business.

Thomas Shafer is a native of Pennsylvania; born in Washington county, on the 1st day of September, 1822. His parents, Abraham and Eleanor (Johnston) Shafer, were both natives of said State. He is the youngest of three children; received a good education; taught school; followed railroading, and subsequently learned the shoemaker's trade. In June, 1845, he was united in marriage with Miss Mary Passimore, also of Washington county. In 1853 he went to Ohio, but did not remove his family to said State until the year following. Here he was engaged in railroading until 1856; then removed to Wisconsin, and from 1857 until 1864 was station agent at Juda station. During this time he also dealt in merchandise, lumber and live stock. Since then he has been operating the Clarksville mill. Mr. Shafer is a democrat in politics, has held local offices, and is a citizen who is highly respected. Mr. and Mrs. Shafer have had nine children, five of whom are now living—William W. B., George P., Thomas T., Mary E. A., now Mrs. William J. Clemmar; and Ortensius D.

ARTISTS.

It cannot be said just when or by whom the first photograph was taken in Clarksville, as for several years every now and then an artist would come along with his gallery mounted on wheels, stop a few days, and go on his way. But in January, 1873, George Fisher located here, and has since continued the business with increasing patronage, and he is therefore the first permanent artist of Clarksville.

George Fisher is a native of Novia Scotia, born on the 12th day of August, 1823. His father, John P. Fisher, was also a native of the Province; but his mother, Agnes (Connelly) Fisher, was born in the State of Pennsylvania. He learned the carpenter's trade, and followed the same near the place of his nativity until 1847, when he came to the United States, and for eleven years was engaged in repairing the machinery of cotton mills in the States of Massachusetts and Rhode Island. In 1858 he commenced his present vocation, and he is therefore one of the few artists whose experience dates back to the days of daguerreotypes. In 1862 Mr. Fisher enlisted in Company F of the Seventh Rhode Island Volunteers, and was wounded at the battle of Fredricksburg, Virginia, December 13, 1862, and was therefore on the 27th day of March, 1863, honorably discharged. He then emigrated to Minnesota, and for two years resumed work at his trade. In 1865 he came to Iowa, and has since been engaged in his present business, being first located at Waterloo, subsequently at Vinton before coming to Clarksville. Mr. Fisher has been thrice married. In 1844 to Miss Mary A. Jenkins. She died in 1858, leaving four children—Robert, Isabelle, Agnes and Jessie. In 1859 he married Mrs. Mary Percival *nee* Falls. She died January 2, 1865, and in June, 1871 he married Mrs. Harriet M. Marsh *nee* Cox, and by this union has one daughter—Lillian.

LUMBER.

The first lumber yard of Clarksville was opened by John Bartlett, in 1870, who conducted the business for three years, then sold to Samuel McRoberts & C. H. Ilgenfritz. The gentlemen under the firm name

G. R. Peet.

HISTORY OF BUTLER COUNTY.

of McRoberts & Co. continued two years. McRoberts then withdrew, and A. J. Ilgenfritz became a partner. Since that time the firm has been Ilgenfritz Bros. The business has been steadily increasing, and it now amounts to about one million feet annually.

A. J. Ilgenfritz is a son of Henry and Ann Ilgenfritz, and was born in St. Joseph county, Indiana, in 1848. He came with the family to Clarksville, in 1863. Previous to his engaging in his present business he was employed in farming. Mr. Ilgenfritz in 1869 married Miss Didama Wamsley, daughter of W. S. Wamsley. They have three children—George, Fred and Belle.

CREAMERY.

The Clarksville creamery was erected in the spring of 1881, by Charles Bulckens, at a cost of about $2,500, and during the first year of its existence manufactured about 500 pounds of butter daily. The creamery has been under the management of Edward Brula, who is a man well qualified for the position. He was born in Dubuque, Iowa, December 15, 1840, and resided under the parental roof until 1867. He then moved to Waverly, where he followed various branches of business until 1880, when he entered the Waverly creamery, and one year later took charge of the one at Clarksville. He was married, in December, 1870, to Miss Edna Ellis. They have one daughter—Nellie.

BUTLER COUNTY BANK.

This institution was founded with M. B. Wamsley, J. Perrin, James Butler, A. Slimmer, S. Lenhart, W. S. Wamsley, N. B. Ridgway and Samuel McRoberts as the principal stockholders. The first officers were: Malon B. Wamsley, president; Jeremiah Perrin, vice-president; Lewis Slimmer, cashier. They commenced business under the name of "Butler County Bank," with a capital stock of $50,000. This same organization continued until September, 1881, when L. and A. Slimmer purchased the stock, and now have full control of the institution. It is called the Butler County Bank of Lewis Slimmer & Co. Correspondence: International Bank, Chicago; First National Bank, Dubuque.

Lewis Slimmer came to Clarksville in 1870, and commenced as clerk in a general store. When the Butler County Bank was organized he was employed as book-keeper, three months later he became its cashier, in which capacity he served until September, 1881, when he became a partner, as already stated, the business being continued under the name of the Butler County Bank of Lewis Slimmer & Co. In 1882 he erected his present spacious and magnificent bank building, which is an ornament to the town, and furnishes him one of the best banking rooms in northern Iowa. The building cost $15,000. Mr. Slimmer is a very idustrious and public spirited citizen, who is ever ready to lend a helping hand to any public enterprise, which will benefit the town in which he resides. He is a man who always meets his obligations promptly. Lewis Slimmer is a native of Prussia, where he was born October 30, 1850. He came to the United States in May, 1867, and first stopped at Berlin, Wisconsin. In 1869 he came to Iowa and dealt in live stock, at Waverly, until he came to Clarksville. On November 15, 1870, Miss Clara F. Root, daughter of Ruluff Root, became his wife, and they now have one son—Ruluff. Mr. Slimmer attended school in his native country until fifteen years of age, and for two years read law. He clerked in Berlin, Wisconsin, for two years, and dealt in live stock until 1870. He is a member of the Masonic fraternity, and is a Royal Arch Mason. He was one of the charter members of the Royal Arch Lodge, and was one of the first officers of the lodge. He has been secretary of the Blue Lodge for several years. He was mayor of the city in 1881. In politics he is a republican, and in religion a liberal.

OTHER BUSINESS INTERESTS.

Henry Ilgenfritz, furniture dealer, established his present business in 1869. He is a native of Easton, Pennsylvania, born in 1820; removed with his parents to Maryland and from there to Ohio, where, in 1843, he married Miss Anna Murray. In 1863 he came to Iowa and settled at Clarksville and first engaged in farming. The children are—Louisa, now Mrs. Samuel McRoberts; Alice M., Alonzo J., Charles H. and Anna A. He was mayor of the city, also one of the councilmen for some time, and a member of the school board for sixteen years.

A. E. Smith, successor to Marion Wamsley, general merchandise, is a native of Adams county, Iowa, born June 2, 1845, is a son of W. T. and Rebecca Smith. In 1871 he went to Jefferson county, remained eleven months and returned to Butler county the following year. Previous to coming west, August 11, 1869, he married Miss Alice Belle Wamsley, daughter of Allen Wamsley. They have two children—Willie C. and George F. Mr. Smith located on section 12, Jackson township, where he now resides, in April, 1878. His mother died in 1865, but his father soon after married Emily Wamsley, and with A. E. came to Iowa in 1869.

Henry Riefe, successor to J. M. Houston, is now carrying one of the largest stocks of general merchandise in the county. Mr. Riefe is a native of Hanover, Germany, born in 1858, emigrated to the United States in 1873 and first stopped in New York, where he engaged as clerk in a grocery store. He subsequently clerked in Brooklyn. In 1875 he came to Iowa and engaged as clerk at Greene, and subsequently at Charles City. In 1879 Mr. Riefe returned to Germany to visit his friends and was absent five months. On his return to the United States he again stopped about three months in the city of New York, then came to Clarksville, and has since been in his present business. In 1879 Mr. Riefe married Miss A. Hoffmann, daughter of C. Hoffmann, of Charles City. They have had one child (deceased). In the winter of 1882-3 he bought the business of J. Cohn, in addition to his other business, and took possession of it January 1, 1883, which was in the large double store owned by Mrs. Walker, and has now the largest and most complete stock of goods in the town. In his native country he was brought up in town and received a liberal education, graduating from the public schools and took a course at the higher school.

The principal blacksmith shop and wagon manufactory in Clarksville is owned and operated by T. E. Kephart. He engaged in business in 1875 in connection with his brother, J. E. Kephart, who then owned the shop. T. E. Kephart subsequently purchased his brother's interest, and has since conducted the entire business; and the "Kephart wagon" now takes the lead in Butler county.

Mr. Kephart is a native of Venango county, Pennsylvania, born November 14, 1848. His father, H. G. Kephart, now resides in Clarksville, and although well along in years, he still follows his trade—that of blacksmith. His mother, Margaret (Berdine) Kephart, died in 1866. When F. E. was yet an infant the family emigrated to Iowa and settled in Dubuque county. J. E. resided here until 1866; he then went to Guttenberg, Clayton county, where he served a three years apprenticeship to the blacksmith and wagon-maker trades, after which he was engaged in business in Deleware county, until he came to Clarksville. Mr. Kephart is an industrious and successful business man, who is highly respected by all who know him. In 1869 he married Miss Catherine Horsch, of Cassville, Wisconsin.

H. F. L. Burton is the sixth of the eight children of Clement N. and Ann (Marryweather) Burton; the former a native of Virginia, and the latter of Kentucky. He was born in Parks county, Indiana, in January, 1834, and was left motherless at the age of six years; but his father subsequently married Mrs. Rachel Taylor *nee* Roby, and in 1853 the family emigrated to Iowa, and settled on section 8 of Butler township, Butler county, where the father died in 1854. H. F. L. Burton helped till the soil; received a good education, and at different intervals taught school. When the rebellion broke out Mr. Burton at once enlisted as a private, but was not accepted on account of his disability. But he was determined to do something for his country, and therefore raised a company—eighty-four men—of which he was chosen Captain. It was mustered into service as Company E of the Forty-fourth Iowa Infantry, and served until the close of the conflict. Mr. Burton then returned to Iowa, and in 1871 purchased the business of W. H. Bettinger, continued the same until 1876, when he closed out the business and again became a tiller of the soil. In 1877 he again engaged in business, and continued alone until September, 1882, when he associated Byron Poisal as partner. Since then the firm has been Burton & Poisal, and is now doing a good business. Mr. Burton has acted with the republican party since 1856, and at different intervals has been chosen to fill local offices. He was married in 1858 to Miss Margaret Edwards, whose native town is Newport, Indiana. They have two daughters—Carrie, now Mrs. A. L. VanHousen and Mary.

The leading livery business of Clarksville is conducted by J. M. Smith, who came to the town in 1880, and on the 11th day of June established his present business, which, under his judicious management, has grown to be one of the leading liveries in this part of the State.

Mr. Smith was born in Onondago county, New York, in 1841, and when ten years of age emigrated with his uncle, H. Sage, to Illinois, where he helped till the soil until 1862. He then enlisted in Company G, Ninety-fifth Illinois, and served three years. In 1866 he removed with his uncle to Iowa and resided at Waterloo. In 1880 he came to Clarksville. Mr. Smith is an excellent horseman, and is therefore a success in his present business. He married in 1870 Miss Susan L. Corey. They have four children—Lettie, Eugene, Edwin and Clayton.

John Hartness became a resident of Clarksville in 1857. He worked at his trade—carpenter—until 1863, when he departed for the mining regions of Idaho. Mr. Hartness was born in Indiana, in about 1827, and resided in that State until his removal to Clarksville. In 1858 he married Miss Susan Bonwell, daughter of John Bonwell; and by this union had three children—Moulton, John C. and Nellie.

Moulton Hartness was born in Clarksville, in 1859. He commenced mercantile life at the age of sixteen years, and has since continued the same. He is a young man who has many warm friends in his native village. He was in business on his own account for about four years, but is now clerking for J. Cahn. His mother is still living in Clarksville. His brother, John C., is in Council Bluffs; his sister, Nellie, is living at home.

E. J. Davis, only son of J. W. and Margaret (Weaver) Davis, was born in Herkimer county, New York, on the 15th day of February, 1852. He came with his family to Butler county and here received a common school education. At seventeen years of age he learned the shoemaker's trade, and followed the same until 1880, since that time he has conducted the business of Hunt & Davis. Mr. Davis is an honest and upright citizen who is highly respected. He is a Royal Arch Mason, and is at present serving his second term as Master of Butler County Lodge No. 94. In politics he is republican. On the 24th day of December, 1874, Miss Frances Maxon became his wife. They have one son—Roy.

A. Seitz established a grocery business in June, 1882, and now is having a good trade in his line. Mr. Seitz was born in Montgomery county, Ohio, in 1843. His parents, Isaac and Elizabeth (Flora) Seitz, were also natives of said state In about 1846 the family migrated to Illinois and settled in Lee county, where the parents died, leaving six children, three of whom are now living—Mary, now Mrs. John Cortright, and Isaac and Abraham, twins; the latter, who is the subject of this sketch, resided in Lee county until 1865, then came to Iowa, and has since been a resident of Butler county. In 1866 he married Miss Sarah Patterson, daughter of William Patterson. He followed farming in Jackson township until he engaged in his present business. The children are —William H., Fredrick O., Forest I., and Frank.

POST OFFICE.

This office was established in 1853, with A. G. Clark as postmaster, who kept it in a little log house just south of the public square. It was then on a mail route from Ceder Falls to Clear Lake and was carried by a man on horseback. In 1855 A. J. Lewellen was commissioned postmaster, but only served for a few months, when J. R. Fletcher was appointed. Next came A. J. Tompkins, then C. W. Wheelock. Afterward Webster Bartlett was appointed and held until August, 1872, when the present postmaster, Mrs. C. M. Mitchell, was commissioned. It is a fourth class office, and the stamps now cancelled annually amount to about $1200.

EDUCATIONAL.

The first school in this vicinity was taught in a log cabin by Miss Malinda Searles, during the spring of 1855. She was afterward married to Valentine Bogle. The next school was taught by Jane Clark. The log building was used for school purposes four or five years, then one was built of "cement," or "concrete," which is still standing, one block north of the D. & D. depot.

On Saturday, the 16th day of May, 1874, an election was held in the school house of sub-district No. 3, at which time the question of organizing independent school districts was submitted. The result was favorable to such formation. When Clarksville was the county seat a large brick court house was erected, 60x40 feet, two stories high. This building was purchased by the Clarksville independent school district, for $2,800, for school purposes. Here was held the first Normal institute in the county, on the 17th day of August, 1874, which proved to be an interesting and instructive session. There were over eighty teachers in attendance. Superintendent Stewart had control, and was ably assisted by a competent corps of instructors, among whom were Professor Stewart, J. E. Davis, Mr. Dodge, Dr. Logan, and Professor McCready. This school has not yet been thoroughly graded or systematized, and no regular course of study adopted and adhered to; otherwise it is in good condition. It is now under the management of N. H. Hineline, principal; M. L. Fowle, assistant; Miss Mary Heery, intermediate department; Miss Clara Lusted, primary. In the higher department there is an attendance of eighty; in the intermediate, of about forty-nine, and in the primary about fifty-six, making a total attendance of about one hundred and eighty-five.

SOCIETIES.

Clarksville Lodge, No. 351, I. O. O. F., was organized August 4, 1876, with the following charter members: J. P. Reed, Thomas Hunt, Charles Fitch, Dan McDonald, Albert Burtch, Peter Poisal and John Palmer. The first officers were: Charles Fitch, N. G.; Thomas Hunt, V. G.; J. P. Reed, P. S.; Albert Burtch, secretary; John Palmer, treasurer; Peter Poisal, warden, and Dan McDonald, conductor.

The present membership is thirty, with the following named officers: Henry Poisal, N. G.; B. L. Poisal, V. G.; J. B. Felters, secretary; Alex. Shannon, treasurer; Ceylon Brown, warden; Marion Wamsley, O. S. .G.; V. L. Rogers, I. S. G.; Peter Poisal, conductor; W. H. Bittinger, R. S. to N. G.; Thomas Hunt, L. S. to N. G.; Moulton Hartness, R. S. to V. G.; Jonathan Harvey, L. S. to V. G.; J. R. Skinner, L. S. S.; J. B. Hickman, R. S. S. The lodge is in good working order and financial condition.

Butler Lodge, No. 94, A., F. and A. M., was organized at Clarksville, June 3, 1857. The first officers were: A. J. Lewellen, W. M.; Thomas Clark, S. W.; Robert T. Crowell, J. W.; J. F. Newhard, treasurer; John Palmer, secretary; G. W. Poisal, S. D.; J. R. Taylor, J. D.; A. Brown, steward; A. G. Clark, Tyler.

The present officers are: E. J. Davis, W. M.; H. F. L. Burton, S. W.; Hiram Newman, J. W.; G. W. Poisal, treasurer; David Moulton, secretary; Frank Hesse, S.

D.; J. J. Eichar, J. D.; John S. McCreary, tyler; J. E. Neal, S. steward; William Tennison, J. steward; B. F. Sherburn, chaplain. The number of members at present is fifty. This is the oldest A., F. and A. M. society in the town and county. The present hall was erected in 1882.

A chapter of the Eastern Star was organized in Clarksville on the 27th of December (St. John's day), 1873, by James I. Enos, Deputy Grand Patron of the State of Iowa. The following were the officers elected: John Palmer, W. P.; Mrs. Sue R. Caswell, W. M.; Mrs. E. C. Newman, A. M.; Mrs. Margaret S. Butler, treasurer; Mrs. M. E. Burton, secretary; Mrs. N. E. Glenn, conductress; Mrs. A. B. Jones, associate conductress; Mrs. L. E. Roberts, warder; Mr. E. A. Glenn, sentinel; Miss Anna A. Ilgenfritz, Adah; Mrs. M. J. Burress, Ruth; Mrs. True J. Neal, Esther; Mrs. Esther Baker, Martha; Mrs. Charlotte T. Baker, Electa. No regular meetings are now held.

Temple Chapter, No. 74, the only Chapter in Butler county, was organized at Clarksville in July, 1874. The first officers and charter members were: Jerome Burbank, H. P.; Malon B. Wamsley, K.; John M. Baker, scribe; Hiram Newman, treasurer; Charles G. Schellenger, secretary; James Butler, N. H. Larkin, Lewis Slimmer, Henry Ilgenfritz, J. R. Jones, Levi Baker, J. Gilbert. M. T. Caswell, G. W. Poisal, J. M. Caldwell, C. H. Forney, H. L. Baker, S. McRoberts, Jr., J. M. Moore, G. P. Babcock, David Moulton, J. A. Carter, J. W. Davis. Present officers: Hiram Newman, H. P.; Malon B. Wamsley, K.; Henry Ilgenfritz, scribe; G. W.

Poisal, treasurer; E. J. Davis, secretary. The present membership is twenty-nine.

Clarksville Lodge, K. of H., No. 40, was organized October 14, 1879, with the following officers: J. O. Stewart, president; J. F. King, vice-president; E. T. DePuy, recording secretary; S. L. Vale, financial secretary; H. M. Rhoads, treasurer; W. R. Cave, chaplain, and a membership of twenty-six. This number increased until, at one time, it reached over thirty. It now has a membership of twenty five. Its meetings are held the first and third Wednesdays of each month. The present officers are, J. J. Eichar, president; H. H. Bettinger, vice-president; W. J. Foster, recording secretary; S. L. Vale, financial secretary; J. F. King, treasurer.

WILLOW GRANGE.

The farmers in this vicinity did not miss the excitement so prevalent in many States years ago in reference to the organization generally known as "Patrons of Husbandry." The plan proposed seemed feasible. A great saving to the producers in cutting off unnecessary expense was promised; the profits of the so-called "middlemen" were to be placed in the pockets of the farmers, and with considerable enthusiasm Willow Grange was organized in February, 1871. On Friday, December 26, 1873, the following officers were elected: J. R. Jones, master; T. G. Copeland, overseer; D. N. Pope, lecturer; H. Atkinson, steward; M. Thorp, assistant steward; W. Woodward, chaplain; W. W. Dunham, treasurer; L. L. Downs, gate-keeper; Miss Carrie Nelson, Ceres; Miss F. Tennison, Pomona; Miss Ada Leet, Flora; Mrs. John Boyd, stewardess. In April, 1874, bids were opened by a committee of this organization for the erection of a "grange warehouse," which were as follows: J. H. & J. A. Leighter, $2,640; Harvey & Newell, $2,098.50; J. A. Shannon, $2,000. The contract was let to the lowest bidder, J. A. Shannon, and the house was at once erected. Matters run smoothly for a time, and prospective gains made things satisfactory. It was not a success, however. The warehouse was sold to Butler & King, and afterwards burned. The organization is now extinct.

DRAMATIC ASSOCIATION.

A society of this character was organized in Clarksville on Saturday, November 15, 1875, with Van E. Butler, president, and Miss Alice E. Ilgenfritz, secretary and treasurer. They decided to make a general *debut* in the drama entitled "Rough Diamond," which they did in due time with credit to themselves. Their success was such that "Ticket-of-Leave Man" and other pieces followed, until quite a local reputation was established. After a few years the organization became extinct, much to the regret of the pleasure-loving public.

LIBRARY ASSOCIATION.

The first organization of this character was merged into the present association, November 23, 1877, at which time a meeting was held at the residence of E. A. Glenn, and the following officers chosen: President, J. R. Jones; vice-president, Mrs. C. M. Mitchell; secretary, J. P. Reed, financial secretary, Mrs. E. A. Glenn; treasurer, Hettie Laus.

At a meeting held December 14, 1877, the following resolution was offered by Mr. McDonald, and adopted by the association:

Resolved, That the Library Association of Clarksville respectfully solicit donations of books, to become the permanent property of said Association.

The following are the by-laws, rules and regulations in force:

BY-LAWS.

I. This society shall be known as the "Library Association of Clarksville."

II. The regular time for each meeting of the society shall be Tuesday evening, once in two weeks, at 7 o'clock, sharp.

III. The object of this society shall be the procuring of a public library, and all money received into the society, shall be appropriated for that purpose.

IV. The admission fee to a membership in this society shall be two dollars for each individual.

V. The officers of this society shall consist of a president, vice-president, secretary, financial secretary and treasurer.

VI. No person shall hold an office longer than three months, unless such person shall be re-elected by the society.

VII. One hour each evening shall be devoted to literary exercises, consisting of readings, essays, declamations, etc. The remainder of the time occupied in social amusement.

VIII. The president shall have the power to assign the literary exercises to whomsoever he may choose, and the nature of these exercises shall be left to his discretion.

IX. The sum of ten cents shall be charged as an admission fee for each evening, in addition to the regular membership fee.

RULES AND REGULATIONS.

I. The library shall be open every Saturday afternoon, from two to five o'clock, for the purpose of drawing and returning books.

II. Books shall in no case be kept more than two weeks, except by application to the librarian, who can extend the time two weeks longer; and any person retaining a book in violation of the above rules shall pay five cents for each day he shall retain the same.

III. All damage for books shall be paid for as assessed by the librarian.

IV. Any person losing a book, or destroying one wholly or in part, shall replace the same.

V. No member shall loan a book belonging to the association.

VI. No person shall be allowed to have more than one book from the library at a time.

VII. All books shall be returned to the library the last week of December, each year.

VIII. Any person neglecting to pay any fine or assessment imposed by these regulations, or to return books at the proper time, shall forfeit the privileges of the library during such refusal or neglect.

IX. The books shall be properly covered by the librarian, and numbered, and a copy of these rules pasted in each book.

X. The librarian shall keep a book in which shall be registered the name and number of each book taken from the library, by whom taken, and date, and price thereof; and when books are returned, shall credit them to the persons returning them, and report from time to time to the association the condition of the library.

XI. The librarian is empowered to issue annual, semi-annual and quarterly tickets, entitling the holders to use of books for time specified; said holders to be subject to all the rules and regulations above specified governing life members.

This institution is self-sustaining, and has a membership of about twenty-five. There are now in the library about four hundred volumes, to which additions are constantly being made. The present officers are: President, E. Fowle; treasurer, J. J. Eichar; secretary, J. O. Stewart.

CLARKSVILLE CORNET BAND.

This organization was effected in the spring of 1874, with Ed. Drake for instructor. Under his efficient leadership rapid progress was made. It is now on a good substantial footing, out of debt and in good condition, and is made up as follows: W. D. Madigan, leader; Homer Sampson, tuba; V. E. Butler, alto; B. Green, tenor; Will Morton, solo alto; L. Schellenger, second alto; Fred Madigan, B flat; S. Byres, bass drum; B. Wamsley, tenor.

PRESBYTERIAN CHURCH OF CLARKSVILLE.

The first services of this denomination were held at the house of David Blakely—who was the first pastor—on the 16th of September, 1854. The first members were, Samuel McCrary and wife, Mrs. Emily A. Strong and David Blakely and wife. Samuel McCrary, elder, was the first officer. Soon afterward the following named became members and active workers for the good cause: William Pringle and wife, John M. Moulton and wife, James Ford, Matilda Hilton, W. H. Van Dyke, John Stevenson, Samuel McRoberts. The first pastor, as stated, was Rev. David Blakely, who continued preaching until 1857. During the years 1858 and 1859 Rev. John Smalley led the services. He was succeeded by Richard Merrill, now deceased, who remained from 1859 to 1864. Then came Rev. George Graham, who is the present pastor.

Services were held in the schoolhouse until 1867, when the present church edifice was erected, at a cost of $2,500, the size of which is 28x44 feet, with a capacity for seating an audience of 160. The principal revivals were held in 1871 and

1879, there being eleven members added at the former and fourteen at the latter. The present membership is fifty; total membership since organization has been about 100. The present officers of the society are as follows: Elders, Samuel McCrery, Christopher Betts and William R. Cave; trustees, Samuel McCrery, William R. Cave, L. M. Downs, Willis Copeland and Henry Ilgenfritz.

A Sunday school was organized in connection with the church, in December, 1867, but has not been in constant working order, there having been intervals when nothing was done. The first superintendent was E. C. Moulton. The present membership is one hundred; average attendance about sixty.

METHODIST EPISCOPAL CHURCH.

A class of this denomination was organized in what is now the city of Clarksville, at the house of Thomas Clark, when the first sermon in the town was preached by Rev. Ingham, in 1853, with the following membership: Thomas Clark and wife, George Poisal and wife, Jeremiah Clark and wife, and Jane Clark. The first officers were: Jeremiah Clark, Thomas Clark and George Poisal, stewards. Services were held every Sabbath, and preaching every two weeks. The society prospered, and the membership continued to increase. Feeling the need of a suitable place of worship this society concluded to build, and in 1864 erected a house of worship 26x48 feet at a cost of $2,000. The different pastors in charge of this church from the date of its organization are as follows: Revs. Ingham, Gough, Burleigh, Holbrook, Swearingen, Henderson, Thompson, Larkin, Waterbury, Smith, Moore, Gould, Sherman, Murphy, Webster, Smedley, Littler, W. W. Smith, Wolf, Shumaker, and McKee, the present minister. The present membership is forty-two, with the following officers: Charles Skillinger, James Stewart and George Poisal, trustees; William Lusted and George Lusted, stewards; William Lusted, recording steward. The church is free from debt and in a prospering condition. In connection with this society a Sunday school was organized soon after the formation of the church, which has continued in existence up to the present time and bids fair to remain a power in the church. The following are its present officers: William Lusted, superintendent; Rev. McKee, assistant superintendent; Mr. Skillenger, secretary; Miss Mary Lusted, treasurer; Edna Pray, organist. There is an attendance of about sixty.

LINWOOD CEMETERY.

This abode for the dead properly belongs to Jackson township. It is under control and direction of the authorities of Clarksville, and is pleasantly situated on the northwest quarter of the southwest quarter of the northeast quarter, and on the north half of the northeast quarter of the southeast quarter of the northwest quarter of section 13, Jackson township. A free lot is one and one-half rods in length by three quarters of one rod in width—all others are fractional. The central road, and circular drives with branches, running westward, from oval to circular driveway, are two rods wide, all other driveways are one rod wide. All the walks are one and one-half rods wide. At each corner of every block a stone is placed permanently in the ground, as also at each corner of the plat. At the corner of each lot a stake is driven into the ground. The blocks are numbered and lettered in black ink. The lots are numbered in red ink. The spaces dotted in red ink are designed for ornamental trees and shubbery. The above described lands were surveyed and platted in accordance with ordinance number 16, passed on the 22d day of February, 1878, by the common council of Clarksville, and are therefore dedicated for cemetery purposes, and for burial of the dead.

The first person buried in these grounds was Daniel, a son of Dr. A. F. Tichnor, April 3, 1878, which occurred before the grounds were regurlarly platted. The cemetery contains an area of forty-three acres, and was purchased from Lewis Slimmer, for $1,000.

BUSINESS OF CLARKSVILLE.

The following is a statement of the present business of Clarksville:

Byres, D. S.—Practicing physician; established 1879.

Bulkins—Creamery.

Burkholder, Albert—Wagon, blacksmith and repair shop.

Bailey—Wagon and repair shop.

Burton & Poisall—Dry goods, boots, shoes and general stock; present firm established August, 1882, in Perrin block; stock, $5500; store-room, 22x60, basement and two floors.

Butler County Bank—Lewis Slimmer & Co.; capital, 50,000.

Camp, M. C.—Physician; practicing since 1871.

Cohn, J.—Millinery.

Cox, M. W.—Livery and feed stable; established two years; has six horses with necessary accoutrements; annual business, $1,383.

Dickinson, H. W.—Physician.

Eichar, J. J.—City mayor and justice of the peace.

Erkenbreck, W. M.—Dentist; established permanently June, 1882; has followed his profession, here and elsewhere, sixteen years.

Fowle, E.—Jeweler, watches, clocks, repairing, etc.; established 1878; stock, $500.

Fisher, George—Photograph gallery.

Gilbert, J.—Drugs and groceries; established many years.

Gilbert, Don—Saw mill.

Hull, L. O.—Publisher and proprietor of the "Clarksville Star."

Hunt & Davis—Boots, shoes, clothing; present firm established in 1880; stock, $5,500; room, 22x50; annual sales about $15,000.

Harrison, D. C.—Drugs, paints, oils, fancy articles, etc.; established in 1878; stock, about $3,000; room, 25x45, with rear room 24x25.

Hornish, H.—Barber.

Hesse, Frank—Hardware, stoves, tinware, etc.; established January 1, 1880; stock, about $2,500.

Ilgenfritz, Henry—Furniture; established many years; stock, about $2,000; room, 24x70.

Ilgenfritz Bros.—Lumber, etc.; stock, about $3,000; annual sales, one million feet.

King & Heery—Elevator, grain, coal.

Kennedy, George—Harness-maker; established nineteen years.

Kephart, T. E.—Manufacture wagons, carriages; has repair, paint shops, etc.; established 1874; a business of about $5,000 annually.

Ladd, Mrs. W. D.—Teacher music, piano and organ.

McMillen, J. N.—Harness shop; established one year.

Morrison, Miss—Dressmaking; established in 1878.

Moyer's Mill—established business 1873; three run burrs; capacity, fifty barrels per day.

Neal Bros'. Feed Mill—Sell flour and feed wholesale and retail; capacity, one car load a day.

Poisall, H. S.—Established four years; manufactures boots, shoes, etc.

Riefe, Henry C.—Clothing, dry goods, boots, shoes, etc.; established January 1, 1883; stock, about $3,500.

Roszell & Shafer—Grist mill.

Rhoads, H. M.—Drugs, school books, medicines, etc.; room, 20x50; stock, about $2,250.

Roszell, C. A. L.—Attorney at law.

Ravenscroft, Benton—Proprietor of the Tremont house.

Shadbolt, A. B.—Shoemaker.

Seitz, A.—Groceries, glassware, etc.; stock, about $700.

Shaw, J. W.—Groceries, confectionery, fruit and flour; established three years.

Smith, John M.—Livery and feed stable; keeps good stock; annual business about $1,500.

Smith, A. E.—Dry goods and groceries, boots and shoes, etc.; established 1881; stock, about $2,000.

Schellenger, C. G.—Groceries, provisions, glassware, queensware, boots, shoes, agricultural implements, farming machinery, etc.; been established about fifteen years; stock, about $5,000.

Salinger, L.—Groceries, boots, shoes, flour, etc.; stock, about $3,000.

Townsend, S. M,—Hardware and agricultural implements; stock, about $12,000.

Tichnor, A. F.—Physician; many years practice here.

Vale, S. L.—Grocery and restaurant; established many years; stock, $1,000.

Virden, Lou and Edith—Millinery and fancy goods; established 1882.

Wamsley, A. M.—Meat market; established September 20, 1882.

The foregoing is not a sufficiently full list to form a perfect directory, but it fairly represents the business of this promising place. Clarksville now has a population of about eight hundred and fifty, with good prospects for the future.

CHAPTER XXII.

COLDWATER TOWNSHIP.

Coldwater is one of the northern tier of townships. It is bounded by Floyd county on the north, Dayton township on the east, West Point on the south and Bennezette on the west. It embraces Congressional township 93, range 17. The greater part of the land is under a high state of cultivation, yielding abundant and profitable crops to the industrious tillers of the soil.

The Shell Rock river runs across the northeastern corner. It is often spoken of as the most bountiful and beautiful region found in Iowa. The valley of the Shell Rock is a continuous garden. The river itself is the gem of the Iowa waters. It flows over a bed of limestone with a steady, even flow which has continued for ages. Its waters are as clear as a mountain brook, and much of the way is outlined by grand ledges of rock and overhanging trees, giving it a poetic charm rarely met with on the prairies. Coldwater creek flows through the township from east to west; south of this is a smaller stream called Dry creek, and north of it one bearing the name of Crab Apple. These creeks are small and are usually dry.

The soil is variable, yet as a rule a rich loam. Along the streams a marked tendency to sandiness is visible, while farther back comes a strip of limestone, and then the wheat lands, underlaid with a subsoil of clay. The township has a greater amount of timber land than Bennezette. The principal groves are Lower, in sections 13 and 14, and Hall's, in section 8, the former being the larger of the two. There is a range of hills in the western part. The highest point is called Mount Nebo. It overlooks the entire surrounding country, giving a general view as far as the eye can reach.

EARLY SETTLEMENT.

The earliest steps leading to the founding and subsequent development of this thriving township were made in the fall of 1851, when Mr. Lacon, or Laken, and "Commodore" Bennett, brothers-in-law, wended their way with teams from their former comfortable homes in the eastern States, and settled in the then unbroken territory of Butler county. Bennett was a single man. Lacon was accompanied by his wife. They located on the banks of Coldwater creek, on section 13, where they erected log cabins. Here they remained for about one year, when, as the country did not settle as rapidly as they had anticipated, they sold their claims to John Hardman and J. H. Miller and removed to parts unknown. These farms are now occupied by William Kingery and Levi Eikenberry.

HISTORY OF BUTLER COUNTY.

William Kingery resides on section 13. He came to Butler county in 1856, and to his present farm in 1865. Mr. Kingery was born in Indiana, in 1828. February 8, 1849, he married Mary N. Etter, a native of Ohio. They have five children—Benjamin, Aaron, Jacob, William and Amos. All natives of Butler county. Mr. Kingery's farm contains about 360 acres.

F. G. Etter resides with his brother-in-law, Mr. Kingery. He was born in Indiana, in 1842, coming here in 1877. He enlisted in 1861, in the Forty-first Regiment, which was also the Second Indiana Cavalry Regiment. He served four years in the Department of the Cumberland. He participated in the battles of Pittsburg Landing, Stone river, Chickamauga, Siege of Atlanta, and Sherman's March to the Sea. Mr. Etter is a blacksmith by trade, and is engaged in business at Greene.

Soon after Lacon and Bennett were settled, in the spring of 1852, John Fox, and his brother-in-law, Lum Coleston arrived, accompanied by their families, and located in the vicinity of section 12, where they erected cabins. In September, 1853, they sold to John M. Hart and John V. Boggs.

John M. Hart, who resides on section 11, is one of the earliest and best known settlers of this township. He located on the farm where he now lives in 1853. When Mr. Hart settled here, Cedar Falls was his nearest post office, and Dubuque and Cedar Rapids were his trading points. Mr. Hart was born in Highland county, Ohio, in 1820. He removed with his parents, John and Margaret Hart, to Indiana, in 1828. Mr. Hart has been twice married. His first wife was Adeline Riley, who died in 1846, and his present wife was Elizabeth Lyons, a native of Virginia. Mr. Hart has one son by his first wife—Francis M.—and seven children by his present wife—Andrew J., Charles L., Sarah M., Martha M., Jane, Lewis W. and Lovina. Mr. Hart has become quite a large land holder, owning at one time about 800 acres, the greater part of which he has divided among his children. His homestead, where he has lived thirty years, contains about 280 acres. Mr. Hart and wife are members of the Christian Church. In politics he is a staunch democrat, and has held local offices.

The next pioneers were James Griffith and family, from Indiana. On September 19, 1852, they settled on section 13 of Coldwater and section 18 of Dayton. The cabin he erected was located just over the line of Coldwater, in Dayton, and consisted of logs, covered with a "shake" roof, and a floor of puncheons hewn from basswood. Mr. Griffith is now in comfortable circumstances, and the little log shanty of olden days has long since been abandoned for his present neat and commodious residence.

Within a short time, John Hardman and family, from Michigan, made their appearance and made a claim on section 13, where they remained some three or four years, when death entered the family and the name of John Hardman was added to the list of "departed."

In June, 1853, John H. Miller and Aaron Hardman, with their families, joined the already busy colony and secured homes in the northeastern part of the township. Mr. Miller remained here until 1856, when he passed quietly to his eternal home.

Mr. Hardman followed him in the latter part of the seventies.

A little later William Hall and family came from Iowa river, bringing considerable stock, and purchased a claim on section 8. They left during the war.

John V. Boggs and John M. Hart arrived in Coldwater at about the same time, in 1853. Both are still in the township—the former in the village of Greene, and the latter upon his original place, on section 11.

William Choate was also one of the arrivals at this time, and claimed a place near where Greene now lies.

David Miller was prominent among the pioneers, coming from Indiana and locating on section 10, where his family remained for a number of years.

In 1854, came Elias Miller. He gave up his life in defense of his country, during the war of the rebellion.

John and William Strong were arrivals of 1854. Both have pulled up stakes, and gone in search of what is hard to find—a "fairer land."

Solomon Sturtz came in the spring of 1855, locating at his present home, on section 11. In the fall of the same year, Philip Moss, a German Baptist minister, accompanied by his wife, came to the township and located on section 13. They both died in 1860.

Felix Landis came with his family in 1856, and located on section 14, his present home. He bought his place of Charles Wood in 1855. Mr. Wood afterward went to California, where he probably died. The log house built by Mr. Wood, and where Mr. Landis lived for many years, is still standing near his residence. Mr. Landis was born in Ohio December 27, 1807. He removed with his parents to Indiana when a young man, and was married in Carroll county, that State, to Leathe Armstrong, a native of East Tennessee, born in 1816. She removed with her family to Indiana in 1831. They have had six children, five of whom are still living—John, Joseph, Emeline, now Mrs. L. M. Lockwood; Rudolph, and Martha, now Mrs. John E. Miller. They lost their fifth child, Mary J., at the age of one year. Mr. and Mrs. Landis are members of the German Baptist Church.

The land began at this time to be taken very rapidly, and the newcomers had to be quick in battling the speculators, or purchase the land they might otherwise obtain free, through the generous laws of Uncle Sam. Many came who could appropriately be termed transients, merely staking out claims and then moving on in search of something better; while others came determined to live down the obstacles in the pathway of civilization. It is impossible to note the arrivals in detail; yet this, with the names of those following, is sufficient to show how the germ—commencing with the two sturdy pioneers who came in 1851—gradually developed into the township of Coldwater, which is to-day among the most prosperous, wealthy and productive townships in the great State of Iowa.

Joseph Miller is one of the earliest settlers of Coldwater township. He was born in Miami county, Ohio, in 1818. In 1845 he removed to Warren county, Indiana; from thence, in the spring of 1856, to Tippecanoe county, coming to this township in the fall of that year. He settled at his present home on sections 5 and 6, which he purchased of the government. He was married in Ohio to Sarah McCollum, born in Washington county, Pennsylvania, in 1818. Mr. and Mrs. Miller have had ten children, to-wit—Cornelius D., Mary C., now Mrs. Linas Greene; Jesse R., Oliver H. P., Margaret; now Mrs. John F. Boldan, and Joseph A. The deceased children are—Francis M., Elizabeth, William A. and Martha. Francis M., their oldest child, enlisted during the rebellion in the Thirty-second Iowa Volunteer Infantry, and died at Cape Girardeau, January 20, 1863. Mr. Miller has held the office of assessor of the township, and is now one of the trustees, and a member of the county board of supervisors. Mr. and Mrs. Miller are members of the U. B. Church.

Samuel McRoberts resides on section 14. Mr. McRoberts was born in county Armagh, Ireland, in 1812. At about the age of thirty he removed to Canada; from thence to Iowa, in 1856. His first settlement in this county was in Butler township, one mile north of Clarksville, where he bought a farm of Mr. Shafer, who entered the same. He bought a quarter section of his present farm of William J. Nettleton. He has now 300 acres of well-improved land. Mr. McRoberts came to America with nothing, but by industry and good management has acquired a competence. He has two brothers living in Canada. Mr. McRoberts was married in Ireland to Mary Quinn. They have four children—Samuel, Margaret, John and Mary Ann. Mr. and Mrs. McRoberts are members of the Presbyterian Church.

Edward S. Tracy resides on section 5. Mr. Tracy is one of the early settlers of this township, having settled on his present farm, which he purchased of the government, August 24, 1857. Mr. Tracy was born in Delphi, Onondago county, New York, in 1835. His father, Samuel Tracy, is a native of Connecticut; he died in Onondago county about 1842. Mr. Tracy came to Dubuque in February, 1857; and to Clarksville the following March. He now has about 200 acres; the original farm contained 117. Mrs. Tracy was formerly Miss Hannah Backus, born in Genesee county, New York. Mr. and Mrs. Tracy have five children—Rachel Ann, now Mrs. Ransom Palmatteer; Charles, Carrie, Jamin and Nettie. Mr. Tracy has been justice of the peace, township clerk, assessor and township trustee.

Emanuel Leybig resides on section 13, where he settled in the fall of 1857. He purchased his farm of unimproved land of Joseph Miller, in June, 1856. He was born in Pennsylvania, in 1827; his father, Jacob Leybig, was a native of Somerset county, that state, dying there in his eighty-seventh year. Mr. Leybig came to Chickasaw county, Iowa, in the spring of 1856. His first wife was Rebecca Shirer, a native of Ohio. She died in 1880. His present wife was a half sister of his first wife. He has eight children by his first marriage—Mary E., Eliza J., Christiana, Jacob V., Carrie, Emma, Elizabeth and Ida. His farm contains 106½ acres.

Abraham Flora resides on section 2, locating here in December, 1862. His farm contains 80 acres, 40 acres of which he purchased about 1860, and the remaining 40, of Benjamin Ellis, several years later. Mr. Flora was born in Preble county, Ohio, in 1836. His father, John Flora, a native of Pennsylvania, removed with his family to Carroll county, Indiana, living there until his death. A. Flora came to Butler county from Indiana, May 17, 1858. His wife, Mary Sarah Ellis, is a native of Indiana. They have seven children—Harvey E., Louisa A., Henry A., Lewis O., Susanna E., William W. and Abraham L.

William Hesalroad resides on section 7. He bought his farm of Mr. Higgins. The farm was first settled by Elias Miller, whose father purchased the land of the government. Mr. Hesalroad settled here in the spring of 1865. He was born in Prussia, in 1833; emigrated to Pennsylvania in 1855, and settled in Somerset county, in that state, where he married Mary Walbring, a native of Prussia, born October, 1830. She came to Pennsylvania in 1858. The parents of Mr. and Mrs. Hesalroad never came to this country, but resided in Prussia until their death. Mr. Hesalroad came to Butler county with his family, in 1861. They have five children—William Wesley, born in Pennsylvania; John, Harriet S., Sarah and Lewis W. They lost five in childhood. Mr. Hesalroad's farm contains 300 acres. They are members of the Christian church.

William Moore resides on section 2, where he settled in 1862. He bought his farm of Benjamin Ellis, but no improvements had been made when he settled there. Mr. Moore was born in Ohio, in 1832, but removed to Indiana with his father's (Johathan E. Moore) family when a child. William Moore came here from Indiana, in the spring of 1858. This was his first settlement. His farm contains 80 acres. His wife was Elizabeth Ellis, a daughter of Benjamin Ellis, who settled in Floyd county, from Indiana, in 1858.

Mr. and Mrs. Moore have three children—Sarah Margaret, John R., and Susan A.

Elihu Moore purchased his present farm, on sections 2 and 3, of S. C. Whittlesy, in 1865. Mr. Whittlesy entered the farm as government land. Mr. Moore was the first resident on the farm. He is a brother of William Moore, of this township, and was born in Carroll county, Indiana, in 1836. He went to Missouri when twenty-one years of age, where he lived about three years, coming to Butler county in July, 1861. His farm contains 160 acres. His wife was Eliza Saulsbury, born in Indiana. They have seven children—Emma, John, Cora, Jesse, Adda, Elizabeth, and Alta. Mr. Moore's father, Jonathan Moore, died at the residence of his son, September 18, 1878.

Solomon Sturtz resides on section 11. Mr. Sturtz was born in Somerset county, Pennsylvania, in 1814. In 1836 he removed to Muskingum county, Ohio. He afterward removed to Carroll county, Indiana, and came to Butler county, Iowa, in the spring of 1865, and settled in his present home in the fall of that year. His farm contains 160 acres, which he purchased of the government. He also owns land elsewhere. His improvements are among the best in the township. He was married, in February, 1836, to Elizabeth Troutman, a native of Somerset county, Pennsylvania. Mr. and Mrs. Sturtz have had nine children, seven of whom are living—Margaret, Catherine, John, Lydia, Benjamin, Elizabeth and Susan. Mr. and Mrs. Sturtz are members of the Presbyterian Church.

Thomas Bettesworth resides on section 19. He bought his farm of R. A. Babbage, in 1870. Mr. Bettesworth was born in Eng-

Solomon Sturtz

land, in 1837. He came to the United States, with his mother— who lives with him— in 1865. His father died in England. Mr. Bettesworth lived in Maquoketa, Jackson county, for some time, coming to Butler county in 1870. He worked on what is known as the "Babbage farm" for about three years before settling on his present place. His wife was Abbie Wright, daughter of Lyman Wright. They have two children—Lyman, and Walter. Mr. Bettesworth's farm contains ninety-two acres.

John F. Richmond resides on section 32. He was born in County Cavan, February 27, 1847. He came to this country in 1851, with his father, Francis Richmond. The family settled in Greene county, Wisconsin, where his father died. Mr. Richmond enlisted, in 1864, in the Sixteenth Wisconsin Infantry, and served until the close of the war. He enlisted as a recruit, joining the regiment at Atlanta. He accompanied Sherman in his famous march to the sea. Mr. Richmond came to this county about 1870, and settled on his present farm in 1872. Mr. Richmond has engaged considerably in teaching, and has taught eight winter terms in this county. His wife was formerly Miss Hattie Mann, daughter of D. E. Mann, an early settler of Grundy county. They have two children—Pearl, and Susie. His farm contains 160 acres.

Isaac Spoor, who resides on section 3, bought his present farm of Messrs. Brooks and Ryner. He was born in Wayne county, New York, in 1829. He moved from Monroe county, New York, to Illinois in the fall of 1856. In 1872 he came to Iowa, and purchased his farm soon after; but did not locate here till 1878. He has 160 acres of prairie, also seven acres of timber land. Mr. Spoor learned the trade of a carpenter, in the State of New York, and worked at carpentering and cabinet-making until he settled here. He was married, December 8, 1862, to Josephine Harris, a native of New York. They have five children— Lillie May, Cora Jane, Carrie E., Marcia Elizabeth, and an infant daughter.

INTERESTING ITEMS IN EARLY DAYS.

The first known birth in Coldwater township, was Margaret, a daughter of Mr. and Mrs. Hardman, in 1854, who resided on section 13. She now resides within a few miles of her birthplace, being now Mrs. M. Bragg, of Dayton township. She had several brothers and sisters, born at an early period.

It is claimed, upon good authority, that the first marriage to take place, united the destinies of Frances Jane Griffith and Martin Van Wamsley. The ceremony was performed by Judge Van Dorne, on the 4th of September, 1856, at the residence of the bride's parents. The bridegroom died in a Texas prison, during the war, in 1864, and the widow has since married Clark Carr, and is now living in Jackson township.

Another early marriage occurred in 1856, the contracting parties being Elias Miller and the "Widow" Miller. The marriage occurred at the residence of Esquire James Griffith, who officiated. Mr. Miller is now dead and Mrs. Miller has again married.

The first death in the township was in 1853, of apoplexy, John Hardman, jr., son of J. Hardman, sr., at the age of thirty years.

Another early death in this vicinity, was on September 20, 1853, Able P. Griffith, of congestive chills, aged eight years.

In early days the settlers here were obliged to go to Ceder Falls for market and mail. On one occasion, late in the fall of 1853, James Griffith and John M. Hart started for Cedar Rapids, a distance of 95 miles, with four horses and a wagon, for supplies, and after much trouble succeeded in making the trip in one week, camping by the wayside. They brought back with them 1,100 pounds of flour, for which they paid one dollar and eighty-one cents per hundred.

AN EMBRYOTIC VILLAGE.

There are probably but few persons now living in the town of Greene that are cognizant of the fact that at a very early day, before Greene was dreamed of, a village plat was laid out, surveyed and recorded just south of the present thriving town. T. T. Rawson was the instigator of this, and the poetic name of "Elm Springs" was bestowed upon it. A post office was established under the same name, which has since been changed to Greene post office. Nothing ever came of the historical enterprise, as the hoped-for railroad did not put in an appearance until after it had become a thing of the past, dim even to memory.

THE TOWNSHIP NAME.

As the name which the township bears is an uncommon one, there has been speculation as to the occurrence which suggested it and as to who was the originator of the eccentric appellation. One idea concerning the matter — and for aught known there may be many theories — is that upon a certain occasion in early days a Kentuckian who had settled on section 8 went to the stream now known by the same name to get a drink of water, and getting down on "all fours" he sucked in draught after draught of nature's purest beverage and got up, exclaiming: "Cold water! cold water!" Hence, it is claimed, the stream first took its name and afterward the township.

OFFICIAL ORGANIZATION.

The clerk's record for the township of Coldwater, embracing the first fifteen years of its official existence, have unfortunately been lost, and therefore anything we might say as to the proceedings of the board during that time would be mere speculation or hearsay.

The first election was held in April, 1855, at the house of John V. Boggs, who lived on section 12, and it is claimed there were less than ten votes cast. The officers elected were: Justice of the peace, James Griffith; constables, A. Hardman and H. P. Balm. Charles Wood was elected assessor, but he did not qualify, and James Griffith filled his place. Thus it was that the township was organized.

Among others who were prominent officers in early days may be mentioned E. S. Tracy, Joseph Miller and Asa Phillips.

The records that have been preserved commence with a session of the board on the 14th of April, 1873, in Greene, at which time William M. Foote was clerk and G. L. Mills, Joseph Miller and John Riner were trustees. Since that time the following are among the gentlemen who have at various times been on the board to oversee public affairs, to-wit: Solomon Sturtz, William Hardman, E. S. Case, William M. Foote, James Griffith, Samuel Thomas, L. Ellis, O. D. Barnum, W. W. Riner, Charles Northfoss, E. J. Moore, W. A. Griffith, John M. Hart, Joseph Miller and Henry Moss. The officers at this writing are: Trustees, Joseph Miller, G. M. Tyler and Samuel Thomas; clerk, W. A. Griffith. The officers elected in November, 1882, to serve in 1883 are as follows: Trustees, William C. Martin, Samuel Thomas and G. M. Tyler; clerk, W. A. Griffith. Meetings are held in the school house of district No. 1.

COLDWATER DURING THE WAR.

This township did its full share in furnishing men to crush the rebellion, and with the exception of one call, men were always ready and waiting to fill the quota assigned the town. The exception mention was in answer to the President's call for men in 1864, when the draft was issued and J. M. Miller was summoned.

Among those who went from this township into the Twenty-first Iowa Regiment were Aaron Moss, Jacob Moss, John J. Sturtz and Francis M. Hart. All of whom returned safe after the war.

The Thirty-second Iowa Regiment numbered among its gallant heroes the following from Coldwater: Solomon Sturtz, Adam Sturtz, Michael Sturtz, James L. Hardman, W. T. Hall, Jacob Leidig, Joel Phillips, Elias Miller, Nicholas Strong, F. M. Miller, John A. Landis and Joseph M. Landis. The latter enlisted in an Indiana Regiment. Of these Adam Solomon and Michael Sturtz, F. M. and Elias G. Miller, and William T. Hall never returned, finding graves in southern soil. J. C. Leidig died after his return, from the effects of injuries received.

EDUCATIONAL.

Originally the entire township of Coldwater was considered an organization, although not active, and was then known, as it yet is, as the District township. About 1854, James Griffith succeeding in having the territory divided into two districts— No. 1 embracing the eastern half of Coldwater, and one mile into Dayton; No 2 consisting of the western half of Coldwater. The first school-house was put up by District 1, shortly after the division, on section 13, and built of logs, which the neighbors all turned out and helped to build. The first school in the township was taught in this building—as soon as it would "hold water"—by Edward Goheen, with five or six scholars. This log house was used for school purposes until the summer of 1865, when the present neat frame building, 22x30 feet, was erected near the old one, at a cost of $700. The last teacher in the log house was Miss Jennie Hart, with twelve juveniles to answer the call.

District No. 2 was not long in following the example of her elder, and in 1865, a log house was constructed by contribution of labor in the center of section 8. The first school was taught by Joseph Miller, with an attendance of eight. The old log cabin was dispensed with in 1868, and the edifice now in use put up on the same site, it being about a counterpart of the house in the above district. Miss Hannah D. Shook instructed the last school held here, being attended by thirty-three pupils.

These two districts did effective service, and answered the requirements until 1866, when, as the population had grown rapidly, District No. 3 was set off and made one of the factors of the whole; and during the same year a log school house was erected near where the present house now stands. The first teacher was Miss Mary Clark; attendance about ten. The present school house is the same that was originally erected, although it has been greatly improved and repaired, and now occupies a site in the northeastern corner of section 35. The last term of school was taught by Irene Ackley; attendance about sixteen.

District No. 4 was made at about the same time, embracing the town of Greene; and the neighbors turned out and put up a little log hut for a school house. This stood a short distance south of the present building. It was used until 1871, when a frame building was erected, at a cost of $800, and the following year, as this did not furnish sufficient room, another frame building of the same size and cost was erected. The first school was taught by Rudolph Landis, in 1865, to an attendance of six. In 1873 this district was re-organized as the Independent School District of Greene, and as this takes it out of the jurisdiction of the township, a further account of it will be found in the history of Greene. W. A. Griffith and J. Zook taught school in this district prior to its independent organization.

District No. 5 was set apart in 1870, from the northwestern part of what was formerly the territory of District No. 1, and during the following year put up their neat school house, on the southeastern corner of section 3; size, 20x28 feet; cost, $600. Miss Kate Ohmert taught the first school, and W. A. Griffith the last; the former having seven scholars; the latter, thirty-one.

District No. 6 was taken from the center of numbers one and two, in 1874, and the same year built a house 20x28 feet, at a cost of $650, which they still use. Miss Ella Clark first called school to order here, with twelve scholars, and Miss Sarah Williams was the last teacher, with an attendance of fifteen.

A district numbered as seven was set off in 1877, which now has the number four to fill the vacancy caused by the independent organization of the Greene school. It embraces sections 17, 18, 19 and 20, and in 1878 constructed a school house in the southeastern part of section 18, size 20x28 feet, at a cost of $600. John Wilson taught the first school in this house, with an attendance of nine, and Sadie Babcock the last, to an attendance of fourteen.

District No. 7 is the youngest district in the township, having been set off in 1879, embracing sections 27, 28, 33 and 34. A house was erected in 1880, size 22x28, on section 33, at a cost of about $550. Miss Sarah Williams taught the first, and Miss Abbie Mabee the last school.

The present school board is composed of the following gentlemen, who represent their various districts, commencing with one, and in sequence up to seven: John M. Hart, J. R. Shaw, A. Wilson, R. W. Crabtree, William Moore, Henry Kohlhaas, William C. Martin; president, A. Wilson; secretary, W. A. Griffith; treasurer, William Moore. Meetings are held in the school house of district one. For the year 1882 there were 219 scholars of school age reported to the secretary. The total value of school property in the township, including Greene, is about $11,950.

TOWN OF GREENE.

This is one of the first towns of importance in Butler county and surrounding country, lying on the banks of the attractive Shell Rock, and is the headquarters of the northern division of the Burlington, Cedar Rapids and Northern Railway. Its location is on section 1 of Coldwater township, and is surrounded by one of the richest and most wealthy farming districts in Northern Iowa. The location is all that could be desired. The Shell Rock furnishes ample and steady water power, which has already been improved to some extent, though but a mere fraction of the power is as yet utilized.

IN EARLY DAYS.

The people of this township almost despaired of railway facilities, as there was a line running north and south both east and west of it, and the probabilities were for a long time unfavorable; but in 1869 prospects of the now flourishing B., C. R. & N. Railway were whispered around and soon brought to a matter of reality by the enterprising managers of that road, which was then called the Burlington, Cedar Rapids and Minnesota Railroad. The tax of five per cent. levied to aid in its construction was paid on the completion of the road into the township, which was in the latter part of September, 1871.

The land upon which the town now stands was purchased in the summer of 1854 by John W. Miller, who died in November, 1856. He put up a log cabin on the bank of the river, near the springs, and kept a "Home for Travelers." He was appointed postmaster, and recommended the name of "Elm Springs," by which name the town site was formerly known, there being some half dozen springs issuing from the roots of as many elm trees. Here many a weary traveler quenched his thirst from the clear, crystal water, and the gypsy-like emigrant went into camp surrounded by scenery unsurpassed. The land finally passed into the hands of the Messrs. Eikenberry (Benjamin and J. E.). The farm house of Benjamin Eikenberry stood where the Ball Hardware Building now is. When the railroad was a substantial reality the company purchased the farm of Benjamin Eikenberry, 120 acres, and 40 acres of J. E. Eikenberry, making 160 acres in all, which they at once laid out into lots and blocks, and recorded as Greene, in honor of Judge Greene, the president of the road. This was done in September, 1871, the purchases having been made in June. The company also purchased a large tract of land on the west side of the river of Mr. Replogle and expected to make a metropolis in this part of Iowa. They had already determined to make this the second division of the road.

The first lots sold by the company were purchased by G. L. Mills, where the Mills store now stands, and O. D. Barnum, where now stands the "Stone Store."

The first preparations for building, was the cellar of G. L. Mills, dug about the 20th of September.

The first building upon the site for business purposes, was the dry-goods and grocery store of Moss & Sturtz, which was moved from near the school house of District No. 1, Lower Grove, where it was built, and a stock of goods moved in the year before. But before they were prepared to sell the Thomas Brothers, who had in the meantime commenced the erection of a hardware store, were selling goods, not waiting for the completion of their building, and they paid the first freight bill, receiving goods on the first day of October.

These were soon followed by the grocery and drug store of Trimble & Spaulding. The stock for the dry goods and grocery store of the McClure Brothers was shipped from Waterloo, on the first day of October, and in one week's time was opened for business. The first store finished in Greene was that of G. L. Mills.

C. T. Sampson erected the first grain warehouse, hauling lumber from Clarksville, before the railroad was completed. Barnum & Case were on the ground at the same time, purchasing the barn of J. E. Eikenberry, to store their grain in. E. S. Case purchased the first produce, and before the cars reached Greene the large barn on the Eikenberry place was well filled with wheat. Mr. A. H. Bell purchased, of the railroad company, the former residence of Mr. Eikenberry, and converted it into a boarding house, Mrs. Bell being the first lady in the village. At this time, says the *Press*, Messrs. Ohmert & Schofield had the contract for building the round house, and employed a good many laborers. It will be remembered that at this time the iron on the railroad was only laid to Clarksville. Those who were here at the time no doubt distinctly remember where the laugh came in, as one after another shook himself from straw-stacks, piles of ties, or out of dry-goods boxes on a cold, chilly morning, slowly and sadly treading their way to Bell's breakfast tables. Mr. Shook, Mr. Earnest, Jesse Ohmert, and E. S. Thomas, together with Bell's boarding house, fed the strangers bountifully, but could furnish no sleeping accommodations.

F. W. Smith put in the first lumber yard. The wagon bridge across the Shell Rock was built in 1871, by A. Spaulding, at a cost of $7,000. The county appropriated $5,000, the railroad company $1,000, and the citizens $1,000.

The first hotel was the Gault House, which was completed about the time the railroad iron was laid. Bradley & Farrell won a high reputation for the house. This is now known as the DeGraw Hotel, and is in every way worthy of patronage. Immediately after its completion, the Bank of Greene, a branch of the bank of Cedar Falls, was opened here, with J. L. Spaulding as cashier. This institution failed in 1875, and the worthy cashier left for parts —"unhung." J. H. Cooksey opened a harness shop; Baughman Brothers, a grocery and fruit store; Gould, a blacksmith shop, and John Reed, a boot and shoe store. A man by the name of Roberts erected a saloon and commenced selling what was extensively recommended as "forty-rod lightning or poison whiskey," but he became disgusted and left. The first millinery store was opened by Mrs. Charles Heath.

Thus the growth of the thriving town commenced, and it was substantial, as will be shown by the following article, clipped

HISTORY OF BUTLER COUNTY.

from the first issue of the *Butler County Press*, and dated August, 1873:

"We now have a town with five hundred inhabitants, one church, a good school house, one drug store, one boot and shoe store, one planing mill, one wagon factory, four dry goods and grocery stores, two harness shops, two hotels, two millinery stores, two banks, two agricultural warehouses, two blacksmith shops, three grain warehouses, two lumber yards, two saloons, and one restaurant. We have a town library containing one hundred and eighty volumes, and constantly increasing. Our freight received during the year 1871, [This is probably a typographical error, and means 1872,] amounted to $13,277.69. Our freight forwarded during the same year, $21,980.73. From January 1, 1873, to August 25, freight received, $13,076.97. Freight forwarded, $16,887.29, and our grain trade not yet fairly commenced. We have one of the finest water-powers in the country; it is now owned by the Cedar Rapids Mill Company. We expect soon to see them at work putting up a three-story mill, with four run of stone. Surrounded as we are, by the best farming country in the northwest, we look forward with great anticipation to the future of our town."

The store building which Moss & Sturtz moved to Greene is now known as the Gates' House, and run by the Gates Brothers. McClure's building was the one which is now occupied by the store of Isaac Russell. The store erected by Trimble & Spaulding was occupied by them for a number of years, then by the firm of Trimble & Strannahan, and was finally purchased by J. W. Osier, who yet continues to handle a large stock of drugs.

The business was established, as already stated, by Trimble & Spaulding in the fall of 1871. They conducted the business about two years, and were succeeded by Trimble & Stranahan. This firm was succeeded by Stranahan & Co.; and they by A. T. Trimble, who was succeeded by the present proprietor, Mr. Osier, September 18, 1881.

Mr. Osier was born in Vermont, in 1857. His father was Joseph Osier. The family removed to Wisconsin, in 1865, and to Coldwater township, Butler county, in the fall of 1874. The father of Mr. Osier now lives in Floyd county. Mr. Osier was engaged as clerk in the drug store of J. S. Cole for five years, beginning with 1876. His wife was Emma J. Burbank, a daughter of Dr. Jerome Burbank, who settled in Waverly in 1865. They were married April 26, 1881. They have one daughter —Maud M.

The hardware store started by Thomas & Co., underwent a number of changes. They run it until about 1875, when it was purchased by M. Ball, who had also been in the field early with a hardware stock. In about one year Mr. Ball sold to P. N. Dellinger, and from him after passing through the hands of Bently & Thomas, and Mr. Barnum, was finally, in 1881, purchased by W. F. Ellis, who still runs it.

J. L. Cole came shortly after Mr. M. Ball, and renting a building of Frank Hotchkiss, opened the large drug store which he still continues.

In 1873, the Butler county *Press* was established, and a history of it will be found in another place.

In 1874, M. A. Gordon made his appearance and opened a general merchandising store, which he continued until 1881, when he moved his goods to Albia, Iowa, and Mr. Feyereisen's large stock now fills the same shelves.

F. D. Mabee, in 1872, opened a restaurant, and is still in the business. He is numbered among the earliest settlers of Greene, locating here in March, 1872. He bought his building, and engaged in his present occupation at that time. Mr. Mabee was born in Canada West, in 1836. He removed to Henderson county, Illinois, in 1860, where he engaged in the insurance business. He was married there to Miss Sarah Tuck, a native of New Hampshire. He has been a resident of Iowa since 1865, when he located at Independence, and engaged in farming, coming here, as before stated, in 1872. Mr. and Mrs. Mabee have five children—Mary Abbie, Charles, Fred, Ella and Myrtle.

At various times since J. A. Yager, Henry Wamsley, J. W. Soesbe, P. Bagley, William Wilson and Charles Gates and brother have been represented in this line, and the last named firm still do a thriving business.

Mrs. C. Fowler is the pioneer milliner of Greene, having opened her store in 1872. Since then a number have come and gone, among whom we notice the names of Mrs. Charles Heath, Miss Feely, Mrs. Riley, Mrs. Luce, Mrs. M. Ball and Mrs. Holstead. Mrs. S. M. Boller opened a stock of this line of goods in 1875, and still does a lively business.

The following list of advertisers in the *Butler County Press* will show to what extent the village had developed at the time of publication—August, 1874—and will furnish a pretty complete directory of Greene at that time, to-wit:

Physicians—C. C. Huckins, V. C. Birney, and W. H. Nichols.
A. Hardman—Drayman.
R. F. Graupner—Barber.
John Collins—Boots and shoes.
J. L. Cole—Druggist.
Charles Northfoss—Door and sash manufacturer.
C. H. Baughman—Architect.
E. Wilson—County recorder.
Theo. Coley—Blacksmith.
Henry Feyereisen—Dubuque Hotel.
Mrs. M. Ball—Millinery.
William M. Foote—Lawyer.
J. W. Gilger—Lawyer.
George W. Long—New hotel.
A. Bradley—Gault House.
S. W. Soesbe—Real estate.
J. M. Wegand—Painter.
E. W. Soesbe—Machines.
S. T. Hotchkiss—General merchandise.
Morris Ball—Hardware.
Bank of Greene—J. L. Spaulding, cashier.
Barnum, Case & Co.—Lumber.
Young & Pope—Furniture.
A. W. Collins—Architect.
W. R. McClure—General merchandise.
J. Pennock—Boots and shoes.
S. Thomas & Co.—Hardware.
L. A. Boller & Bro.—Jewelry.
N. W. Thomas & Co.—Agricultural warehouse.
Johnston & Hill—Wagon and carriage works.
Trimble & Stranahan—Drugs.
D. E. Shook—Machinery.
C. Snyder—Harness.

Frank D. Jackson.

F. D. Mabee—Restaurant.
Trimble & Barney—Livery.
Charles V. McClure—Land office.
E. Jordan—Real estate.
George L. Mills—General merchandise.
T. F. Heery—Lumber.
F. M. Root & Co.—General merchandise.

Andrew J. Burlett, general merchant, also one of the earliest business men of Greene, was born in Switzerland, in 1840; he came to the United States with his parents in 1843. The family settled first in Ohio, and removed thence to Pittsburg, Pennsylvania, finally settling in Indiana. His father was Joseph Burlett and resided in LaPorte county, Indiana, at the time of his death. Mr. Burlett came to Iowa in 1878, and to Greene the following year. He was for some time engaged in the stock and meat business, engaging in merchandizing in 1879. He is an active and successful business man. He keeps a general stock, including clothing, boots and shoes, hats, caps, etc. His wife was Clarrisa A. Shippy, born in Indiana. They have three children—Mary E., Sarah F., and Mildreth E.

Richard Miner, furniture dealer, established business here, May, 1872. He is the only furniture dealer in Greene. Mr. Miner was born in Jefferson county, Ohio, in 1846. His parents were John W. and Rebecca (Dudgson) Miner, and were natives of Ohio. The family came to Shell Rock, Butler county, in the spring of 1865. His father died April 29, 1882. The parents of Mr. Miner had thirteen children, eight sons and five daughters, all of whom are living, and all but two of whom are residents of this county. Richard went to Clay county, in this state, from Shell Rock, where he learned the trade of cabinet making, and engaged there in the business for two years. His wife was Miss Maggie Nary. They have one daughter—Mary D.

GREENE AS A MUNICIPALITY.

Green was incorporated and attained the dignity of a municipal organization in 1879, the town records commencing with the first meeting of the board, on the 20th of September, 1879, the following appearing as the first entry on the books:

"At the meeting of the council of the town of Greene, the following officers elected were sworn in by Justice Riner, to-wit: Mayor, C. T. Lamson; trustees, J. L. Cole, S. W. Soesbe, G. L. Mills, Henry Feyereisen, W. H. Rupert, and R. Miner. On motion, O. D. Barnum was appointed to fill the office of recorder."

The council then adopted twenty-eight rules of order to govern their body, which are yet in force. C. Crocker was elected marshal and street commissioner, and G. L. Mills acted as clerk of the first meeting.

The next session of the council was held on the 22d day of September, 1879, at which various committees were appointed, and William Soesbe was elected treasurer and G. W. Gilger solicitor. At a subsequent meeting it was resolved that both recorder and treasurer be required to give bonds, in the sum of $1,000, each. But at a still later meeting this was reduced to $500.

On the 6th of October, 1879, the proposition of the Butler County *Press*, offering to publish ordinances at fifty cents per square, and the proceedings of the board free, was accepted.

At a session on the 13th of October, 1879, the Mayor appointed a committee, consisting of Messrs. Mills, Rupert and Feyereisen, to see what would be the cost of erecting a "lock-up," and this committee reported on the 20th of the same month, which report was accepted, and they were instructed to proceed to build as soon as possible, letting the job to the lowest bidder. The contract was accordingly let to William Moss; and of furnishing lumber, to Bruce & Co. It consisted of two cells in the back, and the council room in front. 'Squire Foote was allowed the use of the latter for one dollar per month, he to furnish stove, fuel, desk and lights for the use of the council, free of charge.

On January 8th, 1880, a committee of three, Mayor Lamson and Messrs. Mills and Rupert, was appointed to build a ferry-boat. This boat was for the use of the public crossing the Shell Rock, while the bridge was in process of erection.

On the 4th of March, 1880, it was resolved that the mayor, council members, recorder and marshal, receive the sum of fifty cents, for each meeting, as compensation for their services.

The officers for the year 1880 were as follows: Mayor, C. T. Lamson; council, G. L. Mills, J. L. Cole, R. Miner, Henry Feyereisen, S. W. Soesbe and W. H. Rupert; assessor, William M. Foote; marshal and street commissioner, C. Crocker; recorder, O. D. Barnum; treasurer, William Soesbe; solicitor, J. W. Gilger. As Mr. Crocker did not qualify, Mr. Barnum was appointed street commissioner, and H. H. Barnett marshal. In May, W. H. Rupert resigned, and F. D. Mabee was elected to fill his place in the council.

In 1881, Dr. C. C. Huckins was appointed health officer.

The officers in 1882 were as follows: Mayor, C. T. Lamson; trustees, G. L. Mills, J. L. Cole, R. Miner, Mr. Stober, A. J. Burlett, and S. W. Soesbe.

THE POST OFFICE.

As early as 1855 the luxury of a post office was attained by the pioneers of Coldwater, and an office established under the name of "Elm Springs," about this year, with John Miller as postmaster, and headquarters at his residence, just south of the present town of Greene. Later—about the year 1859—a village was platted and recorded under the same name as the post office. A few years later Samuel Earnest was appointed as the person to distribute mail, and the office was removed to his house, south of where the round house now stands. Following him, in 1870, came Jesse Ohmert, who had his office moved to his house, still south of Earnest's. Here it remained until 1871, when the name was changed to Greene post office, and in 1872 it was moved to the Russell building and S. W. Soesbe commissioned. Mr. Soesbe held it for a few months, when E. S. Thomas succeeded him and the office was moved to the hardware store, where it remained until February 10, 1876, when the present affable officer, W. W. Riner, received his commission and removed it across the street to the building it now occupies, adjoining the Gates House. The business of the office for the last year amounted to about $1,600, and the postmaster's salary is $800.

INDEPENDENT SCHOOL DISTRICT.

The territory now comprising this educational sub-division was set apart by the trustees of the district townships, in 1866, as District No. 4, and a short sketch of its early history while under the jurisdiction of these officers, has already been given.

In 1873 it was re-organized as an independent district, with the following gentlemen as officers: Directors, A. Glodery, president; C. T. Sampson, treasurer; T. F. Heery, secretary. Prior to this time the district had erected two frame school houses, each about 24x30, and at a total cost of about $1,600, which accommodated the one hundred and fifty scholars very comfortably for a time. But the school kept increasing until in 1877 it had outgrown the accommodations, and, in answer to the demand for more room, the present school structure was erected. It is an imposing looking building, standing high on the hill, and overlooking the town from the east. O. D. Barnum had the contract for building. It is two stories, frame, with brick vaneering. The cost was $6,000.

The first corps of teachers to instruct the youthful mind, after the district became independent, consisted of J. R. Wagner, principal; Emma J. Burbank, intermediate, and Miss M. F. Petty, primary; their salaries being $65 per month for the principal, and $30 for the remaining two. The principals who have officiated from that time until the present are, J. R. Wagner, C. M. Greene and A. H. Beals. The present efficient corps of teachers consists of: Principal, A. H. Beals; assistant, Emma L. Cole; intermediate, Carrie B. Mills; primary, Flora McCurdy. The salaries have not been altered materially. The report of the 20th of September, 1882, shows two hundred and seventy-six scholars of school age in the district. The present officers are as follows: Board of directors, S. W. Soesbe, president; S. Thomas, W. W. Riner, W. F. Ellis, A. J. Burlett and F. D. Mabee; treasurer, A. Glodery, secretary, William M. Foote.

The principal, Arthur H. Beals, has had the management of these schools since September, 1881. He is a native of Howard county, Indiana; came with his parents to Franklin county, in this State, to Butler county in 1861. Mr. Beals was educated at Cornell college, in this State; began teaching in the winter of 1874-5, in Bremer county. Has taught continually since. He had charge of the grammar department of the Waverly public schools for three years. Mr. Beals is a successful teacher, and devoted to his calling. He is thorough in discipline and his methods of instruction have proved to be the best. The public schools of Greene, under his supervision, have taken an advanced position. His father is a resident of Washington township, Bremer county.

GREENE LIBRARY ASSOCIATION.

The Greene library is one of the institutions to which the citizens point with more or less pride. The organization was effected on the 1st of February, 1873, with about fifteen charter members, an annual membership fee of $2.00 was charged. Many of the members and citizens contributed books, and public entertainments were given, and other means employed to raise the requisite funds, they were quite successful, and a goodly number of books were procured. The first officers were: C. T. Lamson, president, and C. S. Stranahan, secretary. The society grew rapidly, and its library had increased to about 150 volumes, when Judge Greene, of Cedar Rapids, after whom the town was named, donated them $1,200 of stock in Union Savings Bank, of Cedar Rapids, which was to be invested in real estate, and the interest applied to the purchase of books. The association has been unfortunate in some respects, as they were at one time swindled out of $150; but they soon rallied from this, and now have over six hundred volumes—fifty of which have been added this summer—of standard and popular works, and they are extensively read. The yearly membership fee is $1.50, with a membership of about thirty. Books are let to any responsible party, at ten cents per week; yet the rule is not to let books go out to non-members, except on deposit of the worth of the same. The present officers are S. W. Soesbe, president; W. W. Riner, secretary, and Andrew Godery, treasurer. Headquarters at the postoffice.

C. T. Lamson, the first president, was one of the earliest settlers of the town, having located here in September, 1871. No man is more prominently connected with the history of the town than he, having been one of its most active business men, and intimately connected with all enterprises which had in view the best interests of the town.

Mr. Lamson was born in Essex county, New York, in 1823. In the spring of 1844, he removed to Jackson county, Iowa. He was interested in the early history of Maquoketa, and assisted in laying out that town. For many years he engaged in teaching, having prepared himself for college before coming west, intending to enter Middlebury College, Vermont, but circumstances were such that he was obliged to give up the idea. He engaged in teaching before coming to Iowa, and continued in the business after coming west, teaching several terms in Maquoketa, also engaging in farming, having purchased a farm near that village. In 1855, he removed to Anamosa, Jones county, where he taught a graded school four years. He also engaged in the grain business at Anamosa. In fact this has been his principle occupation for many years. Mr. Lamson has always manifested a deep interest in educational matters, and the public schools and the public library of the town owe much of their excellence and success to his influence. He has been mayor of the town ever since its incorporation. Mrs. Lamson was formerly Miss Martha Crane, a native of Michigan, and a daughter of Roswell Crane, of Anamosa. They have adopted two children, both deceased.

Andrew Glodery, general merchant of Greene, was one of the early business men of the town. He engaged in the lumber and coal trade, in 1874, which business he continued until January, 1882. When he first engaged in the mercantile trade he was associated with D. H. Sessions, but has been alone in the business since January, 1882. He was born in France, in 1831; came to this county with his father when a child. The family settled in the State of New York; afterwards he removed to Washington county, Wisconsin. Mr. Glodery came to Floyd county, Iowa, from Vernon county, Wisconsin, in 1872, and purchased a farm on section 36, in Union township, which he recently sold. His wife was Mary E. Morgan. They have two children—Florence and Eugenie.

DELLINGER OR WANATAH FLOURING MILL.

This manufacturing enterprise is one of the most notable and conmendable features of Greene; as it is of that class of industries, around which other business interests cluster. It is the largest mill in Butler county. The name "Wanatah" was bestowed upon it by P. N. Dellinger, in honor of the daughter of Big Thunder, a Sioux chief. The mill was completed by E. Hiller, in 1875; the frame being raised on the 3d of November, 1874. Its size is 40x50 feet, with an office 20x20, a stone basement, and two stories and a half, frame, with a dam eight feet high. The liberal citizens offered to raise $2,000 to assist the building; but it was refused. The mill was equipped with four run of stone, including one for feed, and had a capacity for grinding one hundred barrels per day; the average work being about four hundred barrels per week, and doing the custom business. At the time of erection the cost of the whole property was said to be $18,000. Mr. Hiller was unfortunate with his management, as the high water came upon him and washed out the dam shortly after its completion. This was barely repaired when another fit of anger came upon the powerful Shell Rock, and again the dam went careering down the stream. After this had been repeated several times Mr. Hiller's supply of funds began to run out, so the mill was mortgaged, and then re-mortgaged, until finally Mr. Hiller, in 1877, had to succumb, and the property went into the hands of George W. Dellinger, of Ripon, Wisconsin, who has been in the business since 1844. The dam had in the meantime been put in shape, and the machinery was set in motion by the new management under the most favorable auspices. The dam, while it has never washed out or been rebuilt since 1877, has been greatly repaired and strengthened, being now of crib timber with stone filling, extending all the way from eight to thirty feet below the bed of the river. No race is required, as the mill building is located directly over the dam on the east side of the river. Mr. Dellinger got the property through mortgage; yet it has cost him fully $22,000 in cash. The mill was continued in its original shape until 1882, when it was almost entirely remodelled, the system of burrs being dispensed with, and the patent corrogated roller process introduced; putting in three double sets of rollers; the burrs are now used for grinding rye. The capacity is thus rated at seventy-five barrels of flour, and fifty barrels of rye flour per day, while about two car loads of feed are ground each week. The brands manufactured are the "Roller King" (patent), and "Gilt edge" (straight), for which markets is mostly found in New York and the eastern States. The mill employs six hands, and is ably managed by P. N. Dellinger and his brother, Burt, sons of George W. Dellinger, the owner. P. N. Dellinger, has been a resident of Iowa since 1870, coming here in 1875. His brother, Burt, has charge of the office. Mr. Dellinger was born in Pennsylvania, in 1843; coming to Iowa in 1870, he engaged in milling in Chickasaw county. His wife was formerly Miss Belle Clark, a native of Rhode Island. Previous to the breaking out of the rebellion, she removed with her father's family to Virginia, and, in the early days of the war, the family figured quite conspicuously as Unionists in rebeldom, but finally made their escape to the north. Mrs. Dellinger is a lady of more than ordinary culture and intelligence.

MASONIC.

Alpha Lodge, No. 326, A. F. & A. M., was organized in 1873, with the following gentlemen as its charter members: E. S. Thomas, G. L. Mills, C. S. Stranahan, E. S. Case, W. H. Nichols, E. Jordan, F. D. Mabee, Frank Beals, Charles Klobe, S. T. Hotchkiss, C. C. Huckins, W. H. Smith, A. Glodery, and Hugh Johnson. The first officers of the lodge were as follows: E. S. Thomas, W. M.; G. L. Mills, S. W.; C. S. Stranahan, J. W.; W. H. Smith, Treasurer; C. C. Huckins, Secretary; E. S. Case, S. D.; W. H. Nichols, J. D.; Hugh Johnson, Tyler. The presiding officers, since its organization, have been, in sequence, as follows: E. S. Thomas, three years; E. S. Case, one year; G. L. Mills, two years; J. W. Knisig, one year; W. H. Lyfer, one year, and V. C. Birney, two years, he being the present presiding officer. The order has lost but two members by death, C. P. Leaman and William Young. The total membership, since organization, has been eighty-three. The present membership is fifty. The lodge has been very successful, embracing, as its active members, many of the most influential and respected citizens of Greene and vicinity.

METHODIST EPISCOPAL CHURCH.

One of the pioneer Methodists of Coldwater has kindly furnished the major part of the following historical sketch of this denomination:

In the earlier history of Methodism the northeastern part of this great State comprised what was known as the "Iowa Mission," which was a wild and sparsely settled region, where the weary and lonely itinerants found a laborious task in searching out the settlers. In the year 1853 the Rev. Mr. Ingham was the worker in this field, and Rev. Andrew Coleman—or, as he was usually called, "Father Coleman"—was presiding elder. The latter gentleman died in 1882, after having preached for sixty-two years. In the spring of 1853 Brother Ingham started upon his round of three hundred and fifty miles on horseback, fording and swimming the streams in his course until, on the 18th of June, 1853, he arrived at the cabin of James Griffith, in the northeastern part of Coldwater, and found as hearty a welcome as ever a worn-out preacher enjoyed. He stopped over night and partook of the corn cake and deer meat which Mrs. Griffith knew so well how to cook. Mr. Griffith called in his few neighbors, and the minister preached the first sermon to the settlers of Coldwater in a log cabin 14x16 feet in size. Elder Ingham is now living in Toledo, Iowa.

The next year Rev. William Gough was the preacher on this circuit. He was a noble and zealous worker, and is still living near Bristow, Iowa. He was followed in the year 1855 by the Rev. William P. Holbrook, who was also a hard worker and a zealous christian. He has long since gone to his reward. In this manner preaching was continued at irregular intervals, without local organization, until the town of Greene was platted, when, in the spring of 1872, the Rev. Philip W. Gould organized the "Class of Greene," with the following members: James Griffith and wife, Mrs. Ella Soesbe, Mrs. Mary Spaulding, and Mrs. Courtwright and daughter. J. H. Cooksey was class leader, and James Griffith, steward. During the following year Rev. G. R. Ward was the preacher in charge. His health failing him, he has since quit the ministry. In 1874 James H. Gilruth dispensed the gospel in Greene; but finding that he was out of his element he has quit the business and gone to farming near Davenport, Iowa. He was followed in 1875-6-7 by Rev. Enoch Holland, now in Nebraska. In 1878 and 1879 Rev. George B. Shoemaker, a young man with true and sound religious principles was sent as pastor and did efficient work while here. He is now preaching in Traer, Iowa. Next came David E. Skinner, who filled the pulpit for a time; but his health being poor he left the charge without a pastor, and the presiding elder sent Rev. John A. Brown to fill the vacancy. Mr. Brown is a promising young man, a hard student, a good preacher, and is universally liked. His time expires on the 30th of September, 1883.

The presiding elders since 1871 have been, in succession: John W. Keeler, John Bowman, S. W. Ingham, John T. Crippen, and the present official, Daniel Sheffer.

In 1877 the society erected, in the western part of Greene, a neat little house of worship, size 32x50 feet, at a cost of $3,000. It was dedicated on the 8th of September, 1877, by Elder S. W. Ingham, a little more than twenty-four years after his father had preached in Mr. Griffith's house. The present trustees of the M. E. Church are: Samuel W. Soesbe, William A. Griffith, Henry W. Smith, James Fiddick and Isaac S. McPherson. The society owns a parsonage worth about $500, in trust of Joel Door, James Griffith, F. Delker, H. W. Smith and M. Joslyn.

On the 15th of September, 1877, a Sunday school was organized with forty scholars, which has grown in interest and numbers until there is an enrollment of 100 and an average attendance of seventy. J. S. McPherson was elected the first superintendent, and still occupies the position; Miss Hannah D. Shook is secretary, and S. W. Soesbe, treasurer.

The church has never had a special revival, but is established on a solid basis, and has grown in interest and grace from its original number of ten to a present membership of over fifty.

FIRST PRESBYTERIAN CHURCH.

To get at the foundation of this society, we must go back in date to June, 1863, when the organization was effected of the Presbyterian church of Coldwater. This took place at the Hart school house, on section 13, with the Rev. Richard Morrill officiating, and the following charter members: Solomon Sturtz, Rebecca Sturtz, Henry McNabb, John Sturtz, Emanuel Leidig, Susan Sturtz, Elizabeth Sturtz, Anna E. McNabb, Rebecca Leidig, Sarah C. Sturtz and John McNabb. This organization continued in force until May 19, 1872, when it was re-organized as the First

Presbyterian Church of Greene, by a committee from Waterloo, consisting of Rev. George Graham and Rev. W. R. Smith. Ruling elders, A. D. Barnum and Seman Armstrong, and with the following charter members: Henry McNabb, Solomon Sturtz, Mrs. Rebecca Earnest, Mrs. Sarah C. Hart, Mrs. Ellen Paulsy, Emanuel Leidig, Mrs. Rebecca Leidig, Mrs. Jennie P. Bently. The first ruling elder was Henry McNabb, and the trustees were, Solomon Sturtz, A. D. Barnum and Edward Jordan, of Greene; and Dr. J. F. Eley and W. C. Rowley, of Cedar Rapids; C. H. Bently, secretary. This organization was perfected at the Moore school house, and commenced its good work with the most favorable outlook for the future. The first pastor was the Rev. George Graham, of Clarksville, who preached every alternate Sabbath for five years. He was followed by Rev. David James, who officiated for one year, and in succession came Revs. Joseph Gaslor and E. J. Marshall, each about one year. The latter was drowned in the Shell Rock river, in August, 1882. The Greene *Press*, of August 3, 1882, gave the following account of the sad affair:

REV. E. J. MARSHALL DROWNED IN THE SHELL ROCK RIVER WHILE BATHING.

"Last Tuesday evening, about eight o'clock, a party of bathers, consisting of Rev. E. J. Marshall, pastor of the First Presbyterian church, in Greene, W. C. Fabriz, E. W. Parno, Will Cheeney and George Gates, went in bathing in the mill pond at the north end of S. Thomas & Co.'s warehouse, and all started to swim to the center pier of the bridge, half way across the river. Rev. Marshall was not able to keep up with the rest of the party in the race, and fell behind. When about sixty feet from the shore, he turned around and began to come back. After swimming a short distance he disappeared under the water for a moment, arose to the surface again, and began swimming. He had not proceeded over ten feet before he disappeared a second time, no one realizing that he was drowning. Not coming up again, a boat and grappling irons were secured quickly, and the body of the unfortunate young man recovered by Mr. Fabriz, assisted by L. Downs. About fifteen minutes elapsed before he was taken out. Drs. Huckins, Birney and Johnson were quickly on hand, and with the assistance of many willing and sympathizing friends they worked over the body for two hours in hopes that life might return; but all efforts were fruitless, and the young minister of fine education and much promise, without a relative near, was a corpse in a strange land.

"The appalling news spread like wildfire over our little town, and hundreds of persons collected at the river to get a glimpse of him who, for about five months, had proclaimed to them the unsearchable riches of Christ.

"The deceased was sent to Greene last January, from Chicago, by Rev. Baird, synodical missionary for the northwest. He was unmarried, an Englishman by birth, thirty-two years of age, and had been in America about one year. He was a close student, a deep thinker, and in theology was well versed. He was a graduate of the Manchester and Leeds Colleges, England."

The society, within a year after organization, determined to erect an edifice in which to worship, and accordingly in 1873 their neat building was constructed on the hill overlooking the town from the east, size 40x50 feet, at a cost of $3,500.

The present officers are as follows: Elders, S. Sturtz, O. L. Crandall, and C. H. Bentley; trustees, Solomon Sturtz, C. H. Bentley, A. D. Barnum, J. L. Cole, C. T. Lamson, O. L. Crandall, and James Pennock; secretary, C. H. Bentley; treasurer, S. Sturtz. The society has had no pastor since the drowning of Mr. Marshall. It is in a healthy and growing condition, however, now having a membership of about thirty-six.

A Presbyterian Sunday School was organized in 1879, which is still in a thriving condition, with a membership of about eighty, and an attendance of sixty. A. H. Beals is the present superintendent.

GERMAN BAPTISTS, OR BRETHREN.

The founder of this denomination, in this locality, was Elder Philip Moss, who arrived in Coldwater in October, 1855, from Carroll county, Indiana, settling with his family upon a claim near Greene. The first religious services, to followers of his faith, were held at his house the fall of his arrival, and as soon as the school house, known as No. 1, was completed, preaching was continued during the time of his ministerial labor—a period of about five years, when it was abruptly terminated, March 5, 1860, by the grim messenger of death. At this time the society had a membership of about fifty. An organization was effected in June, 1857, with the following members: John Hardman and wife, Jacob Reprogle and wife, Benjamin Eikenberry and wife, Felix Landis and wife, Jacob Harter and wife, and a few others.

Upon the death of Philip Moss, John H. Fillmore was called to the pastoral duties, and filled the pulpit for about three years. Following him came John F. Eikenberry, who is still in charge, assisted by his brother laborers, Benjamin Ellis, John E. Eikenberry, Humphrey Fallhelm, and others. Special revival services have been held by David Bromer, J. H. Bowman and Eli Grouel, with good success, and large additions were made to the membership.

In 1873, the house of worship was erected in Greene, at a cost of $4,000, size 40x60 feet, being the finest church edifice in this part of the county. The present officers are J. F. Eikenberry, N. Trapp, and E. Moore, ministers; and F. Landis, William Moore and Henry Eikenberry, deacons. The membership is about 104.

A Sunday school was organized in connection with the church in 1873, with N. Trapp as superintendent. The present officer is Elihu Moore. The church has only lost one member by death, Benjamin Ellis, in 1881. Services are held every Sunday.

Rev. John F. Eikenberry, the present pastor of the German Baptist Church, resides on section 19, and is one of the earliest ministers of Butler county. He is a native of Virginia, and was born in 1831. John Eikenberry, his father, also a native of Virginia, removed to Indiana with his family about 1834, being one of the pioneers of that State. Mr. Eikenberry was brought up in Carroll county, and there married Elizabeth Moss. They removed to Butler county in the fall of 1855, and have resided on their present farm since that time. Mr. Eikenberry bought a part of his farm from the government and a part of Mr. John H. Miller. He has been engaged in the ministry since 1861, having been pastor of the society here since that time. Besides attending to his duties as pastor of the church, he has also improved a large farm—leading a life of industry and energy. Elder Eikenberry has eight children—David, William H., Barbara, now Mrs. John Moore; Benjamin F., Mary A., Susan, Minerva, and Edwin. The two oldest were born in Carroll county, Indiana, the others in Dayton township. Mr. Eikenberry has a brother, Elias, who came here at the same time. He now lives on section 18, Dayton township.

Henry Eikenberry, a deacon of this society, has been a resident of Butler county since the spring of 1855. His father, Benjamin Eikenberry, was born and brought up in Preble county, Ohio. He removed to Carroll county, Indiana, where he lived for many years, coming to Coldwater township, Butler county, in 1855, where he purchased a farm of John H. Miller. This farm included the business part of the present village of Greene. His house was just east of the mill, where the stone building called the Centennial Hall now stands. In August, 1871, he removed to Black Hawk county. His wife was Catherine Moss. They had nine children, six of whom are still living—Henry H., Wm. E. H., John E., Mrs. Sarah Sturtz, Levi, and Harvey. Henry H. was born in Carroll county, Indiana, in 1834, and came with his parents to Greene in 1855. He owns a farm adjoining the town of Greene.

His wife was Miss M. L. Harter, daughter of Jacob Harter, a native of Virginia, who settled in Dayton township in 1855, where he still resides. Her mother's maiden name was Jemima Zook, a native of Ohio. Mr. and Mrs. Eikenberry have six children—Amanda E., now Mrs. Charles E. Wilhelm; Francis M., Aaron H., Minerva, Arthur, and George. They lost their fourth child—Charles E.

UNITED BRETHREN IN CHRIST.

This denomination effected an organization in the township of Coldwater in the year 1859, Rev. John Buckmaster and Rev. Israel Shafer officiating. The first officers were—D. W. Miller, class leader, and J. M. Miller, steward. The first services were held at the house of Widow Hall. The presiding elders, since 1860 until the present time, have been in sequence, as follows: David Wenrick, until 1865; G. H. Watrous, until 1868; S. D. Stone, one year; G. H. Watrous, one year; Enoch Fathergill, one year; Israel Shafer, two years; M. S. Drury, three years; M. Bowman, one year; S. Sutton, two years; D. Wenrick, one year; William Cunningham, two years and for the coming year of 1883. The pastors in succession, from 1860, have been as follows: Revs. James Murphy, J. H. Knouse, Simon George, one year; J. Murphy, one year; J. Lash, one year; J. N. Martin, two years; J. Trenholm, one year; J. Baskerville, one year; L. T. John, one year; M. M. Taylor, two years; J. Lindsey, one year, and for the coming year of 1883, George W. Benson.

In the absence of the class record it is impossible to give the membership of the society since its organization. The present officers are: W. A. Keister, class leader, and J. Miller, steward.

NOTES OF INTEREST.

The first birth in the town of Greene was that of a pair of twin girls born to Mr. and Mrs. J. Farrel, of the Gault House.

The first marriage of parties belonging here was that of N. W. Thomas and Miss Lucy Perry. There being no officer here to perform the ceremony, they were married in Clarksville on the 11th of September, 1872. The first wedding was that of Mr. J. Temple, S. W. Soesbe officiating.

The first death in town was that of Willie, son of Frank W. Smith.

PROSPERITY OF GREENE.

In the issue of the Butler County *Press* on the 9th of September, 1874, the editors say: "At no time have we seen a greater degree of prosperity in our town. The number of new buildings in course of erection is great, while all our industries are enjoying a fine degree of growth and enlargement. This state of facts shows that our industries are not of the mushroom sort, but legitimate and demanded by the country."

FIRST FLOUR SHIPMENT.

The first car-load of flour was shipped from Greene on the 15th of April, 1875, and another lot was sent on the following Monday. This was the first lot manufactured by the Dellinger Mill.

DIRECTORY.

A. F. and A. M., Alpha Lodge, No. 326—V. C. Birney, M. W.; O. D. Barnum, Sec.

Beals, Prof. A. H.—Principal Public Schools.

Birney, A. F.—Drugs, paints and oils.

Birney, V. C.—Physician and surgeon.

Brown, Rev. John A.—Pastor M. E. church.

Bruce & VanSaun—Grain.

Bruce, Vehon & Co.—Lumber.

Burlett, A. J.—General merchandise.

Butler County Press—Geo. E. Delevan, editor and proprietor.

City Restaurant—Gates Bros., proprietors.

Cole, J. L.—Drugs, paints, oils, news depot.

Dellinger, B. M.—Flouring mill.

Earnest, I. M.—Agricultural implements.

Earnest, John—Lumber and coal.

Eikenberry, Rev. John—Pastor German Baptist Church.

Ellis, W. F. & Co.—Hardware.

Emmet House—Mrs. V. Morrison.

Fabriz, W. C.—Barber.

Feyereisen, H.—General store.

Fowler, Mrs. C.—Millinery.

Gates House—Gates Bros., proprietors.

Glodery, Andrew—General merchandise.

Green, C. M.—Attorney at law.

Harlinske, F.—Merchant tailor.

Halstead, Miss Myra—Millinery.

Huckins, C. C.—Physician.

Huckins, F. W.—Agricultural implements.

I. O. O. F., Elm Springs Lodge, No. 318—A. J. Burlett, N. G.; M. W. Miller, Sec.

Jackson, Frank D.—Attorney at law.

Johnson, Dr. A. K.—Physician and surgeon.
Kean, R.—Blacksmith.
Kinsey, J. W.—Agent B. C. R. & N. Ry.
Kussel, Isaac—Clothing and gents' furnishing goods.
Lloyd, A. S.—Barber.
Mabie, F. D.—Restaurant.
Madison House—S. Webber, proprietor.
Mills, G. L.—Grain and stock.
Miner, R.—Furniture dealer.
Nevins, Dr. John—Physician.
Osier, J. W.—Drugs, paints and oils.
Parno, E. W.—Dealer in watches, etc.
Pennock, James—Boots and shoes.
Riner, W. W.—Hardware and Postmaster.
Schucknecht, A. C.—General merchandise.
Sessions, E. H. & Co.—Dry goods, boots and shoes.
Shell Rock Valley Bank—C. H. Wilcox, cashier.
Shoemaker, J. F.—Dentist.
Snyder, P. B.—Dentist.
Soesbe Bros.—Lawyers and real estate agents.
Steve, J. D.—Meat market.
Stober, L. J.—Harnessmaker.
Thomas, A. S. & Co.—Farm machinery.
Tyler & Son—Groceries and provisions.
Williams House—G. W. DeGraw, proprietor.
Wilson, E. F.—Livery stable.

CHAPTER XXIII.

DAYTON TOWNSHIP.

This sub-division of Butler county lies in the northern tier of townships, and is among the banner farming localities of Northern Iowa. Floyd county lies on the north; Jackson township on the south; Fremont on the east, and Coldwater on the west. It is a full Congressional township of thirty-six sections, embracing the territory of township 93, in range 16, containing an area of 23,040 acres, a great portion of which is under a high state of cultivation.

The land in Dayton is mostly high rolling prairie of great fertility. It has an excellent soil for mixed farming, and a country admirably adapted by nature for stock raising and dairy purposes. The Shell Rock river traverses the township from the northeast to the southeast, and parallel with it is the Burlington, Cedar Rapids & Northern Railroad. Coldwater creek enters Dayton by way of section 19, and empties its waters into the Shell Rock, in section 29. Flood creek rises in Minnesota and flows in a southerly direction through Dayton, making its confluence with the Shell Rock river in this township. It will thus be seen that the township is well watered, and possesses in a high degree those requisites necessary for manufacturing purposes, which no doubt will be well utilized at some time not far distant. Along the Shell Rock river in places, and at the mouth of Flood creek, are groves of timber.

EARLY SETTLEMENT.

There is some uncertainty as to who was really the first to push their way into the fertile prairies of Dayton in quest of a home. There is abundant testimony, however, that the honor is due to William Goheen, who settled here in March, 1852.

Mr. Goheen was a native of the State of Indiana, and came here with his family, bringing three horses. He entered three forty acre tracts of land in the center of Dayton township. He built a little hewn log house, where he remained braving all the vicissitudes of frontier life, and defending his family from danger and want until June, 1853, when death called him, and left the family to mourn the loss of a brave husband and father. This was the first death in the township.

During the same year James Griffith came with his family, and erected his cabin in southwest quarter of section 18, Dayton township. He is treated at length in the history of Coldwater township.

Among the early arrivals was R. W. Butler, who moved from the Wapsie. Being possessed of some means, by judicious investments and a successful system of farming he accumulated a snug sum, which is now enjoyed by his heirs.

Levi Burress built his cabin on section 27, on the west bank of the Shell Rock. He was a mighty hunter in his younger days, a man of imposing presence, of frank, open bearing, and a voice full of heartiness and good will. His cabin was the stopping place for the many emigrants wending their way north and westward. They will long remember the hospitable Kentuckian.

James Blake, originally from Maine, but by training a Virginian, came in 1854 and entered 320 acres on section 25, where he at once erected a cabin.

Philip J. Ebersold, from New York, was one of the earliest arrivals. He located on the premises now occupied by Mr. McNames, on the banks of Flood creek. He afterward removed about a mile and a half southeast of the old homestead to another farm, which he purchased and brought under a high state of cultivation. He was a reading and thinking man, as well as one used to toil.

In the summer and fall of 1854 came William Gough, Hugh Thomas, P. Ebersold, Delano McCain, and others.

John F. Eikenberry, also one of the oldest settlers, and a preacher of the German Baptist, took a claim and made of it a model farm. He is a man much esteemed wherever he is known, genial in his manner, and honest in all his purposes. He is a fit representative of his faith, of which there are many families settled in this and adjoining townships.

John V. Boggs was another of the first settlers, and was located for years on section 20. He was a member of the old board of supervisors, and a man of sterling rectitude--reliable as the needle to the pole.

Tobias Miller is another of the early settlers of Dayton township—came in June, 1853, and located on the section where Eikenberry now lives. In 1855 he sold out and went to Minnesota.. The last heard of him he was at South Bend, Indiana.

Levi Burris came in 1852, shortly after Goheen, and settled on section 27, living there until his death, in fall of 1882.

Commodore Bennett settled on section 13, the place now owned by Wm. Kingery.

GENERAL ITEMS.

The first religious services in the town was held at the house of James Griffith, in 1854, by Israel Shafer, of the United Brethren denomination. Some meetings were afterwards held at school houses. They generally have a religious service of some character once in two weeks.

The first death was William Goheen, in 1853; he was buried on the banks of Coldwater creek, section 19; afterwards taken up and buried in the Hardman cemetery.

The first school in Dayton was held in the fall of 1858, in a frame building 20x20, costing $500. A winter term was taught by a Mr. Thompson, with an attendance of fifteen.

There are at present ten school districts in the township, with school buildings in each.

The first birth was in 1855, a daughter, Isabella, to J. W. Goheen and Mary (Burras) Goheen. These parties, it is said, were the first couple married in the township.

OFFICIAL RECORD.

The territory now comprising Dayton, on the 6th of February, 1855, was equally divided, the east half being merged into the organization of Butler township, and the west half belonging to Coldwater. In this shape it remained until September, 1860, when Judge Converse set it off and ordered it organized as a separate town from the others, and an election was ordered on the 6th day of November, 1860, at the house of Richard Chellew. At that election C. H. Forney, Abel Eddy and Lemuel Carter were chosen judges; Patrick Hagerty and Phineas Clawson, clerks. The first officers were as follows: Justices of the peace, Hugh Thomas and Levi Burress; constables, Richard Chellew and Reuben Strohecker; supervisor, Thomas Hagerty; clerk, John F. Eikenberry; assessor, Phineas Clawson; trustees, John V. Boggs, Philip J. Ebersold and Lemuel Carter.

The present officers of the township are as follows, elected in November, 1882: Justices of the peace, L. Bragg and F. Morrill, Jr.; township clerk, W. W. R. Shafer; constables, George C. Clark and John Dellker; assessor, W. H. Lyford; trustees, C. H. Forney, George Lathrop, and E. Morrill.

Among others that have held prominent positions in the township are: C. H. Forney, John V. Boggs, John F. Newhard, M. L. Carter, Joseph Packard, E. J. Ebersold, Julius Temple, George Lathrop, and F. Morrill.

DAYTON'S SHARE IN THE WAR.

During the rebellion the township, although sparsely settled, furnished more than its quota of men had it been credited as it should have been.

From the records of Adjutant General Baker we copy a list of those who served in the gallant Thirty-second Iowa Infantry: Phineas Clawson, Joseph Babcock, C. N. Thomas, James Ybright, Wilbur Clauson, Henry Brooks, James Butler, John McCain, Albert Boggs, Isaiah Carter, John Swim, Aaron Harter, John Forney, Roszell Cain, and Sylvester Bragg.

Among other regiments are found the names of the following men from Dayton: Dock Burress, Jasper Blake, and Alex. Forney. The drafted men were Joseph Thornsbrue, Hamilton Brown, and Robert Burress. Among the "hundred-day men" were W. A. Wilkis, John Eddy, and William Carter.

THE FARMERS' CLUB.

The Clarksville *Star*, in its issue of the 20th of May, 1875, contains the following remarks from the pen of Van E. Butler:

"Among the educational institutions of this town is the 'Farmers' Club,' which was organized in 1864, the object being to increase the interest in agriculture, horticulture and floriculture. How much influence it has exerted within a period of ten years is seen by the superior thrift, the intelligence, improved style of farming, and the general neatness of the homesteads of its members. Mutual intercourse and interchange of ideas on farming and other topics have kept its members posted on the issues of the day; and if a stranger should step in when the club is in session he would no doubt conclude that the farmers kept their best stock at home and sent the poorer material to the Senate or Legislature, on the same principle that they select their best seeds for propagation and send the inferior article to market."

CHARACTERISTIC SETTLEMENT.

It has been remarked by some that biographies when published in a work of this kind have a tendency to make the whole matter monotonous and uninteresting, consequently detracting from the interest which otherwise would attach to such a volume. While this in a great measure is true, yet there is no way which will so clearly show the actual character of a settlement. Dayton township has good reason to be proud of her representative people. Among the many deserving of mention, a few are therefore appended.

John N. Boggs is one of the pioneers of Butler county, his residence in the county dating from September 10, 1853. Mr. Boggs was born in Ohio, in 1820. He lost his parents when he was but three years of age, and was brought up by strangers in Henry and Union counties, Indiana. He came to this county with Mr. John Hart, of Coldwater township, and pre-empted a farm adjoining Mr. Hart. He had possession of this farm, only from July 2, 1854, till January 10, 1856, when he sold it for $16 per acre. This was a remarkable price for land at that early day, and the sale was a fortunate transaction for Mr. Boggs. He has owned his present farm in Dayton township since May 1, 1856, buying it of John Hunter, of Janesville, Bremer county. He now has 200 acres. Mr. Boggs has been twice married. His first wife was Susan Lyons, a native of Pennsylvania. She died in 1874. His present wife Mrs. C. (Lence) Hardman, was a native of Pennsylvania, who came to Coldwater township with her husband, Aaron Hardman, in 1853. He died in 1878. Mr. Boggs has three children by his first wife—Albert, Sarah and Joseph P. His first child, Orville, died in 1848. Mrs. Boggs has nine children by former marriage, six of whom are living. In politics Mr. Boggs is a republican, and has held offices of trust.

P. J. Ebersold, a native of the State of New York, was married in New York City to Mary Gihon, who was born in Belfast, Ireland, in 1823, and came to the United States with her mother and brother when she was nineteen years old. She came to Iowa in 1854, and has lived in Dayton township since that time. Mr. and Mrs. Ebersold have seven children—Emily, Katie, David, Lillie, Laura, Sarah J. and Thomas. They lost one child—Alphonse. They have a beautiful home on section 24.

Hugh Thomas, residing on section 24, has been a resident of Dayton township since August, 1854. He was born in Washington county, Pennsylvania, in 1809. When three years of age he removed to Wayne county, Ohio, with his parents. His parents, Michael and Agnes Thomas, lived in Wayne county about nineteen years, when they removed to Hancock county, where his mother died. His father died in Indiana. Mr. Thomas has been three times married. His first wife was Hannah Williams, a native of Pennsylvania; his second wife. was Frances Crawford, and his present wife was Miss Mary S. Arkills, a native of Ulster county, New York, who came to Clarksville with her mother in July, 1867. Mr. Thomas has three sons and three daughters. His oldest son, Hiram, was a member of an Indiana regiment, in the war of the rebellion, and died in the service. His sons, Charles N., and L. D., were also in the service. Mrs. Thomas' parents, Nathaniel and Jane Ann Arkills, removed from the State of New York to Marquette county, Wisconsin, in 1861, where her father died in 1863. Her brother, Charles W. Arkills, served in the war of the rebellion, and now lives in Floyd county. Her mother resides with him. Mr. Thomas' children are—Hiram, (deceased), Asenath, now Mrs. John Duly; Charles N., Liverton D., Amanda A., now Mrs. Charles Surfus; Albert H., and Hattie R. Mr. Thomas has always been identified with the interests of the township, and has seen it change from a wilderness to a well-settled and prosperous county. He was the president of the first school board on its organization, and has held other local offices.

William H. Bonnell resides on section 25. He bought his present farm of F. J. Phillips. His father, Shedrick Bonnell, was one of the earliest settlers of Fremont township. Mr. Bonnell was born in Ohio, in 1851, and came to Butler county, with his father, in 1855. He married Miss Eliza Shannon, daughter of John A. Shannon. They have two children—Amanda E., and Dora N. Mr. Bonnell's farm contains eighty acres.

Lemuel Carter; resides on section 34. Mr. Carter is one of the early settlers of Butler county, coming here in 1855. He was born August 16, 1809, in Geauga county, Ohio; but was brought up in Union, and there married Jemima Orrahood, a native of Virginia. Mr. Carter located upon his present farm upon his arrival, in 1855, purchasing of Mr. Butler. His wife died in August, 1872. His present wife was Mrs. Polly Owens, a native of New York. His children are—Phœbe, wife of C. Wygle; Maria J., wife of Robert Burrass, who died in the service during the war of the rebellion; William and James, who live in Wisconsin. Mr. Carter's farm contains 160 acres. He is now in his seventy-fourth year, and, although he encountered all the privations incident to a pioneer life, yet he is physically well preserved, being hale and healthy for a man of his years. Mr. and Mrs. Carter are members of the M. E. Church.

Charles T. Mather resides on section 33. His father, Dan. Mather, was one of the early settlers of Butler township, and is still living, in his eighty-seventh year. He was born in Otsego county, New York, August 17, 1796, where he was married to Roxanna Underwood. They removed to Warren county, Pennsylvania, in 1825. He was a carpenter by trade, an occupation he followed for many years. He removed from Pennsylvania to Boone county, Illinois, in 1844, and came to Butler county in May, 1854. He was among the earliest settlers of Clarksville, where he was engaged for many years in contracting and building. Among the early buildings which he assisted in constructing was the court house in that village, now used as a public school building. He purchased about 1,000 acres of land of the government, but devoted most of his attention to mechanical pursuits. His specialty for many years was fanning mills. His first wife died October 31, 1856. He afterward married Mrs. Sallie Veber; they now reside in the village of Clarksville. Mr. Dan. Mather had five children, four of whom are now living—Mrs. Maria Nelson, Charles T., Stephen D., who resides in Tennessee, and Milo E., who lives in Kansas. Stephen and Milo served in the war of the rebellion. Charles T. married Caroline Tripp, a native of the State of New York. They have seven children—Jessie, Charles M., Celia, Luella, Nellie, Catherine, and Daniel. Mr. Mather has a large farm, containing a full section of land.

Christian H. Forney is numbered among the farmers of Dayton township. He was born in Tuscarawas county, Ohio, in 1822. When nineteen years of age he removed with his parents, Christian and Christina Forney, to Indiana, where they lived until their death. Mr. Forney moved to Illinois in 1854, onto a farm in Livingston county, near Pontiac. His residence in Butler county dates from July 3, 1856. He bought his present farm from William Mullin and James Blake. Mr. Forney has been twice married. His first wife was Rebecca Prince, a native of Champaign county, Ohio. His present wife was Miss Agnes Burnes, a native of England. She came to the United States when but five years of age, living in Ohio. Mr. Forney had three children by his first wife and has had six by his second, five of whom are living. He is one of the successful farmers of Butler county and is quite an extensive land owner, having five hundred and sixty acres in one body. In 1850 he took a trip across the plains to California and was absent about a year.

John A. Shannon was born near Kingston, in the province of Ontario, in 1826. His parents, John and Samantha (Smith) Shannon, were natives of New York State. Mr. John Shannon was in the war of 1812, and moved to Canada after the close of that war, where he resided till his death.

His wife is still living there. John A. Shannon resides on section 36. He purchased his farm of Andrew Daily, of Bremer county, in the spring of 1862, and settled here several years later. Mr. Shannon went to Michigan from Canada in 1852, and came to Butler county in 1856, settling in Clarksville. He is a carpenter by trade, and assisted in the construction of many of the older buildings of that village, building Peet's Hotel and several of the principal residences there. He married Elizabeth Fisher, daughter of Jeremiah Fisher, an early settler of DeKalb county, Illinois. Mrs. Shannon is a native of Clinton county, New York. They have five children, to-wit: Eliza J., wife of William S. Bonwell; Tina, now Mrs. Schuyler Hardman; Bertha, now Mrs. Charles N. Bonwell; Clara and John L. Their farm contains 160 acres.

Lafayette Bragg resides on section 29. His father, Erastus Bragg, was a native of New York State, and moved to Illinois about 1834. He resided in Illinois and Wisconsin until 1861, when he came to Butler county and settled on section 20 of Dayton township, where he died Christmas, 1874. His wife, Louisa Williams, a native of York State, is still living. She has five children—Lafayette, Clarissa, Sylvester, Roxanna and Martin. She lost two children. Lafayette was born in Illinois, in 1836. He married Jane Burrass, who came to this county with her adopted father, Levi Burrass. Mr. and Mrs. Bragg have four children—Alma, Mary A., Clara and Martin L. Their farm contains 240 acres.

David Ackerman resides on section 28. He bought his farm of 109 acres of Delany McKane, who entered the farm from government land. Mr. Ackerman is a native of New York State, born in 1822. His parents were David and Susanna Ackerman. His father was a native of New York State. His mother was born in Connecticut. They resided in Otsego county until their death. When twenty-five years of age Mr. Ackerman went to Wisconsin and took up land in the town of Rubicon, Dodge county, where he lived for nineteen years; coming to Butler county, November 3, 1866, he purchased his present farm the following spring. His wife was Lucy J. Fairchild, a native of the same county. They have six children—Jane, wife of John Favor, residing in California; Wesley A., Charles D., Lillie A., Byron D. and Mary C. Mr. Ackerman's farm contains 320 acres.

Stephen Fitzgerald resides on section 11. His father, Michael Fitzgerald, was born in Ireland, and came to the United States when twenty years of age, settling in Ontario county, New York. He afterwards removed to Greene county, Wisconsin, being one of the early settlers of that county. In 1867, he came to Butler county, and bought a farm of Mr. Davis on section 11 in Dayton township. In 1874 he sold his farm and moved to Waverly. Mr. Stephen Fitzgerald purchased his place in 1872, of A. Lloyd, who bought of J. J. Wagonseller. The parents of Mr. Fitzgerald had ten children, three sons and seven daughters. Stephen is the only one living in this county. He was born in Canandaigua, Ontario county, New York, in 1846. He married Elizabeth Ashlan, daughter of Lewis and Margaret Ashlan, who settled in McGregor from the State of New York, about 1855, and are now living in Clarksville. Mr. and Mrs. Fitzgerald have three children—Ellen, Lillie M. and Nina.

Joseph Packard purchased his farm on section 22 in 1867. Mr. Packard was born in Wayne county, New York, in 1833. He removed to Michigan with his father, Ira Packard, who died in Lenawee county, that State. Mr. Joseph Packard came to Butler county in 1867. His wife was Helen N. Eddy, daughter of H. S. Eddy. They have two children, Ernest and Ruluff. Their farm contains eighty acres.

Milton R. Root resides on section 22. He is the son of Ruluff Root, of Clarksville, a sketch of whom will be found elsewhere. Milton R. was born in Herkimer county, New York, in 1857; came to Iowa with his parents, who settled in Clarksville. Mr. Root, Sr., resided on the farm, where his son now lives, for several years. It is one of the largest farms in the county, containing 1100 acres. Mr. Root is largely engaged in stock raising. His wife was Mary B. Walker, who died June 13, 1882, leaving one daughter, Fannie.

William W. R. Shafer resides on section 36. His father, Thomas Shafer, purchased the farm of Mr. Gould. Mr. Shafer was born in Washington county, Pennsylvania, in 1846. He came to Iowa with his father, who now lives in Clarksville. W. W. R. purchased his farm, which contains 160 acres, of his father. His wife was Miss L. J. Clemmer, born in Greene county, Wisconsin, in 1848. Her father, Dr. J. N. Clemmer, is still a resident of Greene county. Mr. and Mrs Shafer have six children—Lena L. L., Nettie A., Joseph T., Mary A., George C. and Fred.

George Mason resides on section 16, where he settled in the spring of 1869. He bought his farm of W. H. Bettinger. Mr. Mason was born in Rockingham county, Virginia, September, 1833. When twenty-one years of age he removed to Ohio. His parents, John and Mary Ann (Miller) Mason resided in Rockingham county till their death. Mr. Mason went to Henry county, Indiana, where he enlisted in 1862 in the 84th Regiment Indiana volunteer infantry, and served till the close of the war. He participated in the battle of Chickamauga, was at Chattanooga, &c. During the latter part of the war was on detached service. He has been a resident of this township since 1865. He has been married twice. His first wife was Francis Rife. She died here February, 1874. His present wife was Mrs. Joanna Trimblin. Her maiden name was Flusher. He has six children by first wife. Mrs. Mason has four children by her former husband. Their farm contains eighty acres.

W. H. Price resides on section 7, and has owned his farm since 1870. He is a native of London, England, where he was born in 1837, coming to the United States with his parents when but a child, and resided in New York City, where his father was in business for many years. Mr. Price came to Butler county in April, 1856, and entered into the mercantile business in Clarksville in 1858, where he continued until 1877, when he settled on his farm of 400 acres.

Julius Temple resides on section 20. He purchased his farm of D. and M. V. Bragg in 1871. He was born in Heath, Franklin county, Massachusetts, in 1844. His father, John Temple, died in Massachusetts when Julius was a boy. Mr. Temple came to Waterloo, Black Hawk county, in 1858, with his step-father, James Maxwell. He served six months in the army as a member of the 41st regiment of Wisconsin infantry. After the war he returned to Black Hawk county, from thence removed here. He married Miss B. Minor, daughter of John Minor. They have two children, Jessie and John. Mr. Temple's farm contains 120 acres.

Frederick Morrill resides on section 8. He bought his farm of John Dexter, who, being the first settler, made all the improvements. Mr. Morrill was born in Sebec, Piscataquis county, Maine, in May, 1818. His parents were John and Liberty (Lyford) Morrill. His wife was formerly Miss Diana Lyford, a native of Sebec. Her parents were James G. and Huldah (Spaulding) Lyford. Mr. Morrill came to Floyd county in March, 1873, and settled here the following June. Mr. and Mrs. Morrill have five children—Edwin, Emma M., now Mrs. Harmon Douglass; Minnie, now Mrs. Jacob Montgomery; Frederick, jr., and William H. S.

William H. Lyford came here from Maine, in 1874, and settled on section 6. He is a native of Maine, born in 1831. His wife was Hannah Gould, a native of the same State. Her father settled in Alamakee county, this State, in 1853. Mr. and Mrs. Lyford have four children—Charles W., Hiram G., Cora and Alma. He was the first settler on his farm, and now has 160 acres.

Henry Wamsley resides on section 20. He bought his farm of Martin V. Bragg, in the fall of 1874. The farm was first settled by Douglas Bragg, father of Martin V. Mr. Wamsley has 120 acres. His father, M. B. Wamsley, was an early settler of Butler township; his biography will appear in the history of that township. Mr. Wamsley was born in Ohio, in 1849. Mrs. Wamsley was formerly Miss Ida Hicks, a daughter of John Hicks, of Clarksville. Mr. and Mrs. Wamsley have one daughter—Myrtle.

James W. Williams resides on section 5. He purchased his farm in 1877, of Wm. N. Gaines. Mr. Williams was born in Oneida county, New York, in 1829, and lived many years in Cataraugus county in that State. His father was a native of Wales. Mr. Williams settled in Delaware, Iowa, in 1853, where he lived until coming to Butler county in 1877. His wife was Flora Bush, a native of Chautauqua county, New York. They have three children—Charles H., Anna and Daisy—all born in Delaware county. Mr. Williams' farm contains 240 acres, on which he has made all the improvements.

Jarvis E. Ferguson resides on section 22, which he purchased of J. Perrin in the spring of 1878. A part of his farm was first settled by Z. H. Eddy. Mr. Ferguson was born in Lenawee county, Michigan, in 1837. His father, Joseph F. Ferguson, was a native of Wayne county, New York, and emigrated to Michigan in 1832. Mr. Ferguson first came to Dayton township in 1864, where he resided but two years when he returned to Michigan. In the spring of 1873 he came again to Iowa, and located in Union township, Floyd county, settling in Dayton township in 1878. His farm contains 80 acres. Mrs. Ferguson was formerly Miss Josephine

Mason, daughter of Austin Mason, a native of the State of New York, but an early settler of Michigan.

Charles Ramsy resides on section 15. He bought his farm of Levi Parker in 1880. Mr. Ramsy has been a resident of Butler county since November 3, 1864, and of this township since 1869. He is a native of Pennsylvania, where he was born in 1836. When fourteen years of age he removed to southern Ohio with his parents. He has been a resident of Iowa since 1857. His wife was Margaret J. Gabby, a native of Pennsylvania. They have six children Janette, Agnes, William, John, Charles and Arthur. They lost two children. Mr. Ramsy has 40 acres of land.

CHAPTER XXIV.

FREMONT TOWNSHIP.

The township bearing this name is in the northeastern corner; its east line joining Bremer county; and its north, Floyd county; with Butler township on the south, and Dayton on the west. It comprises township 93, range 15. The soil is rather a sandy loam, and in about one-half of the township is underlaid with a strata of limestone. Those who are familiar with this kind of land know its worth for cereal products. The only timber of natural growth in the township is a five acre tract in the northwestern part. But a large amount has been planted by the enterprising farmers, and is now in thrifty growth. The land is rather rolling, but there is a valley extending from northeast to southeast which is appropriately known as Pleasant Valley. No more beautiful and productive land can be found in the hundred counties that make up the great Hawkeye State. "Beautiful!" "Grand!" is the oft-repeated exclamation of those who look upon the great fields of wheat, corn and oats that extend in every direction. There are no streams, but an occasional spring makes its appearance, and water, as a general thing, can be found in bountiful supply. There is no railroad within its borders, but the facilities for market are excellent. The Burlington, Cedar Rapids & Northern Railroad passes within a half-mile of its southwest corner, with a market point at Clarksville, three miles away. The Illinois Central Railroad runs close to its line on the east, with a station at Plainfield. There is no town or village within its borders.

Withal, Fremont can be considered as among the best farming localities in Iowa.

EARLY SETTLEMENT.

The first steps toward settlement in Fremont were made in 1855, when McCarty Bement came here and located upon a farm, where he resided for many years. He now resides in Plainfield, Bremer county. The same year Shadrach Bonwell, Samuel Lienhart, and James Trobaugh settled in the township.

The following year there were a number of arrivals, among whom were Nelson Bement, a brother of the first settler; James G. Temple, Robert Renfrew, and J. J. Cross. All of this party are yet living in the township, except Lienhart, who now lives in Clarksville, and Nelson Bement, who is somewhere in Minnesota.

William Gilmore and John Saddler, who located on section 6, were also early settlers. No others now remembered came in for several years.

J. J. Cross, who has been mentioned, was one of the very first settlers in the township. He is a son of Asa and Abigail (Cleveland) Cross, and was born in Cataraugus county, New York, July 1, 1829, where he learned the carpenter's trade. In 1853 he emigrated to Wisconsin, living at Madison one year, when he removed to Kane county, Illinois. In 1855 he came to Butler county, and in August of the same year entered his present farm. He then returned to Illinois, and in 1856, with his wife, located in Bremer county, living there one year before settling on the farm. Mr. Cross was married in 1855 to Miss Permelia Ballard. They have had five children, four of whom are living— Frederick W., Carrie L., Cora A., and George.

On the 27th day of September, 1855, S. Bonwell and family arrived in Fremont township, and soon afterward settled in their present home, on the northwest quarter of section 19. Mr. Bonwell relates numerous incidents of the hardships and pleasures of pioneer life; but one will suffice at this place. On the 6th day of January, 1856, he, with his family, attended the funeral of Eliza J. Newhard, at Clarksville. The weather was cold, and the ground frozen so hard that the grave could hardly be dug; it was therefore almost dark before the services were over, and Mr. Bonwell prepared to start homeward. When he arrived at Mr. Leinhart's, a storm was raging furiously, and the folks tried to persuade him to remain all night; but Mr. Bonwell thought it his duty to return and attend to his stock. It was only a half a mile to his home, but there being no road, he missed his house, and soon found that he was lost on the prairie. To remain all night would be death. He, therefore, turned his team about so as to drift with the wind, which was blowing from the northwest, and concluded that in this way he would reach the timber east of Clarksville, which he succeeded in doing just as the storm passed over. After driving a short distance further he found himself at the cabin of Daniel Kinsley, where he remained all night with his family, and in the morning again set out for home. After leaving Mr. Leinhart's, the previous evening, and finding that he had lost his course, he called for aid, which was heard by the neighbors, and they replied by firing guns, etc.; but the wind was blowing such a gale that their answers could not be heard. The next morning the neighbors assembled, and not finding him at home, started in search, following his track over the entire circuit, and were glad to find, upon arriving at Mr. Kinsley's, that all were still alive, as they thought they certainly had perished, or, as one old fellow of the party remarked: "They have, evidently, struck one of the sink-holes on the prairie and all went to h— together." Mr. Bonwell, was born in Brown county, Ohio, October 19, 1825, but removed with his parents to Highland county, where, in 1848, he married Miss Amanda Welch, of Adams county, but a native of Indiana. In the fall of 1852 he emigrated to Illinois, where he resided eighteen months, then moving to Iowa. When the civil war broke out Mr. Bonwell was anxious to go and defend the stars and stripes, but his wife would not consent. In the fall of 1864, however, he was enrolled in Company B Eighth Iowa, and served until the close of the conflict. He has not accumulated a very large fortune, but is in good circumstances, owning 170 acres of well-improved land, clear of debt. In politics he was first a whig, but opposed to slavery. In 1860 he joined the republican ranks, remaining with that party until about 1876, when he joined the greenbackers. The children are—William H., Charles E. Olive J., now Mrs. Charles Owen, and Albert N.

A. W. Lee resides on section 25, where he located in 1861. He was born in Vermont on the 4th of December, 1836. In In 1859 he emigrated to Rock county, Wisconsin, remaining there until he removed to Iowa. In the spring of 1859 he married Miss C. Works, daughter of James Works, a native of Vermont. Mr. and Mrs. Lee own 740 acres of land, and their improvements are among the best in the county. The children are James A., Frank C., Eddie D., and Mattie I.

John Robinson is a native of England, born in Cumberland county in 1817. His parents were Thomas and Elizabeth (Bowman) Robinson. In 1830 the family emigrated to Canada, and in 1834 came to the United States, settling in the Empire State, where Mr. Robinson followed his trade, carpet-weaving, and in 1844 married Miss Emma Ann Darrall. In 1856 he emigrated to Illinois, living two years in Lake county. He then came to Iowa, first settling in Bremer county. In 1861 he came to Butler and settled at his present home. The children are John H., William W., Emma Jane, deceased, and George F. William W. is a Methodist Episcopal minister, but is at present teaching. Mr. Robinson is one of the leading farmers of his township, having a well-improved farm containing 160 acres, valued at $25 per acre. In politics he was an old-time whig, but is at present a republican. He received his education in the common schools of England, Canada, and New York State.

William Cronin, one of the leading dairymen of this county, is living on section 33, Fremont township, where he owns a farm containing 210 acres, and is engaged in the manufacture of creamery butter. Mr. Cronin is a native of Ireland, and was born in 1840, his parents being John and Mary Cronin. In 1847 the father died, and in 1848 the mother, with her ten children, emigrated to Canada, and in 1849 came to the United States, settling at Milwaukee, Wisconsin. William tilled the soil in Wisconsin until 1862, and then emigrated to Iowa, living eighteen months at Cedar Falls. Since that time he has been a resident of Butler county. He was married in 1863, in Fon du Lac, Wisconsin, to Miss Mary Twohig. They have had fourteen children, twelve of whom are now living—Lizzie, John, Bridget, James, Ellen and Hannah (twins), Agnes, May, Katie, Alice, Willie, and Lydia. In politics he is a democrat, and in religion a Roman Catholic.

Samuel Barker is one of the prominent farmers. He resides on section 15, settling there in 1864, and now owns 320 acres of land. Mr. Barker was born in Maine, December 25, 1822. His parents were both natives of England. In 1849, at Shellburne, New Hampshire, he married Miss Betsy Elliott, also a native of Maine. In 1851 they emigrated to Batavia, Illinois, thence in 1856 to Delaware county, Iowa, and from there to Butler county. The children living are Adelia, Emma, S. W., and Ettie. In politics he is a republican, and in religion a Baptist.

William A. Ladd was born in Schenectady county, New York, June 26, 1834. In 1846 he emigrated, with his parents, to McHenry county, Illinois, where he learned the carpenter's trade, and, December 7, 1856, married Miss Eleanor Fox. They are the parents of one child—Ada L. In 1864 they came to Iowa, and, after living a short time in Bremer county, came to Butler and settled in their present home, on section 12, Fremont township.

W. C. Smith was born October 4, 1831, in Harrison county, Ohio. His parents, Jacob and Catherine (Randolph) Smith, were of German descent, but their forefathers were among the early settlers of the United States, and participated in the wars of the Revolution and the second war with England, or the War of 1812. In 1846 the family emigrated to Grant county, Wisconsin, where, in 1853, W. C. Smith married Miss Mary A. Munson. In 1865 he came to Butler county and settled on section 24, Fremont township. Of the ten children born unto Mr. and Mrs. Smith, eight are now living—Walter, Dora, Harland, Eva, Ella, Edward, Parker and Mirt.

John N. Wamsley was born on the 21st day of September, 1830. He came to Iowa, as already stated, with his brother, W. S. Wamsley, and lived with Aaron Moore until 1853; then emigrated to Nebraska; nine years subsequently, to Missouri, and three years afterwards returned to Butler county. Mr. Wamsley was married in 1853 to Miss Wilhelmina Richards, and they now have six children—Frank L., Etta, now Mrs. Albert Thomas; Curzette, Effa, now Mrs. Robert Walch; Lillie, and Rosa May. Mr. Wamsley enlisted in Company I, Sixth Nebraska, and served fourteen months.

Frank L. Wamsley, son of the above, was born in Nebraska, in September, 1858. He always resided with his parents, and October 24, 1882, married Miss Isabella Harvey, daughter of Jonathan Harvey.

Charles N. Thomas is found among the pioneers of 1854, as in that year, with his parents, Hugh and Hannah (Williams) Thomas, he came to Butler county and settled in Dayton township, Hugh Thomas was born in the state of Pennsylvania in 1809; removed with his parents to Ohio, where he married Miss Hannah

Arthur W. Lee

Mrs. A. W. Lee.

Williams. In 1848 he removed to Indiana, from whence he came to Iowa, and settled on section 24, Dayton township, where he still resides. His wife died in 1866. Charles N. is the third of the fourteen children. He was born in the State of Ohio, on the 9th day of September, 1835. Since coming to Iowa he has spent most of his time working at his trade—carpenter. In 1860 he married Miss Susan Lenhart, daughter of E. Lenhart. In 1862 he enlisted in Company G of the 32d Iowa, and served with the same until the regiment was mustered out of service. In 1869 he settled in his present home, on section 29, Fremont township. The children are—Amanda J., now Mrs. A. F. Buchholtz, who was married September 9, 1880, now residing in Calhoun county, Iowa; Asenath, Samuel L., John E., Albert D. and Hugh N.

Alexander Forney, son of C. H. and Rebecca Forney, was born in Wabash county, Indiana, on the 3d day of December, 1847, and came with the family to Butler county. In 1863 he enlisted in Company L, of the Seventh Iowa Cavalry, and served until the regiment was mustered out of service. In September, 1867, he married Miss Ellen Blake, daughter of James Blake. They have two children—Emma and Florence. Mr. Forney now resides on section 16, Fremont township, where he owns a fine farm of 160 acres.

Edward Bennett is a native of England, born July 6, 1831. In 1849 he emigrated to the United States, living one year in Dubuque, Iowa. He then went to Wisconsin, and resided in Marquette county until 1867, when he returned to Iowa, living in Bremer county until 1876, when he came to Butler county, and settled on section 28, Fremont township, where he owns 160 acres of land. In February, 1864, Mr. Bennett enlisted in Company C, of the Twenty-third Wisconsin Volunteer Infantry, and served until the close of the war. Mr. Bennett has been twice married—in 1856 to Miss Elizabeth Ellison, also a native of England. She died in 1857, leaving one child—Elizabeth, now the wife of Albert Shadbolt. In November, 1867, he married Miss Janette Hume, a native of Scotland. They have ten children—James, Sarah A., Edward, Martha V., Maggie, William C., Robert Hume, Cora, Ruth, and Eva.

Wallace E. Balsley was born in Onondaga county, New York, October 26, 1833. In 1853 he moved to Fon du Lac county, Wisconsin, where he resided twelve years, then came to Iowa, living in Chickasaw county until 1871, since which time he has been a resident of Butler county. In 1853 he married Miss Anna Vermilyea. They have seven children—Francis, Alice, Hannah, Cynthia, Melvin, Charles, and Carleton. Mr. Balsley owns 156 acres of land; is a republican in politics, and a member of the Masonic fraternity.

The township is settled in part by Germans, and is the largest foreign settlement in the county. They are very thrifty and go-ahead farmers, and nearly all are in good circumstances. They are just the kind to develop a country. These Germans have a Lutheran church in the township, and besides the English they have a German school to educate their children in their own language.

It was not until after the close of the civil war that this township took such rapid strides in advance. In 1867 its fertile prairies began to catch the eye of those looking for permanent homes. From that time to the present its increase and development have been very rapid. About all the land is now in the possession of residents, who are rapidly placing it under cultivation. Every foot of land is tillable, and the population is now far in advance of the average of country towns. Fremont now has more land under cultivation than any town in the county. The principal productions are wheat, corn and oats.

FIRST THINGS.

The first birth in the township was a son, Harvey Dilman, to Mr. and Mrs. S. Bonwell, born the 6th day of December, 1855, and died in February, 1869.

The first marriage ceremony performed in Fremont occurred December 25, 1859, the contracting parties being Joseph Brownell and Lucy Ballard. They are now living in Manchester, Iowa. The hymeneal knot was tied by Elder David Terry.

The same reverend also preached the first sermon in Fremont. He was a follower of the Baptist faith.

The first death was that of the mother of Robert Renfrew.

THE TOWNSHIP NAME.

There are several different theories as to how and by whom the town of Fremont was named. But the most plausible of all, is that given by a local writer to the Clarksville *Star*, in 1875. The item reads: "'Fremont, free speech and free press,' was what one would hear in the days of 1856, when Horace Greeley, Charles Sumner, and others were rolling the great stone that was to eventually crush out African slavery in the American States. So it was given to this territory of thirty-six square miles." The name was suggested by William R. Phillips in honor of General J. C. Fremont, who was at that time a candidate for the presidency. The name was at once approved by S. Bonwell and the other inhabitants.

ORGANIC.

On February 6, 1855, Judge Palmer divided the county into sub-divisions, and Fremont was merged into Butler township, which at that time embraced 126 square miles. During Judge Converse's administration, Fremont was created and ordered organized. The first election was held on the 11th of October, 1859, at the house of William R. Phillips, which was then in process of erection. When the day came, the voters met, but Phillips had nothing done to his house except the cellar, which he had just finished. The ballot box was accordingly let down in the hole, the voters dropped in their little slips, and the election was held here "with no roof o'er head save the blue canopy of Heaven." However, the day was a pleasant one, and everything passed off nicely. The records have been misplaced, and the officers who were elected have been forgotten, except that J. J. Cross was chosen township clerk. There were sixteen ballots cast, and fortunately we are able to give the voters' names, as follows: James G. Temple, John Boorom, James Trobaugh, William Pringle, M. Bennett, Robert Slaight, John H. Vosler, D. W. Tunsley, S. Bonwell, S. Lenhart, Henry Lenhart, John Lenhart, G.

W. Ellis, Nelson Bement, S. J. Boorom and J. J. Cross.

The people of Fremont township have been fortunate in enlisting the service of honest as well as capable and efficient officers to administer or oversee public affairs. Nothing unusual has transpired to disturb the tranquillity of such matters; there has been no waste of public money nor unnecessary extravagance.

The officers of the township, in the year 1879, were as follows: Township trustees, J. J. Cross, David McSparron and Thomas Edison; town clerk, C. E. Allen; assessor, Charles Fitch; Justices of the peace, W. B. Gillmore and D. Bucholz.

The officers in 1880, were as follows: Township trustees, W. N. Quinn, F. Stuelke and J. J. Cross; town clerk, Myron Temple; assessor, L. Temple.

In 1881, the following were serving: Trustees, F. Stuelke, J. J. Cross and W. N. Quinn; town clerk, C. A. Fulks; assessor, L. B. Temple.

The officers in 1882, were as follows: Trustees; J. J. Cross, W. N. Quinn and Thomas Filkins; clerk, C. A. Fulks; assessor, L. B. Temple.

In the fall of 1882, the following officers were elected to serve in 1883: W. N. Quinn, Jacob Klenskey and W. Bucholz, township trustees; George Sumner, clerk; William Cronin, assessor. They are the present incumbents.

EDUCATIONAL.

The first school in Fremont township was taught by Miss Lucy Ballard, at the residence of James G. Temple. Miss Ballard afterward became Mrs. Joseph Brownell, their marriage being the first in the township.

The first school house was built on the northeast quarter of the northeast quarter of section 11.

There are now the full complement of school districts in the township, which is nine, and educational facilities are second to none of the townships in the county. The school finances are in good condition, and educational matters have been managed with a view to making schools efficient. There is one German school in the town, for the purpose of teaching the children that language.

The township was first organized as a district township, and was continued as such until 1873, when, by a vote of the people, they were all made independent districts, and organized as such during the following spring.

CHAPTER XXV.

JACKSON TOWNSHIP.

This sub-division of Butler county comprises the territory of township 92, range 16, containing a full congressional township of 23,040 acres. It is surrounded by the townships of Dayton, Butler, Jefferson and West Point, respectively on the north, east, south and west. The surface is generally level or gently undulating. The soil is a dark loam with clay subsoil, except the river bottom, which has a sandy subsoil. It is strictly an agricultural township, having no town, postoffice or store within its limits. The population consists of an enterprising industrious class, mostly Americans, engaged chiefly in agriculture, but handle and fatten stock to a considerable extent. The township is mostly prairie and has but one stream of water, the Shell Rock river, which passes through the northeast corner, entering at section 2 and pursuing a meandering course toward the southwest, makes its exit on section 24. Along the banks of this river is found the only timber in the township, consisting of walnut, oak, hickory, ash and other varieties. There are two railroads—the Dubuque & Dakota and the Burlington, Cedar Rapids & Northern—the former passing through the northeast corner, the latter traversing the entire township from east to west. A small portion of the lands are unoccupied by actual settlers, being held by speculators. Although there are no small streams the land is well drained by natural depressions and there is very little waste land. In consideration of the character of the soil and these advantages, this township has possibilities second to none in the county. The trading points are Clarksville, on the east, and Allison, on the southwest, where ready markets are found.

EARLY SETTLEMENT.

The first settler to occupy land in this township was J. B. Hicks, a native of Wisconsin, who made a claim on section 12 during the spring of 1850. Here he remained until 1867 when he went to Kansas, where he remained a few years and again returned to the old place. He did not seem satisfied and started for Mexico, but delayed on the way, on the Solomon river, in Kansas, where he still remains. Meanwhile, his father and brother, Joe, arrived, and took up their abode on the same place, where the old gentleman died and was buried. His remains have since been removed to Linwood cemetery. When he first came he opened a blacksmith shop, and forged the first iron in

HISTORY OF BUTLER COUNTY.

the Shell Rock valley. John still lives in the township.

The next settlers were two brothers, M. B. and W. S. Wamsley, from Ohio. They came in April, 1851, and settled on claims previously made on section 1. They had little property, other than the teams which brought them here. M. B. had his family with him. His brother, W. S., secured land on section 12, and then returned to his native state for a wife. He was there married and the return trip constituted the wedding tour. With his family he still remains upon the place and has a well improved, valuable farm. M. B. Wamsley was president of the Butler County Bank for ten years, and now resides in Clarksville.

In 1852 Seth Hilton and John Baughman, from Illinois, came and selected homes on section 13, near what is now the town of Clarksville, where they remained until 1882, when they sold out and removed to Kansas. Hilton, when he arrived, built a log house upon the present site of Clarksville. They had but little property but accumulated a competence and left in good circumstances.

The next year John Stevenson, John Boyd and E. D. Marquand arrived from Ohio. Stevenson settled on section 36 and remained until his death. John Boyd, his son-in-law, now lives upon the place. Marquand selected a home on section 25, which place he has since occupied. He has a good farm well stocked.

Section 21 received a settler in 1857, by the name of John Klinetob, who came from Illinois. He died there in 1869. Eli Bebee came the same year with his family, making the journey from Ohio with a yoke of cattle, and settled on section 2. He is now in Clarksville. The place is now owned by James Martin. About this time came John H. VanDyke. Henry Newman came also from Ohio and established himself on section 13, near the line, the boundary between sections 24 and 13 being marked by the driveway through his barn. He sold out to S. McCreary in 1871, and removed to Linn county, Oregon.

M. V. Wamsley was an early settler, having made a claim on section 12 in 1851. He enlisted in the army, was wounded at the battle of Pea Ridge, Arkansas, taken to Texas as a prisoner, where he died.

Elisha Doty secured land in this township in 1855, and moved here during the winter of 1861; remained until 1864, when he removed to Tama county. The land is yet owned by the family. Geo. Allen, A. E. Ensley and Richard Keller came about this time from Indiana, and selected homes on section 12. Allen built the first dam across the Shell Rock river in the county, on the section where he settled, and had the first mill. He now lives near Davenport.

Then came Geo. Harkness and John Bonwell and located on section 1, where Bonwell died, in 1875 or 1876. In 1863 Harkness removed to the Pacific coast.

Cyrus Doty came in the fall of 1860. From this time until 1864, settlement was very slow; then, and for a number of years, the township filled up rapidly. Among those who came in were, J. W. Butts and family, A. Sampson and family, R. Sampson and family, Dan Waite and family and A. N. Leet, all from Wisconsin.

ORGANIC.

This township was organized in March, 1858. The following is the record containing a list of township officers for years named:

1858—John Klinetob, John H. VanDyke and John Stevenson, trustees; John Boyd, clerk; Josiah Stevenson and Henry Newman, constables; Samuel Lister, supervisor of roads; John Klinetob, assessor; E. D. Marquand and John Klinetob, justices of the peace.

1859—John Boyd, John Klinetob and John H. VanDyke, trustees; E. D. Marquand, assessor; John Stevenson, clerk; E. D. Marquand, justice of the peace; Josiah Stevenson, constable.

1860—Henry Newman, John Boyd and John H. VanDyke were elected trustees October 11, 1859, but Henry Newman was the only one who qualified, as John Boyd and John H. VanDyke refused. Henry Newman resigned the office the following February, and on the 7th of that month the township clerk appointed Richard Heed, John Klinetob and Joseph Hilton, who served for the ensuing year. Martin V. Wamsley was elected clerk.

1861—Joseph Hilton, John Klinetob and John Boyd, trustees; E. D. Marquand, clerk; John Klinetob, assessor; E. D. Marquand, justice of the peace.

1862—Elisha Doty, John Boyd and Joseph Hilton, trustees; E. D. Marquand, clerk.

1863—Jeremiah Kocher, Elisha Doty and William S. Wamsley, trustees; Cyrus Doty, clerk; John Klinetob, assessor.

1864—Jeremiah Clark, Elisha Doty, trustees; Cyrus Doty, clerk.

1865—G. P. Klinetob, Aaron Doty, Milton Marquand, trustees; Cyrus Doty, clerk.

1866—Aaron Doty, Henry F. Leitz, J. W. Butts, trustees; Cyrus Doty, clerk; John Klinetob, assessor.

1867—Daniel Pope, Jeremiah Kocher, A. Sampson, trustees; G. P. Babcock, clerk; John Klinetob, assessor.

1868—Wm. Neal, Jacob A. Murckley, Jeremiah Clark, J. P. Upp, trustees.

1869—William Neal, Jacob A. Murckley, Samuel McCrery, trustees; J. P. Upp, clerk.

1870—William S. Wamsley, William Neal, Samuel McCrery, trustees; Cyrus Doty, clerk.

1871—William S. Wamsley, F. Thornton, trustees; C. B. Nelson, clerk.

1872—F. M. Russell, A. Sampson, J. H. Hickle, trustees; Cyrus Doty, clerk.

1873—F. M. Russell, A. Sampson, trustees; C. B. Nelson, clerk.

1874—We have no record.

1875—John Boyd, C. B. Wilson, B. Priest, trustees; S. Moyer, clerk; F. M. Russell, assessor.

1876—B. Priest, John Boyd, Aaron Doty, trustees; Cyrus Doty, clerk.

1877—W. W. Hemenway, T. D. Darby, T. T. Miller, trustees; Wilson Bennett, clerk.

1878—E. D. Marquand, F. M. Russell, S. W. Chever, trustees; Wilson Bennett, clerk.

1879—J. Scofield, S. W. Chever, J. H. Hickle, trustees; F. M. Russell, clerk.

1880—The same as 1879.

1881—J. Scofield, F. Patterson, S. W. Chever, trustees; F. M. Russell, clerk.

1882—F. Patterson, T. D. Darby, S. W. Chever, trustees; F. M. Russell, clerk.

EDUCATIONAL.

The first school house in this township was located on section 1, and was built of logs. U. G. Lawrence was the first teacher. The building after a number of years was torn down, and the material used in its construction made into firewood. The first frame school house was built on section 14, in 1855, and George McClellan was the first teacher. It has now been replaced with a larger structure costing $800; and at this time, 1883, Miss Mary Lusted is the instructor. The second frame house for school purposes was erected the same year, on section 25, but was afterwards sold to Mr. Douglas, and used for a dwelling, and a more commodious building erected in its stead. There are now ten school districts in the township, all having good substantial frame houses, well furnished and in good condition. They have in general a competent class of teachers, and the educational advantages and facilities are second to none in the county.

RELIGIOUS.

The first religious service was held in the cabin of Malon Wamsley in the fall of 1851, by Rev. S. W. Ingham, a minister of the Methodist Episcopal Church. But few services were held. In 1852, a Baptist clergyman held service in Seth Hilton's cabin. No organization, however, was effected of any denomination. The churches are well represented in the town of Clarksville, with which many of the people of the township are connected.

GENERAL ITEMS.

The first marriage was that of John Rains and Miss Elizabeth Allen.

The first birth was a son to Mr. and Mrs. Malon Wamsley, born July 30, 1852.

The first death was that of Joseph Kirker, who died and was buried on section 12 without service of any character.

Linwood Cemetry is located in this township on section 13. The first interment therein was a son of Dr. Tichnor, of Clarksville. The grounds are under the supervision of the authorities of the town of Clarksville.

BIOGRAPHICAL.

Herewith a few sketches of the representative men of Jackson township are appended:

Captain Chas. B. Nelson stands conspicuous as one of the defenders of the Union during the bloody days of the rebellion. His father, Charles C., was a native of Vermont; his mother, Laura (Ellsworth) Nelson of the State of New York, and it was in Wayne county of that Old Empire State that on the 11th day of October, 1825, Charles B. Nelson was born. In 1840 the family emigrated to Winnebago county, Illinois, and there continued farming. In 1847, at Beloit, Wisconsin, Captain Nelson married Miss Maria Mathers, daughter of Daniel and Roxana Mathers. In 1861, he responded to the call of his country by enlisting as a private in Company A of the Fifteenth Wisconsin Volunteer Infantry, and was mustered into service September 27. In June 17, 1863, C. B. Nelson was promoted to First Lieutenant, and served in that capacity until January 14, 1864, when the regiment was mustered out of service. But Lieutenant Nelson was not the man to remain at home and see his country in need of help. He therefore within ten days after reaching home had a company of one hundred men enrolled, and on the 2d day of February they were mustered into service as Company H of the Forty-seventh Wisconsin, with Captain Chas. B. Nelson as their leader. This company served until the close of the conflict, being discharged September 13, 1865. Thus it can be seen that Captain Nelson served nearly four years, during which time he was in many hard fought battles, besides numerous skirmishes. At Dallas' Woods, May 28, 1864, he was severely wounded, by being struck in the right shoulder by a piece of shell, thus totally disabling his right arm for three years. He never has regained its full use. After the conflict was ended, Captain Nelson came to Clarksville, as his family had removed to that place, in 1863, and he soon settled on section 3, Jackson township, where he still resides, and will undoubtedly spend the remainder of his life, as he here owns 400 acres of fine land, well improved, and his home is surrounded with all the necessaries of the best social life. Mr. and Mrs. Nelson have had six children. Their oldest daughter died in 1865, and their oldest son was killed by the fall of a limb at Ft. Sill, Indian Territory, in 1877. The four children living are— Lillian, now Mrs. Willis O. Robinson, of Bloomington, Nebraska; Charles, Carrie, now Mrs. Charles Leet, of Santa Barbara, California, and Wesley. The mother of Captain Nelson now resides with him. She has spent the last ten years traveling in various parts of the United States, and although she has now reached her eighty-sixth year, she is in apparent good health, and still enjoys traveling by railroad.

Benjamin Priest was born in Pittsford, Vermont, November 22, 1819. Soon after his birth his parents moved to Mount Holly, Vermont, where Benjamin lived with his parents till twenty-one years of age. He then went to New Hampshire, and worked on a farm for four years, then returned to Mount Holly, where he engaged in the manufacture of butter trays, which business he followed until 1865, when he left Vermont to find a home in the west. He came to Iowa, and purchased 587 acres of land in the township of Jackson, Butler county. On this land he built a large, comodious dwelling house, with all the necessary out buildings. For years he made a specialty of dairy farming, keeping between forty and fifty cows. By careful farming he brought his farm up to a high state of cultivation, second to none in his vicinity. By close application to business he accumulated a handsome property. He was a man held in high esteem by all who ever knew him, either in Vermont or his new-made home in Iowa. He was a member of the Masonic fraternity, and politically was a most decided republican. For some time previous to his death he was in failing health, and on December 11, 1882, he died at his home, surrounded by his family and friends. In March, 1850, Mr. Priest married Elvira Shepard, of Mount Holly, Vermont. She was the daughter of William and Fanny Shepard. Her father was of English, and her mother of Danish extraction. Her father was born in New Hampshire, July 29, 1780, and her mother in New Hampshire, March 4, 1795. They came to Vermont, where they resided till the time of their death. The father died in Wallingford, Vermont, February 18, 1856, and the mother in Rutland, Vermont, October 23, 1843. They reared a family of six children, as follows: William A., born October 29, 1819; Elvira, wife of the subject of this sketch, born April 13, 1822; Dexter C., born April 24, 1825, was a soldier of the Union army, and died at New Orleans, of disease, August 2, 1865; William F., born March 15, 1827; Viana J., born December 1, 1831; Sarah M., born June 18, 1834. Mrs. Priest is a woman held in high esteem by all who ever knew her, for her sterling worth as a woman and a Christian.

Samuel McCrery came to Butler county November 5, 1853, and first stopped at Clarksville. In the following spring he purchased fifty acres on section 7, Butler township, and twenty acres of timber on the Shell Rock, and commenced tilling the soil, residing on said land until 1869. He then sold out, removed into Jackson township, and now resides on section 13, and owns ninety-two acres. Mr. McCrery is a native of Kentucky, born in Jefferson county, on the 26th day of February, 1807. His parents were James and Margaret (Lynn) McCrery. In 1813 the family removed to Washington county, Indiana, and subsequently into Clinton county. Here the father died, having reached the advanced age of seventy-five years. The subject of this sketch is the oldest of eight children. He resided with his parents, and on the 15th day of November, 1836, married Miss Mary B. Shaffer, and continued farming in the Hoosier State until 1853. He then concluded to try the western frontier. Accordingly, he loaded his worldly goods and family, (wife and six children), into two wagons, and started westward on the 4th day of October, arriving as above stated. Mrs. McCrery died on the 16th day of April, 1881. She had twelve children, ten of whom are now living—John, Margaret, Catherine, Jane, Emma, Sarah, Ruth, William L., Martha, and Mary B. Mr. McCrery is a democrat in politics, and a Presbyterian in religion.

William L. McCrery was born in Butler township, March 31, 1857. He has always resided in the county, and September 5, 1882, married Miss S. Nettie Doty, daughter of Aaron Doty. Mr. McCrery is a democrat in politics.

S. W. Cheever resides on the south-west quarter of section eight, Jackson township, where he owns a fine farm of 160 acres. He first came to the county in 1870, but remained only a short time. In 1871 he again came to the county, purchased his present farm and hired 74 acres broke. In the fall of 1872 he brought his family to the county and has since resided on his farm and tilled the same. Mr. Cheever was born in West Moreland, Oneida county, New York, February 11th, 1825. He was reared on a farm, learned the carpenter's trade and followed the same in his native State until 1867, then engaged in farming. In 1852 he married Miss Cornelia E. Foote. She died leaving three children—Francis M, Edward H. and George H. He subsequently married Miss Helen M. Tufts and by this union have four children—John T., James F., Fred, and Roscoe Conkling.

Aaron Doty, son of Elisha and Hannah (Reed) Doty was born in Ogle county, Illinois, January 8, 1836, and resided in that county until 1860. He then married Miss Hannah A. Talbott and soon came to Butler county and he now owns 350 acres in this county and 160 acres in Dakota. The children are—S. Nettie, Martha Etta, and James T. Mr. Doty is a democrat in politics and has held local office.

M. J. Freeman was born in Madison county, New York, April 27th, 1839. His parents were also natives of the Empire State. The father, Benjamin F. Freeman, died about the year 1847. About 1850 the mother, Elizabeth (Holdridge) Freeman, with her three children—A. R., M. J., and D. R., emigrated to Waukesha county Wisconsin. Four years later they went back to Chatauqua county, New York, and remained until 1857, then returned to Wisconsin and settled in Dane county. In 1861, M. J. Freeman enlisted in Company D of the Seventh Wisconsin and served until September 1864. In 1865 he married Miss Lucy Ryan, a native of New York, and in 1866 came to Iowa, lived in Grundy county until 1874, then came to Butler and has since been a resident of Jackson township. Mr. and Mrs. Freeman have had seven children, five of whom are now living—Elton, Elsie, Elmer, Ellis and Elwin.

Clark Carr was born in Bennington county, Vermont, in 1844. While he was yet an infant the family emigrated to Illinois, where he was raised on a farm, and in 1862 enlisted in Company H, of the 127th Illinois, and served three years. He was taken prisoner at Young's Point, near Vicksburg, December, 1862, and confined in Monroe Prison, Louisiana, for two months. Mr. Carr was in many hard fought battles, among which were Chickamauga Creek, Lookout Mountain, Mission Ridge, Kenesaw Mountain, Arkansas Post, Siege of Vicksburg and Siege of Atlanta. In 1866 he came with his parents to Iowa and has since resided in Jackson township. In 1868 he married Mrs. Frances J. Wamsley nee Griffith, daughter of James Griffith and widow of Martin Van Buren Wamsley, and they now have two children, William A. and James L.

Martin Van Buren Wamsley, better known as "Van" Wamsley, was born in Adams county, Ohio, February 9, 1837. He first came to Butler county with William A. Wamsley, but did not remain but a short time. A few years afterward, however, he again came to the county and on September 4th, 1857, married Miss Frances J. Griffith, daughter of James and Elizabeth Griffith. In 1861 he enlisted in company G, 32d Iowa. He was wounded at Pleasant Hill, taken prisoner and died at Tyler prison, Texas, leaving a wife —now Mrs. Clark Carr—and four children, Richard P., S. B., Mary E. and Van Walter.

Charles H. Caswell was born in Boone county, Illinois, November 1842; received a common school education, tilled the soil and in 1868, at Belmont, Wisconsin, married Mrs. Margaret Soin nee Dolan. In the fall of 1871 he came to Iowa, lived in Bremer county until March, 1882, then came to Butler county and has since had charge of the C. T. Allen farm, which is located on sec. 11 of Jackson township. Mr. and Mrs. Caswell have three children, Charles M., Josephine M. and Anna E.

E. E. Mott was born in Wayne county, New York, July 6, 1826. His early life was spent on the farm, but he subsequently learned the carpenter's trade and followed the same in his native State for some years. He emigrated to Illinois and settled in Lake county, where he served as master mechanic for a company of contractors and builders. He then came to Iowa and May 16, 1860, settled at Rockford, Floyd county. Mr. Mott is a sort of a genius and while living in said county worked at various trades,—blacksmith, shoemaker, carpenter, etc., also did some farming. Subsequently he came to Butler county and settled in Coldwater township. He came to Jackson township in 1879 and settled on section 1, where he now resides. Mr. Mott has been married three times. His first wife, Miss Sarah West, died in the State of New York. He married Mrs. Mary Jane Stone *nee* Burnham. She died, leaving two children—Frank and James. His present wife was Miss Cady, They have seven children—Jack, Harry, Ida, Minnie, Jessie, Fred and Kate.

J. Scofield, superintendent of the County Poor Farm, was born in Pennsylvania, in 1843. In 1845 the family migrated to Jo-Daviess county, Illinois, where the father died in 1846, leaving two children—Elizabeth, now Mrs. J. C. Jones, and Josiah, who is the subject of this sketch. He, when five years of age, went to live with one J. W. Marshall, and remained serving him as an errand boy about the store until sixteen years of age. He then worked two years on the C., B. & Q. R. R., after which, in 1861, he enlisted in Company F, of the Twelfth Illinois Volunteer Infantry, and served nearly four years. He then returned to Illinois and engaged in farming. In 1866 he married Miss Mandania Minor, and in 1869 came to Iowa, and has since been a resident of Butler county, and since January 1, 1877, has had charge of the County Poor Farm. Mr. Scofield is a republican in politics, and a member of the Masonic fraternity. The children are —Mary, Charles, Nellie.

C. P. Klinetob is a native of Pennsylvania, born in Luzerne county on the 28th day of April, 1828. His parents were Philip and Elizabeth (Moore) Klinetob. He was bred to farm life, and on the 22d day of June, 1857, married Miss Nancy Hummer, a native of the State of New Jersey. In March, 1860, they emigrated to Illinois; resided in Lee county until 1866; then came to Iowa, and have since been residents of Butler county. He settled on his present farm in 1870. Mr. and Mrs. Klinetob have four children—C. W., John H., Ida J., and Lydia F.

William Patterson was born in Hemensford, Canada, in 1812. His early life was spent on a farm, but he subsequently learned the cooper's trade, and in 1831 married Miss Maria DeLong, a native of the State of New York, born in 1812. They continued to reside in Canada until 1845; then emigrated to the United States; first lived in Kane, and afterward settled in DeKalb county, Illinois. In 1860 Mr. Patterson brought his family to Butler county, and resided in Jackson township until his death, which took place October 22, 1879. Mrs. Patterson still lives on the homestead. She has seven children living —Clarissa, now Mrs. John Hodgson; William H., Charity, now Mrs. Duncan McCray; Frank, Sarah, now Mrs. A. Seitz; Alonzo B., and Abigail E., now Mrs. Albert Neal.

Daniel Wait was born in Orleans county, New York, on the 8th day of April 1833.

His father, Eli Wait, was also a native of the Empire State, but his mother, Abigail (Sprague) Wait, was born in Vermont. Daniel Wait was reared on a farm and in 1856 united in marriage with Betsy Nichols, daughter of Benjamin and Nancy Nichols and continued his residence in his native State until 1861, then came to Iowa and resided in Butler county three years. He then went back to New York, but in 1871 again returned to Butler, and has since been a resident of Jackson township. Mr. and Mrs. Wait have five children— Harriet, Carrie, Fred, Jessie and Edward. Mr. Wait is a republican and a member of the Masonic fraternity.

William Tennyson is a native of England, born in Yorkshire, December 3, 1829, and resided in his native country until twenty years of age. He then emigrated to the United States, and for six years traveled in various parts of the Republic. In 1855 he located at Mt. Vernon, Iowa, and was, therefore, one of the pioneers of Linn county. In 1865 he came to Butler county and settled on section 11, Jackson township, where he still resides. His land is good and his improvements are among the best in the county. He is a democrat in politics, and a Royal Arch member of the Masonic fraternity. At Centerville, St. Joseph county, Michigan, he married Miss Mary Shields. She died in 1877, leaving six children—Florence, Allen G., Robert S., Cora E., Jesse W., and Dan D.

Stephen Barkelew was born in the State of New Jersey, February 17, 1830, and resided in his native state until 1857. He then emigrated with his parents, Stephen and Mary (Dunham) Barkelew, to Coshocton county, Ohio, where he helped till the soil, and in 1860 married Miss Mary E. Coulter. In 1864 he came to Butler county, and has since been a resident of Jackson township. The children are— Charles, Erskine, Edward, James, William, Lillie, and Frank.

E. D. Marquand came to this county in 1855, and in June of said year entered 240 acres of land located on sections 25, Jackson, and 30, Butler townships. He then went back to Ohio and the next year brought his family west and has since resided on the land he first entered. Mr. Marquand organized the township he now lives in and named it Jackson because the township he lived in in Ohio was known by that name, and at the first general election he cast the first and only republican ballot in the township. Mr. Marquand was born in Muskingum county, Ohio, June 28th, 1816. His parents, Charles E. and Nancy Marquand, were natives of France who came to the United States in their youth. He was born on a farm and subsequently was engaged in general merchandise for a period of six years. June 28, 1838, he married Miss Mary E. Barkelew, daughter of Stephen and Mary E. (Dunham) Barkelew. She was born in New Jersey in 1821. They have had twelve children, nine now living—Henriette now Mrs. M. B. Gilbert; Mary E. now Mrs. Jas. W. Winship; Chas. H., Theodore F., Louisa, now Mrs. Geo. R. Copeland; Stephen E., E. D., William and Ellsworth.

Cyrus Doty was born in Ogle county, Illinois, September 3, 1834, and is said to be the first white child born in said county. His parents, Elisha and Hannah (Reed) Doty, first located in the county in

1832, but went back to Peoria on account of the Black Hawk war. In 1834, however, they settled permanently in that county and were, therefore, among the earliest pioneers. In 1841 the mother died, leaving five children, three of whom are now living—Cyrus, Aaron and Louisa. The father subsequently married Miss Catherine Jones and he now resides in Tama county. Cyrus Doty was reared on a farm and resided in his native State until 1860. He then came to Butler county and settled on the southwest quarter of section 11, Jackson township, having purchased the land in 1855, and has since resided on the same and now owns 240 acres. Mr. Doty is a democrat in politics and has held local offices. His religious connections are with the Christian Union Society. In 1856 he married Miss Charlotte Aplington, a native of Brown county, New York, being a daughter of James and Sarah Jane (Anthony) Aplington, and they have reared a family of twelve children, eleven of whom are now living—Samuel N., William N., Mary C., Edith A., Charles B., Nellie M., Rosa A., Simon H., Lillian C., Myrtle and Earl I.

A. B. Patterson is the tenth of the eleven children of William and Maria (DeLong) Patterson. He was born in DeKalb county, Illinois, April 10, 1851. He came with his parents to Butler county, and has since been a resident of the same. In 1873, he married Miss Maggie McDonald, then of Butler county, but a native of Dubuque, and, in 1874, settled on section 23 of Jackson township, where he now resides. In 1877 his dwelling was destroyed by fire. The children are—Lucius, Addie, Rena, and Edna.

John Bonwell settled on section 1, Jackson township, October 31, 1854. He was born in Kentucky, but removed with his parents to Virginia, and there married a Miss Stafford. He then removed to Ohio, where his wife died, leaving seven children, five of whom are now living—James, Arthur, Susan, Margaret, and Elizabeth. He subsequently married Miss Martha Snyder, and removed to Indiana, where she died, leaving three children, one of whom is now living—Charles. He afterward married Miss Elizabeth McKee, and came to Butler county, where he resided until his death, which took place October 2, 1874.

Charles Bonwell was born in Tippecanoe county, Indiana, January 4, 1851. He came to Butler county with the family, and has since resided on the homestead. On May 25, 1881, he married Miss Bertha Shannon, and they now have one daughter—Isa.

John B. Hickman has been a resident of Butler county since 1866. He is a native of England, born in 1838. His parents were Matthew and Frances (Humble) Hickman. In 1854, the family emigrated to the United States, and first located at Kenosha, Wisconsin, but they subsequently resided in Greene county, Wisconsin, Lake county, Illinois, and then again located at Kenosha. In 1866, they came to Iowa and settled in Butler township, where the parents still reside. There are seven children in the family—Mary, Dorotha, John B., Anna, Frances, William and Lucy. John Hickman was married at Kenosha, Wisconsin, in 1865, to Miss Elizabeth Humble, and they now have four children—Frances E., Lucy A., Cora and Roy. Mr. Hickman is a republican in politics,

Baptist in religion, and a member of the I. O. O. F.

Charles M. Ransom is a native of Pennsylvania, born in 1840. In 1850 the family migrated to Carroll county, Illinois, where the subject of this sketch helped till the soil until 1867. He then came to Butler county, and in 1873, settled where he now resides. In 1869, he married Miss Ellen Beetle, daughter of Andrew Beetle, and they now have seven children—Elsie, Andrew, Orval, Susan, Lydia, Mary and Angelina.

John Boyd is a native of Knox county, Ohio, born July 20, 1834. His father, Hugh Boyd, was a native of Pennsylvania, and his mother, Jane (McClain) Boyd, of New Jersey. He was reared on a farm, and resided in his native county until 1857, in which year, on the 7th day of April, he married Miss Maria Stevenson, daughter of John and Sarah Stevenson, and at once, accompanied by his bride and her parents, started westward. On the 24th of May they arrived at Clarksville, and at once settled on section 36, Jackson township, where Mr. Boyd still resides, and now owns 140 acres. Mr. and Mrs. Boyd have four children—James, Albert, Salena, and Florence.

John Stevenson was born in Pennsylvania, on the 23d day of September, 1787. He learned the trade of mill-wright. In 1814, he married Miss Sarah Donovan, a native of Baltimore, born March 19, 1795. In about 1820, he removed with his family to Ohio, and settled in Knox county, where he erected a flouring mill, and run the same until February, 1857, when he traded his mill property for 400 acres of land in Butler county, Iowa. He therefore came west, and resided in Jackson township until his death, which took place July 11, 1876. His wife died April 12, 1879, They reared a family of ten children, but only two survive—Josiah and Maria. Mr. Stevenson was an elder in the Presbyterian church for about sixty years. He was evenly tempered, and one of those straightforward men who are always highly respected.

F. M. Russell resided in his native State until the fall of 1855, then came west as far as Illinois, where he stopped a short time with his brother. Here he made the acquaintance of J. W. Davis, and early in the year of 1856, the two started for Iowa. When they arrived at Dubuque they bid farewell to railroads and continued their journey on foot, and after several days of this mode of travel, they arrived in Butler county. Here Mr. Russell at once resumed his trade—that of a carpenter—and followed the same until the fall, then returned to the Empire State, and in December, 1856, married Miss Sarah A. Caswell. In May, 1857, they came to Iowa and settled at Clarksville. When they commenced life in their new home, their worldly goods amounted to $147.60, but Mr. Russell worked hard at his trade and by being moderately economical, he met with success. He now owns 390 acres of land and is in circumstances which permit him to enjoy life. Mr. Russell is a very ambitious man, and is strictly honest and highly respected. He was born in the State of New York, August 9, 1831. Mr. and Mrs. Russell have one daughter—Mary M., now the wife of J. E. Bickley.

A. C. Wilcox first came to this county in 1860. In said year he also went to the

Rocky Mountains and spent about three months. He then returned to the county, and in August, 1862, enlisted in Company E, Thirty-second Iowa Volunteer Infantry, and served until April, 1864, when he was discharged on account of physical disability. In 1866, he married Miss Martha E. Champlain, and for a few years was engaged dealing in live stock in Black Hawk county. He now resides on section 25, Jackson township, and owns 340 acres of land. Mr. Wilcox was born in Broome county, New York, December 26, 1840. His parents were Austin and Hannah Wilcox. In 1849, the family came to Iowa and settled at Dubuque, where the parents died within a few weeks after coming to their new home. A. C. Wilcox afterwards lived six years with Gregory Berkus, of Jones county. Mr. and Mrs Wilcox have five children—David, Cora, Inzie, and Jay and Jennie, twins.

J. E. Bickley was born in Somerset county, Pennsylvania, January 4, 1857. He is the youngest of the fifteen children of John A. and Anna (Good) Bickley. In 1863 the family emigrated to Iowa and settled at Waterloo, where the mother still resides. The father died in July, 1874. J. E. Bickley was educated at Waterloo, and subsequently taught school. In 1877 he came to Butler county and has since been engaged in farming. He now resides on section 3, Jackson township. Mr. Bickley is an industrious, honest and upright young man, who has good prospects before him. October 25, 1876, he married Miss Medora Russell, daughter of F. M. Russell, and they now have three children—Dora B., Daisy, and Revenell.

A. N. Leet came to Butler county October 26, 1864, and, as he is a man of the strictest honor and integrity, is now one of the most prominent men of the county. He was born in Oneida county, New York, April 24, 1825. His parents, Charles W. and Adaline (Loomis) Leet, were both natives of Connecticut. A. N. Leet learned the carpenter's trade. In 1850, married Miss Abby Button. In 1856 he emigrated to Wisconsin, first lived in Dodge, but afterwards in Dane county, where he continued his trade until he came to Butler county. He is a republican in politics, having associated with said party since its infancy. Has often held local offices, and is at present serving his sixth year as a member of the county board of supervisors. The children are—Charles N., A. Jennie, now Mrs. G. W. Wattles; Addie, now Mrs. Dan. McDonald; Hurley, L. Nellie, Mary E., and Harry.

CHAPTER XXVI.

JEFFERSON TOWNSHIP.

This is one of the center townships of Butler county, its contiguous surroundings being Jackson township on the north, Shell Rock on the east, Albion on the south, and Ripley on the west. It embraces township 91, range 16.

TOPOGRAPHY.

From a Sketch by Van E. Butler.

This township corners with the center of the county. The land is rolling, sloping as a whole to the south and east. Only one stream of importance passes through it—the West Fork—entering on section 36. All the timber in this township lies along the stream, and this is not of much importance, except the many artificial groves that have sprung up about the pleasant farm houses that dot the uplands and valleys. Twenty years ago the major portion of Jefferson township was a splendid specimen of Iowa sloughs. Then a man would hardly have dared to cross it without first making his last will and testament and bidding a kind adieu to his family. How the first settlers ever conceived the idea of founding a city, and the manner of construction of the primitive abodes, will come to light when, like Herculaneum and Pompeii, future generations will exhume from their deep sepulchre all the evidence necessary to a correct conclusion. But what we looked upon as an almost irredeemable portion of the county has become one of the most productive. It takes a longer time to subdue the rich, dark, loam soil, but it makes returns for the extra labor. Much of the land is now under subjection, and the Iowa slough sends its thousands of bushels of cereals to the market towns. No trouble is now experienced in traversing any portion of it. The township is well adapted to stock raising, yet the rich, dark loam, when once subdued, is equal to any locality in the county in the production of cereals.

HISTORICAL ITEMS.

In 1857, the only settlers between Butler Centre and Shell Rock were N. A. Thompson and Henry Trotter. The first house between Butler Centre and Shell Rock was erected, in 1856, on section 14, by Henry Trotter.

The first death in the township was that of Mrs. Fred Berlin, in 1856.

The first birth, was William Marquand, on the 7th of October, 1858.

The first marriage united the future destinies of Noble A. Thompson and Christiana McGregor. The ceremony was performed by Justice Bailey. The couple settled on section 13.

S. M. Balduin.

Cornelia Baldwin.

HISTORY OF BUTLER COUNTY.

ORGANIC.

When, in February, 1855, Butler county, was first divided into townships by the county judge, the territory now comprising Jefferson was embraced in the organization of Beaver. In March, 1856, the latter town was cut in half, and Jefferson was made a part of Shell Rock, which was organized at that time. Thus it remained until 1857, when it assumed its present boundaries.

The first officers, as far as can be ascertained, were as follows: Hugh Mullarky and Albert Cook, trustees; H. A. Shaw, clerk.

Below we give a list of the township officials so far as it is possible to obtain them:

1858—Hugh Mullarky, T. H. Graves and James D. Taylor, trustees; John Braden, clerk.

1859—P. E. Dunson, T. H. Graves and S. L. Scott, trustees; John Braden, clerk; L. P. Mills, assessor.

1860—Hugh Mullarky and Tracy Scott, trustees; John Braden, clerk; Henry Trotter, assessor.

1861—James McGregor, Rawson Owen and P. E. Dunson, trustees; John Braden, clerk; Henry Trotter, assessor.

1862—H. Trotter and William VanVlack, trustees; D. H. Cook, clerk; James McGregor, assessor.

1863—H. Trotter, William VanVlack and Rawson Owen, trustees; Samuel Williams, clerk; W. H. Hoxie, assessor.

1864—W. A. Lathrop, Noble A. Thompson and Louis Rothe, trustees; Samuel Williams, clerk; E. D. Button, assessor.

1865—P. E. Dunson, Fred. Hahn and Noble A. Thompson, trustees; Charles Hyde, clerk, James McGregor, assessor.

1866—W. W. Olmstead, Fred. Hahn and P. E. Dunson, trustees; C. B. Hyde, clerk; E. D. Button, assessor.

1867—N. B. Hendrix, George VanVlack and Louis Hovey, trustees; James McEachron, clerk; Samuel Williams, assessor.

1868—C. M. Allen, N. B. Hendrix and N. A. Thompson, trustees; Samuel Peck, clerk; C. M. Allen, assessor.

1869—N. B. Hendrix, N. A. Thompson and M. J. Upright, trustees; W. H. Fargo, clerk; Lewis Hovey, assessor.

1870—James McEachron, James McGregor and W. H. Beckwith, trustees; F. H. Playter, clerk; Lewis Hovey, assessor.

1871—N. B. Hendrix, S. M. Baldwin and Christopher Rice, trustees; J. W. Jones, clerk; Lewis Hovey, assessor.

1872—N. B. Hendrix, S. M. Baldwin and Christopher Rice, trustees; J. W. Jones, clerk; Lewis Hovey, assessor.

1873—N. B. Hendrix, L. Hovey and Wm. VanVlack; Geo. M. Craig, clerk; Geo. T. Thompson.

1874—Wm. VanVlack, H. Mullarkey, trustees; G. M. Craig, clerk.

1875—S. M. Baldwin, E. F. Mettlen, Levi Elliott, trustees; Wm. VanVlack, assessor; J. M. Jones, clerk.

1876—G. M. Craig, L. Hovey, justices of the peace; Wm. VanVlack, assessor; H. N. Walker, clerk; Ross Lawrence, Geo. Martin, N. B. Hendricks, trustees.

1877—Geo. M. Craig, R. Gonzales, justices; C. B. Hyde, assessor; H. H. Sikkema, clerk; H. Mullarkey, Geo. Martin, T. McCarty, trustees.

1878—Geo. M. Craig, W. H. Irving, (elected but did not qualify and M. Bailey as appointed in his stead,) justices; C. B. Hyde, assessor; H. H. Sikkema clerk; H. Mullarkey, for three years, P. Dunson, for two years, Wm. VanVlack, for one year, trustees.

1879—Martin Bailey, justice; Wm. Van Vlack, assessor; H. H. Sikkemma, clerk; John Costar, trustee.

1880—Martin Bailey, J. W. Davis, justices; Wm. Van Vlack, assessor, for two years; H. H. Sikkema, clerk, for two years; Noble A. Thompson, trustee. H. H. Sikkema resigned and J. D. Anderson was appointed.

1881—C. B. Hyde, H. Mullarkey, trustees; J. A. Trotter, clerk. December 21, J. A. Trotter was appointed justice of the peace, in place of J. W. Davis, removed.

1882—Martin Bailey, W. C. Thompson, justices of the peace; J. A. Trotter, clerk; Bert Chapman, Harry Trotter, constables; A. G. Fellows, assessor; John Costar, trustee.

EARLY SETTLEMENT.

The first settler was H. C. Dawson, who came here in the fall of 1854 and settled on section 33. He afterwards removed to Marshalltown. James D. Taylor also came about the same time, and settled on section 31. He was strongly opposed to the war, and when hostilities commenced, he sold out his property, converting all his earthly possessions, as nearly as possible, into "gold"—having a decided aversion to the "greenback," seemingly quite confident they were not worth "two cents a bushel," as he expressed it—he removed to Illinois, since which time nothing has been heard from him.

William Hays took up his place of abode on section thirty-six, where we now find him, in October 1854. Mr. Hays was born in the State of Virginia, October 17, 1824. He was left motherless when only eight years of age, and in 1840, emigrated with the balance of the family to Illinois, and settled in LaSalle county, where his father died in about 1844. In 1845, Mr. Hays married Miss Rachel White, a native of New York, and in 1854, accompanied by his wife and four children—Robert Olmstead and family, Marshal Kelley and wife, James Hair and family, Myron Hair and his parents, started for Iowa. At Cedar Falls they were joined by Gilbert Knights; they then turned their course up the river and soon arrived in Butler county, where they all settled. Mrs. Hays died in 1863, leaving six children—Elizabeth, Nancy, Calista, Sarah, Tina and Benjamin.

Wm. Mason came to this township during the fall of 1855, and settled on section twenty-eight, where he remained six years; then he removed to Charles City Mr. Whitehead came near the same time and located near what was called New Albion and removed to Missouri in 1863.

A. J. Case came also, in the fall of 1855, and settled near the river, on the northeast quarter of section 30. After a few years, he sold out and went to Waverly.

Robert Armstrong was a settler of 1855, in the same locality, where he remained until his death, which occurred April 1, 1882.

Mr. Stewart was a settler of 1856, and died at Webster City, in 1881.

Joe Santee came to Jefferson township in 1856, and assisted in building the first house in Butler Center, which was of logs. He afterward removed to Ripley township.

Mr. Pennock came near the same time, and built the second log house in Butler Center, which still stands.

O. S. Levis arrived in Jefferson township, and built the first store in the township at Butler Center, and opened up on the 4th of July, 1856, having a stock of general merchandise. He managed the business a few years, when he took in a partner (Dan Mason), to whom he afterward sold, and moved to Shell Rock. This same structure now stands in Butler Center.

H. H. Marsh came to Butler Center in 1856. He was a dentist, and the first in the township. He built a residence, being the third in the place; remained a few years, and removed to Cedar Falls.

Hugh Mullarky was one of the pioneers who came to the county in 1855, and settled at Butler Center in January of that year. Mr. Mullarky is a native of Ireland, born in 1827, his parents being Edmund and Elizabeth (Holliday) Mullarky. In 1839 the family emigrated to the United States, stopping one year in the State of Ohio, thence removing to La Porte county, Indiana, and two years later to Stephenson county, Illinois, where the parents both died, leaving six children, five of whom are now living—Owen, Daniel, Ellen, Anthony, and Hugh, who is the subject of this sketch. In 1857 he married Miss Margaret Giblin, and soon came to Iowa and settled in Butler county, as above stated. Mr. Mullarky has been very successful as a farmer, and now owns 800 acres of land. He is a democrat in politics, and in religion Roman Catholic. The children are—John, Frank, William, Ellen, Margaret, Hugh, Eugene, and Alloisus.

In 1857, C. H. Chamberlain, Dr. Shaw and Enoch George came together, from Ohio, and built a house each in Butler Centre. Chamberlain started a store, but after a few years returned to Ohio. Dr. Shaw was the first practicing physician and after a short time returned to his native State. Enoch George was a house carpenter. He returned to Ohio in about three years.

Thomas Bird arrived and built a store in Butler Center, in 1857. He opened up a general stock, remained three or four years and went to Waterloo. The building still stands.

O. H. Peabird built a residence in Butler Center, soon after his arrival, in 1857. After removing to other points, from which he several times returned, he finally removed to Franklin county, where he now lives. The house still stands.

H. M. Martgretz came in 1856; drove stakes at Butler Center, built the first hotel, where he remained until he enlisted in the army and was killed. The building has since been torn down.

Geo. A. Richmond, a lawyer, put in his appearance in 1857, and bought a one-half interest in the town of Butler Center; was the first lawyer in the township; remained a number of years; removed to Dubuque, and afterward enlisted in the army. He built a large residence, which has been used for a hotel, until the removal of the county seat. It is now occupied as a residence.

F. Digman was first seen in the township in 1857. He bought the Joe Santee building and opened a shoe shop, to which he afterward made additions, and kept a general assortment of dry goods and groceries. He also built a hotel, and finally died here in 1879. The building was moved to Allison, where Mrs. Digman, at this writing, is keeping hotel. Mr. Digman was a live, energetic man, and worked hard for the development of the town.

Other settlers came during and immediately following the foregoing, among whom were Thomas Thompson and two brothers, prominent men in the township.

Thomas Thompson was born in Ireland, December 7, 1799. He learned the shoemaker's trade, and married Miss Phœbe Coulson. In 1850 he emigrated to the United States, following his trade in New York city until 1857, when he came to Iowa, and has since been a resident of Butler county. He still resides on the land he entered. His wife died in 1865, leaving seven children, six of whom are now living—Elizabeth, now Mrs. Henry Trotter; Mary Ann, Irvina, now Mrs. James Trotter; William C., Noble A., and George T.

N. C. Thompson was born in Ireland, September 3, 1834. He came to the United States in 1853. He first engaged as a clerk in mercantile trade, and afterward carried on a tea, coffee and spice trade until 1863, when he came to Butler county, and settled on section 13, Jefferson township, where he now resides. In February, 1864, he was appointed deputy county treasurer, and served in that capacity until January 1, 1872. In the fall of 1871 he was elected county treasurer, and held that office four years. He then followed farming one year in Jackson township, when he again returned to his farm in Jefferson. He owns 240 acres, and is engaged in stock farming. In 1860, in the city of Brooklyn, New York, he married Miss Nannie Reiley, a native of Ireland. She died, in July, 1882, leaving five children—John W., William C., Launcelot, Jane, and Mary.

Noble A. Thompson resides on section 13. He was born in Ireland, June 29, 1839. He came to the United States in 1852, and to Butler county in 1855. The following winter he spent at Cedar Falls, but since that time he has resided in this county. In 1861 he married Miss C. McGregor, a daughter of James McGregor. They have had nine children, six of whom are now living—Alexander, Pierce C., Phœbe, James, George and Charles.

John Braden located, in the spring of 1856, one-half mile from Butler Center. He enlisted in the army and was killed. His body was brought back and buried in the grove west of the house, where all that is left of the earthly nature of John Braden still remains.

S. Williams, a highly respected citizen, came later and is now living on his same place.

Orson Rice, a lawyer, established himself in Butler Center in 1857, where he practiced his profession for several years, when he removed to Clay county and was elected county clerk.

Jule Hale was also an early settler, and the first county treasurer after the county seat was located at Butler Center. He moved to Peterson, O'Brien county.

Albert Cook and others followed. Most of the early settlers in this township remained but a few years when they removed to other parts. The present settlement was made at a later day. Some, however, of the first settlers still remain.

Frederick Berlin, who is a native of Prussia, Germany, born in 1820, came to the United States in 1852, and first settled in DuPage county, Illinois. There, in 1852, he married Miss Amelia Weber, a native of Hanover, Germany. He at once started with his bride for Iowa, making the trip with an ox team, and after a three weeks journey, settled where he now resides. His wife died soon after arriving at her new home. In 1859, Mr. Berlin married Miss Theresa Berger, and they now have two children—Louisa, now Mrs. Fred. Kothe, and John. Mr. Berlin is a successful farmer, a good citizen and is highly respected.

P. E. Dunson, who came to the county February 7, 1856, entered 160 acres on section 29, Jefferson township, and has since resided on the same, making farming a business, and has met with marked success, as he now owns 273 acres. Mr. Dunson was born in Virginia, December 7, 1825. His parents, Abraham and Margaret (Hudlow) Dunson, were both natives of Pennsylvania. In 1833, the family emigrated to Ohio and settled in Shelby county. In 1837, the father died. The mother still resides in Ohio, in said county. Of her eight children, seven are now living—Sarah, P. E., Margaret, Adison, Minerva, Ellen and Amanda. P. E. Dunson was bred to farm life, and in 1847 married Miss Rebecca Skillen. In 1854, he came to Iowa, and resided at Cedar Falls until he came to this county. The children are —Mary E. and Samantha J. Mr. Dunson has been a successful farmer, is a perfect gentleman, and a valuable acquisition to any community.

Henry Trotter, who now lives in Ripley township, owned in an early day considerable land here.

From time to time other settlers came in during these years, many of whom were men of influence and worthy of mention in these pages. Jefferson township has had representative men of the best class, and in this connection a few are mentioned:

Samuel Williams was born in Lewis county, New York, June 7, 1824. In 1844 he emigrated with his parents to Walworth county, Wisconsin, where, in 1851, he married Miss Mary Sewell, a daughter of Jonathan Sewell. In 1855 Mr. Williams came to Iowa and entered 160 acres of the land he now owns. In 1859 he emigrated to Kansas, and from there to Butler county. Mr. and Mrs. Williams have three children—Arthur S., Herbert L. and Ada C. Mr. Williams was early taught the principles of democracy, and adhered to the same until he went to Kansas, where he joined the republican ranks and has since voted with that party. He is well known in the county, as for several years, while residing at Butler Center, his house served as a hotel where the hungry could feed and the weary find rest.

James A. Trotter, son of Henry and Jane (Brown) Trotter, was born in county Antrim, Ireland, August 27, 1830. He came with the family to the United States, and until 1862, served as clerk in a mercantile business in the city of New York. He then came to Butler county, and in 1864, enlisted in Company B of the Seventh Iowa Infantry, and served until the regiment was mustered out of service, since which time he has been engaged in farming in Jefferson township, where he now owns 160 acres of land. Mr. Trotter is a republican in politics. He served as deputy county treasurer nearly eight years, besides holding numerous local offices at different intervals. He was united in marriage, in 1857, with Miss Irvina Thompson, daughter of Thomas Thompson, and they now have eight children—Henry, Lizzie, Mamie, Phoebe, Irvina, Jane, Frances and Mabel.

S. M. Baldwin, one of the largest land owners and leading farmers in Butler county, came here in 1854, and entered land where he now resides. He, however, remained here but a short time, and then returned to Ohio. In 1861, he enlisted in the Eightieth Ohio Volunteer Infantry, and served three years and six months, during which time he saw much hard service. In 1868, he again returned to Butler county, and has since resided on section 8, Jefferson township. S. M. Baldwin was born in Coshocton county, Ohio, March 11, 1825. He is the son of William and Almy (Smith) Baldwin. In 1869, he married Miss Cornelia Baldwin, a native of Massachusetts. They now have two children—William S. and Maro G.

M. B. Speedy was born in Jefferson county, Ohio, March 18, 1838, where he resided until eighteen years of age; then came to Iowa, and first stopped at Shell Rock. In December, 1864, he married Miss A. E. Coats. He followed farming in Shell Rock until 1870. He then carried on a drug and grocery business at Shell Rock until 1878, since which time he has resided in Jefferson township, and now owns a fine farm of 170 acres. The children are—Oscar, Annette, Eva, Ethel and Blanche.

John Giblin was born in Ireland in 1830, and was brought to the United States by his parents when he was only two years of age. The family first stopped in the New England States for about seven years, and then emigrated to Illinois, where the father died in 1880. The mother is still living. In 1850 John Giblin went to California, where he was engaged in mining about two years, and afterward in general merchandising, until 1863, when he went to Idaho Territory, from there to VanCouver's Island, and thence to Montana. In 1867, at Freeport, Illinois, he married Miss Ann Marlow. They now have five children—Emma, Ella, John P., Lizzie and Thomas. Soon after their marriage Mr. Giblin and wife came to Butler county and settled where they now reside. In 1870, however, they removed to Salt Lake City, Utah, and there carried on a general mercantile business for seven years.

Nathan Linn, an early settler in Butler county, was born in Washington county, Maryland, September 26, 1819. When but two years of age his parents emigrated to Knox county, Ohio, where he received his education in the district schools. In 1851 he removed to Illinois and bought a farm near Oxford, Henry county, where he lived until 1854, when he sold his land and started for Iowa. He spent the winter in Carpenter's Grove, and in the spring went to Ripley, entered a claim and went to work breaking; but soon finding that the land overflowed, he left it and went to Monroe, where he took a claim on section 10 and erected a log house. He lived there until 1879, when he sold out and removed to Jefferson, where he bought a farm on section 31, on which he now resides. In 1840 he married Miss Sophia Daniels. They were blessed with six children—Millison A., Rachel, William P., Harriet, Mary and Charlotte. Mrs. Linn was born in Knox county, Ohio, September 5, 1821, and died February 27, 1876, while visiting her daughter in Illinois. Millison A., the oldest child, was born in Knox county, Ohio, June 15, 1841, and died in Henry county, Illinois, in February, 1881.

William Van Vlack entered the land he now lives on in 1857, but did not become a resident of the county until 1860. He first resided on section 36, but only temporarily, as he at once commenced improving his land. In 1862 he settled on the same, and made farming his business until 1869, when he removed to New Hartford, and for two years dealt in agricultural implements, at the end of which time he again returned to his farm. Mr. Van Vlack was born in Albany county, New York, in 1836. He was left fatherless at the age of fourteen years. At the age of nineteen he emigrated to Illinois, and resided in DeKalb county until he came to Iowa. In 1857 he married Miss Rebecca Olmstead, a native of New York. They now have five children—Charles, Eugene and Howell,(twins), Dwight, and Oliver Judd.

R. W. Hunter, son of James and Caroline (Mears) Hunter, was born June 12, 1858. After receiving a good common school education at the home schools, he, in 1875, entered the Lenox Collegiate Institute, of Hopkington, Iowa, where he graduated. He then entered the law department of the Iowa State University, and graduated from it. He is now pursuing his profession in Arberdeen, Dakota. In 1881, October 19, Mr. Hunter married Miss Olive A. Merrill.

BUTLER CENTER.

This town has been considered a point of some importance, being geographically located very near the center of the county, from which fact it derives its name, but at the present writing it seems to be on the wane.

Andrew Mullarkey and Col. Thomas entered the land upon which stands the village, in 1853. The same parties platted the town in the spring of 1855. It is located on the northwest quarter of section 18, township 91, range 16, and is naturally very favorably placed, as far as a site is concerned. At an election called for the purpose, on April 4, 1859, this village had a majority of twenty-one in its favor for the re-location of the county seat, which heretofore had been at Clarksville. Before the records were moved, however, an injunction was sworn out, and the removal was stayed. In July following, the district court adjudged the election void, because of certain irregularities. On the 4th of April, 1860, another election was held, resulting in a majority of eighty votes for Butler Center, and the county seat was removed accordingly. Mr. Mullarkey owned a large amount of land in this vicinity, and was instrumental in accomplishing this result. He was generous and liberal minded, and donated to the county two acres of land upon which he had erected a court house. Induced by these considerations, the apparently probable permanency of the county seat, and the flattering prospects for the future, lawyers, doctors, editors, dentists, representatives of the different professions, exponents of various religious creeds, and other necessary elements of civilization, came together and formed a settlement, and it seemed for a time that Butler Center was certainly destined to become the "future great" of Butler county. But now how changed—the deserted streets, empty houses, vacant lots, dilapidated fences, signs of dissolution and decay, present themselves on every hand, speaking of things that were, suggesting things that "might have been." This change has been wrought mainly by the re-location of the county seat, the lack of railroads being the main factor which occasioned its removal.

Here the county seat remained until the fall of 1881, when it was removed to Allison.

The first business houses have hereinbefore been noticed, in the account of early settlement. After the election which decided upon the removal of the county seat, the town presented much the appearance of a "place on wheels," as house after house made its disappearance and traveled Allisonward.

A newspaper was first published here in 1860 by William Haddock, and was called the *Butler County Jeffersonian*, which was afterward purchased by Martin Bailey, under whose management it appeared the first week in January, 1861. From this time it was called the *Stars and Stripes*. The paper is now defunct and the material removed elsewhere. William Haddock enlisted in the army, raised a company and obtained a commission as captain. Martin Bailey is a resident of Butler Center, and is one of the editors of the agricultural department of the Allison *Tribune*. He has taken an active interest in Butler county since August, 1856. At that time he engaged in general merchandising at New Hartford, and was therefore the first merchant of that place. In 1855 he associated D. N. Root as partner, and the business continued under the firm name of Bailey & Root; but Mr. Bailey soon became convinced that he would never be a successful merchant, and therefore, in the winter of 1858–9, he purchased his partner's interest and closed out the business. In 1859 Mr. Bailey was appointed deputy county clerk and made out the tax lists for that year. In January, 1860, he became deputy county treasurer, removed to Butler Center, then the county seat, and served in that capacity for over two years. On May 1, 1863, he entered the United States service as clerk in the quartermaster's department at Sioux City. In 1865 he was transferred to Dubuque and afterward to Waterloo, where he was discharged October 31, 1865. He then returned to his home, and has since been engaged in farming. He now owns a fine herd of Jersey cattle. His farm, containing 160 acres, lies adjoining the village plat of Butler Center, and his home is supplied with all the necessaries of the best social life. In politics Mr. Bailey was formerly a whig, but in 1856 he joined the republican ranks and has since stood by the same. He has often held local offices, serving as justice of the peace for several years. He is a lover of the public schools, and always takes an active interest in education. He is at present secretary of the school board of this township. Martin Bailey is a son of Joseph and Patty (Tullar) Bailey. He was born in Oswego county, New York, November 7, 1819. His father was a preacher in the Christian Church, and as he was a man of only limited means, Martin worked for other parties during the summer and attended school during the winter seasons. At the age of twenty he commenced teaching, and taught thirteen winter terms. In 1845 he emigrated to Illinois, where, in 1847, he married Miss Mary A. Clark, a native of Vermont, and in 1853 came to Iowa and settled in Black Hawk county. In 1854 he was elected clerk of the court and served one year. When the county seat was removed from Cedar Falls to Waterloo he resigned the office, and was employed in Andrew Mullarky's store one year. He then engaged in general merchandising at New Hartford. Mr. and Mrs. Bailey have had five children, two now living—Celia and Datus.

SALOONS.

Butler Center in its palmy days had its share of drinking places, and those who patronized the same. Upon the principle that a town to build up and secure trade must furnish the necessary inducements, these places were allowed free course, as a general thing, and carried on the business without molestation.

The first place of this order was opened during the war, by Bennett & Embody. They were followed by John Court, who added to the business a billiard hall. Then came James Evans, Crandall and others. There being at times three such places in the village

The true sentiment of the people has been recently manifested at the polls—Jefferson township giving four majority for the amendment.

No saloon has been in the village since the removal of the county seat.

EDUCATIONAL.

The first school was taught by Alzina Waters, in the Lewis building. Martha Niece afterward taught in the house built by Enoch George, and "boarded 'round." There is now in the district containing Butler Center a good school building, the pupils being under the efficient management of Misses Ella and Margaret Mullarky. The former is a graduate of the Normal School at Cedar Falls. There are fifty-five pupils; an average attendance of about forty-five. Including this school house there are six school buildings in Jefferson township.

FIRST THINGS.

Wm. Wright was the first blacksmith.

Nathan Olmstead preached the first sermon in the saw-mill, in 1856.

Charles Stewart, with Andrew Mullarky as chief proprietor, erected the first saw-mill, which was propelled by steam, and "raised" on the 5th day of May, 1856, and by whom it was controlled for four or five years, when it went into the hands of other parties, who conducted the business a number of years, until Yoder & Allen removed the machinery to Cerro Gordo county. The building was then used by Sam Williams for a stable. At length

I. W. Camp bought it for taxes, when it was torn down.

The first burial in the cemetery, located one mile east of the town, was that of Jane Stewart, daughter of Chas. Stewart, in the summer of 1857. The next was John Stewart, son of the same party, about ten days afterward. The next was Freddie Santee, son of Joe Santee, within two weeks of the last named, and soon after, a child of Adam Conn.

The first boy born in the village was a son to Martin Bailey.

The first justice of the peace was H. H. Margretz.

POST OFFICE.

The Butler Center post office was established in 1856, mail being received by carrier by way of Cedar Falls, once a week. The first postmaster was H. H. Margretz, followed by Hugh Mullarkey, W. A. Lathrop, J. H. Plater and H. N. Walker, the present incumbent. It was made a money order office in July, 1875, Geo. M. Craig purchasing the first order, in favor of S. T. McMoran, Saint Paris, Ohio, for $40.00. The first money paid was to R. L. Chase, order issued at Green, Iowa, for $25.64. In 1871, a daily mail was had on the Waverly route by way of Clarksville, afterward by way of Shell Rock. A weekly mail was also received from Parkersburg for two or three years, then tri-weekly and afterward, daily. On the present route from Parkersburg to Allison, there is a daily mail, and a tri-weekly mail from Willoughby.

Butler Centre has now but one store, the business being conducted by H. N. Walker, and one blacksmith shop, the proprietor being John McCarty.

H. N. Walker, the postmaster and storekeeper, is an honest, upright gentleman, social with everybody, courteous to all, whose removal would prove a public calamity. He purchased the business of H. C. Plater, in 1871. He has had several different persons associated as partners at different times, until 1878, since which time he has conducted the business alone. He was appointed postmaster in 1871. Mr. Walker was born in Vermont, January 17, 1830. His parents, Reuben and Lydia (Miller) Walker, were also natives of said State. He was brought up on a farm in the Green Mountain State, where he remained until 1865, when he came to Iowa and engaged in the dairy business at Dubuque until he came to Butler Center. In 1869 he married Miss Caroline French, of Vermont, a native of Pennsylvania. They now have six children—Viola, Lydia, Minnie, Lottie, Abbie and Charles.

PRESBYTERIAN CHURCH.

This church was organized at Butler Center in 1873, by Rev. William Smith, although services had occasionally been held for years previous to this. The first members were, James Barlow and wife, James Hunter and wife, W. C. Thompson and wife, Mrs. B. J. Merrill, Miss Emma Tompkins, James Robbins and wife, Duncan McGregor and wife, and Duncan Stewart and wife. Rev. W. Smith was succeeded, in 1875, by Rev. John Gourley. The society now has a membership of about twenty-five. Meetings have always been held at the court house.

Rev. Richard Merrill, an active and earnest worker in this church, an early settler in Butler county, was county superintendent of schools for a number of years, and is noticed at length in the chapter on that subject.

There has been an organized Sabbath school in Butler Center since about 1864. The first superintendent was George M. Craig, now of Allison. At present there are about forty members of the school, and an average attendance of about twenty-five.

CHAPTER XXVII.

MADISON TOWNSHIP.

This township lies in the western tier of Butler county. On the west lies Franklin county, and the township of Pittsford on the north, Ripley on the east, and Washington on the south. It is a full congressional township, embracing township 91, range 18, containing an area of about 23,040 acres.

The surface of Madison is a rolling prairie. The soil consists of a rich, dark loam, although in places it is inclined to be sandy. The supply of water is very good. There is also a great deal of excellent grass land, and stock raising is carried on very profitably. Through portions of the township, pass the streams of West Fork, Dutchman's Creek and Main's Creek. The valleys of these streams are low and rich, with sandy beds. The timber supply is limited, being mostly confined to Bear Grove.

There are no villages or railroad stations within the limits of the township, and the marketing points are mostly Aplington, Ackley and Dumont. The farmers devote most of their attention to raising corn, wheat, oats and stock. There are many good pieces of land yet for sale in the township, and Madison will be an excellent farming township when fully developed. The population of Madison, according to the census of 1880, was 473. The assessed valuation of personal property is $25,511; of lands, $120,521.

EARLY SETTLEMENT.

To learn with any degree of accuracy the first actual settler of a locality that has been settled for a generation is a more difficult task than would be imagined by one who has never undertaken it, for no matter how authentic the source of information, or how conclusive the evidence brought to bear, there will be some one who will emphatically deny the assertion and bring up another candidate for patri-

HISTORY OF BUTLER COUNTY.

archal honors. It is best, as a rule, in order to avoid any misunderstanding or any chance for dispute, to adopt the order of arrivals, as near as can be ascertained, and the reader can select a first settler to his notion. In the language of Mark Twain, you can "read the facts and take your choice."

The settlement of Madison began in 1854, and the first to put in an appearance for the purpose of making a permanent home was undoubtedly Nicholas Hartgraves, a native of North Carolina. He came to Iowa from Indiana in 1844. In 1852 he came to Butler county and stopped at Beaver Grove, where he remained for two years. In 1854 he pushed his way farther westward and settled in what is now Madison township, on section 17, his present home.

In 1855 Noah Hartgraves, a brother to Nicholas, arrived in Madison, and planted his stakes adjoining his brother, on section 18. He remained here for five or six years, when he moved to Tama county. He is at present living in Osceola county.

A little later in 1855, two more pioneers in search of a home, settled in what is now Madison. They were Ephraim Hizenton and his son, William, from Illinois. William took a claim on section 14, and erected a cabin. In 1858 he died of hydrophobia. The father made a claim on section 15, but did not prove up. He lived on his son's place for a few years, when he removed to Beaver Creek, where he died in 1880.

During the same year—1855—William Mason and Fred Moffatt, natives of England, came here from Massachusetts. Mr. Mason claimed the south half of section 24, and Mr. Moffatt the south half of section 13. In 1866 they traded their property for a woolen mill at Cedar Falls.

Abijah Stacy, a native of Indiana, moved here from Johnson county, Iowa, in the spring of 1855. In the following November, death called him from all earthly labors.

In 1857 Jacob Yost settled on section 16, and remained for a few years. He is now living in Ripley.

Peter Coyle, a native of the loved Emerald Isle, came here in 1858, from Illinois, accompanied by his son-in-law, Thomas Gallagher, and wife. They came with ox-teams, the trip taking about two weeks. Peter Coyle settled on section 10, remaining there until 1875, when he removed to Ackley, his present home. He was a prominent man in public affairs, and for many years was chairman of the board of county supervisors. His son, Edward, now lives on the old homestead.

Thomas Gallagher is now living on section 9. His wife died on November 27, 1872, and left many sincere friends and relatives, who mourn her loss.

James Wilkerson, an Englishman, came here in 1856, and settled upon a farm, on section sixteen, where he remained for about two years, when he removed to Hancock county.

After this, settlement was slow for a number of years, but it revived again after the war. In 1865, a number came from Wisconsin, among whom were Amos E. Hartson, Samuel B. Gordon and Solomon Harvey. Hartson was a native of Pennsylvania, and settled in his present home, on section seventeen. Samuel and Thomas Smith were also natives of the same State. Samuel located on section two. He died in 1871, at the residence of Solomon Harvey. Thomas located on section seventeen, and in 1881 removed to Wright county. Gordon was a native of the same State; he found a home on section twenty, where he remained until 1876, when he removed to Turner county, D. T. Solomon Harvey was a Vermonter. He made a claim on section sixteen, where he continued until 1875, when he removed to his present home in Ackley.

In 1867, Walcott Watson, a native of Connecticut, moved here from Wisconsin, and settled on section twenty-one, where he still "holds the fort."

Elisha Scott also came at an early day, but has since moved from the township and county. At last accounts he was living in Nebraska.

HISTORICAL ITEMS.

The first birth in Madison occurred March 1, 1855, a son, Marion, to Nicholas and Sophia Hartgraves. He is now living in Kansas.

The next birth was on the 26th of November, 1856, a daughter, Melinda, to the same parents. In December, 1878, she married James Harris. They are now living in Keokuk county.

Richard Mertersburg Hartgraves was born July 9, 1858.

The first marriage ceremony in Madison was performed in 1860 by Peter Coyle, at his house, and joined in marriage Elisha Scott and Miss Sally Taylor. It is said that a wedding party had been arranged, a dinner prepared, guests invited, and everything was in order for a good time. When the time arrived a sister of the bride, who was opposed to the match, persuaded her not to go to the wedding. The guests, together with the minister who had been selected, met at the appointed place and hour; but as there was no bride the dinner was eaten and the party dispersed. One of the neighbors went to see the girl and persuaded her to change her mind. In the afternoon she met her affianced, and together they proceeded to Justice Coyle's, where they were made one. Nine years later she was drowned in the West Fork while attempting to cross the river at the time of high water. Her husband was with her, but escaped.

The first death occurred in November, 1855, and Abijah Stacy quietly passed away. He was buried at Beaver Grove without any funeral services. His widow, at last account, was in Wisconsin.

OHIO STOCK FARM.

Some years ago, a stock company was formed in Ohio, under the caption of the Ohio Stock Breeding Association, the parties being John K. Green, of Cincinnati, Judge R. W. Musgrave, and Luther A. Hall, of Tiffin City, Dr. George Sprague and others. The company purchased, through Dr. Sprague, the originator of the concern, 6,000 acres of land, mostly lying in Madison township. He came here at an early day, importing with him a splendid herd of Short Horn cattle. The affair was not a success as the country was not far enough advanced to support such an enterprise. Sprague struggled manfully for a time, but finally gave up and the land was divided among the stockholders. He retained some and J. K. Green got about 3,700 acres. Dr. Sprague, after giving up this idea, removed to Des Moines and started the *Iowa Homestead*, a farm journal of wide reputation and a successful paper. He is still at the head of it, which, with the help of his sons, is making just what the farmers of Iowa are in need of.

ORGANIC.

Prior to its organization as a separate township, Madison composed a part of Ripley, and remained as such from 1855 to 1860. In 1860 it was set off by Judge Converse, and ordered organized. The name of Madison was proposed by Peter Coyle, and it was ratified by a meeting of the citizens.

The first meeting for the election of officers was held at Jacob Yost's house, on section 16, and the following were chosen: Dr. George Sprague, Peter Coyle, trustees; Peter Coyle, justice of the peace; Peter Coyle, assessor. Jacob Yost held some office, but it has been forgotten.

The town matters have been managed in a satisfactory manner. They have no hall, but meetings are held at the school house of District No. 4, on section 17.

Among those who have been prominent in township government, and have held office at various times, are the following: T. W. Smith, Solomon Harvey, J. O. Slade, Jas. Baker, Walcott Watson, Edward Coyle, A. E. Hartson, A. B. Watson.

At the election held in November, 1882, the following officers were elected: G. R. D. Kramer, M. Kirby, justices of the peace; B. J. Ruiter, town clerk; J. Bennett, R. Hartgraves, constables; A. E. Hartson, assessor; John Kirby, trustee.

RELIGIOUS.

The first Catholic services held in the township were held in 1865, at the house of Peter Coyle, and presided over by Father Shields, of Waverly. A child of John Cunningham was baptized at the time. Quite a number of meetings were subsequently held at the same place.

The Methodists, in 1867, held services in the school house of District No. 4. The first to officiate was Rev. Captain Williams, of Ackley, who was also an auctioneer. No organization was attempted at this time. In 1871 a society organization was effected by Elder Wakely, with a small membership. The following are among the ministers who have officiated here: Revs. Bargelt, Bodgett, Smith, Murphy, Cooley and Sproul.

A Sabbath school was organized in the summer of 1867, with N. R. Carpenter as superintendent. This school was continued for a year or more.

In the summer of 1882, a school was again started with about thirty scholars. Miss Aggie McMurray, a teacher in District No. 4, was superintendent.

EDUCATIONAL.

The first school house in the township was erected in 1860, on section 14, in District No. 1. The old school house was moved away in 1870, and in 1872 a board shanty was erected, in which one or two terms of school were held. The present school house was built in 1873, at a cost of about $400. It is located in the southwestern part of section 13. Miss Carpenter was the first teacher in the township.

In 1868 District No. 2 was organized, and a school house erected, on section 16, at a cost of $600. The house is still in use. Miss Helen Slade was one of the first teachers in this district.

District No. 3 was set off in 1875, and in 1876 the school house was erected on section 8, at a cost of $425, including cost of land, surveyor's fees, etc. Miss Mary Johnson, Alice Hurley, and Mr. George Palmer were among the first teachers in this house.

District No. 4 was set off from No. 2 in 1864, and a house was constructed, in 1865, on section 16, at a cost of $409. In 1868 the school building was moved to section 17, its present location. Thomas W. Smith was the first teacher.

District No. 5 erected their first house early in the "sixties." In 1881 this house was sold to K. S. Greene, and it is now used as a dwelling by some of his tenants. The present house was erected in 1881, on section 26, at a cost of $450. The first to teach in it was Miss Maggie Miscoll.

District No. 6 was organized in 1870, and the neat frame house was erected the following year, on section 32. Mr. Thomas Butler was one of the first teachers.

ISLAND GROVE POSTOFFICE.

A postoffice under this name was established in Madison, in 1858, with Dr. George Sprague as postmaster, with the office at his house on section 35. It was on the mail route from Cedar Falls to Hampton, and later on the route from Aplington. The office was discontinued about 1868.

BLACKSMITH SHOP.

The industrial enterprises have not been very well represented in Madison. Some years ago Albert Schmitz purchased the pioneer school house, and moved where he started a blacksmith shop, which he ran for about one year. Schmitz is now engaged in the mercantile business at Dumont.

PATRONS OF HUSBANDRY.

The Madison Grange, No. 214, was chartered on the 28th of February, 1872, with thirty-one charter members. The first officers were as follows: Edward Coyle, master; Walcott Watson, overseer; Jacob Brooks, lecturer; Jesse Baker, assistant; Frank Beack, secretary; J. B. Gordon, gate-keeper; Ella Harvey, Ceres; Mrs. E. C. Brooks, Pomona; Mrs. Julia Baker, Flora; Mrs. Emma Harvey, assistant steward.

The meetings were held at the school house on section 17, and for a time it was successful, the membership increasing to fifty. But interest finally began to wane, and on the 11th of February, they surrendered their charter and sold the property at auction.

The last officers were as follows: A. E. Hartson, master; A. B. Watson, overseer; J. O. Slade, steward; G. W. Watson, assistant steward; T. W. Smith, lecturer; W. Watson, treasurer; N. Long, secretary.

MADISON CEMETERY.

This cemetery was platted in 1873, by M. D. L. Niece, under the auspices of the Madison Cemetery Association. This association was composed of the leading citizens of the town, among whom were, W. Watson, J. Baker, S. Harvey, T. W. Smith, J. Brooks, M. Harvey, J. O. Slade, J. Kalabarer, A. Schmitz, Frank Beach, P. Long and P. Pfaltgraftz. The officers were, W. Watson, president; J. O. Slade, vice-president; J. Baker, treasurer; T. W. Smith, secretary; and seven trustees. The first burial here was of the remains of Mrs. Jacob Kalabarer.

In 1881, the grounds were given to the township. There are now but three members of the association left in the township.

PROMINENT CITIZENS.

In this connection is presented the personal history of a few of Madison's representative men. Of course, want of space forbids giving biographical sketches of all the citizens, even though it be the most interesting of all history; yet it is hoped that enough will be given to show the kind of men who are now the bone and sinew of Madison.

Nicholas Hartgraves, a pioneer of Butler county and the first settler in Madison, was born in North Carolina, August 18, 1817. When three years of age his father died; his mother soon married again. In 1827 the family moved to Indiana and settled in Washington county. In July, 1831, his mother lost her second husband. When he was twenty-one years of age he went to Kentucky and there engaged in farming for four years, when he returned to Indiana. In the summer of 1846 he came to Johnson county, Iowa, living there until 1852, when he moved to Butler county, being the third settler in Beaver Grove. In 1854 he sold his claim and came to Madison, taking a claim on section 18, where he built the first house in the township. His present home is on section 17. He was married in March, 1844, to Miss Sophia Stacey, a native of Indiana. They have had fifteen children; ten are now living—Delila, Clarissa, Marion, Melinda, Richard, Sinie A., Henrietta, Ellen, Estella, Virgil. Ulysses S. G. died in 1871, in his seventh year; the other four died in infancy.

Peter Coyle is a native of Monaghan county, Ireland, born Nov. 27, 1802. He married, Oct. 9, 1827, Mary McAntee, and in 1847, emigrated with his family to America. He entered a machine shop in Auburn, N. Y., living in that city until 1855, when he moved to Amboy, Illinois, and engaged in the same business. Here he bought land and built a house. In 1858, he traded his property for land in Butler, Howard, Blackhawk and Chickasaw counties. That summer he came to Butler county and settled in Madison, on section ten. In 1875 he moved to Ackley, having previously built a house there. He has eight children—Catherine, Edward, Ellen, Rosa, Ann, Mary; two died in infancy. He was the first justice of the peace elected in the township. He was elected a member of the board of supervisors in 1861, and was chairman of the board for five years.

Edward, son of Peter Coyle, was born in Monaghan county, Ireland, December 8, 1830, and was there reared to agricultural pursuits. In 1848 he came to America; landed at New York, June 13, going directly to Auburn, where his father had lived one year. He remained there until the spring of 1850, when he moved to Patterson, New Jersey, where he served an apprenticeship in the New Jersey Machine Company's shops. In 1854 he went to Chicago, where he was engaged by the Illinois Central Railroad Co., working for them in Chicago until 1856, and at Amboy until 1859. He then engaged with the Rock Island Railroad Co., one year; then with the Chicago and Northwestern, eighteen months. In July, 1863, he entered the government service as machinist, and went to Nashville. He was there at the time of the battle before Nashville. Just before that the machanics were called out to help throw up earthworks. He was discharged from the service, and returned to Chicago, where he engaged with the Illinois Central Railroad for a few months. In March, 1866, he started for Iowa, landing at Ackley the 21st of March. He went to Madison and settled with his parents, on section 10, and has since devoted his time to farming. In 1874 he built his present frame house. He was married in 1877, to Miss Margaret Jordan. They have three children—Mary J., Charles F., and Edward Jordan.

Kelsey S. Green was born in Cincinnati, Ohio, October 1, 1843. When he was fourteen years old the family moved five miles into the country. In 1865 he came to Iowa, to take charge of the farm lately owned by the Ohio Stock Breeding Company. He has already improved 2,000 of the 3,400 acres contained in the farm, which is the largest in the county. He has three hundred head of horned cattle, forty head of horses, and three hundred hogs. He has lately added to his stock two Clydesdale stallions, one of them being imported from Scotland. He was married in 1869, to Miss Ella Hageman. They have four children—Clara, John, Archie and Frank. The children are attending school at Cedar Falls.

Amos E. Hartson is a native of Pennsylvania, born in Luzerne county, March 26, 1843. When he was five years of age his parents moved to Wisconsin, and settled in Randolph, Columbia county. In 1859, he went to Woodford county, Illinois, and there was employed in farming one year. He went trapping two years, on the Illinois river, and then returned to Wisconsin, where he engaged in the pineries two winters. In the spring and fall he drove rafts down the Wisconsin and Mississippi rivers, as far as Rock Island. The years of 1863-64, he made his home with his father, who still lives on his original claim. In 1865, he came to Iowa, and bought land in Madison township, on section 20. He now has 320 acres, and lives on section 17. He married, in 1876, Samantha, daughter of Solomon Harvey, and widow of Samuel Smith. They have two children—Bert and Minnie Belle.

Wolcott Watson was born in Middlesex county, Connecticut, July 11, 1821. When twenty-one years of age, he engaged on a vessel for a whaling voyage. He went to the Pacific ocean—was absent one and one-half years. In the spring of 1844, he engaged with the Middlesex Quarry Co., at Portland, Conn. In 1848, he moved to Columbia county, Wisconsin, and bought land in Courtland township, where he built a house. In 1867 he sold out, and came to Butler county, Iowa, buying land on section 21, Madison township. He has improved the land, and in 1867 built the frame house in which he lives. In 1880 he built a barn. In 1882 attached a stable, 14x32, and a shed 24x90. He now has a farm of 270 acres. Mr. Watson commenced farming by raising wheat. He has now abandoned that, and turned his attention to stock raising. He has about thirty head of horned cattle, seven horses and about ninety hogs, and has as well appointed a place as any in the township. Mr. Watson was married in September, 1845, to Miss Albatina Polly. They have six children—Gilbert N., Elizabeth, Alvin B., Henry C., Frank W., Leveret O. Mr. Watson has been elected to offices of trust in the township, and is the present treasurer.

Wilhelm Stock, a native of Prussia, was born on the 6th of July, 1833. When seventeen years of age he engaged in a brick yard in Hanover. In 1866 he emigrated to America, and settled in Ogle county, Illinois, where he engaged in farming until 1869, when he moved to Iowa, and bought land on section 19. He has improved the land, and, in 1879, built his present home. He married, in 1860, Miss Franka Rippentrop. They have had three children but all died in infancy. They have an adopted son of Mrs. Stock's sister, whose mother died when he was two weeks old. His name is Wilhelm. Mr. Stock has filled offices of trust in the town, and was a member of the last board of trustees.

Perry Long, a pioneer settler in Fillmore county, Minnesota, was born in Somerset county, Pennsylvania, February 5, 1827. In 1840 he moved to Alleghany county, Maryland, and in 1855 he came west to seek a home, and settled in the township of Preston, Fillmore county, Minnesota, where he took government land one mile south of the county seat. He improved the land, built a house, and lived there until 1869, when he sold out and came to Iowa. He bought 340 acres of land in Madison township, on section 15, where he built a house. In 1872 he sold this farm, and bought 160 acres on section 20. He has improved this land. He married, in 1849, Miss Savilla Engle. They have seven children living — Norman, Simon, Cornelia, Marshall, Melissa, Laura, and Alvin.

Norman, son of Perry Long, was born in Alleghany county, Maryland, March 13, 1850. When but five years of age his parents moved to Fillmore county, Minnesota. In 1869 they moved to Iowa, settling in Madison. Norman received his education in the district schools of Minnesota and Iowa. He married Miss Rebecca Eleanor Hazlett. They have one child— Perry Roland. He lived with his parents until 1875, when he moved to his farm on section 7.

Samuel Smith was born in Orange county, New York, February 2, 1838; died in Madison, Iowa, March 4, 1871. When quite young his parents moved to Pennsylvania, where they lived until he was sixteen years of age, when they moved to Columbia county, Wisconsin. He married in June, 1861, Miss Samantha Harney. They had three children—Willie, Fred and Cassius. In 1865, he came to Iowa and settled in Madison, buying land on section 3, which he sold six months later, and bought on section 22. In 1869, he moved to section 16, where he died after an illness of more than two years, leaving a widow and two children to mourn his death. His widow married Amos D. Hartson, in 1876. The children lived with her.

Alvin, son of Walcott Watson, was born in the city of Columbus, Columbia county, Wisconsin, September 27, 1850. In 1867, his parents came to Iowa, and settled in

Madison. He married November 18, 1874, Miss Cornelia, daughter of Perry Long. They have two children—Clio S. and Jessie A. He now occupies his farm on section 8, and is the secretary of the school board.

George K. D. Kremer was born in Hanover, Germany, August 8, 1844. He graduated from the high school when eighteen years of age; then engaged as overseer on a large farm. In 1868, he came to America to view the country with the intention of settling. He came to Iowa and stopped at Ackley, where he had friends. In 1870, he took a trip to the Pacific Slope, visiting San Francisco, Los Angelos, Portland, Oregon. Returning to Iowa, he bought land in Madison, on section 28, and has since made that his home. He married, in 1871, Miss Louisa Sonnema. They have six children—Anna, John, Sebo, Elise, Henry and George.

Fred Pfaltzgraff was born in Alsace, September 20, 1819, where he attended school. When twenty-one years of age he joined the French Army and served twelve years, the last ten as a musician. In 1852 he was joined in marriage to Miss Magdalena Schnelberger, and in 1854 left his native land to find a home in America. On landing at New York he went to Rochester, where he was engaged in a nursery two years; then removed to Illinois and engaged in farming thirteen miles south of Chicago. In 1869 he came to Iowa and bought land on section 23, Madison township, where he was engaged in raising grain and stock. In 1879 he built his present frame house, and two years later a barn. They have had eight children, seven of whom are now living —Philip, George, Lizzie, Hellena, Fred, Charlotte and Jacob. One child died in infancy.

Friedrich Bomgardner, a native of Switzerland, born November 26, 1843. He attended school until twelve years of age and then entered a slate quarry. In 1861 he left his native land for America. On landing at New York he started for Wisconsin and rented land in Monroe, Greene county. In 1869 he came to Franklin county, Iowa, and in 1872 moved to Madison and bought land on section 8. He has improved the land, and in 1879 built the house in which he now lives. In 1869 he married Miss Fredrick Zell, a native of Germany. They have four children— John, Bertie, Amanda and Fred.

August Zell is a native of Germany, born December 7, 1834, where he attended school until fourteen years of age. In 1863 he emigrated to America. On landing at New York, he started directly for Wisconsin and there bought sixty acres of land in Dodge county of an old settler who sold to remove to Iowa. He lived there until 1868, when he sold out and came to Iowa, buying a farm near Ackley, where he lived two years, then sold out and went back to Wisconsin, buying a farm in Green Lake county. In 1876 he sold that and came to Madison township, buying land on section 5. In 1882 he built the farm house in which he lives. He married, in 1863, Miss Wilhelmina Miller. They have had one child which died when six weeks old. They have two adopted children—Mary and Herman.

Henry Messerschmidt is a native of Germany, born at Hanover, June 13, 1837. In 1867 he left his native land and came to America. On landing at New York, he went directly to Freeport, Ill., where he engaged in farming, until 1876, when he came to Franklin county, Iowa. In March, 1882, he came to Madison and bought his present farm on section fifteen. He married, April 17, 1862, Louisa Hakot. They have had four children—August, Lisa, Augusta and Lena. Mrs. Messerschmidt died Febuary 18, 1879, of typhoid fever, after an illness of two weeks. He married his second wife, Louisa Liatirits, February 26, 1880. They have had two children—Ernst and Ida.

CHAPTER XXVIII.

MONROE TOWNSHIP.

This is one of the southern tier of townships of Butler county, lying within one of the western boundary. Grundy county lies on the south; on the north, east and west are the townships of Ripley, Albion and Washington, respectively. In this, as in all the sub-divisions of Butler county, the integrity of the government survey has been maintained, embracing the territory of township 90, range 17, containing an area of about 23,040 acres.

Monroe is a prairie township, its surface is undulating. The soil is a dark loam, slightly mixed with sand; it is rich and well adapted for grazing, and all kinds of the cereals. Wheat formerly was the chief article raised, often yielding from thirty to forty bushels per acre, which was marketed at Cedar Falls. At present writing but little wheat is raised, corn, flax and hay being the chief products. There are also a few good orchards. The farmers are engaged quite extensively in stock raising. The whole township is well watered, and adapted to stock raising. Beaver creek crosses it from west to east, and, although it is generally a very moderate stream, sometimes it "gets on a tear"—to use the expression of the settlers —overflows its banks, and, in early days, it often forced the settlers to abandon their little log cabins, and seek safety on the high land. The banks of Beaver creek are skirted with timber, consisting of poplar, cottonwood, maple, walnut, ash, elm, and oak. A wet strip of land, known as Beaver slough, extends across the township from west to east, and when filled with water, presents a formidable appearance to the traveler.

EARLY SETTLEMENT.

The first settlement in this township was made in 1844, by Walter Clayton, a native of Saratoga county, New York. He had lived in Wisconsin for several years, when, in 1853, he started, with his family, for Iowa, with a wagon and yoke of oxen. After about three weeks' travel he reached Butler county, and took a claim on section 30, township 90, range 16, now known as Albion. He built a house and broke some of the land. Not understanding the law, he did not enter the land, but a man at Cedar Falls entering it notified him to leave, he, however, paid him $150 for his improvements. In April, 1854, he again started west, going about five miles, when he made a claim in town 90, range 17, now known as Monroe, on sections 21 and 28. He erected a log house on the northwest quarter of section 28, covering the roof with shakes, and, with an ax, split the boards from basswood logs to make the floor. In this humble abode the first white child in this township was born. This was also the first hotel in this part of the county. It was called the Half Way House, being half way between Cedar Falls and Iowa Falls. A basswood board, with the name "Half Way House" written upon it with red chalk, was nailed to a stake in front of the house. In 1856 he built another log house, with two rooms on the ground floor and two above. This was made a stage station that same year. An elk horn was procured and put up over the porch, and this was known as the Elk Horn Tavern. He ran this tavern until the cars passed through. He made great improvements, and in 1868 built a large frame house, where he lived until his death, which occurred in 1870. His family now occupy the homestead.

Walter Clayton was born in Saratoga county, New York, December 6, 1817, and died in Monroe, January 9, 1870. When quite young he married and moved to Walworth county, Wisconsin, being among the early settlers of that county. There his wife died, and he married his second wife, Miss Rachel Beals, of Oswego county, New York. They moved to Illinois, lived one year in Jo Daviess county, and then moved to Waupaca county, Wisconsin. In 1853 they came to Iowa and settled in Butler connty, first taking a claim in township 90 north, range 16 west. He lived there about a year, then sold his improvements for $150 and removed to township 90 north, range 17 west, making a claim on section 28. He sent $150 to DesMoines by a young man with which to enter the land, but he ran away with the money. They then saved $353, which they had made by keeping travelers, and that was stolen from them. But still they persevered and made money. He first built a log house, in which he kept hotel some years, and in 1868 erected a large frame house, where he lived until his death. He left a widow and eight children to mourn his death. The children were Henry C., Daniel W., Winfield S., Roxie A., Earnest G., Durilla R., Nettie L. and James W. Winfield S. was born June 10, 1855, and died February 6, 1871. Mrs. Clayton married Richard Clarke, September 18, 1876.

Another settler of 1854, was Solomon Cinnamon, a native of Massachusetts. He took a claim on section 36, living there for several years. He is now in Nebraska, and his family are in Parkersburg.

In September, 1864, James Monroe Caldwell and Thomas Nash, came from Henderson county, Illinois, and took claims. Mr. Caldwell, a native of Georgia, selected for his future home a portion of sections 19 and 30. Mr. Caldwell was born in Troup county, Georgia, June 10, 1826. When but six years of age his parents moved to Tennessee, and lived in McMinn and Bradley counties. At seventeen years of age he was apprenticed at Cleveland to a tanner, one Isaac Low. He served three years, and then returned to Georgia with a drove of horses; there he engaged with Robert Shugart, in Troup county, and worked at his trade one and a-half years. He then returned to Cleveland; while there he was sick for some time. Upon recovering he went to Columbus, twelve miles distant, and there worked at his trade. In 1844, he started on horseback for Illinois, stopping in Henderson county, he engaged with Anthony Howard to work at farming at twelve and one-half cents per day. He married, August 30, 1859, Miss Sarah Howard. They made their home in Henderson county, Illinois, until 1853. In September, 1854, he came to Iowa, and made a claim in Butler county, town 90, north range 17 west, now known as Monroe. In October he returned to Illinois, and there spent the winter, returning in the spring accompanied by his wife and some friends. He settled on his claim on section 30. He has improved the land, and erected a good house and barn. He is engaged to quite an extent in stock raising. Mr. Caldwell is a democrat in politics, and has been the candidate of his party for the State Legislature.

Thomas Nash took as his claim portions of sections 19, 29 and 30. In October they returned to Illinois, sold their real estate and bought stock, and in 1855 started back to their new homes. In company with them came quite a colony of pioneers, consisting of Anthony Howard and his son Robert, Jefferson G. and George W. Caldwell, Silas Bebee, and Jonathan Gee. They came with three horse and five ox-teams, bringing their cooking utensils and camping on the way. Their trip took about sixteen days.

J. M. Caldwell settled upon his present farm, on section 30, where he has erected a good set of buildings, and is in comfortable circumstances. He is one of the most prominent old settlers in the county, and we append to this a sketch of his life.

Mr. Nash settled also on section 30. In 1858 he sold his land to Zenas Aplington, and returned to Illinois; but his land, through some cause, fell back into his possession, and in 1861 he returned to Monroe township, and made this his home until his death, in 1865.

George M. Caldwell took a good farm on section 32. He was married in 1856, and in the following year sold out and returned to Illinois. In 1863 he enlisted in the Thirty-second Illinois Regiment, and in the battle of Lookout Mountain was slain among the thousand other heroes in blue.

Silas Bebee made himself at home on section 29. He made but a short stop, and is now at home in Henderson county, Illinois.

J. G. Caldwell did not make a claim.

This concludes the history of the little colony from Illinois that settled in Monroe township. The others settled in Washington township.

During the following year a number of pioneers swelled the little settlement thus started. Among the first was Nathan Lynn, a native of Maryland, who started from Illinois, in the fall of 1854, and soon reached the confines of Butler county. He first stopped at Carpenter's Grove, where he lived for a couple of weeks in his wagon; he then moved into a vacant log cabin, in the grove, and there spent the winter. In the following spring, of 1855, he pushed his way westward, and made a claim in what is now known as Ripley township. Soon after that he came to Monroe township, locating on section 2. Here he erected a log house, and commenced improvements. In 1879 he sold his farm and removed to Jefferson township, where he now resides.

He had been but a short time on section two when a native of the same State made his appearance and located on the northwest quarter of section one. This was Daniel Peterson. He remained here until 1858, when he sold out and went to Missouri. He is now living in Kansas.

Another prominent settler of 1855, was Peter McMahon, a native of Ireland, but had been living in Pennsylvania a number of years. In 1855 he started with his family, by team, for the far west. At Cleveland he took the cars for Chicago, arriving there they again took to their teams, forcing their way through the great waste of Illinois and on with their tedious journey through the eastern part of Iowa, to the valley of the Cedar and the Shellrock rivers. When near Butler Center they stopped and asked to be kept over night, but were told that they could not be accommodated. Mrs. Nathan Lynn chanced to be there at the time and told them to move on as they (Lynn's) often kept land seekers. Pushing onward they arrived at Lynn's; there they found a little log house without a floor, the front of which was chinked with chips. In the absence of a door a blanket was hung up to keep out the wolves. Here they were made heartily welcome. Mr. McMahon then made a claim on section four, and rented a cabin in Butler Centre, where they lived until he was able to erect one for himself. This was soon completed and he commenced the improvement of the farm which they still occupy, living in a neat frame house erected a few years since.

Two others who arrived in 1855, were Lycurgus P. Hazen and Recellus R. Horr, both natives of "good old York State." Hazen claimed the southwest quarter of section 24, and sold one-half of it to Horr, who was yet too young to make a land entry. Hazen was a school teacher and surveyor. He was married in March, 1857, to Miss Sarah J. Quinn. In 1858 he removed to Kansas. He is now county surveyor of Brown county, that State. Horr lived upon his farm until 1881, when he removed to Parkersburg, where he now lives. He still owns the land bought of Hazen and has purchased adjoining land.

Wells A. Curtis, a native of Ohio, was another of the pioneers of '55. He laid claim to a tract of 160 acres on section 25. In the fall of 1881 he went to Colorado, and is still there.

Joseph Embody came the same year (1855) and planted his stakes around a farm on section 3. He remained but a few years. He is now living in Montana Territory.

Just about this time quite a party put in an appearance, which broke up the monotony of early settlement. This company consisted of Thomas Conn, an Irishman, with his three sons—Joseph, Moses and Samuel—together with Joseph, William and Alexander Hopley. They stopped for a time in Delaware county, where they left their families while they came on to Butler county in quest of land. Thomas Conn made a claim on the southeastern quarter of section 1, but soon sold to his son Joseph, with whom he made his home until the time of his death. Joseph still occupies the now well-improved farm. Moses made a claim, but it had been previously entered. He is now living south of Aplington. Sam took his claim of government domain from section 12. The Hopleys, Joseph and William, made claims on sections 2 and 3. Samuel Conn did not settle upon his place, but traded for an improved farm near New Hartford. He now lives in Jefferson. They all spent the winter in Delaware county, moving to their claims in the spring. Joseph Hopley is still living on section 2. In 1866 William removed from section 3, and is now living in DesMoines.

Still another is remembered as having made his ingress into Monroe in 1855. This was Montford S. Wightman, a native of New York State. He made a claim on sections 25 and 26, going to DesMoines to enter it, and made the trip from Cedar Falls to that place on foot. He then returned to New York and spent the winter. In the spring of 1856, with his family, he moved to his wild prairie home.

He has erected a good set of buildings on section 26, his present home.

At about the same time, in 1855, James Gillard, a native of England, made a claim on section 14. In 1874 he moved to Rock county, Minnesota, where he is yet living.

Benjamin Inman was a prominent arrival of 1856. He settled on section 36, where he lived for a number of years; he is still a resident of the county.

Samuel Gillard came also in 1856; he made himself at home on section 23. In 1873 he removed to Kansas.

In 1857, W. H. Bebee made his appearance. He was a native of New York State, but came here from Polo, Illinois; a blacksmith by trade; he has since tilled the soil and followed his trade. He is now living in Aplington.

There were many other arrivals this and subsequent years, but the above is sufficient to show the class that inaugurated civilization in Monroe.

A biography of Peter McMahon, who is still living in the township, is here presented:

Peter McMahon, one of the pioneers of Butler county, was born in Ireland, June 29, 1823. In 1840 he left his native land for America. On landing at New York, he engaged in a livery stable on Brower street. In 1841 he moved to Pennsylvania, and was there employed on the Reading Railroad four years, when he went to the north branch of the Susquehanna Canal, where he worked that following winter. He was then engaged in farming in Schuylkill county a few months, when he moved to Canada, where he was employed in a quarry, getting out stone for the Welland Canal. He soon returned to

Pennsylvania, and there worked on the Erie Canal. On September 22, 1845, he married Miss Hannah Gillespie, a native of Allegheny county. That same year he bought a farm in Pamatoning township, where they lived until 1855, when they started west to seek a home. They came to Butler county, Iowa, taking government land on section 4, township 90, north range 17, west, now known as Monroe township. He there built a log house. In 1866 he built another of logs, and, in 1875, attached a large frame house to them. They have had fifteen children, ten of whom are now living—John S., Mary A., Thomas F., Peter F., Francis G., Edward, Joseph, Margaret, Stephen E., and Andrew P. Mr. McMahon is generally called Uncle Peter. He was the first treasurer of the school board.

J. H. Kerns, an early settler in the township, was born in Schenectady county, New York, June 1, 1831. In 1843 his parents moved to McHenry county, Illinois, where he received his education in the district school. At the age of twenty-one he removed to Elgin, and was there employed in a livery stable three years. In October, 1855, he came west, and through the winter engaged in a livery stable at Cedar Falls. In the spring, with a team, he took the engineer of the Dubuque & Pacific Railroad the length of the State, on the proposed route to Sioux City. At that time there was but four houses and one tent there. On his return he engaged with the Western Stage Co. to drive on the route between Dubuque and Ft. Dodge. He continued with them six years. In 1862, he went to Wisconsin to visit his mother, and there enlisted on the 5th of September, 1862, in the Thirty-first Wisconsin, Company B. They joined Sherman at Marietta, Georgia, and were present at the Siege of Atlanta. He was taken sick at Stone Mountain, Georgia, and sent to the hospital at Jeffersonville, Indiana. He re-joined the army at Fayetteville, N. C., and was with the regiment until the close of the war, and was honorably discharged, July 6, 1865. He returned to Iowa and engaged in farming in Grundy and Osceola counties until 1876, when he moved to Aplington, where, in September, 1882, he bought the Quinn Hotel property, his present home. He married in 1862, Miss Julia Bisbee, of York State. They have two children—Mary C. and Ella M.

PERSONAL HISTORY.

It can be said that a work of this kind would be incomplete without giving in detail the geneology and the personal trials and disadvantages under which some of the now prominent citizens of the township labored. This matter will be found of much interest, not only to the relatives, but also to all who are acquainted with the subjects of the various sketches. It is to be regretted that space forbids dealing with every citizen of the township in a like manner.

Thomas Nash, one of the early settlers of Monroe township, was born in Ohio, May 7, 1815, and died in Monroe township, May 1, 1865. He was brought up on a farm. When a young man he moved to Illinois, and there lived in Warren and Henderson counties. There he enlisted and served three months in the Black Hawk war. In 1834 he returned to Ohio, and there, on March 5, married Miss Isabelle Booth. They made their home in Greene county until 1847, when they moved to Illinois, where he bought a farm in Henderson county. In 1854 he came to Iowa, selecting a claim in Monroe township, and brought his family in the spring of 1855. In 1858 he returned to Illinois, remaining there until 1861, when he came again to Iowa and occupied his farm on section 20 until the time of his death. His widow is still living on the old homestead. They had fifteen children, seven of whom are now living. Mr. Nash was long connected with the Methodist Episcopal Church, had always been a consistent member, and personally identified with its interests. He held the position of class leader continually during his residence in Iowa, and held the same position many years while a resident of Illinois.

Rollin P. Mead was born in Franklin county, Vermont, April 3, 1837, where he received his education in the district school. When nineteen years of age he visited Illinois, and there worked at farming one year, when he returned to Vermont. In 1861 he came to Beaver Grove, Iowa. September 20, 1862, he enlisted in the Thirty-second Iowa, Company E, going to New Madrid, thence to Fort Pillow, then to Vicksburg, where they joined Sherman's command, and was with him on his Meridian raid. They joined Smith's command at Columbus, and was with the Red River expedition, under Banks. Mr. Mead was wounded in the arm at the battle of Pleasant Hill, Louisiana, April 3, 1864. He walked one and one-half miles, to the hospital, where his arm was amputated that evening. He arose early the next morning; on being told that the army was going to retreat, he started on foot with them, rather than be left in the hands of the enemy. After walking about two hours, he secured a ride on the cassion of a battery, and afterwards in an amunition wagon. He entered the hospital at New Orleans and remained there three weeks, when he was transferred to Memphis, and was there honorably discharged, September, 1864, and then returned to Iowa, living for some months with his brother, in Monroe. He married, February 26, 1866, Miss Selinda Goodsell, and the same year moved to section 8, where he had previously bought land. He made his home there until 1882, when he traded for land on section 20, at the same time buying his present farm on section 17, and now has about 280 acres of land. Mrs. Mead was a native of Pennsylvania, born in Wyoming county, December 21, 1848; died in Monroe township, January, 1871. He married his second wife, Miss Fannie E. Goodsell, sister to his first wife, November 11, 1873. They have two children—Herbert A., and Mary A.

Joseph Linn was born in Franklin county, Penn., July 28, 1834. He received his education at a district school, three miles from the farm. He was married in 1856 to Miss Mary Mogart. They went to St. Louis by water then took a wagon for Springfield, Ill., where they arrived with just sixty-five cents. He there found employment farming. His wife died there in 1859, aged 20 years and 5 months. His second wife was Miss Rachel Linn, whom he married February 26, 1861. In April, 1861, he enlisted at the first call for troops in the Forty-first Illinois, Company I, and participated in the battle of Fort Donelson. Soon after that he was sent back on account of disability and was appointed Provost Marshal at Camp Butler, and served until Jan. 1, 1864, when he started for Iowa overland, taking his stock with him; he was thirteen days on the way. He located on section 1, Monroe township. In 1874 he bought the northwest quarter of section 2. In 1877 he built his present home. His first wife had two children, the first—Martha Ellen—died in infancy. Andrew J. died August 26, 1878, in his nineteenth year. His present wife has been the mother of eight children, four of them are now living—Florence M., Mabel Edith., Joseph J. and Mary E.

William Wright, the son of an English soldier, was born in Woolege Barracks, County Kent, England, December 7, 1815. The spring after the battle of Waterloo his father was honorably discharged from the army and settled at Golspey. William Wright married Miss Elizabeth Dring in 1844, and soon after engaged as a shepherd. In 1855 he emigrated to America. On arriving at New York he went to Somerset Corners and there worked at farming one year, when he came to Iowa and rented land in Dubuque county. In 1865 he came to Butler county and purchased land in Monroe township, where he engaged in raising grain and stock. Here he set out an apple orchard, which is now in good bearing condition. In 1876 he bought land in Ripley, and now has nearly 400 acres. His first wife died in 1864, aged forty years. She was the mother of eight children. His second wife, to whom he was married June 24, 1868, was Mrs. Susan Petheran, daughter of John Connell, one of the early settlers of Butler county. In 1870 Mr. Wright bought ten acres of land and made it an addition to Parkersburg.

Alvinzi Straight was born in Delaware county, New York, August 10, 1821. When quite young his parents moved to Chenango county, then to Broome county, where they lived until he was fourteen years old, when they moved to Allegany county. On October 19, 1842, he married Miss Rosila Bryant, a native of Chemung county, New York. In 1843 he bought a farm in Allegany county, in the town now known as Alma, where they lived until 1865, when he sold and came to Butler county, Iowa, and bought a farm on section 2, Monroe township, his present home. In the winter of 1882-3 he built a large frame house. They have six children—Wallace R., Willard F., Waldo M., Betsy K., Wesley A. and Warren S. Willard F. enlisted, October 5, 1862, in Company H, One Hundred and Sixtieth New York Regiment, and was killed on Banks' Red River expedition, in April, 1863, when but eighteen years of age. Warren died October 5, 1859, aged four years, and Waldo died in April, 1862, aged thirteen years.

A. C. Warner was born in Strafford, Vermont, May 30, 1824. He was the son of a merchant tailor. He attended school until he was seventeen years of age, when he went to York State and engaged as clerk in a large general store in Clintonville, remaining one year when he returned to Vermont and attended school another year. In 1843, he started west and stopped for awhile in Kane county, Ill., where he was engaged for a short time as clerk in a store, after which he worked at farming. In

1845, he went to JoDaviess county, where in company with his brother, he bought an improved claim and built a large frame house. A year later he was joined by his parents. He married June 29, 1848, Miss Mary Hannah Welty, who was born at Gettysburg, Pennsylvania. In 1852, he moved to Nora, a town about three miles distant from his farm, and there engaged as carpenter and joiner. He bought town property and built an octagon brick house, lving there until 1868. In 1867, he came to Aplington, where he worked at his trade through the summer; in the fall he returned to Illinois. In the spring of 1868, he sold his property in Nora and moved to Aplington, where he lived a year. In the meantime he built his present house on section 10, on land which he had previously bought. He has improved the land, and has a fine orchard of about 300 trees. He is the father of seven children—Francis H., George A., Eunice Kate, Goodrich W., Effie J., Mahlon W. and Bessie M. Mr. Warner has a twin brother named Goodrich, now living at Nora, Illinois.

C. H. Hill settled in Monroe township in 1868. He was married that year, to Miss S. J. Brown, of Wisconsin. They have had six children, two of them are living—Frank H., and Mary J. They lost two children from that dread disease, diphtheria—Minnie, who was born February 8, 1872, died November 27, 1881, and Edwin, who was born March 1, 1874, died two days later; two other children died in infancy. Mr. Hill was born in Washington county, Vermont, June 15, 1837. At twenty years of age he started out to see the world. He first went to Wisconsin, and worked at farming in Columbia county two years. In 1861 he went to the Rocky Mountains, where he engaged in freighting two years. He then started traveling with fast horses, visiting the horse fairs in different States, until he settled in Monroe township, and bought his present farm on section 17. In 1868 he built his fine residence. He still retains his love for good horses, and has now two fine stock horses.

Michael Nugent was born in Ireland, in 1832, and made his home there until 1852, when he started for America. He engaged in railroading in Marathon, Courtland county, New York, a few months, then engaged on the Erie Canal, in Medina county. In 1853 he came to Iowa, and engaged with the Dubuque and Sioux City Railroad. In the fall of that year he went to Memphis, working that winter on the levees. In the spring he returned to Dubuque, and there married Miss Kate Flannigan. In the fall they went south, remaining there during the war. In 1864 they returned to Iowa, where he worked on the railroad at Waterloo. In 1866 he engaged to work for the Illinois Central Railroad Company, and came to Butler county. He was in their employ constantly until 1880. The first two years he lived at Parkersburg, then moved to Aplington. In 1877 he bought a farm on section 28. In 1879 the family moved on to the farm. In 1882 he built his present frame house. They have had nine children, seven of whom are now living—John, Thomas, Bridget, Patrick, Michael, Margaret and Mary. Catherine E. died in infancy. Honora died, with diphtheria, February 2, 1882, aged five years, four months and twenty-six days.

Michael Logan is a native of Canada, born in Montreal, January 1, 1846. When quite young his parents moved to New York, settled near Buffalo, and engaged in farming, living there until 1860, when they moved to Stephenson county, Illinois. In 1863 Michael went to Pennsylvania, living in the oil regions about a year, when he returned to Illinois. In 1865 he came to Iowa and spent a few months, then went to St. Louis and spent the winter, returning to Illinois in the spring. In 1869 he returned to Iowa, and bought land on section 2, Monroe township. He has improved the land, and in 1880 he built his large frame house. He married, April 17, 1867, Miss Kate Dailey, of Stephenson county, Illinois. They have had eight children, seven of whom are now living—John H., Edward P., Bernard, Agnes E., Frank T., Annie E., and Eliza A.

Charles Caul is a native of New York, born in Jefferson county, August 28, 1837. He received his education in the district schools. When twenty years of age he went from home, and engaged in farming, working for one man, in the town of Antwerp, eight years. He married, December 28, 1861, Miss Sarah Wells; after that he rented a farm. In 1869 he came to Iowa, and bought a quarter of section 34, in Monroe township, a part of which had been improved. There was a log house on the place, where he lived until 1877, when he built his frame house. He has set out a large number of shade and ornamental trees, and now has one of the most tasty farm residences in the county. Mr. Caul has two children—Archile W., and Charles Emery. He has taken a lively interest in township affairs, has filled offices of trust in the town, and is a member of the present board of trustees.

James Brook is a native of England, born in Kent county, September 25, 1828. When eighteen years of age he went to London and engaged to learn the trade of plasterer and stone mason. He worked there ten years, then came to the United States, first living at Mansfield, Ohio, one year; he then went to Foreston, Illinois, where he lived until 1870, working all the time at his trade. In February of that year he came to Iowa, and settled in the township of Monroe, Butler county, where he had bought land the fall before. He there built his present house. He has since worked at his trade in this vicinity, the most of the time in Parkersburg, while his sons have carried on his farm. He was married in 1852 to Miss Frances Ward. They have three children—Helen, Charles, and Jesse.

Henry Dreyer was born in Germany, October 19, 1852, where he received his education. In 1865 he came with his parents to America, and settled in Stephenson county, Illinois, where he engaged in farming. In 1869, he and his brother started with three teams, overland, for Grundy county, Iowa, where his father had bought land. They broke several acres, and returned to Illinois. In the fall of that year the family moved to Grundy county. In 1874 he entered Monee College, in Will county, Illinois, attending two years, when he received a certificate as teacher, and engaged teaching in the schools of Grundy county. In 1877 he came to Aplington, and engaged as clerk in G. B. White's store; was with him until 1879, when he engaged in the lumber and grain business, in company with Robert Wright, and continued with him one year. In 1880 the firm of H. Reints & Company was formed, Mr. Dreyer being one of the firm.

Edward Owens was born in Ddohhydefed Mills, Montgomery county, Parish Lanver, township Hennaith in Wales, January 13, 1776. He succeeded his father in the management of the mills, and lived there until 1834, when he emigrated to America, settling in Pike township, Bradford county, Pennsylvania, where he bought a farm. He died there September, 1861. His son, John E., was born in the same building as his father, on December 19, 1827; and was but seven years of age when his father emigrated to America. He attended school until seventeen years of age, when he engaged with his uncle, John Morris, to learn the trade of carpenter and joiner, serving three years. He then entered the office of Upjohn, the architect, in New York City, and was with him three years. He then made a contract with the Erie Railroad Company to build bridges. In 1854, he built the Catholic Church at Penn Yan, New York. In the fall of that year he built the Baptist Church at Elmira; also the Brainard House. In the spring of 1855, he made a contract with the Delaware & Lackawana Railroad Company to build bridges. In the fall of that year, in company with two other men, he made a contract to build three churches in Scranton, Pennsylvania, and one at Wilkes Barre. He married, in 1856, Miss Anna Eliza Morgan. In July of that year he came to Dubuque, and with his brother engaged as architects and builders. In 1857, he engaged with the government in the construction of the custom house. In 1858, he engaged in mining five miles northwest of Dubuque. That year he struck what is well known as the Owens Lead, which yielded over a million pounds of ore. During the war he went to Cedar Falls and engaged in the livery business, buying horses for the government. In 1863 he went to Wisconsin and bought 3,000 sheep, which he brought to Iowa and sold among the farmers; some of which he sold in Butler county. In 1865 he came to Monroe township and bought a farm on section 26. He engaged in building bridges in Butler, Hardin and other counties, in payment of which he took indemnity scrip. Mr. Owens is at present engaged in farming, stock raising and dealing in real estate. He has four children — Hazel C., Robert Dale, Etta L. and Ann Eliza.

Ottze Otthoff came to Monroe township from Grundy county in 1872. He was born in Germany, August 28, 1845. He attended school until he was fourteen, when he engaged in farming. In 1869 he left his native land for America, settling in Grundy county. In 1872 he came to Monroe township, where he bought wild land on section 6. He has improved the land, and in 1874 built his present house. In 1874 he married Miss Gesine Janssen. They have four children—John, Henry, Louis and Ottze.

P. Nichlaus came to Butler county in 1874. He was born in Germany, March 15, 1831, and in 1856 emigrated to America. He first settled near Galena, Illinois, where he rented land, and from there came to Monroe, Butler county, buying land on section 10. He now has one of the largest farms in the township. He was married in 1855, and has four children—Peter, George, Joseph and Annie.

HISTORICAL ITEMS.

The first birth in the township was a son—Winfield Scott—to Walter and Rachel Clayton, on the 10th day of June, 1855. He died February, 1871.

Burt, a son of Joseph and Annie Embody, was born on the 22d of August, 1856. The last heard of him he had gone west with his parents.

Peter F., a son of Peter and Hannah McMahon, was the next birth, born August 29th, 1856. He is still living at home.

About the next birth occurred on the 10th of August, 1858, a son—Harvey Nash—to Thomas and Isabell Nash. In January, 1879, he was married to Miss Maggie Carney. They have had one child.

The first marriage in Monroe township was celebrated on the 10th day of July, 1856, and united Richard Parriott and Lillie M. Caldwell. The bridegroom enlisted in the Union Army and was killed at the battle of Murfreesboro, on December 1st, 1863. They had three children, two of whom are still living. His widow is now the wife of Lewis McDaniel, who lives in Washington township.

On the 16th day of November, 1856, the second marriage ceremony was performed, the contracting parties in this case being George W. Caldwell and Lucinda Parriott. The year following their marriage they moved to Illinois, where he enlisted in the Thirty-second Illinois Regiment in 1863, and was killed on the 19th of October, 1863, at the battle of Lookout Mountain. His widow is now the wife of S. B. Findley, of Aplington.

On the 14th of October, 1859, there were two deaths in Monroe township—Catherine, the wife of Samuel Bisbee, aged twenty-two years; and Sarah, wife of Anthony Howard, in her seventy-second year. They were both buried on the same day in Aplington cemetery.

The next death occurred on the 27th of November, 1859, when Adelia, the wife of M. S. Wightman died.

ORGANIC.

This township was organized in 1856, and included what is now Monroe and Washington townships. James Monroe Caldwell proposed the name of Monroe, which was adopted at the first town meeting held in his house. At that meeting, an oyster can was used for a ballot box. The following persons were elected as the first officers of the township:

Robert Howard, justice of the peace; Jonathan Gee, clerk; J. Monroe Caldwell, constable; Thomas Nash, supervisor of roads; R. R. Parriott, Peter McMahon and Robert Howard, trustees.

The last annual meeting was held at the Tremont House. The officers for 1883 are as follows: Peter McMahon, Charles Caul, John P. Ahrens, trustees; Charles Fitzpatrick, clerk; Dr. E. L. Blackmore, secretary of school board; E. A. Gilman, justice of the peace; Edwin McFarland, assessor.

EDUCATIONAL.

This township was organized as a district township in 1856. The first school was held during the winter of 1856-7, in a small log shanty that belonged to J. M. Caldwell, on section 19, with L. P. Hazen as teacher. The next school was held during the winter of 1857-8, at the residence of Walter Clayton, which had formerly been used as a hotel; Morris F. Whitney being teacher.

In 1859 there were two school houses erected, one at the point of Parriott's grove, on section 30, and the other in the eastern part of what was the village plat. The one in the village was not completed until about two years later, and W. C. Garrison was the first teacher. In a few years the house was too small for the increasing attendance, and the primary class met in the bar-room of Quinn's Hotel for several terms; after that, over one of the stores. The present school house at Aplington was erected in 1877. It is a commodious structure, situated on a rise of ground, in the southern part of the village, between Ninth and Tenth streets. William Hunter was the first principal in this house, with Miss Jessie Hemenway assistant. The old school house is now owned by L. M. Swan, and is used as a granary.

The school house which was erected on section 19, was used as a school house but a few years, when it was sold to Whitney & Streeter, trustees, for the Methodist Episcopal Church; but the society would not accept it, and it was afterward bought of Mr. Whitney and moved to Aplington, where it is now used as a private residence.

The districts in the township number from one to six, the number of the village districts being four.

The first school in District No. 1 was taught in Joseph Conn's house, on the southwest quarter of section 1, by Thomas Conn. The school house was erected in 1863, or '64, on section 2, and a Mr. Hawkins taught the first school in it.

In District No. 2 the school house was erected in 1865, on the northwest corner of section 15, and Miss Sarah Smith was the first teacher. An addition was made to the house in 1877.

District No. 3 erected its house in 1872, on the western part of section 8. George C. Mead was the first teacher in the district.

The first school in District No. 5 was held in a little shanty on section 34, and next in Mr. Miller's house, on section 27. Mrs. Miller taught the first school. The school house was erected on section 27, in 1871, or 1872.

The first school in District No. 6 was taught by Wells A. Curtis, at his house, on section 25, in the winter of 1858–9, there being quite a large attendance. The following winter the school was taught in M. S. Wightman's house, by George Russell. In the spring of 1861 the school house was erected on the northeastern part of section 26, where M. F. Whitney taught the first school.

RELIGIOUS.

The early religious services were held in a building put up for a stable. The quarterly meetings were held in Mr. Caldwell's barn. The first, or among the first, sermon ever delivered in the neighborhood is a reminder of the old dissenters who posted their sentinels among the rocks. The good women of the neighborhood, having long been denied the privilege of hearing the word of God, proposed to their husbands to have a sermon from some source. The religious enthusiasm of the men had been overcome by a pressing necessity for active physical labor. A minister to perform regular service every sabbath could not be supported, consequently a discourse from a minister from Hardin county, who could come no other time than through the week, was agreed upon. Mr. Parriott mounted a horse and hied himself off for the Rev. Mr. Crippin. The signal for his return on the following day, was to be a blast from the dinner horn of Mrs. Parriott's, in order to call in the hands, busy at work in the fields. The sound of the horn on the following afternoon, apprised the settlers that their messenger had appeared in sight. Oxen and horses were turned to graze and rest, while the barefooted, ragged and dusty yeomanry assembled to hear the word of the Holy One expounded. Such a luxury could not often be indulged in, consequently the more appreciated. It is merely a single instance among thousands of a similar character which occur in the first settlement of a country.

As early as 1856, he house of Thomas Nash, on section 30, was used for religious services.

In 1860, the society that had been organized at the residence of R. R. Parriott, met at the school house in Aplington to worship—Father John Connell being the preacher. In 1869, Elder Gossard started the project of building a church, and solicited subscriptions in the fall of that year. He was succeeded by Elder Kerr. Mr. E. Y. Royce donated land, and the church was erected in 1870. It was dedicated to the worship of God, on December 18th, of that year, by Elder Kindig, of Dubuque, who came here for that purpose; Rev. Platt being the pastor in charge at the time, and Llewellyn House and Solomon B. Findley, class leaders. The church is located in Aplington, on the corner of Howard and Ninth street. The present officers are as follows: H. Barglet, S. G. Smith, O. H. Sproul, George Elliott, S. Sherin, J. G. Williams, J. M. Hedges and W. F. Barclay. Rev. G. W. Ballou is the present pastor. This society belongs to the Upper Iowa conference, and helps make up the Parkersburg circuit.

PRESBYTERIAN SOCIETY.

This denomination effected an organization in 1868-9, with the Rev. Mr. Boaz for pastor. The first elders were G. B. Smith and Julian Winnie. Meetings were held in the school house at Aplington. Rev. Doolittle was the last pastor, having charge in 1880.

CATHOLIC CHURCH.

Father Shields was the first priest to celebrate mass within the limits of Monroe township. He was located at Waverly, and had under his charge quite a number of counties in this region, where he held mass. Services were held at Peter McMahon's and other private houses. In 1872, E. Y. Royce donated to the society two lots on which to erect a church edifice. The subscription paper for the building was started by Father Murphy, and the same year the building was erected on the corner of Eleventh and Nash streets. The first mass was said in it by Father Murphy, in December, 1872.

GERMAN BAPTISTS.

The followers of this faith have at various times held services in the school house of District No. 3. Elder Schroder, of Washington township, officiated, in 1874, and was the first minister. At present the members of this society attend at the Pleasant Valley church, in Grundy county, but are about to build a church in Aplington, on lots donated them by E. Y. Royce. Rev. John Engleman is the present pastor in charge.

APLINGTON CEMETERY.

This burial ground was laid out in 1857, the land being given for that purpose by Thomas Nash. It is located on section 19. The first interment here was of the remains of Sarah A. Howard, of Washington township, in July, 1857.

TOWN OF APLINGTON.

This is the only town in Monroe township, and is situated a little west of the center, on the Beaver creek. In is on the line of the Iowa division of the Illinois Central Railroad, and is surrounded by a good farming country. It does a thriving trade.

The village was platted in the summer of 1857-8, and recorded on the 2d of February, 1858, by the proprietors, Thomas Nash, R. R. Parriott, Zenas Aplington and Theodore A. Wilson. There was at this time, one house on the site, which was put up by Charles Savage, a New Englander, who stayed but a short time.

The first store in the village was opened in 1856; Zenas Aplington put up the building and furnished the goods. It stood on the south side of Parriott street, between Ninth and Tenth. George W. Hunter ran the store for Aplington for about one year, when Chester Stilson, who is now recorder of Black Hawk county, succeeded him, and clerked for about eighteen months, when the store was closed. In 1864 Isaac Hall opened a general merchandise stock, in the same building, which he had moved. He continued until 1866, and then sold to C. S. Prince, who, in less than a year, sold out at auction.

The railroad was completed this far in the summer of 1865. A. McKey was the first station agent, with the office at his store. In 1867 the company erected a depot building, a part of which is now used for freight.

Mr. McKey came here in September, 1865. He erected the first warehouse in the village, and engaged in buying grain. In 1860 he made an addition to the warehouse and put in a stock of goods, which, after running a few months, he sold to James Dobbins. He kept the building until 1870.

In April, 1868, Alexander Chrystie opened a store on Ninth between Ellis and Parriott streets, and in 1870 moved his goods to a building on Parriott between Ninth and Tenth streets, and in 1872 he removed to his present location, on the corner of Ninth and Parriott streets. He keeps a general stock of dry goods, boots, shoes and groceries.

In June, 1868, Lynd & Wright opened a general merchandise stock in the old building on Parriott street. In 1869 they erected a building on Tenth between Ellis and Parriott streets, but sold out within a year, and the stock of goods was moved away.

Dr. Whitfield opened the first drug store in 1868. He ran it a few months and then sold to Charles Prince, who soon formed a partnership with Dr. Waterbury, but it was soon dissolved. Mr. Prince sold a part of the stock to Lynd & Wright, who moved the goods to their store on Tenth street. A. M. Whaley was the next proprietor. In 1873 he sold the stock to the present proprietor, L. M. Swan, who has added a stock of general merchandise.

In 1869 A. S. Burnham started a furniture and hardware store, and during the following year his brother, J. J. Burnham, joined him. In 1872 J. J. withdrew from the firm, and in 1873 A. S. sold the establishment to James Dobbins, who finally closed out.

William Bisbee was one of the first to enter into business in Aplington. In 1857 he opened a blacksmith shop for Zenas Aplington, working for that gentleman about one year. Since then he has run a business for himself, except the time spent in the army. At present there are three blacksmith shops in the village.

George Lefaver opened a wagon shop here in 1877, which he still runs.

Joseph Kellogg established a hardware store here in 1875, which he sold the same year to William R. Cotton. The store is now run by C. M. Cotton.

In 1868 E. Y. Royce opened a land office here, which he still continues.

In 1878 Arends & Raus opened the hardware store which is now under the proprietorship of John P. Arends.

Mr. Farland opened his grocery store in 1882. The large store of H. Reints & Co. was opened in 1880, on Parriott street. The company formed consisted of H. W. Reints, N. H. Reints, Henry and Harmon Dreyer. The Reints brothers have charge of the store, in which they keep a large stock of general merchandise. The Dreyer brothers have charge of the grain and lumber business and have an extensive trade.

As stated above the railroad was completed through Monroe township in 1865, and A. McKey was the first station agent. To show, by way of comparison, the increase of the business transacted by this office, we present a few items. For the month of January, 1868, the tariff on freight forwarded from Aplington amounted to $165.32; during the same time the tariff on freight received amounted to $15.85. Ten years afterward, for the month of January, 1878, the tariff on freight forwarded amounted to $6,341.46, and on freight received, $619.15. W. G. Bolser is the present station agent, telegraph operator and is also agent for the American Express Company. His assistant is C. A. Bozarth.

FIRST BLACKSMITH SHOP.

A blacksmith shop was erected in the village by the father of Charles Savage, and was the first in this part of the county. The shop was built of sod and had no roof, but the old pioneer withstood the weather for a short time and forged the first iron in the Beaver Valley.

HOTELS.

The first hotel in the village was built in 1858, by Mrs. Rachel Quinn, on Nash street, between Sixth and Seventh streets. In 1866 she sold to E. Y. Royce. Edward Bourns bought it in 1867, and run it a few years. It was always known as the Quinn Hotel. It is now owned by Henry Kerns, and occupied by him as a private residence

Luther Finney remodeled a store building, on Tenth street, in 1872, and opened a hotel. It changed hands two or three times, when, in 1878 or 1879, Edward Bourns bought it. His widow now runs it; it is the only hotel in the place, and is called the Tremont House.

POST OFFICE.

The post office was established in 1858: Chester Stilson was appointed postmaster, and kept the office at Aplington's store. In 1859 Harvey Quinn was appointed, and the office was moved to Quinn's hotel. He enlisted in 1861, and his sister, Maria, was appointed to fill his place. Isaac Hall, who succeeded her, was succeeded by A. McKey, and he by James Dobbins, who was succeeded by the present postmaster, Alexander Chrystie, in 1869. The office is at his store, on Parriott street.

ELEVATORS.

The first elevator in the village was erected in 1865 by Alonzo McKey, and usually goes by the name of the "Old Elevator." It is now run by C. M. Mead.

The next was erected by Wright Brothers, and has a capacity of 8,000 bushels. It was run by them until 1877, and has since changed hands several times. The Dreyer Brothers are the present proprietors.

The third was built by S. L. Kemmerer, in 1872. having a capacity of 10,000 bushels. A. M. Whaley, the present proprietor, purchased it in 1876.

Chrystie & Prince erected the fourth and last elevator in 1879. In 1880 they sold to Mr. Willis.

APLINGTON MILLS.

A number of years ago Edward Hiller came to Aplington from Hardin county, with plans laid for the erection of a mill. He bargained for forty acres of land of J. M. Caldwell, on section 20, and commenced digging a tail race; but not being able to secure the right of way on reasonable term, he finally gave up the scheme.

In 1872, John Matthews & son, of Jackson county, came here with the intention of erecting a mill. They formed a stock company, with a capital of $14,000, fixing shares at $25 each. Matthews & Son took $4,000 worth of the stock, and the balance was mostly disposed of in the neighborhood. The present mill building was erected and enclosed, its size being 32x40 feet, three and one-half stories high, with a stone basement. Before it was completed some of the stock-holders refused to pay assessments, and operations were blocked for a time. The Matthews finally sold their interest to William Dobbins, who secured a controlling interest in the stock, and then sold to A. L. Morris & Son. This firm put in three run of burrs, three reels, and a purifier, and had the mill in running order in September, 1877. They continued until September, 1880, when they sold to Dr. E. L. Blackmore and J. M. Groat; the latter sold his interest to the former; and Dr. Blackmore is still proprietor. He has added two reels, a separator, a new smutter, and a cockle machine. The mill does custom and mercantile grinding.

SPRING HILL CREAMERY.

This enterprise was started early in the spring of 1881, by Markley & Dodswell,

HISTORY OF BUTLER COUNTY.

and is located on section 20. It is conveniently arranged, and employs in the busy season, three teams to gather cream; the routes extending through Butler, Hardin and Grundy counties. During the year ending December 31, 1881, 65,840 pounds of butter were churned; and for the year 1882, amounting to 100,000 pounds.

VILLAGE NAME.

The village was named by its proprietors, when laid out, in honor of Zenas Aplington. The gentleman was never a resident of the village, but was interested financially in its welfare and growth. He was a native of Illinois, where he lived. He was a soldier in the war of the rebellion, losing his life in the service.

REPRESENTATIVE CITIZENS.

Here are presented the personal sketches of a few of the representative men of Aplington, and the matter will be found of much interest to all readers:

William Bisbee, an early settler in Aplington, was born in Herkimer county, New York, August 29, 1828. When quite young his parents moved to Delaware county. At eighteen years of age he commenced to learn blacksmithing, and worked at that trade in Delaware county until 1856. In the spring of 1857 he came to Aplington, where he was engaged to run a blacksmith shop. At the breaking out of the rebellion he responded to the first call for troops. He was mustered into the service in August, 1861, in the Ninth Iowa Regiment, Light Artillery, as chief artificer. He served through the war, participating in many engagements; was honorably discharged in October, 1865, and returned to Aplington, where he has since been engaged at his trade. He was married in 1867 to Miss Maria Quinn. They have had three children—Clara L., Edith M. and Frank A. Edith May died in infancy.

Alexander Chrystie, a prominent citizen of Aplington, was born in Franklin county, Vermont, October 4, 1830. He received his education in the district schools. When a young man he learned the carpenter's trade of his father. In the spring of 1850 he came west, locating at Portage, Wisconsin, where he worked at his trade until fall, when he went to California, and there worked at his trade. In the following spring he returned to Wisconsin. In 1861 he raised a company of volunteers, of which he was elected Captain. He was discharged, in April, 1864, and engaged in mercantile business. In 1865 he returned to Wisconsin. In 1866 he came to Waterloo, and engaged in mercantile business for two years. In 1868 he came to Aplington, and opened his store. He was appointed postmaster in 1869, an office which he now holds. He has taken a lively interest in county, as well as town affairs. He was elected county commissioner in 1870, an office which he held nine years. He married, in 1855, Miss Elizabeth Hogan. They have five children—Alice, Eliza, John A., Isabelle May, and Clara A.

Solomon B. Findley, a prominent member of, and class-leader in the Methodist Church was born at Green, Monroe county, New York, Aug. 25, 1837. His father, whose name also was Solomon B., was a practicing physician. He was born at Tolland, Conn., Sept. 13, 1788, and graduated from the Hartford Medical College, at Hartford, Conn. He commenced practice in Livingston county, New York; from there he came to Monroe county, where he died, June 6, 1843. Solomon B., Jr., made his home with his mother until 1857, when he went to Illinois. He attended Marengo College eight months; he then entered the Garret Biblical Institute, at Evanston, Ill., to study for the ministry, but his health failed and he went to Union, Ill., where he engaged in mercantile business, until 1865, when he sold out and came to Iowa, engaging in the same business at Tipton, Cedar county, until 1869, when he again sold out and came to Aplington. He bought land in Grundy county, near Aplington, which he has improved. He has since bought property in Aplington and has bought and improved land in Butler county. He was married June 13, 1876, to Mrs. Lucinda Caldwell. They have had three children. The oldest one—Lizzie P.—was born Dec. 1877, and died Jan. 26, 1882, of diphtheria. Mr. Findley's mother made her home with her son at Aplington, until the time of her death, Oct. 29, 1877, at 77 years of age. His sister Polly makes her home with him.

Charles S. Prince was born in Cumberland county, Maine, seven miles from Portland, July 7, 1828. When but two and one-half years old his father died, and when four years old his mother moved with her children to Franklin county, where he lived until eighteen years of age, when he went to Lowell, Massachusetts, and found employment in the Middlesex Mill for eight months. He then engaged in the Lowell Machine Shops one year, when he went to Virginia. He was there employed as overseer on plantations, excepting in the winter seasons, when he engaged in getting out ship timber. In 1853 he went to California via the Nicaraugua route. He there engaged in mining and fluming in Tuolumne county for four years, when he returned to Maine and was married there, February 9, 1858, to Miss Elizabeth Allen, of Franklin county. The next fall he bought a saw mill there, which he ran for two years. He then sold it and engaged in buying stock and shipping it to Portland until 1865, when he came to Iowa and settled in Aplington. He bought real estate, engaged in mercantile business for a short time, and built several houses which he has since sold. In 1878 he built his present residence. Mr. Prince has been quite a prominent man, and has filled offices of trust in the town. He has two children living—Birdie S. and Eva. Mr. Prince met with great trouble, which was keenly felt, in the loss of his only son, Walter, who was a promising young man. Walter H. was born in Franklin county, Maine, December 28, 1860, and died in Aplington, November 24, 1877. Their first child, Cora, died in infancy.

G. B. Smith was born in England, November, 1805, where he received a good education. He studied medicine with the intention of practicing. When about twenty years of age he came to America, and settled in New Jersey, where he engaged in teaching. He was married there to Miss Eliza Prall. They had seven children, six of whom are now living—Sheridan, Sarah M., Jane H., Mary P., Lydia F., and Charlotte A. His children were all teachers. The daughters are now married, and live in Butler county, while the son is engaged in mercantile business in Traer, Tama county. In 1851 Mr. Smith returned to England, and visited the world's fair at London, returning to New Jersey, after an absence of about six months. In 1853 he moved to Madison, Wisconsin, and taught there in the city schools. In 1861 he moved to Illinois, living in Lee and Ogle counties until 1866, when he moved to Aplington, where he has since been engaged in teaching and practicing medicine. Mrs. Smith was born in Hunterdon county, New Jersey, August, 1809; died in Aplington, in June, 1882. Mr. Smith makes his home with his children.

John P. Arends settled in Butler county in 1870. He is a native of Germany, born June 1, 1853. When fourteen years of age he came to America with his parents. They settled in Stephenson county, Illinois. In 1870 they moved to Iowa, settling in Monroe township, on section 34. He engaged in farming in this neighborhood till 1875, when he went to Ackley, and engaged in selling farm machinery. In 1876 he came to Aplington, and engaged with John Rays in the same business. In 1878 they added a stock of hardware to their business. In January, 1883, they dissolved, and Mr. Arends now runs the business. He married, in October, 1878, Miss Greetje. They have two children—Arend, and Gertie. Mr. Arends is a member of the present board of trustees, and is village assessor.

Henry W. Reints, of the firm of H. Reints & Company, was born in Germany, May 31, 1851. His early life was spent in acquiring an education. In 1868 he came to America, and settled in Illinois, where he was employed in farming until January, 1872, when he started back to Germany. The September following he returned to America with his parents. They came to Iowa, and settled in Butler county, Washington township. Two years later, he entered Monee College, at Will county, Illinois. After six months of study he was examined, received a teacher's certificate, and commenced teaching in the schools of Grundy county. He went to Nebraska and taught two terms. In 1880 he came to Aplington, and engaged in mercantile business, as a member of the firm of H. Reints & Co.

William R. Cotton, one of the early settlers of Butler county, was born in Onondago county, New York, May 13, 1813. His father was a blacksmith, and he early learned that trade, of which he was a master. In 1853, he came west to seek a home, and took a claim in Black Hawk county. He brought his family in the fall of 1854. In 1855, he went to Janesville, Bremer county, where he worked at his trade one year. In 1856, he went to Willoughby, in Butler county, where he bought a farm, which he traded the next year for property in Shell Rock, where he engaged in keeping hotel and in the mercantile business until 1861, when he sold out and went to Waverly. After this he engaged in farming in Jefferson awhile, then came to Butler Center and engaged at his trade three years. He then went to Albion and tried farming again. In 1873, he moved his shop from Butler Center to Aplington, and there worked at his trade until 1875, when he bought out a hardware store here and carried on the business until the time of his death, which occurred July 12, 1881. He was married at Port Gibson, New York,

November 4, 1835, to Miss Aurelia Harris, of Wayne county.' Mr. Cotton filled offices of trust in the county, and was the last county assessor. Mrs. Cotton now makes her home with her son, Charles, at Aplington. Charles M. was born in Niagara county, New York, May 11, 1838. His younger days were spent acquiring an education, after which he engaged in teaching. In 1854, he came west with his parents. In 1861, he enlisted under Captain M. M. Trumbull, in Company I, the first company organized in Butler county; joined the Third Iowa, and was with Grant in his Tennessee Campaign, and at Vicksburg; was with Sherman on his Meridian Raid; in Banks' Red River Expedition; joined the Seventeenth Corps under McPherson at Memphis; was in the Atlanta Campaign, and with Sherman in his March to the Sea; thence to Washington, and was honorably discharged the 26th of May, 1865. He returned to Iowa and engaged in farming. He married December 25, 1865, Miss Louise, daughter of Lorenzo Perry, one of the early settlers of Albion. They had one child, which died in infancy. In 1882, he came to Aplington, where he succeeded his father in the hardware business.

George Lafaver was born in Ontario, Canada, January 26, 1843. When but a boy he was employed in blacksmithing, and followed that trade seven years, but his eyes failed him, and he went to Illinois, where he engaged to learn the wagon-maker's trade, at Oregon, Ogle county, working there two and one-half years, when he returned to Canada, and there engaged in farming two years. He then resumed his trade, at Gananoque, two and one-half years, when he went to Brookville, and engaged in a car-shop one year, then worked in an agricultural implement factory one year, after which he again tried farming. In the spring of 1877, he came to Iowa, and stopped in Butler Center. In the following December, he came to Aplington, where he opened the wagon shop which he now runs. In 1878 he bought land in the east part of the village, and built a house; living there awhile, he sold the land, and moved his house nearer to the business portion of the town. In 1882 he bought a house and four lots, on Nash street, his present home. He married, in 1870, Miss Lucy A. Cochrane. They have four children—Harvey M., Herby F., Hiram W., and George R.

Ferdinand E. Dahn, a native of Germany, was born August 15, 1845. At fifteen years of age he was apprenticed to a harness-maker to learn the trade, and served three years. When twenty years old he joined the German army; was in the war between Germany and Austria; participated in several battles, serving three years, and then resumed his trade. In 1870 he came to America; located in Stephenson county, Illinois, where his brother was living, and there engaged in farming. In the spring of 1875 he came to Aplington and worked at his trade. In 1876 he worked at Ackley. In March, 1877, he returned to Aplington and started a harness shop in the building first used in this town for a store, where he still carries on a successful business. In 1878 he bought property on the town site; built a barn in 1879, and in 1882 erected the neat frame house where he now lives. In 1877 he married Mrs. Minnie Lichtenburg. They have two children—Cora and Frank.

Charles S. Root, deputy sheriff of Butler county, was born in Orleans county, New York, January 27, 1827. In the fall of 1858 he moved to Marquette county, Wisconsin, taking government land. In 1854 he sold out, and the following year came to Butler county, Iowa, and bought 1,080 acres of land on sections 10, 11 and 12 of Albion township. In 1857 he moved to the east end of Beaver Grove, where he bought 360 acres of land, which he still owns. In 1858 he was elected town clerk of Beaver. He was appointed enrolling clerk to enroll the State Militia, in June, 1862, and in the fall of that year was appointed deputy provost marshal for Northwestern Iowa, with Fort Dodge as headquarters. In 1864 he returned to his farm. He was appointed deputy sheriff in Jan., 1880, and is now serving his fourth year. In 1851 he married Miss Mary Burgess. They have three children—George W., Emma J. and Katie E. Mr. Root now lives in Parkersburg.

CHAPTER XXIX.

PITTSFORD TOWNSHIP.

The first settlers in what now constitutes Pittsford township were John Boylan and James Matterson Park, who, together with their families, settled on portions of sections 13, and 24. Both families were former residents of Bureau county, Illinois. They located here in the fall of 1852.

The next settlers were Samuel Moots and family, who settled, and built a cabin in the eastern part of the township, some time in the winter of 1852-3. At that time there had been no entries made of government lands in the township, and the probability is that no entries had then been made in the west half of the county; but at the same time there were what was called settlers' claims, which were generally made by laying a foundation, constructed of four logs, and sometimes, in addition, the claimant's name cut on a tree. There were some such claims made soon after Boylan and Parks settled, but mostly by transient men, who soon returned to the haunts of civilization, and the bosoms of their families, perhaps never to return.

The first prairie broken was in 1853, on land now owned by James Logan, on section 13. Some time in 1853, a man by the name of Maxwell settled in the township, making his home with Mr. Parks and family, who, it is believed, entered forty acres of land on section 24, in the spring of 1854. Maxwell left for other parts, and has never returned.

During the winter of 1852-3, there were large numbers of buffalo and elk in and about what is called Upper, and Lower Boylan's Grove. Boylan and Parks embraced the opportunity to kill large numbers of both, and, so far as meat was concerned, fared sumptuously every day. Buffalo and elk never were so plenty afterward, and, since the winter of 1856-7, none are known to have been in the township. Up to that time, elk were tolerably numerous and deer very plenty; but during that winter snow fell until it was something over three feet deep on the level, and a crust on the top strong enough to bear up a man on foot, but not sufficiently strong to carry a horse.

The condition of the snow, and the crust upon it, was such that a deer or elk, endeavoring to run on the snow, would break through the snow crust, which at once impeded their progress, and made them fall an easy prey to hunters, dogs and wolves. Consequently, nearly all the deer were destroyed that winter. There was, by actual count, thirty-two deer killed at what is known as Jamieson Grove, within the space of two miles up and down the West Fork of the Cedar. The elk were also fearfully slaughtered, not being able to run on account of the snow, one man being enabled to kill one with a hatchet, without the aid of dogs or gun. Since that time but very few deer, and no elk, have been seen in the township. Wolves, said to be plenty wherever deer are, have not been so numerous since the extermination of the deer and elk. It may be mentioned here that in addition to the destruction of the deer and elk, there was another cause for a decrease of the wolves in the township, which was, that in the latter part of the winter of 1856-7, or in the beginning of the winter of 1857-8, two men, Jacob Yost and Joseph Riddle, killed a large number of them by the use of strychnine, which depleted their numbers very much, but still they were not entirely annihilated, and now the prairie wolves are becoming more numerous than is desirable. It is not certain that any of the species of the wolf called timber wolves have ever been seen in the township. Among other wild game found here at an early day was bear, lynx, gray foxes, wild cats, gray and black timber squirrels, pocket gophers, gray and striped gophers, ground hogs, chipmunks, rabbits, weasels, raccoons, otter, beaver, muskrats, minks, prairie chickens, pheasants, partridges, wild turkeys, geese and ducks, together with numerous other beasts and fowls. Bear, elk, deer and otter seem to be almost extinct, but the other wild game, both beast and fowl, remain in greater or less numbers.

But to return to the first settlers, John Boylan, one of the first settlers named, was a midde aged man of some energy, and quite a good talker. He was married to Miss Haunk Demoss, and raised quite a numerous family, who as they became old enough, all in turn married. On the death of his wife, some years subsequent to his first settlement here, he re-married with a widow Haskins, which proved to be rather an unhappy marriage, when after a short time they separated, and he and his sons and sons-in-law, together with their families, all removed to Kansas.

James M. Park was married to Eliza Boylan, an only sister of John Boylan.

HISTORY OF BUTLER COUNTY.

Park was a very quiet, civil, inoffensive, good citizen, who also raised a large family, sold out his farm, and all removed to Kansas.

Samuel Moots and family were from Indiana. Moots married Miss Molly Oxford, a sister of Eliss Oxford, and Mrs. Betsy Rush, both lately deceased. The Moots family were very civil, quiet citizens. The oldest daughter, Sarah Ann, married Jonathan Armstrong. This probably was the first marriage in the township, as it must have taken place in the fall or winter of 1853. John Moots, the oldest son inter-married with a daughter of Thomas Hewitt, and resides near Bristow, in West Point township, and is the oldest settler that now remains. Marion, the second son, is somewhere in Iowa, and is still unmarried. The second daughter, Martha M. Moots, married James W. Boylan, is the mother of a large family, and has also the honor of being the oldest settler now residing in Pittsford township.

The next settler was Isaac Boylan, who came, together with his family, sometime during July or August, 1853.

With Isaac Boylan's family came Jonas Demoss, a brother of Mrs. Boylan. He was a single man, has never been married, and is still a member of the family. Isaac Boylan's three daughters, by his first marriage, were all married; one to John Wilkes, one to Isaac Neal, and the youngest, Hannah, to Serling Gibson; all of the daughters are now dead. The oldest son, William, married a daughter of Barnet Neal, and now resides in Kansas.

W. R. Jamison and family were the next to settle in the township. His family consisted of a wife and five children, four boys and one girl; which has since increased by the birth of three girls and one boy. One of the girls died when a few weeks of age. He has five boys and three girls now living, and all married, leaving him and his wife where they first started, without family, under the disadvantage of being older. Early in July, 1853, Mr. Jamison, in company with two other gentlemen seeking location, came to Boylan's Grove, which is a tract of timber containing, at that time, about one thousand acres, and a smaller grove about one mile north, located in Pittsford township. At that time there had been no entries of land made in Pittsford, and probably not in the west half of Butler county. It is true that all the land in both groves, and, in fact, all the land in the township, was open to entry, not even a homestead or pre-emptom having been made, but as the settlers then in both groves had, as they said, claims for themselves, and also claims for all their relatives and friends, both present and absent. The settlers were then expected, before making entries, to buy the claims, either real or imaginary, before making an entry, under pain of an unpleasant reception into the little community. Mr. Jamison was not anxious to seize either horn of the dilemma, and being informed by John Boylan that he knew of a grove of good timber near by, where there were no claims or homesteads, he concluded to investigate the matter. So, in company with Mr. Boylan, and the two other land lookers mentioned, he set out to view the grove referred to, which was afterward called Jamison's Grove. The day proved to be wet and disagreeable, but still they persevered.

Mr. Boylan, not being able to read or write, could give no information in relation to numbers or description of the land. Mr. Jamison was obliged to find the traces of the lines as blazed through the timber, by which means he was enabled to find the lay of the land and also the corner-post at the northeast corner of section 19. This corner-post being recently placed he was enabled to get the numbers in a satisfactory manner, of all the land he wished to locate at that time, being 320 acres—120 acres in section 19, and 200 acres in section 20. The land selected proved to be nearly all good timber, there being, perhaps, corners of prairie land on it amounting to 20 acres. Mr. Boylan seemed somewhat anxious to have Mr. Jamison not locate on Boylan's Grove unless he would purchase claims, and was happy to have him make his selections where he did, which was perhaps a fortunate circumstance for both parties, as the timber on the premises proved to be quite valuable. On the 11th day of August, following, (1853,) Mr. Jamison made entry of the half section of land above mentioned, at the land office at Des Moines, Iowa, being the first original entry of land in the township, and probably in the west half of the county, the dividing line between the Dubuque and Des Moines land districts being on the range line between ranges 16 and 17, and it is believed that all entries made in the county had been made in the Dubuque land office. About the first of September, 1853, W. R. Jamison, with his family, moved from Buchanan county, Iowa, into this township, and stopped in a log cabin on the land now owned by M. D. L. Niece, where he remained until the next March, when he removed into a log cabin which he had built on section 19; he afterward sold it to John Harlan, Sr., in 1855.

When Mr. Jamison came into the township he brought the first span of horses and two-horse buggy, harness, and also the first two-horse covered carriage that was brought into the township. He likewise brought a fine stock of Berkshire hogs with him. Some of the earlier settlers fairly hooted at him for bringing hogs, as there was so much wild meat which could be so easily obtained that he would not need any pork. No doubt they had a vivid recollection of the large number of elk, buffalo and venison so easily obtained the previous winter. It so happened, however, that the buffalo and elk stayed away, and even the deer were rather scarce that winter, so that those settlers who hooted at their being any necessity for the use of pork had to be satisfied most of the time to feed on opossum, raccoon and such small game as they could obtain. During the winter Mr. Jamison sold his covered carriage for cash and traded his span of horses for two yoke of oxen. In the spring he had a man by the name of Hitchcock to make him a breaking plow, and with his oxen and plow he broke 65 acres of prairie ready for the crops the next spring.

In the spring of 1854, Rev. Richard Merrill, his brother Joseph, Ephriam and James W. McKinney, Henry A. Early and Seth Strong all came into the township and entered land. They all moved their families in at once, except the Merrills. While here at that time Rev. Richard Merrill, being a Presbyterian minister, preached at the house of John Boylan the first sermon ever preached in the township. All either bought or built cabins as soon as possible after stopping.

About the month of May, 1854, James Woods and family moved in, from Strawberry Point, in this State. Mr. Woods camped out until he broke prairie and planted corn. He then went to work, and built a log cabin. After having resided in the township several years—raising a large family of boys and girls—and after all the daughters had married and left the homestead, Mr. Woods and his wife, by mutual agreement seperated, he keeping the property, and paying her a certain amount in money. In the course of a year Mr. Woods sold the farm to a Mr. Griffin, and finally went to Kansas, where he soon after died. The widow and her two sons, neither of whom are married, still live in the township, respected members of society.

About the month of May, or June, 1854, a German, by the name of Kniphals, came into the township, and entered a quarter section of land. His family consisted of one daughter, Catherine, and one son, Henry. He worked at smithing; built a cabin, and improved his land. In 1855, he sold his land to Mr. Ahrens, who moved on it with his family. Mr. Kniphals entered another 160 acres of land, which he improved some, and then sold it to R. W. Butler, and removed to Kansas, where he soon after died.

In the winter of 1854–5 a German named Peterson, with his wife, moved into the township, but in about a year they removed to Cedar Falls.

About July, 1854, Comfort Williams and a woman he lived with came from about Cedar Rapids and settled in the township. Williams had some children that came with him, among whom was a grown-up daughter. A few months after Williams came Greenbury Luck, also from Cedar Rapids, who soon after married Miss Williams. The wedding took place at Clarksville, and the marriage license was the second one issued in the county. Mr. Williams and the lady that lived with him were guests at the wedding, and perhaps thinking it altogether proper and right, procured a license and were joined in marriage the same day. These were the first and second marriages of persons living in the township. Williams and his wife soon after removed to Cedar Falls. Luck and his wife still reside in the southern part of Butler county.

In the early settlement of the township the Winnebago Indians frequently passed through Boylan's and Jamieson's groves in going to and from James Newell's, on the Cedar river, to Hewitt's, at Clear Lake, in Cerro Gordo county, both Newell and Hewitt being great favorites with the Indians at that time. Next came the Sioux Indians, who traveled through on about the same routes. Of late years they have not put in an appearance. The Misquaka tribe, who have a reservation in Tama county, generally come through about once a year, hunting, fishing and begging. The Indians mentioned have always been civil and inoffensive when in and passing through the county.

About the first of July, 1854, some ill feeling existing between the Winnebago and Sioux Indians, one of the Sioux shot and killed a boy belonging to the Winnebago tribe, at Clear Lake, in Cerro Gordo county, Iowa; the boy was on horseback and dropped off dead, which appears to have ended the trouble. Nothing further occurred between the tribes, only that thereafter, the Winnebagos seem to have abandoned their former haunts and routes to the Sioux, who since, seem also to have quit this section of the country. The killing of the boy at Clear Lake got up an excitement which soon created a panic, the citizens of this township not escaping. When taking counsel of their fears, they banded together and moved in a body to Janesville, Bremer county, where defensive works were immediately erected by way of a slab stockade. W. R. Jamieson and family and the family of James Woods only remained in the township, Woods at the time being away at mill. It was soon ascertained that the scare was groundless, but in the meantime the water had risen in the Shell Rock river so that it could not be forded, there being no bridges across the stream at that time; consequently the refugees were obliged to wait several days for the water to subside in the river, so that they could return to their abandoned homes. During the stay of our worthy absentees at Janesville, Orson Rice, mentioned in the general history of this county as a lawyer, first made his appearance among them and interested them by bragging on his rifle and other things, and shooting at a mark at eighty rods, having a dry goods box for a target. Rice came into the township with the returning absentees. On coming here he either preempted or entered eighty acres of land, which Nat. G. Niece afterward owned and on which he lived and died. Parting with that land, Rice entered another eighty acres and built a cabin on it and lived there for a short time, when he went to Clarksville and read law with M. M. Trumbull. [See bar history.]

During the latter part of 1854 several other parties settled in the township, among whom were David and Elizabeth Rush. Mrs. Rush entered a considerable amount of the public domain. Her husband also made some entries of land. Previous to her death Mrs. Rush had accumulated quite an estate. David Rush was a good citizen. He has been dead several years.

Thomas Jackson, who married a sister of James W., and E. McKinney, came into the county in 1854. He was something of a nimrod, and made the principal part of his living by hunting, trapping and fishing. They had no children. In the course of a year or two she died, and he left. There also was a family named Frazier came in, but only remained a short time. A family by the name of Calkins moved in. Mr. Calkins soon died, and the family left. The death of Mr. Calkins was the first to occur in the township. Perhaps the death of Mrs. Jackson, above named, was the third.

During this year, James W. Boylan, Wm. H. Boylan, Asa Boylan, and Thomas and Nelson Demon, came into the township. James W. Boylan still remains in the township. William H. Boylan volunteered, and died in the military service. Asa Boylan, with his family, has removed to Kansas. Thomas Demon married, and still remains, one of the good citizens of the township. Nelson Demon came in 1853, at the time Isaac Boylan and family came. He married Miss Surfus, and lives in West Point township.

It is believed that George W. Parker and his family came here in the summer of 1855. His family consisted of himself and wife, four grown sons, three grown daughters, one or more younger daughters and a minor son named Greene. They came from Ohio. The old gentleman built a house and resided where Samuel K. Hazlett now lives, bordering on Pill Town (Boylan's Grove). His oldest son, Dan, was married when he came here; the ext son, Asakel, married Achsah Needham; Iva, the fourth son, married Miss Caroline Brotherton, from whom he was afterward divorced; George, the third son, never married; Mary E., the second daughter, married O. C. Smith, and has since died; Aurilda, the third daughter, married one Levi Cronkhite, and is now dead. They all sold their property, except Mary E., who remained here. She died while on a visit to Kansas. All the others moved to Kansas, where the father and two daughters died.

During the winter of 1854 Hiram Brotherty and family moved in and entered land. He had some means and was industrious, besides being a good manager, and as a consequence prospered. Some years afterward he built a new house on the Franklin side of the county line and moved into it, thereby becoming a resident of Franklin county, where he now resides.

The Wickham's, Lester and Abisha, together with their wives and children, came, perhaps, in 1855. Lester and his wife had two children—a daughter named Hetty and a son named Irwin. Hetty married Nathan Ball before coming here, and they accompanied the Wickhams. Abisha and his wife raised one son, Thomas, who is now married and a respectable citizen. Irwin, Lester's son, died in early manhood. The wives of both Lester and Abisha are dead, and both men are now widowers and stay with Thomas. The Wickhams are good, honest, civil citizens. They located south of the South Fork, and were almost isolated for some time, not having any near neighbors; but of late years quite a number of Germans and others have improved farms near by, and now there is quite a settlement.

Charles F. Kleever, a German, was the first to settle there after the Wickhams. He is a good citizen, and has a very intelligent and industrious family. Mr. Kleever has been very industrious in the pursuit of happiness.

About the month of May, 1855, John M. Nichols came and settled in the township, but prior to that, during the winter, or perhaps fall of 1854, Elias Oxford came from the State of Indiana and settled in the township. Oxford was a brother of Mrs. Rush, and an uncle of John M. and William R. Nichols, also of Nancy J. Getchels. He and his wife brought up a large family, who have all married. Nearly a year since, Oxford died, his widow still survives and stays with one of her sons-in-law. John M. Nichols came from Indiana to Illinois, where he stopped one winter, moving here the next spring. He is a fair-minded intelligent man and has held the office of constable, justice of the peace and county supervisor, and now holds the office of road supervisor. Being economical and industrious he has accumulated considerable property, and now lives at ease on one of the best farms in the township. He and his wife have raised a large family, most of whom are grown to maturity and a majority of them married.

Sometime during 1855 or 1856, Ben. C. Needham came into the township and became the owner of all of section 9. Later in 1856 he moved in with his wife and children. Soon after, his father, B. C. Needham, Sr., moved here, also his uncle, Azariah Needham, and a brother, Silas T. Needham, who all became settlers. Ben. C. Needham, Jr., soon after divided up his section of land and conveyed a portion to B. C. Needham, Sr., a part to his uncle Azariah, a part to Samuel Overturf, a portion to Rev. H. H. Janes, and 160 acres to his son Perin O. Needham.

P. O. Needham, son of B. C. Needham, Jr.; R. H. Needham, son of Azariah Needham, and W. H. Boylan, son-in-law of Azariah, all volunteered, and went into the military service, on the part of the Union, during the rebellion. Both R. H. Needham and W. H. Boylan died in the service of their country, but P. O. Needham, at the end of his term, came home all right. B. C. Sr., and Azariah Needham, after living to a good old age, have both died. Benjamin C. Needham, Jr., still resides on, and owns a portion of his original purchase, where he is seemingly contented and happy.

Silas T. Needham and wife are comfortably situated, on a good farm, which they own, in the township, and have reared a respectable family, who are all married but one daughter. Both of these parties are mentioned at length elsewhere.

In the latter part of June, or early in the month of July, 1855, John Harlan, Sr., moved from Ohio into the township, and became a settler. His family consisted of his wife, four sons and one son-in-law, five daughters and one daughter-in-law. Mr. Harlan, Sr., bought eighty acres of land, partially improved, on which there was about thirty acres of timber, of W. R. Jamieson, on which he resided. He also furnished money to enter his three oldest sons eighty acres of land each, also the same amount to his son-in-law, Samuel A. Dearmaun, and entered eighty acres for himself. Nearly all his children settled near him. These parties are treated at length in this chapter.

Some time, perhaps in 1856, W. R. Nichols came into the township. He soon became the owner of considerable real estate, and in a few years married Miss Oxford, and settled down to farming, in which occupation he has ever since been engaged, except that he has, occasionally, taught school. He is now well situated in life, owning considerable real and personal property. He is principally engaged in farming, raising and dealing in stock. He has held several minor offices, such as constable, township clerk, town trustee, township assessor and justice of the peace.

After 1855 Ancil Durank and M. D. L. Niece came from Ohio and settled here. M. D. L. Niece was a single man, and has never married. He has a good education, has taught school several terms in the township, and has held several small offices, such as township assessor, and, perhaps, clerk, and was once appointed to fill a vacancy in the office of county superintendent of schools. He was also once elected to the office of county surveyor.

John Harlan

Ancil Durand's first wife was a sister of Nat G. and M. D. L. Niece, and was a lady of fair mental culture; had a good common-school education. She raised a family of two children—two girls and two boys. Both the boys are unmarried and reside about Bristow. Soon after coming into the township he was elected justice of the peace, running in opposition to Orson Rice, and the contest was a lively one. He has subsequently been elected several times to the same office in the township. He has also held the office of supervisor of roads and that of township clerk, and at one time was elected county judge. He is now holding by appointment the office of marshal of the incorporated town of Bristow.

Seth Strong, one of the settlers of 1854, did not remain in the township long. His first wife dying, he re-married about the winter of 1855-6 with Mary Canon, a widow and one of the Demoss sisters, and finally went to Black Hawk county, where he and his wife are supposed to still remain.

Henry A. Early and his wife remained in the township until the fall of 1882, when, having sold out his farm near Bristow, he bought another farm in West Point township, where he removed and soon afterward died. His oldest son, W. F. Early, married, and now resides in La Porte, Black Hawk county. He has held the office of township assessor, justice of the peace and some other offices in West Point township. Thomas M. Early, the second son, is noted at length elsewhere. John, the third son, has recently been married. Orra, the fourth son, married a Miss Hall. Tooker, the fifth and youngest boy, still remains unmarried. They had but one daughter—Elizabeth, who married John Hewit. The old gentleman and lady were always looked up to, and were very much esteemed and respected. He, in his time, was elected to several township offices.

In the spring of 1866, Samuel Overturf and family moved into the township. His wife died a few years ago. He still remains a widower, resides in the township, and is a respected member of society.

Soon afterward James Logan removed here with his family, consisting of his wife, one son and four daughters. All his daughters are married—Eliza J. to John Jamison, Bina to L. J. Austin, Martha M. to Ross Jamison, and Lizzie to Jasper M. McCormick. David, the only son, unfortunately, was deprived of his eyesight when about fourteen years of age. He is unmarried and stops at home with his father's family.

Soon after Logan came, the widow Powell and two daughters moved from Buchanan county into this township. The old lady is dead. One of the daughters, Mary Jane, married Thomas Demoss. The other daughter, Rachel Ann, remains single and resides with her sister, Mrs. Demoss.

H. H. Janes came into the township at an early day. He was a preacher of some prominence—a Second Adventist. He took well with the people, and prospered for a time, until the decease of his wife. He afterward married a widow, who was also a preacher, when things did not go so well with nim, and soon after they separated. Her present whereabouts is not known to the writer. It is understood that the elder is soon to remove to Nebraska. In 1856, '57 and '58, many others came to the township.

ORGANIZATION.

At the first county election W. R. Jamison drove an ox team to Clarksville, to attend the election, and was the first resident of Pittsford township to cast a vote. In February of 1855, John Palmer, county judge, made an order making all the west half of the county, except, perhaps, the territory now embraced in Coldwater township, into one township, to be called Ripley, and appointed W. R. Jamison to call an election for the purpose of electing township officers, and organizing said township, which was done in April of that year, the election being held at the house of Henry A. Early, in what is now Pittsford. There was a full board of township officers elected; Henry A. Early and W. R. Jamison being elected the two first justices of the peace in the township. In the subsequent divisions of the county into townships, the name of Ripley was given to a township south of West Point, and this township received the appellation of Pittsford, by an order of County Judge Converse, at the suggestion of Azariah Needham and other Vermonters.

The first lawsuit in the township was before Henry A. Early, justice of the peace, wherein W. R. Jamison was plaintiff, and Orson Rice defendant; judgment in favor of plaintiff, for which decision Rice so abused the justice that he resigned his office.

SCHOOLS.

In the winter 1854-5, application was made to the school fund commissioners of Butler and Franklin counties for a school district, or rather a sub-district to be formed of the west half of Pittsford and the east half of Ingham township, in Franklin county, which was granted. In the meantime another sub-district had been applied for and formed, including the east half of Pittsford and the west half of West Point township, which was called Sub-district No. 1. The sub-district in the west half of the township was named No. 2. In the spring of 1856, a log school house was erected in each of the sub-districts. In sub-district No. 1, Martha J. Niece taught a summer school and Miss Melissa M. Overturf a summer school in sub-district No. 2. These were the first schools ever taught in these townships.

There were several changes in the sub-districts from time to time, as the law and wants of the people seemed to require, until September, 1866, when P. O. Needham and W. R. Jamison were appointed by the board, a committee to report a plat and plan of re-districting the township, which they did, and the board immediately confirmed and adopted the report. This divided the township into five sub-districts, which still exist with very little change or alteration. One change made was the formation of sub-district No. 6 out of territory attached to sub-district No. 2, which is generally known as the Keaver district. Another change was made at an adjourned meeting of the board, in the fall of 1882, attaching the southwest quarter of section 27 to sub-district No. 2, making No. 2 about six miles long, which John W. Stewart, county superintendent, decided, on an appeal, to be wrong. With these exceptions, no changes have been made in the boundaries of sub-districts since 1866.

There are six sub-districts and seven school houses in the township, which were erected at an average cost of about $800 each, or perhaps a little more.

The board of directors consist of five sub-directors, all republican.

FIRST THINGS.

The first death in the township was a man by the name of Calkins, who died soon after coming here. The second death was that of John Harlan, Sr., who died December 19, 1855, as previously stated, of dyspepsia; his disease was of long standing. The third death was that of Mrs. Jackson, before mentioned.

Hannah Boylan was the first child born in the township, a daughter of Isaac Boylan and wife. She, after attaining womanhood, became the wife of Mesling Gibson, and soon after died of consumption. She was born in the fall of 1853.

Henrietta Wood was the second birth in the township, born in the summer or fall of 1854, and is now the wife of Aaron Joy, and the mother of a large family of children.

The third birth in the township was that of William Brotherton, in the fall of 1855. He was one of a pair of twins, the other twin died when a few weeks old. William became a resident of Franklin county, and is still unmarried.

The first marriages in the township have already been stated.

The first sermon preached was by the Rev. Richard Merrill, in the spring of 1854. As there is a chapter being prepared for insertion in this history, in relation to the Presbyterian Church, we shall not here enter into the matter. There has been a good deal of religious excitement and zeal exhibited in the township at times, by different denominations and persons of a devout turn of mind. Among others, the Advent Church flourished for a time, but is almost dormant at present. The United Brethren also run well for a time but there is no organization in the township at present. The Methodists have had several organizations in the township. Soon after the first settlement of the township, the Methodist church commenced to hold revival meetings each winter in the old school house at Boylan's Grove, in the east part of the township, which were kept up yearly as long as the old school house remained standing. Other denominations generally participated, until all seemed to have turned from the error of their ways, but it is said, by the time the next winter came, they generally were all to warm over again, the work done on each winter requiring repair by the succeeding winter. It is, however, thought that the citizens of Pittsford will compare favorably with the adjoining townships both in religion and morals.

DESCRIPTIVE.

There are three streams of water running through Pittsford, to-wit: Boylan's creek on the east and northeast; the west fork of Cedar river running from the northwest to the southeast; and Thorp's or Dutchman's creek running from west to east in the south part of the township. The West Fork and Thorp's creek were formerly skirted with timber as far as they run through the township, but by degrees it has been nearly all appropriated by the settlers of this and other townships, but there still remains in the township, upper and lower Boylan's Grove and Jamieson's Grove, besides some other timber, making in all something over fifteen hundred acres of timber land in the township.

There is nothing in the township, which can, in reality, be called a slough, but the West Fork and Thorp's creek are bordered by extensive bottoms, which sometimes overflow. These bottom lands afford a large amount of pasturage and hay each year, and could readily be made to produce tame grass. The tillable land in the township is of a superior quality, and for agricultural and stock raising purposes, Pittsford, it is thought, is not to be surpassed by any township in the county.

As to stone quarries, there are many superior quarries of both lime and sandstone found on Boylan's creek and other places, which are being extensively worked, one quarry and a lime kiln being used by Elias Frick. The quarry and kiln are both located on the D. & D. Railroad, by which Frick ships large amounts of building stone and lime. The lime burnt is of a superior quality.

The Dubuque and Dakota Railroad passes through the township from east to west, leaving Bristow on the east, and passes through Dumont toward the west part of the township. There was a township tax of five per cent. voted in favor of this road about ten years ago. Considerable work was done, by way of grading the road, soon after. The company finally failed to finish the road, as stipulated, and, as a consequence, the tax was forfeited. The road changed hands, as well as name, and was completed through the township in the summer of 1879. In the meantime, the township voted another tax of five per cent., to aid in building the road, which, it is thought, is all paid. Bristow and Dumont stations on the road, furnish sufficient market facilities for produce of all description in the township.

As to towns, Bristow is an incorporated town, on the east line of the township, partly in Pittsford and partly in West Point townships. The Bristow depot is located on the West Point side of the township line. Bristow furnishes a market for all in the eastern portion of the township, and Dumont furnishes a market for all in the western part, and all others that see proper to patronize it.

The present population is about 725, being an increase of about 25 per year since the first settlement, and the voters are estimated at about 183.

The present assessed value of personal property is $26,301, and the assessed value of lands is $114,261; but it is to be remembered that the assessed value of property, for the purpose of taxation, is only about one-third of the real value in money.

The first settlement of the township only dating back to the fall of 1852, it will be preceived that both settlement and improvment have been very rapid. Those settling in this township are a mixture of English, Irish, Germans, Hollanders and others; however, citizens of the United States predominate.

Joseph Merrel, one of the early settlers, still remains a resident of the township. His first wife died and he then married a

HISTORY OF BUTLER COUNTY.

Miss McKinney. They have a large family of children. Jo. is an honest man and minds his own business.

During the war of the rebellion there was an organization called "The Union League," formed in the township. It was for a time well patronized, and, being a secret organization, it is not for this historian to state what good or harm it did, if any. But it was rather short lived, and dropped out of existence quietly.

MAILS AND POSTOFFICES.

In the first settlement of the township most of the settlers received their mail at Janesville, in Bremer county. Subsequently, about 1854 or '55, the settlers, having more business at Cedar Falls than Janesville, had their mail ordered to Cedar Falls, distant about thirty-six miles. At an early period there was a postoffice established at Clarksville, Butler county, but as the mail was only carried, when carried at all, once a week, and there being two streams to cross—the West Fork and the Shell Rock—over which, at that time, there were no bridges, and, in fact no road leading to Clarksville, it may well be conjectured that no one in the township patronized that office. At that time the mail was only supplied to Waterloo, Cedar Falls and Janesville, once each week, and carried on horseback.

Some time during the latter part of 1855, or the first part of 1856, George A. Richmon, then a resident of Butler Center, in this county, having secured some influence with the Postoffice Department, at Washington, managed to have Henry A. Early appointed postmaster. Mr. Early resided in the east part of the township, near Bristow, then named West Point; there being already one postoffice in the State called West Point, it was suggested by W. R. Jamison that the office be named Boylan's Grove, which was agreed to. Mr. Early acted as postmaster for some time. The postoffice became permanently located at West Point, now Bristow, and is still known as Bristow postoffice.

Shortly after the appointment of Mr. Early as postmaster in the east part of the township, Isaac Stover, who resided just over the line in the east edge of Franklin county, applied to the same, George A. Richmon, who succeeded in getting a postoffice established, named Union Ridge, and Stover appointed postmaster. So started the Union Ridge postoffice; but at that time and for some time afterward there was no mail route to or past either office, the postmaster sometimes carrying the mail himself on foot, and at other times the patrons of the office would contribute and hire some one to carry the mail once per week. Mails were very light at that time.

The Union Ridge office was supplied from Geneva, Franklin county, Al Benson, postmaster. In a few years Mr. Stover, desiring to remove to some other place, the Postoffice Department directed him to notify the patrons of the office to meet and select by ballot the person whom they wished appointed postmaster. The election was called and held at the house of Mr. Stover. There were two candidates for the position. James Harlan had some friends who wished him elected, and W. R. Jamison also had friends who wanted him elected. The contest was quite animated, and the contestants were about to come out a tie, when Mrs. Stover came in and decided the matter by casting her vote for Mr. Jamison, who was accordingly declared the victor, and duly appointed postmaster at Union Ridge. He held the office some time, carrying the mail from Benson the greater part of the time, or having it done at his own expense. Afterward Samuel Jamison, Isaac Stover and James Harlan were in turn appointed postmaster at Union Ridge. James Harlan was appointed in 1862, and held the office six years. By that time there was a mail route established, and mail carried twice a week.

In 1868 H. J. Playter established a general variety store at Jamison's Grove, on section 20. Mr. Harlan, weary of being postmaster, had Mr. Playter appointed, who held the office until 1869 or 1870, when he resigned. Ross Jamison was then appointed postmaster, and held the office until April 28, 1875, when W. R. Jamison was appointed the second time, and held the office until some time in the latter part of 1877, when he resigned in favor of James Harlan. But there being other aspirants for the office, A. L. Bickford was appointed postmaster. This caused the site of the post office to be removed about four miles southeast of Union Ridge, to the town of Dumont, and Mr. Bickford has since been postmaster.

OFFICIALS.

The following named persons have held office higher than township office:

Ancil Durand has held the offices of county judge, postmaster and notary public.

M. D. L. Niece has held the offices of county superintendent and county surveyor.

W. R. Jamison has been elected prosecuting attorney and county supervisor, and twice appointed postmastet at Union Ridge, and is now a notary public.

James Harlan has been postmaster at Union Ridge, and once elected county supervisor.

John M. Nichols has once been elected county supervisor.

S. B. Dumont has held the office of county supervisor, and has represented the county for two terms in the lower branch of the legislature, and is now acting in the capacity of a notary public.

Henry C. Brown has been elected a member of the board of county supervisors and also a member of the lower branch of the State legislature, which last named term of office has not yet expired.

Gilbreth Hazlett has held the office of county supervisor, and also that of sheriff, to which office he has been re-elected, and is now serving his second term.

Henry A. Early, now deceased, has held the office of postmaster.

Henry J. Playter has been postmaster.

A. L. Bickford has been postmaster, and still holds the office.

PROMINENT CITIZENS.

In this connection we present the sketches of the personal history of a few of the prominent citizens of Pittsford township, arranged with regard to the date of their arrival in this locality. Space forbids giving a personal history of each citizen in the township, even though it does furnish very interesting reading, but enough is given to illustrate the kind of men Pittsford of to-day has.

James W. McKinney is one of the pioneers of Pittsford township, where he has lived since May 7th, 1854. He was born in Ohio, in 1823, and remained there until fourteen years of age, when his parents emigrated to Indiana. He returned to Ohio after several years, and coming back to Indiana was married to Emma Beedle, a native of that State, and they came to Butler county in May, 1854, as above stated, and entered the farm on which he has since lived on the 11th of that month. He was accompanied to this county by an older brother, Ephram, with his family, who located upon a farm adjoining, where he lived until the spring of 1882, when he sold to Lewis Austen, and removed to Nebraska. Mr. and Mrs. James McKinney have been blessed with eleven children, six sons and five daughters. They lost their oldest child—Mary E.—by death. The two oldest children were born in Indiana and the balance are native born of Butler county. Mr. McKinney is of Irish descent, his great grandfather having come from the "land of the Shamrock." His grandfather, Ephram, assisted in the building of the first house where Cincinnati now stands, and was a soldier in the war of 1812. His father, John S. McKinney, died in Indiana where he had lived many years.

T. M. Early, farmer and justice of the peace, resides on section 35. He was born April 3, 1840, in Florence, Stephenson county, Illinois. His parents were both natives of Kentucky, who came to Illinois about the year 1830. They remained there until 1854, then came to Iowa, and bought 180 acres of choice land near where the village of Bristow now stands. The subject of this sketch remained with his parents, on the farm, until he was twenty-one years of age. On September 10, 1861, he enlisted as a soldier in Company E, Twelfth Iowa Infantry. He remained in the army until February 23, 1862, when he was honorably discharged for disability. After partially regaining his health he commenced farming for himself, and we now find him owning 160 acres of choice farm land, with good buildings. He is doing general farming. On December 16, 1863, he was united in marriage with Rhoda A. Overturf. She was born March 7, 1844, in Elk county, Pennsylvania. They have seven children—Alma E., born September 15, 1864; Clara F., born April 8, 1866; Ornell J., born May 29, 1868; Norman A., born March 23, 1879; Vernon C., born April 5, 1881. Mr. Early belongs to the Order of Odd Fellows, and is also a member of the Grand Army of the Republic. He has held the office of justice of the peace for the past ten years. During these ten years of actual service, he has had but a single case reversed in the higher courts. Politically he is a republican. His post office address is Bristow, Butler county, Iowa.

James Harlan, another of the pioneers, was born in Richland county, Ohio, in August, 1829. He was married to Matilda Crissinger, a native of Pennsylvania. Her parents were John and Catherine Crissinger, who removed from Pennsylvania to Ohio. They had sixteen children, and Mrs. Harlan is the only one of whom settled in this State. James Harlan's father,

John Harlan, was born in Virginia in 1792, but removed to Ohio with his parents when twelve years of age. He was married in the latter State to Susannah Moore, born in 1807. They resided for many years after marriage in Richland and Crawford counties, and came to Butler county July 3, 1855. The old gentleman purchased 80 acres of W. R. Jamieson, which he intended for a homestead, but died the following December. He was an elder in the Presbyterian Church and an upright, honorable man. His wife survived him fifteen years, and both died at the age of sixty-three. They had fifteen children, eight of whom are still living—Esther, James, George, Jehu, Elizabeth Allen, Susannah Allen, Nathan, and Clarinda, now Mrs. Elias Bell—all born in Ohio. James came here at the time of his parents, and has owned the 80 acres upon which he now lives ever since his first advent to the county. His entire farm contains 176 acres. Mr. and Mrs. Harlan have six children—Jehu, Catherine, now Mrs. Jasper Cannon, Hannah J., John C., James T. and Olie Day. They have lost three children. Mr. and Mrs. Harlan are members of the Presbyterian Church at Bristow, he being an elder in that organization. He is one of the township trustees, and has been for several years; was one of the first constables of the town; was justice of the peace two years, and was second lieutenant of the Home Guards in war times. Mr. Harlan was a delegate to the General Association of the Presbyterian Church which met at St. Louis in 1874. He is also vice president of the Old Settlers' Association for Pittsford township.

Jehu Harlan, son of Jehu Harlan, senior, resides on section 19. A part of his farm was entered by his father in 1855. The north part he purchased of Greenbury Luck. He has 150 acres. Mr. Harlan was born in Richland county, Ohio, in 1834. He was brought up in Crawford county; came to Butler county with his parents in 1855. He has been a resident of this township since that time, except a few years, which he spent on the Pacific coast. In fact, he has been quite an extensive traveler in the territories of the west. He went overland to California in 1860, his journey consuming 135 days. He engaged in mining; also spent some time in mining and prospecting in Idaho and Montana. He returned in 1866. He went to the Black Hills in 1874; but the Indian troubles prevented his remaining there; this was about the time of the massacre of General Custer and his command. He went to Leadville in 1879, but was absent but a short time. He married Isabelle Hartgraves, daughter of J. R. Hartgraves, an early settler of Ingham township, Franklin county. Mr. and Mrs. Harlan have six children—Carrie A., James E., Cora A., John R., May, and Maggie Belle.

Samuel R. Dearmoun resides on section 19, and is one of the pioneers of Butler county, his residence here dating from July 3, 1855. He entered his present farm a few days after arriving, coming with his father-in-law, Mr. Jehu Harlan, Sr. Mr. Dearmoun put up a temporary residence near his claim, of forked stakes and poles, which he covered with clapboards or "shakes." In this house his family and that of James Harlan resided until the following October, when he put

B. C. Needham.

up a log house on the site of his present residence, which he occupied for twenty-four years, although he built a frame addition in 1871. His present house was erected in 1879. Mr. Dearmoun was born in Huntington county, Pennsylvania, in 1819, and his father, William D., was also a native of Pennsylvania. The subject of our sketch went to Ohio about 1844, where he was married in 1848, to Esther Harlan daughter of Jehu Harlan, and they have been blessed with seven children—Cinderella, now Mrs. Oscar Chambers; William J., who married Laura Richard; Nancy Ann, wife of John Harper; Alice A., wife of George B. Sutton; J. Harvey, Ida Belle, and Alva M. The old homestead contains 120 acres, of which he entered 80. They are members of the M. E. Church.

Benjamin C. Needham is one of the well-known old settlers of Pittsford township. His date of arrival was June, 1856. Mr. Needham was born in the town of Wilmington, Essex county, New York, in 1814. His parents were Benjamin C., and Achsah (Thair) Needham. His father was born in the town of Pittsford, Rutland county, Vermont. His mother was a native of Essex county, New York. B. C. Needham, Sr., was a soldier in the war of 1812. He came to Butler county in 1856 with his son, and settled on section 9. He died at Parkersburg, in this county, September 17, 1880, in his eighty-seventh year. He lost his first wife, and married again. His second wife is also deceased. Mr. Needham, Jr., was married to Charlotte Bowers, born in Addison, Addison county Vermont. They removed from Vermont to Kane county, Illinois, and thence to DeKalb county. They came to Butler county, as stated above, in 1856. Mr. Needham has resided where he now lives since he first came to the county. He made all his improvements, being the original settler on the place where he now lives. His first wife died here in July, 1859. His present wife was Mrs. Harriet Barrett, born in Addison county, Vermont. Her maiden name was James. Her first husband was Richard Barrett. Mr. Needham had eight children by his first wife, only two of whom are living—Perrin and Charles W., both of whom live in Nebraska. He has a daughter by his present wife—Emma Alice, now Mrs. T. U. Dubois. Mrs. Needham has a daughter by her former marriage—Ellen, now Mrs. Albert Austen. Mr. Needham's farm contains 145 acres. He and his wife belong to the M. E. Church.

Silas Needham, a brother of B. C., resides on section 15. He was born in Essex county, New York, in 1817. He, also, came here in 1856. His wife was Susan Dunning, daughter of Loam Dunning, a Butler county settler of 1856.

Henry Ahrens resides on section 30. His father, Jacob Ahrens, bought the claim of this farm, where he settled, in 1855. Henry came in 1856, and has lived on this farm since that time. His father died here in 1859; he was born in Germany in 1800, and came to the United States with his family in 1853. He lived at Davenport, this State, two years before he came here. His wife still lives with her son. The parents of Henry had five children, two of whom are living — Louise, a sister, wife of George Miller, of Cedar Falls. Mr. Ahrens was born in

Germany, in 1830; he was married at Davenport, to Louise Dahl, born in Germany. Mr. and Mrs. Ahrens have four children—Theodore, James, William, and George. They have an adopted daughter, Louise. Mr. Aherns has 400 acres of land, on which he has made all the improvements. He and wife belong to the German Evangelical Church.

Silas Needham resides on section 15. He is a brother of B. C. Needham, and came to the township at the same time. He was born in Essex county, New York, in 1817; was brought up in Addison county, Vermont; married Susan Dunning, a daughter of Loan Dunning. He settled on his present farm the same year he came to the county—1856. The log house, which was his first residence here, was the first dwelling on the prairie, and the first election held in the township was held at that house. Mr. Needham has four children—Edward E., Melville S., Leslie B., and Lillian. His farm contains 120 acres.

James Logan resides on section 13. He owns one of the very earliest located farms in this township. He purchased his place of Madison Parks, in 1856. Mr. Logan was born in Tuscarawas county, Ohio, in 1812. His parents were John and Jane Logan, natives of Virginia. Mr. Logan was married in Ohio, to Margaret Ann Icenoggle. His settlement in Iowa dates from 1845. In that year he started for Buchanan county to locate on a farm which he had entered two years previous. He took a steamer at Wheeling, West Virginia, for St. Louis, where he changed steamers and in due time landed safe at what is now Muscatine. But he was destined to meet with a sad misfortune at the beginning of his career as a pioneer of Iowa. At Muscatine, he started with his family in a wagon for his future home in Buchanan county, but on the second day of the journey, his wife and child, an infant one year old, were attacked by that dreadful disease cholera, and both died in about forty-eight hours after being taken sick. They were buried near the place where they died, which is somewhere on the site of the present city of Marion, Linn county, but the exact spot is unknown. Mr. Logan with the remainder of his family, continued his journey to Buchanan county. He was married to his present wife in Buchanan county. Her maiden name was Clarinda Powell, daughter of William and Elizabeth Powell. She also was born in Ohio; her father died in Indiana. Her mother, with her family, went to Buchanan county in 1850, and came to Butler county and settled in this township in 1856. She died about 1863. Mr. Logan had five children by his first wife, four of whom are living, viz: David, who lost his sight when a boy; Eliza Jane, now Mrs. John Jamieson; Sabina, Mrs. L. J. Austen;—the last two named are twins,—his youngest daughter, by first marriage, was a twin sister of the child that died of cholera, she is now Mrs. Ross Jamieson. Mr. Logan has a daughter by his present wife—Lizzie, now Mrs. McCormick.

Thomas Demoss settled in this township in June, 1857. He bought a part of his farm of Daniel Parker; the north eighty of Melvin Rush. Mr. Demoss was born in Vermilion county, Illinois, in 1836. He came to Butler county from Fulton county, in that State. Mr. Demoss was married in this county to Miss M. Powell, born in Indiana. They have two children—Charles L. and Thomas Addison. Mr. Demoss' farm contains 160 acres. He enlisted in 1861, in the Twelfth Regiment, Iowa Volunteer Infantry, and served in the army two years. He participated in many important engagements, including Forts Henry and Donelson, battle of Corinth, etc. His brother, James, enlisted at the same time in same company, and was mortally wounded at the battle of Corinth, serving the engagement but eight days.

Alexander Cline resides on section 1, and his residence in this township dates from August 24, 1858. He was born in Columbia county, Pennsylvania, in 1829. His parents moved to Lycoming county of that State when he was a child, and here he was brought up. His parents, John and Margaret Cline, resided in that county until their decease. Alexander was married in Pennsylvania to Elizabeth McCollum, also a native of Columbia county. Her parents, Ephraim and Ann McCollum, were born in the same county, where they died. Mr. Cline came here with his family, as stated, in 1858, and entered a fractional quarter on sec. 3, and another on sec. 1, embracing 109 acres, which constituted his original farm. In 1864, he purchased 40 acres, which was the first addition to his original farm, having now 569 acres. Mr. and Mrs. Cline have been blessed with eight children, who are yet alive—Francis M., John C., Ephraim E., Martha J., Western M., Milan S., Mary A. and Lilly A. They have lost two children, their oldest—Esther, and the youngest, an infant.

Albert Austen resides on section 9, where he located in March, 1866. He was born in England in February, 1842. His father, Peter Austen, came to this country with his family in the fall of 1844, locating at Cleveland, Ohio, where he resided until his death. The family consisted of seventeen children, eight of whom are living. Two of these, Lewis and Alfred, served during the war in Company A, Seventh Ohio Infantry, enlisting the second day after the firing on Fort Sumpter, the latter losing his life in the battle of Ringold. Lewis served over two years, and came to Butler county in December, 1874. Albert bought his farm of 160 acres in 1865. He was married to Ellen A., daughter of Richard Barrett, a native of Vermont. Her mother is now Mrs. B. C. Needham.

William P. Woodworth was one of the early settlers of Bennezette township. He now resides on section 22, Pittsford township, on the farm formerly owned by Gilbraith Hazlett, which he has owned since November, 1877. He was born in what is now Cameron county, Pennsylvania, in 1828. He came to Iowa from Bennezette township, in that county, with Samuel Overturf, and settled in what is now Bennezette township, in this county. They named the township, then known as Coldwater precinct, from Bennezette, Pennsylvania. Mr. Woodworth entered the southwest quarter of section 35, Bennezette township, which he improved, and where he lived for ten years. He then removed to Marble Rock, Floyd county, and soon after to Nora Springs, where he built a store and was engaged in the mercantile business about six months. He then came to Pittsford township and settled on section 23, where he was for a time engaged in the nursery business. He sold his nursery stock to Mr. Ferris and returned to his native county in August, 1873, where he remained four years. He returned in 1877 and settled where he now lives. His wife was Jane Miller, born in Pennsylvania. They have two adopted daughters—Mary S. and Lucy Brockway.

Lewis J. Austen resides on section 14, of Pittsford township, where he owns a farm containing 120 acres, which is one of the oldest settled farms in the township, having been settled by Ephram McKinney, in 1854, from whom Mr. Austen purchased it, in March, 1882. Mr. Austen was born in county Kent, England, in December, 1846. His parents, John and Helen Austen, with the family, emigrated to the United States, in 1849, and located at Cleveland, Ohio. The family consisted of the parents and three sons, and, at the latter place, the parents and one son, Daniel, died of cholera the following summer. After this, Lewis J. Austen made his home with relatives until 1866, when he came to Butler county, arriving here in March. He has been a resident of this township since April 2d, of that year. He lived on section 9 for two and one-half years; then on section 13, with his father-in-law, for thirteen years, and then purchased eighty acres, on section 10, where he built a good house and made other valuable improvements, and sold out to John Morford and bought his present farm. He married Sabine Logan, daughter of James Logan. They have two children—Mary J. and Josephine. Mr. Austen is the present assessor of Pittsford township, and is now serving his fifth year in that capacity. His brother, George, returned to England, after the death of his parents, and is now a resident of Gravesend, England, where he owns an extensive brick manufactory.

S. W. Ferris resides on section 26, where he located in June, 1866, and is the first settler upon this farm. He was born in Broome county, New York, in 1841. His father was John Ferris, who removed with his family to Kane county, Illinois, in 1846. Here the subject of our sketch grew to manhood, and on the 1st of January, 1862, enlisted in the Second Illinois Light Artillery, and served for about six months, when in May, 1863, he was discharged for disability, and came to this township the same year. He has a farm of about 520 acres, and is also extensively engaged in stock raising. For a number of years he devoted considerable attention to the nursery business. An account of his nursery appears in connection with the article upon industrial enterprises. His wife was formerly Maude Hazlet, a daughter of S. K. Hazlet. Their marriage has been blessed with one son—Earle, who is yet living, and daughter—Conchita, who died at the age of twelve years.

William R. Johnson is one of the arrivals of 1869, and resides on section 11. His father, Job Johnson, was a native of Pennsylvania; his mother was formerly Margaret Ray. They were married in Philadelphia, and lived at Schuylkill Falls, near that city, for many years, his father doing business in Philadelphia. He died there about 1864. His mother came here with her family in 1869, and purchased the farm on section 11, which is now owned by the subject of our sketch. His mother, Margaret Johnson, had four children, two of whom are living—William R., and John

R. One son—Jerome, died in Philadelphia, and the other—Joseph, died here.

John Miles was born in Caledonia county, Vermont, in 1827; his parents being Martin and Mary (Jennings) Miles. His mother died in Vermont, and his father removed to Massachusetts. The subject of this sketch, in the fall of 1850, came to Linn county, Iowa, and shortly after went to Bremer county and made a claim in Jefferson township, where he removed his family the following spring, and were among the first settlers of that county, and was one of the judges of the first election held in the county, at which there were twenty-five votes cast. He sold that claim the following fall, and entered a farm in Washington township, near the present city of Waverly. In 1855 he went to Rice county, Minnesota, where he made a claim, which he purchased when the land came into market, and remained there for about twelve years, when he removed to Missouri, and after three years came back to Bremer county; but settled in Shell Rock in 1871. He lived in this vicinity for about eleven years, and in August, 1881, he purchased his present farm of William Brett. Mrs. Miles was a native of Rensselaer county, New York, where she was born in 1824; her father died while she was yet in infancy, and in 1838, her mother removed to Adams county, Ill., with her family, and to Johnson county, Iowa, in 1842. Several of Mrs. Miles' brothers had settled in that county some years prior to this, one of whom still resides there. Mr. and Mrs. Miles have four children—Calista, now Mrs. R. A. DeWitt, of Mason City; Charles H., John M. and Ida J. Besides they have lost four children.

Samuel Overturf resides on section 9. He was one of the early settlers of Bennezette township. Mr. Overturf was born in Union county, Pennsylvania, 1812. He removed with his parents, Henry and Maria Overturf, to Clearfield county, when a boy, where his parents lived until their decease. His father was a soldier in the Revolutionary War, in which he served from the age of sixteen to twenty-one. Mr. Overturf came to Butler county in the spring of 1857, and settled in what is now Bennezette township. Mr. Overturf and Wm. P. Woodworth called the township Bennezette, from the name of the township where they formerly lived in Pennsylvania. Mr. Overturf has lived in Muscatine county, Iowa, and in Will county, Illinois, for about eight years since his first settlement in Bennezette. He was married to Olivia Woodworth, a sister of Wm. P. Woodworth. She was born in Clearfield county, Pennsylvania, March 23, 1821. They have had seven children, five of whom are now living,—Alonzo, Rhoda, Ann, Helen, Isaac, Osler and Willis.

TOWN OF DUMONT.

This pleasant little town is situated in the southern part of Pittsford township, on section 28, on the line of the Dubuque and Dakota Railroad, the plat containing about 80 acres. It is admirably laid out with streets 80 and 102 feet wide, and alleys not less than 30 feet. It is located high and dry upon a beautiful knoll between the two streams described in the township history. During the past year many trees have been set out, and as time flies and they grow up and mature the place will each year grow in beauty. The surrounding country is about the best farming and stock locality in the county, and this being tributary, Dumont can truthfully be said to be one of the best of trading points, while its future is assured. Good water is within easy reach, and a water power of thirteen-foot fall can at a moderate expense be brought right to the town by means of tail-races. A project is now on foot to secure and make this available, which, if carried out, will be of material benefit to the town.

Dumont was named after its founder, Hon. S. B. Dumont, who still owns one-half interest and makes this his home. Each alternate lot is owned by the railroad company.

The land upon which Dumont stands was originally entered by a man named Young, about 1856, but who never did anything toward improving it. In 1864 S. B. Dumont arrived from Dubuque, bringing his family, and purchased this land and much land adjoining, being a man of means. Shortly after his arrival he erected the first house upon the site, in which he still lives, it being located directly in the center of Main street. The place remained as a farm until 1879, when the Dubuque and Dakota Railroad was constructed through the township, and then Mr. Dumont had the village platted and recorded.

The first business started was by the same gentleman, who, in the fall of 1879, erected an elevator and commenced business. In 1882 he sold this to A. A. Robertson, of Iowa Falls, who still conducts it in a business-like manner. About the same time Mr. Dumont commenced the lumber business and that fall sold one hundred car loads.

From the time the village was platted, in the fall of 1879, until the close of the year, about thirteen buildings were erected. Mr. Dumont furnishing nearly all of the means. His son T. A. Dumont, M. D., opened the drug store which he still runs.

The Smith Brothers opened their general merchandise store about the same time, and are yet doing a thriving business.

Martin Griffith put up a building, which S. B. Dumont occupied with a stock of hardware.

O. A. Chambers erected a dwelling in the fall of 1879, and opened a small stock of groceries in a building which S. McMannes had erected. He has gone to his farm in Franklin county.

William Schulnborg, the carpenter; John Ryan, J. Kruse, A. N. Arnold and James Stewart, all put up dwellings, while Nic. Hess put up a building for a saloon, and A. L. Bickford, son-in-law of Mr. Dumont, put up a store building—all in the fall of 1879.

During the year 1880, the advance was very rapid. Early in the spring, William Francher removed an elevator from Waterloo, which he still manages.

S. McMannes opened his furniture store. W. T. Scott erected a dwelling. Hotchkiss & Eikenbery, A. L. Bickford, and Mr. Lutz, were all instrumental in building up the place; while S. B. Dumont put up a fine brick block, with eighty-four feet front, arranged for a hotel and two store rooms—public hall over head.

Patterson & Cole came in the fall of 1882, and now do a fair business.

Dr. T. A. Dumont is still running the drug store.

Smith Brothers also in the general merchandising business.

S. B. Dumont still manages the lumber trade and does an annual business of $25,000.

S. McMannes in the furniture trade.

W. T. Scott, meat market.

A. A. Robertson handles grain and stock.

Moses Barnes and S. E. Allen do the blacksmithing.

Charley Coryell attends to the livery business.

D. W. Williamson and Philip Pfaltzgraff represent the hardware trade.

I. M. Nichols handles all kinds of agricultural implements.

A. L. Bickford, stock buyer.

D. Richmon is the shoemaker.

Robert Schmitz, justice of the peace and collection agent.

M. S. Needham is the accommodating landlord of the hotel and gives good satisfaction.

Nick Huss and William Schulnborg, saloons.

O. S. Rowley is depot agent.

W. R. Jamison was the first lawyer here. T. A. Dumont, M. D., was the first doctor.

The first death in the village was the demise of Mrs. Sarah F. Townsend on the 3d of January, 1880, aged eighty-nine years.

The first birth was of a child of Nick Huss, early in 1880.

A neat school building was put up in the fall of 1882, at a cost of about $1,000, although the district only had to pay about $800 of it, S. B. Dumont furnishing the balance.

Samuel Beekman Dumont was born September 14, 1823, in Somerset county, New Jersey, near the village of Harlingen. His father, Abraham I. Dumont, was born in the same county in 1799, and for a number of years was engaged in mercantile pursuits. Subsequently, he was judge of the county court, and held other prominent positions in the county, until he removed to Philadelphia, in 1843. His grandfather, Abraham Dumont, was also born in the same county, near the town of Somerville, on the Rariton river. The family originally came from France, and were Hugenots. Mr. Dumont's mother, whose maiden name was Ann Ten Brock Beekman, was the youngest daughter of Captain Samuel Beekman, whose ancestors were among the original settlers of New York City, then called New Amsterdam. The branch of the family to which Captain Beekman belongs left New York and settled in Somerset county, New Jersey, in 1720. The Captain was a soldier in the Revolutionary War. Her mother, the grandmother of S. B. Dumont, was a Ten Brock, also one of the old Hollander families who first settled in New Amsterdam. The old homestead which was built before the Revolutionary War, in 1760, near Harington, in which S. B. Dumont and his mother were born, is still standing and in a good state of preservation, and has many marks in its doors from bayonet thrusts and musket shots, made during the Revolutionary War, when this house was attacked by the Hessians after the battle of Trenton.

At the age of fourteen years—in 1838—S. B. Dumont left home for New York city, and was then a stranger in a strange land. He commenced life in that city as errand boy in a store. New York at that day was not the New York of to-day. Bleeker street was up town, Union Square was out of town, Stewart's was opposite the park, near the Astor House; Captain Cornelius Vanderbilt ran a steamboat from New Brunswick to New York. New Brunswick was then the terminus of the railroad, from whence you took a stage to Washington and Philadelphia. What a change in forty-six years! It is scarcely to be realized, yet nothing, compared to what has taken place, in one-half of that time, in the West. S. B. Dumont left New York in 1843, and settled in Philadelphia, where he lived until 1856, except the years 1846 and 1847, during which time he was in business in Salem, New Jersey, where he became acquainted with Caroline F. Townsend, daughter of Captain Jonathan Townsend. They were married, on June 28, 1847. Mrs. Dumont was born in Philadelphia, January 26, 1829. They have two children. Their daughter, Matilda, is married to A. L. Bigford, and lives in the town of Dumont. Their son, Thaddeus A. Dumont, also lives in Dumont, where he is practicing as a physician and druggist. The mother of Mrs. Dumont—Sarah Fries—was born in Salem county, New Jersey, and belonged to the old Holland stock of Fries, the first settlers in the county, near Alloways town.

S. B. Dumont moved west with his family and landed in Dubuque in April, 1856, where he engaged in mercantile business until 1864, when, his health giving way from long-continued close confinement to business, he was compelled to try out-door life. He chose Butler county, Iowa, as his future home, and moved there with his family and mother-in-law. He had about all the advantages and disadvantages of a pioneer life. He settled on section 28, township 92, range 18, west of the fifth principal meridian, on raw prairie land. The beautiful grove which now surrounds his prairie home was planted by himself and son, Dr. T. A. Dumont. Here the family have since resided, Mr. Dumont engaging in farming until 1879, at which time the Dubuque and Dakota Railroad was built and the town of Dumont located on his farm. Since 1879 he has devoted his time and means to build up a prosperous town and a successful lumber business. Mr. Dumont has frequently been honored by his fellow citizens with offices of trust, serving the township of Pittsford in several positions. For four years he was a member of the county board of supervisors, three years of which time he was chairman of the board. He was a member of the House of Representatives from the Sixty-first district, composed of Butler and Grundy counties, in the Twelfth General Assembly, and also of the Thirteenth General Assembly, when Butler county comprised a district. He was again a member when the new code of 1873 was adopted. Mr. Dumont has been a successful man in life, his success being brought about by push, perseverance and energy.

S. McMannes, who is mentioned prior to this, is comparitively a late settler in Pittsford. He was born in Mearsville, Crawford county, Pennsylvania, but was brought up in Mercer county of that State. His residence in Iowa dates from 1849, when he came to Dubuque, and from thence to Grant county, where he engaged in mining. He has been a resident of this township since 1874, and is at present engaged in the furniture business, having served an apprenticeship at the cabinet business in his native town, and followed that business while in Dubuque. Upon coming to Pittsford, he purchased a farm on section 29. He now owns one on section 28. He was married to Mary Kline, of Pennsylvania, and they have five children —James N., Margaret A., Mary J., John W. and Bertha.

Hon. Henry C. Brown, of Dumont, has been a resident of Pittsford township since March 1867. He was born in Belknap county, New Hampshire, in 1831, January 1st. He was reared to the occupation of farming. He served during the last year of the rebellion in the First New Hampshire Heavy Artillery. Before locating in Butler county, he spent a short time in Black Hawk county, where he purchased land, locating here as before mentioned, in March, 1867. Mr. Brown is chiefly engaged in agricultural pursuits. He is a large land owner, possessing the whole of section 33, in this township; 200 acres in another part of the township. He owns altogether about 1,500 acres in this county. Mr. Brown is one of the prominent citizens of Butler county. He was one of the county supervisors for five years— from 1871 to 1876. He is the present member of the legislature from this district, having been elected to the General Assembly in the fall of 1881. Mrs. Brown was formerly Miss Mary F. Bickford, daughter of Arthur Bickford. They have two children—George S. and Anna. They lost their youngest child, Clara.

Philip Pfaltzgraff is another of the business men of Dumont. He is a native of France, where he was born in 1852. His father, Frederick, emigrated to this country, from France, in 1854, and settled in Chicago. He came to Butler county in 1869, and settled on section 23, in Madison township, where he purchased a farm of Henry and N. Daniel. When the town of Dumont was started, Philip came to the new town and engaged in the hardware business. His wife was Anna, daughter of Henry Miller.

CHAPTER XXX.

RIPLEY TOWNSHIP.

The sub-division of Butler county bearing this name, lies adjoining West Point on the north, Jefferson on the east, Monroe on the south and Madison on the west. It embraces the territory known as township 91, north, range 17, west of the fifth principal meridian.

The area of the township is abundantly watered. The West Fork, one of the principal streams of the county, enters on section seven, making confluence with Dutchman's Creek within half a mile of the town line, and taking an easterly course, bearing to the south, crosses the town and makes its exit on section 24, entering Jefferson township. Right here however, an abrupt southward curve is made, and the stream, bearing to the west again enters Ripley, to leave on section 25. On section 23, it is joined by Bates' Creek, a stream which rises in West Point township, takes a southerly course, enters Ripley in section 4, and finally makes a junction with the West Fork as above stated.

The natural timber, in a body, follows these streams. The general inclination of the surface is rolling, but a large area of it lies along the West Fork bottoms, which is rather low and wet, yet it furnishes plenty of pasturage, which is covered with a heavy growth of nutricious indigenous grasses, for the stock grower of whom there are a number. The soil is principally a black loam with a clay sub-soil. Some good stone is found and excellent water is plenty within a reasonable depth.

This is wholly a farming community, and has no town or village, no railroad, and only one post-office. It is probably best adapted to stock raising, yet it is being rapidly brought to a cultivated state. A considerable amount of wild land owned by non-residents is found, but is fast being transferred to those who will put it under cultivation.

EARLY SETTLEMENT.

The honor of the first settlement in the township belongs to George McConnell, who in May, 1854, pushed his way within the limits of Ripley, and planted his pioneering stakes around an excellent farm on section 15. He remained for some time, and then sold, removing from the county. He afterwards returned, however, and was called from earthly labors in 1862 or 1863, while at the house of Nathan Linn, in Monroe township. The land which he claimed now belongs to H. C. Mead. Mr. McConnell was for years known far and near as the "Old Bach," and his house was headquarters for everybody, no matter who, that came in search of land.

The second settler in the township was James Hunter, who settled in November, 1854, spending the first winter with Mr. McConnell, and in the spring of 1855, taking up a claim on section 13. He arrived here on the fifth of April, from Waterloo, after making the third attempt to reach the town, but failing each time on account of high water in the streams. He still lives in the township, and is the oldest living settler.

In July, 1855, came J. C. and Christian Hites, and were among the first to cast their lot here for a home. J. C. Hites made a claim on section 20, where he still remains, a prominent and well-to-do farmer. Christian Hites settled on section 28, where he remained until 1861, when he was called from earthly labors.

During the month of August, in 1855, Andrew Hesse settled where he yet lives, on section 20, in comfortable circumstances.

Nathan Linn was the third settler of Ripley, coming during the summer of 1855, and locating on section 14. He remained for about six years, when he moved to Monroe, and now lives in Jefferson township.

About the same time Michael Consodine, with his family, came from Nova Scotia, and located on section 9, upon land now owned by Edwin Kincaid. Soon afterward a Mr. Ulery, coming from Boone county, Illinois, took up a claim upon the land now owned by O. Porter. Ulery is now living in California.

In September, 1856, section 4 received a settler. This pioneer was John G. Moorehead, who now resides on section 9. He is one of the earliest settlers in the township.

J. G. Moorehead, one of the early settlers of Butler county, was born in County Tyrone, Ireland, in 1820. When twenty-seven years of age he came to America, and after engaging in lumbering, at St. Johns, New Brunswick, for two years, removed to New York city, where he engaged in railroading for some time, and then farmed in that State for about two years. Upon leaving there, he removed to Philadelphia, where he continued to live until 1854. At that date he came west, and after spending two years in Cedar county, Iowa, came to Ripley township, and settled on section 4, where he now lives, and owns 360 acres of land. Mr. Moorehead has held the offices of assessor, trustee, and school director. He was married, in June, 1850, to Miss Martha Taylor, a native of Londonderry. Three children have been born to them, of whom one—William G.—is now living. Charlotte died on the 28th day of January, 1872, and the other died in infancy.

Geo. W. Stoner came to this township in 1855. He died several years since. His sons are now living on the place.

In 1856, Geo. Monroe made his appearance, and settled about two and a half miles from Butler Center.

About the same time a Mr. Elmore, having a tract of land near the creek, sent his brother-in-law, Mr. Fortner, to his place, furnishing necessary means to carry it on. Fortner engaged to a limited extent in the manufacture of Limburger cheese. He did not prove to be a success, and in a short time sold his brother-in-law's team, and pocketing the proceeds, went to California.

In 1857, Daniel Haynes selected section 16, moved his family on to it, but was drowned out by the repeated overflow of the West Fork, and purchased another place in the southwest part of the township. He went into the army; has returned to his family a number of times, but not to remain permanently. His wife and boys carry on the farm with success, and are highly respected by the entire community.

Edwin Kincaid, who has been mentioned heretofore, is a son of James and Hepsey (Pierce) Kincaid, and was born in Somerset county, Maine, April 25, 1825. He passed his youth on his father's farm, and lived in that county until twenty-three years old. When of sufficient years, his winters were spent in the pineries of that State. In 1848, he removed to Illinois, locating in Winnebago county, where he engaged in teaming; and after some years located in Juneau county, Wisconsin, where he followed farming. During the year 1860, Mr. Kincaid came to Butler Center, Iowa, and in April, 1862, settled on his farm on section 9 (which farm was known as the Consodine place), and now owns 540 acres in Ripley township. He has held the office of township trustee. In the year 1848, he was married to Miss Catherine Kershner, who also is a native of Somerset county, Maine. They have nine children living—Lewis, Aurilla, wife of Charles Yost; William, Myrta, wife of William Reed, and now living in Bennezette township; Jessie F., wife of John Randolph, of Washington Territory; Eugene, Laura, wife of William Moorhead; Clara and Ella.

One of the prominent early settlers was Henry Trotter, born in County Farmauch, Ireland, March 20, 1824. When nineteen years old he joined the constabulary, and after serving nine years resigned and crossed the ocean to America. Soon after arriving in New York he entered the employ of Holstead, Haines & Co., dry goods merchants. At the end of three years, however, he was obliged to resign that position on account of failing health, after which he came west and located in Cedar Falls, Iowa, where he built a small house, and during the summer of 1855 made a claim on section 14 of Jefferson township. The following year he settled on this claim, camping out until he could get his breaking done and a house erected. After improving that piece of land Mr. Trotter moved to Ripley township, Butler county, and settled on section 24, where he now owns 166 acres of land. He has held nearly all the town offices, and is at present justice of the peace. He also was one of the supervisors of the county at an early date. During the year 1849 he was joined in wedlock with Miss Elizabeth Thompson, who is also a native of Ireland.

Joseph L. Santee was born in Steuben county, New York, October 8, 1827. Five years after his birth the family removed to Luzerne county, Pennsylvania, where they lived but a short time, however, and then continued west until reaching Ohio. There they settled, and Joseph remained at home until 1855, at which time he came to Butler county, Iowa, settling in Butler Center, where he built the first house in the village and also assisted in erecting the steam mill of that place. In 1859 he removed to Ripley township, locating on section 8, where he lived for about two years, and then settled on section 19, where he now resides and owns 270 acres of land. Mr. Santee has held the office of justice of the peace for several years. In 1858 he was married to Mrs. Jane Moorehead. They have five children—George A., James N., Charles B., Robert A. and Carrie M. The subject of this sketch was one of three to stake out the road from Butler Center to Shell Rock, July 4, 1855.

Jacob Yost was born in York county, Pennsylvania, on the 9th day of October, 1809, and is a son of Jacob and Mary Ann (Kauffman) Yost. During his youth he learned the shoe-maker's trade, of his father, and when nineteen years old, removed to Maryland, where he remained a short time, and thence to Crawford county, Ohio, locating in Bucyrus, the county seat, where he followed his trade until 1853. In June of that year, he came to Iowa and settled in Linn county, twelve miles east of Cedar Rapids, and engaged in farming. The following year he removed to Toledo, Tama county, where he worked at his trade two years, and thence to Franklin county, where he resided one winter, and then removed to Madison township. In August of 1865, he settled on section 8, of Ripley township, and now owns 120 acres of land. Mr. Yost has held the office of school director. In 1857 he was joined in wedlock with Miss Eveline B. Scott, a native of Jefferson county, New York. Ten children have been born to them, eight of whom are now living—Jacob Butler, who lives in West Point township; George W., Elmer Elisha, Sherman Sheridan, William Lincoln, Luther Henry, Cornelius Ezra, and Rachel May. Mr. Yost has also four children, by his former wife—Mary Ann. Josiah W., Sarah Jane, Charles Kauffman, and Sherlania E.

Robert McKernan, a native of county Tyrone, Ireland, was born in the year of our Lord, 1827. When twenty years of age he came to America, and after remaining in Philadelphia, Pennsylvania, one year, engaged in draying, removed to New Jersey, where he followed farming. In March of the year 1868, he came to Iowa, and settled on section 10, of Ripley township, Butler county, where he now lives and owns a fine farm of 120 acres. Mr. McKernan has held the offices of president, secretary and treasurer, of the township schools. He was married in the state of New Jersey, during the year 1867, to Miss Mary Maloney, a native of county Shigo, Ireland. They have one child—Margaret.

Geo. W. Monroe, Jr., an early settler of Butler county, was born in Ithica, New York, March 2d, 1840, and is a son of George W. and Caroline S. (Ryan) Monroe, who are also natives of New York State. About the year of 1846, his parents removed to Albany county, New York, where they lived until 1850, and then located in the State of Ohio. During the year of 1855, they came to Butler county, Iowa, settling in what is now Monroe township; where his father entered land. George W., Jr., received a good common school education, supplemented by an attendance at an academy in New York State. In 1869, he removed to section 15 of Ripley township, where he has since resided, with the exception of ten years spent in Knoxville, Illinois, and Davenport, Iowa. His farm consists of 135 acres of excellently improved land, on which are comfortable buildings. During the year of 1877, he was united in marriage with Theresa Matthew. They have one child—George Frederick. Mr. Monroe's parents are residing in Jackson, Butler county.

FIRST THINGS.

The first white child born in the township was Allen, son of Mr. and Mrs. James Hunter, who was born on the 2d of August, 1856. Allen now lives in Jefferson township. The first death in the township was a child of Samuel Kimmel, in the fall of 1855. The remains were deposited in the cemetery on section 29.

The first couple to be united in marriage was Richard Davenport and Miss Susannah Kimmel. The ceremony was performed at the house of the bride's parents, Samuel Kimmel, by J. J. Criswell. This took place in the fall of 1859; the parties now reside at Parkersburg.

The first bridge across the West Fork, in Ripley township, was built on section 15, in 1860. There are now two bridges across this stream.

The first election held in the township was at a sod house, owned and built by Moffatt and Mason. They were factory men from New York. There were not, at this time, settlers enough to fill the offices, and one man was obliged to bear the honors of two or three.

John Hites was the first township clerk.

The present town officers of Ripley are: Clerk, Jerry Margretz; trustees, A. C. Stoner, Jonathan Hites, and Joe Santee; assessor, Ed. Crosier.

RELIGIOUS.

The first religious services in Ripley were held at the school house on section 15, by the Rev. Richard Merrill, in September, 1860. Mr. Merrill was of the Presbyterian faith, and was quite a prominent man in the county. He was county superintendent of schools for several years, and is noticed at length in that connection.

A Methodist Episcopal Church was organized, by Rev. J. Rowen, in 1868, in a school house, then on section 20. Among the first members were, Minnie and Maggie Moorehead, Jerry Needham, J. J. Criswell, wife and daughter. The church continued, in a flourishing condition, for some years, services being always held in the school house mentioned. The organization is still in existence, but has no regular preacher. Among the ministers who have officiated here, are, the Reverends Cooley, Embrey, S. G. Smith, Henry Borgelt, O. H. Sproul, George Murphy, L. Winsett, and W. S. Robinson.

HITESVILLE POST OFFICE.

This post office was established in July, 1871, and J. S. Margretz was appointed the first postmaster, the office being located at his house on section 19. It was then on the mail route from Aplington to Bristow. It remained as such while the route was changed from Aplington to Hitesville. Mr. Margretz has since held the office and is the present postmaster. The office took its name from the Hites family or families, there being several of them among the first settlers of this part of the township.

J. S. Margretz was born in Union county, Pa., September 29, 1838, and is a son of Herman H. and Sarah (Stumpff) Margretz. During his early life he learned the miller's trade in his native county, and while there was also engaged in clerking for some time. In 1856 he came to Butler county, Iowa, passing the first summer in Albion township, and the following winter removing to Butler Center, where he worked in the steam saw-mill. On the 27th day of September, 1861, he enlisted in Company E, Twelfth Iowa Volunteers, and served until mustered out, January 20, 1866. At the battle of Shiloh, April 6, 1862, he was wounded in the left arm and also taken prisoner by the confederates. After remaining in different southern prisons until October 17, 1862, he was exchanged and returned to his regiment. Soon after Mr. Margretz's enlistment he was appointed corporal and afterward sergeant. Upon again entering civil life he returned to Butler Center, where he farmed for one year, and then came to his present location on section 19, where he now owns 160 acres of land. He has held the office of town clerk for eleven years, and has been justice of the peace three years. In 1879 he was appointed postmaster of Hitesville, and still retains that office. Mr. Margretz was joined in wedlock, December 5, 1869, with Miss Mary E. Dunson, a native of Shelby county, Ohio. Five children—Herman E., Guy C., Lotta B., Ella E. and Lloyd R.—have been born to them.

CEMETERY.

A cemetery is located on the northwest corner of the northeast quarter of section 29. This was used for this purpose at a very early day. The first interment was of the remains of a deceased daughter of Mr. and Mrs. Samuel Kimmel, in October, 1855.

FIRST SCHOOLS.

The first school in the township was taught in a building, erected for the purpose, on section 20, by Miss Susanna Kimmel, during the summer of 1858. Miss Kimmel is now the wife of Richard Davenport.

The next school was taught in the summer of 1859, by Miss Charlotte Levis, in a frame building, erected for the purpose, on section 15; James Hunter donating an acre to the district. Among the first scholars were the children of James Hunter, and George McCoy.

At present the township, being organized as a district township, is divided into seven sub-districts, and educational facilities here are good and efficient. The sub-districts are numbered from one to seven, and embrace territory as follows:

District No. 1 embraces sections 1, 2, 11, 12, 13, and 14, and has a school house on the eastern part of section 11, which was erected at a cost of $600.

District No. 2 is comprised of sections 3, 4, 9, 10, 15, and 16, having a $600 school house on the northwestern part of section 10.

District No. 3 embraces section 5, and a portion of sections 6, 7, and 8, and has a school house, on the latter section, which cost $600.

District No. 4 comprises sections 29, 30, 31, and 32, and parts of sections 19, and 20, having a school house on section 30, which cost $750.

District No. 5 is composed of sections 21, 22, 27, 28, 33, and 34. Its school house is located on section 28, and cost $600.

District No. 6 contains sections 23, 24, 25, 26, 35, and 36, having a school house on section 36, which cost, when erected, about $600.

District No. 7 embraces portions of sections 7, 8, 19, and 20, and all of 17, and 18.

Their school house was erected, on the southwestern part of section 17, in 1880, at a cost of $600.

CHAPTER XXXI.

SHELL ROCK TOWNSHIP.

This township derives its name from the Shell Rock river, and comprises township 92, range 15. Its contiguous surroundings are, Bremer county, on the east; Jefferson township, on the west; Butler township, on the north; and Beaver township, on the south. The township is a continuous garden, and the farmers here are quite prosperous.

The Shell Rock river enters on section 2, and, crossing sections 11, 12 and 13, leaves to enter Bremer county. Along the banks is to be found a heavy growth of timber; the balance of the township is made up of a rolling prairie, and is better adapted to raising the cereals than for stock.

There are two railroads crossing the township, the Burlington, Cedar Rapids & Northern, and the Dubuque & Dakota; the former on the west side of the river, the latter on the east.

The land in the northeastern part is of a sandy nature, and somewhat broken, as it lies on both sides of the river; but as you go southward from the stream, the land becomes rolling and the soil changes to a rich dark loam.

EARLY SETTLEMENT.

The first settlement made in this township was made in 1851, by two brothers, Harrison and Volney Carpenter, who had been here the year previous. They were hunters, and had come from Linn county. A little log cabin was erected which was used as a sort of hunters rendezvous, until Volney, who was a married man, brought on his wife. D. C. Finch was also in some manner associated with their settlement. Most of their time was spent in hunting and trapping, as this region abounded with game of all kinds, and the fur trade was good. Their claim was made on section 1. Volney's land included the old town plat of Shell Rock. In 1852, he sold it to Alexander Glenn, who is still a resident of Butler county. Volney then took up a tract of land northwest of Shell Rock, which has lately been occupied by Heman

Wm. Adair.

Hunt. He only remained here a short time, and his whereabouts at present are unknown. Shortly after the arrival of Mr. Glenn, in 1852, Daniel Myers put in his appearance and purchased Harrison Carpenter's place on section 1. Myers remained here a number of years. Harrison then removed to the West Fork—still in the same township—and took another claim, which, in 1854, he sold to A. Smith.

In the spring of 1853, George W. Adair came looking for a home. He stopped at Mr. Glenn's, and the latter gentleman sold him forty acres on the east side of the river on section 11, where the town of Shell Rock now is, which was all heavy timber, except that taken up by the bed of the river.

George W. Adair was born in Lexington, Virginia, October 31st, 1813. Shortly after his birth, his parents moved to Ohio and in that State his early life was passed. When he was seventeen years of age, the family moved to La Grange county, Indiana. Here he continued his education in the common schools, and helped his father work their farm. At the age of twenty-six, he moved to Iowa and settled near Muscatine. At that place he was married, January 17th, 1841, to Miss Elizabeth Smith, who was a native of Ohio. In 1853, as before stated, they came to Shell Rock, being the first settlers on the town plat, and moved into their log cabin on the first day of June. Soon after their settlement here, Mr. Adair began the erection of a saw mill, and in the fall of 1854, laid out the village of Shell Rock, he having entered the land upon which it now stands. He was of the democratic party, and although not caring for office, he always took an active part in his country's politics. Mr. Adair, in company with others, built both grist mills of the town and his great aim in life was the building up of a village of which he was the founder and pioneer settler. He died while on a visit to Kansas, on the 4th day of September, 1879. His wife still survives him and is the oldest living settler of the village. Nine children were born to them —Mary Jane, now the wife of Ephraim Town; John, now living in Winnipeg; Lucy A., now the wife of R. D. Bowen, of Kansas; George, living at Shell Rock; Walter, living in Clarinda, Iowa; Elizabeth, now the wife of Allen Allburn, of Sioux City; Sadie, Blanche and Nettie.

In the fall of 1853, Heman Hunt came and commenced working in the saw-mill which Adair built. Mr. Walters came the next year, and at about the same time came Messrs. Hawker, Compton, Dewy and Smith. In the fall of 1853, came Charles and Henry Sweitzer. In 1854 the other settlers came in rapid succession, among whom were, Hiram Ross, Messrs. Cram, Eastman and Hitchcock. The Newcomb brothers came in fall of 1855.

In the western part of the town the settlement began in 1853-4, and was close to the West Fork. Harrison Carpenter was about the first to stop here, as already stated. Others who were among the pioneers in this locality were, Michael Hollenbeck, D. White, R. L. Town, G. Shannon and T. Marslin.

D. White died some time since, leaving a nice property to his wife and children.

Shannon was unfortunate. At the time of his settlement quite a Mormon sensation was stirred up, and a Mormon preacher coming through, stopped with him. Shannon proposed to build a Mormon Tabernacle, in this vicinity; but before he had time to mature his plans and accomplish anything, his wife became too Mormonistic, and eloped with the preacher to Salt Lake.

Mr. Marslin went to Fort Randall during the war, and has not been heard of since.

REPRESENTATIVE SETTLERS.

It would be desirable, if possible, to here notice every settler in this township; but such a course adopted in each township throughout the county would enlarge this work to such an extent as to make it cumbersome and unwieldy, without adding to its value. We therefore herewith append a sufficient number of sketches concerning prominent citizens to fully represent the character of this settlement.

Frederick Frowe was born in England, February 11, 1827, and is a son of John and Mary Ann (Wood) Frowe, who are natives of England. When he was six years of age his parents came to the United States and settled in New York State, where they remained until 1849, and then came west and settled in Rockford, Illinois. Here Frederick engaged in farming for five years. In 1854 he came to Butler county, Iowa, and settled on section 29, Shell Rock township, where he now owns 200 acres of land. He was married in 1850 to Mary Ann Gunsalus. Seven children have been born to them. five of whom are now living—Ada Isabel, wife of William Mason, of this county; Antoinette, wife of James Mason; Effie, wife of Theodore Graham, of Grundy Center; Minnie, wife of John Walker, of Shell Rock, and Marchia. Mr. Frowe's mother died in 1872, and his father followed her two years later. Mrs. Frowe was born on the Illinois river on a raft. Mr. Frowe built his fine house in 1871.

H. L. Sweitzer is a son of Levis and Susan (Leverich) Sweitzer, and was born in Indiana in November, 1832. Four years afterward his parents moved to Iowa and settled on a farm in Cedar county, where they still reside. The son remained at home until 1854, when he came to Shell Rock, and soon after his arrival purchased a farm near Clarksville. This homestead he sold in 1865, and he now owns 220 acres of land in Butler county. Mr. Sweitzer has held several of the town offices at different times, and is a member of the village board at the present date. He was married in January, 1860, to Cynthia Bussey. Their children are: Dellis, Willie and Mary.

Asa Stannard was born in Monroe county, New York, February 10, 1827, and is a son of John and Phoebe (Norris) Stannard. His father was born in Vermont, and his mother, in New York. He remained in his native county until twenty-six years of age, with the exception of a few years passed in Gates county attending the Starkey Seminary; then went to Orange county and engaged in farming two years. In the spring of 1855, he came to Butler county, Iowa, and entered 160 acres of land on section 17, Shell Rock township. Here he lived for nine years, and then settled on section 16, where he now owns 80 acres. Mr. Stannard has held the offices of township assessor and trustee. He was married in 1853, to Miss Cynthia Cook, who is a native of Oswego county, New York. Eight children have been born to them, of whom seven are now living—Carlon Asa, Miriam C., Calisto E., Melissa F., Ida Arvilla, Phares Cook and Lydia P.

J. D. Landphere was born in Wyoming county, New York, November 6, 1836, and is a son of Ezra and Mary Ann (Wood) Landphere, who were both natives of that State. He remained in the county of his birth until six years of age, and then moved with his parents to Elkhart county, Indiana. Here they lived three years, and then moved to Kane county, Illinois, and afterwards to Will county. In 1856, they came to Butler county, Iowa, and settled on a farm in Beaver township. Mr. Landphere's mother died July 5, 1852. His father is still living in Denver, Colorado. He was married November 5th of the year 1857, to Hester A. Leslie, who was born in the State of Ohio, Licking county. They are the parents of one son—Claude L. Claude Leslie lives at home.

Amos Ressler is a son of Jacob and Esther (Roads) Ressler, and was born in Strasburg, Lancaster county, Pennsylvania, November 5, 1828. He grew to manhood in his native county, and there learned the carpenter's trade. In March, of the year 1856, he came west, and settled in Butler county, Iowa, and immediately began working on the steam mill at Butler Center. At this place he continued laboring for some time, and then rented a farm in Jefferson township, and took up the occupation of a "tiller of the soil." In 1862 he purchased forty acres of land in Shell Rock township, and now owns a fine farm of 160 acres. On it are good buildings, all of which he has erected since his residence there. Mr. Ressler has held a number of school offices at different times. His father died in 1880, on the old homestead, in Pennsylvania, where he had lived fifty-six years. His mother, also, died there in March, of the year 1838, at the age of forty-one years. Mr. Ressler was married in July, of the year 1854, to Miss Albertina Margretz, who was born in Union county, Pennsylvania, March 17, 1836. She is a daughter of Herman Henry and Sarah (Stumpff) Margretz. Her mother is a native of Pennsylvania, and her father, of Germany. The latter was killed on the battlefield, near Jackson, Tennessee, on December 17, 1863. Her mother still lives in Ripley township, Butler county. Ten children have been born to Mr. and Mrs. Ressler, of whom eight are now living—Adeline M., now the wife of J. W. Metzger, of Shell Rock; Amanda L., now the wife of Franklin Rice; Emma C., Mary J., Carrie A., Ellen S., Fred A., and Lottie E.

John Drum was born in County Westmeath, Ireland, in the year of our Lord, 1822. He came to America in 1849, and lived in the city of Detroit, Michigan, during the first winter after his arrival. He then moved to Genoa, Illinois, where he remained eight years. At the expiration of this time, he came to Iowa, and settled in Butler county, on section 25, of Shell Rock township, where he now resides, and owns 120 acres of land. Mr. Drum has held the office of school director and school treasurer. He was married, in 1857, to Miss Bridget Leary, who is, also, a native of Ireland. They are the parents of three children—Mary, Margaret, and Rose.

Martin Gleason was born in Ireland, in November, 1829. In 1848 he came to America, and first located in Orange county, New York, where he remained until the spring of 1855. He then came west and settled in Dubuque county, Iowa, where he lived three years, and in the spring of 1858, moved to Butler county, with an ox team. He traded his property in Dubuque county for 120 acres of land on section 34 of Shell Rock township. During the summer of 1858, he built a small log house on his place, in which the family lived for fourteen years, and it was then supplanted by his present fine residence. Mr. Gleason now owns a fine farm of 400 acres. He was married in 1855 to Miss Anna Barry, who is a native of Ireland. Eight children have been born to them of whom only one—William Lewis—is now living.

G. C. Hawley is a son of L. P. Hawley, and was born in Wayne county, Ohio, January 11, 1836. He remained in his native county until 1855 and then spent two years in Michigan. His mother died in 1844 and his father in 1852. In March of the year 1857, he came to Butler county, Iowa, and began working by the month. In 1862 he enlisted in Company F, Bissell's Engineer Regiment, afterwards consolidated with the First Missouri Engineer Corps, and served until honorably discharged at the close of the rebellion. Upon again entering civil life, he returned to Butler county and located on section 4, of Shell Rock township, where he now owns 100 acres of land. He was married in 1866 to Miss Eliza Adams, who is a native of Linn county, Iowa. In 1872 Mr. Hawley went to Montana, where he remained two years, working at his trade.

O. J. Wheeler was born in Chatauqua county, New York, in July of the year 1845, and is a son of Miles and Fanny (Pitcher) Wheeler, who were also born in New York State. When the son was twelve years old, the family moved west, and lived for one year in Janesville, Bremer county, Iowa, but at the end of that time, they moved to section 2, of Shell Rock township, and settled on a farm entered by the father, October 18, 1851. Mr. Wheeler's mother died in 1874, and his father followed one year later. He was married in April of the year 1877, to Ida Sewell, and they live on the old homestead.

Sylvester Rice is a son of James and Olive (Hall) Rice, and was born in Livingston county, New York, December 25, 1829. He remained in his native county until he was thirty years old. He was reared on a farm and followed that occupation while in the State of New York. His education was received in the common schools and in the State Normal school, of New York, from the latter of which he was the recipient of a first grade certificate. In 1860 he came to Waverly, and the following spring settled in Shell Rock. Mr. Rice belongs to the republican party, and has taken a great interest in the county and town politics; having held nearly all of the town offices. Mr. Rice has been a member of the Baptist Church since he was twenty-two years of age, and has taken an active part in the building up of that church, in Shell Rock. He was married in 1864, to Miss Carrie M. Dean, who was born in Michigan, Lenawee county. He has been trustee, assessor, treasurer, etc. His fine house was built in 1860.

Joseph Walker was born in England, January 5, 1835, and is a son of Joseph and Ann (Hall) Walker, who were both natives of England. He came to America in 1850 and made his home for some time in Rock county, Wisconsin, working at various occupations. In 1863 he came to Butler county and settled on section 34 of Shell Rock township, where he now resides and owns a farm of 120 acres. Mr. Walker was married in 1856 to Lecha Molloy, who is a native of Ireland. They have six children—Edwin, John, Alonzo, Anna, Kate and Arthur.

James Whitehead was born in Oneida county, New York, September 14, 1843, and is a son of Jeremiah and Harriet (Kellogg) Whitehead. His father was a native of Kent, England, born March 9, 1809, and came to America in 1835; and his mother was born in Herkimer county, New York, May 7, 1818. In 1850 the family moved to Oswego county, New York, and in 1855 to Milwaukee, Wisconsin. In October, 1861, his father enlisted in Company I, First Wisconsin Cavalry, commanded by Colonel Daniels, and served nearly two years. He was taken prisoner at Jonesborough, Arkansas, and was paroled and honorably discharged in 1863. He then returned to Wisconsin, and came to Shell Rock in 1864, where he died August 17, 1881. Mr. Whitehead's mother is still living and resides in Shell Rock, near where he now lives. Upon his arrival here he bought a farm of 80 acres, and now owns 160 acres. He was married, November 6, 1869, to Miss S. A. Ernst, a native of Sycamore, DeKalb county, Illinois. They are the parents of five children—Carrie, Bertie, Hattie, Freddie and Florence. Mrs. James Whitehead died January 3, 1883,
at the age of thirty-two years, five months and twenty-eight days.

J. W. Allen is a son of Isaac and Sarah (Blaisdell) Allen, and was born in Chatauqua county, New York, on the 10th day of August, 1846. Seven years after his birth his parents came west and located in Kendall county, Illinois, where they remained a short time, and then moved to Greene county, Wisconsin. In 1865 they came to Iowa and settled in Shell Rock township, Butler county. His mother died in Wisconsin, and his father is now living in Dakota. Mr. Allen now resides on section 17, where he owns 160 acres of land. He has held the office of assessor several times. In 1873, he was united in wedlock to Miss Ellen N. Varier, who is a native of Ohio. Three children have blessed this union—Dora, Ina and Addie.

Henry Nettleton is a son of Samuel and Elizabeth (McCauley) Nettleton, and was born near Prescott, Canada West, on the 1st day of January, 1836. In 1854, the family came to the United States and settled in Ogle county, Illinois. Here Henry remained until 1865, and then came to Iowa and settled on section 36, Shell Rock township, Butler county, and now owns 480 acres of land. Mr. Nettleton has been a member of the school board and a trustee of the town. He was married in 1860, to Miss Sarah C. Dillworth, who is a native of Canada. They are blessed with six children—Nora E., Laura J., Carrie A., Viola M., Irene B., and Ollie B. Mr. Nettleton's mother died when he was a child, and his father died in Shell Rock township in 1878. Mrs. Nettleton's father, Wm. Dillworth, died in Cook county, Illinois.

Her mother, Jane Dillworth, is living in Winona county, Iowa.

Phineas Weed is a son of Joshua and Abigail Weed, and was born in Wayne county, Ohio, November 7th, 1824. Here he lived until his father died—which event occurred about five years after Phineas' birth—and then he moved with an uncle to Cincinnati. In that city he received his education, and when old enough, learned the printing business. In 1840 he moved to Detroit, Michigan, where he followed his trade for some time and then returned to his native county, and there remained until the year 1865. During the years of the rebellion, Mr. Weed was engaged in furnishing horses for use of the government. At the close of the war he came to Butler county, Iowa, and settled in Shell Rock, and became largely engaged in sheep raising. In 1867 he returned to Ohio and spent two years in the city of Worcester, and then came back to Shell Rock and settled on the farm where he now resides. While the woolen mill of this place was in operation, Mr. Weed owned a half interest in it. He was married in 1864 to Miss Philomel S. Scobey, who is a daughter of Dr. John Scobey. Six children have been born to them, four of whom are now living—Florence, now the wife of Charles D. Henry, who is assistant cashier of the First National Bank of Waterloo, Iowa; Jennie, now the wife of J. D. Powers, a hardware merchant of Spencer, Iowa; Wallace P. and Jessie S.

Lawyer W. Howard was born in Broome county, New York, December 31st, 1834, and is a son of Samuel and Nancy (Rogers) Howard, both natives of that State. When he was fourteen years of age, the family moved west and settled in Jefferson county, Wisconsin, on a farm. Here the son grew to manhood, and two years after reaching his majority, was married to Miss Harriet Hoskins, who is a native of the State of Ohio. In 1865 they came to Butler county, and settled on section 14 of Shell Rock township, where they now own a farm of eighty acres. Mr. Howard is at present a member of the board of trustees and has served in that capacity several years. He has also held other school and town offices. His father died during the year of 1874. His mother is still living and resides in Wisconsin. Seven children have been born to the subject of this sketch, of whom four are now living—Frank Elmer, Fred Lincoln, Samuel Whiting and Nancy Irena. Mrs. Howard died December 11th, 1882, at the age of fifty-four years and seven months. While not a member of any church she was a kind, loving woman, a good wife and a loving mother.

G. G. Blake was born in Ireland, July 9, 1835. He is a son of Robert and Maria (McWilliams) Blake. His mother was a native of England, and his father of Ireland. Five years after his birth, the family came to the United States, and first settled in Waukesha county, Wisconsin, where they remained eight years, and then moved to McHenry county, Illinois. Here his mother died, in 1862, and his father, in 1875. During the first year of our rebellion Mr. Blake enlisted in Company E, Ninety-fifth Illinois Infantry, as a non-commissioned officer, and served until honorably discharged, at Springfield, Illinois, at the close of the war. Soon after returning to civil life he came to Iowa, and bought his present farm, of 240 acres, in Shell Rock township, Butler county, and in the spring of 1866 settled on it. He has held the office of school treasurer for the past ten years. He was married, in 1859, to Miss Mary Little, who is a native of Scotland. They have six children—Jeannette, now the wife of H. O. Smith, of Boone county, Nebraska; Clara, Minnie, Abbie, Robert and Julia. Mr. Blake went to Minnesota, in 1853, and settled on the present site of the city of St. Peter.

John Bowen is a son of Peleg and Rachel (Burnett) Bowen, and was born in Elk Creek township, Erie county, Pennsylvania, March 30, 1826. The family remained in that county but a short time after John's birth, when they moved to Middlebury, Summit county, Ohio. Here he grew to manhood, and when sufficiently old, learned the trade of boiler making, in Nilestown, Trumbull county, Ohio. He was chief engineer one year in the rolling mills at Nilestown. In 1853 he came to Iowa, and located in Farmers' Creek township, Jackson county, where he entered fifty-six acres of land, which he lived on and improved, nine years. He then spent two years in Linn county, and, in 1866, came to Butler county, first locating in Butler township. The next year, however, he settled on section 3, Shell Rock township, where he has since resided. In 1849 he was united in wedlock to Miss Mary A. Carns, who is a native of Mercer county, Pennsylvania. Six children have been born to them, five of whom are now living —Samuel D., Emma J., Harriet A., Otto A., and S. J. Mr. Bowen's father died in April, of the year 1879. His mother is still living.

Joseph R. Gibson was born near Prescott, Canada, on the 1st day of October, 1841, and is a son of Joseph G. and Charlotte (Wood) Gibson. His father was born in Edinburg, Scotland, and his mother in Canada. In 1852 the family came to the United States, and settled on a farm in Ogle county, Illinois. Here the son lived until the opening of the war, when he enlisted, October 8, 1861, in Company E, Forty-sixth Illinois Infantry. He served as a non-commissioned officer until honorably discharged, March 21, 1866, at Springfield, Illinois. In 1863 he re-enlisted as a veteran, and served until discharged, as stated above. Upon receiving his dismissal, he went home, and in July of the same year came to Butler county, Iowa, and settled in Beaver township. Here he remained until 1869, and then lived near Butler Center one year, after which he settled on section 33, of Shell Rock township, where he now owns 80 acres of land. Mr. Gibson has held the office of road supervisor. He was married December 25, 1866, to Miss H. R. Bass, who is a native of Illinois. They have three children—Charles Henry and Pearly Jane, twins; and James W. Mr. Gibson's mother died in the spring of 1859. His father still lives, in Ashton, Lee county, Illinois.

Colonel H. Greene is a son of John and Orphy (Slayton) Greene, and was born in Claybourne county, Tennessee, January 16, 1837. Two years after his birth, the family moved to Rockcastle county, Kentucky, where they lived about seventeen years, and then moved to Scott county, where the Colonel lived two years. He then moved to Owen county where he remained until the opening of the war of the rebellion. September 25, 1861 he enlisted in Company K, Fourth Kentucky Infantry, and served until honorably discharged December 29, 1863, at Chattanooga, Tennessee. Upon returning to civil life he came to Bridgeport, Indiana, where he remained until 1864. In the spring of that year he moved to Piatt county, Illinois, where he engaged in general work until 1866. From there he moved to Bremer county, Iowa, and afterwards to Butler township, Butler county; and in 1873, he settled on his present farm on section 28 of Shell Rock township, where he now owns 160 acres of land. He was married in 1861, to Miss Susan A. Bassett. Seven children have been born to them, of whom four are now living—Amanda, Mason, Adelbert and George P.

Charles Johnson was born in England, February 2, 1822. He came to America in 1840, and after spending two years in New York State, located in Walworth county, Wisconsin, where he bought 160 acres of land and improved it. For some years afterwards he engaged in freighting between Milwaukee and Watertown. In 1851, he settled on the farm he had previously purchased, and there lived for ten years. At the expiration of that time he moved to Sheboygan county, and, after living there four years, went to Chickasaw county, Iowa, and one year later came to Butler county, Iowa, and settled on section 23 of Shell Rock township, where he lived until the fall of 1882, when he moved into the village of Shell Rock. In 1851, he was united in marriage with Margaret Culbert. Three children—William, Mary and Ella—have been born to them.

Washington Tharp was born in Indiana, October 24, 1831. He is a son of Andrew and Jane (Ryan) Tharp. His mother is a native of Kentucky, and his father was born in North Carolina, near Guilford Court House. Shortly after their son's birth the parents moved to Central Indiana; first located in Rush county; then moved to Henry, soon afterward to Hancock, and then to Hamilton county. In the latter place his father entered some land, and there they lived three years and then moved to Hancock county, where they remained some time, and then returned to Rush county and still later to Hamilton. In 1853 they came to Iowa and located in Bremer county. Here they lived on a rented place for a year and then purchased and improved a farm. Washington remained at home until June 10, 1863, when he enlisted in Company G, Eighth Iowa Cavalry. He entered the army as a private, but was soon afterward promoted to commissary sergeant. He was taken prisoner at Newman, July 26, 1864, and carried to Andersonville, where he remained until September 15, 1864. He was then taken to North Carolina, where he was held prisoner until March 3, 1865. At this time he was restored to the Union army and was placed in a hospital on account of sickness, where he remained until able to return home. He was honorably discharged at Clinton, Iowa, June 16, 1865. In the fall of 1866 he settled on the farm on section 13, Shell Rock township, where he now resides and owns 135½ acres. He was married March 1, 1866, to Miss Mary

Jane White, of Waverly, a native of Delaware county, New York. They are the parents of five children—Frank, Ezra W., Roy F., Leta Eliza and Ray. Mr. Tharp's mother died during the year 1863, and his father passed away February 6, 1878. He bought his farm in Butler county in 1854, and holds a patent from the government for his land in Shell Rock township.

John Christy was born in Crawford county, Pennsylvania, October 15, 1827, and is a son of Henry and Margaret (Douglas) Christy, who were both born in Pennsylvania. He was reared on a farm and received a common school education in his native county. In 1855 he came west and located in DeKalb county, Illinois, where he lived five years, and then to McHenry county, for eight years. In 1868 he came to Butler county, Iowa, and settled on section 7, of Shell Rock township, where he has since resided. He was married, February 23, 1860, to Miss Julia Ann Dugan, also a native of Pennsylvania, born in 1826. They have one child—Mary B. She is living at home. Mr. Christy was elected justice of the peace, but refused to serve. He has a farm of 120 acres of land. His father died in December, 1867, and his mother in 1858. Mrs. Christy's father died in 1851, and her mother in 1870.

Benjamin Robbins was born in Herkimer county, New York, November 13, 1817, and is a son of Jacob and Lois (Mack) Robbins. His father was born in the State of Connecticut, and his mother in Massachusetts. Benjamin remained in his native county until he had attained his majority. He obtained a thorough education in the common schools of that section, after which he entered Hamilton Institute, Hamilton, New York, where he studied for four years, and in that time finished the academic and began the theological course, but was unable to complete the latter on account of his failing health. In 1839 he came west and located on a farm, in Trumbull county, Ohio, in the western reserve. This occupation he followed until the second year of the rebellion, at which time he enlisted in Company D, Sixth Ohio Cavalry, as a commissary sergeant, and served until honorably discharged, in August of the year 1863. Upon returning to civil life, he came to Bremer county, Iowa, and settled on a farm of forty acres, in Washington township. Here he remained until 1868, and then settled on section 10, of Shell Rock township, where he now owns a farm of 80 acres. In politics, Mr. Robbins belongs to the republican party, and is a member of the Christian Church. He was married, in 1842, to Sarah P. Leavitt, who died in 1852. Two children were born to them—Leavitt W., who is now living in Shell Rock township; and Lester C., who was killed at Atlanta, Georgia, September 4, 1864, while on picket duty, serving with the Twentieth Ohio Volunteer Infantry. Mr. Robbins was again married, in 1854, to Elizabeth Petitt. This union has been blessed with four children—Sarah, now the wife of Joseph Pease; Parintha A., now the wife of Robert Hunter; Frank W., and Burton B., who lives in Dakota. Frank W. was married, in November, 1881, to Nora Nettleton.

E. B. Corson is a son of Peter and Margaret (McCarty) Corson, and was born in Lycoming county, Pennsylvania, December 11th, 1844. Two years after the son's birth, the father died, but the mother is still living. E. B. remained in his native county eleven years and then came west with the family and settled in DeKalb county, Illinois, where he was reared on a farm and grew to manhood. In 1869 he came to Butler county, Iowa, and settled on section 1 of Jefferson township. Here he remained eight years and then, in October of the year 1882, settled on section 23, Shell Rock township. He lived in the village of Shell Rock three years previous to his settlement on section 23. Mr. Corson was married in January, 1871, to Miss Rachel Soach, who is a native of Westmoreland county, Pennsylvania. They are the parents of four children—Milton M., Estella May, George Ellis and Pearl Belle.

John H. Meade was born in Saratoga county, New York, January 14th, 1828, and is a son of Charles and Abigail (Owen) Meade. His father was born in Vermont, and his mother in Massachusetts. When John was sixteen years of age, his parents moved to Oneida county, New York, where he received his education. Four years later the family moved to Wisconsin, Sheboygan county, where he lived until the year 1870. In May of that year, he came to Butler county, Iowa, and settled on section 18 of Shell Rock township. There he lived for nine years and then moved to section 8, where he now owns 160 acres of land. Mr. Meade has held the office of township trustee, and has been a member of the school board. He was married in 1852, in the month of January, to Miss Sarah Albright, who is a native of New Jersey. Four children have been born to them, of whom three are now living—George E., who lives in the village of Shell Rock; Amy E., now the wife of William Johnson, of Shell Rock township; and Mary E. Mr. Meade's mother died in 1869, and his father in 1882, in Wisconsin.

Elias Ressler is a son of Jacob and Esther (Roads) Ressler. He was born in Lancaster county, Pennsylvania, August 27, 1823. He was reared on a farm, and his education was received in the common schools of his county. At the age of eighteen he began learning the blacksmiths' trade, and after his apprenticeship was served, he followed that occupation while living in that State. In 1865 he came west, and located at Sterling, Whiteside county, Illinois, where he remained six years. While there he worked in a machine shop. In 1871 he came to Butler county, Iowa, and settled on section 14, Shell Rock township, where he now owns forty acres of land. Mr. Ressler has held the office of school director. He was married, in February, 1852, to Miss Hannah Pennepecker, who is a native of Montgomery county, Pennsylvania, and is a daughter of Henry and Catherine (Hornsher) Pennepecker, natives of the same county. Her mother died in 1859, and her father in 1875. Seven children have been born to them, five of whom are now living—Emma, Melinda, now the wife of Roland Nettleton, of Shell Rock; Franklin J., Charles, and Minnie May. Mary Elizabeth died October 26, 1855; Thaddeus Stevens, died October 17, 1872. Mr. Ressler's mother died in 1838, and his father, in 1880.

Gasper T. Husband was born in Westmoreland county, Pennsylvania, June 27,

1829. He is a son of John and Margaret (Tarr) Husband, who, also, were natives of Westmoreland county. In 1857 he came to Washington county, Iowa, where he engaged in farming until the first year of the rebellion, when he enlisted in Company H, Second Iowa Infantry. He served in that company one year, and then served for two years in the Fourteenth Iowa Infantry, Company B. He was honorably discharged at Davenport, Iowa, November 16, 1864. Upon receiving his dismissal from service he returned to Washington county, and there remained until 1866. In the spring of that year he moved to Bremer county, and located in Sumner township, where he lived until 1874. At this time he went to California, on a visit, where he spent one summer, and then returned to Iowa, and settled on section 6, of Shell Rock township, where he has since resided. He was married, October 31, 1876, to Mary L. Hunt, who is a daughter of Samuel Hunt, of Trumbull county, Ohio.

Charles A. Jones is a son of Dr. Daniel and Mary (Barrett) Jones, and was born in Windsor county, Vermont, November 21, 1848. When he was six years of age the family moved to Bureau county, Illinois, where they were among the early settlers of that section of the country. While in school Charles used his time to the best advantage and thus was enabled, even in the frontier State of that country, to enter manhood's estate with a good education. He was reared on a farm. In 1876 he came to Butler county, Iowa, and settled on section 6, Shell Rock township, where he now owns 800 acres of land. He was married in 1876 to Miss Nancy A. Hammer, who was born in Cook county, Illinois. They are the parents of three children—Daniel, Louis and Joseph.

METHODIST EPISCOPAL CLASS.

A class of this denomination was organized in the spring of 1871 at Norton's Corners, on section 32, by the Rev. L. Cooley. The first members were: William Bass and wife, J. R. Gibson and wife, G. W. Bunn and wife, C. S. Simonds and wife, C. S. Norton and wife, J. B. Ressler and wife, J. M. Knight and wife, and R. Hughes and wife. The first class leader was R. Hughes, who has acted in that capacity ever since. The stewards are G. W. Bunn and J. R. Gibson. Services have been held every two weeks in the school house, and the membership has increased to thirty.

A Sunday school was also organized in 1871, with R. Hughes as superintendent, who held the position for six years. He was succeeded by G. W. Bunn, who was in turn by J. R. Gibson, and then R. Hughes again. They have an average attendance of thirty at the Sunday school.

SUNDAY SCHOOL ASSOCIATION.

The Shell Rock Sunday School Association was organized in June, 1878, with R. Hughes, president, and S. Rice, secretary. The presidents in sequence have been S. Rice, J. W. Phillips and R. Hughes. The object of the association is to advance the Sunday School work, its efficiency and interest. Meetings are held twice a year, alternately in the Baptists and M. E. Churches.

PLEASANT VIEW CREAMERY.

The starting point of this enterprise was a cheese factory which was commenced and operated in 1879, by a stock company. In 1880, it was purchased by J. H. Kublank, who added the creamery machinery and commenced work in February, 1880. The enterprise is located upon section 17; both butter and cheese are manufactured. Mr. Kublank also manages a farm of 80 acres in connection.

MURRAY'S CREAMERY.

In the winter of 1882, W. W. Murray established this on section 9. It occupies a building 20x40 feet, one story high, and is propelled by a five-horse steam power.

ORGANIC.

When the county was first divided into townships, in February, 1855, the territory now comprising Shell Rock was made a part of Beaver township, which, at that time, embraced, in addition to its present limits, Shell Rock, Jefferson and Albion. In March, 1855, another division took place, and the township of Shell Rock was created as embracing its present limits and the town of Jefferson. In March, 1857, Shell Rock was made to comprise its present territory, Jefferson being created and organized.

At the November election, in 1882, the following officers were elected, and are the present incumbents: Justices of the peace, E. Wilson and R. Hughes; township clerk, George VanVleck; constables, C. H. Lanning and W. J. Reed; assessor, J. D. Branum; trustee, L. Howard.

TOWN OF SHELL ROCK.

This is the only town platted in the township. It is very pleasantly located on both sides of the Shell Rock, one of principal streams in Iowa, and which furnishes an almost unlimited water power, and is almost ten miles from the junction of this stream with the Cedar river.

The town is one of those points that seem to be indicated by nature for an important commercial center, surrounded, as it is by an excellent farming country, whose farmers are thrifty and in good circumstances; and furnished by nature with one of the best water powers in Iowa, capable of propelling a vast amount of machinery. The site for the town could hardly be bettered, and there is no reason why the future of Shell Rock should not rank it high among the inner cities of the great Hawkeye State. The Burlington, Cedar Rapids & Northern Railroad, and the Dubuque & Dakota Railroad, both run within easy reach of the main part of the town, and make it a good shipping point.

There has been, in the minds of many, even in the minds of some old settlers, the false impression that the town was platted in 1853, but the following entry on the books of the county court will set that right.

"March 29, A. D., 1855.

"On this day, George W. Adair and Elizabeth Adair presented the plat of the town of Shell Rock, in the county of Butler, situated on the northwest quarter of section 11, in township 91, range 15, west of the fifth principal meridian, and having acknowledged the same as required by law, it was ordered that the whole be recorded as the law directs.

JOHN PALMER,
County Judge."

It is but just to say that some claim the town was platted in 1854, but the plat was not recorded until 1855. Additions which have subsequently been made, have extended the town westward, until the west side of the river is the largest and has the greatest number of inhabitants.

EARLY SETTLEMENT.

When the Carpenter brothers first came here, in 1850, and, in fact, when it passed into the hands of George W. Adair, the founder of the town, the site, and all along the stream, was covered with a heavy growth of timber, which was almost impenetrable; but this belt of timber has been cut away even faster than time has cut away the first settlers that have so often crept beneath its shadows. A thrifty little city has grown up over its decayed roots, and all that is left of the giant forest, is the scattering shrubs that shoot upward here and there, as if in defiance of the work of former years.

The first settlers here were Harrison and Volney Carpenter, above mentioned. Following them came Alexander Glenn; then George W. Adair. The latter platted the town.

Among others of the early comers here were, the Newcomb brothers, Messrs. Hiram Ross, the Switzers, Cram, Eastman, Hitchcock, John Leverage and John L. Stewart.

O. L. Eastman was born in Orleans county, New York, January 10, 1836. He is a son of Jeremiah and Caroline (Dodd) Eastman. His father is a native of Vermont and his mother of New Hampshire. In 1838 his parents moved to Will county, Illinois, and here the son received a good common-school education, and when old enough learned the trade of blacksmithing. In October, 1855, he came to Cedar Falls, Iowa, and in the spring of 1856 removed to Shell Rock and opened a blacksmith shop. In this business he has since been engaged, with the exception of three years spent in farming and sheep raising. In 1867 Mr. Eastman added agricultural implements to his business, and now occupies himself with the two branches of trade. He was married in 1860 to Miss Constansia A. Scobey, who is a daughter of Dr. John Scobey, of Shell Rock. They have been blessed with one child—Maud —who is now the wife of C. S. Eastwood, of Spirit Lake.

J. L. Stewart is a son of William M. and Ann (Laughlin) Stewart, and was born in Bond county, Illinois, February 28, 1824. Here he remained until 1832, when his parents moved to Putnam, Illinois, where they remained until May of the year 1839; they then moved to Muscatine connty, and afterward to Johnson county, Iowa. In this latter county Mr. Stewart's mother died, in 1848. His father still survives her, and is now living in Washington Territory, and on the 24th of April, 1882, he reached his eighty-eighth year. J. L. remained in Johnson county until 1844, and then moved to Linn county, where he lived for about nine years. In 1853 he came to Shell Rock, Iowa, and worked at mill-wrighting, on the old saw mill. However, he did not move his family here until 1855. He continued working in the mill until 1870, when he opened a wagon shop, and since that time has been in business for himself. Mr. Stewart was a delegate to the convention that led to the establishment of the first mail route through the village. He was married in Johnson county, Iowa, September 22, 1844, to Miss Maria Ann McCorcle, who is a native of Piketon, Ohio. Only one child has been born to them, and it died in infancy. His father is a Presbyterian preacher. J. L. is a worker in the M. E. Church.

The first goods were sold by Mr. Cram, in a hotel building erected by him in 1855.

O. S. Newcomb went into business at an early day and opened a stock of goods on the east side of the river, in the building where Mr. Town afterward resided. He is of the firm of Newcomb & Carter, and truly one of the pioneer merchants of Shell Rock. He was born in the town of Middlefield, Geauga county, Ohio, May 20, 1830, and is a son of Orin and Parmelia (Robinson) Newcomb, who are both natives of the State of Connecticut. Mr. Newcomb's youth and the first few years of his manhood were passed in the vicinity of his birthplace. In 1855 he came to Iowa and settled in Shell Rock. Soon after his arrival he opened a store here, and has since been in trade at this point. In 1862 he enlisted in Company E, Thirty-second Iowa Infantry, and served until honorably discharged at Davenport, at the close of the rebellion. He was captured at Pleasant Hill, Louisiana, during the battle there, and was carried a prisoner by the enemy to Camp Ford, Texas. Here he remained in prison for thirteen months and eighteen days, and his food consisted of corn meal and poor beef, without salt, and no cooking utensils save a small kettle for fifty men. As soon as peace was declared Mr. Newcomb returned to his home and business in Shell Rock, and since then has given his undivided attention to his chosen branch of trade. While in prison he became a convert to religion, and has since been a member of the Disciple Church. He was married in 1855 to Miss Huldah C. Carter, a native of Parkman, Geauga county, Ohio. They have been blessed with five children, of whom Frederick O., Minnie C. and Mabel Estella are now living. Frederick O. is financial manager of the Iowa City *Republican*, and a graduate of the State University. Minnie C. is now the wife of Thomas S. Kenyon, of Grundy Center.

George W. Adair erected a small log house on the east side of the river, and moved his family in during July, 1853. During the summer of that year he erected a saw mill, the millwright being Hiram Ross, which stood the sunshine and tempest for twenty-five, and was then—in 1878—torn down. George W. Adair also built the first dam at this point, in 1853. This was partially washed away in 1855, by a freshet, and soon afterward the present dam was constructed by George W., and William Adair.

FIRST THINGS.

The first house in Shell Rock was erected in the spring of 1853, and was a little log structure on the east side of the river. The first frame house was built in 1854, by Elias Walter, and also stood on the east side of the river.

The first store was opened by R. D. Cram, in a room of the building now owned and occupied by E. Town, on the east side of the river. This took place early in the fall of 1855.

O. S. Newcomb came at about the same time, and erected a small building, for store purposes, on the same side of the river, and, on the 1st of October, 1855, opened up a small stock of general merchandise. This building is now occupied by Jerry Evarts, as a dwelling. Mr. Newcomb remained there until the spring of 1859, when he removed to the west side of the river, and opened up in a log school house. In the fall of that year he moved to the present location of Newcomb & Carter. He then took T. G. Copeland as a partner, and, in 1860, J. H. Carter purchased that gentleman's interest, so that the firm has since been known as Newcomb & Carter. They do a large business, and are among the "solid" men of Butler county.

The first birth was Frank Walter, a son of Elias Walter and wife, and was born in January, 1855. He is now living at Waterloo, Iowa.

The first marriage was Elias Walter to Miss Rachel Billhimer, at the house of the bride's parents.

The first wagon-maker to locate at Shell Rock was John L. Stewart, who opened up for business near the site of his present shop in 1854.

The first blacksmith was John S. Robbins, who opened a shop on the east side, where Ralph Town's residence now stands, in the fall of 1854. He sold to George Hawker in 1855. Hawker died in 1863.

The first shoemaker was T. G. Copeland, who opened a shop on the west side in Newcomb & Copeland's store, in 1859. He remained one year, and is now at Willoughby, in this county.

The first furniture store was established by L. F. Bristow.

The first drug store was opened by Dr. E. L. Thorp.

In 1859, Philip Bemler opened the first hardware store in town, and after remaining two years he moved to Cedar Falls.

The first photograph gallery was established by Henry Apfel. He was born in Sultz, France, on the first day of April, 1838. Two years after his birth, his parents came to the United States, stopping at Syracuse, New York for a short time, and then settling in the city of Chicago, where his father formed one of its early settlers, and he continued to live there until his death, which occurred in 1879. Henry grew to manhood in the city, and when old enough, learned the trade of photography in E. L. Brand's studio. He continued to make Chicago his home until 1870, when he came to Iowa and located at Waverly, during which time he lost his property by the Chicago fire. Here he remained four years and then returned to Chicago, where he lived for one year, and again came to Iowa, and settled in Shell Rock, where soon after his arrival, he opened his present business. He was married in 1865, to Miss Minnie Toll. They are the parents of four children—Walter, Alfred, Elmer and Robert.

The first agricultural implement warehouse was established by O. L. Eastman in 1867.

The first burial in the cemetery, which is located just north of Shell Rock on the west side of the river, was the wife of Charles Leverich, who was called from earthly labors on the 18th of June, 1855.

HOTELS.

The first hotel in Shell Rock was erected by R. D. Cram, during the spring of 1856, and was opened by him in connection with his store. It afterward became the property of W. R. Cotton, and was called the "Butler House." This is now known as the "Revere House,"

G. W. Adair, who platted the town of Shell Rock, opened the second hotel in the place, on the east side of the river, in 1867, which was called the "Shell Rock House." He continued this business for about thirteen years, when, his health failing, he took a trip to Kansas, hoping thereby to be benefited. He died while in that State.

The "Central House" was erected in 1878, by Boomer Brothers & Phillips. It was afterwards purchased by J. W. Phillips, and finally came into the hands of John Speaker, the present proprietor. The hotel is a neat, two-story frame building; size, 36x80 feet.

John Speaker was born in Seneca county, Ohio, on the 8th day of April, 1832. He is a son of John and Sobina (Speaker) Speaker, who were natives of Maryland. He remained in his native county until 1845, when he, in company with his parents, moved to Winnebago county, Illinois. Here he remained until 1865, when he moved to Waverly, Bremer county, Iowa, where he engaged in the hotel business, and subsequently, in the grocery trade. In April, 1878, he came to Shell Rock and took the proprietorship of the Central House, and is now its genial landlord. He was married, in 1860, to Miss Mary Jane Cowan, who was born in Canada. Four children have been born to them, three of whom are now living—Orilla, wife of J. F. Cole, who now holds a government position in China; Carrie, and Ralph.

LEGAL PROFESSION.

The first lawyer to locate here was Orson Rice, in 1855, and who remained about five years. William Norval came soon after. There are no practicing attorneys here at present, although several have come and gone in the meantime. The attorneys are treated at length in the chapter upon the history of the bar.

MEDICAL PROFESSION.

The first physician was Dr. John Scobey, who came in May, 1856, and who practiced medicine here until 1875, when he retired from practice. He is still a resident and an honored citizen. The present members of the medical profession are Drs. E. H. Dudley, W. H. Smith, E. L. Thorp and E. E. Sill. These gentlemen are sketched in the proper chapter.

SCHOOL MATTERS.

The first school in Shell Rock was taught by Mrs. Nancy McAllister in a room of the dwelling of Ebenezer Walter, during the summer of 1855. The Methodist Church was afterward used for school purposes, and Ozro R. Newcomb taught the second term. The town is now divided into two independent districts, one on each side of the river, respectively called the East and West Shell Rock districts.

In 1862 a school house was erected on each side of the river, and these were used until 1874, when the present school buildings were erected, each costing $3,000.

POST OFFICE.

The postoffice of Shell Rock was established in the summer of 1855, in a building now owned and occupied by J. W. Stewart as a residence. The first postmaster was George Hawker. Mail was, at this time, brought by carrier from Janesville; but the town was afterward on the route from Cedar Falls to St. Ansgar, Minnesota. It was then a weekly mail, but was changed to a daily upon the arrival of the railroad in 1871. For some time previous they received three mails per week.

In 1856, O. S. Newcomb was appointed postmaster, and the office was moved to his store. He was succeeded by John Smith; he by James Leverick; then came Wm. R. Cotton, J. H. Carter, Wm. Mullen, James Leverick, E. L. Thorp and A. G. Stonebreaker, the present incumbent. It was made a money order office July 1, 1877, and the first order was drawn July 2, 1877, Dr. E. H. Dudley being the remitter, in favor of E. F. Ingalls, of Chicago, to the amount of $2.00. The first order paid was to Minerva Wellman from W. H. Cramer, of Galena, Illinois, July 13, 1877, for $3.00.

MILLS.

George W. Adair erected the first grist mill on the west side of the river in 1856, but did not commence operations until 1857. It is now known as the Shell Rock Mills. The mill was built at a cost of $10,000, and was 30x40 feet in size and three stories high, containing two run of stones. In June, 1857, it became the property of John F. Wright, and he afterward sold a one-third interest to the Overman Brothers, and also a like share to Sheldon Fox. In 1866 Wright purchased one-half of Overman's interest and Fox possessed himself of the remainder. Soon afterward Fox sold his interest to Francis Levins, and in 1868 this interest became the property of C. H. Parsons, subject to a mortgage to the Dean estate. This half was finally divided between the estate and Benjamin Levins. In 1878 John Ray purchased the half in question, and Mr. Wright having retained his interest, the firm of Wright & Ray have since been owners. Its size is the same as when first built; it now has three run of stone.

J. F. Wright, of the milling firm of Wright & Ray, is a son of Dan. and Ruby (Fellows) Wright. He was born in Maryland, Otsego county, New York, on the 12th day of July, 1828. He remained in his native State until nineteen years of age, and then made a trip to Wisconsin, where he spent one year. He then returned to the State of New York, and engaged in millwrighting, which work he followed in that State until 1855. In September, of that year, he came west to Cedar Falls, Iowa, and there remained till June, of the year 1857, when he removed to Shell Rock, and bought an interest in the flouring mills of this place. On August 13, 1862, he enlisted in Company E, Thirty-Second Iowa Volunteers, and was commissioned Second Lieutenant. He was wounded at the battle of Pleasant Hill, Louisiana, taken prisoner, and remained in rebel prisons about three months. From the effects of his wound he has never entirely recovered, and now receives a pension therefor. At the close of the rebellion he was honorably discharged, at Clinton, Iowa, and, in September, 1865, returned to Shell Rock, where he has since been actively engaged in the milling business. In 1867 Mr. Wright was elected county treasurer, and on the 1st of January, 1868, entered upon his new duties. He was re-elected in 1869, and continued to fill that office until January 1, 1872. He was married, in 1871, to Miss Anna J. Follett, who is a native of Otsego county, New York.

ROCKLAND MILL.

This flourishing mill was erected by George W. Adair in company with Emanuel Metzger, on the east side of the river, in 1870, at the cost of $18,000. It was a two-run mill, propelled by water power, the building being the same as at present, a four story frame structure. In 1872 the builders sold it to Robert McDonald, who added another run of stone in 1874, and in 1879 sold to the present proprietors—the Haynes Brothers. In 1880 another run of stone was added.

Thomas L. Haynes, of the firm of Haynes Brothers, is a son of Thomas and Hannah (Lester) Haynes, and was born in England on the 29th day of March, 1849. When he was eleven years of age his parents came to the United States. They first located in Milwaukee, Wisconsin, but after living there a short time, left for Waukesha county, where they resided for many years. In 1869 Thomas left home and engaged in milling at different points for the space of ten years, after which time he and his brother William bought the Rockland Mill at Shell Rock, Iowa, and here he has since lived. He was married in the year 1880, to Miss Kate Robinson, who is a native of Menasha, Wisconsin. Mr. Haynes is a Master Mason, a member of Escollop Lodge, No. 263.

William H. Haynes, of the firm of Haynes Brothers, was born in England, December 2, 1853, and is a son of Thomas and Hannah (Lester) Haynes, who are both natives of England. Seven years after William's birth his parents left their home for the United States, and upon reaching the new land started westward until they came to Milwaukee, Wisconsin. Here they stopped a short time and then went to Waukesha county, where they found themselves a good home and settled. In 1873 W. H. left his parents' roof and engaged in milling at different points for six years. In 1879 he came to Shell Rock, and in company with his brother Thomas bought the Rockland Mill of this place.

WAGON AND FURNITURE MANUFACTORY.

A wagon and furniture manufactory was built in 1858 on the east side of the river by Ross & Town. This building was changed to a woolen mill in the spring of 1868, and Hard & Royce became owners, where they carried on a general manufacture of all kinds of woolens. Mr. Hard sold his interest to James A. Morrison in 1869. Royce, Morrison & Mason were the next owners, who ran the mill two years, when Morrison sold to Phineas Weed, and he afterward to D. P. Holt, who afterward bought the whole mill. The machinery was taken out and the manufactory abandoned in December, 1877. The building is now used as a feed mill.

THE HAWKEYE CREAMERY.

This enterprise was established at Shell Rock, during the winter of 1878, by W.

W. Murray and Charles Austin. During the first year 50,000 pounds of butter was manufactured. In July, 1881, the firm changed, and W. W. Murray owned the property, retaining it until November, 1881, when Charles Austin became proprietor. In April, 1882, Samuel Kennedy purchased a half interest, and the firm has since remained Austin & Kennedy. They manufacture an average of 200,000 pounds of butter a year, employing six teams and nine men to gather cream throughout the surrounding country. The propelling power is an eight horse steam engine. In connection with their butter business, the firm handles 20,000 dozen of eggs monthly, shipping to eastern markets.

W. W. Murray was born in Franklin county, Ohio, October, 1844. He remained in his native county until he was sixteen years of age, and then came west and settled in Woodford, Illinois. In 1861 he enlisted in Company K, Ninth Illinois Cavalry, and served until honorably discharged, in October, 1865. He enlisted as a private, but was afterward made a sergeant. Upon returning to civil life, he came to Linn county, Iowa, and engaged in merchandising at Palo. There he remained until 1869, and then spent some time in Missouri. In 1874 he came to Shell Rock, Butler county, and opened a hardware store. This business he followed some time and then farmed for two years; after which he again opened a store at Shell Rock. After continuing in business here for some time, he went to Walker, and engaged in trade, and in November, 1878, he opened the Hawkeye Creamery, and there did business until the fall of 1881, when he sold it and rented the Hall factory, and engaged in the manufacture of butter and cheese. During the winter of 1882, he opened the creamery on his farm. Mr. Murray was married in October, 1874, to Miss Emma Hollenbeck.

G. P. GREEN'S STOCK EXCHANGE.

One of the leading and most important industries in the business of Shell Rock is the Stock Exchange of G. P. Green; and there is probably no one branch of industry that brings trade to the town as this does. G. P. Green established the business here in 1871. In 1873, seeing the necessity for better facilities, he built his present commodious yards, which are well worth a visit. To give a complete description and a correct idea of the amount of business can hardly be done. Suffice to say that they were erected at a cost of $8,000. In the building and under one roof is, first, the scale house and office. Back of these come the main stock sheds, which are mainly used for swine. This shed is 18x220 feet in length, and is divided into pens large enough to accommodate twenty hogs each. Running through the center of this building is an alley, and by an ingenious arrangement in the shape of a gate the swine can be separated with but little trouble. Connected with the building and under the same roof is a slaughter house and a store room 18x54 feet. This part of the building is two stories, the upper one being used for offices, scale house, cook room (for cooking feed), store room, wagon house and horse barn. Underneath is another lot of pens and a stable for fattening cattle. Underneath the building is a well which supplies the whole building with water, by means of a pipe running the entire length of the building and out into the yards. The power used is a windmill, and by turning a faucet the stock can be watered in any part of the grounds, or by attaching a hose the stables can be cleaned. The building is located on the banks of the Shell Rock, so that all refuse matter can be carried away. Mr. Green does a business of $200,000 annually. In connection with his business here he also has stock yards at Allison, Bristow and Dumont. During four months of the summer of 1882 he shipped 106 carloads of stock from this point.

G. P. Green is a son of Lewis and Nancy (Lewis) Green. He was born in Erie county, Ohio, December 23, 1837. He remained in the county of his birth until twenty-five years of age, and then moved to Huron county, Ohio, where he lived one year. From Huron, he moved to Loraine county, where he remained two years, and from there to Wood county, where he made a stay of four years. During these years he was engaged in buying and selling horses. In 1869 he came to Butler county, Iowa, and, soon after, embarked in stock trade, in which business he has since engaged. He was married, in 1860, to Miss Julia Cain, who is a native of Ohio. Mr. Green began life with nothing, and, by perseverance, good management and strict attention to business, has accumulated a large property.

THE SHELL ROCK BANK.

This banking institution was established, in September, 1876, by Boomer Bros. & Phillips, with Benjamin Boomer, president; J. H. Boomer, vice-president, and J. W. Phillips, cashier. On the 15th of May, 1878, it was purchased by Fairfield & Phillips, and started in present management with Clark Fairfield, president, and J. W. Phillips, cashier. The bank does a good business, and is of sound financial standing. Its correspondents are Preston, Kean & Co., Chicago; National, of New York, and the First National Bank, of Dubuque.

INCORPORATION.

The town of Shell Rock was organized as a distinct municipality, under the special laws of Iowa, in 1873. The first election was held in 1875, when the following officers were elected: Mayor, E. Town; trustees, R. McDonald, J. G. Rockwell, C. Sweitzer, Orville Jones and A. G. Stonebreaker; recorder, R. D. Prescott; treasurer, J. W. Phillips.

In 1876, the officers were: Mayor, R. D. Prescott; trustees, H. L. Sweitzer, John Williams, A. G. Stonebreaker, Orville Jones, W. C. Eastwood; recorder, N. Johnson; treasurer, J. W. Phillips; marshal, C. S. Simons.

The officers for 1877 were: Mayor, R. D. Prescott; trustees, W. C. Eastwood, E. Town, H. L. Sweitzer, G. O. VanVleck and John Williams; recorder, N. Johnson; treasurer, J. W. Phillips; marshal, W. J. Reed.

The officers for 1878 were: Mayor, J. H. Carson; trustees, H. L. Sweitzer, J. W. Ray, M. B. Speedy, John Williams, James H. Graham; recorder, Anson Peck; treasurer, J. W. Phillips; marshal, E. Winship.

In 1879 the officers were: Mayor, John Jamison; trustees, John Williams, A. G. Stonebreaker, J. H. Graham, E. Town and Robert McDonald; recorder, J. S. Auner;

treasurer, J. H. Carson; marshal, E. B. Morill.

In 1880 the officers were: Mayor, E. M. Jones; trustees, E. Town, G. P. Green, C. Sweitzer, R. Wilford, J. A. Graham and John Williams; recorder, R. W. Fulton; treasurer, J. H. Carson; marshal, E. B. Morill.

In 1881 the officers were: Mayor, John Hamilton; trustees, W. C. Eastwood, W. W. Murray, E. Town, G. P. Green, R. Wilford and John Williams; recorder, E. D. Ross; treasurer, J. H. Carson; marshal, J. W. Walter.

The officers for 1882 were: Mayor, Richard Hughes; recorder, E. D. Ross; trustees, W. C. Eastwood, J. P. Reed, H. L. Sweitzer, R. Wilford, J. A. Graham, G. P. Green; treasurer, J. H. Carson; marshal, James Jerolaman.

PRESENT BUSINESS OF SHELL ROCK.

Of the present business men of Shell Rock a great deal could be said, and deserving commendation be bestowed. They are a live and energetic class, made up of men who are of standing in the commercial world, and who are recognized as honorable and upright. They established their various branches of business as follows:

J. L. Stewart commenced his wagon trade in 1854.

The business of Newcomb & Carter was established in 1855, by O. S. Newcomb, and they now do an annual business of $30,000.

J. H. Carter was born in Parkman, Geauga county, Ohio, on the 4th day of April, 1837, and is a son of James H. and Caroline G. (Burgess) Carter, who were natives of Vermont, and early settlers of Ohio. His educational advantages were, first the common schools and afterward two years at Hiram College, under James A. Garfield. In the spring of 1857, he came to Shell Rock, Iowa, and after remaining about two years, returned to Ohio. In 1862 he made a second trip to Shell Rock, and this time entered in partnership with O. S. Newcomb, with whom he has since been associated. In politics he is a republican, and during late years, has taken an active part in the politics of the county. He has always taken great interest in the building up of the town of Shell Rock, and has left no stone unturned by which he could further its advancement. He is a genial, whole-souled gentleman, and esteemed by all who know him. In 1863 he was united in marriage to Miss Kate J. Nash, who was born in the State of Ohio. They have two children—Carrie H. and James H.

O. L. Eastman engaged in blacksmithing in 1856. In 1870 he put up his present establishment, 25x65 feet, and does a general blacksmithing business, employing three men. He also, in 1867, established an agricultural warehouse.

T. S. Walter commenced business in the harness trade in 1868.

L. F. Bristol established himself in the furniture trade in 1871, and in 1882 changed to undertaking goods exclusively.

Fairfield & Phillips, in 1871, established their lumber yard, and also erected a warehouse with a capacity of 10,000 bushels of grain.

The following year J. P. Bement commenced the grain trade.

HISTORY OF BUTLER COUNTY.

J. P. Bement is the son of J. C. and Frances E. (Cornell) Bement, and was born July 13, 1836, in Niagara county, New York. Here he received an academic education, and remained in his native State until twenty-two years of age. In 1858 he came west and settled in Waverly, Bremer county, Iowa, where he engaged in farming three years, drugs one year, and after that in the grain business. In 1872 he came to Shell Rock and started in the lumber and grain trade, which branches of business he now follows. While living in Waverly Mr. Bement went back to his native State and spent two years among old friends. He was married in 1867, to Miss Mary E. Taber, who is a native of Wisconsin. They have two children—Charles P., and Frank T. Mr. Bement's parents are now residents of Iowa. Commencing as weigher in a warehouse, he worked up till he now is proprietor of an elevator and lumber yard. He spent one winter buying grain at Ackley.

The same year—1872—W. C. Eastwood opened his boot and shoe store and shop, in which he now does an annual business of $15,000. He was born at Brockville, Canada West, March 30, 1817. He is the son of Amos and Sarah Eastwood, of Connecticut. At the age of fifteen he removed to St. Lawrence county, New York. At the age of twenty he married Mahala Dayton, of Rossie, St. Lawrence county, New York. He was engaged in the hotel business until 1840, when he moved to Brockville, Canada West. He remained in Canada until June 10, 1849, when he removed to Sheboygan Falls, Wisconsin. On the 7th of April, 1859, his wife died. They had seven children, five of whom are still living—Mary J., wife of J. B. Kelsey, of Shell Rock, Iowa; Charlotte, wife of W. P. Cary, of Sheboygan Falls, Wisconsin; Harriet A., wife of Frank Wesenfelder, of Sheboygan Falls, Wisconsin; Edgar O., resides at Chicago, Illinois, and Elvoretta, who resides at home. In 1875 Mr. Eastwood married a Mrs. Hurd, of Shell Rock, Iowa.

D. J. Gould commenced doing business in his shoe shop in September, 1874.

In November, 1874, J. R. Clawson commenced business in the hardware trade, and the business now amounts to $30,000 annually.

Dudley & Stonebreaker, in 1875, commenced business in the drug line.

A. G. Stonebreaker was born in Cattaraugus county, New York, October 25th, 1840. Here he remained until fifteen years of age and received a good common school education. In 1855 he moved with his parents, Peter and Julette (Reed) Stonebreaker, to Kenosha, Wisconsin, where he remained until he entered the army. He enlisted in Company K, First Wisconsin Heavy Artillery, in 1863 and served as a non-commissioned officer until honorably discharged at Milwaukee, Wisconsin, at the close of the Rebellion. Upon his return to Kenosha, he engaged in stock buying, which business he followed until 1874, when he came to Shell Rock, Iowa, and opened a drug store. He was appointed postmaster of Shell Rock, December 25, 1875, and fills that position at the present time, besides doing a good business as a druggist. He was married in October, 1861, to Miss Addie Bristol, who died in 1863. He again united himself in marriage to Miss Lucy M. Upson, in August, 1866. They have had three children, two of whom are now living—Ellen A. and Grace Edna.

Wright & Ray, the same year, took charge of the Shell Rock Mills, as elsewhere stated.

The photograph gallery was established in 1875, by H. Apfel. This was in August.

J. H. Carson, in 1876, opened his store with a stock of $700, which by close application to business has increased until he now carries a stock of $7,000, and does an annual business of $25,000.

In January of the same year, the opening of C. W. Bishop's jewelry store took place.

J. P. Bement established his lumber yard in 1877.

The millinery store of Mrs. H. Apfel was opened in the spring of 1878.

J. H. Paley's boot and shoe shop was opened in September, 1878, and now does a thriving business. He was born in Saxony, Germany, October 11, 1833. Here he passed his youth, and, in the course of time, learned the shoemaker's trade. When twenty-one years of age he came to the United States, and after remaining in New York State a short time, went to Wisconsin. He made short stays at different points in this State until 1857, when he located at Lake Mills, Wisconsin, and worked at his trade for some time, and then moved to Columbus, Wisconsin, where he remained nine years. At the expiration of this time he went to Tomah, Wisconsin, where he lived eight years. In 1876 he came to Shell Rock, Iowa, and worked two years for W. C. Eastwood, and then opened his present shop. He was married in 1857, at Lake Mills, Wisconsin, to Amelia Bartel. They have had eight children, seven of whom are now living—Matilda, now the wife of Augustus Werehran; Amelia, now the wife of A. Baker; Emma, Gustave, Frances, Otto and Bertha.

In 1879 Haynes Brothers took charge of the Rockland mills, a history of which appears elsewhere.

J. E. Patton opened his harness shop for trade in July, 1880.

Graham & Jerolaman established themselves in the stock trade in 1880, and now do an annual business of $30,000.

E. J. Young opened up in the furniture business, in February, 1881. He is a native of Oswego county, New York, born June 15, 1858. He is a son of Frederick and Sarah (Hawthorne) Young. When he was seven years of age, his parents moved west, and settled in Shell Rock, Iowa, where he grew to manhood. In February, 1881, he embarked in the furniture trade, and now carries a fine, and well-assorted stock of goods. He was married, September 27, 1882, to Miss Jennie B. Dean, of Waverly, Iowa. His parents are living in Shell Rock.

During the winter of 1881, J. B. Kelsey established his grocery store.

J. M. Longfellow commenced in the hardware trade in May, 1882, and does a thriving business.

About the same time Graham & Jones took charge of the general merchandise establishment, formerly conducted by Kothe & Graham. This store now does an annual business of $20,000.

In October, 1882, W. F. Stoddard established his grocery store, which has a healthy and growing trade.

The firm of Austin & Kennedy took charge of the Hawkeye Creamery in 1882.

Samuel Kennedy was born in Ireland, November 19, 1843. He was educated in the common schools of that country, and at the age of twenty-one years came to the United States and located in Brooklyn, New York, where he engaged in the dry goods business, and there remained until 1865. At this time he came west and settled in Sheboygan county, Wisconsin, on a farm, where he lived for five years, and then engaged in general merchandising, which business he followed until 1875. He then resumed farming for five years, and in the spring of 1880 came to Shell Rock, Iowa, and engaged in the meat and egg trade. In this branch of business he continued for some time, and then formed a partnership with Charles Austin and became one of the proprietors of the Hawkeye Creamery. He was married in 1867 to Miss Amy Smith, who is a native of England. They have been blessed with five children—Job, Robert, Kenneth, Joseph and Annie.

SOCIETIES.

Escallop Lodge, No. 261, A. F. & A. M., was granted a charter by the Grand Lodge of the State of Iowa, June 8, 1870, and the Lodge was organized on April 22, 1869, and first meeting held at that time.

The first officers were as follows: Asa Lowe, W. M.; Julius Preston, S. W.; G. C. Hawley, J. W.; E. W. Metzger, Treasurer; J. G. Scobey, Secretary; O. S. Eastman, S. D.; Charles Hitchcock, J. D.; Alonzo Coates, Tyler.

The presiding officers since organization are as follows: In 1869 and 1870, Asa Lowe; 1871, J. G. Scobey; 1872, J. C. Ross; 1873, Hiram Ross, 1874, J. G. Scobey; 1875 and 1876, Hiram Ross, 1877, J. C. Ross; 1878, W. W. Pattee; 1879, E. M. Jones; 1880, J. C. Ross; 1881 and 1882, E. M. Jones. The present officers are as follows: E. M. Jones, W. M.; E. D. Albright, S. W.; R. Hughes, J. W.; J. A. Graham, S. D.; H. Meyer, J. D.; E. D. Ross, Secretary; W. H. Haynes, Treasurer; John Caley, R. Wilford, Stewards; A. Coates, Tyler.

The total membership since organization has been 99, with a membership at present of 67. Of members there has occurred only one death, Jacob S. Paris, who died at Ashland, Nebraska, June 4, 1882. The condition of the Lodge is flourishing.

KNIGHTS OF HONOR.

Charity Lodge, No. 1,538, Knights of Honor, was organized April 8, 1879, by H. S. Albert, Deputy Grand Dictator of the State of Iowa. The charter members were John W. Stewart, R. D. Prescott, C. H. Lanning, J. R. Clawson, J. H. Mullen, J. H. Carson, A. H. Hitchcock, Henry Barr, J. H. Paley, Robert McDonald, Lewis Larkin, William VanVleck, L. F. Troutman, W. A. Doran, L. H. Mead, J. E. Jewell, H. D. Perry, C. D. Mead, J. P. Reed, G. O. VanVleck, J. A. Bass, J. P. Bement, E. H. Dudley, F. L. Matheson, J. A. Graham, J. K. Hotchkiss, and A. G. Stonebraker. The presiding officers have been R. D. Prescott, W. A. Doran, L. F. Troutman and J. P. Bement. The total membership of the lodge has been twenty-eight, with a membership now of sixteen. The lodge is in rather a dormant condition. The present officers of the lodge are as follows: J. P. Bement, Dictator; J. R. Clawson, Vice Dictator; J. H. Paley, Assistant Dictator; G. O. VanVleck, Reporter; J. R. Clawson, Financial Reporter; J. H. Carson, Treasurer; J. A. Graham, Guide; J. E. Jewell, Guardian; J. D. Landphere, Sentinel, and W. H. Smith, Medical Examiner.

INDEPENDENT ORDER OF ODD FELLOWS.

Shell Rock Lodge, No. 270, I. O. O. F., was instituted January 26, 1874, by a charter granted by the Grand Lodge of the State. The first officers were as follows: F. Mason, N. G.; R. D. Prescott, V. G.; L. F. Bristol, Secretary; J. D. Powers, Treasurer; J. Mullen, O. G.; J. H. Mead, I. G. The total membership since its organization has been one hundred and ten, with a membership at present of sixty-six. The lodge is in a flourishing condition. The N. G. chair has been held by F. Mason, R. D. Prescott, E. D. Albright, R. Hughes, John Miles, J. W. Phillips, W. C. Eastwood, J. H. Law, C. E. Patchen, J. H. Mullen, R. D. Prescott, G. O. VanVleck, J. E. Jewell, R. Hughes, W. J. Reed and J. L. Couch. The officers at the present time are as follows: J. L. Couch, N. G.; S. March, V. G.; G. O. VanVleck, Recording Secretary; R. Hughes, Permanent Secretary; W. C. Eastwood, Treasurer; J. E. Jewell, R. S. N. G.; A. L. James, L. S. N. G.; Peter McGregor, Warden; C. E. Patchen, Conductor; S. J. Conn, R. S. S.; W. J. Hunt, L. S. S.; J. H. Mullen, O. G.; J. K. McCague, I. G.; E. H. Dudley, R. S. V. G.; U. D. Myers, L. S. V. G.; D. J. Gould, Chaplain.

Morton Encampment, No. 98, I. O. O. F., was instituted January 16, 1878, under a dispensation of the Grand Encampment of the State of Iowa, and a charter was granted October 16, 1878. The charter members were Anson Peck, R. D. Prescott, John Miles, J. E. Jewell, J. A. Bass, E. H. Dudley and F. K. McCague. The first officers were: A. Peck, C. P.; R. D. Prescott, H. P.; John Miles, S. W.; E. H. Dudley, J. W.; J. A. Bass, Scribe; J. E. Jewell, Treasurer. The total membership since organization has been forty-seven. This includes those who have been made members to organize other encampments. The present membership is twenty-five. It is in a flourishing condition. The present officers are: R. Hughes, C. P.; P. McGregor, H. P.; S. March, S. W.; J. E. Jewell, J. W.; C. E. Patchen, Scribe; G. O. VanVleck, Treasurer.

WOMEN'S CHRISTIAN TEMPERANCE UNION.

This society, for the purpose of aiding in the work of temperance, was organized on the 7th of December, 1876, with twelve members. The first officers elected were as follows: President, Mrs. C. Sweitzer; vice-presidents, Mrs. S. H. Mitchell and Mrs. W. S. Skinner; corresponding secretary, Mrs. E. Bristol; recording secretary, Mrs. Kate J. Carter; treasurer, Mrs. R. D. Prescott. The presidents during the various years since organization have been Mrs. C. Sweitzer, Mrs. Kate J. Carter and Mrs. H. C. Newcomb.

The present officers of the Union are as follows: President, Mrs. H. C. Newcomb; vice-presidents, Mrs. F. E. Brasted and Mrs. M. Eastwood; recording secretary and treasurer, Mrs. R. D. Prescott; corresponding secretary, Mrs. Kate C. Carter. Other active and earnest workers in the cause have been Mrs. F. E. Brasted, Mrs. M. Couch, Mrs. J. Densmore, Mrs. W. W. Murray, Mrs. Abbie Bristol (deceased), Mrs. N. Landphere, Mrs. Knickerbocker, Mrs. H. Winship, Mrs. A. J. Rockwell, Mrs. S. Kennedy, Mrs. L. Stonebreaker and others. The only death of a member since organization occurred in May, 1880, and Mrs. Abbie Bristol, a beloved and worthy woman, was added to the host of departed.

The society was the first organization of the kind in the county and has been very active. It has had a total membership of fifty and at present enrolls twenty-five. Meetings are held weekly and union meetings monthly, when lecturers are engaged. A great deal of work was done previous to the amendment election, by circulating literature and employing noted lecturers. The good result was shown in the fact that Shell Rock gave the largest majority for the amendment of any township in Butler county.

RELIGIOUS.

The people of Shell Rock are evidently a God-fearing class, judging from the houses of worship. The first religious service was held at the house of G. W. Adair, in the fall of 1854, by Rev. Mr. Burley. The second religious services in town were held, in 1855, in the house of Hiram Ross, and the Rev. Mr. Burley preached the gospel.

FIRST METHODIST EPISCOPAL CHURCH.

This was the first religious society organized in Butler county, filing articles of incorporation on the 26th of June, 1855. The first religious services for this society were held, as stated, by Rev. Burley, he being of this faith. A revival was held, commencing in February, 1855, the reverend gentleman named being assisted by Rev. Kendall and Abram Myers, at which there were thirty members added to the society. In the spring of 1856 a church was erected on the east side of the river, on the site of the present building. Services were continued as a class until 1871, when the society was re-organized. The officers then were, H. L. Sweitzer, William Adair, William Steward, E. W. Metzgar, John Leverich, A. Meyers, and H. D. Hunt.

The first regular pastor, was Rev. J. W. Gould, who came, in 1869, and remained two years. In 1871, Rev. L. S. Cooley came, and filled the pulpit for two years, when he went to New Hartford, and is now in Fayette county, Iowa. Then, in order, followed: Rev. Eugene Sherman, one year; Rev. Timothy Anderson, six months; Rev. A. Critchfield, one year; Rev. W. S. Skinner, two years; Rev. C. M. Wheat, two years; Rev. S. Knickerbocker, one year; Rev. G. L. Garrison, two years; and then, the present pastor, Rev. S. Sharon.

Their present house of worship was erected in 1872, at a cost of $3,500, and is located on the east side of the river. The parsonage was constructed, in 1878, at a cost of $1,200.

The present officers of the church are as follows: Trustees, E. Town, C. Austin, J. W. Phillips, William Adair, T. H. De-Witt, J. R. Clawson, Dr. W. H. Smith; Stewards, C. Austin, J. W. Phillips, William Houghsteader, and A. L. James; Recording Steward, R. Hughes; Leaders, A. H. Benjamin, and Mrs. Landphere.

The society is out of debt, and is in a most healthy and flourishing condition, having a membership of 130.

The Sunday School connected with the society was organized at the time of the institution of the class. Its present officers are, C. Austin, superintendent; William Hunt, assistant superintendant; Ezra Moyer, secretary; Mary Phillips, treasurer. The average attendance is about 90.

FIRST REGULAR BAPTIST CHURCH.

This society was organized January 18, 1864, by Rev. Samuel Sill, assisted by Rev. Wm. Wood. The first members were, Rev. Samuel Sill, Mary E. Sill, Menzo Best, Emily L. Best, Roxy Couch, Minerva Couch, James Chaffin, Deborah Chaffin, J. W. Whittaker, Nancy Whittaker, Serepta Copeland, Fanny Helason. The first officers were, Rev. Samuel Sill, pastor; Menzo Best, deacon; J. W. Whittaker, clerk.

The first religious services of the denomination were held in O. L. Eastman's stone building, on Main street, by Rev. I. R. Dean, a brother of Mrs. S. Rice, in 1858. He was the second county superintendent of public schools. He came here from Kalamazoo, Michigan, and went from here to Pike's Peak, and died on his way back.

The first regular pastor was Rev. Samuel Sill, whose biography appears elsewhere in this volume. He resigned March 5, 1869. Then came Dr. J. Hall, formerly of Kalamazoo, Michigan, who supplied the pulpit and afterwards became pastor. He was founder of the Kalamazoo Baptist College, and was afterward president of Grandville College, Grandville, Ohio.

The first revival services were held by Rev. William Wood, assisted by Rev. Samuel Sill, during the winter of 1868-9, when there were forty-two additions by baptism. The next revival was held by Rev. B. H. Brasted, an evangelist, during the winter of 1875-6, when there were added fifty members. The lots and a good share of the lumber used in this church building were bought by the Ladies' Mite Society. The church was built at a cost of $5,500. In size it is 35x60 feet.

The present officers of the church are: J. J. McIntyre, pastor; S. Rice, A. Soash and Elias Wightman, deacons; H. I. Scribner, clerk; J. E. Patton, treasurer; E. Johnston, S. Rice and Amos Ressler, trustees. Since organization the church has had a membership of 245;—with a membership at present of 105. The present condition of the church is prosperous.

They have a Sunday school in connection with the church which is in a prosperous condition. The present officers are: S. Rice, superintendent; E. J. Young, assistant superintendent; Maynard Farr, secretary; Minnie Patton, assistant secretary; Mary Young, treasurer. The school has an enrollment of 125, and an average attendance of 75.

PERSONAL MENTION.

In a town like Shell Rock, where a considerable amount of business is transacted, many persons come and go, engaging frequently for a time in some branch of trade. Mention is made here of a number who have been more or less prominently identified with the business interests of the town:

William Adair, one of the pioneers of this part of Butler county, is the fourth son of William and Mary (Rollston) Adair, and was born near Lexington, Virginia, on the 8th day of April, 1818. In 1826 the family moved to Jefferson county, Ohio, where they remained three years and then located in La Grange county, Indiana, and here his mother died of consumption in the year 1831. During the year 1837, the family came west and settled in Cedar county, Iowa, where Wilton Junction now stands and in this year also, his remaining parent died. William remained here two years and then located near where Cedar Rapids now stands, west of Marion. However, at that time there was not a house in the place, and the only building at Marion was one log cabin. Here he lived until the spring of 1855, when he came to Shell Rock. The fall before he had entered land on section 10 and soon after his arrival, he in company with his brother George W., built the first grist mill erected in the town. Ever since his settlement here, Mr. Adair has closely identified himself with the interests of his chosen town, and has spent both time and money in procuring its advancement. He is a member of the Methodist Episcopal Church and has ever lent a helping hand in the building up and strengthening of this, his favorite place of worship. He was married December 17, 1840, to Miss Sabrina Williams, and ten children have been born to them, four of whom are now living—Mary, now the wife of James Graham, of Shell Rock; Sabrina, wife of Andrew Countryman, of Ida county, Iowa; Phoebe, wife of William Fields, of Marshaltown; Etta, now teaching at Clear Lake, Iowa. Mrs. Adair died February 17, 1863, and Mr. Adair subsequently married Miss Sarah E. Leonard. They have one child—Viola, now at home.

E. Town is a son of E. and Jane (Willis) Town. He was born in Franklin county, Vermont, April 15, 1832. He was brought up on a farm, and followed that occupation until 1855. In December, of that year, he arrived at Shell Rock, Iowa, and, during the remainder of the winter, worked in the old saw mill. The next spring he began working, as a millwright, in the grist mill. In 1873 he embarked in the hardware trade, followed that business three years, and then engaged in the lumber and grain business for the same length of time. Mr. Town has held the offices of mayor and justice of the peace. He was married, in 1860, to Miss M. J. Adair, a daughter of George W. Adair. They have been blessed with seven children, five of whom are now living—Charles O., Ella L., Willis W., Dana E., and Flora E.

Jacob R. Myers is a son of Jacob and Mary (Conrad) Myers. He was born in Westmoreland county, Pennsylvania, June 5, 1813. He was reared as a farmer, and followed that occupation while living in his native county. In 1854 he came west, locating in Washington county, Iowa, where he remained two years, then moved to the village of Shell Rock, Butler county, and became engaged in the work of masonry, which occupation he has followed the greater part of the time since. Mr. Myers also owns a farm of eighty acres, in Shell Rock township. He has, since his residence here, owned over 600 acres of land. He was married, in February, 1837, to Miss Maria L. Ragana, who is, also, a native of Westmoreland county. Ten children have been born to them, of whom six are now living—Alexander W., Uriah D., Marion, Joseph, Frances, and Harriet.

J. M. Mullen, "the wide awake restaurant man," is a son of J. H. and Ann (Williams) Mullen, and was born in Henry county, Indiana, in April, 1858. When J. M. was eight years old the family came to Iowa, and settled in Shell Rock, Butler county, and here the son received his education and passed his youth. His first business enterprise was the opening of a restaurant, in Parkersburg, in 1878. One year later he launched in the same business at his old home, where he still continues, and enjoys a liberal patronage. In 1881 he was married to Miss Maggie Brock, of Waverly.

Rev. Samuel Sill was born in Cattaraugus county, New York, on the 30th day of May, 1823, and is a son of Deodatus and Margaret (McNett) Sill. His father was a native of Connecticut, and his mother of New York. His early educational advantages were the common school, but upon reaching the age of twenty-one, he entered a seminary, in Allegany county, New York, where he studied three years. At the age of thirty he began work in his native county, as a minister of the gospel; and after doing good work there for three years, he came west, and spent three years in Walworth county, Wisconsin, where the fields were large and the laborers few. He arrived in Shell Rock, Butler county, Iowa, in 1863, and immediately began the organization of the Baptist Church; and the neat church edifice of that village, is largely due to his untiring efforts. After the society was organized, he was their pastor for six years. Since that time he has been pastor of numerous churches. He spent two years at Strawberry Point; three years at Janesville; two years at Plainfield; two years near Marble Rock, and three years near Clarksville. On account of failing health he has been compelled to give up the ministry, and therefore, in 1873, and since that time, he has attended to the many duties of a farmer. He was married in 1850, to Miss Mary Pierce, who is a native of Madison county, New York. Three children have been born to them— Eddy Eugene, who is now practicing medicine at Shell Rock; Susan E., and William Sanford. Mr. Sill has done much missionary work, holding services in almost every school house in the county.

W. H. Graham is a son of Cornelius and Elizabeth (Alexander) Graham, and was born in Butler county, Pennsylvania, April 26, 1852. Seven years after his birth his parents moved west and settled in Greene county, Wisconsin, where the son received a good common-school education. In 1865 they came to Butler county, Iowa, and here Mr. Graham farmed until 1877. At this time he went into the hardware business, in company with J. R. Clawson. He was afterward engaged in the drug business for Dudley & Stonebreaker, and in September, 1880, engaged in the general merchandise business on his own account. He was married, December 15, 1880, to Miss Esther Blaisdell.

R. Hughes was born in Oneida county, New York, January 26, 1833, and is a son of Owen and Ann (Williams) Hughes, who are both natives of Wales. Soon after his birth the family moved to Herkimer county, New York, where he remained until 1852. He then settled in Courtland county, New York, where he lived for twelve years. Mr. Hughes was raised on a farm, and followed that occupation while in the State of New York. In 1866 he came to Shell Rock, Iowa, and settled on section 31, Shell Rock township, on a farm which he still owns. In 1875 he began handling agricultural implements, and also embarked in the insurance business. Mr. Hughes has held the office of justice of the peace for eight years, and in 1882 was elected mayor of Shell Rock. He was married in 1854 to Miss C. T. Blanchard, who is a native of Courtland county, New York. This couple have six children—Owen C., Orville E., Milford, Alvah, Seabury, and Mary. During the prohibitory movement Mr. Hughes was a strong advocate, and devoted his whole time to the interests of the question that agitated the public minds. He was secretary of the Butler county prohibitory organization.

J. H. Mullen was born in Hamilton county, Ohio, June 25, 1836. When he was ten years old the family moved to Henry county, Indiana, where he grew to manhood, and learned the cooper's trade. He moved to Shell Rock, Iowa, in 1866, and began working at his trade. For the past ten years, however, he has been engaged in painting. In 1856 he was united in marriage to Miss Ann Williams, who was, also, born in the State of Ohio. Two children have been born to them, of whom one—James M.—is now living.

J. E. Patton is a son of David W. and Jane (Patton) Patton. He was born, in Fayette county, Pennsylvania, August 14, 1831. He received his education in Pennsylvania, and also learned the trade of harness making, in the county of Westmoreland. In 1866 he came to Shell Rock, Iowa, opened a harness shop, worked for eighteen months, then returned to Pennsylvania, and engaged in the lumber business, and gardening, in the Allegheny Mountains for the space of twelve years. In July, 1879, he returned to Shell Rock, and opened a second harness shop, where he now does a thriving business. During Mr. Patton's first residence in Shell Rock, he was trustee of the town. He was married, in 1860, to Miss Mary Elliott. She died, in Shell Rock, in 1867. Three children were born to them, two of whom are now living—Wallace J., and Minnie.

G. O. VanVleck was born in Schenectady county, New York, May 30, 1844. He is a son of A. C., and Belinda A. (Radnor) Van Vleck, who are both natives of New York. He remained in the county of his birth until eleven years of age, and then moved, with his parents, to St. Joseph county, Michigan, where he grew to manhood. His educational advantages were such as the common schools afforded. He was reared on a farm. In 1866 he came to Butler county, Iowa, and located in Shell Rock township, on a farm on section 19. This occupation he followed for ten years. He has since been engaged in the insurance business, in the village of Shell Rock. Mr. Van Vleck has held the offices of assessor trustee, town clerk, and is the present clerk of the township. He is a member of the society of Odd Fellows—both Subordinate

HISTORY OF BUTLER COUNTY.

and Encampment—and is Secretary of the Lodge. He is also a member of the Knights of Honor, of which he is also an officer. In 1868 he was married to Miss E. P. Chapin, who is a native of the State of Michigan. Three children have been born to them—Frank A., Fred W., and Jennie E. The parents of Mr. VanVleck still reside in Michigan. Mr. VanVleck sold his farm, in Shell Rock township, in the winter of 1882.

J. A. Graham was born in Butler county, Pennsylvania, July 25, 1843. He is a son of Cornelius and Elizabeth (Alexander) Graham. He remained in Pennsylvania until 1857, when he, in company with his parents, moved to Greene county, Wisconsin, where he lived until the opening of the war. On the 4th day of September, 1861, he enlisted in the Fifth Wisconsin Light Artillery, and served, as a non-commissioned officer, until honorably discharged, at Madison, Wisconsin, June 15, 1865. In the meantime, his parents had left Wisconsin, and settled in Butler county, Iowa, near Shell Rock. The son, upon receiving his dismissal from the army, followed them, and, after remaining home a short time, left for Montana, in which Territory he spent the years 1866-7, mining. During the latter year his father died, and he returned home to take charge of the farm. He continued in this occupation until 1876, when he embarked in the stock business. He was married, in 1869, to Miss Mary Adair, a daughter of William Adair, of Shell Rock. Three children have blessed this union—Cora, Gertie, and Leon.

John S. Auner was born in St. Joseph county, Michigan, January 23, 1842, and is a son of Philip and Mary (Dugan) Auner, who were born in the State of Pennsylvania. His father was of German descent, and his mother of Scotch-Irish. In 1853, the family moved to Waverly, Bremer county, Iowa, and settled five miles east of there, on a farm which his father entered during that year. His father died on the place in August, 1877, but his mother still lives there. John grew to manhood on the homestead, and received a good common school education. During our late rebellion he enlisted in Company B, Fourteenth Iowa Infantry, but shortly afterwards was taken sick, and had to be discharged. He then returned to his home, and during the winter worked on the place, and also studied under Hon. Matthew Farrington. At twenty-two years of age he moved to Wisconsin, and was there engaged in a store at Sun Prairie, and after working in the capacity of a clerk for two years, was taken into partnership. One year afterwards he sold out and went to Kansas, where he remained until 1870, and then returned to Iowa and embarked in the insurance business at Shell Rock. For the past ten years he has been engaged with the State Insurance Company of Des Moines, and during the last three years he has had charge of the northern half of the State. In April, 1871, he was united in marriage to Miss Helen M. Allen, who was born in the State of Ohio. They have one son—Jay Frank.

George E. Meade is a son of J. H. and Sarah (Albright) Meade, and was born in Greenbush, Sheboygan county, Wisconsin, November 23, 1853. He remained in his native county until 1870, when the family moved to Shell Rock, Iowa. Upon their arrival the subject of this sketch worked on his father's farm until about 1875, when he commenced to learn the trade of blacksmithing. In 1880 he was taken in partnership with W. J. Reed, under the firm name of Reed & Meade. He is a single man.

W. J. Reed is a son of Hiram and Susannah (Campbell) Reed, and was born in St. Lawrence county, New York, May 12, 1850. Shortly after his birth the family removed to Winnebago county, Wisconsin, and there the son remained until 1865. On the first day of that year he enlisted in Company A, Fiftieth Wisconsin Infantry, and served until honorably discharged at Madison, Wisconsin, in 1866. Upon receiving his dismissal from the army he settled at Belvidere, Illinois, and there learned the blacksmith's trade. In 1870 he came to Shell Rock, Iowa, and has since followed his trade. Mr. Reed was married to Miss E. J. Skelton, a native of Ohio, in 1870. They are the parents of three children — Herbert William, Carl Basil and Garfield. He was the first marshal of the village, a member of the school board for three years, and constable. Mr. Reed was away in 1877-8 to Washington for one and one-half years, when he returned to Shell Rock, and has been in business in this place ever since.

J. G. Rockwell was born in Madison county, Vermont, February 23, 1830, and is a son of Joesph and Mary (Chamberlain) Rockwell. His father was a native of Canada, and his mother of Massachusetts. In 1837 his parents moved to Watertown, New York, and here he spent his early life. When a young man he went to Canada and entered a college at Montreal, where, after some months of close study, he graduated in the civil engineering department. After receiving his diploma he occupied a position as civil engineer on the Grand Trunk Railway for some time, and then spent two years in his native county. From there he went to Onondago county, New York, where he engaged in manufacturing until 1860. He then spent ten years in Courtland county, New York, and in 1870 came to Shell Rock, Iowa, where, for the first five years, he was engaged in farming. In 1872 he was elected county surveyor, which office he held with credit until January 1, 1882. Mr. Rockwell is now engaged in the insurance business. He was married in 1860 to Miss Amanda Jane Wilder, who is a native of New York. They have one daughter—Belle, now the wife of C. J. Alderson.

Robert McDonald was born in Tyrone county, Ireland, July 7, 1833. Here he received a good common school education. In 1850 he came to America, located in New York State, and engaged in milling business at Rochester. In 1854 he came west and located near Monmouth, Warren county, Illinois. In 1856 he moved to Camden Mills (now Milan), Rock Island county, Illinois, where he was engaged in milling business until 1861, when he bought the property known as Jack's Mills, near Oquawka, Henderson county, Illinois. Since 1861, R. McDonald has owned and operated six flouring mills in the States of Iowa and Illinois, his last purchase being the Rockland Mills, located at Shell Rock, Butler county, Iowa, which he owned and operated from 1873 until 1879, when he sold to Haynes Brothers of

Wisconsin, the present proprietors. R. McDonald was married June 6, 1857, to Mary E. Hartley, of Rock Island, Illinois.

J. H. Carson is a son of D. M. and M. J. (Robinson) Carson, and was born in Augusta, Maine, May 14, 1840. Nine years after his birth his parents moved to Wisconsin, and settled in Sheboygan county. He was reared on a farm, and received an excellent common school education; after which he taught school fifteen terms. Mr. Carson's father died in Sheboygan county, July, 1881; his mother still resides there. In 1876 he came to Shell Rock, and engaged in trade, and has since been one of the leading business men of the place. He was married, in November, 1867, to Miss Celesta C. Mansfield. They are the parents of two children—Lillian E., and Carlos M. He does a business of about $25,000 a year, which is steadily increasing.

Professor W. T. Hunt was born in Butler township, Butler county, Iowa, December 1, 1875, and is a son of H. D. and Sarah A. (Husband) Hunt, who were early settlers of this county. His education was received in the district schools of his native county, supplemented by four terms at the State Normal School, and two years at Cornell College. His first school was taught in Jackson township, before he was eighteen years of age. Since that time he has taught fourteen terms. In the fall of 1882 he was appointed principal of the West Shell Rock Schools, and in the winter of 1882-3 was engaged to teach a district school, in Shell Rock township, some five miles from the village.

J. H. Kublank is a son of John and Silbene (Hartung) Kublank, and was born in Cook county, Illinois, on the 5th day of August, 1856. He was reared on a farm, but during the last six years, in his native county, was engaged in cheese-making. In 1877 he came to Albion township, Butler county, Iowa, and worked in Hall's Creamery until September of that year, Afterwards he was engaged in creameries in different parts of the county, until he purchased the Pleasant View Creamery, in 1880. Mr. Kublank was married in 1879, to Miss Mary Nagle, of Illinois. They have two children—Florence and Sarah.

CHAPTER XXXII.

WASHINGTON TOWNSHIP.

The township bearing this familiar name is in the southwestern corner of Butler county, lying contiguous to Madison township on the north, Monroe on the east, Grundy county on the south and Franklin county on the west. It embraces the territory of township 90, range 18, and contains an area of about 23,040 acres.

728   HISTORY OF BUTLER COUNTY.

The surface is a rolling prairie, and the soil a rich dark loam with a sandy mixture. Beaver creek passes through the township from west to east. The North Branch of the Beaver enters the township from Franklin county and makes junction with the creek in section 23. There is a good supply of timber, mostly in a grove in the eastern part of the township, which contains about 800 acres, and consists chiefly of oak, the heaviest of which has been cut. There is another grove on section 32, called Island Grove. There is an abundance of excellent water within easy access, and through the township there are a number of springs which bubble up clear, sparkling water. The largest one is in section 33, and is known by the name of "Big Spring." In an early day, emigrants on their way west would invariably inquire for the "Big Spring," as it was a favorite camping ground.

The settlement of Washington township was very slow as the greater portion of the land fell into the hands of speculators, and settlers coming in as late as 1870, found a good share of it a wild unbroken prairie. Most of the improvements have been made since that time. It is now one of the best farming townships in the county, and is populated by an industrious and thrifty people, who are engaged quite extensively in stock raising in addition to their agricultural pursuits. It is strictly a rural township, there being no store, post office or railway station within its limits, although the line of the Illinois Central Railroad passes through the township from east to west, having been constructed in 1865. The farmers find good market points within easy access: Aplington for the east, and Ackley for the west, the latter being but a few miles from the southwest corner. According to the last census the population of Washington township was 766. Assessed value of personal property, $25,941; of lands, $120,521.

EARLY SETTLEMENT.

The first settlement in this locality appears to have been made in the spring of 1853, by two brothers,—Elery and Reuben Purcell,—who made a business of going just ahead of the line of settlement and selecting the most valuable claims; then when a good opportunity offered,—when those in quest of permanent homes reached them,—the claims would be sold at a good figure, and the adventurers would again move toward the setting sun to repeat the scheme. Reuben claimed the southwest quarter of section 24, and Elery took the west half of the northeast quarter of section 25. Elery put up a little log house and broke about eight acres, on which he raised a fair crop of corn. This was the first breaking in the township; the first sod turned, and the first article raised on Washington soil. Early in the spring of 1854 he sold his claim to Roby R. Parriott, and again started on his endless westward march. Mr. Parriott, whose name is indissolubly connected with the settlement and early days of this region, was a native of Virginia, and came here from Stephenson county, Illinois. He came here in the spring of 1854, and purchased the land as stated, and in June returned to Illinois. On the 4th of July he started back for his new home, accompanied by his family, coming overland with seven yoke of oxen, three horses, three wagons and a top carriage, and were one month on the way. He found upon his arrival that the little log hut was too small for his family, which numbered thirteen, and he therefore erected another log house, 16x24 feet, with a "lean-to" 12x24 feet. This was the first and only hotel ever kept in the township, and in 1855 it was made a stage station. Mr. Parriott made great improvements, and in 1868 he erected the frame house in which he lived until the time of his death in 1871.

REPRESENTATIVE SETTLERS.

Notwithstanding Washington township lands have been to a great extent in the hands of speculators who early saw its advantages, yet rapid strides have been made in its development, which fact speaks well for the character of the citizens, who are a wide-awake, go-ahead class of people. All cannot be mentioned, but we present sketches of a few, from which may be determined the kind of people who have had something to do in making Washington what it is.

Elisha Tobey is a native of the Bay State, born near New Bedford, April 22, 1821. His younger days were spent in school and on the farm. When sixteen years of age he engaged to learn the painter's trade, serving four years, when he started on a whaling voyage. He sailed around the world and returned to his home after an absence of thirty-one months, after which he resumed his trade. In 1854 he came to Iowa and purchased land in Jones county, four miles from Monticello. In the fall of 1855 he returned to Massachusetts; worked at his trade in North Bridgewater one year, and then went to New Bedford, where he lived one year. In 1857 he returned to Iowa and lived in Monticello township four years, when he went to Alamakee county, where he had traded for land. He lived there two years, and then went to Bowen's Prairie, where he lived one year. He then bought a farm in Delaware county, where he lived until 1871, when he came to Butler county and bought 320 acres of land on section 11, Washington township. In 1879 he rebuilt the house in which he now lives. In 1880 he built a barn 32x60 feet, with a stone basement, and a shed 20x98. He was married in 1845 to Miss Jane F. Knight. She had two children—Elisha and Mary. Mrs. Tobey was born in Hull, Massachusetts, February 22, 1812, and died April 7, 1852. He married for his second wife, Miss Love D. Butler, in the fall of 1852, by whom he had eight children— George H., Tristram P., Abby J., Charles S., William E., Franklin J., Zenas W. and Ella T. One child died when quite young. Mrs. Tobey was born at Martha's Vineyard, June 10, 1825, and died February 22, 1868. His third wife was Lydia S. Whitcomb, a native of New Hampshire.

Mrs. Rachel Quinn, an early settler of Washington township, came from Warren county, Illinois, in 1856. She was a daughter of William Nash; was born in Pennsylvania, February 19, 1807. She was married, May, 1827, to John Quinn, who was born in Virginia, May 22, 1800. They settled in Warren county, Illinois, where he engaged in farming until May, 1850, when he started for California, overland. When near his destination he was stricken with cholera and died; he was buried on the plains. He left a wife and ten children to mourn his death. In 1856 Mrs. Quinn took her family and started west to seek a home. She bought land in Washington township, Butler county, where she lived until 1858, when she came to Aplington, where she built the first hotel in the village. She kept that until 1866, when she sold out, and went onto a farm, on section 23, where she lived with her sons, James and John, until her death, December 26, 1878. Her son James was born in Warren county, Illinois, March 24, 1842, where his early days were spent in school. He came to Iowa and made his home with his mother; enlisted July 12, 1862, in the Thirty-second Iowa, Company E; went south, and joined Smith's command at Columbus, Kentucky; was in Banks' Red river expedition; was taken prisoner at Pleasant Hill, Louisiana, remaining in the hands of the enemy thirteen months and eighteen days. At the close of the war he returned home. He was married November, 19, 1879, to Miss Cora Fabes, of Massachusetts. They have one child—Edna May. In April, 1882, he opened a livery stable, which he now runs.

Thomas Clark settled in Washington township in 1868. He was born in Allegany county, New York, September 23, 1826, and was raised on a farm. In 1847 he moved to Wisconsin, and settled in Dane county, and there engaged to learn the carpenter's trade. He bought land there which he improved, besides working at his trade. In 1863 he took up the wagon-maker's trade. He sold out there just previous to his coming to Washington, where he bought land on section 12, southwest quarter. During the spring and summer of 1869 he worked at wagon-making in Ackley. Since then he has divided his time between farming and carpentering. He was married in 1846 to Miss Ann Neal. They have four children—Martha, Henry, John, and Mary.

James Keenan, a native of County Laugh, Ireland, was born in June, 1819, and was there raised on a farm. In 1840 he emigrated to the United States, landing at New York. He lived in Livingston and Genesee counties, except one month in Jefferson county, until 1848, when he went to Allegany county. While in New York he was engaged in farming. In 1868 he came to Iowa, and settled in Butler county. He bought wild land in Washington township, section 31. He has improved the land, and in 1875 built the house in which he now lives. He married Miss Julia Ward in 1839. They were blessed with two children—George and John. Mrs. Keenan died in Jefferson county, New York, in 1845. He married for his second wife Miss Mary Welch. They have been blessed with eight children—James, Mary, Peter, William, Thomas, Michael, Stephen, and Patrick. John was born in New York in 1845, and died in Texas in 1873. William was born in Wisconsin in 1859, and died in Franklin county, Iowa, in 1872.

Patrick Kenefick came to Washington in 1868 from Wisconsin. He was born in Ireland, in 1820. When but eight years of age he came to America with his parents, who settled in the Province of Quebec, Canada. He made his home there until 1855, when he went to Wisconsin and bought 120 acres of improved land, in Fon du Lac county, where he lived until

1868, when he came to Washington and settled on section 19. In 1869 he built the house in which he now lives. He has a farm of 320 acres. He was married in 1879 to Miss Sarah Coyle, who has borne him thirteen children, six are now living —John, William, Margaret, Michael, James and Thomas. Thomas died when eight years and eight months old. Mary died when eight years and six months old.

Henry Austin is a native of England, born Oct. 27, 1844. When but two years and a half old, his parents emigrated to America and settled in Michigan, where they lived five years, then moved to Wisconsin and settled in Grant county. His younger days were spent in school and on a farm. In 1868 he came to Iowa, and bought wild land in Butler county, section 21, township of Washington. He returned to Wisconsin. In the spring of 1869, he came back with a team and broke ninety acres of land. In 1870 he settled on the land. In 1872 he built the frame house in which he now lives. In 1882 he built a barn 40x88 feet, with a stone basement. He was married in 1871 to Miss Sarah M., daughter of G. B. Smith. The fruits of their union are three children—Walter G., Alice E. and Clarence W. Mr. Austin not only manages his farm but deals largely in cattle and hogs.

His brother, William Austin was born in England, February 6, 1847. He was but six weeks old when his parents started for America. He made his home with his parents in Michigan and Wisconsin until 1870, when he came to Washington. In 1873 he bought wild land on sections 21 and 22. In 1876 he built the house in which he now lives, on section 22. He was married September 7, 1876, to Miss Charlotte, daughter of G. B. Smith. Mr. Austin has 320 acres of land.

Daniel Beninga was born in Germany April 17, 1825; went to school there; when fifteen years of age he engaged on the canal shipping. In 1846 he joined the army; after serving fifteen months he got a leave of absence for six months; he then joined again and served seven months, when he was relieved again for seven months. He was then called upon again, and served five months, when he was discharged from the service, and resumed work on the canal. In 1857 he came to America; landed at New York; went to Freeport, Illinois, and engaged on a farm near that place, for two years; he then went to Springfield and worked at farming. He married, in 1863, Miss Etje Bagger, daughter of one of the early settlers of Freeport, Illinois. They have seven children—Kate, John, Jacob, Mary, Henry, Daniel, Ubbe. In 1869 he came to Iowa, and bought land in Washington township, that formerly belonged to the Ohio Stock Breeding Association, on section 2. In 1875 he built the house in which he now lives; he has also built a nice barn.

Hugh G. Scallon, secretary of the school board, was born in Province of Quebec, Canada, August 16, 1840, where he was raised to agricultural pursuits. In 1855 he came to the United States with his parents, who settled in Waushara county, Wisconsin. He made his home there until 1869, when he came to Washington township, and settled on section 20, on land that he had bought the year before. He has improved the land, and in 1879, he built a barn 48x80, with stone basement. In 1869 he built a frame house, to which he made an addition in 1876. He married, February 15, 1876, Miss Elizabeth Kenefick. They have four children—Hubert W., Mary M., Mary J., and John J.

Jurian Winne is a native of New York, born in Albany county, September 16, 1843. In 1853 his parents moved to Illinois, and settled in Boone county. His younger days were spent in school and on his father's farm. He made his home in Illinois until 1869, when he came to Butler county, Iowa, and spent the winter in Aplington. He bought land in Washington township, on section 10, built a house, and moved there, in 1870. This part of the township, at that time, was very little settled. In the fall of 1875 he went to Chicago, where he was foreman in the Cottage Grove Avenue Railway stables. He lived there until 1882, when he returned to Washington township, and built a house on his father's homestead, on section 3, where he now lives, and has a farm of 240 acres of land. On September 23d, 1866, he married Miss Alice J. Tripp, a native of Boone county, Illinois, born March 6, 1847. They have two children—Frank J., and Ira T.

Patrick Parker was born in the Province of Ontario, Canada, March 13, 1839. He was raised to agricultural pursuits. In 1857 he came to the United States, and settled in Grant county, Wisconsin, where he engaged in farming until 1862, when he went to Eau Claire, and engaged in the lumber business until 1870, when he came to Iowa, and settled in Butler county, buying land on section 16, in Washington township. He has improved the land, and built the frame house in which he now lives. He married, July 3, 1869, Miss Carrie Ulrich. They have five children—Flora A., James L., Leo. E., Julia B., and Mary E.

Julius J. Burnham was born in Addison county, Vermont, April 1, 1845. When young he attended the district school, and advanced his education by two terms at the academy at Mankton Ridge and one term at Barre Academy. When seventeen years of age he commenced teaching. In 1870 he came to Iowa and settled in Aplington, and there bought an interest of his brother in a furniture and hardware store. They also run a dairy, keeping from forty to sixty cows, and started a cheese factory in Aplington. In 1871 he traded the cows for land on section 26, Washington township, and in the spring of that year moved there, and the first two winters was engaged in teaching. He was married in June, 1872, to Miss Mary Smith. They have been blessed with two children—Freddie and Ena Mabel. Freddie was born January 2, 1876, and died in March, 1878. They have an adopted son named Forrest. Mr. Burnham was town clerk six years and secretary of the school board seven years. He was elected member of the board of supervisors in 1879.

Samuel Croot is an Englishman, born in Devonshire, June 10, 1835. He received his education in the Sabbath school. In 1857 he came to the United States, landing in New York, and went to Columbia county, where he engaged in farming for three years. He then went to New York city and engaged in a pickle factory seven years, when he returned to England. He returned to the United States, after a visit of eighteen months, and settled in New

HISTORY OF BUTLER COUNTY. 733

Jersey, where he engaged in farming until 1871, when he came to Iowa and bought land on section 10, Washington township. He has since improved the land and rebuilt the house in which he now lives. In 1861 he married Miss Sarah J. Fallen. They have but one child—Sarah. They have three adopted children—Thomas, Charlie and Christopher.

E. Wiechman, a member of the present board of trustees, settled in Washington in 1875. He is a native of Germany, born September, 1848. When but eight years of age his parents emigrated to the United States, and settled in Ogle county, Illinois, where he lived until he moved to this township, where he bought land in section 35. He has improved the land, and built the house in which he now lives. He was married in 1871 to Miss Cornelia Hayenga. They had three children—Cornelius, Kate and Annie.

P. DeVries is a native of Holland, born November 2, 1823. He attended school from six until he was fourteen years of age. In 1843 he joined the German army, and served four months. In 1868 he came to America, and settled in Illinois, where he lived until 1872, when he came to Iowa and settled in Butler county, Washington township. He bought a farm on section 33, where he now lives. He was married in 1857, and has five children.

Frank Parker, a member of the board of trustees, was born in the Province of Ontario, Canada, March 12, 1848. In 1860 his parents came to the United States, and settled in Grant county, Wisconsin, where he lived until 1872, when he came to Iowa and settled in Butler county, and bought land in Washington township, section 16, where he now lives. He was married in 1875 to Miss Ellen Kenefick. They have five children—Mary, Martha, Leonard, Edmund A. and John C.

Captain M. D. Eustis, of Company K., Fifty-seventh Illinois Volunteer Infantry, enlisted September 25, 1861. He was mustered into the service as fourth sergeant; was promoted to orderly sergeant, June 20, 1862; was promoted to captain, April 30, 1864. He served five years, was honorably dismissed, and mustered out November 6, 1866. He participated in several engagements, the most notable of which were, Fort Donelson, Shiloh, siege and battle of Corinth, Iuka and Nashville. He was born in Kenebeck county, Maine, March 26, 1840. In 1854 his parents moved to Illinois, and settled in Boone county, where he made his home until the time of his enlistment. When discharged from the service he returned to Illinois. He married, May 5, 1869, Miss Sarah McKey, a native of Boone county. In 1873 he came to Butler county, Iowa, and bought land on section 3, Washington township, where he now lives. His father died in 1869. His mother lives here with her son. She is now in her eighth-eighth year.

Lafayette Levally was born in Oswego county, New York, October 19, 1836. When sixteen years of age his parents moved to Wisconsin, and settled in Walworth county. He enlisted there August 29, 1862, in the Thirteenth Wisconsin Infantry, Company C. He served with the regiment until the close of the war, and was honorably discharged June 13, 1865, and returned to Wisconsin. He made his home there until 1875, when he came to

Iowa. He bought land in Washington township, section 4, where he now lives. He married, in 1856, Miss Mary J. Flansburgh, a native of Schoharie county, New York. They have been blessed with nine children—Julia C., Eva M., Ada E., Frank E., Alfred W., Elizabeth, Tina B., Daniel J., and Ethel May.

Harrison Combs is a native of Pennsylvania, born in Tioga county, March 10, 1827. His younger days were spent in school, and later he worked on the farm during the summer season and lumbering in winter. In 1854 he went to Wisconsin prospecting. He spent the summer on the Wisconsin River, and in the fall he returned to Pennsylvania, In 1856 he moved to Wisconsin and engaged in the lumber business. He rented a saw-mill for a few years. He built a saw-mill that was run by water power, at a place now called Merrill, in Lincoln county. In 1875 he bought a farm in Washington township on section 24, and erected a large brick house. In 1880 he moved here with his family and now makes this his home. He has now 600 acres of land in this township. In 1882 he built a barn 36x92, with a stone basement, on section 14, also a frame house. He has now a hundred cows on this farm. He was married in 1851 to Miss Elvira Niles. She bore him three children—Helen J., William H. and Albert. Mrs. Combs was born in Pennsylvania, October, 1829, and died in Wisconsin, October, 1872. His second wife, Mrs. Dora Stickler, widow of Jacob Stickler, bore him one child. She was a sister of his first wife, born in Pennsylvania, September, 1842, and died in Wisconsin, February, 1877. She had one child by her first husband—William. His third wife was Annie L. Showers; they have had one child—Jerome B.

Robert Martin came to Washington township in 1870, from Lafayette county, Wisconsin, where he had lived since 1855. He was born in Crawford county, Pennsylvania, June 29, 1828, where his younger days were spent in school and on the farm. He made his home there until his removal to Wisconsin. He lived but two years in Washington township, on section 22, when he removed to the Clayton farm, in Monroe township, and lived there one and one-half years; then back to Washington township, where he lived nine months, on section 32; then moved to the Greene farm, in Madison township, where he lived seven years. In 1881 he bought a farm on section 2, Washington township, and moved there in April of the same year. He was married in 1857, to Miss Ziza Fulp, a native of North Carolina. They have five children — Mary, James V., Charles R., William W., and Cora.

Roby R. Parriott was born in Tyler county, Virginia, February 2, 1808. In 1827 he emigrated to Vermilion county, Indiana. He was married to Miss Abigail Howard, in 1831, by whom he had eleven children—nine sons and two daughters—six of whom are now living, He removed to Porter county, Indiana, in 1836, and from thence to Stephenson county, Ill., in 1840, where he remained until 1854, when he located in Washington township, Butler county, Iowa. He was the first postmaster in this part of the county. He lodged the passengers on the stage that made the first trip west of Waterloo. He was the owner of the present site of the

J. M. Early.

city of Ackley, and conveyed to the Dubuque and Sioux City Railroad Company one half of the town site, or every alternate lot. The Company conveyed their interest to William J. Ackley, of Waterloo, hence the town derived its name. He was, at one time the owner of 2,500 acres of land in this part of the county. He gave to the Dubuque and Sioux City Railroad the right of way through his entire tract of land, and worked earnestly for the establishment of the road. He was also liberal in donating to the Iowa Central Railroad Company.

Richard, his oldest son, was born in Vermilion county, Indiana, in 1829. He married Miss Lillie M. Caldwell, July 10, 1856. In 1859 he moved to Illinois and settled in Henderson county. In August, 1862, he enlisted in Company G, Eighth Illinois Volunteer Infantry, went south, and was killed at the battle of Murfreesboro, Tennessee, December 1, 1863. He left a wife and two children to mourn his death.

Anthony, his second son, was born in Vermilion county, Indiana, in 1830. He married, August 7, 1856, Miss Melinda Spangler, and settled in Ackley. He moved to Sac county in 1870, where he died December 28, 1878, leaving a wife and eleven children to mourn his death.

Owen, the third son, born in Indiana, was never married. He died in 1872 at his brother Wesley's. He enlisted in the army in 1864 and served until the war closed.

Newton, the fourth son, was born in Porter county, Indiana, February 14, 1837. He married Miss Margaret Vance in 1865. She lived but a few months. His second wife was Miss Susanna Sharpe, who was a native of the North of Ireland, born May 13, 1847. She came to America in 1871 and lived for a while with her cousin in Washington; went to Franklin county and was married December 9, 1873. She now occupies the farm of her late husband on section 32, Washington township.

Lucinda, the oldest daughter, who first married G. M. Caldwell, is now the wife S. B. Findley, and lives at Aplington.

Roby, the fifth son, returned to Illinois in 1860. In 1861 he enlisted in the Eleventh Illinois Cavalry, and re-enlisted at the expiration of his time, serving through the war. After his honorable discharge he settled on section 32, Washington township, and lived there until 1882, when he moved to Laverne, Rock county, Minnesota, where he is dealing in grain.

Marion, the sixth son, was born October 10, 1841. He made his home with his parents until 1860, when he went to Illinois. He enlisted in the Seventy-first Illinois, Company B. He was honorably discharged at the expiration of his term, and came to Iowa on a visit. He then went to Wisconsin, where he engaged in farming for one year, and then returned to Butler county. He was married February 15, 1871, to Miss Cordelia Galloway, of Canada. They have been blessed with four children—Byron, Clarence, Bertie J. and Edith P. He settled on the farm that he now occupies in November, 1873. He now has 218 acres of land. He built the house in which he now lives in 1882.

Louisa, the youngest daughter, was married April 12, 1870, to George Huey, a native of Edinburg, Scotland. He died January 19, 1873. She married her second husband, R. R. Horr, October 9, 1878. Has two children—Jennie E. and Annie E.

Jasper enlisted July 12, 1862, in the Thirty-second Iowa, Co. E. He was killed in the battle of Pleasant Hill, Louisiana, April 9, 1864.

Wesley now lives in Hamilton county, where he is engaged in farming.

William enlisted in the regular army in 1867, and served three years. He now lives in Ohio.

A man named Craw, generally called "Doc" Craw, also came in the spring of 1854, and made a claim on sections 24 and 25. In the spring of 1855 he sold the improvements to Robert Howard, a native of Ohio, who came from Henderson county, Illinois, in company with J. M. Caldwell and others, who settled in Monroe. Mr. Howard improved the land on section 24, until 1863, when he sold out, and removed to Johnson county, Nebraska, where he now lives.

These were about all the settlers of 1854. Early in 1855, William, the eldest son of Charles Stockdale, a native of Scotland, made his appearance, and planted his stakes on the southeast quarter of section 23, where he built a log house, and improved the land. In 1862 he enlisted in the Thirty-first Iowa Regiment, and died, while in the service, at Mound City, Illinois, on the 31st of March, 1864, at the age of thirty-nine years. His remains were brought back, and interred in the Aplington cemetery.

Charles Stockdale, Sr., one of the early settlers of Washington township, was born in Scotland, in 1802. When but two years of age his parents moved to the northern part of Ireland. He was married there, in 1822, to Miss Margaret A. Sharpe. They were blessed with eight children—William, Thomas, James, Eliza, Margaret A., Steward, Jane, and Charles. In 1854 he emigrated to America, and settled in Onondaga county, New York, where he lived until 1856, when he came to Iowa, and settled in Washington township. He made his home with his son, William, until the time of his death, which occurred December 9, 1859, aged fifty-seven years. Mrs. Stockdale died June 14, 1871, aged sixty-eight years. The oldest son, William, who settled here in 1855, enlisted in the service, in 1862, and died, while in the service, at Mound City, Illinois, March 31, 1864, aged thirty-nine years. Eliza died September 24, 1861, aged twenty-nine years; Stewart died April 15, 1860, aged twenty years; Margaret died April 12, 1858, aged twenty-four years. Thomas, James, and Jane now live in Franklin county. His youngest son, Charles, was born in 1846. He came to Iowa with his parents, where he received his education in the district schools. He attended the first school taught in this township. In 1871 he married Miss Lydia F., daughter of G. B. Smith. They have six children—Mary F., Charlotte J., Charles J., Archie E., and Grace and Guy, twins. In 1870 he built the house in which he now lives, on section 26. He has been a very successful farmer, and now has 850 acres of land. He has been quite an extensive dealer in live stock. He has taken quite an interest in township affairs, and has been repeatedly elected to offices of trust in the township. James married in 1864, Sarah F. Liddy, a native of Pennsylvania. He lived in Washington township until the summer of 1873, when he removed to

Franklin county. His wife died in 1866. He was again married in 1871, to Elizabeth Sharpe. They have five children.

Jonathan Gee, a native of Tennessee, also came in the spring of 1855, with the company from Henderson county, Illinois, the most of whom settled in Monroe township. He laid claim to a farm on section 23 and 24, and erected a log house besides making other improvements, but sold his claim the following year without proving up. He now lives at Biggsville, Illinois.

Morris F. Whitney was another settler of 1855. He was a native of New York and placed his sign manual upon papers for a place in section 24. He was a school teacher by profession and divided his time between teaching and farming. In 1870 he sold his place and went to Cherokee county, but has since died at Waterloo.

In 1856 Charles Stockdale, a native of Scotland, came from New York with his family. He and his son James entered a farm on section 23, He made his home with his son William, who is mentioned above until the time of his death in December, 1859. His son James now lives in Franklin county.

James Gray came here from Illinois, in 1856, and bought out Jonathan Gee. He soon sold that place and lived in various parts of the township until he finally removed to Missouri where he now lives.

Wesley Long, a native of Ohio, came from Davenport, this year and settled on section 23, on land he had traded for.

Alfred Munson, a southerner, came here in 1858 and boarded with R. R. Parriott. He owned large tracts of land in the western part of the township and built a house on section 31. He went south about the time the war broke out and served in the rebel army. He has since disposed of his land here.

HISTORICAL EVENTS.

About the first birth in the township was that of Genevra, a daughter of Anthony and Melinda Parriott, who was born on the 19th of May, 1857.

On the 19th of December, of the same year, Sarah Florence, a daughter of Richard and Lillie M. Parriott, was born. She died on the 9th of May, 1860, in Henderson county, Illinois.

The first marriage in the township, united the destinies of Anthony J. Parriott and Melinda Spangler, and dated August 7th, 1856. Mr. Parriott died in Sac county, Iowa, December 28, 1878, leaving a widow and eleven children to mourn his loss. The widow now lives in Webster City.

Lycurgus P. Hazen was married to Miss Sarah Quinn, in March 1857, and they now live in Brown county, Kansas.

The first death in the township occurred in the fall of 1853, and was an infant child of Elery Purcell. It was buried on his farm. This was among the first deaths in the county.

The second death was that of Sarah Ann Howard, daughter of Robert Howard, who departed this life July 3, 1857. The remains were interred in Aplington cemetery, it being the first burial there.

Margaret, a daughter of Mr. and Mrs. Charles Stockdale, died on the 12th day of April, 1858, aged twenty-one years. She was buried in the Aplington cemetery.

Another death occurred this year, in June, and Sarah, daughter of Robert and

Jane Howard, paid the debt of mortality. She was also buried in the Aplington cemetery, Elder John Connell officiating.

The demise of Charles Stockdale, Sr., was another early death, occurring in December, 1859, he being fifty-seven years of age.

ALGONQUIN POST OFFICE.

This office was established in 1855, with R. R. Parriott, who is mentioned prominently in early settlement, as postmaster. The office was kept at his hotel. In 1857 the office was removed to Aplington and the name changed.

OFFICIAL.

According to the first division of Butler county into townships, the territory now comprising Washington was made a part of Ripley township. This division took place in 1855. In March, 1856, another division occurred, and Washington was thrown into the organization of the new township of Monroe. In 1857, under the judgeship of Alonzo Converse, it assumed its present boundaries. It was organized by Wesley Long. The first officers elected were: Robert Howard, justice of the peace, and Silas Beebe, constable.

The last annual election was held at the school house of District No. 8, in November, 1882, and the following officials were chosen: Town clerk, Robert Waudby; trustees, David Wheatman, Frank Parker and Leonard Crosby; justice of the peace, Robert Waudby; constables, John Clark and Thomas Waudby; assessor, John Kennefick; clerk of school board, Hugh Scallon.

RELIGIOUS.

The first religious services in the township were held at the house or hotel of Roby R. Parriott, during the winter of 1854-5, with Elder Crippin, of Hardin county, as preacher. A society was organized in 1855, by Elder Stewart, from Hazel Green, Hardin county, with Robert Howard as class leader. They afterwards held meetings in Anthony Howard's log stable, which had been fitted up for school purposes. This society now worship at Aplington. An interesting anecdote of one of the early meetings of this society is given in connection with the history of Monroe township.

The German Reformed Church of Washington was erected in 1881, and was dedicated on the 25th of November, of that year, by Rev. Mr. Decker. Rev. Paul Schüelke is the present pastor. Services were formerly held in Madison township.

EDUCATIONAL.

The first school in the township was taught by Mrs. Chichester at Morris Whitney's house on section 24, in the summer of 1857, and was a select school. The next school was kept in Anthony Howard's log stable, and S. B. Decker was the teacher. This was in the winter of 1857-8. The first school house was built in 1863, in the northwestern corner of section 25. David Washburne was the first teacher in the school house. This was in what is now District No. 1.

The first school in District No. 2 was held at a private house on section 31. The school house was erected, on the same section, in 1869, and Mary McGill was first to call school to order in the new house.

The first school in District No. 3 was held, in 1870, in William Kenefick's granary, and his daughter, Nellie, was the first to teach. The school house was put up, in 1872, on section 19, and here Miss Cynthia Bird was first to handle the ferule.

There was a board shanty put up in District No. 4, on section 7, about 1868, which was used for school purposes until 1873, when the present house was erected on the same section.

District No. 5 was formerly a part of No. 1. In 1869 the district furnished lumber, and the citizens of the northern part of the district put together a small board shanty on the line of sections 11 and 12, where Miss Martha Clark taught the first term of school. In 1872 the present neat frame house was erected, on the northeastern part of section 11, at a cost of about $840. E. A. Whitcomb was the first teacher in the new house.

The school house in District No. 6 was erected, in 1876, on section 27, and Miss Emma Wright was the first instructor.

The school house in District No. 7 was built in 1878, on the northeastern part of section 10. During the summer of 1878 school was held in a board shanty on the hill south of where the school house now stands. Miss Anna Ford was teacher.

District No. 8 erected their school building in 1880, and Miss Bertha Brace was the first teacher.

BLACKSMITH SHOP.

The first, and we believe the only blacksmith shop ever started in the township, was in 1857. A man named Shaw, from Waterloo, was the proprietor. R. R. Parriott furnished him with logs with which to build a shop, and he put them together on the northwestern part of section 25. He did not stop long, as he did not find much work to do. This shop was afterward used for school purposes, and Samuel Burke and Augusta Arnold, of Iowa Falls, were among the first to teach in it.

CHAPTER XXXIII.

WEST POINT TOWNSHIP.

This township is surrounded by Coldwater, Ripley, Jackson and Pittsford, respectively, on the north, south, east and west. It embraces township 92, range 17, and contains an area of about 23,040 acres.

The general surface is rolling, sloping toward the south. Its soil is of a dark loam, under laid with a sub-soil of clay. There is no native timber within the borders of West Point township, but there are many fine domestic groves, which the farmers have set out and cultivated. The nearest natural timber is Boylan's Grove, which touches the western boundary. There is no stone to speak of and no lime stone—at least none has been quarried. As the soil is of such a nature, it was originally inclined to be wet, but as the case in all such localities, cultivation makes it drier, and as it progresses, will eventually be all subject to the plow.

There is but one stream passing through West Point township, called Dailey Creek, which finds its source on sections 9 and 10, and takes a southerly course, leaving by way of section 33, to make a junction with the West Fork in* Ripley township. Though running water is not plenty, good water can be found in nearly all portions at a reasonable depth from the surface. The peculiar adaptability of the soil to indigenous grasses, renders stock raising a most profitable business, and already farmers are turning their attention to it extensively with good success. Most of the farmers have excellent meadows of tame grass. There are many fine farms—West Point territory making some of the best agricultural land to be found in Butler county.

There are two towns in West Point township, Allison, the county seat, and Bristol, which will receive due attention further on. They are both situated on the line of the Dubuque & Dakota Railroad, which was graded through here in 1875 by the Iowa and Pacific Railroad Company. The iron was laid by the present company in 1879.

EARLY SETTLERS.

The earliest settlement of West Point township commenced in the western part, in the vicinity of Boylan's Grove.

Isaac Boylan came here in 1852, settling just over the line in Pittsford township. A number of the Boylan brothers—John, James and Asa—came about the same time. The Grove was named in honor of them.

Mr. Parks came here in 1856 and took a claim in the western part of the township, near Bristow.

Isaac Boylan resides on section 18. He is one of the earliest settlers of Pittsford township, having settled there in 1852. But two families—those of his brother John and James M. Park—had preceded him in that township. The former now lives in Oregon and the latter in Kansas. Mr. Boylan was born in Muskingum county, Ohio, in 1823, but removed with his parents to Fulton county, Illinois, when he was a boy. His father, William Boylan, resided in Fulton county until his death. Isaac Boylan entered his land on section 24, Pittsford township, walking all the way to DesMoines to accomplish it. The country was very sparsely settled at that time, and he met only a few settlers on the route. He resided in Pittsford township about ten years, when he exchanged for his present farm with his brother-in-law, James M. Park. Four of the Boylan brothers, with their mother, settled in Butler county. John came in the fall of 1851, Isaac in 1852, and the mother, Jane Boylan, with three sons, came several years later. The mother has been dead for several years. The sons who came with her were Asa, now in Kansas; James, in Pittsford township, and William, who died in the army during the rebellion. Isaac Boylan has been twice married. His first wife was Catherine Demoss, who died in 1871, and his present wife was Mrs. Jane Morris, sister of his first wife. He had six sons and three daughters by his first wife and a son and daughter by his second. His daughters by the first wife are all dead. Mr. Boylan belongs to the Church of the United Brethren.

Louis Kilson was also an early settler, residing on section 29. He was born in the District of Bergen, Norway, October 30, 1807. He received the advantages of education in his native land, which were common in those days. Mr. Kilson was confirmed in the Lutheran Church; married in June, 1838, and came immediately to America, landing in New York City the first day of the following September, soon after starting for Cincinnati, a journey which was a great undertaking in those days. His route was via the Hudson river to Albany; to Buffalo by the Erie canal; to Cleveland by boat on Lake Erie; thence by the Ohio canal to Portsmouth on the Ohio river, and to Cincinnati on a flat boat. Soon after reaching Cincinnati he was sick for about three months. On his recovery he started for Quincy, Illinois, going by water. He settled in Adams county, where he lived about twelve years. In 1851, he went to Dane county, Wisconsin, remaining about one year, thence to McHenry county, Illinois. In 1855, he came to Butler county, and has been a resident of West Point township. He entered 240 acres of land, which still constitutes a part of his homestead. Mr. Kilson, losing his first wife at Quincy, Illinois, was married in Dane county, Wisconsin, to Carrie Nelson, in 1852. She died November 10, 1881. Mr. Kilson had six children by first wife, only three of whom are living—Anna L., now wife of Silas F. Woodworth, residing in Placer county, California; Albert M., living in Kansas, and Martha M., wife of John Wilkes. He had five sons and one daughter by second wife, of whom four sons and one daughter are living—Franklin S., George E., Charles G., Walter Louis and Alice L. The name of the deceased son was Albert Oscar. Mr. Kilson's farm contains 320 acres; he has also 43 acres of timber land in Pittsford township. Mr. Kilson has been an extensive reader, and is possessed of much general information. He has always been a student of history, and excells in a knowledge of the history and literature of his native land.

Ancil Durand came about the same time, and landed in Pittsford. He was elected county judge, and is noticed in that connection.

John Hewitt, Philip Miller, Mr. Daily and Mr. Surfus are four more pioneers of West Point. They all know the struggles of pioneer life in a wild country.

John Hewitt is living on section 20. He was born in Marion county, Ohio, in 1827. His father, Thomas Hewitt, was a native of Pike county, in that State, but for many years a resident of Indiana, who came to Linn county, Iowa, in 1854, and to Butler county, the following year, settling in West Point township. He and his wife now live in the village of Bristow. They have five children, two sons and three daughters, all of whom are living in Butler county, except the youngest, who resides in Kansas—Catherine N., wife of C. L. Jones; Jane C., wife of John Moots; Mary, wife of Thomas Boylan; John, and Levi. Mr. John Hewitt's first settlement was on section 19, in the fall of 1858. He settled where he now lives in 1865, buying his farm of W. F. Early. He married Elizabeth Early, a daughter of Henry A. Early, who settled in Pittsford township in 1854, a native of Kentucky, and one of the well known early settlers of the township. Mr. and Mrs. John Hewitt have nine children, two boys and seven girls—Edward L., Edith M., Ida L., Elsie V., Alta L., Ocea A., Myrtie I., Riva L., and Charles F. Their farm contains 120 acres; they also have another farm containing a quarter section. Mr. Hewitt has held most of the township offices; has been township clerk for several terms, township trustee, and assessor for the township the second time after organization.

Philip Miller and George Lash were the earliest settlers of West Point township. They were brothers-in-law, and came here about the same time. Mr. Lash is now a resident of Story county, Iowa. Mr. Miller was born in Germany, in 1828, and came to the United States with his parents when ten years of age. The family settled in Stark county, Ohio. His parents, Henry and Eve Miller resided in Ohio until their death. Philip Miller came to West Point township in the fall of 1854, and pre-empted eighty acres of land on section 20, which is a part of his present farm. His residence is located on this eighty. Mrs. Miller was Miss Catherine Lash. When Mr. Miller came here his family consisted of himself, wife and two children. Their entire worldly possessions consisted of a team and twenty-five dollars in money. He exchanged his horses and harness for forty acres of timber land. This was previous to the pre-emption of his first eighty. As a business man Mr. Miller has been very successful. From the small beginning mentioned, his possessions have grown to the magnitude of 1,000 acres of good land, being one of the finest stock farms in Butler county. Mr. rnd Mrs. Miller have six sons and two daughters—James T., Milo L., Walter P. and Mary C., (twins), Henry, Laura, Anthony, and Lawrence.

Mrs. Emily Daily, widow of Christian Daily, resides on section 22. Christian Daily was born in Pennsylvania in 1803. He moved to Ohio with his parents, when a boy, and there lived until manhood, when he married Miss Emily Neighman. After their marriage they removed to Indiana, where they remained twenty years. They came to Butler county in 1857, and settled on section 22, on the farm which Mrs. Daily now owns. Mr. Daily died in 1875. Mrs. Daily was born in Portage county, Ohio, in 1813. Her father, Adam Neighman, was one of the pioneers of that State. Mrs. Daily has three sons and one daughter—Anthony, in Sheffield, Iowa; Lydia, now Mrs. S. E. Crosby; Christian, in Waterloo, and P. F. Daily, who resides at the homestead. She lost five children, three sons and two daughters, all but one of whom reached maturity.

Charles V. Surfus resides on section 30. He is the son of William Surfus, who came to Butler county, from Indiana, in the fall of 1856, and settled in this township, being one of its earliest settlers. His first settlement was on section 18, and in 1864 settled where his son now lives. He after-

J. M. Fisher

Mary J. Fisher.

ward returned to Indiana, where he died in 1878. The father of Mr. Surfus had thirteen sons and one daughter, by first wife, and two by his second marriage. The daughter and five sons of the former, are living, and one of the latter. Charles V. and his sister are the only ones living in this county. The family of Mr. Surfus was largely represented in the Union army during the rebellion; five of the sons entered the service; three were members of the Twelfth Regiment Iowa Volunteer Infantry; one served in the Second Iowa Cavalry, and one in the Forty-fourth Indiana. Two of them, Emanuel and Nathaniel died in the service. Charles V. was born in Indiana, in 1838; came to this county with his father; he enlisted in the Twelfth Iowa Regiment, and served from September 29, 1861, until January 26, 1866. He participated in many battles; was taken prisoner at the battle of Shiloh, and remained such nearly six months and a-half. He bought his present farm, of 160 acres, of his father. His wife was Amanda Thomas. They have three children—Anthony L., William H., and Stella E.

Samuel Moots, from Indiana, located on section 19, in 1854, where he built a log house. He now lives in Pittsford township.

Then came John Lash, William and Adam Sarbee and Seth Strong. John Lash made selection on section 19, George Lash on 18, and Adam and William Sarbee on 18.

At a later date a large number arrived and took up residence, among whom were Messrs. Ray, Smith, Gough, Wilkes, Trindle, Bell, Thompson, Bornell, Neal and Cass.

Robert Smith was born in the north part of Ireland in 1820. His father, William Smith, died in that country, and his mother and seven children emigrated to the United States in 1834. Four of the children came first, and the mother and other children later, one of whom is the subject of this sketch. The family settled in Philadelphia. Mr. Smith is the only surviving member of the family. He came to Butler county from Ohio in 1861 and settled in Pittsford township. He now resides on section 6, settling there about 1866. His farm contains 240 acres, 80 of which he obtained as a homestead, buying the remainder of Mr. Underwood. Mr. Smith and wife belong to the Presbyterian Church at Bristow. He is one of the original members of the church, one of the most liberal contributors to the building of the church edifice, and among the most generous supporters of the Gospel. He married Miss Phœbe Given, a native of Ireland. They have six children— three sons and three daughters.

William Gough is one of the early settlers of Iowa, his residence dating from March, 1852, when he came to Jones county, and thence to Janesville, Bremer county, in October, 1853. His residence in Butler county dates from the fall of 1854, residing on section 4. Mr. Gough is a native of Gloucestershire, England, where he was born in 1817, residing there until thirty-five years of age. He is best known as a minister of the Methodist Episcopal Church. Mr. Gough entered the ministry as a local preacher when about twenty-seven years of age. He came to the United States in 1850, settling in Illinois, but transferred it to Jones county, Iowa, in

1852, and thence, as dictated by the conference, to Bremer and Butler counties. Mr. Gough was for many years an itinerant minister of his church, and enjoyed all the experiences incident to the life of a Methodist preacher on the frontier. A portion of his time has been devoted to farming. He entered a farm in Dayton township, north of Clarksville, about 1853. He was married in Pittsfield, Pike county, Illinois, in 1852, to Susanna Walsh, born in County Galway, Ireland, June 23, 1822. She came to the United States in 1848. Mrs. Gough has been a member of the Methodist Episcopal Church since she was six years of age. She is a woman of great energy, excellent memory, of a poetical turn of mind, and for the advantages she had, of good literary attainments. She is a sister of Thomas Walsh, of this county. Mr. and Mrs. Gough have six children—Caroline A., now Mrs. Jacob Kephart; William C., George W., Joseph J., Thomas A. and Elizabeth J. They lost two children while living at Clarksville.

John Wilkes resides on section 18, West Point township. He has been a resident of Butler county since 1863. He was born in Morgan county, Ohio, in 1838. His father, Ira Wilkes, was a native of the State of New York. John Wilkes was a Union soldier during the War of the Rebellion, serving in Company C, Ninety-seventh Ohio Volunteer Infantry, for over a year, when he was discharged by reason of disability. He bought his present farm of Johnson Lawyer. The farm was first settled by William Sarver. He has eighty acres of land. Mrs. Wilkes was formerly Miss Martha Kilson, daughter of Lewis Kilson. Mr. Wilkes has been twice married; his first wife was a daughter of Mr. Isaac Boylan. He has one child by first marriage.

George Trinde resides on section 31. He was born in Fairfield township, Westmoreland county, Pennsylvania, in 1826. He removed to Wisconsin and settled in Dodge county in 1855, coming to Butler county in 1863, and settled in Boylan's Grove, Pittsford township. Mr. Trinde lived where he first settled eight years, settling where he now lives in 1871, purchasing the farm of Mr. Joseph Merrill. He has 160 acres of land. His wife was Miss Sarah McDowell, born in Pennsylvania. They have six children—William, Susan M., Almira, James, Emily and Lewis.

Hiram Bell resides on section 33, coming to Butler county in 1870. He settled where he now lives, two years later, making his present improvements. Mr. Bell was born in Rensselaer county, New York, in 1832. He went to Columbia county from the State of New York, and resided near Fall River for the fifteen years previous to his coming here. His wife was Elizabeth Carmford, born in the State of New York. They have had five children—Walter S., John A., Martha E., Willie J. and George H. Mr. Bell's farm contains 160 acres.

Charles Thompson is a native of England, having been born at Yorkshire, in 1836, coming to the United States in 1854. He resided in Johnstown, Cambria county, Pennsylvania, until 1856, when he removed to Dubuque, Iowa. Mr. Thompson is well known as the former superintendent of the Babbage Farm, properly the Iowa Central Stock Farm. He came to Butler county for the purpose of opening this farm for Mr. Babbage, in 1868. The real object was to make improvements, and to bring into market the land which now comprises this farm; but it was afterward decided to make a stock farm of the land. A history and description of the Iowa Central Stock Farm is given elsewhere. Mr. Thompson remained its superintendent until the fall of 1871. In 1870, he purchased the farm on section 33, where he now resides. He has about 300 acres of land. His first wife was Mary Ann Brimskill, a native of England. She died in 1874. His present wife was Miss Maggie Wray, a native of Pennsylvania. Mr. Thompson has four children by his first wife—James L., Simon G., Charles H. and Ralba E. He has three children by his present wife.

E. Bomell resides on section 15. Mr. Bomell was formerly a resident of Black Hawk county. He was born in Massachusetts, in 1815, where he lived until eighteen years of age. In the fall of 1833, he went to Ohio with an uncle, continuing his visit to Illinois the following spring, where he lived until 1864. He then came to Iowa and settled in Black Hawk county, where he lived two or three years; then removed to Bremer county. He came to West Point township in 1870, and purchased his present farm of 160 acres. His wife was Savina Howell, a native of Pennsylvania. They have eight children, five sons and two daughters. One child died in infancy.

Joseph N. Neal resides on section 16. He is one of the largest and most successful farmers in Butler county. His farm consists of about 1,100 acres. He was born in Pennsylvania, but removed to Ohio, where he lived about twenty years. He was brought up to the business of farming, and follows the occupation from choice. He has been a resident of West Point township since 1869. The improvements on his farm are among the best in the township, and were all made by himself. He devotes his attention principally to stock raising. His wife, formerly Miss Elizabeth Mitchell, is a native of Ohio. They have six children—Thomas M., Barnet, John H., Mary E., Joseph N., and Maud I. They lost one son.

Hollis Cass resides on section 16. His farm was entered by William Linderman. Mr. Cass purchased it in 1871, of Henry Linderman. He was born in New Hampshire, but removed to Caledonia county, Vermont, with his parents, when a boy. He was a soldier in the Union army during the rebellion, enlisting in the Eighth Regiment Vermont Volunteer Infantry, serving nearly four years. He participated in some of the most important battles of the war, including the siege of Fort Hudson, battles of Fisher Hill, Cedar Creek, etc. At the close of the war he returned to Vermont, soon after emigrating to Boone county, Illinois, coming to Butler county, in the fall of 1871. He has resided in this township since that time. Mrs. Cass was Miss Lefie Latham, born in Vermont. They have three children—Hollis L., Grace A., and Ella M. They lost their third child, Charles H. Mr. Cass has 160 acres of land in the farm where he resides, and 80 acres on section 19. Two brothers of Mr. Cass also came to Iowa, Henry, who came two years earlier, now living in Boone county, Illinois, and Welcome, who settled near

Charles City. He is now a resident of Minnesota, on the Northern Pacific Railroad.

B. F. Garrett was an early settler who took an active interest in the affairs of the town, and was a member of the board of supervisors for a number of years. He left early in the seventies for Kansas.

ORGANIC.

When the county was first divided into townships, on the 6th of February, 1855, by Judge Alonzo Converse, West Point was made a part of Ripley, which, at that time, embraced the entire western half of the county, except the town of Coldwater. W. R. Jamison, on the 26th of February, was authorized to organize the township of Ripley, which he did, holding the election on April 2, 1855. This was the organization until March 3, 1856, when Judge Converse again divided the territory forming West Point, which embraced its present territory and that of Pittsford. The first voting was held at the old school house near the line in Pittsford township, where Mr. Early resides, and Benjamin Needham was elected justice of the peace.

In the fall of 1857, Pittsford township was set off from West Point by another sub-division.

At the election held in November, 1882, the following officers were elected for the ensuing term: Justices of the peace, E. S. Thomas and R. B. Lockwood; clerk, L. L. Hatch; constables, G. E. Martin and S. B. Myrick; assessor, W. A. Smith; trustee, C. V. Surfus.

HISTORICAL EVENTS.

The first birth in this township was Orrin, a son of George and Margaret Lash, who was born in November, 1855. He removed to Storey county with his parents at an early day.

The first death was Mrs. Seth Strong.

The first marriage occurred in January, 1856, uniting the destinies of Seth Strong and Miss Mary Cannon; W. R. Jamison officiating.

Another early marriage was that of C. L. Jones and Miss Catherine Hewitt; the ceremony being preformed by Ancil Durand, October 5, 1856. Mr. Jones is still a resident and engaged in the hardware trade at Bristow.

The first school in the township was taught during the winter of 1859-60, at the house of Thomas Hewett, by Miss Mary A. Rich, with an attendance of about fifteen scholars.

The first attorney was D. F. Ellsworth, from Eldora, Hardin county. He came in 1874, remained a few years and then went to Allison.

The next representative of the bar was John Jamison, who removed to Greene and thence to Belmont, Wright county.

The first hotel was a log house built by George Lash in 1854.

POST OFFICE.

The first post office in this vicinity was established on section 24, Pittsford township, with H. A. Early as postmaster, under the name of "Boylan's Grove." The office remained here for some time when it was removed to West Point, and Julius Hoffman received the appointment, who remained in charge until October 10, 1862, when he was succeeded by C. L. Jones, who continued until October, 1864, when A. Durand, was commissioned and the office moved back to its starting point, where it remained until James Butler became postmaster, then the location was changed to West Point. He discharged the duties of the office until 1868, when he was succeeded by H. J. Playter, who held the office only during the winter of 1868, when J. C. Underwood received the appointment, and was followed in turn by F. H. Playter. The name of the office was changed from "Boylan's Grove" to "Bristow," in 1876.

RAILROADS.

An election waa held in this township on the 11th day of February, 1871, at the school house in District No. 2, on the question of aid to the Dubuque & Dakota Railroad. The assistance was refused by a majority of nine votes. Nothing was accomplished by way of securing a railroad, until 1879, when a special election was called, and a five per cent. tax voted to aid the D. & D. Railroad, with the conditions that the road should be completed through the township by the following fall. The road was graded, the track laid, and a train run into Bristow, July 12, 1879.

TOWN OF ALLISON.

This is the county seat of Butler county. It is laid out upon the east half of section 25, in the township of West Point, one mile north of the geographical center of the county. The plat is well drawn, with wide streets. In the center of the plat is laid out Court House Square, embracing ten acres. The ground is slightly elevated, and in the center stands the court house of Butler county.

Allison lies in the midst of an excellent farming country, on the line of the Dubuque & Dakota Railroad, and will ever be a good point for trade. This, taken with the advantages secured by the county seat, and its future is assured.

EARLY DEVELOPMENT.

Allison does not furnish much of a field for the historian, as it is the youngest town in the county.

In 1875, the Iowa and Pacific Railroad was surveyed through Butler county, and a road bed graded. About this time a village was platted by Mr. Babbage—who owns the stock farm—and called "Maudville," lying almost, if not wholly, on the south side of the railroad track. Only one lot was sold, that to M. B. Hendricks, of Butler Center, who commenced building a house, but never finished it. He moved the frame to Butler Center. It has since been removed to Allison. The lot was sold back to the founder of the village.

The Iowa and Pacific Railroad Company did not at once commence laying iron, but subsequently broke up. The Dubuque and Dakota Railroad company was then formed, which, in 1879, laid iron over the road bed, and commenced running trains in June of that year.

In the meantime a partnership had been formed among prominent capitalists of Dubuque, known as the Allison Town Company, which, in August, 1879, platted the present village of Allison, naming it after one of Iowa's United States Senators. The members of this company were John R. Waller, General C. H. Booth, R. E. Graves, Frank D. Stout and James Stout, all of Dubuque. The business was mostly attended to by John R. Waller. The first local agent was George M. Craig, while living in Butler Center. When the hotel was opened, in January, 1880, C. W. Corwin was installed as agent, and still acts in that capacity. The Town Company at once commenced the erection of the Allison Hotel.

The first settler upon the town site was George E. Martin, who had lived upon a farm a short distance from town. On the 10th of September, 1879, he moved his family into his house in town. He went into the livery business, and is still living in the house which he originally built.

The second settler was Charley Waters, who came in the latter part of September, and at once opened a lumber yard. He erected a number of the first buildings in town.

The next settler to arrive was Frank Elliott, a Canadian, who had been living, for some time, at Butler Center. He moved his family into one of the Waters' houses, the house now used by Charles Franklin.

Soon afterward, J. J. Cleaver, a painter, moved his family into one of the Charley Waters' houses.

L. E. Lincoln, a farmer, living a short distance south of Allison, erected a substantial house in Allison, and, in December, 1879, became a resident of the town. Mr. Lincoln is one of Allison's carpenters. He still occupies the house he first built.

George Woodward, of Minnesota, came soon after. Mr. Woodward first took charge of the elevator erected by the Town Company, and purchased the first grain marketed at Allison. This was early in January, 1880. James Dobbins now has charge of the elevator.

Early in the year 1880, arrived C. B. Bishop, J. K. Winsett, C. W. Corwin, Michael Weires, Louis Pharo, Harry Daggett, Mr. Sweely, James Gillan, and others, who are noted elsewhere.

In the fall of 1880, by vote, the county-seat was changed from Butler Center to Allison, and the county records moved here on the 7th of January, 1881. This gave Allison quite a boom, and about that time the Digman Hotel, two houses belonging to S. S. Burroughs, one house of C. H. Ilgenfritz's, one of Sheriff Hazlett's, one of Mrs. Craig's, two of E. Wilson's, lumber office of Mr. Barlow, and the law office of Lathrop & Davis, and other buildings were moved from Butler Center to Allison.

BUSINESS INTERESTS.

The first to commence business on the site of Allison was George E. Martin, who brought several teams and opened a livery stable, which is now kept by the firm of Martin & Dopking.

George M. Dopking was born in Crawford county, Pennsylvania, April 16, 1835. When quite young his parents moved to Erie county, New York. He attended school in the city of Buffalo until thirteen years of age. In 1848 his father, Nathan Dopking, moved his family to Lafayette county, Wisconsin, and settled on the farm where he still resides. George made his home with his parents until nineteen years of age, when he went to Illinois and engaged with the Illinois Central Railroad Company. The following spring he returned to Wisconsin. In 1855 he went to New Orleans and engaged as watchman on a steamer. In the fall of 1856 he came to Iowa, prospecting and gunning, making his way on foot across the State to Minnesota as far as the Blue Earth river, and returning to Wisconsin that winter. In the spring of 1857 he started with ten yoke of oxen and two plows for Iowa, where he engaged in breaking the prairie sod in Black Hawk, Bremer and Butler counties until July, when he sold his teams and engaged in the livery business at Cedar Falls. The following winter he sold his business and returned again to Wisconsin. In the spring of 1860 he went to Colorado and engaged in mining, returning the following winter. In 1862 he came to Iowa and with Holmes, Keeley & Kay engaged in a flour and saw mill business for one year. He enlisted in 1863 in the Forty-third Wisconsin Volunteers, Company E, and went south to Nashville, where he joined General Thomas' command. He was with the regiment until the close of the war, and honorably discharged in July, 1865. Returning to Wisconsin he bought a farm near his father's, which he sold in 1870, and went to Harrison county, Iowa, where he engaged in farming, also keeping a hotel, the Clinton House, at Magnolia, for about one year. He then went to Tripoli, where he took a contract to carry the United States mail between Waverly and West Union, afterward between Waverly and Old Wine, and also between Waverly and Butler Center. After running that five years he came to Shell Rock and engaged in the livery business with C. E. West, continuing until 1880, when he removed to Allison and engaged in the same business with George Martin. In 1857 he married Miss Abigail Jarvis, a native of Ashtabula county. They have been blessed with six children, four now living—Lewis, Annie, Fred and Homer.

Early in the fall of 1879, the railroad company erected a neat and substantial depot, over which Harry Daggett was placed in charge. Harry went from here to Hampton and his father, J. M. Daggett, is the present agent. He came here April 8th, 1880. He is a native of Maine, born in 1818. When but a boy he engaged on a sail vessel for a whaling voyage. He has sailed around the world a number of times. He settled in Linn county, Iowa, in 1853, and went to Dubuque in 1860. He located at Allison as stated, April 8, 1880.

The first to enter into mercantile business was the firm of Fletcher Moore and Charles Grasley, who rented a small building just south of the Allison Hotel, and on the 20th of January, 1880, opened for business with a small stock of general merchandise, mostly groceries. Mr. Moore now carries on the business, occupying his own corner block, and doing a thriving trade in groceries and farming machinery. He is a young man who has the confidence of the people, born at Belvidere, Illinois. He was engaged as clerk for one year in a dry good store at Harvard, Illinois, coming to Butler county November 1, 1879. His father, Francis Moore, was an early settler of Boone county, Illinois.

The first building expressly for mercantile purposes was that of J. K. Winsett and the Parris Bros., erected in the spring of 1880 by C. B. Bishop. It was first occupied as a hardware and grocery store; but the latter trade has been abandoned.

The firm of Winsett & Burnham now carry on the hardware business, on the east side of Main street.

J. K. Winsett was born in Indiana in 1845, and removed to Black Hawk county, with his parents, when a child, where he resided until he came here, in May, 1880, where he engaged in the grocery and hardware business. He closed out the grocery, and continued the hardware trade. His partner, Edward H. Burnham, was born in Richland county, Wisconsin, in 1859. Before coming to Allison he was engaged for some time as clerk for Foote & Mott, of Parkersburg, this county. His father, A. G. Burnham, settled in Richland county about 1857.

During the summer of 1880 the buildings now occupied by Fletcher Moore, J. A. Riggs & Co., Donald Bruce & Frank Elliott, and the McLeod buildings were erected, making an improvement upon the appearance of Main street.

The first dry goods store was opened by C. D. Williams, who commenced doing business in the summer of 1880, in the McLeod building, keeping a general merchandise stock. He erected the store now occupied by W. W. Pattee, where he continued the business for a time, finally closing out his stock of goods, selling the buildings to Craig & Smith.

In February, 1881, the Birkbeck Brothers opened one of the finest stock of goods in the county, and still continue in the trade with growing patronage. They came from Etna, Lafayette county, Wisconsin, where Turner, the elder of the brothers, was associated with his father in merchandising. J. T. Birkbeck, the father of the Birkbeck brothers, was born in Yorkshire, England, in 1825, emigrating to Grant county, Wisconsin, in 1850. He resided in Grant and Lafayette counties, Iowa, for a number of years. He spent several years in California; dying at his old home in Etna, Wisconsin, October 7, 1880. Mrs. Birkbeck was born in England, in 1831. Their children are—Turner, John W. and Anna; the latter born in Lafayette county, in 1868. The family all reside at Allison. Turner, of the above firm, was born in England, in 1858, and John W. in 1863. The Birkbeck brothers are young men of energy, and by enterprise and attention to business, are building up a fine trade in the promising town of Allison.

In November, 1881, G. M. Stockwell, in company with Emmett Laughlin, started a general merchandise store in the *Tribune* Building, No. 287, owned by the Dodge Brothers. They did a fair business for about one year, when they were closed by mortgages.

This stock was purchased by W. W. Pattee, who still continues to supply a large trade from the Craig & Smith building. Mr. Pattee is county recorder. A biography of him will be found in the article under that head.

Anderson & Harbert came from Shell Rock in the spring of 1881, and opened a stock of dry goods, groceries, clothing, boots and shoes, in the building now occupied by the restaurant. They moved to the Burbank Block on its completion, and at present handle clothing and boots and shoes.

The first drug store was started in 1880, by Dr. J. S. Riggs, who erected the neat store and office just opposite the Allison

Frank L. Dodge

Mrs Frank L. Dodge.

Hotel. In 1881 he took his brother, John A., as a partner in the business, and continued until September, 1882, when he sold his interest to Dr. S. E. Bourroughs, late of Grundy county. The firm name is J. A. Riggs & Company.

Dr. Burbank & Son started their drug store in the fall of 1882, erecting one of the best business houses in town, known as "Burbanks' Corner Block." One half of this is used by the drug store, and the other rented to Anderson & Harbert. Both of the drug stores carry a good stock and do a good business. The doctors are noted in the medical chapter.

The elevator was commenced early in January, 1880, by the Town Company, and completed early in the spring. George Woodward, of Minnesota, was first placed in charge, and, as stated, purchased the first wheat marketed at Allison, which was stored in the elevator. Mr. Woodward has removed to Dakota Territory, and at present James Dobbins has charge of the elevator.

The first blacksmith in Allison was Michael Weires, who commenced work April 8, 1880, and is still faithfully working at his trade. Another blacksmith came here for a time but has since removed.

Louis Pharo, from Galena, Illinois, was the first wagon-maker, and still continues this business here.

The first barber shop in town was opened by F. J. Smith. In the fall of 1882 he left for a new location in the northern part of the State. He is now in Waverly. Frank Elliott is the present knight of the razor.

The first furniture dealer in the town was John Bell. He was succeeded by C. B. Bishop, who still represents the trade, carrying a heavy stock and doing a good business. He settled here October 14, 1879. There was but one residence here at that time—that of George Martin. He was born in Cattaraugus county, New York, in 1842. When nine years of age he removed with his parents to Canada, and thence to Winona, Minnesota, in 1852. There was at that time only one house in that flourishing city. In the fall of the same year he moved to Wisconsin. His father, Jonas B. Bishop, now resides in Wood county, Wisconsin. Corydon B. Bishop enlisted in 1861 in Company F, Seventh Wisconsin Volunteer Infantry, and served in the Iron Brigade for three years. He participated in the principal battles of the Army of the Potomac until the battle of the Wilderness, including the second Bull Run, South Mountain, Fredricksburg, Chancelorville and Gettysburg. He was wounded at the battle of the Wilderness. He went to Minnesota after the war, coming to Iowa from Wisconsin in 1868. He located at Osage and engaged in the business of joiner and carpenter. He lived for a time in other parts of the State, coming to this place from Nashua in October, 1879; and was the first carpenter and builder to locate here. He was in partnership with M. B. Butler in the building of the court house at Allison. He engaged in the furniture business in February, 1882, succeeding John Bell. His wife was Miss Hattie Bunder, born in St. Lawrence county, New York. They have three children—Lottie, Lulu N. and Gilbert Haven.

Early in the summer of 1881 Levi Baker opened the restaurant which he still runs.

The first harness shop was started by R. Pond & Company, and conducted by Henry Farnum.

The first millinery store was opened, and is still continued, by Mrs. Anna Myers. Business was commenced in May, 1881.

The abstract firms are Lathrop, Hyde & Levis, and Geo. M. Craig & A. I. Smith; the former being formed in 1880, and the latter in July, 1881.

The legal profession is represented by Lathrop & Davis, Craig & Smith, George A. McIntyre, and O. H. Scott, who are all noted at length in the History of the Bar.

Mettler & Elliott were among the first masons. Pattee & Levis opened an insurance office. C. B. Bishop was the first contractor and builder. E. S. Thomas, Esq., dealt out justice. J. B. Combellick started the first meat market in the winter of 1880–81.

HOTELS.

The first stopping place in Allison was at the residence of George E. Martin, who accommodated the weary traveler while the hotel was in process of erection; but he did not make it a business. There are, at present, two hotels in the town, the Allison House and the Digman House.

THE ALLISON HOUSE.

This was one of the first buildings erected in the village. It was built by the Allison Town Company, the contractor being Mr. M. Flick, of Dubuque, one of the most extensive hotel builders in Iowa. The architectural design was drawn by F. D. Hyde, of Dubuque. The building was commenced in September, 1879, and finished, as originally designed, just before Christmas, of that year. Its size was then 32x36 feet, three stories high, with Mansard roof, and had cost about $5,000. On the 2d day of January, 1880, the house was opened to guests, by C. W. Corwin, of Waterloo, who arrived and took charge of it. The house remained as originally built until August, 1881, when an addition was made to it, doubling its former size. The addition is 32x50 feet, three stories high, with Mansard roof, and a kitchen 20x28 feet, one and one-half stories high. These improvements cost about $6,000; the house was furnished at a cost of $2,000, making the total cost about $13,000. The interior of the hotel is admirably arranged, containing twenty-two sleeping rooms, of which eight are large double ones. The lower floor is divided into a ladies' parlor, office, sample rooms, wash room, and dining room, and all have been very tastily furnished by the company. The entire house is furnished with water by means of a force pump. In February, 1880, an excellent barn was erected at a cost of $1,000.

C. W. Corwin came to Allison and opened the Hotel, January 2, 1880, two weeks after it was completed. The house in general structure, excellence of finish, number of rooms and general convenience, is not excelled in this part of the State of Iowa, and does credit to the new and thriving town of Allison. Mr. Corwin is a native of Tompkins county, New York, where he was born in 1834. His parents removed to Schuyler county, in that State, when he was a boy, and thence to Lake county, in 1847. The family removed to Black Hawk county, Iowa, and settled on a farm in Fox township. His father,

Joshua C. Corwin, afterward removed to Waterloo, where he resided until his death. A brother of C. W. Corwin, I. T. Corwin, settled in Poyner township several years earlier. He was quite prominent among earlier settlers of Black Hawk county; he was one of the supervisors and justice of the peace of that county, for many years. He is now a resident of Sioux county and an extensive land owner near the town of Rock Valley. Mr. Corwin was deputy sheriff of Black Hawk county under sheriff W. F. Brown for several years, and was also notary public and collector. He is at present agent for the town lot company, at Allison. Mrs. Corwin was formerly Miss Alice McStay, born in the State of New York. They have one son—Williard H., and a bright little daughter—Daisy Pearl. Mr. Corwin is a genial popular landlord, and the Allison House, under his charge, has established an excellent reputation.

THE DIGMAN HOUSE.

This popular house was first built in Butler Center, by Franz Digman, now deceased. It was removed to Allison, after the re-location of the county seat, in the summer of 1881, and late in the fall opened to guests. Mrs. Digman is proprietress and Carl Frank, clerk. They are accommodating and pleasant and the house is justly popular.

BANK OF ALLISON.

This institution was organized on the 4th of April, 1880. The founders were, Ridgeway, Perrin and Slimmer. Messrs. Ridgeway and Slimmer, of Waverly, and Mr. Perrin, of Clarksville. The capital of the bank was nominally $7,000, yet was really unlimited. The bank was first opened in the drug store of J. A. Riggs & Co. The present bank building was soon after erected. It is a neat and tasty building, with glass front, standing nearly opposite the Allison Hotel. I. E. Lucas was the first and is the present cashier; a more accommodating and capable cashier never signed a draft. He was born in Carroll county, Indiana, in 1846, coming to Bremer county with his father, Parker Lucas, who settled on a farm in Lafayette township, in that county. Mr. Lucas was brought up on a farm, attending the public school at Clarksville for three years, and for one year a student at Osage College, in this State. He was engaged for a number of years in teaching in Bremer and Butler counties. For three years he was principal of the school at Clarksville, where he was formerly a student; also principal for a time of the school at New Hartford. On the organization of the Bank of Allison, April 4, 1881, he was made cashier. Mr. Lucas was a very successful teacher. Politically he is a republican.

Irving M. Fisher, the superintendent of the Iowa Central Stock Farm, lives in this township. He was born October 2, 1839, in Williamstown, Massachusetts. He is the son of Minot and Mary (Austin) Fisher, natives of the same State, but of English origin. His mother died when he was but five years of age. He then lived with an aunt two years. His father being again married, he returned home and remained there until thirteen years of age, during which time he attended school in his native State and also in Union village,

New York. Leaving home he went to Vermont, there making his home with Colonel Baker, attending school during the winter months and assisting on the Colonel's farm during the remainder of the year. In the spring of 1857 he removed to Columbus, Wisconsin, with Henry Baker, a son of the Colonel, with whom he remained until the following October, when he went to Bradford, Chickasaw county, Iowa. Here he remained two years. He then went to Nashua, in the same county, and was there when the rebellion commenced. On the 8th day of July, 1861, he enlisted in Company B, Seventh Iowa Volunteer Infantry. With his regiment he participated in the battle of Belmont and sieges of Forts Henry and Donelson. He was honorably discharged on the 22d of March, 1862, on account of disability. Recovering his health, on the 13th of October, 1862, he enlisted in Company C, Fourteenth Iowa Volunteer Infantry, and was one of the sergeants of the company. He was in the ordnance department with General A. J. Smith in the Red River expedition. At the close of the service he was again honorably discharged and returned to Nashua. On the 1st day of January, 1867, he was united in marriage at Bradford, Iowa, with Mary J., daughter of William and Elizabeth Biggar, a native of Huntingdon county, Pennsylvania, but of Scottish descent. Mrs. Fisher received an academic education, and while attending school ranked first in all her classes. She has taught in some of the best schools in Chickasaw county, and was a teacher in the public schools of Bradford at the time of her marriage. She still retains an interest in schools and school work. On the 6th day of January, 1875, Mr. Fisher removed to the Central Iowa Stock Farm, of which he has since been manager. Thrown upon his own resources at the age of thirteen, he has had a struggle in life, but success has crowned his efforts. He now owns a farm of 280 acres one and one-half miles from Allison. Mrs. Fisher also owns a small farm in Chickasaw county, three miles from Nashua. Mr. Fisher's father died in 1879 in his native State. Mr. and Mrs. Fisher are members of the Congregational Church. In politics he is a staunch republican and a worker in the cause.

POST OFFICE.

The post office was established during the winter of 1879–80. The office was kept at the depot, with J. M. Daggett, postmaster, who was the father of E. W. Daggett, station agent. In May, 1881, the office was removed to the Williams building, just opposite the north of Burbank's corner block. On the first of November, 1881, E. S. Thomas was appointed postmaster, and on the first day of December, 1882, removed the office across the street, to the old office of the clerk of the courts. Mr. Thomas is still the incumbent, and makes a most accommodating and satisfactory officer. He was treasurer of Butler county four years. A sketch of him appears in connection with the article upon county officers. The office is a fourth class one, the business amounting to about $1,300 per year. About $900 worth of stamps are cancelled annually. It was established as a money order office in August, 1882.

INCORPORATION.

Allison was organized as a city municipality in the summer of 1881, the election for the city officers being held on Saturday, August 13, 1881. The campaign was quite active, the canvass showing eighteen candidates for official honors. The successful candidates and first officers were: Mayor, W. A. Lathrop; recorder, George A. McIntyre; trustees, George M. Craig, W. W. Pattee, Louis Pharo, J. K. Winsett, D. K. Harbert, and George Woodward.

The city council assembled for the first time, at the auditor's office, on August 22, 1881, with the following members present: Mayor, W. A. Lathrop; recorder, George A. McIntyre; W. W. Pattee, George M. Craig, Louis Pharo, George E. Woodward, J. K. Winsett. Mr. Craig moved that the recorder be instructed to draft rules and regulations for council meetings, to be presented at the next session. The motion prevailed.

The mayor appointed committees as follows: Ways and means—Pattee and Winsett; claims—Harbert and Woodward; streets and alleys—Craig and Winsett; ordinances and printing—Craig and Harbert; health—Pattee and Pharo; offices and accounts—Woodward and Winsett; supplies—Harbert and Pharo; judiciary—Craig, McIntyre and the mayor.

At the next meeting on August 29th, Levi Baker was appointed city marshal.

At the election in March, 1882, the following officers were elected and are the present incumbents: Mayor, W. A. Lathrop; recorder, George A. McIntire; council, W. W. Pattee, George M. Craig, Louis Pharo, Turner Birkbeck, J. K. Winsett and Charles Franklin; marshal, George Dopking. Meetings of the council are held at the office of Mayor Lathrop.

MASONIC.

Opal Lodge, A. F. and A. M., was instituted under dispensation, on the 1st of September, 1881. W. W. Pattee made W. M.; E. S. Thomas, S. W.; J. W. Ray, J. W.; C. H. Ilgenfritz, Treasurer; J. M. Daggett, Secretary; Levi Baker, S. D.; J. W. Davis, J. D.; and G. M. Dopking, Tyler. The charter members aside from the above named officers were, H. Farnum, James Scofield, A. I. Smith, A. G. Fellows, I. E. Lucas, J. W. Spencer, and G. M. Craig. The first meeting of the lodge was held on the 6th of October, 1881, and the following were raised under dispensation: J. K. Winsett, J. S. Riggs, George A. McIntyre, John A. Riggs, G. E. Franklin, W. A. Lathrop, Frank Baker, C. W. Lewis and Edward H. Burnham. A charter was granted the lodge in June, 1882, and A. I. Smith was appointed D. G. M. He called the lodge together, and it was organized under the charter on the 6th of July, 1882, at which time the following officers were elected: W. W. Pattee, W. M.; E. S. Thomas, S. W.; J. W. Ray, J. W.; C. H. Ilgenfritz, Treasurer; and J. M. Daggett, Secretary. The W. M. appointed L. Baker, S. D.; J. A. Riggs, J. D.; J. K. Winsett and C. W. Davis, Stewards; and Frank Baker, Tyler; all of whom were installed.

The regular meetings of the lodge are held on the Thursday night on or before the full moon, in each month. A commendable interest is manifested, and it is in a flourishing condition.

BRASS BAND.

The Brass Band of Allison was organized in August, 1881, consisting of the following musicians: F. L. Dodge, leader, E flat cornet; G. L. Anderson, first B flat cornet; Henry Farnum, second B flat cornet; C. W. Levis, first alto; Will Corwin, second alto; M. Weires, first tenor; Will Daggett, second tenor; W. E. Hyde, baritone; Ed. Lincoln, tuba; James Gillen, bass drum; Zena Thomas, snare drum.

The officers of the organization were as follows: President, G. L. Anderson; vice-president, Henry Farnum; secretary, W. E. Hyde; treasurer, C. W. Levis.

There has been but little change in the band, and its members have become very proficient in the use of their instruments.

PROHIBITION CLUB.

This club was organized during the agitation of the constitutional amendment. It had fifty members to commence with. The officers were: J. W. Davis, president; F. L. Dodge, vice-president; Mrs. G. M. Craig, secretary; Turner Birkbeck, treasurer. When the amendment was carried the work of the club ceased.

TERPSICHOREAN CLUB.

Early in December, 1882, a dancing club was organized with George A. McIntyre, president; F. L. Dodge, secretary; E. H. Burnham, treasurer; J. W. Spencer and O. E. Mullarkey, managers; J. W. Spencer, O. E. Mullarkey and J. K. Winsett were made a committee on membership and invitation. The Parkersburg Orchestra were engaged to furnish music for a series of five parties which it was proposed to hold during the winter.

CHORAL CLUB.

This musical society effected an organization on the 13th of October, 1882. George A. McIntyre was elected president; Mrs. J. W. Davis, vice-president; Mrs. Frank Burbank, secretary; Miss C. Daggett, treasurer; Mrs. Beck, Mrs. Evans and Mrs. Dodge, committee on meeting; and F. L. Dodge, musical director. Thursday evenings were decided upon for the meetings of the club.

METHODIST EPISCOPAL CHURCH.

This society was organized on the 15th of August, 1880, with the Rev. Laban Winsett officiating, and the following members: D. Bruce, Flora Bruce, F. Moore, C. B. Bishop, Hattie Bishop, Catherine McCleod, Christian McWilliams and Mary Cleaver.

The first officers were: Leader, D. Bruce; stewards, D. Bruce, F. Moore and C. B. Bishop; trustees and incorporators, I. M. Fisher, D. Bruce, C. B. Bishop, F. Moore, J. K. Winsett and C. W. Corwin. The first religious services for the denomination were held at McCleod's Hall, by Rev. Labon Winsett, who after filling the pulpit for about three months was succeeded by Rev. W. H. Records, who remained one year, and was followed by the present minister, Rev. J. M. Hedes. The neat church building was erected in the summer of 1881, at a cost of $2,200, and is a frame building, 30x50 feet in size.

The present officers are: Class leader, D. Bruce; stewards, John Bell, Mrs. Bell, T. Birkbeck, Mary Cleaver, Mrs. M. J. Davis; trustees, W. A. Lathrop, D. Bruce, F. Moore, C. B. Bishop, John Bell, T. Birkbeck, J. K. Winsett, F. L. Dodge and J.

W. Davis. The present membership of the church is sixteen. All the incumbrances or indebtedness is provided for, and the society is in a most flourishing and prosperous condition, with a future before it full of promise that much good will be accomplished.

The M. E. Sunday School was organized in May, 1880, with C. B. Bishop as superintendent, and has grown in interest from the first until it now has an enrollment of 70 scholars and an average attendance of about 30. The present officers are as follows: T. Birkbeck, superintendent; Frank Elliot, assistant; F. Moore, treasurer; L. Davis, secretary.

The church building was dedicated on the 14th of May, 1882, Rev. L. D. Parsons officiating.

FIRST OCCURRENCES.

The first birth within the thriving town of Allison, occurred on the 24th of April, 1880, a son to Frank and Mary Jane Elliott. The boy was christened Frank Allison, in honor of the town. The happy father is the genial barber of the town.

The first death occurring in Allison was that of a child of Mr. and Mrs. George M. Craig, on Tuesday night, August 16, 1881, the remains were taken to Butler Center for interment.

The first marriage of parties belonging in Allison, occurred in Waverly, and joined the future destinies of Michael Weires, of Allison, and Miss Nellie Morrow, of Wisconsin. Their child, Frank, was the third birth in town.

Charles Grasley, of Allison, was soon after married, in Waterloo, to a lady of that city. They now live in Waterloo.

The first marriage ceremony performed in Allison, was that uniting Mr. and Mrs. Coonley, of Bristow.

TOWN OF BRISTOW.

This town was formerly called West Point. George Lash and H. A. Early entered the land on which the place now stands. The original town was platted by them, consisting of 10 acres on section 18 and ten acres on section 19. The situation is a pleasant one on the Dubuque and Dakota Railroad, and on the west line of West Point township. The first business building was erected here in 1860, by Julius Huffman. It was a frame log house, in which, for about two years, he kept a small stock of goods, when he removed to Cedar Falls, and thence to Ackley, where he still remains.

The next party to embark in mercantile business at this point was James Butler, from Clarksville, who purchased a small dwelling house, converted it into a store, and opened a stock of goods in 1866. Like his predecessor, he remained but a short time, as in June, 1868, he sold out to H. J. Playter, and returned to the place from whence he came, where he died in 1880. Mr. Playter carried on the business until 1871, when he went to Butler Center. He returned, however, the following season and resumed business. In the fall of 1874, he again removed and tried Aplington as a business point for a season; but 1875 found him again at the old place in Bristow engaged in business with his son. They remained until 1877, when they closed out entirely. The son is still a resident of the town.

Henry J. Playter is station agent on the Dubuque and Dakota Railroad. He was born in England, in 1821. He has been a resident of Bristow since 1868. He went to Buffalo, New York, from Canada, in 1843, and removed to Dubuque in 1856. He was, for some time, in the service of the Union, during the war of the rebellion. He assisted in raising and organizing Company H, of the Twelfth Volunteer Regiment, and commanded the company in the field for about two years. On coming to Bristow he engaged in mercantile business, which he followed for several years. He has been station agent at Bristow since the railroad was completed. H. J. Playter, on the 1st of December, 1882, received an appointment as clerk in the war department, at Washington, where he now resides. His wife was born in the State of New York. They have three sons—Frank H., John B., and Edward A.

In 1872 Colvin & Arnold opened a general stock of merchandise. In 1874 this partnership was dissolved, Mr. Colvin remaining at the old stand, Mr. Arnold building, and opening a stock of his own. During the spring of 1880, Mr. Colvin closed out his stock, and removed to Plainfield, Bremer county. He is now in Dakota. After the dissolution of the old firm, Mr. Arnold formed a partnership with Mr. L. L. Hatch. This firm is yet in the trade.

Following them came Duboys Bros., who commenced business in 1878. They remained in the trade but a short time, when they made an assignment.

E. M. Haven came, also, about this time. He remains, and carries a general stock.

In 1882 H. A. Wheeler engaged in general merchandising, and still continues.

The harness trade was first represented by Kocker & Lichty, in August, 1878. This partnership continued until 1879, when Mr. Kocher purchased the interest of his partner and associated with him Mr. Holtz, who remained his partner until 1880, when the interest he represented was purchased by Mr. Kocher, Sr. This establishment is now doing business under the firm name of Kocher & Son.

The next to engage in this line of trade were Hoffman & Laster, from Waverly. They continued here in business about two years, when they removed their stock to Sumner, Bremer county.

Following them were Hultz & Connelly, who commenced business in October, 1880. They were in business but a short time, when C. L. Jones purchased the interest of Mr. Hultz. They are still in the business, under the firm name of Jones & Connelly.

Kocher & Kocher, father and son, dealers in hardware, at Bristow, entered into business here in 1879. Jeremiah Kocher was born in Luzerne county, Pennsylvania, in 1822. He removed to Dixon, Lee county, Illinois, in 1856, where he engaged at the trade of carpenter, and came to Butler county with his family in 1861, settling on a farm in Jackson township, three miles west of the village of Clarksville, purchasing the farm of Joseph Crawford, of Dixon, Illinois, continuing on the farm until 1880. He has seven children. John W., a partner with him in the business, was born in Luzerne county, Pennsylvania, in 1848, and came to Butler county with his father. John W.'s wife was Miss Ida A. Ripsom. They have four children. J. W. Kocher is a tinner by trade and carries on that line of business in connection with the hardware trade.

James Connolly, of the firm of Jones & Connolly, hardware dealers, is a native of Wellington county, Canada, where he was born in 1849. He came to Bristow in 1869. He is a blacksmith by trade, and was engaged in that business for ten years previous to engaging in his present business. His wife is a native of Pennsylvania, and a daughter of W. W. Royer, of West Point township. The firm of Jones & Connolly was formed in October, 1881.

Charles L. Jones, of the firm of Jones & Connolly, is one of the early settlers of West Point township. His residence in this county dates from November 27, 1855. He was born in Elmira, Chemung county, New York, in 1836. In 1852 he removed with his father's family to Linn county, this State, and came here in the fall of 1855, as stated. Mr. Jones purchased a farm of Mr. John Hewitt, on section 30, in this township, and engaged in farming until February, 1864, when he entered the army, as a member of the Second Iowa Cavalry. He served in the army until September, 1865, participating in a number of general engagements. He enlisted as a private, but later, was made sergeant. Mr. Jones resumed farming on his return from the army, which he continued until 1879, when he engaged in the sale of farm machinery, and in the fall of 1880, added the hardware trade to his business. Mrs. Jones, formerly Miss Catherine Hewitt, was a daughter of Mr. Thomas Hewitt. They have four children—William E., Eugene A., Elmer S., and Annie L.

Frank A. Jones, a brother, came several years later, and bought the farm of George Lash. This was the first farm settled in West Point township; a part of the plat of Bristow is included in this farm. He engaged in farming, and also in keeping hotel. He built the hotel known as the Jones House, in 1878. Another brother, Edward F., came here in 1867, and purchased a farm, which he sold in 1872, and removed to Jackson county, Kansas. Mr. Jones' mother died in Marion, Iowa, after which his father, H. Jones, returned to the State of New York, where he died in 1864.

A drug store was opened by D. F. Ellsworth, who remained in the business a short time, going to Dakota in 1881.

John B. Playter established his business in September, 1875: He is a son of Henry J. Playter, was born in Buffalo, New York, in 1855. He was educated at Cornell College, Iowa. He was married to Miss Mary Betzer, daughter of Peter Betzer, of West Point township. Mr. Playter is a gentleman of more than ordinary attainments, is a careful and competent druggist, and possesses in the highest degree the esteem and confidence of the public.

The first blacksmith shop was opened by Mr. Hepner, who remained until 1865, and went to Cedar Falls. Barnett Neal was next to follow this business. He remained about one year. Then came Mr. Wagoner for a short time, when he removed to Pittsford township. During this time, 1869, James Connolly, from Canada, opened a shop but in 1882 he sold it to G. G. Coonly, who had been in business in another shop since 1876; he is still following the trade. Henry Underkafer came in 1879 and engaged in the same business which he continues.

On the 16th of November, 1881, an order was issued by the district court, appointing H. J. Playter, S. B. Uyrick, R. B. Lockwood, James Connolly and L. L. Hatch, a board of commissioners, to call an election for the purpose of ascertaining the views of the people as to incorporation. An election was therefore called for the 15th of December, 1881, at which time the incorporation was decided upon, and the following officers were, on the 10th of January, 1882, elected: Mayor, T. E. Newbury; recorder, W. F. Early; trustees, Wm. Arnold, J. W. Kocher, James Connolly, A. H. Hitchcock and S. Gibson; treasurer, J, W. Kocher; marshal, S. Kennison; street commissioner, John Boston. At this election there was a tie vote for mayor, Mr. Newbury and Mr. Durand each having received thirty votes. The question was decided by drawing apples from a box, the one drawing the last apple being the successful candidate.

At the annual meeting held on the sixth of April, 1882, the following officers were elected: Mayor, F. E. Newbury; recorder, W. F. Early; trustees, W. B. Dubois, James Connolly; treasurer, C. T. Coonly; assessor, L. L. Hatch; street commissioner, John Boston; marshal, S. Kennison. The recorder left the town shortly after the election, and F. H. Playter was appointed to fill the vacancy.

EDUCATIONAL.

Upon the organization of school districts, Bristow was included in the territory comprising the entire township. An independent district was formed, June 26, 1876, and comprised four sections of land—17, 18, 19, and 20. The southeast quarter of section 13, and the northeast quarter of section 24, of Pittsford township, was annexed during the winter of 1881-2, by a special act of the legislature. The first school house, a frame building, 18x24 feet, was erected on the northeast of section 19, on land owned by F. E. Newbury. This building is still used for school purposes.

The second building erected was a structure of more importance, arranged for two departments, and desirable in all its appointments. It cost $2,200, and was completed in 1880. The first school in this building was taught by O. H. Scott, as principal, assisted by Miss Ella Gibson in the primary department. Mary Mellenger taught the school in the old building during the same time. There was an attendance of 41 in the higher department, 34 in the primary, and 25 at the old house, making a total attendance of 100. School is in running order, in all these departments, the present winter—1883—with Miss Hattie Ripson, principal; Miss Jennie Wray, assistant, and Mrs. Ella Gibson in the old building. There is an attendance of 119.

The schools are in a flourishing condition, and the educational facilties of this town speak well for the place.

HOTELS.

"Farmers' Home" was the title of the first place for entertainment in Bristow. This house was opened by George Trindal, in the fall of 1863. He continued as landlord until 1870, when he sold to Joseph Merrill, and moved on a farm, on section 31, where he still lives. The building is now used as a farm house.

The next hotel was kept by John A. Weeks, in 1865. It was, in part, built of logs, by George Lash, in 1856. Mr. Weeks continued here until 1869, when he moved to Cedar Falls. He now lives in Dakota. He was succeeded by F. A. Jones, who purchased the property, and fed the hungry within its walls until 1878, when he erected a more commodious structure, now called the Jones House. He rented the same to F. A. Newbury, the present proprietor.

The Eagle House was built and opened during the fall of 1878, with E. J. Stoddard as landlord. He continued in the business until the spring of 1880. He was succeeded by William Refsnider, who remained until the fall of 1880, then Stoddard again had control until 1882, when the house was closed, and is now used as a residence.

F. E. Newbury, who succeeded Mr. Frank Jones as proprietor of the Jones Hotel in Bristow, on March 16, 1881, was born in Kenosha county, Wisconsin, January, 1845, where he was brought up. His father, Henry A. Newbury, still resides on the farm where he settled when Wisconsin was still a territory. Mr. Newbury was a soldier in the army during the war; enlisting in Company G, Forty-third Wisconsin Infantry, in 1864, and serving until the close of the struggle. He has been a resident of this county since 1867, settling on a farm on section 19, which he still owns. His wife was Sophia Pierce, a daughter of Carleton Pierce, of Kenosha county, Wisconsin, where she was born. They have two children—Henry and Floyd. Mr. Newbury keeps a good hotel, and is a popular landlord.

Among other prominent business men and influential citizens in this thriving town are S. Kenison, H. A. Wheeler, J. H. Neal, Emmett M. Haven and Robert B. Lockwood.

Dubois & Kenison, lumber dealers in Bristow, are the successors of W. P. Smith, whom they succeeded November 7, 1881. Sevedra Kenison is the son of John Kenison, who was born in Canada, and removed when a young man to Illinois; thence to Alamakee county, in this State; thence to Grundy county, and finally to Butler county, in 1865, settling in West Point township on a farm now owned by Joseph N. Neal. He afterwards removed to Pittsford township, where he resided until his death. His wife is also deceased. They had six children, all of whom are living. Sevedra Kenison was born in Freeport, Illinois, and came to Butler county with his parents, and has been a resident of this county since that time.

Horace A. Wheeler, general merchant at Bristow, commenced business April 22, 1882. Mr. Wheeler was born in Boone county, Illinois, October 14, 1847. He came from Illinois to Butler county in 1872 and purchased a farm in West Point township of L. H. Yamwell, of Pittsfield, Massachusetts. He sold to Benjamin Bates and engaged in business as above stated. His father is Adam Wheeler, of Clarksville. His wife was Lucy Arnold, born in the State of New York. They have three children—Cora, Harmon, and Leon.

John H. Neal, harness-maker, Bristow, succeeded M. B. Wilson in the fall of 1881. He learned his trade with Mr. Wilson, who is now a resident of Wright county, Iowa. Mr. Neal is a son of Joseph N. Neal, of West Point township. He was born in Monroe county, Ohio, in 1857. His wife was Miss Mary Hatch, of Bristow.

Emmett M. Haven, general merchant, of Bristow, established a grocery business here in November, 1879, and engaged in general merchandising in April, 1881. Mr. Haven was born in Illinois, and brought up in Rockford, Floyd county, Iowa. He has always been engaged in his present business, having been for many years a clerk. He first came to Butler county in 1870, and was a resident of Clarksville for about five years. Mr. Haven keeps a full assortment of general merchandise, has established a good business, and is having an excellent trade. His wife was Miss Sarah E. Hull, of Jones county, Iowa.

Robert Barrett Lockwood, of Bristow, was born in Durham county, England, in 1816. He resided in London for many years, where he held for some time the position of notary public, and was engaged in the practice of law for many years. He emigrated to the United States in 1857, settling on a farm in Dubuque county, Iowa. He was engaged in the cultivation of his large farm in that county for many years. Mr. Lockwood was a member, for some time, of the board of supervisors, of that county. He came to Butler county in 1875, and again located on a large farm, but has now retired. Mr. Lockwood is a gentleman of good education; has read extensively, and is possessed of much general information. He has twice married; his first wife died in Dubuque county. His present wife was Mrs. Chapline, widow of Charles J. Chapline, a prominent citizen of Dubuque. Mr. Lockwood has five children, two sons and three daughters. Mrs. Lockwood has three sons by her first marriage.

RELIGIOUS.

The Methodist Episcopal Church was organized during the summer of 1855, by Rev. Mr. Swearingen, from Clarksville. Among the first members of this class were John Lash and wife, P. Miller, and Mr. and Mrs. George Lash. Rev. Mr. Swearingen continued in charge, holding service once every two weeks, until 1857, when Rev. Alva Freeman, from Franklin county, ministered to the spiritual wants of the people, and a parsonage was erected for his use. He remained two years, when he removed to Grundy county. The society was then left without a pastor for some time. Afterward the United Brethren sent Rev. I. Shafer here, who remained for a time. They still have an organization, with Rev. George Benson as pastor, with a membership of about twenty-five, holding service once every two weeks in the Presbyterian Church.

Rev. George Benson was born in Genesee county, New York, in 1844. When three years old he went with his parents to Wisconsin, where receiving a good common school education, he grew to manhood. He engaged in the ministry in 1873, and in 1880 came to Bristow. Mr. Benson was married, in April, 1866, to Miss Millie A. Pond. They have two children, both of whom are members of the United Brethren Church.

The first Presbyterian Church was organized in Jamison's Grove, on the 31st day of October, 1857, and called the Pisgah Church, which name it still retains.

Rev. Williston Jones, a missionary from Iowa Falls, officiated on this occasion. The original members of this church were: Samuel Armstrong and wife, John A. Staley and wife, Mrs. Susanna Harlan, Henry Myer and wife and their two sons, Henry and Frederick; Mrs. Brotherton, Mrs. Hannah Moore, Mrs. Isabella Jamison, and Mrs. Diantha Wickham. Lemuel Armstrong was chosen ruling elder, and the church was connected with the Cedar Valley Presbytery. The first sacramental service was observed on the 27th day of December, 1857.

The first death was that of Diantha Wickham, April 18, 1858. The funeral service was conducted by Rev. Williston Jones. This pastor officiated twice each month and served the church for two years. On the 1st day of October, 1859, Rev. G. G. Renshaw was sent to administer to the wants of this people. He was in poor health and died in about one year. After this the church was without a pastor for two years. On June 2, 1862, a supply was found in Rev. Richard Merrill, who continued with this people for about six years. He was followed by Rev. George Graham, from Clarksville, and he in turn by Rev. German H. Chaterson on February 11, 1871. Then in June, 1871, came Rev. W. R. Smith. In 1872 this organization consolidated with the church at Butler Center, and both societies were incorporated as one, under the name of Pisgah Church, with the following officers: Francis McGeachy, A. Woodley and Lewis Nelson, trustees; Robert Smith, treasurer; Robert Given, secretary. In 1873 they built a church 42x60 feet, at an expense of $2,400, in the town of Bristow, the young people of the community donating a bell. The present officers of the church are: Francis McGeachy and Robert Smith, trustees; Charles H. Stewart, secretary and treasurer; James Harlan and William Wray, elders; Rev. John Gourley, pastor. There have been seventy-four members of this church, and at this date (January, 1883) but thirty-six. There was a Sabbath school organized during the spring of 1858 in a log school house located on section 19, with Lemuel Armstrong as superintendent and John A. Staley, assistant. Afterward, sessions of this school were held in another larger school house on section 20.

The first Sabbath school of Pisgah church in the town of Bristow, elected William Ray, superintendent; H. J. Playter, assistant; George Given, secretary and treasurer; William Smith, librarian. This organization was effected in 1874. There is now an average attendance of forty-five. The following are the officers: J. M. Graham, superintendent; H. J. Playter, assistant; J. W. Dubois, secretary; W. W. Robinson, organist.

GOOD TEMPLARS.

The Bristow Lodge, No. 33, I. O. G. T., was instituted March, 1882, under the direction of George Fisher, of Clarksville, with the following charter members: H. J. Playter, Mr. and Mrs. C. T. Coonley, Mr. and Mrs. G. G. Coonley, Mrs. F. H. Playter, F. P. Hurlbut, O. D. Miller, E. L. Turner, Mrs. M. Murphy, Mrs. R. E. Murphy, Lewis Coonley, S. G. Welcher, G. S. Welcher, Mrs. L. L. Hatch, Miss May Hatch and J. H. Neal. The first officers of the order were as follows: C. T. Coonley, W. C. T.; Mrs. L. L. Hatch,

W. V. T.; E. L. Turner, W. S.; F. H. Playter, I. W. C. T.; J. H. Neal, W. M.; O. D. Miller, W. F. S.; and Miss May Hatch, W. T. The office of President has been filled one quarter by C. T. Coonley, and two quarters by F. H. Playter. There has been but one death, which occurred in October, 1882—Mrs. G. G. Coonley. The present roll shows sixty-five members, which is the largest number since it has been instituted. The success of the lodge has been very good, far above the average of such societies, and the present condition of affairs is very encouraging.

ODD FELLOWS.

Garfield Lodge, No. 436, I. O. O. F,, was instituted at Bristow, November 17, 1881, by S. G. Blythe, D. D. G. M., with the following charter members: Peter Ebling, Jacob Krebbs, C. H. Wilbur, C. W. Smith and John Cline. Peter Ebling was elected N. G.; C. H. Wilbur, V. G.; J. Krebbs, Recording Secretary; W. R. Nichols, Treasurer, and T. M. Early, Permanent Secretary. These gentlemen held their offices until the first of July, 1882. At the election for the second term of 1882, the same persons were re-elected. The total membership since organization has been 43; the present membership is 42. The lodge has been a success both fraternally and financially, and is in a prosperous and growing condition, having within a year accumulated a fund of $62 for the widows and orphans.

Surfus Post, No. 105, G. A. R. was organized at Bistow, October 18, 1882, by Horace G. Wolf, Mustering Officer, Department of Iowa, with the following charter members: H. J. Playter, William Jay, H. H. Cass, F. E. Newbury, J. A. Fisher, S. W. Ferris, Peter Ebling, T. J. Hart, L. L. Hatch, L. Austin, Isaac Grove, S. B. Myrick, C. L. Jones, G. P. White, J. Davis, A. Moore, C. V. Surfus and C. Coonly. The following officers were duly installed: Lou Austin, P. C.; C. L. Jones, S. V. C.; T. J. Hart, J. V. C.; L. L. Hatch, Adjt.; S. W. Ferris, Q. M.; F. E. Newbury, Surg.; C. V. Surfus, Chap.; Peter Ebling, O. D.; C. T. Coonly, O. G.; James Fisher, S. M.; John Wicks, Q. S. M. Post meets every Wednesday evening in I. O. O. F. hall. The officers for 1883, were the same as those for 1882. The membership January, 1883, is twenty-six, with recruits coming in at nearly every meeting.

PROFESSIONAL.

This vicinity for a number of years was dependent upon Clarksville and Butler Center for medical treatment. Dr. Cline administered to these wants for a short time. He made his home with H. A. Early. The first regular practicing physician locating here was Charles McCormick, of the homœopathic school, who came in 1870, and remained until 1879, when he removed to Kansas. He was followed in professional labor here by E. L. Turner, M. D., who came in 1874, and still remains. In 1881, J. Krebbs, M. D., commenced practice here and still remains.

CHAPTER XXXIV.

MISCELLANEOUS.

This chapter contains a few historical items, too short for a chapter, but of sufficient importance to be incorporated in the work.

THE STORM KING.

One of the worst storms in this section of Iowa, swept over the northern part of the county, on the evening and night of the 4th of June, 1878, carrying with it destruction of life and property. The *Butler County Press*, in speaking of it says: "During the afternoon a heavy black cloud lay in the north, and at about 7 o'clock in the evening a great bank of clouds came sweeping down the country, bringing wind and deluges of water. The wind blew terrifically for over an hour, and the rain came in torrents until late in the night. The water in the river rose rapidly. S. Thomas & Co. worked hard all night to secure their machinery. By 9 o'clock the water had reached its highest point, coming within about five inches of the high water mark of 1875. John Feyereisen's house, west side, was struck by lightning, and damaged somewhat, but no one was injured. The ice break above the mill was torn away by the angry elements as though it were but a toy; and much damage done to minor obstacles. The dam did not go out, but sustained considerable damage.

"West of the village the storm seems to have been still more severe. In Bennezette township, a house of Levi Sheets was unroofed, and his goods scattered. A granary of W. S. Starkweather was broken in, and about 500 bushels of oats blown away."

One of the saddest results of the storm was the drowning of Elias German and wife. The Greene *Press* describes the affair as follows: "Their house stood on the Coldwater bottoms of Walnut Grove. The creek rose suddenly and in a very short time was as high as the top of the stove in the room, when an attempt was made to leave the house in a wagon by Mr. German and wife, their two sons, and Andrew Anderson, son of Nelson Anderson, of this vicinity. In doing so the road was missed and the wagon upset. The oldest boy swam ashore. The younger swam and caught hold of a tree, when he asked his brother what to do, and was told to throw off his clothing and swim to where he heard his voice, as it was so dark that nothing could be seen. Anderson clung to the wagon box while it floated down some two or three miles, where it lodged and he was rescued the next morning. His escape is considered miraculous, as he could not swim and was subjected to frequent severe immersions during his perilous journey in the dark among the trees and stumps. The neighbors state they heard him crying for help in the night, but were powerless to render him any assistance. He was rescued by means of a raft, and was found to be all right, though thoroughly chilled from being in the water so long. Mr. German and wife were drowned, and no one can tell of their efforts to escape. The team was also drowned at the same time by becoming entangled in the harness. The body of Mrs. German was not found until Monday, and Mr. German's not until some time after."

George Beaver's house was blown down, and catching fire from an overturned stove, burned.

William Lovell's barn was blown to pieces, and two of his horses killed.

John Schimmerhorn lost a valuable horse by a rail being driven into the barn and through the animal.

The top of P. J. Thornton's granary was blown off, and a quantity of grain scattered. W. Thields also lost a lot of grain in the same manner.

A house belonging to a Mr. Berry was blown down in such a manner as to leave him and his wife sitting in their chairs on the floor. The contents of the house were carried off and destroyed.

Philip Lovell's barn, containing eight horses, was blown away. The next morning all of the animals came back to the house uninjured. A wagon tire was blown off the wheel of Mr. Lovell's wagon. These two items are given on good authority.

Shepard Berry had a narrow escape from drowning. He was returning from work with a team of horses when the storm struck him; and in endeavoring to cross a stream, his horses became unmanagable; he was thrown into the current, and as he could not swim, would probably have drowned had he not fortunately grasped one of the horse's tails, and thus pulled ashore in an exhausted state.

Fred Smith's new two story house was blown over, also a two story house of Isaac Dubois, who lives just over the line in Coldwater township. Fred Schuman's house was taken off its foundation.

A great many bridges were carried away, among them the one across the Coldwater, west of town. It stood about twenty feet above low water mark.

In Scott township, Floyd county, a great amount of damage was done by the same storm, and several persons badly injured, a babe fatally. Mr. John Johnson, who lives in that vicinity, gave the following particulars:

Mr. Church's house was torn to pieces by the gale, and everything they had swept away. All the members of the family were more or less hurt, some of them quite seriously.

The destruction of property on John Waller's place was very great. Four of his tenant houses blew over, together with a large barn. A German, living in one of the houses, had his leg broken in two places. His wife's jaw sustained a double fracture, and two of their children were badly hurt, the younger so much that it died on Tuesday morning.

The wing of Mr. Oaks' house was torn away and his sulky plow carried a mile distant.

The large school house in District No. 17, was carried over ten rods from its foun-

R. Prist.

dation. Trees four inches through were twisted off like pipe stems.

A house belonging to Mr. Johnson, a Swede, was prostrated, and he was caught by some of the timbers and seriously injured.

East of Greene the storm was also quite severe. The upper story of Thomas Montgomery's house was torn away and several of the remaining windows broken by large hail.

The house of James McAbee, who lives on Flood Creek, was torn all to pieces. The inmates miraculously escaping.

On the Root farm, south of town, the water ran so high that it carried off several thousand tons of hay, entailing a heavy loss to the owner, Mr. Bedlong.

Richard Kival, who lives a few miles northwest of town, had a lively time when the storm struck his place. The boys were just coming in from milking; before reaching the house the roof went off and part of the building was carried over, upsetting a stove, which set fire to the floor.

A man in Bennezette was going home with his team of horses hitched to a wagon, and seeing the storm approaching, unhitched his team and got under the wagon box. When the wind struck, it turned the wagon over several times, but he hung on and came out uninjured. The wagon was blown against some trees, where it lodged. His horses went with the gale.

On the Iowa Central at Rockwell, a great amount of damage was done and several lives lost. A railroad bridge was swept away and a freight train coming along shortly afterwards, went headlong in to the abyss, with the exception of a few rear cars. The engineer, fireman and front brakeman jumped into the stream and succeeded in escaping with their lives.

Thomas Federspiel's house was destroyed, himself badly injured, and his youngest child killed. His wife and hired man also sustained severe injuries. G. N. Brough's house was turned over and set on fire by the stove. The furniture and everything was burned.

CONSTITUTIONAL AMENDMENT.

The constitutional amendment, section 26, is as follows: "No person shall manufacture for sale, sell, or keep for sale, as a beverage, any intoxicating liquors whatever, including ale, wine and beer. The General Assembly shall, by law, prescribe regulations for the enforcement of the prohibition herein contained, and shall thereby provide suitable penalties for violations of the provisions hereof."

The vote in Butler county on the adoption of the amendment, stood as follows:

Townships.	For.	Against
Fremont	46	60
Dayton	70	26
Coldwater	130	130
Bennezette	88	17
Pittsford	99	40
West Point	189	45
Jackson	90	36
Butler	174	73
Shell Rock	270	66
Jefferson	60	56
Ripley	35	23
Madison	19	54
Washington		
Monroe	112	49
Albion	180	63
Beaver	170	24
Totals	1,632	762

Majority in county for amendment..........875

BIOGRAPHICAL.

Dr. A. O. Strout, of Parkersburg, is a native of Maine, born in Durham, September 29, 1849. He worked on his father's farm in summers, and attended school from eight to ten weeks each winter, till the fall of 1865, when he taught a term of school in Pownal, Maine. In the fall of 1866, he removed to Indiana, where he taught school the greater part of the time during the first year. In the fall of 1868 he entered the Cook County Normal School, then situated at Blue Island, Illinois, and graduated from that institution, July 3, 1871, when he entered upon the active duties of a professional teacher, at Forty-seventh street, Chicago, Illinois. During the first year he employed three assistants, and had 225 pupils in attendance. In two years the school had increased to over 600 pupils, and ten assistants. The second year he ran this large school, he commenced the study of medicine. In September, 1873, he entered the Chicago Medical College, graduating therefrom March 16, 1875. In the fall of 1875, he located at Anamosa, Iowa, where he soon acquired a large practice. On the first day of April, 1876, he was appointed prison physician for the State penitentiary, located at Anamosa, which position he held till the spring of 1879, when he resigned. He settled in Parkersburg the following fall, since which time he has continued in the active duties of his profession. Dr. Strout is the present Master of the Masonic Lodge at Parkersburg, one of the strongest in this section of the State. He has been twice elected town councilman.

Milton Wilson was born at the village of Wilson, Niagara county, New York, July 22, 1826. The place of his birth was first settled by his grandfather, Reuben Wilson, in 1810. Reuben Wilson was the father of twelve children, six sons and six daughters. Three of the sons are yet living, but the daughters all died before reaching the age of twenty-five. Calvin Wilson, the father of Milton, was born in Canada West, in 1800, and died in 1878. His mother, Hannah (Sherwood) Wilson, was born in Vermont, in 1804. and is yet living Her parents, Nathaniel and Lucinda Sherwood, located at Wilson in 1813. Her father died there at the age of fifty-six, and her mother at the age of seventy-six. Calvin and Hannah Wilson were the parents of thirteen children, four sons and nine daughters. The sons are all living, and four of the daughters. Milton was the third child, but first son. He was reared on a farm, and spent his entire life in his native State engaged in agricultural pursuits, with the exception of two years in the city of Lockport, where he was in the mercantile trade. In 1850 Milton Wilson and Adaline Freer were united in marriage. Mrs. Wilson was born July 25, 1829. Her father, Solomon Freer, was born in Ontario county, New York, in 1799, and in 1824 married Mary Ann Snyder, who was born in 1808, in Ontario county. In 1826 they moved to Niagara county, New York. where they located, and raised a family of nine children, two sons and seven daughters, all of whom are living, save one daughter. Mr. Freer died in 1879; Mrs. Freer in 1878. In the fall of 1856, Mr. Wilson sold his farm in, Niagara county, New York, and on the 26th of May, 1857, with his family, started west. [See page 476.]

DIPHTHERIA.

In the spring of 1878 this dread disease broke out in Greene and for some time continued to rage. The physicians were of the opinion that it originated from a local cause, as the town was not at the time entirely free from filth, and from the few cases thus produced was carried on by contagion. About the first case was that of Charles H. Fugle, on the 20th of March, and although severe, was not fatal. Soon after this the family of C. H. Stranahan was taken down, and within a few weeks his wife and two of his three children were taken away by the hand of death. Edward Jordan's family were sick, but all recovered. The home of Mr. Atherton was invaded and two children taken. About the same time Charles Ramsey lost two of his children.

After this there seemed to be a lull in the ravages of the disease for several months, and no very violent or fatal cases appeared until late in the fall, when cold weather began to set in. Then it again appeared, and the family of G. B. Lathrop, in Dayton township, lost two of its members; eight of Henry Wagner's family had the disease, one proving fatal; Robert Prindle's household was despoiled of two of its members, and many others were taken with the disease. It is claimed that within two months there were as many as seventy-five cases in Greene and vicinity. In May, 1879, it broke out in the family of W. H. Crouse, west of Greene, leaving only two of the family of six children.

About the last cases were Pearlie Samson, Anna Harlinske and Minnie Sutton who contracted the disease at the same time, while attending a public gathering, and all died. A rigid quarantine was then established throughout the town, the schools were closed, public gatherings of all kinds were prohibited and it was finally brought under subjection. The last case was in March, 1879.

It is estimated that there were about two-hundred and fifty cases in all, of which at least seventy-five proved fatal. This estimate includes the town of Greene and surrounding country within reach of the practice of Greene physicians, who were at the time, Doctors C. C. Huckins, V. C. Birney and William Young.

Surname Index

ABBOTT, 531
ABERNETHY, 277
ABRENS, 408
ABRENSO, 388
ACKERMAN, 397 584 David 584
ACKERSON, 406
ACKLEY, 558 737
ADAIR, 252 273 388 406 693 695
 706-708 710-712 720 722 725
 George W 695 William 722
ADAMS, 285 318 351 481 484 486
 698
AHERNS, 678
AHRENS, 647 661 677-678 Henry 677
AINSWORTH, 272
AKERS, 285 377
ALBERT, 718
ALBRIGHT, 397 704 718-719 725
ALDERSON, 726
ALDRICH, 254-255 398
ALDRIDGE, 272
ALEXANDER, 406 723 725
ALFORD, 343
ALLBRIGHT, 459
ALLBURN, 695
ALLEN, 252 257 262 274 282 300
 397-398 408 434 439 444 450 508
 597 599 601 604 615 623 654 683
 699 725 J W 699
AMSDEN, 446
ANDERSON, 276 285 342 371 371-372
 375 378 398 439 506 616 720 756
 761 766 777 John D 371
ANDREWS, 359 377
ANGEL, 262 517
ANGELL, 244 528
ANTHONY, 607
APFEL, 709 717 Henry 709

APLINGTON, 274 408 607 636 650-
 651 653
ARENDS, 651 655 John P 655
ARKILLS, 580
ARMSTRONG, 236 262 496 528 572
 616 659 775
ARNOLD, 682 741 768 772-773
ARTLIP, 310
ASHLAN, 584
ASHTON, 474 M W 474
ASPREY, 397
ATHERTON, 783
ATKINSON, 504 504-505 527 540
 Henry 504
ATWATER, 340
ATWELL, 463
AUNER, 714 725 John S 725
AUSTEN, 673 677-680 Albert 679
 Lewis J 680
AUSTIN, 358 402 667 713 718 720-
 721 731 763 776 Henry 731
 William 731
AUYER, 315-316 322 415
BABBAGE, 552 751 753
BABCOCK, 249 398 406 411 420 423
 425 433 435 540 558 579 600
BACKUS, 551
BAGGER, 731
BAGLEY, 453 562
BAILEY, 238 272 275 280 308 363
 413 436 446 450 462-466 546 610
 616 622 622-624 Martin 622
BAIRD, 232 493 572
BAKER, 282 365 377 406-408 436
 540 578 628-630 717 761 764-765
 Otis 436
BALDWIN, 612-613 615 620 S M 620
BALL, 561-562 663

BALLARD, 281 588 596-597
BALLHAUSEN, 450
BALLHOUSEN, 434
BALLINGER, 275
BALLOU, 649
BALM, 556
BALSLEY, 595 W E 595
BANKS, 504
BANNO, Charles A 332
BANNON, 253 255-256 272 293 299-
  300 323 328 330 332 335 398
BARBER, 364
BARCLAY, 446 649
BARGELT, 446 628
BARGETT, 465
BARGLET, 649
BARKELEW, 606 Stephen 606
BARKER, 233 270 272 275 300 420
  429 449 590 John 420 Samuel 590
BARLOW, 378 624 754
BARNARD, 311 507 527
BARNES, 683
BARNETT, 481 484-485 485 566
  Benjamin H 485
BARNEY, 565
BARNHOUSE, 299
BARNUM, 285 366 557 559-562 565-
  567 572-573 575
BARR, 718
BARRETT, 514 677 679 705 A C 514
BARRICK, 232 252
BARRY, 698
BARTEL, 717
BARTHOLOMEW, 249 296 397 443 450
BARTLETT, 364-365 481 532 538
BASKERVILLE, 574
BASS, 298 425 435 450 701 705
  718-719
BASSETT, 702
BASY, 299
BAUGHMAN, 236 241 560 562 599
BAWN, 449
BEACH, 629
BEACK, 629
BEALS, 290 376 378 567 570 573
  575 635 A H 567
BEARD, 236 496 527
BEASMONT, 281
BEAVER, 778

BEBEE, 599 636 638
BECK, 275 282 311 766
BECKWITH, 388 396 450 466 615
BEDELL, 376 378
BEDLONG, 781
BEEBE, 388 526 740
BEECHER, 398
BEEDLE, 673
BEEKMAN, 683
BEEMER, 436
BEETLE, 608
BEETLES, 398
BELDEN, 470 502
BELL, 560 674 749-750 761 766
  Hiram 750
BELLOWD, 464
BELLOWS, 376 378 445 E C 445
BEMENT, 237 378 588 597 715-719 J
  717
BEMIS, 280-281
BEMLER, 709
BENEDICT, 435
BENINGA, 731
BENJAMIN, 454 720
BENNETT, 237 368 548-549 578 595
  595-596 600 623 628 Edward 595
BENSEN, 403
BENSON, 441 574 671-672 774
  George 774
BENTLEY, 573
BENTLY, 561 572
BENTON, 274
BERDINE, 537
BERGER, 619
BERKUS, 609
BERLIN, 610 619 Frederick 619
BERRY, 778
BEST, 262 515 721 A 515
BESWICK, 466
BETTENGER, 508
BETTESWORTH, 552 555 Thomas 552
BETTINGER, 537 540 585
BETTS, 506 545
BETZER, 771
BICKFORD, 672 682-683 685
BICKLEY, 608-609 609 J E 609
BICKNELL, 419 424 426 429
BICKSBY, 465
BIGELOW, 289 419 433

BIGFORD, 684
BIGGAR, 764
BILLHIMER, 262 397 519-520 520
  525 525-527 709 Christopher 525
  Henry 520
BILLINGS, 422 422-423 440 James V
  422
BILLSEN, 473 475 G W 473
BILSON, 460
BIRD, 388-389 397 408 450 617 741
BIRKBECK, 756 765-767 Brothers
  756
BIRNEY, 352 562 570 572 575 783 V
  C 352
BISBEE, 408 641 647 651 653
  William 653
BISHOP, 252-254 269-275 289 297
  323-324 398 717 754-755 761-762
  766 C B 761 W H 297
BISSELL, 275 277
BITTINGER, 539
BLACKMAN, 280 397 408
BLACKMER, 358 358-359 E L 358
BLACKMORE, 280 647 652
BLAISDELL, 513 513-514 699 723 E
  B 513
BLAKE, 237 244-245 323 577 579
  583 595 700 G G 700
BLAKELY, 237 262 542
BLAKENSHIP, 406
BLAKLEY, 496
BLANCHARD, 724
BLASS, 397 408 419
BLIM, 282
BLYTHE, 776
BOARDMAN, 281
BOAZ, 649
BODGETT, 628
BOGGS, 237 242 258 270 300 323
  398 549-550 556 577-579 579-580
  John N 579
BOGLE, 539
BOHALL, 434 450
BOLDAN, 551
BOLLER, 562
BOLSER, 651
BOLTON, 397 465 470 472 J F 470
BOMELL, 751 E 751
BOMGARDNER, 633 F 633

BOND, 402
BONE, 277
BONESTEIN, 514
BONNELL, 237 580 William H 580
BONORDEN, 286
BONWELL, 254-258 413 538 584 588
  588-589 596 599 607 S 588
BOOMER, 311 330 342 710 714 J H
  342
BOON, 398 411
BOORAM, 257-258 386 408
BOOROM, 596-597
BOOTH, 641-642 753
BORGELT, 690
BORNELL, 749
BOSS, 453
BOSTON, 772
BOTTENFIELD, 377
BOUCHER, 359 361
BOURGUIN, 397
BOURNS, 651-652
BOURQUIN, 459 462-463 463-466
  471 Eugene 463
BOURROUGHS, 761
BOWEN, 695 701 John 701
BOWERS, 677
BOWMAN, 571 573-574 589
BOYD, 453 460 474 480 516 540
  599-600 608 John 608 John E 474
BOYER, 422
BOYLAN, 237 262 272 300 388 397
  657-664 669 742-744 750 Isaac
  742
BOYNTON, 446
BOYRIE, 459
BOYS, 351
BOZARTH, 651
BRACE, 741
BRADEN, 272 323 396 408 615 618
BRADLEY, 238 272-274 300 323 459
  462 560 562
BRAGG, 555 578-579 584 584-586
  Lafayette 584
BRAINARD, 273
BRAND, 709
BRANDON, 237 496 529-530
BRANLON, 495
BRANNIC, 397
BRANNOM, 276

BRANUM, 706
BRASTED, 719-721
BRECKENRIDGE, 445
BREEN, 490
BREMER, 241 330 343 343-344 John 343
BREMERMANN, 286
BRETT, 681
BRIGGS, 482
BRIMSKILL, 751
BRINK, 262
BRISTOL, 406-407 459-460 715-716 719-720
BRISTOW, 709
BROCK, 341 723
BROCKWAY, 680
BRODTBECK, 389
BROMER, 573
BRONSON, 286 464-465
BROOGG, 398
BROOK, 645 James 645
BROOKMAN, 397 408
BROOKS, 398 555 579 629
BROOKSLAND, 408 411
BROQUE, 397
BROTHERS, 560
BROTHERTON, 663 669 775
BROUGH, 781
BROWER, 359 361
BROWN, 241 258 262 272 277 280 283 285-286 289-290 378 397-398 408 419-420 423-425 429 450 455 525 527 539 571 575 579 619 644 672 685 763 H C 685
BROWNELL, 490 596-597 Joseph H 490
BROWNWELL, 388
BRUCE, 367 506 566 575 756 766
BRULA, 535
BRUTLEY, 446
BRYANT, 507 643
BUCHANAN, 384
BUCHHOLTZ, 595
BUCHOLZ, 597
BUCKMASTER, 574
BUDLONG, 515
BUELL, 390
BUFLEB, 474
BULCKENS, 535

BULKINS, 546
BULLIS, 257 277
BUNDER, 761
BUNDY, 311
BUNN, 422 705
BURBANK, 349-350 350-351 351 540 561 567 761 766 F E 351 Jerome 350
BURCH, 465
BURDICK, 280 282 297 324 330 344 386 443 446 449 459 W H 297 344
BURGER, 397
BURGESS, 397 408 657 715
BURGOYNE, 340
BURHAM, 397
BURK, 333 John E 333
BURKE, 274 365 505 505-506 741 James E 505
BURKET, 501
BURKHOLDER, 546
BURLEIGH, 426 545
BURLETT, 565 565-567 575 A J 565
BURLEY, 720
BURNELL, 330 342
BURNES, 583
BURNETT, 461 473 701 Herman D 473
BURNHAM, 258 282 434-435 450 605 651 732 756 765-766 J J 732
BURNS, 421
BURRAS, 578
BURRASS, 583-584
BURRESS, 237 243 323 540 577-579
BURRIS, 578
BURROUGHS, 349-350 350 525 754 S E 350
BURROWS, 262
BURT, 435-436 436 443 T J 436
BURTCH, 539
BURTON, 232 236 250-252 257 262 264 269 296 365 398 406 408 496 516 519 527 529 537 539-540 546 H F L 537 W E 296
BUSH, 445-446 450 586
BUSHNELL, 240
BUSSEY, 364 696
BUSWELL, 432
BUTLER, 236-237 244-245 251 276-277 285 308-309 343 398 535 540-542 577 579-580 610 629 661

BUTLER (cont.)
  729 753 767
BUTTERFIELD, 270 299 503-504
BUTTON, 277 280 300 481 609 615
BUTTS, 267 599-600
BYERLY, 440 450 O 440
BYRES, 352 542 546
BYWATER, 323
CADY, 605
CAHART, 432
CAHN, 538
CAIN, 579 714
CALDWELL, 237 277 280 407 413 464
  540 636 647-648 652 654 737-738
  J M 636
CALEY, 718
CALKINS, 662 669
CALVERT, 481 514
CAMERON, 460
CAMP, 352 519 546 624
CAMPBELL, 281-282 359 388 460 463
  481 726
CANBY, 396 406 504
CANFIELD, 274
CANNON, 262 674 752
CANON, 667
CANTONWINE, 402
CARD, 276
CARMFORD, 750
CARNEY, 647
CARNS, 701
CAROWAY, 493
CARPENTER, 235 275-277 485 628
  692 695 707 Harrison 235 Volney
  235
CARR, 368 555 604 Clark 604
CARSON, 714-715 717-719 727 J H
  727
CARTER, 364 388 398 413 540 578-
  580 583 708-709 711 715 719
  Lemuel 580
CARTNER, 435 443
CARY, 716
CASE, 272 280 309 557 560 562 570
  616
CASEY, 285
CASS, 479 749 751 776 Hollis 751
CASTERLINE, 251 323
CASTLOW, 388

CASTO, 455 462-464 466
CASWELL, 480 540 604 608 Charles
  645
CATTELL, 271-272
CAUL, 645 647 Charles 645
CAVE, 540 545
CAVO, 398
CAYWOOD, 422 471 David 422
CHAFFIN, 721
CHAMBERLAIN, 257 358 466 617 726
CHAMBERLIN, 479 484-485 Cyrus D
  479 Ira A 479
CHAMBERS, 677 682
CHAMPLAIN, 411 609
CHAMPLIN, 398
CHANNOCK, 435
CHAPEL, 424 Thurman S 424
CHAPIN, 357 506 725 F W 506
CHAPLINE, 343 774
CHAPMAN, 273-274 436 461 464 473-
  474 474-475 616 Chauncey 474
CHARNOCK, 433 443
CHASE, 271 280-281 289 293 297
  444 449 476 624
CHATERSON, 775
CHEENEY, 572
CHEEVER, 603 S W 603
CHELLEW, 578
CHESLEY, 262 419 423 426
  Nathaniel 419
CHEVER, 600-601
CHICHESTER, 740
CHILDS, 462 464-465 471
CHITESTER, 397
CHOATE, 242 550
CHRISTIAN, 402
CHRISTY, 703 John 703
CHRYSTIE, 258 277 281 378 650
  652-653 653 Alex 653
CHURCH, 778
CHURCHILL, 398 454-455
CINNAMON, 272 429 635
CLARK, 232 236-237 250-252 262
  267 269-270 285-286 290 294
  303-304 398 408 485 496 501 530
  538-539 545 558 570 578 600 623
  730 740-741 A G 294
CLARKE, 250 276 357 413 635

CLARKSON, 273 290
CLAUSON, 579
CLAWSON, 398 411 578-579 716 718-720 723
CLAYTON, 246 398 414 635 648 Walter 414 635
CLEAVER, 754 766
CLELAND, 280
CLELLAND, 285
CLEMMAR, 532
CLEMMER, 585
CLEVELAND, 588
CLIGGET, 280
CLIGGETT, 285
CLINE, 398 679 776 Alexander 679
CLOUKEY, 505
CLOUSKY, 386
CLUKEY, 480
COATES, 718
COATS, 620
COCHRANE, 656
CODNER, 244 275 397-398 416-417 417-418 425 Joseph 417
COFFIN, 444
COHN, 536 546
COLDWELL, 262
COLE, 274 277 354 378 561-562 565-567 573 575 682 710
COLEMAN, 570
COLESTON, 237 549
COLEY, 562
COLLAR, 257 363-364 413 453 455-456 459-460 James 453
COLLIER, 490
COLLINS, 398 440 440-441 443 445 449-450 456 459 464 562 Joseph 440
COLSTON, 368
COLTON, 388
COLVER, 406
COLVIN, 768
COMBELLICK, 762
COMBS, 734 Harrison 734
COMER, 267
COMPTON, 695
CONGER, 282 286
CONKLING, 321

CONN, 276 300 419 433 439 441 446 450 475 624 638 648 719 Thomas W 439
CONNELL, 246 426 431 450 643 649 740
CONNELLY, 532 768
CONNER, 397
CONNOLLY, 771-772 James 771
CONRAD, 722
CONSADINE, 388 396
CONSIDINE, 398 411
CONSODINE, 687
CONVERSE, 238 253-254 258 260 270-272 274-276 290 293 304 327-328 330 339 341 397 454 456 459 464 484 578 596 628 668 740 752 Alonzo 341
COOK, 280 287 378 396-397 516 615 618 696
COOKSEY, 560 571
COOLEY, 431 450 628 690 705 720
COON, 416-417 417-418 426 465-466 August 417
COONLEY, 767 775-776
COONLY, 771-772 776
COOPER, 446 493 514
COPELAND, 257 273 277 300 363 397 470 540 545 606 709 721 T G 470
COREY, 527 538
CORNELL, 716
CORNWALL, 455
CORNWALLIS, 340
CORNWELL, 456 459-461
CORSON, 703-704 E B 703
CORTRIGHT, 472 472-473 538 S S 472
CORWIN, 454 754 762-763 766 C W 762
CORYELL, 418 449 683 G J H 418
COSSON, 398
COSTAR, 616
COTTLE, 395
COTTON, 270 300 386 388 396 651 655 655-656 710-711 William R 655
COUCH, 397 470 719-721
COULSON, 618
COULTER, 389 606
COUNTRYMAN, 722

COURT, 285 623
COURTRIGHT, 285 330 344 436 443
COURTWRIGHT, 295 312 344 571 O B 344
COUSINS, 466
COVEY, 473
COWAN, 710
COX, 464 532 546
COYLE, 254-257 413 467 626-630 630 731 Edward 630 Peter 630
CRABTREE, 485 491 558
CRAIG, 275-277 294 330 343 345 615-616 624-625 754 756 762 765-767 George M 343
CRAM, 695 707-708 710
CRAMER, 237 249 352 407 416-417 417 425 440 443 711 James D 440 Miss Dr 352 Samuel 417
CRANDALL, 573 623
CRANE, 405 465 568
CRAW, 738
CRAWFORD, 580 768
CRIPPEN, 571
CRIPPIN, 649 740
CRISSINGER, 673
CRISWELL, 256-258 690
CRITCHFIELD, 720
CRITZMAN, 285 460 474 August 474
CROCKER, 565-566
CROMWELL, 382
CRONIN, 589 589-590 597 William 589
CRONKHITE, 663
CROOKS, 370
CROOT, 732 Samuel 732
CROSBY, 364 386 740 744
CROSIER, 690
CROSS, 237 275 339 515 588 596-597 J J 588 Solomon C 515
CROSSETT, 450
CROUSE, 484-485 490-491 491 783 William F 491
CROWELL, 232 235 235-236 250-251 262 267 269 297 436 493 501 505 539 R G 235
CULBERT, 702
CULLISON, 281
CULP, 423 Joshua R 423
CUMMINGS, 449 485 Edward 485

CUMMINS, 397
CUNNINGHAM, 407 574 628
CURRIER, 450 464
CURTIS, 244 254-255 350 398 449 637 648 W A 350
CURTISS, 254 450
CUSTER, 674
DAGGETT, 754-755 764-766 J M 755
DAHL, 678
DAHN, 656 F E 656
DAILEY, 486 645
DAILY, 406-407 473 584 743-744 Christian 744
DANIEL, 685
DANIELS, 273 407-408 411 413 416 416-417 425 446 455 460-461 470 621 699 Richard 416
DARBY, 600-601
DARRALL, 589
DARROW, 473
DAVENPORT, 690-691
DAVIDSON, 401-402
DAVIES, 403
DAVIS, 254-255 262 265 271 273-277 287 290 296 324-327 330 339 339-340 359 363 371 383-384 398 408 411 413 421-422 443-445 459 481 527 529-530 538 538-540 546 584 608 616 754 762 765-767 776 E J 538 James W 339 Timothy 287
DAWSON, 397 408 420-421 425 429 616
DAY, 258 277 281 298 449 515
DAYTON, 276 716
DEAN, 271 285 369 424 455 463-464 698 711 717 721
DEARMAUN, 664
DEARMOUN, 674 677 S R 674
DECKER, 450 740
DEERING, 280 282 285 288 N C 288
DEES, 433 442
DEGRAW, 576
DELAVAN, 318
DELEVAN, 575
DELKER, 571
DELLINGER, 561 569 569-570 575 P N 569
DELLKER, 578
DELONG, 605 607

DEMMICK, 432 442
DEMMON, 474
DEMON, 662
DEMOREST, 435
DEMOSS, 388 411 658-659 667 678-679 743 Thomas 678
DENISON, 277
DENSMORE, 720
DEPEW, 450
DEPUY, 540
DERR, 286
DEVIN, 281
DEVOE, 464
DEVRIES, 733 P 733
DEWITT, 386 407 411 681 720
DEWY, 695
DEXTER, 233 366 586
DICKENSON, 352
DICKERHOFF, 470
DICKINSON, 546
DICKISSON, 262 398
DIGMAN, 272 290 296 617-618 763
DILLON, 273 276
DILLWORTH, 699-700
DILMAN, 596
DILTZ, 460-461 466
DINGMAN, 426
DIXON, 262 440 465
DIXSON, 514
DOBBINS, 388 406 650-652 754 761
DOCKSTADER, 398 408 411
DODD, 455 475 707
DODGE, 316 318 322 376 398 411 442-443 445 449-450 539 756 758-759 766 Frank L 622 Fred A 316
DODSWELL, 652
DOERR, 277
DOLAN, 604
DOLLISON, 270 502 530-531
DONOVAN, 608
DOOLITTLE, 285 649
DOOR, 571
DOORE, 352
DOPKING, 754 765 George M 754
DORAN, 718
DORSEY, 446
DOTTY, 282

DOTY, 285 364-365 398 413 599-600 603 603-604 606 606-607 Aaron 603 Cyrus 606
DOUGHERTY, 282
DOUGLAS, 271 371 495 528 601 703
DOUGLASS, 586
DOUNS, 277
DOW, 343
DOWD, 455
DOWN, 446
DOWNEY, 330 344 420-421 421 425 443 445 Daniel 421
DOWNING, 366 481 484-485 489 507 507-508 John E 489 Simeon 507
DOWNS, 341 435 540 545 572
DRAKE, 542
DREW, 424
DREYER, 645 645-646 651-652 Henry 645
DRING, 643
DRUM, 697 John 697
DRUMMOND, 290
DRURY, 282 341 574
DRYER, 262
DUBOIS, 677 772-773 775 778
DUBOYS, 768
DUDGSON, 565
DUDLEY, 354 357 357-360 710-711 716 718-719 723 E H 357
DUGAN, 703 725
DULY, 580
DUMONT, 247 258 276 290 672 682-684 S B 683
DUNBAR, 274
DUNCAN, 277 529
DUNCOMB, 272-273
DUNCOMBE, 274
DUNGAN, 282
DUNHAM, 388 407 435 464 540 606
DUNLARY, 276
DUNNING, 398 677-678
DUNSON, 270 275 277 615-616 619 691 P E 619
DUNTON, 358
DURAND, 237 262 272-273 293 328 667 672 743 752 772
DURANK, 664
DURHAM, 286 289
DWIGHT, 460 464 472

EADS, 241
EARLEY, 272 300
EARLY, 237 270 273 660 667-668 671-673 735 744 752 767 772 776 T M 673
EARNEST, 491 560 566 572 575
EASTMAN, 273 357 695 707 709 715 718 721 O L 707
EASTWOOD, 707 714-717 719 W C 716
EBERHART, 398 400 403 405
EBERSOLD, 237 244 577-578 580 P J 580
EBERSOLE, 286
EBLING, 484-485 776
ECK, 508
EDDY, 406 578-579 585-586
EDE, 398
EDISON, 597
EDMONSON, 449
EDSON, 406
EDWARDS, 262 286 315-316 322 386 537
EICHAR, 237 262 274 365 413 496 502 513 527 529-531 540 542 546 J J 502
EICHER, 529
EIKENBERRY, 237 548 559-560 573-574 574-575 577-578 J F 574
EIKENBERY, 682
ELAM, 236 251 261-262 496 527
ELCHLEFF, 450
ELDER, 280
ELEY, 572
ELLIOT, 276 767
ELLIOTT, 273 275 281 445-446 517 590 615 649 724 754 756 761-762 767
ELLIS, 253 270 300 398 535 551-552 557 561 567 573 575 597
ELLISON, 595
ELLSWORTH, 277 330 342 601 752 771 J F 342
ELMORE, 687
ELWOOD, 271-272
EMBODY, 262 623 637 647
EMBREY, 690
EMERSON, 421
ENGLE, 632
ENGLEMAN, 650

ENOS, 464 540
ENSIGN, 237 323 354-355 406 413 436 453-454 454-456 459-466 470 470-471 Charles 454 E W 470
ENSLEY, 236 495-496 599
ERB, 450
ERBOECK, 281
ERKENBRECK, 546
ERNST, 699
ETTER, 549 F G 549
EUSTIS, 733 M D 733
EVANS, 257-258 479 484 623 766 Oliver 479
EVARTS, 709
EWALD, 466
FABES, 730
FABRIZ, 572 575
FAGUE, 262 406
FAILING, 317 330 336 C M 336
FAIRCHILD, 584
FAIRFIELD, 274 276 324 418 714-715 W B 324
FALLEN, 733
FALLHELM, 573
FALLS, 470 532
FALSOM, 397
FARGO, 615
FARLAND, 651
FARLOW, 237 261-262 272 398 406 411 496 514 527
FARNSWORTH, 281 454
FARNUM, 762 765-766
FARR, 721
FARRAR, 312-313
FARREL, 575
FARRELL, 560
FARRINGTON, 281-282 725
FARRIS, 241
FARTHAN, 366
FASSETT, 525 R E 525
FATHERGILL, 574
FAULKNER, 514
FAVILLE, 271 274
FAVOR, 584
FAX, 483
FAY, 483
FEDERSPIEL, 781
FEELY, 562
FELCH, 422 425

FELLOWS, 616 711 765
FELTUS, 525 525-526 George 525
  James 526
FERGUSON, 322 586 Jarvis E 586
FERRIS, 398 411 443 450 680 776 S
  W 680
FETTERS, 456 460-461 470 Samuel
  470
FEYEREISEN, 562 565-566 575 777
FIDDICK, 571
FIELDS, 722
FIFIELD, 469 J R 469
FILKINS, 386 597
FILLMORE, 573
FINCH, 235 692
FINDLEY, 647 649 653 653-654 737
  S B 653
FINK, 426
FINNEY, 652
FISHER, 275 289 502 529-530 532
  546 584 746-747 763-764 775-776
  George 532 Irving M 763
FISK, 424
FITCH, 272 280-282 365 434 453
  456 459-460 539 597
FITZGERALD, 270 584 584-585
  Stephen 584
FITZPATRICK, 647
FLANNIGAN, 644
FLANSBURGH, 734
FLAVIEN, 446
FLETCHER, 255-257 273 277 289 293
  323 328 330-332 332 335 364-365
  538 J R 332
FLICK, 762
FLINN, 454
FLOOD, 262 398 517 William 517
FLORA, 538 551 551-552 Abraham
  551
FLUSHER, 585
FOAK, 489
FOLEY, 286
FOLLETT, 712
FOLSOM, 408
FOOTE, 286 300 330 336 433-434
  434 450 556-557 562 566-567 603
  756 S A 434 William M 336
FORD, 251 542 741
FOREMAN, 274 276 280 285

FORKNER, 519
FORNEY, 257 277 281 323 365 386
  398 413 540 578-579 583 595 C H
  583
FORREST, 394
FORTNER, 687
FORTNEY, 366
FOSTER, 286 289 398 459 540
FOWLE, 257-258 378 495 529-530
  539 542 546
FOWLER, 257 562 575
FOWLES, 529
FOX, 237 368 549 590 711
FRANCHER, 682
FRANCIS, 308 502
FRANK, 434 450 763
FRANKLIN, 754 765
FRAZIER, 662
FREEMAN, 604 774 M J 604
FREER, 476 782
FREMONT, 513 596
FRENCH, 475 624
FRICK, 670
FRIES, 684
FRISBIE, 482 490
FROWE, 696 Frederick 696
FRY, 280
FUGLE, 783
FULKS, 597
FULP, 734
FULSOM, 406
FULTON, 715
FUNK, 436
GABBY, 518 526 587 A M 526 Thomas
  B 526
GAGE, 423
GAINES, 586
GALIPO, 480
GALLAGHER, 626
GALLARD, 446
GALLASPIE, 271
GALLOWAY, 737
GALPIN, 450
GARDNER, 426
GARFIELD, 282 369 486 715
GARNER, 277
GARRETT, 258 752
GARRISON, 648 720
GASLOR, 572

GASTON, 286
GATES, 340 366-367 507 561-562
    572 575 Johnson 507
GAYLOR, 290
GAYLORD, 249 282 291-292
GEAR, 281
GEE, 636 647 739
GEER, 282
GEORGE, 574 617 623
GERMAN, 397 777-778
GETCHELL, 386
GETCHELS, 663
GIBBONS, 281
GIBBS, 435 464
GIBLIN, 617 620 John 620
GIBSON, 423 459 659 669 701 705
    772 J R 701
GIHON, 580
GILBERT, 254-255 257 273 386 397
    405-407 507-508 530 540 546 606
GILE, 397
GILGER, 330 336 341 343 562 565-
    566 J W 336
GILLAN, 754
GILLARD, 244 638
GILLASPY, 276
GILLEN, 766
GILLESPIE, 641
GILLETT, 289-290
GILLMORE, 597
GILMAN, 647
GILMORE, 342 406 588
GILRUTH, 571
GIVEN, 749 775
GLASNER, 465
GLASS, 238
GLASSNER, 446
GLEASON, 424 424-425 434 697-698
    Charles L 424 Martin 697
GLENN, 236 323 364-365 397 493
    529 540-541 692 695 707
GLEW, 342
GLODERY, 567-568 568 570 575
    Andrew 568
GODERY, 568
GOHEEN, 243 262 274 557 577-578
GOLACHALK, 275
GOLDTHWAITE, 472
GONZALES, 276 615

GOOD, 324 609
GOODALE, 433 443-444 446 450
    Jonathan 433
GOODHUE, 388 398 406
GOODSELL, 642
GORDON, 461 562 626-627 629
GOSSARD, 649
GOTTSCHALK, 272
GOUGH, 237-238 545 570 577 749-
    750 William 749
GOULD, 295 545 571 585-586 716
    719-720
GOURLEY, 624 775
GRADY, 460
GRAHAM, 275 370 370-371 542 572
    696 714-715 717-719 722-723 725
    775 George 370 J A 725 W H 723
GRANDON, 424 452
GRANT, 276 315 387 389
GRASLEY, 755 767
GRAUPNER, 562
GRAVER, 398
GRAVES, 330 339-340 340 408 615
    753 Zur 340
GRAY, 286 739
GREELEY, 596
GREEN, 542 575 627 631 713-715 K
    S 631
GREENE, 252 330 341 345 377 551
    559 567-568 629 701 714 C M 341
    G P 714 H 701
GREETJE, 655
GREGG, 528
GRIFFIN, 530 661
GRIFFITH, 232 237 242-243 250 258
    262 267 269 368 398 413 549
    555-558 570-571 577-578 604 682
    James 368
GROAT, 258 286 439 450 459 652
    James M 439
GRONENEG, 280
GROUEL, 573
GROUT, 464
GROVE, 776
GROWER, 292
GUE, 274 370 W H 370
GUNN, 446
GUNNISON, 454
GUNSALUS, 696

GURTHIE, 300
GURTHRIE, 273
GUTHRIE, 275 290 406 459 464 466
GUY, 397
HADDOCK, 308 622
HAGEMAN, 631
HAGERTY, 274 578
HAGEY, 353 359 462 466 William H
    H 353
HAGGARTY, 254-255 276 290
HAGGERTY, 257
HAHN, 615
HAINE, 397-398
HAINES, 688
HAIR, 616
HAKOT, 634
HALE, 271-272 274-275 277 294 618
    J H 294
HALL, 258 262 276 282 312 397-398
    408 417 446 456 459 479 507
    527-528 550 557 574 627 650 652
    667 698-699 721 J R 507 Jacob
    417
HALSTEAD, 411 575
HALSTED, 397
HAMBLIN, 483-484
HAMILTON, 274 289 715
HAMMER, 276 705
HAMMON, 272
HAMMOND, 237 317 407 456 459 464
HANCOCK, 282
HANNANT, 398
HANNOM, 277
HANSBERRY, 527
HARBERT, 756 761 765
HARD, 254-257 456 712
HARDMAN, 237 259 323 398 548-550
    555-557 562 573 578-579 584
HARDY, 237 251 496 530
HARE, 397 455-456 459-460 463
HARKNESS, 599
HARLAN, 262 323 413 660 664-665
    669 671-674 677 775 James 673
    Jehu 674
HARLINSKE, 575 783
HARLON, 257
HARMON, 407 459-460 471 C R 471
HARNEY, 632
HARPER, 517 677

HARRIS, 275 406-407 555 627 656
HARRISON, 398 546
HART, 237 242-243 323 397 413 486
    549 549-550 556-558 572 579 776
    John M 549
HARTER, 398 491 573-574 579 Aaron
    M 491
HARTGRAVES, 262 267 452-453 626-
    628 630 674 N 630
HARTLEY, 727
HARTMAN, 398
HARTNESS, 530 538 538-539 John
    538 Moulton 538
HARTSON, 626 628-629 631 631-632
    A E 631
HARTUNG, 727
HARVEY, 268 272 274 306 539 541
    590 626-629 631
HARWOOD, 463
HASKIN, 459
HASKINS, 460-461 658
HASSELL, 366 484
HASTINGS, 290
HASWELL, 330 344
HATCH, 752 768 772 774-776
HAVEN, 768 773-774 E M 774
HAWKER, 271-273 298 503 695 709
    711
HAWKINS, 648
HAWLEY, 408 698 718 G C 698
HAWTHORNE, 717
HAY, 507
HAYDEN, 397 408
HAYENGA, 733
HAYES, 238 280 313
HAYNES, 687 712 717-718 726 T L
    712
HAYS, 616 William 616
HAZELET, 280
HAZELETT, 530
HAZELTON, 453
HAZEN, 441 472 637 647 739 L P
    637
HAZLET, 258 282 299 312 680
HAZLETON, 358
HAZLETT, 285 299 632 663 672 679
    754 Gilbert 299
HEAD, 485
HEATH, 560 562

HEDES, 766
HEDGES, 446 450 649
HEDRICK, 398
HEED, 600
HEERY, 235-236 366 496 502-503 531 539 546 565 567 John 502
HELASON, 721
HEMENWAY, 600 648
HEMMINWAY, 344
HENDERSHOTT, 273 285
HENDERSON, 286 288 288-289 386 398 407 411 426 545 D B 288
HENDRICKS, 615 753
HENDRIX, 615
HENNEY, 526
HENRY, 343 369 481 700
HEPNER, 771
HERD, 274
HERSEY, 258 422 William 422
HESALROAD, 552 William 552
HESETROAD, 481
HESS, 682
HESSE, 398 411 508 529 539 546 687
HEWART, 460
HEWETT, 465 752
HEWIT, 667
HEWITT, 659 661 743-744 752 771 John 743
HICKLE, 364-365 407 505 513 600 John 505
HICKMAN, 539 607 John B 607
HICKS, 235 235-237 251 364 492-493 586 598 Joseph 235
HIGGINS, 275 552
HIGH, 398
HILL, 562 644 C H 644
HILLER, 366 434 441 569 652
HILLMAN, 495
HILLS, 322 341
HILLUSTED, 388
HILTON, 236 250-253 262 267 269-272 294 303-304 406 496 528 530 542 599-601 D C 294 Seth 236
HINELINE, 376 378 539
HINKLE, 397-398
HIRAM, 663
HITCHCOCK, 290 660 695 707 718 772

HITES, 257 398 411 687 690
HIZENTON, 626
HOBSON, 469
HODGSON, 407 411 519 519-520 525 527-528 605 Asa 519
HODSON, 519 James 519
HOEY, 441
HOFFMAN, 254-257 752 768
HOFFMANN, 536
HOGAN, 653
HOISINGTON, 323 388
HOLBROOK, 261 274 545 570
HOLCOMB, 262
HOLDRIDGE, 604
HOLLAND, 285 571
HOLLENBECK, 257 262 273-275 280 297 297-298 470 695 713 Michael 297
HOLLIDAY, 617
HOLMES, 272-273 276 281 462 755
HOLSTEAD, 562 688
HOLT, 712
HOLTZ, 768
HOOD, 406 504
HOODE, 262
HOOKER, 282
HOOVEY, 429 Lewis 429
HOPKINS, 407 411
HOPLEY, 638
HORNISH, 546
HORNSHER, 704
HORR, 441 446 637 738 R R 441
HORSCH, 537
HORSINGTON, 411
HORTON, 513
HOSKINS, 700
HOSTETLER, 506 506-507 David 506
HOTCHKISS, 561-562 570 682 718
HOUCK, 398 460 527
HOUGH, 398 411 433
HOUGHSTEADER, 720
HOUSTON, 519 536 J M 519
HOVEY, 424 429-430 615 Elias S 424
HOWARD, 398 636 647 650 700 706 734 738-740 L W 700
HOWE, 378 518 John 518
HOWELL, 751

HOWENSTEIN, 432-434 434-435 439 444-446 450 W M 434
HOXIE, 615
HUBBARD, 272 274-275 288 388 419 A W 288
HUCKINS, 352 366 562 566 570 572 575 783 C C 352
HUDLOW, 619
HUEY, 737
HUFFMAN, 767
HUGHES, 353 364 705-706 715 718-720 723-724 R 723
HULL, 281-282 286 309-310 310 320 546 774 L O 310
HULTZ, 768
HUMBLE, 607
HUME, 595
HUMMER, 605
HUMPHREY, 354
HUNT, 262 270 376 407 514 519 519-520 522-523 527 538-539 546 692 695 705 719-721 727 H D 519 Thomas 514
HUNTER, 286 295 376 394-395 407 464-465 475 579 621 624 648 650 687 690-691 703 R W 621 W M 475
HUNTINGTON, 440
HUNTLEY, 463
HURD, 716
HURLBURT, 387 393
HURLBUT, 775
HURLEY, 629
HUSBAND, 520 704-705 727 G T 704
HUSH, 262
HUSKINS, 366
HUSS, 683
HUTCHINSON, 469
HYDE, 296 339 408 615-616 762 766 Willis 296
ICENOGGLE, 678
ILGENFRITZ, 280 282 285-286 297 365 495 529-530 532 535 535-536 536 540-541 545-546 754 765 A J 535 C H 297 Henry 536
INGALL, 417
INGALLS, 711
INGHAM, 250-251 545 570-571 601
INGLIS, 385
INGRAM, 570

INMAN, 388 396-397 406 411 481 638
INSLEY, 432
IRISH, 281
IRVING, 616
ISHERWOOD, 359 361
IVERSON, 383
JACKSON, 281 330 341 418 431-432 450 452 563 575 662 669 Frank D 341
JAMES, 243 281 308 530 572 719-720
JAMIESON, 473 482 661-662 664 674 678 L W 473
JAMINSON, 270
JAMISON, 237 252 254-255 259 262 271 275 300 323 330 334 334-336 373 413 460 659-660 667-668 671-672 683 714 752 775 W R 334
JANES, 664 667
JANSSEN, 646
JAQUIS, 420-421 421 Elihu 421
JARDEE, 463
JARVIS, 755
JAY, 446 776
JEFFERSON, 381
JENKINS, 419 532
JENNINGS, 681
JENSEN, 450
JEROLAMAN, 715 717
JEROME, 272 406 459
JESSUP, 281
JEWELL, 718-719
JOHN, 574
JOHNSON, 277 290 330 344 353 366 388 393 396 411 425 436 442-443 445-446 450 570 572 576 629 680 702 704 714 778 781 A K 353 Charles 702 N T 344 William R 680
JOHNSTON, 532 562 721
JONES, 258 271 275 277 280-282 285-286 293 298 298-299 299-314 314-343 343-365 365-391 391-397 397-398 398-413 413 415-462 462-463 463-503 503-504 518 540-541 605 607 615 705 714-715 717-718 744 752 768 771 773

JONES (cont.)
  775-776 Charles A 705 Charles L
  771 Frank A 771 John R 298
JORDAN, 280 282 565 570 572 631
  783
JOSLYN, 571
JOY, 669
JUDSON, 446 449
KALABARER, 629-630
KALTENBACH, 396
KANE, 398 527
KARK, 419
KATH, 490
KAUFFMAN, 689
KAY, 755
KEAN, 576 714
KEELER, 571
KEELEY, 755
KEENAN, 730 James 730
KEISTER, 258 476 482 484-485 575
  William A 476
KEITH, 282
KEITT, 385
KELLAR, 262
KELLER, 398 599
KELLEY, 420 479-480 616
KELLOGG, 433 442-443 450 506 651
  699
KELLY, 397 408 411
KELSEY, 716-717
KEMMERER, 292 415-416 416 425 440
  446 652 Jacob 416
KENDALL, 720
KENEFICK, 258 730 732-733 741
  Patrick 730
KENISON, 407 773 Sevedra 773
KENNEDY, 282 433 440 443 450 546
  713 718 720 Samuel 718
KENNEFICK, 740
KENNISON, 772
KENSLEY, 269-270 300
KENT, 490 515 F P 490
KENYON, 708
KEPHART, 365 530 536 536-537 547
  750 T E 536
KEPHERT, 365
KERNS, 641 651 J H 641
KERR, 446 649
KERSHNER, 688

KETCHEM, 397
KETCHUM, 249
KIENTZ, 450
KILLEN, 489 Gawn S 489
KILNETOB, 605
KILSON, 743 750 Louis 743
KIMMEL, 397-398 411 690-691
KIMMINS, 298 517 527 John 517
KINCAID, 687-688 Edwin 688
KINDALL, 262 353
KINDIG, 465 649
KING, 343 461 465 540-541 546
KINGERY, 476 481 548-549 549 578
  William 549
KINNE, 285
KINNEY, 351
KINSEY, 576
KINSLEY, 261-262 398 527 588-589
KIRBY, 628
KIRKER, 237 494 601
KISSELL, 276
KITTEL, 312
KIVAL, 781
KLEEVER, 663
KLENSKEY, 597
KLINETOB, 599-600 605 C P 605
KLOBE, 570
KNAPP, 232 277 281 422 422-423
  452 520 526 Horace 520 J 422
KNICKERBOCKER, 720
KNIGHT, 398 705 729
KNIGHTS, 616
KNIPE, 453 460 471 471-472 474
  484 Jacob M 471
KNIPHALS, 661
KNISIG, 570
KNOUSE, 574
KNOX, 526
KOCHER, 600 768 772 Jeremiah 768
KOCKER, 768
KOHLHAAS, 558
KOTHE, 619 717
KRAMER, 628
KREBBS, 351 776 Jacob 351
KREMER, 633 G K D 633
KRUSE, 682
KUBLANK, 489 706 727 J H 727
KUSSEL, 576
KUSTER, 481

KYLE, 489 Adam 489
LACEY, 357
LACON, 548-549
LADD, 515 547 590 William A 590
LAFAVER, 656 George 656
LAHR, 434 443 450
LAINHART, 237
LAKE, 474
LAKEN, 237 548
LAKIN, 368
LAMB, 425 446 513
LAMKIN, 464
LAMSON, 565-566 568 573 C T 568
LANDIS, 237 323 368 550 557-558 573 Felix 550
LANDPHERE, 697 719-720 J D 697
LANE, 280
LANGDON, 397
LANNING, 706 718
LARKIN, 258 365 540 545 718
LARNE, 388
LASH, 237 269 273 323 574 744 749 752 767 771 773-774
LASHBROOK, 420
LASTER, 768
LATHROP, 255-257 273 275-276 290 296 325 330 337 339 339-340 370 377 578 615 624 754 762 765-766 783 W A 339
LAUGHLIN, 707 756
LAURENCE, 449
LAUS, 541
LAW, 719
LAWRENCE, 601 615
LAWYER, 257-258 750
LEAMAN, 570
LEARY, 697
LEAVENS, 518 Bainbridge 518
LEAVITT, 703
LEE, 394 396 453 589 592-593 A W 589
LEET, 258 281 285 365 540 599 602 609
LEFAVER, 651
LEFFINGWELL, 271
LEFFLER, 407 420
LEIDIG, 557 571-572
LEIGHTER, 541
LEITZ, 600

LEMON, 426 429
LENCE, 579
LENHART, 398 517 535 595-596 Samuel 517
LEONARD, 503 722
LESLIE, 296 421 697
LESTER, 712
LETT, 609 A N 609
LEVALLY, 733 Lafayette 733
LEVERAGE, 707
LEVERICH, 251 262 271 297 388 397 411 696 709 720
LEVERICK, 297 711 James 297
LEVINS, 711
LEVIS, 296 339 617 691 762 766
LEWELLEN, 323 538-539
LEWIS, 369 397 411 454-455 459 471 491 525 714 765 Baldwin D 471
LEYBIG, 551 Emanuel 551
LIATIRITS, 634
LICHTENBURG, 656
LICHTY, 768
LIDDY, 738
LIENHART, 588
LIGHT, 490
LINCOLN, 273 383-385 425 754 766
LINDERMAN, 275 751
LINDSEY, 574
LINGLEBACK, 450
LINN, 445 469 620 620-621 642 686-687 Nathan 620
LISTER, 600
LITCHFIELD, 470
LITTLE, 424 701
LITTLER, 545
LIVINGSTON, 489
LLOYD, 576 584
LOBDELL, 425 442-443 443-444 450
LOCKWOOD, 366 481 483 483-484 550 752 772-774
LOGAN, 352 482 539 645 657 667 678 680
LONG, 254-256 397 411 474 562 629 632 632-633 739-740
LONGFELLOW, 717
LONGUEVILLE, 342
LOOMIS, 253 282 339 529 531 609
LORAH, 271-272

LOVELL, 486 778
LOW, 254 262 407 636
LOWE, 271-272 300 718
LOWMAN, 262
LUCAS, 289 312 364 366 463 763 765
LUCE, 562
LUCK, 238 261 661 674
LUSH, 407 529
LUSTED, 323 539 545 601
LUTZ, 682
LYDIG, 366
LYFERD, 570
LYFORD, 578 586
LYLE, 258
LYND, 650-651
LYNN, 449 464 603 637
LYON, 463 518
LYONS, 549 579
MABARY, 485
MABEE, 558 562 565-567 570
MABIE, 576
MACK, 418 703
MACREADY, 281
MACY, 402
MADIGAN, 542
MAFFIT, 398
MAHANKE, 316 435 450
MAIN, 408 516
MAJOR, 519
MALONEY, 689
MANLEY, 354 431-432 432 442 446 450
MANLY, 432
MANN, 262 406-407 555
MANNING, 285
MANSER, 422
MANSFIELD, 358 727
MANWAIRN, 388
MARCH, 397 525 527 719
MARGARETZ, 407
MARGRETZ, 272 333 388-389 624 690-691 697
MARGRITZ, 397
MARKLE, 520 525
MARKLEY, 282 450 652
MARLOW, 620
MARMADUKE, 390 394 398 400
MARQUAND, 260 407 599-600 606 610

MARQUEST, 269
MARRYWEATHER, 537
MARSH, 532 617
MARSHALL, 572-573 605
MARSLIN, 455 695-696
MARTGRETZ, 617
MARTIN, 262 347-348 386 397-398 408 411 454 519 527 557-558 574 599 615 734 752 754-755 761-762
MARTS, 330 336
MARYATT, 463-464
MASON, 270-271 273 275 330 335 342 369 383 388 411 585 585-587 616-617 626 690 696 712 719
MAST, 506
MATHER, 236-237 251 406 496 501 501-502 505 528 583
MATHERS, 601
MATHESON, 718
MATHEWS, 285
MATTHEW, 690
MATTHEWS, 276 652
MAXON, 538
MAXWELL, 407-408 435 459-460 463- 465 469 471 481 486 586 657
MAYBERRY, 490
MAYNARD, 388
MCABEE, 781
MCALISTER, 397
MCALLISTER, 710
MCANTEE, 630
MCBARNARD, 527
MCCAGUE, 719
MCCAIN, 237 398 411 577 579
MCCARTY, 276 615 624 703
MCCAULEY, 699
MCCLAIN, 608
MCCLELLAN, 262 270-273 300 305 398 601
MCCLELLAND, 526
MCCLEN, 406
MCCLEOD, 766
MCCLINTOCK, 271
MCCLURE, 253 267 460 560 562 565
MCCOLLUM, 551 679
MCCOLUM, 513
MCCONNEL, 527
MCCONNELL, 686-687
MCCORCLE, 708

MCCORMACK, 308 351
MCCORMICK, 667 678 776
MCCOY, 691
MCCRARY, 542
MCCRAY, 605
MCCREADY, 539
MCCREARY, 540 599
MCCRERY, 323 515 545 600 603
MCCURDY, 567
MCDANIEL, 647
MCDONALD, 397 482 527 529 539 541 607 609 712 714 718 726-727
MCDOWELL, 750
MCEACHRON, 258 615
MCELVAIN, 281
MCELWAIN, 460 463 466
MCEWEN, 417 426
MCEWING, 262
MCFARLAND, 647
MCGEACHY, 775
MCGEE, 465 481
MCGILL, 464 740
MCGLATHERY, 271-272 324
MCGREGOR, 610 615 618 624 719
MCINTIRE, 765
MCINTOSH, 276-277 281-282 286 300 459-461
MCINTYRE, 299 330 342 345 504 721 762 765-766
MCJUNKIN, 280-281
MCKABE, 446
MCKANE, 584
MCKEE, 465 545 607
MCKENNIE, 275
MCKERNAN, 689
MCKEY, 650-652 733
MCKIM, 465
MCKINNEY, 237 270 323 479-480 482 660 662 671 673 680
MCLEAN, 407 442
MCLEOD, 306
MCMAHON, 637-638 638 641 647 649
MCMANNES, 682-684
MCMILLAN, 517
MCMILLEN, 547
MCMORAN, 624
MCMURRAY, 628
MCNABB, 571-572
MCNAMES, 577

MCNEIL, 400
MCNETT, 723
MCPHERSON, 285-286 402 571 656
MCREADY, 280'
MCROBERTS, 364 532 535-536 540 542 551
MCSPARRON, 597
MCSTAY, 763
MCWILLIAMS, 700 766
MEAD, 397 406 423 642 648 652 686 718-719
MEADE, 378 704 725-726
MEARS, 475 621
MELINDY, 420
MELLENGER, 772
MENINGA, Daniel 731
MERIFIELD, 386
MERREL, 670
MERRICK, 366
MERRILL, 272-276 369 542 621 624-625 660 669 690 750 772 775
MESSERSCHMIDT, 633 633-634
METTLEN, 615
METTLER, 762
METZGAR, 273 275 300 720
METZGER, 697 712 718
MEYER, 490 718
MEYERS, 388-389 720
MICHEL, 449
MILES, 681 719
MILLEN, 473
MILLER, 237 242-243 253 255 257-258 262 269-272 277 300 328 398 411 413 446 449 476 480 484 491 548-550 550-552 555-557 559 566 574-575 578 585 600 624 633 648 677 680 685 743-744 774-776
MILLIER, 403
MILLS, 406 479-480 556 559-560 565-567 570 576 615
MINER, 565 565-566 576
MINOR, 586 605
MISCOLL, 629
MITCHELL, 446 480 484 506 538 541 719 751
MIX, 386 397-398 405 408 411
MODLIN, 398
MOFFATT, 626 690
MOGART, 642

MOLLOY, 699
MOLSBERRY, 493
MONETON, 530
MONROE, 274 687 689-690
MONTE, 435-436
MONTGOMERY, 286 297 330 342 345 586 781
MONTY, 450
MOON, 272
MOORE, 262 270 282 336 494-495 501 516 527-528 528-530 540 545 552 557-558 573-574 590 605 674 755-756 766-767 775-776
MOOREHEAD, 687 689-690
MOORHEAD, 688
MOOTS, 270 657 659 744 749
MORFORD, 680
MORGAN, 318 569 646·
MORILL, 715
MORRILL, 571 578 586
MORRIS, 282 454 479-480 646 652 743
MORRISON, 314 440 462 508 529 547 575 712
MORROW, 527 767
MORSE, 249 257-258 422 425 442 450
MORTIN, 277
MORTON, 232 237 252 267 269-270 300 369 453 496 542
MOSHIER, 525
MOSS, 397 481 490 550 557 560-561 566 573-574
MOSSER, 471
MOTT, 433-434 434-435 450 604 604-605 756
MOULTON, 526 529 539-540 542 545
MOWER, 395
MOYER, 353 547 600 721
MUFFLER, 398
MUFFLEY, 275 481 484
MUFLEY, 476
MULLARKEY, 615-617 621 624 766
MULLARKY, 237 282 305 376 378 414 426 615 617 623
MULLARPY, 246
MULLEN, 711 718-719 723-724
MULLIN, 250 583
MULLINS, 408

MUMM, 277
MUNCY, 450
MUNDINGER, 423
MUNSON, 590 739
MURCKLEY, 600
MURDOCK, 341
MURPHY, 262 274 300 465 545 574 628 649 690 775
MURRAY, 280 443 472 508 525 536 706 712-713 715 720
MURRY, 388
MUSGRAVE, 627
MYER, 775
MYERS, 250-251 386 388 397 411 525 695 719-720 722 762
MYRICK, 752 776
NAGLE, 727
NARY, 565
NASH, 237 280 282 636 641 641-642 647 649-650 715 729
NEAL, 495 508 525 529 540 547 600 605 659 730 749 751 771 773 775-776
NEEDHAM, 237 254 397 418 663-664 668 675 677-679 683 690 752
NEFFORD, 429
NEGUS, 275 280
NEICE, 274
NEIGHMAN, 744
NELSON, 262 365 502 540 583 600-601 601-602 743 775
NETTLETON, 257-258 459 551 699 703-704 Henry 699
NEVINS, 352-353 576
NEWBORN, 481
NEWBURY, 772-773 776 F E 773
NEWCOMB, 397 470 695 707-711 715 719 O S 708
NEWELL, 235 339 492 503 541 661
NEWHARD, 258 323 539 578 588
NEWMAN, 507 518 529-531 539-540 599-600 Hiram 518
NEWTON, 335 518
NICHLAUS, 646 P 646
NICHOLAS, 305
NICHOLS, 237 257 352 358 417 562 570 606 663-664 672 683 776
NIECE, 271 300 369 416-417 417 482 491 623 629 660 662 664

NIECE (cont.)
  667-668 672 M D L 369 Michael 417
NILES, 734
NOBLE, 277 282 289
NORRIS, 273 431 433 439 439-440 450 456 696 Robert 439
NORTHFOSS, 557 562
NORTON, 259 270 300 456 526 705 Selden 526
NORVAL, 330 710
NOURS, 272
NUGENT, 644 Michael 644
NUTTING, 406 411
NYE, 433
OAKS, 778
O'BRIEN, 479-480
O'CONNER, 275-277
ODELL, 271
OHMERT, 558 560 566
OLIVER, 513
OLLINBURG, 525
OLMSTEAD, 237 260 262 270 272 300 397-398 411 433 452 452-453 453 455-456 459 461 464 470 615-616 621 623 Aaron 453 Nathan 452
ORCUTT, 464
ORMSBEE, 351
ORR, 277 288 Jackson 288
ORRAHOOD, 580
ORVIS, 323 330 339-340 340-341 397 406 L A 340
OSIER, 561 576
OSTERHOUT, 298
OTTERBURN, 440
OTTHOFF, 646 Ottze 646
OVERACKER, 406 408 420 425
OVERCRACKER, 273
OVERMAN, 232 252 267 296 711
OVERTURF, 254 479-480 484 667-668 673 679 681 Samuel 681
OWEN, 246 323 408 419 425 444 446 450 589 615 704 Henry 419 L D 419
OWENS, 408 453 580 646 Edward 646
OXFORD, 273 659 663-664
PACKARD, 274 366 460 578 585 Joseph 585
PAGE, 298

PALEY, 717-719 J H 717
PALMATIER, 366
PALMATTEER, 551
PALMER, 232 237-238 240 250-252 254 258-259 262-264 269-270 272-275 286 290 292 294-295 299 308 311 323-324 327 330 332 344 357 378 388 483 496 529-530 539-540 596 629 668 706
PANLEY, 411 506
PARCUPILE, 388
PARIS, 718
PARISH, 423 481
PARK, 397 657-659 742
PARKER, 237 246 249 262 416 416-417 425-426 431 433 435-437 441-442 442-443 446 449-451 520 587 663 678 732-733 740 Frank 733 J D 442 James F 442 Pascal 416 Patrick 732
PARKS, 237 386 411 493 658 742
PARNO, 572 576
PARRIOT, 254
PARRIOTT, 237 257 262 270 272 274 411 441 647 649-650 728-729 734 739-740 R R 734
PARRIS, 433 440 443 445 451 755 Brothers 433
PARRISH, 446
PARROT, 311 398
PARROTT, 413
PARSONS, 531 711 767
PARTHEMER, 406
PARVIN, 271 449
PASSIMORE, 532
PATCHEN, 719
PATTEE, 267 276 282 285 295-296 406 718 756 762 765 William W 296
PATTEN, 340
PATTERSON, 351 538 600-601 605 607 682 A B 607 William 605
PATTON, 717 721 724 J E 74
PAULEY, 388
PAULGER, 466 469 John 469
PAULSY, 572
PAYNE, 232 252
PEABIRD, 617
PEASE, 703

PECK, 398 615 714 719
PECKHAM, 456
PEEBLES, 403 473
PEET, 364-365 530 530-531 533
    George R 530
PELTON, 326
PENNEPECKER, 704
PENNOCK, 562 573 576 617
PERCIVAL, 532
PERKINS, 451 469
PERRIN, 236-237 413 495 495-496
    498-499 516 527 535 586 763
    Jeremiah 495
PERRY, 420-421 429 434 450 575
    656 718
PETERSON, 637 661
PETHERAN, 643
PETTERS, 455
PETTIT, 703
PETTY, 567
PFALTGRAFTZ, 629
PFALTZGRAFF, 633 683 685 Fred 633
    Philip 685
PHARO, 754 761 765
PHELPS, 471 501
PHILLIPI, 398
PHILLIPPI, 411
PHILLIPS, 262 273 398 407 529
    556-557 580 596 705 710 714-715
    719-721
PHILO, 464
PICKEREL, 440
PICKETT, 459 461 464
PIERCE, 358 398 412 450-451 460
    503 688 723 773
PINGREY, 446 449
PITCHER, 698
PLANT, 262
PLATER, 624
PLATT, 446 649
PLAYTER, 281-282 289 300 615 672
    753 767-768 771-772 775-776 H J
    768 John B 771
PLUMMER, 398 463
POISAL, 232 250 252 262 269-270
    277 303 328 331 412-413 501
    501-502 515 515-516 527 529 537
    539-540 545 Byron L 515 George
    W 501

POISALL, 236 398 496 546-547
POLLY, 530 632
POMEROY, 276 288 388 Charles 288
POND, 762 774
POPE, 365 540 562 600
PORCUPILE, 451
PORTER, 281 404 406 687
POWELL, 667 678-679
POWERS, 274 281-282 290 344 354
    359-360 432-436 444 449 700 719
    M I 354
PRALL, 654
PRATT, 288 317 464-465 Henry O
    288
PRAY, 275 545
PRESCOTT, 330 342 714 718-719 R D
    342
PRESTON, 258 714 718
PRICE, 395 405 504 525 585 W H
    585
PRIEST, 600 602 602-603 779
    Benjamin 602
PRINCE, 464 583 650-652 654
    Charles S 654
PRINDLE, 783
PRINGLE, 542 596
PROBASCO, 519 525 527
PROCTOR, 277 425
PURCELL, 728 739
PUTNAM, 398
QUACKENBUSH, 471
QUILLEN, 407
QUIMBY, 398 454
QUINN, 237 398 408 551 597 637
    651-653 729-730 739 Rachel 729
RADNOR, 724
RAGANA, 723
RAID, 270
RAINS, 601
RAMSEY, 526 783
RAMSY, 587 Charles 587
RANDOLPH, 590 688
RANKIN, 275-277
RANSOM, 608 C M 608
RAUS, 651
RAVE, 439
RAVENSCROFT, 529-530 547
RAWSON, 237 251-252 269-270 496
    556

RAY, 282 285 296 321 425 435 443 451 463 501 501-502 680 711 714 717 749 765 775 John 501 John W 296
RAYMOND, 274 471
RAYS, 655
RECORDS, 766
REED, 289 299 314 504 539 541 560 603 606 688 706 714-716 718 726 J P 314 W J 726
REFSNIDER, 773
REID, 271
REILEY, 618
REINIGER, 280 285 329
REINTS, 646 651 655 H W 655
REMILEY, 473
RENFREW, 237 588 596
RENKEN, 435-436 436 439 442-443 451 R G 436
RENSHAW, 775
REPROGLE, 573
RESSLER, 697 704-705 721 Amos 697 Elias 704
REYNOLDS, 135 526
RHETT, 385
RHOADS, 540 547
RHODES, 464
RICE, 254-255 269 271-272 286 324 330-332 332-333 364 615 618 662 667-668 697-698 705 710 721 Orson 332 Sylvester 698
RICH, 752
RICHARDS, 330 344 350 435 446 450-451 494 590 677
RICHARDSON, 276 332 408 515
RICHMON, 671 683
RICHMOND, 260 270 324 330 333 555 617 George A 333 John F 555
RICKS, 464
RIDDLE, 262 658
RIDEN, 505 510-511 W A 505
RIDENOUR, 280
RIDGEWAY, 763
RIDGWAY, 535
RIEFE, 536 547 Henry 536
RIEFFE, 519
RIFE, 585

RIGGS, 306 349 349-350 756 761 763 765 J S 349
RILEY, 323 420 549 562
RINER, 317-318 556-557 565-568 576
RIPLEY, 285
RIPPENTROP, 632
RIPSOM, 768
RIPSON, 376 378 772
RIX, 443 445 451
ROADS, 697 704
ROBBINS, 267 446 464 624 703 709 Benjamin 703
ROBERTS, 398 420 513 540 560
ROBERTSON, 321 344 682-683
ROBEY, 516
ROBIN, 272
ROBINSON, 359 398 518-519 589 602 690 708 712 727 775 John 589
ROBISON, 386
ROBY, 537
ROCKWELL, 280-282 300 398 714 720 726 J G 726
ROGERS, 463 474 539 700
ROLLSTON, 722
ROLSTON, 423
ROOT, 253-254 272 280 282 285 323 450 455-456 459-460 462 465-466 515 535-536 565 585 622 657 781 Milton R 585 Ruluff 515
ROSEBRAUGH, 273 459
ROSEBROUGH, 257 454
ROSECRANS, 504
ROSENCRANS, 274
ROSS, 695 707-708 712 715 718 720
ROSZELL, 232 250 269 272 275 280 290 303-304 330 332 335 339 342 398 502 531 547 C A L 335
ROSZELLE, 276 281
ROTHE, 615
ROTHROCK, 281 527
ROWEN, 690
ROWLEY, 572 683
ROYCE, 397-398 417 439 649-651 712 Orlin 417
ROYER, 771
RUDDICK, 276-277 280 285 324 329 344
RUDE, 453-454 456

RUITER, 628
RUNNELS, 281
RUNYON, 281
RUPERT, 565-566
RUSH, 659 662-663
RUSSELL, 237 418 441-442 450-451 561 600-601 608 608-609 648 F M 608 George L 418 Thomas 418
RUST, 237
RUTHERFORD, 281
RYAN, 446 604 682 689 702
RYCKMAN, 525
RYNER, 555
SACKETT, 466
SADDLER, 588
SAGE, 537
SAINTJOHN, 388
SALES, 275
SALINGER, 547
SAMPSON, 542 560 567 599-600
SAMSON, 783
SAMUELS, 271 288
SANTEE, 616-617 624 688 690 Joseph L 688
SARBEE, 749
SARVER, 750
SAULSBURY, 552
SAVAGE, 313 316 330 344 450 463 650-651
SAYRE, 402
SCALLON, 731 740 H G 731
SCHELLENGER, 508 513 540 542 547 C G 508
SCHELLINGER, 529
SCHIMMERHORN, 778
SCHMITZ, 629 683
SCHNEE, 505
SCHOFIELD, 560
SCHOOLCRAFT, 435 439 442 449 D W 439
SCHRODER, 650
SCHUCKNECHT, 576
SCHUELKE, 740
SCHULNBORG, 682-683
SCHULTZ, 451
SCHUMAN, 778
SCNELBERGER, 633

SCOBEY, 276 346 354 357 386 700 707 710 718 John 354
SCOBY, 257-258 277
SCOFIELD, 268 600 605 765 J 605
SCOTT, 275 330 343 386-387 398 403 504 615 627 647 683 689 762 772 Oscar H 343
SCRIBNER, 406 721
SEARLES, 238 262 366 539
SEAVER, 474 J W 474
SECOR, 280
SEEVERS, 280 286
SEICHTG, 502
SEITZ, 538 547 605 A 538
SELLS, 271
SENNETT, 274
SESSIONS, 282 568 576
SEWELL, 262 508 619 698
SEYMOUR, 273 276
SHADBOLT, 516 547 595 Jerome 516
SHAFER, 507 529-532 532 547 551 574 578 585 774 Thomas 532 William W R 585
SHAFFER, 262 276 323 432-433 436 603
SHANNON, 365 539 541 580 583 583-584 607 695-696 John A 583
SHARON, 720
SHARP, 388 506
SHARPE, 737-739
SHAUNTZ, 446
SHAVER, 277 436
SHAW, 238 257 273-274 404-406 456 462-465 519 547 558 615 617 741
SHEEON, 277
SHEETS, 777
SHEFFER, 398 412 571
SHELDON, 481
SHEPARD, 464 602
SHERBURN, 540
SHERIN, 649
SHERMAN, 280-281 285 292 393 403 503-504 545 641 656 720
SHERRIN, 446
SHERWOOD, 782
SHIELDS, 289 446 525 606 628 649
SHIPPY, 565
SHIRER, 551
SHOEMAKER, 571 576

SHOOK, 557 560 562 571
SHOWERS, 734
SHUGART, 636
SHULTZ, 402
SHUMAKER, 545
SHUMWAY, 515
SIKKEMA, 615-616
SILL, 354 358 710 721 723 E E 358
  Samuel 723
SIMMONS, 464
SIMONDS, 705
SIMONS, 449 714
SIMPSON, 407
SIMS, 294
SKELTON, 726
SKILLEN, 482 619
SKILLENGER, 545
SKILLINGER, 545
SKINNER, 357 539 571 719-720
SLADE, 628-629
SLAID, 378
SLAIGHT, 596
SLAYTON, 701
SLIMMER, 515 529 535 535-536 540
  546 763 Lewis 535
SLOAN, 396
SLOSSON, 518 Henry 518
SLY, 446
SMALLEY, 542
SMART, 261
SMEDLEY, 545
SMELTZER, 277
SMITH, 258 262 270 273-277 280
  292 298 323 330 343 345 354 358
  358-359 366 388-389 394-395 398
  403-407 412 425 430 439 443 446
  459-460 462 464-465 471-472 472
  479-480 480 483 491 501 513 518
  536 536-537 537-538 545 547 560
  570-572 575 583 590 620 624 626
  628-632 632 642 648-649 654
  654-655 663 682-683 690 695 701
  710-711 718-720 730-732 738 749
  752 756 761-762 764-765 773
  775-776 778 A E 536 A J 343 G B
  654 J M 537 L L 472 Orrin C 480
  Robert 749 Samuel 632 W C 590 W
  H 358
SMOKE, 514

SNYDER, 352-353 353 562 576 607
  782 Peter B 353
SOACH, 704
SOASH, 721
SOESBE, 317 330 336 339 562 565-
  568 571 575-576 E W 339 S W 336
SOIN, 604
SOLOMON, 557
SONNEMA, 633
SOULE, 405
SOWASH, 398
SPANGLER, 737 739
SPAULDING, 336 366-367 560-562
  571 586
SPAWN, 406
SPAWR, 396
SPEAKER, 710 John 710
SPEARS, 388 412
SPEEDY, 281 397 620 710 714 M B
  620
SPENCER, 282 285 293 293-294 321
  440 765-766 A M 440 James W 293
SPERNIER, 285
SPERRY, 398 412
SPICER, 446
SPINCER, 273
SPOONER, 359 361 445
SPOOR, 555 Isaac 555
SPOWAR, 262
SPOWER, 262
SPRAGG, 449
SPRAGUE, 237 464 606 627-629
SPROUL, 314 446 482 628 649 690
  Rev O H 1314
SPURLIN, 402
STACEY, 630
STACY, 262 626-627
STAFFORD, 471 607
STALEY, 775
STANLEY, 397 455 460-461
STANNARD, 271 696 Asa 696
STANTON, 463-464
STARKWEATHER, 777
STEARNS, 345-346
STEELE, 402
STEPHENS, 525
STERN, 273
STETSON, 294
STEVE, 576

STEVENS, 272 462-463
STEVENSON, 542 599-600 608 John 608
STEWARD, 720
STEWART, 280-282 309-310 318 363-365 370 370-371 377 388 397 408 539-540 542 545 616 623-624 668 682 707 709 715 718 740 775 J L 707 John W 370
STIBBS, 393-394
STICKLER, 734
STICKNEY, 352
STILES, 275 277
STILSON, 650 652
STINE, 275
STOBER, 566 576
STOCK, 632 Wilhelm 632
STOCKDALE, 275 412 738-740 Charles 738
STOCKUALE, 398
STOCKWELL, 756
STODDARD, 275 717 773
STONE, 262 274 298 386-387 432 446 481 574 605
STONEBRAKER, 718
STONEBREAKER, 711 714 716 720 723 A G 716
STONER, 254-256 323 687 690
STOUGHTON, 335 William 335
STOUT, 753
STOVER, 671-672
STOW, 276
STRACHAN, 400
STRAIGHT, 643 A 643
STRANAHAN, 562 568 570 783
STRANNAHAN, 561
STRATTON, 507
STRAUM, 398
STRAWHACKER, 525
STREETER, 648
STRICKLAND, 351-352 469 R D 469
STRINGER, 417
STROHECKER, 578
STRONG, 237 262 269 388 454 464 496 531 542 550 557 660 667 749 752
STROOT, 427

STROUT, 354 354-359 359-365 367-427 427-432 432-436 436-443 443-450 450-782 A O 354-782
STRUTZ, 398
STUART, 421
STUBBS, 281
STUBENRANCH, 280
STUELKE, 597
STUMPFF, 690 697
STURDEVANT, 406 412
STURTZ, 397 412 491 550 552 552-553 557 560-561 571-574 Solomon 552
SULLIVAN, 474
SUMNER, 398 596-597
SUNDERLAND, 449
SURFUS, 275 388-389 398 407 409 412 580 662 743-744 749 752 776 C V 744
SUTCLIFFE, 505
SUTTON, 574 677 783
SWAIN, 285 454
SWAN, 282 439 508 648 651 H M 508
SWEARINGEN, 545 774
SWEELY, 754
SWEITGER, 276
SWEITZER, 281 378 695-696 714-715 719-720 H L 696
SWERINGEN, 281
SWIGGETT, 342
SWIM, 398 412 493 579
SWISHER, 336
SWITZER, 707
TABER, 716
TABOR, 470 481
TALBOTT, 604
TAMMEN, 436 439 443 Mr 439
TANNER, 432
TARR, 705
TAYLOR, 236 254-257 262 298 418 418-419 425 451 455 465 472 480 495-496 508 516 519 525 527-528 537 539 574 615-616 627 687 J R 516 Morrison A 236 Sylvanus H 418 W R 519
TEMPLE, 237 262 575 578 585 585-586 588 596-597 Julius 585
TEMPLIN, 400
TENENT, 435

TENNISON, 540
TENNYSON, 365 606 William 606
TERRY, 596
THAIR, 677
THARP, 407 702-703 Washington 702
THAYER, 353
THIELDS, 778
THOMAS, 237 262 280-281 295 295-296 303 396 398 412 426 452 455 504 557 560-562 566-567 570 572 575-580 580 590 621 627 749 752 755 762 764-766 777 Charles N 590 Edward S 296 Hugh 580
THOMPKINS, 254 273-276 293 328
THOMPSON, 253 273-275 282 286 295 300 323-324 324 335 530 545 578 610 615-616 618 620 624 688 749-751 Charles 750 J D 324 N A 618 N C 618 Thomas 618
THORINGTON, 287 James 287
THORNSBRUE, 579
THORNTON, 600 778
THORP, 312 354 357 540 709-711 E L 357
THORPE, 343
TIBBLES, 406
TICE, 291
TICHENOR, 352
TICHNOR, 546-547 601
TILDEN, 280
TILFORD, 517 J Y 517
TINDAL, 490 John 490
TINDALL, 482
TOBEY, 729 Elisha 729
TOBIAS, 473
TOLL, 709
TOMPKINS, 257 293 538 624 A J 293
TOWN, 364 695 708-709 712 714-715 722 E 722
TOWNSEND, 254 273 300 323 441 455 529 547 683-684
TRACEY, 551 Edward S 551
TRACY, 274 290 551 556
TRAPP, 573
TRENHOLM, 574
TRIMBLE, 274 282 560-562 565
TRIMBLIN, 585
TRIMMER, 515
TRINDAL, 772

TRINDE, 750 George 750
TRINDLE, 749
TRIPP, 583 732
TROBAUGH, 588 596
TROTTER, 245-246 258 300 413 610 615-616 618-619 619-620 688 Henry 688 James A 619
TROUTMAN, 552 718
TROWBRIDGE, 388
TRUMBULL, 237-238 241-242 251-252 271 289 323 330 330-331 333 340 386 465 496 656 662 M M 330
TUCK, 562
TUCKER, 257
TUFTS, 603
TULLAR, 623
TUNSLEY, 596
TUPPER, 389
TURNER, 351 359 361 386 388 398 414 414-415 425-426 775-776 Abel 414 E Leroy 351
TURTELOTTE, 350
TUTTLE, 273 275 290
TWINING, 446 449
TWOHIG, 454 590
TYLER, 557 576
ULERY, 687
ULRICH, 732
UNDERKAFER, 771
UNDERWOOD, 502 583 749 753
UPP, 600
UPPS, 398
UPRIGHT, 615
UPSON, 716
UPTON, 424
UTLEY, 396
UYRICK, 772
VALE, 529 531 540 547
VANANDA, 274
VANBUREN, 351
VANBUSKIRK, 481
VANCE, 737
VANCUREN, 296
VANDERBILT, 684
VANDEVEER, 271
VANDEVER, 287 400 William 287
VANDORN, 232 237 251-252 262 269-270 293 299 323 327 425 496
VANDORNE, 555

VANDYKE, 260 542 599-600
VANGUNDY, 505
VANHOUSEN, 537
VANSAUM, 367
VANSAUN, 575
VANVLACK, 615-616 621 724 William 621
VANVLECK, 706 714 718-719 724-725 G O 724
VANWAMSLEY, 555
VARIER, 699
VEASEY, 517
VEBER, 583
VEHON, 575
VERMILYEA, 595
VIM, 262
VINCENT, 237 253 262 323 332 459 496 502
VIRDEN, 547
VOLNEY, 235 692
VOLTZ, 407
VONCOELIN, 282
VONCOELLN, 281
VONCOLLN, 280
VOOGD, 433 451
VOSLER, 596
WADE, 451 481 489 Michael 489
WAGNER, 281 317 567 783
WAGONER, 771
WAGONSELLER, 584
WAIT, 605 605-606 Daniel 605
WAITE, 599
WAKELY, 628
WALBRING, 552
WALCH, 590
WALDEN, 276
WALKER, 238 253-254 270 280 282 285-286 296 323 326 346 352 426 530 536 585 615 624 696 698 H N 624 Joseph 698
WALLACE, 273 357 435
WALLER, 306 753-754 778
WALRATH, 297 514 519 James 514
WALSH, 750
WALTER, 407 519-520 520 708-710 715 Elias 520
WALTERS, 520 695
WALWORTH, 527

WAMSLEY, 236-238 251-252 257-258 262 269 274-277 280 303-304 323 493 493-495 502 513 520 525 527 529-530 535-536 539-540 542 547 562 586 590 599-601 604 Henry 586 John M 590 M B 493 M V 604 W C 513 W S 493
WAMSLY, 398 412
WARD, 253 465 480 482 571 645 730
WARNER, 386 388 398 460 643 A C 643
WARREN, 421 446
WASHBURNE, 740
WATERBURY, 545 651
WATERS, 398 406 408 412 415 417-418 418 420 426 449 623 754 Isaac 418
WATROUS, 574
WATSON, 527 613 627-629 631-632 632 Alvin 632 Wolcott 613
WATTLES, 609
WAUDBY, 740
WEAVER, 282 408 455 464 538
WEBBER, 576
WEBER, 619
WEBSTER, 397 545
WEED, 357 371 700 712 Phineas 700
WEEKS, 343 423 772-773 Henry 423
WEGAND, 562
WEICHMAN, 733 E 733
WEIRES, 754 761 766-767
WELCH, 463 589 730
WELCHER, 775
WELLER, 282
WELLMAN, 711
WELLS, 262 275 408 645
WELTY, 644
WEMPLE, 267 406-407 415 419-420 424 435 449 Henry B 415
WENRICK, 574
WEREHRAN, 717
WERNER, 436
WESENFELDER, 716
WESLEY, 552
WEST, 605 755
WETSEL, 397
WHALEY, 281 285 290-291 291 301 651-652 A M 291
WHALY, 282

WHEAT, 720
WHEATMAN, 740
WHEELER, 313 398 407 451 474 518 698 768 773 Horace A 773 O J 698
WHEELOCK, 538
WHELAN, 515
WHIPPLE, 472 Nelson H 472
WHITCOMB, 729 741
WHITE, 311-312 369 432 463 482 616 645 695 702-703 776
WHITEHEAD, 616 699 James 699
WHITFIELD, 435 650
WHITNEY, 258 344 398 648 739
WHITTAKER, 721
WHITTED, 398
WHITTER, 398
WHITTLESY, 552
WICK, 353 359 361 466 D M 353
WICKER, 445
WICKHAM, 663 775
WIECHMAN, 733
WIEKS, 776
WIESER, 407
WIGHTMAN, 638 647-648 721
WILBUR, 237 415 426 776
WILCOX, 352 386 388 398 407 517 529 576 608 608-609 A C 608
WILDER, 386 726
WILFORD, 715 718
WILHELM, 502 574
WILKERSON, 626
WILKES, 659 743 749-750 John 750
WILKINS, 484
WILKINSON, 268 446 520 525 E A 520
WILKIS, 579
WILLARD, 469
WILLETT, 407
WILLIAMS, 238 261 271-272 324 333 386-387 398 408 415 431 436 446 455-456 459 466 471 481 507 558 580 584 586 590 595 615 618-619 619 623 628 649 661 714-715 722-724 756 E H 324 James W 586 Samuel 619
WILLIAMSON, 276 285-286 683
WILLIS, 406 652 722
WILSON, 237 249 254-258 274-276

WILSON (cont.)
280 282 285 294 294-295 339 364 366 378 398 412-413 417 440 459 476 476-479 479-481 481-483 483-484 484-485 485-558 558-562 562-576 576 578-600 600-650 650-782 Elwood 294 Milton 476-782
WINCHELL, 243 397 412
WINNE, 277 732 Jurian 732
WINNIE, 649
WINSETT, 690 754-756 765-766 J K 756
WINSHIP, 388 400 606 714 720
WINTER, 472
WISSLER, 482
WOLCOTT, 464
WOLF, 285 344 446 451 545 776
WOLFE, 435 450
WONDERLY, 446 451
WOOD, 275 323 450 459-460 464 466 550 556 669 696-697 701 721
WOODLEY, 775
WOODLIN, 352
WOODLING, 353
WOODS, 330 335 342 389 394 396 495 516 661-662
WOODWARD, 540 754 761 765
WOODWORTH, 479-480 484 679 681 743 William P 679
WOOSTER, 418
WOPPLE, 262
WORKS, 589
WRAY, 378 484-485 751 772 775
WREY, 491 William 491
WRIGHT, 262 273-277 295 397 407-408 426 429 555 623 643 646 650-652 711-712 717 741 J F 711 William 643
WYANT, 286
WYATT, 354
WYGLE, 583
WYKOFF, 494 518
WYLIE, 514
YAGER, 562
YAW, 398
YBRIGHT, 579
YEOMAN, 282
YOCUM, 408

YODER, 623
YONKER, 421
YOST, 398 626 628 658 688-689
   Jacob 689
YOUNG, 280 352 359 361 432 436
   562 570 682 717 721 783 E J 717
   William 352

YOUNGER, 530
YOUNKER, 415 415-416 420 426
   George 415 William F 415
ZELL, 633 August 633
ZELMER, 398
ZOOK, 558 574

CPSIA information can be obtained
at www.ICGtesting.com
Printed in the USA
FSHW021940040219
55478FS